PRACTICAL ETHICS

THOMAS REID

Practical Ethics

*Being Lectures and Papers on
Natural Religion, Self-Government,
Natural Jurisprudence, and
the Law of Nations*

EDITED FROM THE MANUSCRIPTS
WITH AN INTRODUCTION AND
A COMMENTARY BY
KNUD HAAKONSSEN

Princeton University Press

Copyright © 1990 by Princeton University Press

Published by Princeton University Press, 41 William Street,
Princeton, New Jersey 08540
In the United Kingdom: Princeton University Press, Oxford

All Rights Reserved

Library of Congress Cataloging-in-Publication Data

Reid, Thomas, 1710–1796.
Practical ethics : being lectures and papers on natural religion, self-government,
natural jurisprudence, and the law of nations / Thomas Reid ; edited from the
manuscripts, with an introduction and a commentary, by Knud Haakonssen.
p.   cm.   Bibliography: p.   Includes index.
ISBN 0–691–07350–3 (alk. paper)
1. Ethics—Early works to 1800. I. Haakonssen, Knud, 1947–
II. Title. B1533.R38 1989   170–dc19   89–30633

This book has been composed in Linotron Baskerville

Clothbound editions of Princeton University Press books
are printed on acid-free paper, and binding materials are
chosen for strength and durability. Paperbacks, although satisfactory
for personal collections, are not usually suitable for library rebinding

Printed in the United States of America by Princeton University Press,
Princeton, New Jersey

DESIGNED BY LAURY A. EGAN

For Lisbeth

Contents

Thomas Reid
Lectures and Papers on
Practical Ethics

Commentary
BY KNUD HAAKONSSEN   301

AUTHOR'S NOTE

THIS BOOK is both by and about Thomas Reid. The centerpiece is an edition of Reid's manuscripts on practical ethics, which are preserved in the Aberdeen University Library in Scotland. Reid's text (pp. 101–299) is preceded by an Introduction and followed by a detailed Commentary on the text by the editor. At the back of the volume are a scholarly apparatus of Textual Notes, a Bibliographic Index of authorities cited in the Introduction and the Commentary, and a General Index.

In order to use this edition properly, it is important that the reader consult part 4, pp. 86–94, of the Introduction. This is followed at pp. 95–96 by an Index of Manuscripts in this volume. The note indicators in Reid's text refer the reader to the Commentary. The Textual Notes are identified by page and line number. Manuscript and folio numbers for Reid's original manuscripts are printed in the margin of Reid's text.

ACKNOWLEDGMENTS

NOBODY is now learned enough to produce a book like this without help from other scholars, and I have incurred a considerable number of debts to colleagues around the world, debts that it is a pleasure to acknowledge, however briefly.

I owe special thanks to J. C. Stewart-Robertson for suggesting that I participate in the planning for publication of Thomas Reid's unpublished papers and for our subsequent exchanges of first transcriptions of the manuscripts.

Elizabeth Short has once again proved to be as nearly the ideal research assistant as her other duties would permit. Her help with both the first transcription of a number of manuscripts and the final presentation of the volume has been considerable.

David Fate Norton has, with a willing suspension of disbelief, supported my attempt at scholarship with the voice of experience. J. B. Schneewind and M. A. Stewart read the whole of the manuscript in its second last form and flattered me by finding it worth their criticism. I am grateful also to those who read and commented on various parts of the manuscript: James Moore, John Passmore, and Paul Wood.

My belief in the international community of scholarship was reinforced by the many who responded so willingly to specific inquiries. I thank all who answered my calls for help—in particular, Hans Aarsleff, Robert Barnes, Robert Brown, Conal Condren, David Daiches, Colin Davis, Gordon Donaldson, Karsten Friis-Johansen, William M. Gordon, Thomas S. Hall, John Henry, Dorothy Johnston, D. H. Kelly, Douglas E. Leach, Klaus Luig, Geoffrey MacCormack, Neil MacCormick, Thomas Mautner, Fiammetta Palladini, John Passmore, Alan Saunders, Werner Schneiders, John Shy, Michael Silverthorne, Andrew Skinner, and Donald Winch.

The whole of this volume was written and several times rewritten in a handwriting as difficult to decipher as Reid's at his worst, but somehow Wendie Hare managed to produce typescripts of each successive version without once complaining about the lack of a word processor. Occasional secretarial assistance was lent by Vibeke Wetselaar, Beverley Shallcross, Anna Moran, and Colette Keith. To them all my best thanks.

A large part of the required library resources were available in the Australian National University Library and in the National Library of Australia, to whose helpful staff I owe many thanks. I am particularly grateful to the Australian National University Library's Law Library and Inter-Library loan service.

The History of Ideas Unit within the Research School of Social Sciences at the Australian National University is an ideal place for humanistic scholarship, not least because its head, Eugene Kamenka, knows how to encourage his colleagues without distracting them from the pursuit of their work. Even so, the present work required much travel overseas, and I am greatly indebted to several funds and institutions for financial and other assistance and to individual colleagues for undertaking the arrangement of visits. In 1982 and 1983 I extended my knowledge of natural law in the Herzog August Bibliothek in Wolfenbüttel, thanks to its director and to Sabine Solf, and in the Max-Planck-Institut für Geschichte in Göttingen, thanks to its director and Hans E. Bödeker and to Hans Medick, with the assistance of the Fritz-Thyssen-Stiftung. In 1983 and 1984 I visited the University of New Brunswick, thanks to J. C. Stewart-Robertson, with the assistance of the Social Sciences and Humanities Research Council of Canada and the University of New Brunswick. In 1985 I had the use of the fine library facilities in the Faculty of Law at Aarhus University, the Statsbibliotek in Aarhus, the Royal Library in Copenhagen, and the Aberdeen University Library, thanks to Stig Jørgensen, Mogens Blegvad, the assistance of the Scandinavian Cultural Fund for Australia and Aarhus and Copenhagen universities. In 1986 the British Council and my fellowship in the Institute for Advanced Studies in the Humanities in Edinburgh enabled me to put some of the finishing touches to this work in the midst of the full and very successful program of Scottish Enlightenment events which was organized by Peter Jones and his staff. Finally, I can see the work through the press from my privileged vantage point as a fellow in the Wilson Center in Washington, D.C. On each of these occasions I was able to leave Canberra with the blessing and often the support of my university.

My final thanks go to the librarian of the Aberdeen University Library for his kind permission to print the manuscripts in his custody.

Washington, D.C.
1 September 1988

ABBREVIATIONS

FULL DATA for the following abbreviations are in the Bibliographic Index at the end of the book.

WORKS BY THOMAS REID:

A.P.	*Essays on the Active Powers of Man*
H.M.	*An Inquiry into the Human Mind*
I.P.	*Essays on the Intellectual Powers of Man*
Orations	*The Philosophical Orations of Thomas Reid*, edited by D. D. Todd

WORKS BY ADAM SMITH:

LJ (A) and (B)	*Lectures on Jurisprudence*
TMS	*The Theory of Moral Sentiments*
WN	*An Inquiry into the Nature and Causes of the Wealth of Nations*

MISCELLANEOUS:

AUL   Aberdeen University Library, Aberdeen, Scotland

Introduction

by Knud Haakonssen

1. Reid's Reputation

Thomas Reid spent most of his long life in church and university, holding no significant public office and, other than family life, engaging in few activities that were not related directly or indirectly to his position as a minister of the Church of Scotland and subsequently as a university teacher at Aberdeen and Glasgow. In modern terms, he was a purely professional man, though this label is misleading when dealing with men of the Enlightenment like Reid. First, it is characteristic of the Enlightenment to resist any simple correlation between specialization of knowledge and of occupation. Second, in following such professions as preaching and teaching, the man of the Enlightenment was, in Scotland, understood to be fulfilling a public office—not just in the trivial sense of an office controlled by the public authorities, but in the moral sense of one contributing to the formation of proper citizens.

Both points are important for an understanding of Reid. Although the longest and most distinguished part of his career was as professor of moral philosophy, the moral philosophy he professed was only part of a wider concern with human knowledge, aimed as much at the formation of character as at the imparting of knowledge. Indeed, the latter was seen as the most valuable means to the former. For a proper appreciation of Reid's moral philosophy, that philosophy must therefore be set in its wider intellectual and historical context, and this introduction attempts to provide that setting.

This is all the more necessary because the common picture of Reid tends to preclude such a wider perspective. In many histories of philosophy, as well as in more specialized discussions, Reid is seen as a primarily negative or critical philosopher who only developed a philosophy of his own to the extent required by his refutation of Humean skepticism.[1] If we concentrate on Reid's published works, we

---

[1] An associated problem is the tendency to see Reid as the founder of Common Sense philosophy in reaction to Hume. This error has been thoroughly corrected in David F. Norton's study of the development of Common Sense theory from the Moral Sense tradition of Shaftesbury through Hutcheson, Butler, Turnbull, Hume, and Kames: "From Moral Sense to Common Sense" (1966). (Full bibliographic details for all authorities cited are provided in the Bibliographic Index.)

can come to understand in part how this image was formed, especially because it was already present in the first and very influential
general presentation of Reid's philosophy by his disciple Dugald
Stewart.[2] However, Reid's Common Sense philosophy, in its narrow
context as an answer to Hume's skepticism, though important, is only
part of a wider intellectual framework, access to which is facilitated
by Reid's considerable manuscript *Nachlass*. Through this and other
contemporary sources, we can place Reid in his contemporary philosophical scene more justly than the debate on Humean skepticism
would allow and so perhaps also come to a more adequate appreciation of the latter. There are two areas in particular where Reid's manuscripts significantly alter his conventional image: natural philosophy
or the sciences, and moral philosophy in the sense of practical or normative ethics. Reid was both an epistemologist exploring the possibility of knowledge and a natural and moral philosopher contributing
to the general stock of knowledge even though, measured by some
absolute standard of originality and importance, his contribution in
the former role was far more significant than in the latter. There is,
however, reason to believe that Reid's self-assessment was different
and not entirely reflected in what he chose to publish. Certainly if our
concern is with historical intelligibility—perhaps as a precondition for
the assessment of argumentative originality and force—then the
whole of Reid's oeuvre must interest us.

As far as natural philosophy and the accompanying mathematics
are concerned, an important recent study has shown that these were
among Reid's earliest intellectual pursuits and a lifelong concern of
his. Although Reid was neither a scientist nor a mathematician of the
first rank, his achievement was of a high order and well beyond that
of the amateur dabbler.[3] This concern grew not merely from the requirements of his teaching, but also out of his belief that it was the
philosopher's task to explore the providential order of creation in all
its aspects. We shall discuss this theological framework for Reid's
thought briefly below.

While the manuscripts clearly show that Reid's interest in natural
philosophy dates back to his student days, the situation regarding
moral philosophy is very different. We can document that from the
age of about twenty-six or twenty-seven Reid had some interest in
moral epistemology and psychology and in metaphysical problems
with moral implications, especially the moral implications of the

[2] Dugald Stewart, *Account of the Life and Writings of Thomas Reid* (first published in
1803). Stewart's one-sided view of Reid has been corrected by Paul Wood, "The Hagiography of Common Sense" (1985).
[3] See Paul Wood's valuable "Thomas Reid, Natural Philosopher" (1984).

problem of free will, but apart from an obvious interest in political theory there is little evidence that before 1764, when as professor of moral philosophy at Glasgow University he began to give the course that is reconstructed below, he took more than a cursory interest in what he then called "practical ethics." The lectures and papers he wrote over the next five or six years, supplemented with a few later papers, constitute a full system of practical ethics, which is here presented for the first time.

2. Reid's Life and Career

Student and Minister

THOMAS REID was born on 27 April 1710, the son of the minister of Strachan in Kincardineshire.[1] Through his mother he was related to the Gregorys, well-known mathematicians and scientists. From the Kincardine parish school and Aberdeen Grammar School he entered Marischal College in Aberdeen in 1722, where he undertook the four-year arts course that generally preceded the professional courses, in Reid's case theology. He completed his studies in 1731 and was then admitted to the ministry of the Church of Scotland. After a brief spell as presbytery clerk, he became the librarian at Marischal College from 1733 to 1736 and afterward took a lengthy tour of England. On his return to Scotland in 1737, Aberdeen's senior university, King's College, presented Reid to the ministry of New Machar, then in their gift, where he spent the next fourteen years until called to King's College as regent in 1751. Reid married his cousin Elizabeth Reid in 1740.[2]

Any attempt to trace the development of Reid's intellect and character during the first half of his life is frustrated by a dearth of sources, but we know enough to identify him as a type and to add some distinguishing characteristics. In general, Thomas Reid resembles the members of the slightly younger clerical circle remembered as "the Moderate Literati" of Edinburgh—namely, Hugh Blair, John Home, William Robertson, Adam Ferguson, and Alexander Carlyle.[3] Although he was an Aberdonian, Reid's background, like theirs, was

[1] Reid's life has not been well explored until recently. Apart from brief notices, the first biography of Reid was an anonymous pamphlet published in the year of his death, *Sketch of the Character of the Late Thomas Reid. . . .* The next and by far the most influential biography was D. Stewart's *Account.* A. Campbell Fraser's *Thomas Reid* (1898) contained some new material, but was on similar lines. The first really scholarly examination of Reid's life was Wood's "Thomas Reid, Natural Philosopher," part 1, to which I am greatly indebted for many of the external circumstances of Reid's life.

[2] See Wood, "Thomas Reid," pp. 38–58, and the sources referred to there.

[3] This group has recently been the subject of one of the finest general studies of the Scottish Enlightenment, Richard Sher's *Church and University in the Scottish Enlightenment: The Moderate Literati of Edinburgh* (1985).

Whig and Presbyterian, not Jacobite and Episcopalian, and his moral and intellectual outlook was apparently decisively influenced by a university training broadly similar to theirs. At Edinburgh the arts curriculum had been modernized in 1708 by the appointment of specialist professors in separate subjects, but Marischal College, like King's College, retained the regent system, under which first-year students were taught by one specialist professor of Greek, Latin, and Hebrew and for the remaining three years had one teacher, a regent, in all arts subjects: logic, history of natural philosophy, ethics, metaphysics, and particular sciences. In addition, the professor of mathematics taught elementary arithmetic and geometry in the first two years.[4] Even so, Marischal College had undergone a considerable intellectual renewal just before Reid's arrival. All the staff, except the principal, were recent appointees following a purge of the college for suspected Jacobite sympathies in the 1715 uprising.[5]

Of the young and newly recruited teachers, the most important here is George Turnbull, whose second and last regency (1723–26) included Reid as a pupil.[6] Turnbull's central message to his class, as set out in his graduation orations, was a providential naturalism according to which a scientific analysis of the phenomena of this world would show the hand of Providence in the regularities exhibited. The most complete example of this was Newtonian physics, but as Newton himself had pointed out, the method could and should be extended from physical phenomena to moral phenomena. Thus, contrary to the Marischal curriculum, natural philosophy would become an introduction to and an exemplar for moral philosophy, the completion of which was natural theology. Empirical investigation of the nature of the world and especially of man's mental and moral faculties would show that there are things that are inherently good and bad, and the supreme will disclosed by the providential order of the world would put man under a moral obligation to follow the laws of nature. The natural jurisprudence that Turnbull presumably outlined to his students on this basis shows only slightly in a few theses at the end of his graduation oration for Reid's class in 1726, from which the graduands were to choose their topics of disputation: (1) the right to do or not to do something derives as much from God as the similar obligation to do or not to do something—that is, there are purely permissive laws of nature; (2) all rights over things and over people de-

---

[4] See Wood, "Thomas Reid," p. 59.   [5] Ibid., pp. 38–39.

[6] In fact, Turnbull absented himself from his class for the first months of Reid's final year in order to study with Jean Barbeyrac in Groningen. The class may have been taught by Robert Duncan, also Barbeyrac's student. See M. A. Stewart, "George Turnbull and Educational Reform" (1987), p. 97.

rive from God; (3) man is created for society and (in the similar theses
for 1723) the state of nature is not completely lawless; (4) no natural
rights can be contractually alienated, and in cases of the utmost necessity the individual has a right to the property of others; (5) without
divine grace no man can be good, pious, and upright.[7] Although
these theses do not establish Turnbull's precise jurisprudential line at
the time, it is very likely that they reflect his teaching and are therefore evidence that Reid was introduced by Turnbull to some central
issues in contemporary natural law, especially the debate about voluntarist versus realist bases for ethics. It is not clear how far Turnbull
spelled out the theologico-political implications of his views, but it
must soon have become evident to his students that, if the laws of
morals could be arrived at independently of dogmatically enshrined
religion, there was no justification for clerical authoritarianism and
that the proper role of the preacher was that of a teacher of morals.[8]
Further, if independent moral character could be formed by a liberal
education, then this was the proper foundation of the virtues of citi-
zenship and, by extension, of a political system of liberty. In short,
although full documentation is impossible, it seems reasonable to assume that from Turnbull Reid not only learned a providential naturalism, with its methodological and pedagogical implications, but also
acquired some idea of modern natural jurisprudence, a polite
Shaftesburian Stoicism and a humanism with "republican" or Commonwealth leanings, though one in which education in a more or less
formal sense had become the primary means to a full and active citi-
zenship.

  [7] See Turnbull, *Theses academicae de pulcherrima mundi cum materialis tum rationalis constitutione* (1726), esp. p. 12; and idem, *Theses philosophicae de scientiae naturalis cum philosophia morali conjunctione* (1723). Later works of Turnbull's that are relevant here are
The Principles of Moral (and Christian) Philosophy (1740–41), which derives from his lectures in Aberdeen; *Observations upon Liberal Education* (1740); and his translation of
Heineccius, *Elementa juris naturae et gentium*, which is used extensively in the Commentary below. Turnbull also wrote on theology and art. On Turnbull, see James McCosh,
Scottish Philosophy (1966), pp. 95–106; David Norton, *David Hume: Common-Sense Moralist, Sceptical Metaphysician* (1982), pp. 152–173; M. A. Stewart, "Berkeley and the Rankenian Club" (1985), esp. pp. 31–34; idem, "George Turnbull and Educational Reform"; J. C. Stewart-Robertson, "The Well-Principled Savage, or the Child of the
Scottish Enlightenment" (1981); and K. A. B. Mackinnon, "George Turnbull's Common Sense Jurisprudence" (1987).
  [8] Elements of this general outlook were already current at Marischal. Shaftesbury's
ideas had been introduced a couple of years before Turnbull's arrival by David Verner
(see M. A. Stewart, "Berkeley and the Rankenian Club," p. 32); Turnbull corresponded
with Robert Molesworth, and in 1728 Colin Maclaurin, the professor of mathematics,
was in touch with an old Glaswegian fellow student, Francis Hutcheson, who was then
(in the 1720s) associated with the Molesworth circle in Dublin (M. A. Stewart, "George
Turnbull").

We know little of the moral philosophical influences to which Reid was exposed for the next twenty-odd years, after his studies with Turnbull, or of Reid's reactions to them, and we know almost nothing of his theological training. But we do know that in the winter of 1736–37 he was active in a philosophical club that, according to his brief minutes, discussed theories of human nature (apparently John Locke's and Francis Hutcheson's), free will, self-love and benevolence, the passions (probably Hutcheson's theory), and, most significant here, the divine government of moral agents through law.[9] There is further evidence of Reid's interest in these topics at this time, especially an eight-page "Abstract of Dr. Clarke's Notion concerning Liberty, Collected from his Papers upon that Subject Published Ao. 1717."[10] After visiting England in 1736–37, Reid wrote to an unknown host in London, discussing the passions, and from 1738 we have notes on Peter Browne's *The Procedure, Extent, and Limits of the Human Understanding.*[11]

Much more important than any of this is a twenty-page abstract of Joseph Butler's *Analogy of Religion* dated November 1738.[12] In it Reid follows Butler's text and its emphases without offering any comments of his own, but in view of the many similarities between the two thinkers' moral philosophy, and considering Reid's high regard for Butler throughout his life, this early and close reading of the *Analogy* indicates a formative influence.[13] At the most general level, Butler reinforced the providential naturalism to which Reid would have been introduced by Turnbull. At the same time, Butler clearly practiced the idea that the teaching of moral philosophy should aim primarily

[9] See 2131/6/1/17. Unless otherwise noted, all such references to Reid's manuscripts are to the manuscripts in the Birkwood Collection at Aberdeen University Library. The first four digits (2131) are common to all the Reid manuscripts in that collection and will be omitted hereafter. Manuscripts from other collections are referred to by library and number in the usual manner. The relevant minute referred to here is quoted in the Commentary, p. 306 n. 5.

[10] 3/II/8. See also 6/1/34–35 concerning free will. Also relevant are some seven pages of notes on the Clarke-Leibniz correspondence (3/II/7). Neither of these manuscripts is dated, but the type of paper and the handwriting both point clearly to the 1730s. The reference is Clarke's *Collection of Papers, which Passed between . . . Mr. Leibnitz, and Dr. Clarke in the Years 1715 and 1716* (1717).

[11] See 3/III/7 and AUL (Aberdeen University Library) MS. 3061/10,1r–2v.

[12] AUL MS. 3061/10,3r–12v. Apparently anticipating a later need to use the abstract, Reid paginated it separately from the surrounding notes in the manuscript.

[13] For Reid's later appreciation of Butler, see also n. 39 below. As late as 22 August 1781, Reid was "revising Butler's Analogy" and discussing problems of probability arising from the introduction to the work (AUL MS. 3061/12,2r). For Reid, both analogical and probable reasoning remained important topics; see esp. *Inquiry into the Human Mind* (1764), p. 201b ff., and *Essays on the Intellectual Powers of Man* (hereafter I.P.), I.iv and VII.

at inculcating morals and that theorizing about morals had little relevance to practice because the ordinary person's moral faculty sufficed for the latter. The purpose of moral theory was mainly to stave off moral skepticism.[14] As we shall see, all of this remained basic both to Reid and to many other moralists of the time. More distinctly important to Reid was Butler's criticism of the moral skeptics for reducing morals to self-interest and of Hutcheson for reducing it to benevolence. According to Butler, in order to understand the complexity of morals we must acknowledge the variety of "internal principles" in human nature, which experience reveals. First there are the "particular passions, appetites and affections"; second, there is the "general affection or principle of self-love," which moralists have not commonly distinguished from the former; third, there is the principle of benevolence; and fourth, there is conscience, under whose authority the other principles stand.[15] It is difficult to avoid the impression that this pluralistic theory had a significant influence on Reid's account, many years later, of the hierarchy of active powers, and there is nothing closer to his idea of the moral faculty than Butler's notion of conscience.[16] It should also be noted that in his abstract of the *Analogy* Reid pays attention to the argument in the appended dissertation "Of Personal Identity"—namely, that personal identity is presupposed in the operations of consciousness and not constituted by the latter.[17] If this argument were applied to those who try to disprove personal identity, it would be a form of the reflexivity or self-refuting argumentation that we shall meet in Reid below, and it is Butler who may have inspired Reid to think along those lines.[18]

The letter to Reid's London host, mentioned above, also introduced his friend David Fordyce, who had taken the Arts and Divinity

---

[14] These aspects of Butler are perhaps clearer in his *Sermons* than in the *Analogy* (in Butler, *Works*). I do not know of any direct evidence that Reid read the *Sermons* (the *Analogy* was better known throughout the eighteenth century), but D. Stewart says so (*Account*, p. 318) and in view of his high regard for Butler it is reasonable.

[15] The *locus classicus* for conscience is Butler's dissertation II, "Of the Nature of Virtue," which is appended to the *Analogy* and was particularly valued by Reid, according to D. Stewart (*Account*, p. 318). The other principles are treated more distinctly in Butler's *Sermons* (nos. 1, 2, 3, and 11), but see also the *Analogy* (*Works*, 1:5).

[16] For brief but perceptive remarks on the relationship between Butler and Reid, see J. B. Schneewind, *Sidgwick's Ethics and Victorian Moral Philosophy* (1977), pp. 63–74; and for Butler's notion of conscience, see idem, "The Use of Autonomy in Ethical Theory" (1986).

[17] See dissertation I, "Of Personal Identity," in the *Analogy*.

[18] For Butler's direct influence on Reid's theory of personal identity, see I.P., pp. 350a–353a, and Terence Penelhum, *Butler* (1985), pp. 132–133. Penelhum's is the most important modern discussion of Butler's philosophy.

courses at Marischal a couple of years after Reid. The trip on which Fordyce carried Reid's letter, presumably in 1737, probably also took him for a time to Northampton Academy, which under Philip Doddridge was one of the notable dissenting academies.[19] Thus, when Fordyce eventually returned to Aberdeen as regent at Marischal in 1742, he strengthened the already significant links between the liberal Presbyterian intellectuals there and various groups of English dissenters and set about giving an account of their common educational ideas in his *Dialogues concerning Education* (1745) and his later writings.

From the end of the period under consideration we find two further indications of Reid's interest in moral philosophy. His first publication, "An Essay on Quantity," was presented to the Royal Society in 1748 and appeared in its Transactions for that year.[20] It contains a brief criticism of Hutcheson's "Attempt to introduce a Mathematical Calculation in Subjects of Morality" and seems to stem from his critical reading of Hutcheson's *Inquiry* prior to 1738.[21] As far as I know, this is the only concrete evidence that Reid in this entire period read anything directly concerned with the central problems peculiar to natural jurisprudence, and there is no suggestion that he took any interest in these.[22]

Finally we have two-and-a-half pages of reading notes from Arrian's arrangement of Epictetus, probably made in 1750, which confirm Reid's familiarity with ancient Stoicism. In view of the eighteenth-century tendency to link Socrates and Stoicism and to adapt both to the framework of rational Christianity, it is of interest that the notes on Epictetus are followed by a few lines on Xenophon's

[19] See Peter Jones, "The Polite Academy and the Presbyterians, 1720–1770." Reid's letter, though undated, seems to have been written soon after his return from England in 1737, which makes this the most likely date for Fordyce's own departure for England (see ibid., p. 161). On Fordyce, see also the literature referred to in ibid., p. 177 n. 9; McCosh, *Scottish Philosophy*, pp. 106–107; Stewart-Robertson, "The Well-Principled Savage"; W. H. G. Armytage, "David Fordyce: A Neglected Thinker" (1956); Fordyce's main works are *Dialogues Concerning Education* (1745), I–II, and *Elements of Moral Philosophy* (1748); the latter will be encountered in the Commentary below.

[20] Reprinted in Reid, *Philosophical Works* (hereafter *Works*), pp. 715–719.

[21] The quotation is from the subtitle of the first edition of Hutcheson's *Inquiry*. Hutcheson removed the mathematical material from the fourth edition of 1738. Wood dates the first of two early sketches of Reid's "Essay" to the 1730s on grounds of orthography and paper size (5/1/20; Wood, "Thomas Reid," pp. 55–56). The second manuscript (5/1/22), also undated, is entitled, "Essay Concerning the Object of Mathematics occasioned by reading a piece of Mr. Hutchesons where Virtue is measured by simple & Compound Ratios."

[22] I refer to section VII of Reid's *Inquiry into the Human Mind* (hereafter H.M.), entitled "A Deduction of some Complex moral Ideas, viz of Obligation, and Right, Perfect, Imperfect, and External, Alienable, and Unalienable, from this moral Sense."

defense of Socrates's religion as being in accordance with accepted doctrine.[23]

As far as we can tell from the meager sources, Reid's discharge of his ministry at New Machar was fully congruent with the moral and theological outlook outlined above. The description of his sermons indicates that they were lectures on morals rather than a preaching of the faith. The suggestion of a morality-centered rational Christianity is further strengthened by his use of the sermons of Samuel Clarke, John Tillotson, and John Evans, the Dissenter. As Paul Wood says, quoting Ramsay of Ochtertyre's claim that "a very great majority of northern ministers were the earliest and steadiest supporters of the moderate party":

> Although Reid's party affiliations within the Kirk at this time are unknown, his theology is perhaps best characterised as that of the Moderates. That is, he too probably emphasised the moral and practical aspects of Christianity, the use of reason in the examination and defence of the fundamentals of faith, and the toleration of doctrinal differences. . . . As far as can be determined, Reid's religious outlook was, therefore, similar to that of the "Neu lights and Preachers-legall," the generation of Moderate clergy trained at Edinburgh under Professor William Hamilton which included Patrick Cuming, William Leechman, James Oswald, Robert Wallace, and William and George Wishart.[24]

This view is also supported by Reid's willingness to receive his charge through patronage. Since its reintroduction by law in 1712, the patronage system had in a number of cases become a vehicle for the appointment of what might be called intellectuals to the ministry of the Kirk, often against the wishes of presbyteries and parishioners, and this was a most important precondition for the formation of the Moderate party in the Kirk.[25] The exercise by King's College of its right of patronage was very unpopular; Reid was received with hostility and physical violence at New Machar. However, his intellectualism was sufficiently meliorated by his moral character to make him at last eminently acceptable to his flock.[26]

This sums up Reid's involvement with moral philosophical ideas

---

[23] See 3/11/4. Concerning Reid's later use of Epictetus and Arrian, see the Commentary below at p. 305 n. 3, pp. 307–308 n. 10, and esp. p. 377 n. 2. The notes on Xenophon, which are dated September 1750 and are clearly later than those on Epictetus, concern "Memorabilium Lib. 5," generally known as the *Oeconomicus*.

[24] Wood, "Thomas Reid," pp. 48–49. The quotation from Ramsay is from *Scotland and Scotsmen*, 1:302. Concerning the transition from older to younger Moderates, see Sher, *Church and University*, pp. 152ff.

[25] Sher, *Church and University*, pp. 45–64.   [26] Wood, "Thomas Reid," pp. 47–48.

directly relevant to what is here called "practical ethics," before his removal to King's College in 1751. Moral philosophy was plainly not his main interest; his primary concern was with a range of mathematical and scientific problems, especially in astronomy, and with problems of epistemology and the philosophy of mind. He was clearly engaged with the theory of ideas, where he seems to have taken a Lockean rather than a Berkeleian line.[27] There is also in the manuscripts a discussion of the self which, as Paul Wood points out, is important for two reasons: it provides a slight indication that Reid took any interest in Hume at this stage, and it foreshadows the form of argumentation so characteristic of his later philosophy—namely, that certain basic notions, such as "self," are necessarily presupposed in all cognition.[28]

Regent at King's College, Aberdeen

In 1751 Reid succeeded Alexander Rait as regent at King's College. He took over Rait's class from its third year to the completion of the course in 1753 and subsequently completed three full regencies and two years of a fourth before moving to Glasgow in 1764. Reid's life in Aberdeen was a busy one, dominated by his involvement in the business of his college. Apart from teaching, he was active in the administration of King's, serving on several committees, apparently looking after the college finances during part of the period, and on several occasions representing the college in the General Assembly of the Church of Scotland. He was involved in planning an amalgamation of the two Aberdeen colleges, which in the end came to nothing.[29] Most significant, Reid took part in important educational reforms at King's College that, as we shall see, tell us something about the structure of his teaching.

Most of Reid's activities outside King's College were intellectual in character, and most of his associates had links with either King's College or Marischal College. Of particular importance is the Aberdeen Philosophical Society, better known as the Wise Club, which he helped to found in 1758. Among its first members were his kinsman John Gregory; his friend and fellow student of Newton John Stewart; another close friend, the physician David Skene; a minister, Robert Trail; and another minister and future principal of Marischal College, the philosopher George Campbell.[30] To this society, soon joined

[27] Ibid., p. 52.
[28] See 6/1/18 and Wood, "Thomas Reid," p. 53. See nn. 17 and 18 above.
[29] Wood, "Thomas Reid," pp. 65–66.
[30] See ibid., pp. 86–87 and W. R. Humphries, "The First Aberdeen Philosophical Society" (1938).

by, among others, Alexander Gerard and James Beattie, Reid presented many of the ideas that he subsequently published. He was also, though more sporadically, involved in agricultural improvement through the Gordon's Mill Farming Club, founded in 1758, an interest that he was later to share with his noble patrons, Lords Deskford and Kames.[31]

Reid's recent biographer has meticulously traced the fragmentary evidence of the circles in which Reid moved and shown how Reid during his thirteen years at King's College became "an established member of the landed, professional and commercial élite of Aberdeen,"[32] one who could discuss mathematics and science with the Gregorys and Skenes, talk farm improvement with the landed gentry and nobility, and share with them all a general assumption about man as a "progressive," educable species. Reid was an unprejudiced, "liberal" man who moved freely among Episcopalians and Quakers,[33] a man with social concerns and compassion; a sociable man who could talk to children while observing their minds; a politic though not political man with a realistic appreciation of the role of patronage in the social and intellectual life of Scotland, as his own appointment to the chair at Glasgow would show; but first and last a man of intellect, not only in the obvious sense that he was an intellectual and an academic, but in the sense that for him an understanding of the human intellect was the key to understanding all human activity.

We have two major sources for Reid's intellectual development during these thirteen years, the graduation *Orations* that he delivered at the conclusion of each of his regencies in 1753, 1756, 1759, and 1762, and the *Inquiry*, which was published in his last year in Aberdeen and was the main fruit of his work there. Together with a variety of minor sources they show that it was in Aberdeen that Reid's general philosophical outlook, his epistemology and metaphysics,

[31] Wood, "Thomas Reid," pp. 116–119.
[32] Ibid., p. 127.
[33] Ibid., pp. 120–123. Reid's distance, in Aberdeen, from the evangelical side of Scots Presbyterianism is evident in his reaction to the different atmosphere in Glasgow. Soon after his arrival in Glasgow he was writing to his friend Andrew Skene: "The common people here have a gloom in their countenance, which I am at a loss whether to ascribe to their religion or to the air and climate. There is certainly more of religion among the common people in this town than in Aberdeen; and, although it has a gloomy, enthusiastical cast, yet I think it makes them tame and sober." The following year David Skene received this outburst: "I think the common people here and in the neighbourhood greatly inferior to the common people with you. They are Boeotian in their understandings, fanatical in their religion, and clownish in their dress and manners. The clergy encourage this fanaticism too much, and find it the only way to popularity. I often hear a gospel here which you know nothing about; for you neither hear it from the pulpit, nor will you find it in the bible" (Reid, *Works*, p. 41b).

took shape and developed, while foreshadowing his approach to normative moral philosophy.

As regent at King's College, Reid had to take his students through the whole Arts curriculum, except first-year Greek, and thus he taught mathematics, natural history, natural and experimental philosophy, and "the Philosophy of the Human mind and the Sciences that Depend upon it" [i.e. moral philosophy],[34] which a curriculum regulation at King's College, of which he was co-author, described as follows:

> By the Philosophy of the Mind is Understood, An Account of the constitution of the Human mind, and of All its powers and Faculties, whether Sensitive, Intellectual or Moral. The Improvements they are capable off, and the Means of their Improvement; of the Mutual Influences of Body & Mind on each Other; and of the knowledge we may acquire of Other Minds and Particularly the Supreme Mind. And Sciences depending on the Philosophy of the Mind, Are Understood to be Logic, Rhetorick, The Laws of Nature and Nations, Politicks, Oeconomicks, the Fine Arts and Natural Religion.[35]

Reid's *Orations* show how far he followed this curriculum.

Undoubtedly the philosophy of mind, or pneumatology, was central to Reid's teaching of philosophy both at Aberdeen and at Glasgow and was seen as the foundation for all other sciences inasmuch as it demonstrated the possibility of knowledge. His approach to it was designed to show that the experimental and inductive method, which he saw as a coherent Baconian-Newtonian one, could be as successful in mental science as in physical science and led to the conclusion that the empirical method showed that while the physical and the mental worlds are equally law-governed they are inherently disanalogous. This was the basis of Reid's rapidly developing criticism of the theory of ideas and Humean skepticism. With this went the articulation of Reid's own philosophy, and especially the theory of the First Principles of Common Sense as the undeniable presuppositions for all knowledge and thus for all science, as we shall see below, where the theological framework of Reid's philosophy will also be touched on.

Reid's constant pursuit of natural philosophy and mathematics during these years has been definitively treated by Wood, but what about all those sciences, the moral sciences, directly dependent upon

[34] See AUL MS. I.43, p. 373, as quoted by Wood, "Thomas Reid," p. 62.
[35] Ibid., p. 395, as quoted by Wood, "Thomas Reid."

the philosophy of mind which are more directly relevant in the context of the present volume—"The Laws of Nature and Nations, Politicks, Oeconomicks"? In his *Orations* Reid mentions thinkers whom he thinks are particularly important for his students as they go out into the world, and there is not a single natural lawyer among them, nor any other evidence from this period that Reid had an interest in natural jurisprudence. As for "oeconomicks," we cannot be entirely sure what the term meant. In his Glasgow lectures he used the label "oeconomical jurisprudence" for the jurisprudence of the household (Greek: *oikos*). The clue is Reid's fondness for Xenophon's *Oikonomika*. As we saw above, he took notes from this work in September 1750, and in his first *Oration* he again refers to it.[36] This receives confirmation from the "scheme of a Course of Philosophy" from 1752, to be quoted below, which gives a brief outline of a kind of Xenophontian moral and material economy of the household, called oeconomicks.

Taking the *Orations* as probably a reliable guide to what was emphasized, Reid's Aberdeen lectures on morals concentrated on the basic principles of moral knowledge, on classical notions of virtue and duty, and on "Politicks."[37] We find the first indications of Reid's notion of First Principles in morals, which became central to his mature moral philosophy:

> what has been established first in mathematics, then in physics, . . . we hope will be established in other parts of philosophy as well, that is that they will be built in an orderly fashion upon common notions and phenomena. Nor have I . . . found any cause which would make this hope impossible. For there are axioms and phenomena in ethics and politics no less than in physics on which all right reasoning in these sciences depends.[38]

Morals is a matter of common sense, so already in 1753 Reid rejected any theorizing about morals:

> those, either among the ancient or the modern writers, who have tried to philosophise about the causes, origin, and nature of virtue . . . beyond the common sense of mankind in general, have made little progress and rather have rendered a subject, clear and obvious to the multitude, obscure and doubtful by their phil-

[36] See n. 23 above and Reid's *Philosophical Orations*, ed. Todd (hereafter *Orations*), pp. 936–937.

[37] Even these topics disappear from the 1759 and 1762 *Orations*, which may be an indication that they received less and less attention in Reid's course.

[38] *Orations*, pp. 955–956.

osophical subtleties. However, in this matter Joseph Butler . . .
has been seen to wrest the palm.[39]

Moral philosophy should rather seek to "strike the minds of men with
the importance of the subject matter and move their hearts."[40] Accordingly, we should turn first to Socrates, especially Xenophon's
Socrates, and second to Stoicism, especially Cicero's *De officiis*, both of
which apparently manifest the moral essence of Christianity.

Reid's brief remarks about politics are of great interest because
they foreshadow much of his later thought. The authors referred to
represent a constellation of republican, utopian, and constitutional
elements, to be unraveled at the end of the next section. Reid's views
on Hume's politics at this time (1753) remain a puzzle, but he makes
it clear that he himself saw politics as the explanation of means,
technē, rather than the determination of aims. Montesquieu emerges
as the greatest political genius of all time, the high priest of the British constitutionalism that finally checked Reid's utopian leanings:

> The chief figures of the Socratic school, Xenophon, Plato, and
> Aristotle, have also treated in a distinguished fashion politics, the
> most noble part of philosophy. . . . Among modern philosophers
> Machiavelli, Harrington, and David Hume, who have been
> taught by the experience of past ages and by the fate of the gov-
> ernments of both ancient and modern peoples, have made
> strong progress in this part of philosophy. The most illustrious
> leader, Montesquieu, however, is seen to outstrip all philoso-
> phers by a long distance; he is by nationality a Frenchman, by his
> character and zeal, a Briton. This man, instructed by the learn-
> ing of the whole of history, with the keenest judgment, with Attic
> wit, and with Laconic brevity and weight of diction, has set forth
> most lucidly the causes, principles, and effects of laws, morals
> and politics, from the first beginnings of human nature. From
> the British race in particular he has well deserved the name
> Briton because he has taught us, who are blessed with a form of

[39] Ibid., p. 937. Reid's Latin is ambiguous here ("In hac parte tamen Josephus Butle-
rus . . . palmam praeripere visus est" [*Philosophical Orations*, ed. Humphries, p. 14]) and
misled the translator into thinking that Reid was claiming preeminence for Butler
among the obscurantists (see *Orations*, p. 937n.). The point is that Butler has wrested
the palm from those who have gone beyond common sense. From his 1738 notes on
the *Analogy* (see n. 12 above), Reid's comments on Butler are consistently favorable,
and D. Stewart (*Account*, p. 318) confirms his high opinion of Butler. Even if Reid in
the early 1750s wavered in his assessment of Butler, it is quite unlikely that he would
single out the bishop in a graduation speech and hand him the palm for obscurantism
in morals—in Reid's eyes a fiercely competitive field.

[40] *Orations*, p. 935.

government surpassing all the governments which either history
has shown forth or imagination has contrived and who are exceedingly fortunate, to recognize our own blessings and to value
them highly.[41]

The curriculum regulation and the brief passages from the *Orations*
should be supplemented by the four-page "Scheme of a Course of
Philosophy," drawn up in 1752, for a fuller picture of Reid's moral
ideas in the 1750s.[42] After a two-page outline of the various branches
of natural philosophy and mathematics, Reid sketches "The other
Grand Branch of human Knowledge . . . the Mind," later called
pneumatology. The remainder of the manuscript is concerned with
natural theology, "Ethicks," "Oeconomicks," and "Politicks" and is of
interest for his eventual system of practical ethics, making clear the
providential framework of his moral thought and emphasizing a divine government by law:

> Next to the History of the Human Mind and its operations &
> Powers   The Knowledge of God and of his Natural Govern-
> ment. The Laws by which he Governs Inanimate Matter Brutes
> & Men. Our Capacity of Moral Government. The Indications of
> our being under it and of our State here being a State of Disci-
> pline & Improvement in order to another.
> The Natural Immortality of the Soul.[43]

Reid's remarks on morals show that he inculcated virtue in a setting
of household economy inspired by Xenophon, which he took to be
the proper foundation for civic life, and a concern with honor and a
hostility toward "Riches," as well as the classic alliance of politics,
arms, and rhetoric:

> Ethicks Oeconomicks Politicks. The Grand Instruments of Gov-
> ernm⟨ent⟩ Authority acquired by the opinion of Wisdom of
> Goodness of Right   Courage & Military Skill Eloquence.
> The Scale of Human Life.
> Some Things are attainable by all Men & make up the Duties
> of Low Life. To live virtuously keep a Good Conscience towards
> God and Man   to provide for ones family by some honest Em-
> ployment such as Husbandry Manual Arts Traffick. Those
> who exercise these Employments honestly & make profit by them

---

[41] Ibid., pp. 937–938. In the only other passage of direct political interest in the
Orations (the fourth, 1762), Reid illustrates the very wide meaning of "idea" as "the
offspring of the human mind" by these examples: "the *Utopia* of More, or the *Oceana*
of Harrington, the ideas of forms of government, are called ideas" (ibid., p. 982).
[42] See 8/v/1.   [43] 8/v/1,2r.

are usefull Members of Society   those who improve them by
new Inventions deserve Honour & Publick Reward.

2 There are Some professions that belong to Middle life & are
more Honoura⟨ble⟩   Publick Instructors in Religion or the Liberal Arts   Physicians Lawyers   Judges.

Thirdly there are some things still of a Higher Degree   the
Government of Large Bodies of Men by means of Political or
Military Skill or Eloquence.

The Prerogatives of human Nature or the Chief Excellencies
of one Man above another. The things which ought to be the
objects of Ambition which claim Honour & Respect from others
and make a Man great   usefull & raise him above the herd of
mankind may be I think reduced to these two Classes Power &
Virtue. Virtue is the principle of all real Excellence   Power its
instrument. Virtue is the Soul & Spirit   & Power the Organ by
which Virtue accomplishes its Ends and Purposes. . . . Power has
various principles that deserve to be particularly Enumerated 1
Riches which is in itself among the lowest & most despicable Species of Power. 2 Authority . . . 3 . . . Memory   Judgment
Wits   Good Manners . . . 4 Prudence . . . 5 Operative Habits
and . . . Skill in Arts   6 Many Virtues Such as Courage

Temperance   Meakness   Industry are likewise kinds of Power.

7 Eloquence.

Reid's final note foreshadows his later most important concept of offices in life:

A View of the Different Stations in Life & the Qualities of Body
& Mind & Fortune necessary to the proper Duties of them.[44]

Outside the classroom, Reid developed a number of his moral philosophical ideas in the Aberdeen Philosophical Society. The society's
activities were divided between the presentation of formal discourses
and the introduction of questions for discussion, and it is interesting
to note that, while Reid used his discourses to develop leading themes
of the *Inquiry*, his moral ideas were always aired in the form of questions. This custom, which he generally followed in the Glasgow College Literary Society, probably reflects the view that morals and politics are conversational matters. As he wrote to Andrew Skene years
later:

I wish often an evening with you, such as we have enjoyed in the
days of former times, to settle the important affairs of State and

44 8/v/1,2r–v.

Church, of Colleges and Corporations. I have found this the best
expedient to enable me to think of them without melancholy and
chagrin. And I think all that a man has to do in the world is to
keep his temper and to do his duty.[45]

In assessing Reid's utopian leanings, this attitude should be borne in
mind.

In his first paper to the new Aberdeen Society, on 22 November
1758, Reid introduced a question that remained central to his critical
concerns thirty years later in the *Active Powers*, "Whether justice be a
natural or artificial virtue?"[46] In 1759 he asked "Whether mankind
with regard to morals always was and is the same?" and in 1760 he
asked "Whether it is proper to educate children without instilling
principles into them of any kind whatsoever," topics that recurred
constantly in his later published work.[47] Clear evidence that Reid's
central ideas on moral judgment and human agency were already
taking final shape is provided by his discussions in 1761 and 1763:
"Whether moral character consists in affections, wherein the will is
not concerned; or in fixed habitual and constant purposes?" and
"Whether every action deserving moral approbation must be done
from a persuasion of its being morally good?"[48] Finally we see that
his demographic interests, apparent in the lectures below, were being
formulated at this time: "Whether by the encouragement of proper
laws the number of births in Great Britain might not be nearly dou-
bled or at least greatly increased?"[49]

Reid's first major publication, *Inquiry into the Human Mind, on the
Principles of Common Sense* (1764),[50] is a work on epistemology and

[45] Reid to Andrew Skene, 30 December 1765, in Reid, *Works*, p. 43b. The fullest list
of the society's "questions and discourses" during the period of his membership is provided by Wood, "Thomas Reid," appendixes I and II.

[46] In *Essays on the Active Powers of Man* (hereafter A.P.), Reid says that the chapter
with that title, together with the three other chapters that conclude the book, were in
substance "wrote long ago, and read in a literary society" (p. 645b). An earlier version,
perhaps very close to the original paper, is in the Birkwood Collection (6/I/9).

[47] See, e.g., H.M., pp. 200b–201a; I.P., pp. 439b–441a; A.P., pp. 529b–530b, 578a–
579a, 595a–596b. See Stewart-Robertson, "The Well-Principled Savage," which provides a useful discussion of the theory of education developed by Turnbull, Fordyce,
and Reid.

[48] The first of these was put five years later to the Glasgow Literary Society, and
Reid's treatment of it at some stage is in 2/II/13 and 6/I/12 while his answer to the latter,
at some stage before A.P., may be found in 2/II/12.

[49] See Reid's manuscript below, pp. 225ff. It may be Reid's discussion paper that is
preserved as 2/11/17.

[50] For the history of its composition and publication, see Wood, "Thomas Reid," pp.
95–98, and his "David Hume on Thomas Reid's *An Inquiry into the Human Mind, on the
Principles of Common Sense*: a new letter to Hugh Blair from July 1762" (1986).

especially on sensation. It is also important for an understanding of his moral thought because it fixes the theological framework and associated methodological principles for philosophy in general and, more particularly, presents the refutation of epistemological skepticism as fundamental to the criticism of moral skepticism, but these topics are best dealt with in the systematic exposition of Reid's philosophy in part 3 below.

We may tentatively conclude that, by the time Reid left for Glasgow in 1764 many of the basic features of his moral thought were more or less formed and in varying degrees articulated. They included the metaphysical and theological foundations for morals, the methodological principles by which philosophical inquiry in general should be conducted, the dependence of the moral sciences upon the philosophy of mind, the notions of moral agency and moral judgment, the refutation of moral skepticism as represented by Hume, a view of the teaching of moral philosophy as the practical inculcation of morals, a concern with the connection between moral education and the proper conduct of civic life understood in a Christian-Stoic perspective, and an interest in classical republican, utopian, and constitutional writers. When seen against the background of moral thought during the preceding 150 years, the one great and surprising omission is natural jurisprudence. There is barely a trace of interest in, and certainly no evidence of work on, any topic in natural law. This was soon to be changed.

In Glasgow

The Glasgow chair of moral philosophy, which Thomas Reid took up in the autumn of 1764, had achieved a more than national reputation through three of its previous four occupants—Gershom Carmichael, Francis Hutcheson, and Adam Smith—but Reid himself was no small contributor to its distinction. Reid's *Inquiry* had been widely noticed, favorably on the whole, and went through four editions in his lifetime. His later *Intellectual Powers* and *Active Powers* not only confirmed Reid's reputation but ensured that he would be seen as the founder of a school.

It was, however, neither Reid's proven ability nor the fact that he was by far the strongest candidate, that alone secured him the Glasgow chair.[51] As usual in eighteenth-century Scotland, Reid also needed patronage—in his case that of Lords Deskford and Kames. One of his opponents within the university was apparently the pro-

---

[51] For the story of Reid's appointment, see Wood, "Thomas Reid," pp. 130–133.

fessor of law, John Millar, a disciple of Adam Smith and a former protégé of Kames.[52] There seems to be no evidence that Millar's opposition was based on intellectual grounds, though it may have been. In metaphysics, where Reid had so recently shown his hand, Millar was in the opposite camp, being a devotee of "the true old Humean philosophy," and in later years they certainly did dispute about this.[53] In politics they were both liberal Whigs, but the philosophical bases for their political positions were utterly incompatible.[54]

If Reid's new colleagues were less than unanimous in electing him they seem on the whole to have received him well, and he was soon heavily involved in the administration of the university, serving on committees, as quaestor of the library, as vice-rector appointed by Edmund Burke when he was rector in 1784–85, and twice as the university's representative to the General Assembly of the Church of Scotland.[55] However, this aspect of Reid's life was badly marred by his unavoidable involvement in the internal squabbles of the faculty, which plagued the university for much of the century and reached new heights during Reid's time in office. It was a struggle for administrative control between the university's two main bodies, the Senate and the Faculty, essentially about the extent of the principal's power.[56] Though Reid generally supported Principal Leechman's main opponent, the professor of natural philosophy John Anderson, he had none of Anderson's passion for academic politicking. For him the faculty was very much a learned and collegiate society in which administration was a necessary burden to be carried collectively.

This collegiate ideal was underpinned by Reid's notions of the methodological coherence of all the sciences, their common theological framework and joint social aims (the promotion of politeness and virtue), and their pedagogical coherence as determined by the natural progress of the mind. From the tangible world treated by natural philosophy, our understanding proceeds via the more elusive world of the mind, demanding maturer observational powers, to those abstract sciences dependent upon the philosophy of mind, including

---

[52] See W. C. Lehmann, *John Millar of Glasgow, 1735–1801* (1960), pp. 17–18; and I. S. Ross, *Lord Kames and the Scotland of His Day* (1972), pp. 95–97.

[53] See John Craig, "Account of the Life and Writings of John Millar" (1806), pp. lxi–lxii.

[54] This is provided that one accepts the interpretation of Millar suggested in K. Haakonssen, "John Millar and the Science of a Legislator" (1985); see also Duncan Forbes, " 'Scientific' Whiggism: Adam Smith and John Millar" (1953–54).

[55] See Wood, "Thomas Reid," p. 133.

[56] Ibid., pp. 134–140.

the most abstract of all, logic, which depends upon the ultimate mental faculty, namely, pure reason, to mature.[57]

In pursuit of these ideals and his multifarious scientific interests, Reid did not confine himself to the subjects he professed, but sought his friends among his scientific colleagues. He even attended Joseph Black's chemistry lectures in two successive years.[58] Perhaps his most important friendship was with Lord Kames, with whom he corresponded at length, mainly on metaphysical and scientific topics, and on whose estate he and his family spent many summer holidays. He also contributed an appendix entitled "A Brief Account of Aristotle's Logic" to Kames's *Sketches of the History of Man*, and he read Kames's works in manuscript.[59]

Reid remained attached to his old city, revisiting it periodically in the holidays, and he kept in touch with his friends there, both those who remained in Aberdeen and those who had left: John Stewart, the Skenes, John Gregory, and others.[60] As their numbers dwindled, by the early 1780s, his obvious gift for intellectual friendship was bestowed upon two much younger men: James Gregory and Dugald Stewart. James Gregory, John Gregory's son, was also a medical man, successively professor of the institutes of medicine and of the practice of medicine, in succession to William Cullen, at Edinburgh University.[61] Reid, who had lost his own three sons, took an almost paternal interest in the young Gregory, but the most striking feature of the relationship was Reid's ability to accept a younger man as his intellectual equal—proof not only of a notable generosity of mind and heart but also of a remarkably undiminished intellectual agility and passion for new ideas. In the case of Gregory, the result was a fruitful intellectual exchange ranging widely over scientific and philosophical matters, much of which can be followed in the surviving correspondence. Dugald Stewart, who studied with Reid in 1771–72, on the recommendation of his Edinburgh professor Adam Ferguson, himself an ardent admirer of Reid, similarly became a disciple and friend

[57] The connection between Reid's idea of mental development and his notion of the ideal academic curriculum is quite rightly stressed by Wood, ibid., e.g., pp. 63 and 194–196.

[58] Ibid., pp. 143–146.

[59] See Ross, *Lord Kames*, pp. 356–362; and "Unpublished Letters of Thomas Reid to Lord Kames, 1762–1782" (1965).

[60] See the correspondence printed in Reid, *Works*. Concerning David Skene, see also Alexander Thomson, *Biographical Sketch of David Skene* (1859), esp. p. 7.

[61] For James Gregory, see Michael Barfoot's pioneering study "James Gregory (1753–1821) and Scottish Scientific Metaphysics, 1750–1800" (1983), which includes material on Reid.

and more than anyone created the image of a Common Sense school of Scottish philosophy and spread its fame abroad, especially to France and to North America. But Stewart also created the image of Reid as a rather narrow philosopher's philosopher, a distortion that has only recently begun to be corrected.[62]

As in Aberdeen, a significant factor in Reid's life was the local learned society, the Glasgow College Literary Society.[63] Although the society had its basis in the university, it included some nonacademic members and, as modern research has shown, was very alert to the practical problems of the day, especially those of a growing commercial center. Reid himself took an interest in matters of economic policy. In 1767 he introduced the question "What are the most proper means to be used by a state in order to prevent the necessarys of life from rising to too high a price?" and in 1778 he contributed to the debate about the Corn Laws in a paper providing balanced support for the merchants against the landed interest in the prohibition of the storing of imported corn: "Whether the storing or warehousing foreign grain or meal for exportation be highly prejudicial to the interest of this country and whether it ought to be prevented if possible?"[64] Later in the same year he preempted parts of Jeremy Bentham's argument in the *Defence of Usury*: "Whether it is proper that the interest of money should be regulated by law in cases where the parties have contracted?"[65] Finally, in an undated paper, Reid took up an issue on which he touches below in the traditional natural law framework: "What are the bad consequences of the diminution of our coin by wearing?"[66] These papers belong with the section on "Police" in Reid's lectures on politics.

[62] Stewart's perception of his relations with Reid can be gauged from his *Account*; see also John Veitch, "A Memoir of Dugald Stewart" (1858), ch. 1, and esp. Wood, "Hagiography of Common Sense." For Ferguson's appreciation of Reid, see D. Stewart, *Account*, p. 261, and for the philosophical connection, D. Kettler, *The Social and Political Thought of Adam Ferguson* (1965), ch. 5.

[63] Wood, "Thomas Reid," pp. 175–178. Wood lists such questions and discourse titles of Reid's as have been preserved in the now patchy records of the Literary Society (see ibid., appendix III).

[64] There is a useful brief analysis of this paper (AUL MS. 3061/3) and its background in Wood, "Thomas Reid," pp. 178–181. Reid himself described his effort to Lord Kames: "I have read three Discourses this Winter in our Society. One upon a Clause of the last Corn Act about Warehousing Grain, a Clause which some meetings of the Landed Gentlemen have resolved to be prejudicial to the Country, I think unjustly" (Ross, ed., "Unpublished Letters," pp. 31–32).

[65] AUL MS. 3061/5. See Reid's comments on Bentham, ten years later, in a letter to James Gregory (Reid, *Works*, p. 73a), quoted in the Introduction below, p. 65 n. 82.

[66] See Reid's manuscript below, pp. 165–166. Reid's fascination with money and especially with coinage is also seen in his reproduction of tables from the well-known work on

Reid also discussed in the Glasgow Literary Society two topics of direct importance to practical ethics. On 1 April 1768 he introduced the question "Whether the supposition of a tacit contract at the beginning of societies is well founded?" The paper printed in this book as Section XV is almost certainly either his paper on this occasion or closely related to it. On 28 November 1794 he gave a discourse that, while occasioned by contemporary political upheavals, is at the same time Reid's political testament: "Some Thoughts on the Utopian System." This important paper is printed below in Section XVIII.

This aside, Reid obviously used the Glasgow Literary Society to try out material for inclusion in his later books, as the titles and in some cases the surviving manuscripts show. In metaphysics he not only developed a number of central doctrines for the *Intellectual Powers*, but also argued strongly against Hume's skepticism and Joseph Priestley's materialism and necessitarianism. Of special relevance to "the theory of morals" are the following: the question on moral character, 1766, which he had introduced in Aberdeen in 1761;[67] "Whether moral obligations are discerned by reason or sentiment?" in 1769;[68] in 1776, "Discourse on active power," and the following year another well-known theme, "Have we any reason to ascribe active power to beings not endowed with understanding and will?"; and in 1778 "Discourse on the principles of action in the human mind."[69] Reid undoubtedly presented other discourses and questions on both moral theory and practical ethics, but there are significant gaps in the records of the society's proceedings. Apparently he gave his last discourse to the society, on the muscular motions of the human body,[70] on 27 November 1795, a year after his Utopia paper, showing that he retained his wide-ranging interests to the last.

Reid's concern with public matters, noted above, is also evident in his support for various humanitarian and social reform schemes. Wood has documented his generosity toward and practical support of charitable causes, the new Glasgow infirmary (he had also supported the plan for an Aberdeen infirmary), prison reform, and William Wilberforce's antislavery movement.[71] Though not unusual in a man of general liberal-Whig inclinations, these things are significant because they fit in not only with Reid's view of the proper role of a private man of upright character but also with his views on the

---

English coinage (4/III/22) by Martin Folkes, whom Reid had met on his English tour in 1736–37, and in the correspondence with Kames (Ross, ed., "Unpublished Letters," p. 27).

[67] See n. 48 above.   [68] See 8/III/4.
[69] See 2/I/8–10 and 2/I/12–13.   [70] AUL MS. 3061/2.
[71] Wood, "Thomas Reid," pp. 188–191.

proper aims of public policy. Basic material security, health, the reformation of the delinquent, and the treatment of all as moral agents are all ingredients in the notion of the public good that, as we shall see, stands at the center of Reid's political philosophy.

While Reid led a busy and useful life in many spheres, his chief concern remained the profession of philosophy, both in the classroom and in his writings. For sixteen years he gave the two traditional courses: from about 10 October until about 10 June[72] he lectured to the "public" class prescribed by the Arts curriculum, on Mondays to Fridays from 7:30 to 8:30 in the morning, and between 11:00 and 12:00 he "examined" part of the same class. From some time in November until probably the beginning of May[73] he gave a more advanced series of lectures (the "private" class), which was not prescribed for the Arts degree, three days a week from 12:00 noon to 1:00 P.M.[74]

We know little of the students to whom Reid delivered his lectures.

[72] We cannot be entirely sure of the termination of the course. In his *Statistical Account of the University of Glasgow*, Reid says, "The annual session for teaching, in the university, begins, in the ordinary *curriculum*, on the tenth of October; and ends, in some of the classes, about the middle of May, and in others continues to the tenth of June" (*Works*, p. 733b). It seems clear that in his first year at Glasgow, 1764–65, Reid completed his course on 17 May: the last dated lecture-notes are from this day and are on the topic that his course outline for Politics indicates as the last (4/III/10,2r and 4/III/1,2r). But it is unlikely that in subsequent years he would have been able to complete the course so early because he extended both the Pneumatology and Practical Ethics parts by more than a fortnight and began Politics only in early May. See Reid's remark in a letter of 8 May 1766: "My class will be over in less than a month . . ." (*Works*, p. 46b).

[73] These dates are doubtful. The quotation from the *Statistical Account* in n. 72 above continues: "The lectures, in all other branches, commence on the first of November, and end about the beginning of May." Whether these lectures included the private class of the professor of moral philosophy is unclear but seems likely. However, in the letter of 14 November 1764, quoted in n. 74 below, Reid says that his advanced class will begin in a week or two. If the same class is meant, two possible explanations for the discrepancy spring to mind: either Reid was running late in his first year in Glasgow, or the timetable had changed between 1764 (the letter) and 1794 (the year Reid probably wrote the *Statistical Account*). As far as I know, the only evidence that Reid ended his advanced class in early May is the passage quoted above.

[74] In a letter to Andrew Skene of 14 November 1764, shortly after Reid had taken up his new duties, he described his schedule and classes as follows: "I must launch forth in the morning, so as to be at the College (which is a walk of eight minutes) half an hour after seven, when I speak for an hour, without interruption, to an audience of about a hundred. At eleven I examine for an hour upon my morning prelection; but my audience is little more than a third part of what it was in the morning. In a week or two, I must, for three days in the week, have a second prelection at twelve, upon a different subject, where my audience will be made up of those who hear me in the morning, but do not attend at eleven" (*Works*, p. 39b).

They were young, generally in their early teens, when they started. Most of them repeated his class; in the first year they followed the "public" lecture and the "examination," in the second year they followed the "public" and the "private" lectures. The lectures were given an element of maturity by the fact that "Many attend the Moral Philosophy class four or five years; so that I have many preachers and students of divinity and law of considerable standing, before whom I stand in awe to speak without more preparation than I have leisure for."[75]

Those who intended to become ministers of the Church of Scotland had to take the arts curriculum before beginning their divinity studies; divinity students with other plans and students of law and medicine seem often to have taken at least some part of the arts curriculum before entering their professional course. Other students simply followed classes for a year or two, to complete their schooling instead of in preparation for a career. Because of this relatively loose structure and the fact that most of a professor's income came from class fees and not the small fixed salary, lectures had to attract students, and student numbers provide significant evidence for this. Reid's class was always well-attended; two years after his installment in Glasgow he was boasting that "Dr. Smith never had so many in one year," though the year before he had had to admit that Ferguson, in the larger Edinburgh University, had more than twice his numbers.[76] Many students were also poor, some very poor, but class fees were low (one-and-a-half guineas for the "public" class, one guinea for the "private"), and living expenses were so low that "it was possible to obtain a University education at an expenditure in cash of as little as about £5 sterling a year."[77] Some university training was thus possible for the middle classes and for tenant farmers, whose sons formed the majority of Glasgow students during Reid's tenure, while the attendance of even very poor boys was helped by a number of bursaries. Since the divinity course, unlike law and medicine, was free, the typical upward path for the poorer students was to scrape through the arts curriculum and then train for the ministry.

Nearly half the students came from west-central Scotland and more than one-fifth came from Ireland. In his first year Reid estimated the latter to be "Near a third part of our students" and, like Hutcheson before him, he found them a nuisance:

[75] Ibid., p. 40a. Reid points out that the students "pay fees for the first two years, and then they are *cives* of that class, and may attend gratis as many years as they please" (ibid., pp. 39b–40a).

[76] Ibid., pp. 47b and 42b.

[77] W. R. Scott, *Adam Smith as Student and Professor* (1965), p. 29.

The most disagreeable thing in the teaching part is to have a great number of stupid Irish teagues who attend classes for two or three years to qualify them for teaching schools, or being dissenting teachers. I preach to these as St. Francis did to the fishes. I don't know what pleasure he had in his audience; but I should have none in mine if there was not in it a mixture of reasonable creatures.[78]

Two of Reid's most outstanding students have given us brief glimpses of his class. In Dugald Stewart's account of Reid's lectures they are lent a stiff and stuffy earnestness that is difficult to reconcile with the quiet and often ironical humor and the lively spirit that otherwise comes across so clearly:

In his elocution and mode of instruction, there was nothing peculiarly attractive. He seldom, if ever, indulged himself in the warmth of extempore discourse; nor was his manner of reading calculated to increase the effect of what he had committed to writing. Such, however, was the simplicity and perspicuity of his style, such the gravity and authority of his character, and such the general interest of his young hearers in the doctrines which he taught, that by the numerous audiences to which his instructions were addressed, he was heard uniformly with the most silent and respectful attention. On this subject I speak from personal knowledge, having had the good fortune, during a considerable part of the winter of 1772, to be one of his pupils.[79]

One suspects that Stewart had little appreciation of understatement and simple matter-of-factness and that, at a distance of thirty years, he used the standard of his own flowery oratory somewhat unfairly to judge a very different man in different circumstances. Stewart is almost certainly wrong in saying that Reid always read his lectures; many parts of Reid's course exist only as brief notes, and there is nothing to suggest that fuller texts ever existed.[80] In spite of these

[78] Reid, *Works*, pp. 40a and 43. See a letter of Hutcheson's printed in McCosh, *Scottish Philosophy*, p. 464. Apart from sources already cited, the following have been used in this brief sketch of the Glasgow students: James Coutts, *A History of the University of Glasgow* (1909); J. D. Mackie, *The University of Glasgow* (1954); W. M. Mathew, "The Origins and Occupations of Glasgow Students, 1740–1839" (1966); David Murray, *Memoirs of the Old College of Glasgow* (1927); R. N. Smart, "Some Observations on the Provinces of the Scottish Universities, 1560–1850" (1974).

[79] D. Stewart, *Account*, p. 264.

[80] In his mode of delivery Reid probably tried to facilitate the student's taking of notes, a practice he strongly encouraged; see his inaugural lecture in Glasgow, 4/II/ 9,3v.

reservations it seems clear that Reid's style was conversational rather than declamatory. This may have made his "examination" class more agreeable than his "public" lecture, and it may explain the rather different impression of Reid's pedagogy preserved by George Jardine, who became his colleague in logic in 1774. Jardine graduated in 1765, so his experience probably refers to Reid's first year in Glasgow:

> I remember well the striking effect produced on the minds of his students, by an instance of great simplicity and candour, on the part of the late venerable Dr. Reid, when he was professor of moral philosophy in this university. During the hour of examination they were reading to him a portion of Cicero de Finibus; when at one of those mutilated and involved passages which occasionally occur in that work, the student who was reading stopped, and was unable to proceed. The doctor attempted to explain the difficulty; but the meaning of the sentence did not immediately present itself. Instead, however, of slurring it over, as many would have done, "Gentlemen", said he, "I thought I had the meaning of this passage, but it has escaped me; I shall therefore be obliged to any of you who will translate it". A student thereupon instantly stood up in his place, and translated it to the doctor's satisfaction. He politely thanked him for it; and further commended the young man for his spirited attempt. This incident had a powerful effect upon the minds of the other students, while all admired the candour of that eminent professor; nor was there a single difficult passage which was not afterwards studied with more than usual care, that the next precious opportunity for distinction might be seized.[81]

Reid's private class was concerned with the implications of the basic theory of the mind that he had expounded in Aberdeen and now developed further in his public class in Glasgow. In its early form the course was divided into these sections:

> I intend in these Lectures to treat first of the Culture of the human Mind. Secondly of the Connexion between Mind and Body and their mutual Influence on one another, which will make way for some observations on the fine Arts and Chiefly on Eloquence with which we shall conclude.[82]

This was how Reid saw it on 16 December 1765; over the following two decades both the arrangement and the content were endlessly

[81] George Jardine, *Outlines of Philosophical Education* (1825), pp. 263–264.
[82] See 4/1/31,1r.

refined and changed. Some of the material ended up in the *Intellectual Powers*, some did not. Taken as a whole, the manuscripts are a record of subtle philosophizing that deserves publication.

The concentration on the philosophy of mind in the private class was a novelty in Glasgow. Hutcheson had lectured mainly on the ancient moralists, while Smith taught rhetoric and belles lettres.[83] Reid's break with tradition was probably felt more strongly in the public class. Since the days of Carmichael the backbone of the course had been natural theology and moral-philosophy-cum-natural-jurisprudence; from Hutcheson's time on, less attention was given to the former, and political theory had grown into an independent segment.[84] Reid changed all this. His public course, as explained in his Introductory Lecture (Section I, below), was divided into pneumatology, ethics, and politics. Of these, pneumatology, as the most important, was allocated the most time, from early October until early March. Ethics—that is, the Practical Ethics here presented—ran through the rest of March and April, while politics took up May and probably the first few days of June. In this arrangement pneumatology covered not only the general theory of the mind but also what Reid called "the theory of morals," which we should call moral psychology and epistemology, and that part of natural theology concerned with the existence and nature of the divine mind. Moral theology, a part of traditional natural theology, became the opening section of Practical Ethics, on "Duties to God." Much of traditional moral philosophy was compressed into the "Duties to Ourselves," while the rest of Practical Ethics, or normative ethics, was treated as a system of natural jurisprudence under the general heading "Duties to Others."

While the emphasis on the theory of the mind resulted from Reid's methodological commitment to the empirical, antispeculative study of mental phenomena, the development of Practical Ethics as an intricate system of duties was implicit in his substantive moral philosophy, as shown in part 3 below.

[83] Concerning Hutcheson's class, see William Leechman, "Account of the Life, Writings, and Character of the Author [Hutcheson]" (1755), p. xxxvi; and W. R. Scott, *Francis Hutcheson* (1966), p. 63. On Smith, see ibid., p. 63. See also Adam Smith, *Lectures on Rhetoric and Belles Lettres* and the Introduction therein by J. D. Bryce, pp. 7–23.

[84] On Carmichael, see Robert Wodrow, *Analecta* (1842–43), 4:95–96; Murray, *Memoirs*, pp. 506–508; Hans Medick, *Naturzustand und Naturgeschichte* (1973), pp. 299ff.; James Moore and Michael Silverthorne, "Gershom Carmichael and the Natural Jurisprudence Tradition in Eighteenth-Century Scotland" (1983); idem, "Natural Sociability and Natural Rights in the Moral Philosophy of Gershom Carmichael" (1984). On Hutcheson, see Leechman, "Account," p. xxxvi, as well as his textbooks, *Synopsis metaphysicae, Logicae compendium*, and *Philosophiae moralis institutio compendiaria* (translated as *A Short Introduction to Moral Philosophy*). On Smith, see the editors' introduction (1978) to his *Lectures on Jurisprudence* and the literature cited there.

The third part of the course, Politics, is sharply distinguished from Practical Ethics in the Introductory Lecture (Section I, below). Practical ethics, in modern terms, is a normative discipline and has a branch "which is very properly called political Jurisprudence," as Reid explains at the beginning of his politics lectures. "The Object of this Branch," he continues, is "The Rights & moral obligations that arise from the political Union."[85] Politics is quite different: "It is not . . . the business of politics to show how men ought to act, that belongs to Morals, but to show how they will act when placed in such circumstances and under such Government."[86] Politics, however, is not simply an explanatory science—that would be an anachronistic description—but rather a traditional *technē*: "as an expert Physician ought to understand the nature and Effects of Poisons as well as Medicines; so an able Politician ought to understand the nature & Effects of all kinds of Government the bad as well as the good."[87]

Politics is divided into two parts. The first and most important is the forms or constitutions of government, which has itself two facets. On the one hand it concerns the natural effects of given forms of government; on the other it specifies which of these are best suited in given circumstances to achieve whatever ends are set for the exercise of government, a question that, as we have seen, lies outside the scope of politics. The second part is "Police," which presupposes those "subordinate ends of Political Society the attainment of which tho not necessary to the being or continuance of it may yet conduce greatly to its well being and Prosperity. The proper means of Promoting these are likewise an object of the Science of Politicks."[88] Reid, however, never managed to keep practical ethics and politics entirely separate, and there are in the politics lectures various elements of importance to an understanding of practical ethics, which we will draw into the general interpretation of Reid below.

The manuscript lectures, Literary Society papers, and other material, especially Reid's scientific writings, from the Glasgow years constitute by far the largest part of the Reid *Nachlass*. When organized and presented in coherent and legible form, as in the present volume, it will be possible to investigate in detail Reid's intellectual development from the *Inquiry* to the two *Essays* and beyond. In pneumatology, in particular, the material is so rich that one can follow closely Reid's elaboration of the fundamental metaphysical, epistemological, and methodological ideas that he adopted in Aberdeen.

---

[85] 4/III/3,1r (5 May 1766).

[86] 6/I/31,1r. See A.P., p. 591b. Reid sometimes uses "morals" instead of "practical ethics" as a contrast to "the theory of morals."

[87] 4/III/3,1r.

[88] 4/III/9,1r (6 May 1765).

There is much less on practical ethics, and Reid's development of this topic falls conveniently into two parts: first, the immediate results of the move from Aberdeen to Glasgow and, second, developments in the Glasgow period. Undoubtedly, Reid's great "discovery" here was modern, Protestant, natural jurisprudence.[89] Though Reid was exposed to it under Turnbull, there is nothing to suggest interest in natural law, or indeed in law at all, while Reid was in Aberdeen. Reid's earlier Practical Ethics seems to have been a fairly common-place Stoic-Christian doctrine of virtue, coupled with some interest in classical republican, utopian, and Whig constitutional political themes, though his line on these is unclear. It may be merely symbolic that his development from a traditional doctrine of virtue to a modern juridical system of duty parallels his move from a large rural center to a larger commercial center, and he never showed any appreciation of the lawyers' law usually associated with Edinburgh.

Reid's "discovery" of natural jurisprudence clearly necessitated considerable readjustment to repair his previous neglect. In the letter to Andrew Skene of November 1764, mentioned above, Reid complains of lack of time and expresses some apprehension about his audience, and in his opening lecture he asked for notes of the lectures of his predecessor Adam Smith.[90] It is unlikely that either pneumatology or politics would have caused him any problems, but it is understandable that having to produce at short notice a two-month course in natural law, which had been the central theme of Smith's lectures, might cause some diffidence. There are other signs of Reid's initial insecurity: in his first year he failed to treat "Duties to God" and "Duties to Ourselves" in any systematic way, and "Rights and duties of states" (here printed in Section VIII as "Duties to Others: States") was covered, if at all, only perfunctorily. Most significant, Reid, in the jurisprudence parts of his first course in Glasgow, is more dependent on a textbook—namely, Hutcheson's—than in any other part of his course or at any other time.[91] This is documented in detail in the Commentary to Reid's text below.

[89] For brief surveys of the Scottish connection with modern natural law, see Duncan Forbes, "Natural Law and the Scottish Enlightenment" (1982); idem, *Hume's Philosophical Politics* (1975), chap. 1; Haakonssen, "Natural Law and the Scottish Enlightenment" (1985); idem, "Hugo Grotius and the History of Political Thought" (1985); D. N. MacCormick, "Law and Enlightenment" (1982); Peter Stein, "From Pufendorf to Adam Smith" (1982); and the papers by Moore and Silverthorne cited in n. 84 above.

[90] The passage is quoted in the Introduction below, pp. 91–92 n. 12.

[91] There is one partial exception to this. In natural theology Reid claimed to follow Hutcheson's "plan," but this does not seem to apply to the content. Since the "tract" by Hutcheson to which Reid refers his students must be the *Synopsis metaphysicae*, part

Once Reid had, with Hutcheson's help, mastered natural jurisprudence, he clearly took to it and made it his own, recognizing its congruence with his own theological ideas, and the adaptability of the Stoic-Christian doctrine of virtue to a theory of duty consistent with both his notion of divine law and his theory of moral judgment. The result was the coherent system of practical ethics set out below. On the question of how Reid developed this system, the manuscript record is little help. Most of the manuscripts written after his first year at Glasgow are undated; those that are date from the 1760s, with only occasional additions in 1770 or 1771. It seems probable that by the end of the 1760s Reid had essentially completed his Practical Ethics on lines taken over from Hutcheson and Pufendorf and that it never changed. Certainly there are few differences between his own notes and those of his students from 1776 (Robert Jack) and 1779–80 (George Baird),[92] and the parts that Reid chose to include in his *Active Powers* (1788) can all be traced back to his earlier lectures. The only exception is his idea of contract, and especially his criticism of Hume's theory, which was an extension of his criticism of Hume's notion of the artificiality of justice. After Reid's address to the Literary Society in 1779, he continued to be occupied by this issue which is understandable because promises and contracts were intimately connected with his theory of language, which he constantly discussed with James Gregory.[93]

On the boundaries of practical ethics and politics, Reid most probably continued to work on the proper balance between those elements in his political thought identified earlier in his Aberdeen work and interpreted in part 3 below on their last appearance in the paper on the utopian system (Section XVIII below).

Reid retired from teaching at the age of seventy, in 1780, and left his classes to his assistant and eventual successor, Archibald Arthur.[94] Though Reid lacked the charisma of Hutcheson or the popular touch

---

III, "De Deo," this is quite understandable; in several respects it would have been too "scholastic" and Augustinian for Reid, but it does present the tripartite division he wants—namely, God's existence, his nature and attributes, and his works. See George Baird's notes from Reid's lectures (1779–80), 5:19; and Hutcheson, *Synopsis metaphysicae*, p. 85. It is difficult to judge Reid's natural theology because his own lecture notes on that subject apparently have not survived and we must rely on students' notes.

[92] See the Bibliographic Index.

[93] See the correspondence with Gregory in Reid, *Works*, and the brief but helpful discussion in Barfoot, "James Gregory," pp. 150–154. See also the Commentary below at pp. 402f. n. 4.

[94] Wood, "Thomas Reid," pp. 169–170. On Arthur, see also William Richardson's biographical account in Archibald Arthur, *Discourses on Theological and Literary Subjects* (1803).

of John Millar, he was obviously a respected and successful lecturer, whose audiences and fees steadily increased.[95] He was certainly comfortably off and could practice one of his favorite arguments for private property—that it made possible the exercise of generosity and charity. Nor did Reid have heavy family expenses. Death was a constant visitor with the Reids, and of his nine children only one survived him, four dying in infancy and four in early adulthood.[96]

We do not know why Thomas Reid retired when he did. One motive may have been his increasing deafness,[97] but he was probably also moved by a desire to write up his philosophy systematically. He divided the work into two parts, perhaps fearing that he might not live to complete it, yet in 1785 the *Essays on the Intellectual Powers of Man* appeared, and three years later the *Essays on the Active Powers of Man*. They were well received on the whole, and within a generation, together with the works of Dugald Stewart and to a lesser extent those of James Beattie and James Oswald, they had created the general idea of a coherent Scottish school of Common Sense philosophy.[98]

Throughout the nineteenth century, Reid's position in Scottish philosophy—as the generally acknowledged leader of the school—was assured. In England Reid's views were treated seriously by William Whewell and Henry Sidgwick and given fresh prominence by John Stuart Mill's *Examination of Sir William Hamilton's Philosophy* (1865), which effectively divided the field into "empiricists" and "intuitionists." With the gradual amalgamation of English and Scottish philosophy, Reid's name survived into the twentieth century in the work of G. E. Moore and others, and recent years have seen a remarkable revival of interest in Reid's ideas. Reid's influence outside Britain is well established, particularly in North America, where his writings, together with Stewart's, were so widely used as textbooks that philosophy and Common Sense became virtually synonymous for much of the nineteenth century. Reid also influenced Charles Peirce's pragmatism. While it is well-known that Reid's influence on nineteenth-century France was equally important, his impact on Germany, together with that of other Common Sense philosophers, has only recently been recognized.[99]

[95] Wood, "Thomas Reid," pp. 168–169.   [96] See Fraser, *Thomas Reid*, p. 32.
[97] See Wood, "Thomas Reid," p. 168.
[98] For the composition, publication, and reception of the two *Essays* see ibid., pp. 169–175.
[99] There is no general study of the influence of Reid or the Common Sense school, but for some brief outlines see Ronald E. Beanblossom's Introduction to Reid's *Inquiry and Essays*, ed. R. E. Beanblossom and K. Lehrer (1983); and Selwyn Grave, *The Scottish Philosophy of Common Sense* (1977), esp. pp. 1–10. The following works, each in their field, will supply some beginnings: McCosh, *Scottish Philosophy*; Henry Laurie, *Scottish*

In this legacy something was lost. Grand in scope though they are, the two *Essays* do not fully convey the vision of the interdependence of all human knowledge held by the Glasgow Professor of Moral Philosophy. Reid's concern with science is nowhere apparent, and his idea of the coherence between natural philosophy and his well-known theory of the mind has only now been retrieved from the manuscripts. As far as Reid's Practical Ethics is concerned, a few elements appear as three brief chapters in the *Active Powers* but give little idea of the full system as Reid presented it to his class.[100] No reasons for this are given, but he may have considered the system, both as a whole and in part, as too derivative to warrant full publication. In this he was probably justified. At this distance the situation looks very different. The main difficulty in understanding the ideas that past thinkers have thought original enough to justify publication is precisely the retrieval of the background ideas that were too common to be worth publishing but that have now been lost sight of. In the case of the *Active Powers* there is certainly little prospect of fully understanding the selected normative themes without a prior acquaintance with the full system of practical ethics from which they derive. Much the same applies to the remarks on politics scattered throughout Reid's published work that presuppose his lectures on "political jurisprudence" and on "Politicks" proper.

After the publication of his two great works, Reid continued to busy himself with social causes of the sort mentioned above, with politics, especially after the outbreak of the French Revolution (see part 3 below), with the Glasgow Literary Society, and with his correspondence—first and last with ideas. In these final years he manifests an extraordinary intellectual energy and a passion for knowledge that, while he makes the complaints to be expected of old age, give him an

---

Philosophy in Its National Development (1902); George Davie, *The Social Significance of the Scottish Philosophy of Common Sense* (1973); Schneewind, *Sidgwick's Ethics*, esp. chs. 2 and 3; Henry Sidgwick, "The Philosophy of Common Sense" (1895); S. V. Rasmussen, *Studier over William Hamiltons Filosofi* (1921); G. E. Moore, "Nature and Reality of Objects of Perception" (1960); Beanblossom, "Russell's Indebtedness to Reid" (1978); Keith Lehrer, "Reid's Influence on Contemporary American and British Philosophy" (1976); R. Peterson, "Scottish Common Sense in America, 1768–1850" (1972); J. D. Hoeveler, Jr., *James McCosh and the Scottish Intellectual Tradition* (1981); Emil Boutroux, *De l'influence de la philosophie écossaise* (1897); Manfred Kuehn, *Scottish Common Sense in Germany, 1768–1800* (1987); T. T. Segerstedt, *Moral sense-skolan och dess inflytande paa svensk filosofi* (1937).

[100] On natural philosophy, see Wood, "Thomas Reid," and R. Olson, *Scottish Philosophy and British Physics, 1750–1880* (1975). On ethics, see A.P., essay v, chs. 1–3; chs. 4–7 deal mainly with criticism, especially of Hume, but also cover special points originating in the lectures on practical ethics.

air of mental timelessness, of looking ahead to the future. His mind never seems to have become retrospective. This is of course a matter of tone and mode of feeling, not of opinion, and it is perceived partly in his letters—in some ways Reid's best writing—and partly in his last published piece, the *Statistical Account of the University of Glasgow*.[101] As part of the *Statistical Account of Scotland*, Reid's essay is dry and schematic, yet it has some interesting personal touches. Apart from the expected thoroughness, fairness, and clarity, Reid's judgments are notable for their openness to novelty;[102] there is a readiness to assess each new institutional development on its merits, more usually associated with middle age, when all is still in the future. Coupled with this is an enthusiasm for the probable growth of knowledge, especially in the sciences, and a pride in the university as a moral pillar of decent society, a society in which the common good, comprehensively conceived, is a matter of civic duty. This presupposes free moral agency, which the university recognized by not requiring religious or similar tests for entry and which might be improved by the moral instruction conveyed in a system of practical ethics.

In addition to Reid's accepted intellectual and moral qualities, I would like to emphasize also the sheer good humor and sense of irony that Reid shared with his great intellectual opponent, David Hume. Reid's good humor, which like Hume's was often applied to himself and his own circumstances, has a pleasant tendency to break through and lighten the studied Christian Stoicism that was the conventional reaction of his intellectual peers to the vicissitudes of life. There is a glimpse of this in his letter to Dugald Stewart after his wife died in 1792:

> By the loss of my bosom-friend, with whom I lived fifty two years, I am brought into a kind of new world, at a time of life when old habits are not easily forgot, or new ones acquired. But every world is God's world, and I am thankful for the comforts He has left me. Mrs. Carmichael has now the care of two old deaf men, and does everything in her power to please them; and both are very sensible of her goodness. I have more health than at my time of life I had any reason to expect. I walk about; entertain myself with reading what I soon forget; can converse with one person, if he articulates distinctly, and is within ten inches of my left ear; go to Church, without hearing one word of what is said.

[101] This was probably written in 1794 and published in 1799 in the *Statistical Account of Scotland*, vol. 21. See now, Reid, *Works*, pp. 721–739.

[102] See a passage in a letter to James Gregory from 1788: "I comfort my grey hairs with the thoughts that the world is growing better, having long resolved to resist the common sentiment of old age, that it is always growing worse" (Reid, *Works*, p. 72b).

You know, I never had any pretensions to vivacity, but I am still free from languor and *ennui*.

If you are weary of this detail, impute it to the anxiety you express to know the state of my health. I wish you may have no more uneasiness at my age.[103]

Thomas Reid died on 7 October 1796 after a brief illness, having been active in his garden and in higher mathematics almost until the end. "In apparent soundness and activity of body, he resembled more a man of sixty than of eighty-seven," says his disciple. Sir Henry Raeburn's splendid portrait of 1794 confirms this.[104]

[103] D. Stewart, *Account*, pp. 312–313. Mrs. Carmichael was Reid's only surviving child. She had married the son of one of Reid's predecessors, Gershom Carmichael—hence the "two old deaf men."

[104] Ibid., p. 314. Raeburn's portrait is in Fyvie Castle in the care of the National Trust for Scotland. It is reproduced well in Duncan Macmillan, *Painting in Scotland: The Golden Age* (1986), color plate 24, and on the dustjacket of the present book.

3. Reid's Philosophy

To provide a framework for the manuscripts and the unavoidably fragmented Commentary that follows, this portion of the introduction sets out first to give a brief survey of Reid's general presuppositions and then to interpret his moral philosophy as systematically as possible.

Human Knowledge

Given Reid's presuppositions, the argumentative coherence of his moral thought is tight and systematic. The cardinal themes are the possibility of knowledge and, deriving from this, the possibilities in knowledge. The philosophy of mind shows what knowledge, including moral knowledge, is possible for man, and practical ethics shows what possibilities this gives man as moral agent. The basic presuppositions are theological and may, as mentioned earlier, be characterized as providential naturalism, a term also used of George Turnbull and Lord Kames, Reid's principal mentors along with Butler in this regard.[1] For Reid—as for Turnbull, Kames, Butler, and most of their contemporaries—the world in both its material and immaterial aspects was a well-organized whole whose parts by their coherence indicated an intelligent, purposeful mastermind. The existence within creation of the human mind, with its apparent cognitive powers, thus gave rise to the presumption that the purpose of the mind is to explore the created world as it is presented to these powers. However, the world appears to us not as a coherent whole but as piecemeal, as discontinuous events and things, and we must therefore study it piecemeal, noticing similarities and regularities as they appear. If we go beyond this and form "hypotheses" about connecting links outside our field of experience, we are in effect exceeding our cognitive brief and prying into God's affairs. In other words, there is strong theological sanction for the inductive method suggested by Francis Bacon and, in Reid's view, definitively developed and explained by Newton.

[1] See Norton, *David Hume*, ch. 4. For Reid's natural theology, see esp. vol. 5 of Baird's notes. Reid's defense of the argument from design is in I.P., pp. 457b–461b.

This method had been applied to the physical world with extraordinary results, but moral philosophers still employed it with what Reid considered insufficient stringency, thereby often being involved in unnecessary and dangerous problems. Modern philosophy—from Descartes via Nicholas Malebranche, John Locke, and George Berkeley—had made the possibility of knowledge more and more incomprehensible, until Hume finally drew the full skeptical conclusions.[2] Reid's interpretation of the course of modern philosophy soon became the textbook version and, as still surviving today, it must be conceded to be his most lasting influence on Western thought. Fortunately, modern scholarship has begun to reject his simplification of the history of philosophy, but we should not forget that such simplification was an important argumentative or polemical move. We may say briefly that Reid concentrated the battle against skepticism on one front by viewing epistemological skepticism as fundamental to all forms of skepticism and as pervading the whole of modern philosophy.

At the heart of the sorry confusion that was modern philosophy lay a general tendency to adopt a totally misleading analogy between body and mind in an attempt to replicate in moral philosophy the success of natural philosophy.[3] Treatment of the mind as analogous to material mechanisms was naturally suggested and supported by the physical expressions ordinarily used to refer to its workings. Consequently the mental world was seen as composed of certain basic entities—namely, simple ideas that were imparted to the mind by its surroundings in the form of sense impressions and from which complex ideas of things, events, and so on, were composed. The materialist and mechanistic analogy for the mind thus led directly to that

[2] In general, see H.M., ch. 1. See also Norton, *David Hume*, pp. 171–173 and 189–203.

[3] The following sketch of Reid's epistemology and its critical implications is based mainly on the *Orations* of 1759 and 1762 and on H.M., ch. 1, with occasional reference also to the *Intellectual Powers of Man*. The critical literature on Reid's epistemology and metaphysics is extensive. There is no general bibliography, but the following together substantially cover the field: Nina Mikhalevsky, "Bibliography" (1976); R. A. Legum, "An Updated Bibliography of Works on the Philosophy of Thomas Reid" (1978); and the bibliography in Louise Marcil-Lacoste, *Claude Buffier and Thomas Reid* (1982), pp. 209–220. The most comprehensive English survey of Reid's basic philosophy is still Selwyn Grave, *The Scottish Philosophy of Common Sense* (1977), but see also E. Griffin-Collars, *La Philosophie écossaise du sens commun* (1980), and M. F. Sciacca, *La filosofia di Thomas Reid* (1963). In addition, there is an extensive literature of dissertations and articles, including the *Monist* issue on Reid, and Barker and Beauchamp, eds., *Thomas Reid*, and Marcil-Lacoste's enlightening comparison of Buffier and Reid (cited earlier in this note). See also McCracken, *Malebranche and British Philosophy* (1983), and J. W. Yolton, *Perceptual Acquaintance: From Descartes to Reid* (1984).

other basic error of modern philosophy, "the theory of ideas," as
Reid called it—that is, the theory that ideas, not the objects of ideas,
are the immediate objects of the mind's apprehension.

All this, for Reid, was fundamentally wrong. In fact, it rested on a
total disregard of sound empirical method in the interests of formu-
lating a purely speculative "empiricist" (as it was to be known) philosophy. There was no empirical evidence to support the analogy between mind and body, and uncontaminated Common Sense clearly
showed that the mind was in its nature quite different from and not
comparable to the physical world. It is true that sensation suggests
the presence of an object and occasions many of our ideas, but for
many very important ideas—such as those of space, time, and
power—this is not so. Furthermore, the process of perception, from
sensation to idea, cannot be understood as a causal chain, like a physical process, for not only are mental "images" of a totally different
nature from that of their objects in the material world, but the mind,
far from being a passive recipient, is in fact active insofar as even
simple perception is judgmental in character, judging *that* something
is the case. Finally, it is empirically false that complex mental content
is composed of simple ideas; on the contrary, even casual reflection
shows that the mind spontaneously apprehends complex objects,
which may subsequently be subjected to analysis. Reid even suggests
that there is no empirical evidence whatever for the existence of
ideas, in the sense of mental objects immediately present to the mind.
Instead of acknowledging things and events of varying complexity
that common experience shows to be present to the mind, philosophers have speculatively created an intervening phantom-world of
ideas.

Reid believed this was not only false but also dangerous, as leading
to skepticism. In order to solve their self-created problem of the epistemic adequacy of the ideas through which the mind is supposed to
apprehend the world, philosophers have had to embark on a wild-
goose chase in search of proof of such adequacy. However, because
all suggested guarantors of our ideas—such as Berkeley's God—can
be apprehended only through ideas or are in some other way subjective in character, the inevitable conclusion is that each person lives in
his own world of ideas with no means of knowing that there is either
a physical world or other minds or a God around him. This progressive impoverishment of the world reaches the height of absurdity
with Hume's argument, as Reid understood it, that we do not even
know that there is a self because we can form no idea of it.

Reid's various arguments against the theory of ideas are further
buttressed by the well-known "reflexivity argument," as we may call

it, that skeptics like Hume are entirely inconsistent because in the practice of living they presuppose the reality of all those things of whose existence their theory of ideas denies them knowledge. Even in writing down their skeptical ideas and addressing them to others they are affirming what their words deny—a line of argument well-known to Hume himself.[4]

If we abandon the materialist and mechanistic view of the mind as a passive recipient of ideas causally implanted by sense perception, we have, according to Reid, cleared the way for a proper empirical investigation of the mind. This reveals that the mind is by its very nature constituted as a highly active cognitive agency. Apart from the operations that it acquires or learns (habits), the mind is provided with various innate powers, among them instincts and such faculties as the ability instantly to form judgments or shape beliefs about objects of perception—that is, without learned process of reasoning. Finally, the mind is issued a large number of "first principles of common sense, common notions, self-evident truths" or, in other words, "intuitive judgments . . . which are no sooner understood than they are believed."[5] These naturally absorbed First Principles are not subject to proof, but themselves unquestionably supply the starting-point for all further cognitive activity:

> In every branch of knowledge where disputes have been raised, it is useful to distinguish the first principles from the superstructure. They are the foundation on which the whole fabric of the science leans; and whatever is not supported by this foundation can have no stability. In all rational belief, the thing believed is either itself a first principle, or it is by just reasoning deduced from first principles.[6]

The First Principles of human knowledge are of two kinds: "They are either necessary and immutable truths, whose contrary is impossible; or they are contingent and mutable, depending on some effect of will and power, which had a beginning, and may have an end."[7] The former are divided into six categories: principles of grammar, logical axioms, mathematical axioms, axioms of taste, first principles of morals, and first principles of metaphysics.[8] The contingent truths are not organized, but they are illustrated by twelve examples, demonstrating that they basically guarantee our knowledge of our own

---

[4] For further discussion of this, see Marcil-Lacoste, "The Seriousness of Reid's Sceptical Admissions" (1978), and Lobkowicz, *Common Sense und Skeptizismus* (1986).

[5] I.P., p. 434b.

[6] A.P., p. 637a. For the role of First Principles in general, see I.P., vi.iv.

[7] I.P., p. 441b.   [8] Ibid., vi.vi.

mental world, our personal identity, the content of our memory, ourselves as free agents, the external world, other minds as intelligences and free agents, the uniformity of nature, and reliable signs and evidence. These principles, together with the intellectual powers that harbor them, are what Reid calls Common Sense.[9]

As we have seen, the defense of Common Sense is that its principles are inescapable or incontestable, a view often expressed in the familiar reflexivity argument *ad hominem*. This is repeatedly reinforced by the theologico-teleological argument that because Common Sense is part of our natural constitution it is, like nature in general, instituted to fulfill its ostensible function in creation by helping us to survive and lead human lives by supplying us with knowledge. Its truthfulness is therefore part of the providential arrangement of nature.[10]

Human Agency

The foundations of Reid's providential naturalism and its methodological implications were laid early, in Turnbull's classroom. They were probably reinforced by later reading of Turnbull's *Principles of Moral Philosophy*; Hutcheson's *Inquiry* and probably his other works; and not least Butler's *Analogy* and subsequently Kames's *Essays on the Principles of Morality and Natural Religion*. By the time of his graduation *Orations* at King's College, it is clearly the framework for Reid's developing theory of Common Sense as the answer to skepticism. That theory itself was long in the making, and it is quite likely that the characteristic reflexivity argument—that all claims to knowledge, including skeptical claims that appearances of knowledge are deceptive, necessarily presuppose the principles of Common Sense—had been developed before the theory of ideas was identified as the source of the skeptical malaise. There are already clear traces of this argument in the 1730s, which together with Reid's interest at the time in the notion of human agency make it possible that Reid was then using the reflexivity argument to show the reality of human agency. If so, then he may have begun to see epistemological skepticism as fundamental to moral skepticism and consequently Common Sense as the answer to both, before the publication of Kames's arguments in his *Essays* of 1751. Certainly he was prepared for Kames's theory and thoroughly absorbed it, including many of the key elements in

---

[9] Ibid., VI.v. See also Reid, "Cura Prima. Of Common Sense," ed. Norton, in Marcil-Lacoste, *Claude Buffier and Thomas Reid*, appendix.

[10] See Norton, "From Moral Sense to Common Sense," pp. 53–54.

the Common Sense solution to the problems of skepticism, particularly the First Principles.[11]

In any case, whatever the chronology or origin of the view, by the time of his *Inquiry* (1764) Reid had clearly come to see the struggle against moral skepticism in the tradition of Shaftesbury, Hutcheson, Butler, and Turnbull as a mere side-skirmish in the general battle against epistemological skepticism, with Hume as the principal antagonist on both fronts. This polemical narrowing of the idea of skepticism in general and of Hume's skepticism in particular may well be Reid's second most significant legacy, and again one making more argumentative sense in his problem situation than its historical accuracy would lead one to believe.

The central problem was the concept of human agency. If the mind did not have direct access to the objects of cognition except as a sequence of discrete ideas, as Reid's reading of the theory of ideas would have it, then not only were causal connections between events unintelligible, but it would also be impossible to ascribe actions to agents or indeed to have an idea of continuous and coherent agency whether in oneself or in others. Consequently it would be impossible to ascribe moral qualities, such as virtue and vice, to agents on the evidence of their behavior, and it would make no sense to hold a person responsible for his actions. Hence, reward and especially punishment would be impossible and there would in general be no foundation for the enforcement of law or the upholding of society. As Reid says in explanation of the wider perspective of the *Inquiry*'s otherwise narrow refutation of epistemological skepticism,

> upon this hypothesis ⟨the theory of ideas⟩, the whole universe about me, bodies and spirits, sun, moon, stars, and earth, friends and relations, all things without exception, which I imagined to have a permanent existence, whether I thought of them or not, vanish at once. . . . I thought it unreasonable . . . upon the authority of philosophers, to admit a hypothesis which, in my opinion, overturns all philosophy, all religion and virtue, and all common sense.[12]

More specifically directed against Hume, on the lines indicated above, we find this remarkable, ironic aside:

> We were always apt to imagine, that thought supposed a thinker, and love a lover, and treason a traitor: but this, it seems, was all

---

[11] For an incisive comparison of Reid and Kames, see Norton, ibid., esp. pp. 271ff., and idem, *David Hume*, pp. 189–191.

[12] H.M., p. 96.

a mistake; and it is found out, that there may be treason without
a traitor, and love without a lover, laws without a legislator, and
punishment without a sufferer . . . or if, in these cases, ideas are
the lover, the sufferer, the traitor, it were to be wished that the
author of the discovery had farther condescended to acquaint us
whether ideas can converse together, and be under obligations
of duty or gratitude to each other; whether they can make promises and enter into leagues and covenants, and fulfil or break
them, and be punished for the breach. If one set of ideas makes
a covenant, another breaks it, and a third is punished for it, there
is reason to think that justice is no natural virtue in this system.[13]

For Reid, as for so many of similar moral and theological outlook,
such as the "Moderate Literati" and the moderate clergy in general,
it was of the utmost importance to establish the reality of free human
agency. While Butler in the *Analogy* had asserted free will and agency,
he had neither explained it nor defended it. After Hume, this was
badly needed, because it was seen as the necessary precondition for
the possibility of morals. Without it, moral education seemed a mere
illusion and social improvement through education, in the widest
sense, was impossible. Moral freedom was the necessary presupposition of moral personality seen as the basis of civil society, the unit of
which social structure and political institutions were composed. Ultimately moral freedom was at the heart of a vision of humanity as
God's moral vicegerents on earth, set there to realize a moral potential both in each individual life and in the collective life of society and
the species as a whole.

In its context the doctrine of moral freedom was a two-edged
sword.[14] On the one hand it was, as we have shown, directed against
modern philosophy's materialist analogy of the mind, seen as neces-
sitarian, whose logical conclusions were perceived to be moral skepticism and a Godless universe; of this Hobbes and Hume were seen
as the chief representatives. On the other hand, the notion of moral
freedom and its attendant ideas indicated above flew in the face of
traditional Calvinist necessitarianism with its emphasis on election
and justification by faith alone.

Reid's solution to the problem of moral freedom should be viewed
partly against the background of classical determinism as represented

[13] Ibid., p. 109b.

[14] The following outline of Reid's theory of free moral agency is based upon A.P.,
essay IV; the letters to James Gregory (Reid, *Works*, pp. 62–89) and to Kames (ibid., pp.
50–52); and "Unpublished Letters of Thomas Reid to Lord Kames," pp. 48–51. In the
critical literature, I am especially indebted to Barfoot, "James Gregory," pp. 135–158,
and J. A. Weinstock, "Reid's Definition of Freedom" (1976).

by Hobbes and its continuation, for Reid, in Hume's notion of "free-dom," partly as a response to a controversy of the 1750s. Stated briefly, the problem is as follows. Hobbes, like many simpler minds, had held that moral freedom simply meant freedom to act as one willed. However, if one adopted a determinist theory of the will, as Hobbes did, this definition of freedom seemed quite inadequate to most moralists, because determinism was held to make ideas of moral worth and moral responsibility, and thereby morality as such, mean-ingless. On the other hand, it was difficult to make sense of moral freedom as freedom of the will, because this was thought to lead to an infinite regress of acts of will: one is free to will, because one can will to will, ad infinitum—a point made by Locke.[15] In his *Essays* Kames tried to solve this problem within a determinist framework by arguing that, although our acts of will, like all other natural events, are determined, we do in fact have an illusory sense of power over our will. Furthermore, because we have this natural though false be-lief in the freedom of will, we naturally ascribe moral worth and moral responsibility to ourselves and others, and these moral notions thus become part of the causal determinants of our will.

Despite his misguided attempt, using Jonathan Edwards as repre-sentative, to present this view as compatible with Calvinist doctrine, it caused Kames considerable trouble with great numbers of the clergy and led to charges that he was, like Hume, a skeptic and an infidel, although one of his principal aims in the *Essays* had been to refute Hume's views. After protests from Jonathan Edwards too, Kames dropped his theory from the second edition of the *Essays* (1758),[16] but Reid took up the issue by offering an alternative analysis of the con-cept of power over one's will. Put simply, Reid broke the infinite re-gress of acts of will, mentioned above, by his insight that power over one's will is not itself an act of will but rather the ability to judge rationally of what it is that one wills. Thus animals, small children, and people whose minds are permanently or temporarily defective may certainly be said to act according to their will, but they cannot therefore be said to act with moral freedom and responsibility be-cause their willing is deficient, inasmuch as their judgment of what it is that they will is either lacking or very imperfect or distorted. Moral freedom is therefore a matter of being able or competent to judge of what it is that one is willing, especially to judge in terms of the First Principles of Common Sense and thus to control the will. Because the

---

[15] See Weinstock, "Reid's Definition of Freedom," p. 98.

[16] Concerning the whole episode, see ibid., p. 101 n. 27; Ross, *Lord Kames*, ch. 8; and Sher, *Church and University*, pp. 65–74. Reid's interest is underlined by his four-page abstract of Jonathan Edward's *Freedom of the Will* (1754); see 3/11/6.

exercise of judgment does not presuppose an act of will, the infinite regress does not arise. Furthermore, once willing is seen to be linked with the power of judgment, the issue of determinism or necessitarianism is simply sidestepped, since judgment as a mental activity cannot be understood in mechanistic causal terms but must be seen as *sui generis*.[17] Put another way, Reid is not in fact maintaining the freedom of the will as such, because it is determinable by judgment. However, this determining power of judgment cannot meaningfully be talked about in causal terms, as for instance being "determined" by this or that motive. When we are talking about agency, "causality" is simply a category mistake.

Principles of Moral Judgment

Reid's doctrine of moral freedom and free moral agency (or active power) as a power of judgment over the will is vastly more complicated both in what Reid says about it and more especially in what it presupposes or implies. The brief outline given here should, however, suffice to indicate how knowledge in the form of judgment is determining for moral action. The general possibility of knowledge, or of epistemically adequate judgment, has already been outlined in the discussion of Common Sense, particularly its First Principles. It remains to apply this specifically to moral knowledge, to show how moral judgments are available to determine the will of moral agents. It is this combination that makes moral *action* possible, and it is the possible world of moral action that is charted in the Practical Ethics of this volume.

As so often in Reid, his own theory of moral knowledge is reached through criticism of the theories of others. Reid's main targets are Hutcheson and Hume, and the starting-point is Reid's general criticism of the empiricist theory that all simple ideas stem from sense or feeling while all complex ideas are constructed by the mind from simple ideas. This, according to Reid, is as false of moral knowledge as of all other knowledge, first, because the moral faculty in fact begins with complex ideas and only by analysis reaches simple ones and, second, because such analysis reveals the presence of ideas—for example, the moral First Principles of Common Sense—which are not derived from any form of sensation but rather from the native operations of the mind. Furthermore, attention to the actual workings of the moral faculty shows that these are not simply a matter of

[17] The latter seems to be overlooked by Weinstock, but I do not deny his charge ("Reid's Definition of Freedom," pp. 97 and 99) that there is some confusion in Reid between the issue of moral freedom and the issue of determinism.

feeling but a matter of judgment. When we make moral judgments, as the familiar term significantly has it, of our own or others' behavior, we are directly conscious that we not only have a feeling but are also asserting a proposition that in contrast to a feeling, may be true or false, and that this proposition is about the behavior not about the feeling.

> That other men judge, as well as feel, in such cases, I am convinced, because they understand me when I express my moral judgment, and express theirs by the same terms and phrases. Suppose that . . . my friend says—'Such a man did well and worthily, his conduct is highly approvable'. This speech . . . expresses my friend's judgment of the man's conduct. . . . Suppose, again, that in relation to the same case, my friend says—'That man's conduct gave me a very agreeable feeling'. This speech, if approbation be nothing but an agreeable feeling, must have the very same meaning with the first. . . . But this cannot be, for two reasons.
> *First*, Because there is no rule in grammar or rhetoric, nor any usage in language, by which these two speeches can be construed so as to have the same meaning. The *first* expresses plainly an opinion or judgment of the conduct of the man, but says nothing of the speaker. The *second* only testifies a fact concerning the speaker—to wit, that he had such a feeling.
> Another reason why these two speeches cannot mean the same thing is, that the first may be contradicted without any ground of offence, such contradiction being only a difference of opinion, which, to a reasonable man, gives no offence. But the second speech cannot be contradicted without an affront: for, as every man must know his own feelings, to deny that a man had a feeling which he affirms he had, is to charge him with falsehood.[18]

So far from being constitutive of the operation of the moral faculty, feeling is in fact causally dependent upon our judgment: it is the judgment that some act or person is good or bad that causes certain feelings about it.

Reid's principal antagonist, Hume, would not of course have denied that judgment is relevant to the formation of our moral sentiments, commonly termed "judgments," nor that the relationship is often a causal one. Thus the judgment that A is a means to B leads to an evaluation of A, if B is already considered to have some value or other. Such relational judgment may again lead to the evaluation

---

[18] A.P., p. 673.

of B in relation to C. But this process will have to stop somewhere, with something considered of value in itself and not simply a means, and Reid believed that this consideration was for Hume a matter of feeling and not of judgment. This was how he understood Hume's maxim that reason is and ought to be the slave of the passions, a maxim that Reid rejected:

> among the various ends of human actions, there are some, of which, without reason, we could not even form a conception; and that, as soon as they are conceived, a regard to them is, by our constitution, not only a principle of action, but a leading and governing principle. . . . These I shall call *rational* principles; because they can exist only in beings endowed with reason, and because, to act from these principles, is what has always been meant by acting according to reason.[19]

Foreshadowing a later point, we may say that for Reid relative value-judgments imply not facts (such as feelings) but judgments of facts—that is, *moral* facts. Such judgments are arrived at by the application of his "rational principles" or ends, of which there are two—"to wit, *What is good for us upon the whole*, and, *What appears to be our duty*."[20] The former, also called prudence, is a principle of cool, rational self-interest. It presupposes that we are creatures with a complex of animal principles, desires, and aims in life, whose immediate or long-term satisfaction or disappointment suggests to us a plurality of goods and evils. Prudence or "practical reason," as it is also called,[21] is a judgment on the best attainable balance of these, based on past experience and a reasonable assessment of the future. This can plainly not be calculated on some simple, unitary scale but, though sometimes approaching value-pluralism, it cannot be denied that Reid's concept of "our good upon the whole" depends on a teleological concept of the true nature (purpose) of human personality.

This is particularly clear in the *Lectures* below, where Reid treats "prudence" as our duty to ourselves or the duty of self-government. The proper exercise of prudence, he thinks, will show, as most ancient moralists, particularly the Stoics, had pointed out, that our good upon the whole consists in the exercise of three of the four classical virtues—prudence, temperance, and fortitude—and indirectly leads to the fourth, justice:

> according to the best judgment which wise men have been able to form, this principle leads to the practice of every virtue. It leads directly to the virtues of Prudence, Temperance, and For-

---

[19] Ibid., p. 580.   [20] Ibid.   [21] Ibid., p. 582a.

titude. And, when we consider ourselves as social creatures, whose happiness or misery is very much connected with that of our fellowmen . . . from these considerations, this principle leads us also, though more indirectly, to the practice of justice, humanity, and all the social virtues.[22]

It is of the utmost importance to realize that, as was usual in late seventeenth- and eighteenth-century moral thought, when Reid talks of duty he adopts the Stoic (Ciceronian) concept of *officium* and adapts it to Christian beliefs by adding the notion of being called or appointed to the offices of one's life, as indicated by a natural power to fulfill these. By the same token, we are called upon to know and worship the Creator and to promote the "good upon the whole" of the rest of creation. Consequently Reid's lectures on our duties to ourselves are preceded by a discussion of our duties to God and followed by an elaborate treatment of our duties to others. In other words, the language of virtue, as the exercise of natural powers of moral judgment, and the language of duty, as the fulfillment of appointed offices, are one and the same and are seen to be so.[23]

The ancient tripartite division of man's duties had become an accepted part of contemporary teaching and lecturing practice, especially after Pufendorf adopted it in his *Duty of Man*.[24] However, because the English word "duty," unlike *officium*, had lost the sense of a prudential duty to realize one's "good on the whole," the *utile*, and retained only the sense of *honestum*—that is, the performance of one's duties to others—Reid in his published work dropped the organization of the lectures and restricted "duty" to the latter use.[25]

This led Reid on to the further point that although prudential regard for our good on the whole is a basic end or principle of practical reason, it is not a genuinely moral one; only *duty* is that. Reid acknowledges that the two are so similar in their effects on human life that they lend plausibility to the attempts by "many of the ancient philosophers, and some among the moderns, to resolve conscience, or a sense of duty, entirely into a regard to what is good for us upon the whole."[26] In fact, as he points out, if the regard to our good on

[22] Ibid., p. 584. See ibid., pp. 581–584 and 638.

[23] This was not a new idea for the time, but it is particularly clear in Reid. For discussions of how Hutcheson in particular prepared the way for it in Scottish moral philosophy, see Haakonssen, "Moral Philosophy and Natural Law: From the Cambridge Platonists to the Scottish Enlightenment" (1988); idem, "Natural Law and Moral Realism: The Scottish Synthesis" (1989); idem, "Natural Jurisprudence in the Scottish Enlightenment. Summary of an Interpretation" (1989).

[24] See the Commentary below at p. 305 n. 1.

[25] A.P., p. 588a.   [26] Ibid., p. 582b.

the whole is fully developed it will produce the same behavior as a regard to duty. The problem is that few, if any, can "attain such extensive views of human life, and so correct a judgment of good and ill, as the right application of this principle ⟨of prudence⟩ requires."[27] Consequently the principle of duty is necessary as the foundation of morals. Furthermore, even when truly virtuous behavior arises from a prudent pursuit of our good on the whole, it is not considered as meritorious as when it arises from a sense of duty:

> Our cordial love and esteem is due only to the man whose soul is not contracted within itself, but embraces a more extensive object: who loves virtue, not for her dowry only, but for her own sake ... who, forgetful of himself, has the common good at heart, not as the means only, but as the end.[28]

Finally, the direct pursuit of our own good as the ultimate end, which Reid now polemically tends to identify with happiness,[29] is generally counter-productive, leading instead to "fear, and care, and anxiety."[30] The performance of duty for its own sake alone gives real and lasting happiness. Duty as a contribution to the common good is what man is charged with as a moral being, while his ultimate happiness is God's reward.[31]

All this seems to Reid to indicate that regard to our good on the whole and regard to duty are two very different ends or principles of practical reason, that the latter cannot be reduced to the former, and that duty is the only properly moral principle:

> This principle of honour, which is acknowledged by all men who pretend to character, is only another name for what we call a regard to duty, to rectitude, to propriety of conduct. It is a moral obligation which obliges a man to do certain things because they

---

[27] Ibid., p. 584b.

[28] Ibid., p. 585. For Butler's somewhat different emphasis, see "Of the Nature of Virtue" in his *Analogy*, pp. 333–335.

[29] A.P., pp. 585–586.   [30] Ibid., p. 585b.

[31] Ibid., p. 586a. The idea that the piety derived from the insights of natural religion is the necessary premise for and completion of morals is forcefully stated in ibid., pp. 598b–599a: "if we suppose a man to be an atheist in his belief, and, at the same time, by wrong judgment, to believe that virtue is contrary to his happiness upon the whole, this case, as Lord Shaftesbury justly observes, is without remedy. It will be impossible for the man to act so as not to contradict a leading principle of his nature. . . . This shews the strong connection between morality and the principles of natural religion; as the last only can secure a man from the possibility of an apprehension, that he may play the fool by doing his duty. Hence, even Lord Shaftesbury, in his gravest work, concludes, 'That virtue without piety is incomplete.' Without piety, it loses its brightest example, its noblest object, and its firmest support."

are right, and not to do other things because they are wrong. . . .

Men of rank call it *honour*. . . . The vulgar call it *honesty, probity, virtue, conscience*. Philosophers have given it the names of *the moral sense, the moral faculty, rectitude*. . . .

What we call *right* and *honourable* in human conduct, was, by the ancients, called *honestum* . . . ⟨and they⟩ distinguished the *honestum* from the *utile*, as we distinguish what is a man's duty from what is his interest.[32]

He goes on to make the point noted above, that "duty"—the English rendering of the Latin *officium* (which in Latin includes the sense of *utile*)—is commonly restricted to *honestum*. The basis of all morality is thus the doing of duty in the sense of fulfilling one's office for its own sake, and the moral faculty, by whatever name it is commonly known, is the sense of duty or conscience.

Reid, as we have seen, has no objection to calling the moral faculty a "sense," provided this is understood, as in ordinary usage, to include judgment.[33] But two kinds of judgment are required of the moral faculty.[34] First, it must assent to the First Principles of morals previously referred to, of which Reid, in the *Intellectual Powers*, gives the following examples.

That an unjust action has more demerit than an ungenerous one: That a generous action has more merit than a merely just one: That no man ought to be blamed for what it was not in his power to hinder: That we ought not to do to others what we would think unjust or unfair to be done to us in like circumstances.[35]

In the *Active Powers* the sample is more extensive and is divided into those principles which "relate either to *virtue in general*, or to the different particular branches of virtue, or to the *comparison of virtues* where they seem to interfere."[36]

Second, the moral faculty judges the moral worth of particular actions by relating such actions to the moral end—duty—through subsuming them under the relevant First Principle or Principles.[37] Following ordinary usage, Reid commonly calls this form of judgment moral judgment. While the First Principles of morals constitute certain knowledge to any competent moral judge, the particular moral

---

[32] Ibid., pp. 587a–588a.

[33] Ibid., pp. 589b–590. See also Butler, "Of the Nature of Virtue," p. 329.

[34] Reid is not able to distinguish the two clearly, as D. D. Raphael has pointed out in a searching discussion, *The Moral Sense* (1947), pp. 172–189.

[35] I.P., p. 453b.   [36] A.P., p. 637.   [37] Ibid., pp. 589b–591a.

judgments are inherently fallible because we can never have perfect knowledge of the "real essence" of contingent beings such as those related in moral judgments—namely, particular agents and their particular behavioral circumstances.[38] He often muddles this point badly when, by a confused and rhetorical use of "axiom" for First Principles as well as for particular moral judgments, he transfers the certainty of the former to the latter.[39] The necessity and importance of the point is, however, quite clear when he insists that the self-evidence of First Principles does not dispense with the need for moral education or vitiate the role of moral experience in such education. This would not be intelligible if particular moral judgments had the same epistemic standing as moral First Principles, for it is the ease of error in the former that often obscures the latter. Despite lapses, Reid manages to avoid the common error in responses to skepticism of trying to prove too much.[40]

Duty and Virtue

Turning now from moral judgment to the objects of moral judgment, we must make explicit what has already been hinted at. Reid acknowledges that in ordinary language moral judgments concern the moral quality of either actions or agents or duty. However, Reid believes that philosophical scrutiny will make it clear that an action considered in abstraction from an agent and his motives can have a moral "quality" only in the sense that it is a *duty* either to do it or to avoid it. As we shall see, this is the crux of his criticism of Hume. If we judge a particular action as resulting from the agent's motive, we are judging the merit or demerit of the agent.[41] However, since the exercise of virtue is a duty, all judgments of moral merit ultimately depend on judgments of duty. Even when a moral quality like benevolence is the ostensible object of a moral judgment, we must understand that it derives its moral status from the fact that it is a duty.

Thus, because all moral judgments are ultimately about duty, their objects must be relational in character:

[38] I.P., p. 579b.
[39] See Raphael, *The Moral Sense*, pp. 175–176.
[40] A.P., pp. 640b–643a. While Reid, in accordance with his rational religious outlook, maintains that revelation must be consistent with reason, he also subscribes to the not uncommon view that the moral teaching of revelation may lead corrupted mankind to *see* the moral First Principles, which are used by reason. This is clearly how he saw the work of Christ. See ibid., p. 641b. For a similar view of revelation, see Butler, *Analogy*, II, ch. 1.
[41] A.P., p. 649a. There are lively discussions of this in the manuscripts; see esp. 7/v/17. For Butler's similar standpoint, see "Of the Nature of Virtue," p. 330.

If we examine the abstract notion of Duty, or Moral Obligation, it appears to be neither any real quality of the action considered by itself, nor of the agent considered without respect to the action, but a certain relation between the one and the other.

When we say a man ought to do such a thing, the *ought*, which expresses the moral obligation, has a respect, on the one hand, to the person who ought; and, on the other, to the action which he ought to do. Those two correlates are essential to every moral obligation; take away either, and it has no existence. So that, if we seek the place of moral obligation among the categories, it belongs to the category of *relation*.[42]

Judgments are moral in character when they express a duty relationship; a man is virtuous because he does his duty, and actions are good because they are duties to be done by people in particular circumstances.

We have already seen that Reid's theory of the moral sense as a faculty of judgment constitutes a break with Moral Sense theory, especially as formulated by Hutcheson, though it may be smaller than Reid thought and rather less dramatic than most scholars would have it. Hutcheson has generally been presented as an affective subjectivist for whom moral judgments were expressions of certain affections of the moral sense. In line with some recent studies, I incline to believe that he was a "moral sense cognitivist" and a "moral realist," who saw the moral sense as a cognitive faculty perceiving moral qualities.[43] He had been forced, by a complicated set of problems arising out of the debate on Pufendorf's voluntaristic natural law theory, into trying to show that morality concerned personal qualities, that were empirically ascertainable by the moral sense, a view that helped ensure that much eighteenth-century Scottish moral thought was couched in the language of *virtues*.[44]

This makes the real nature of Reid's break with Hutcheson clear. It was a division not between subjectivism and realism but between two kinds of realism, two kinds of cognitivism, and two kinds of moral judgment. For Hutcheson the moral world consists of qualities

---

[42] A.P., pp. 588b–589a.

[43] See Norton, *David Hume*, ch. 2; idem, "Hutcheson's Moral Realism" (1985); W. Leidhold, *Ethik und Politik bei Francis Hutcheson* (1985), ch. 4. This interpretation of Hutcheson is, however, controversial and has been criticized by, among others, K. Winkler, "Hutcheson's Alleged Realism" (1985).

[44] See Haakonssen, "Natural Law and Moral Realism." I cannot here go into the vexing question of Locke's role in this problem situation, but see James Moore, "Locke and the Scottish Jurists" (1980), and for a brief account of Locke's duty-based ethics see Ryan, "Locke on Freedom: Some Second Thoughts" (1988).

that are perceived by the Moral Sense and ascribed to people in moral judgments. For Reid the moral world consists of relations that are judged to be the proper ones between particular people and actions in the light of the First Principles of morals. For the former, the language of virtue is the primary one; for the latter, the language of duty is primary.

It appears that Reid was precluded from an adequate appreciation of the relationship between his own Common Sense theory and the classical formulation of the Moral Sense theory by his reading of Hume. Like most of his contemporaries, Reid understood Hume as being a self-confessed skeptic for whom morality was entirely a matter of subjective states and not a body of objective knowledge. Once skepticism was seen as the result of Moral Sense theory, the possibility that the moral sense was a cognitive faculty giving access to an objective moral world was lost from sight and only its affective side was remembered.[45]

Leaving aside the adequacy of Reid's interpretation of Hume, we may elucidate the central point of his criticism.[46] He starts from the question, "Whether an action deserving moral approbation, must be done with the belief of its being morally good,"[47] his affirmative answer to which introduces his criticism of Hume's theory of the artificial virtues. As Reid and most other readers have understood him, Hume maintains that it makes sense in ordinary language to say that the motive for an action is good because the action itself is good. This assumes that of certain categories of action, typically acts of justice, we can say why in the final analysis it is good. However, moral goodness cannot rest in the external action as such, but must depend upon a morally good motivation, so we are in effect arguing in a circle: the motive is good because the action is good, and the action is good because the motive is good.[48] Hume breaks the circle with his well-known argument that when actions of the justice type in general are performed within a group this contributes to the common good of the group, whether or not this was the intention. Because of our sympathy with the public good, we approve of such actions, and this becomes their "artificially" engendered *moral* motive, turning them into proper acts of justice.[49]

---

[45] See I.P., p. 421b.

[46] This is part of the critical reflection contained in the last four chapters of *Active Powers*, which have the character of appendixes rather than integrated parts of the systematic exposition; see Reid's remarks about their origins, A.P., p. 645b.

[47] Ibid., p. 646a.

[48] Hume, *Treatise*, III.ii.1, esp. pp. 479–480. Reid quotes the central passages (A.P., p. 648a).

[49] *Treatise*, III.ii.1–2.

Reid has several criticisms of this theory, but behind them all is one arising from the ideas discussed above. Hume's alleged circularity of motive and action, Reid declares, is false; it never existed, and his elaborate scheme for breaking it is therefore futile. We are perfectly entitled to say that a man's motive is good or virtuous if it intends a good action, for the goodness of the action itself does not depend on the motive. We must distinguish between the goodness of the doer of a specific good action, and the goodness of the act considered in abstraction from its being done at a particular time by a particular person. Goodness in the latter case simply derives from the fact that the action in the abstract is a type or category of action that is a *prima facie* duty for *any* moral agent:

> what do we mean by goodness in an action considered abstractly? To me it appears to lie in this, and in this only, that it is an action which ought to be done by those who have the power and opportunity, and the capacity of perceiving their obligation to do it. . . . And this goodness is inherent in its nature and inseparable from it. No opinion or judgment of an agent can in the least alter its nature.[50]

As I understand it, this is just another way of saying that the judgment that an act considered in the abstract is good is a moral First Principle and, further, that when a particular act of this kind is related to an agent by his application of this First Principle, that is, by his judging that the particular act is his duty—then his motive is morally good. If the same action is related to the agent by sheer coincidence or by some nonmoral principle of practical reason, such as self-interest, then there is no "transfer" of moral goodness from the action to the agent.

This interpretation hinges upon the identification of actions in the abstract as the subjects of moral First Principles. It seems to be borne out by Reid's example of an action considered abstractly, "that of relieving an innocent person out of great distress";[51] that this is a duty is clearly a principle that could take its place among Reid's explicit First Principles of morals. His criticism of Hume thus rests upon the idea that there are such undeniable First Principles that make actions good and obligatory independently of the motive of the agent.[52]

[50] A.P., p. 649a.   [51] Ibid.

[52] We cannot here consider all the moralists subjected to Reid's critical analysis, especially in the manuscripts, but some who influenced the early Reid may be mentioned. Reid's general criticism of the "selfish" system is well-known, but not his opinion that John Gay refined on it (7/v/14). Reid's elaborate criticism of Smith's system of sympathy as essentially a variant of the same was published in 1980 and 1984 by J. C. Stewart-Robertson and D. F. Norton, "Thomas Reid on Adam Smith's Theory of Mor-

I have stressed Reid's switch from a theory of virtue to a theory of duty, in the sense of offices, partly because this is an often neglected structural feature of his basic moral philosophy, as published in the *Active Powers*, and partly because it is a precondition for an adequate understanding of his Practical Ethics, as published here. As we have seen, there are rules of translation between the two languages, of virtue and of duty, so that either can be used for normative and didactic purposes—that is, in Practical Ethics. Even so, Reid considers "duty" more proper and natural than "virtue" in this regard also, and he arranges his lectures accordingly, as this volume demonstrates:

> Morals ⟨practical ethics⟩ have been methodized in different ways. The ancients commonly arranged them under the four cardinal virtues of Prudence, Temperance, Fortitude, and Justice; Christian writers, I think more properly, under the three heads of the Duty we owe to God—to Ourselves—and to our Neighbour. One division may be more comprehensive, or more natural, than another; but the truths arranged are the same, and their evidence the same in all.[53]

This brings us to the final point to be made here concerning the primacy of duty in Reid's theory. We saw earlier that, considered as virtues in the traditional sense of qualities of persons, even the cardinal virtues were not properly *moral*, but only *prudential* ends or principles of practical reason. However, if the same behavior is considered as *duty*, then not only the other-regarding justice but also the prima facie self-regarding prudence, temperance, and fortitude are properly

---

als." Against Hutcheson, Reid argues with Butler that benevolence is not the only ultimate moral principle, and this is incorporated into the following summary of Reid's criticism of Clarke, William Wollaston, and Shaftesbury: "As that System which places Virtue solely in disinterested Benevolence narrows the foundation too Much So all the three Systems of S. Clarke, Wollaston & Shaftesbury make the foundation too broad and lead us to ascribe Virtue or moral Worth to actions no wise intitled to that Character. . . . It is . . . a bad definition of Virtue to say that it is acting according to Reason, because though every Virtuous Action is according to Reason. Yet every Action that is agreeable to Reason is Not virtuous" (8/III/10,1r). Elsewhere Reid spells out what he only hints at here, that Shaftesbury's definition of virtue as "the Conformity of our Actions & Affections to the fair & handsome, the Sublime & Beautifull of Things," suffers from a similar weakness and that the systems of both Shaftesbury and the intellectualists "tend to confound two things which are really distinct and which the french Language distinguishes more accurately than ours to wit Manners & Morals, les manniers, & les moeurs" (7/V/1,14r). In a brief note dated 22 February 1768, Reid again touches on this topic, this time bracketing John Balguy, Richard Hooker, and Richard Price with Clarke (4/I/21).

53 A.P., p. 642b.

moral principles. Accordingly, the last three are included in Reid's Lectures as "duties to ourself," alongside "duties to God" and "duties to others" (justice).

The apparently paradoxical notion of duties to ourselves is explained by the fact that these duties are only prima facie self-regarding. We have a duty to cultivate the cardinal virtues of prudence, temperance, and fortitude because we are created with a moral nature and have been given a divine brief to develop it to the best of our ability. The duties to ourselves are thus really owed to God, and their value to ourselves can only be seen as a moral good insofar as it is a contribution to the good of the world as a whole, the striving for which is a duty imposed by God upon mankind individually and collectively.

This religious perspective is very important. Not only does Practical Ethics presuppose the pneumatological explanation of the divine as well as of the human mind, but practical ethics itself has as its fundamental first part "duties to God." As Reid explains it in his published work: "That conscience which is in every man's breast, is the law of God written in his heart, which he cannot disobey without acting unnaturally, and being self-condemned" and again, "Right sentiments of the Deity and of his works, not only make the duty we owe to him obvious to every intelligent being, but likewise add the authority of a Divine law to every rule of right conduct."[54] The ultimate foundation of morality is divine law, and we can thus appreciate why Reid generally respected the traditional distinction between duty and obligation.[55] Morality is a matter of duties imposed, not of obligations undertaken; obligations, like virtues and all other moral categories, presuppose duty and law. Remembering the inspiration Reid derived from the Stoics, we may also say that morality is an elaborate network of "offices" of greatly varying extent to which God has appointed us.

Pneumatology explains the appointed place of mind within the creation and the cognitive powers and epistemic principles that make knowledge possible to the mind. The theory of morals is the part of pneumatology that explains how the mind is an active power: it has moral (and metaphysical) freedom to act and the power of judgment to guide its action, and it can acquire the moral knowledge to guide its judgment. Practical ethics, or morals, is not in the same way explanatory; it is, rather, a taxonomic discipline that systematically ar-

[54] A.P., pp. 638b and 639b.
[55] The distinction had become obscured, and Reid occasionally confuses the subjective and objective concepts, though mostly using "obligation" either for the subjective state of the person who has a duty or for obligations undertaken, e.g., by contract.

ranges the principles of our duty and thus provides a map of the network of typical offices that constitute the moral world.[56] We must take it that the world that is thus depicted is not the actually existing moral condition of mankind but rather that which, given the moral powers of man, is possible in principle and a guiding ideal in practice. In this sense, "systems of morals" are supportive of our haphazard moral judgments of our duty. This is what Reid understood by Practical Ethics.

Natural Jurisprudence

We have already seen that in the lectures on practical ethics Reid adopts both of the traditional divisions of morality to structure his course: the three duties (to God, to ourselves, and to others) and the four virtues (prudence, temperance, fortitude, and justice). The three duties provide the basic structure of the lectures, and of these the last is by far the most extensive; duties to ourselves consist in the exercise of the three virtues of prudence, temperance, and fortitude, while the fourth, justice, applies to our duties to others. Reid often reserves the label "natural jurisprudence" for the justice section of his course. The opening discussion of duties to God is brief, drawing on the pneumatology lectures on natural religion, and is generally organized around the traditional distinction between internal and external worship. Together with the lectures on the duties to ourselves, it presents an integration of Christian and Stoic ideals, now sometimes called Christian Stoicism, which was a common theme in the moral thought of the period. The important point here is the analysis of the classical theory of virtue in terms of a Christian theory of duty and law within a teleological framework.

The section on natural jurisprudence, or duties to others, is by far

[56] As he once defines it: "Ethics the knowledge of these Rules or Laws by which men ought to regulate their Actions" (6/ıv/2,1r). See also A.P., p. 642b: "A system of morals is not like a system of geometry, where the subsequent parts derive their evidence from the preceding, and one chain of reasoning is carried on from the beginning; so that, if the arrangement is changed, the chain is broken, and the evidence is lost. It resembles more a system of botany, or mineralogy, where the subsequent parts depend not for their evidence upon the preceding, and the arrangement is made to facilitate apprehension and memory, and not to give evidence." This point is central to his claim that morals, or practical ethics, in contrast to the (pneumatological) "theory of morals," is not a matter of reasoning in the sense of deductive inference, but is open to any ordinary intelligence (see Raphael, *The Moral Sense*, pp. 165–172). "Morals" is thus not an *inference* from "the theory of morals." The latter explains how morals is possible for man, but that is a point never doubted by anyone in the practical conduct of life, and the only practical implication in demonstrating it is to rebut skeptical metaphysicians, whose sophistries might otherwise derange the moral Common Sense of some people.

the most extensive in Reid's course on practical ethics. The basic division of the topic is between the rights and duties of individuals and those of societies. While he draws the traditional parallels between the two groups, Reid is careful to point out the significant differences, which fully justify the separate treatment of international law. The tripartite division of the law of nature pertaining to individuals is again entirely traditional. In "private jurisprudence" we consider the individual in isolation from any organized society and in that sense in a state of nature, whereas the other two sections deal with the individual's rights and duties within the household and within civil society. Though Reid adopts the old use of "oeconomical" as the adjectival form of *oikos* and operates with the familiar extended concept of the household, as indicated here by the third of the three oeconomical relations, he is well aware that historically the juridical roles of the household are steadily being transferred to the state. Finally, political jurisprudence deals with rights and duties between rulers and the ruled in civil society and between citizens qua citizens.

Basic to Reid's idea of natural jurisprudence is the concept of natural law. In common with all modern natural lawyers, he sees this as God's command to man, apprehended by human reason (as opposed to revelation), and he identifies it simply as the precept of our moral power or conscience. It is worth noting that Reid does not take this opportunity to revive the old dispute about a voluntarist versus a realist foundation for the obligation to natural law, which had played a significant role in modern natural law, dividing Grotians from Pufendorfians.[57] The law of nature so orders the moral world of human actions into rights and duties that for every right there is a corresponding duty, whereas there are some duties that cannot be claimed as rights.[58] This applies most obviously to our duties to ourselves but also to some other cases, which we shall look at below. Ignoring duties to God and to ourselves, Reid in the *Active Powers* takes the systems of rights and of duties to be alternative ways of dealing with morals, but more judiciously, in the lectures he sees them as complementary.[59] This is not just or even primarily because of the odd status of duties to God and to ourselves, but because the law of nature in some cases appoints the rights as primary and the matching duties as consequent upon them, whereas in others the reverse is true. Thus our

[57] See Haakonssen, "Natural Law and the Scottish Enlightenment" and "Natural Law and Moral Realism."

[58] Below, pp. 143ff. Page references not otherwise identified are to the manuscripts printed below in this volume as Reid's Lectures and Papers on Practical Ethics.

[59] A.P., pp. 643–645. See below, p. 202, where Reid explicitly excepts duties to ourselves.

rights of liberty (to be and to do, put simply) and our "real" rights (our rights in things, i.e., property) are primary, and it is as a consequence of granting us those that the law of nature appoints duties to respect them. Our "personal" rights (i.e., our rights to some performance by other persons, usually contractually established), on the other hand, are derived from the duties imposed by natural law on those others.[60] The important thing is that, irrespective of what in this sense is primary and what is secondary, the law of nature maintains the correspondence between natural rights and duties.[61] Reid believes that the moral world is in principle well ordered by a natural law whose relationship to natural rights and duties is analogous to the relationship between positive law and legal rights and duties.

My emphasis here on the role of natural law may meet with some skepticism, as being far too voluntaristic for a moral realist like Reid. And so it would be if we stopped there, but when we look at the concept of the common good I hope that such skepticism will be reassuringly mitigated.

Apart from the divisions of rights according to their "nature" (liberty-rights, real rights, and personal rights), and according to their "relations" (private, oeconomical, and political), Reid uses a couple of other devices from jurisprudential architectonics. He divides rights according to "subject," into private, public, and common, of which the first pertain to individuals, the second pertain to any social grouping, and the third pertain to mankind as a whole. This he mentions only in passing.[62] More important, he divides rights, according to their "source" or "foundation," into innate or natural and adventitious; sometimes he adds acquired rights as a third category, sometimes instead he subdivides adventitious rights into original and derived.[63] It is interesting to note that in the *Active Powers* Reid introduces the concept of rights as deriving from that of injury, a traditional notion that Adam Smith had developed into a highly orig-

[60] See below, p. 199.

[61] It has been suggested that Reid's assertion of this correspondence is mistaken in one important respect: Liberty-rights are not matched by duties on the part of others; the only logical connection between liberty-rights and duty, it is said, is "that my ⟨liberty⟩ right to do X entails my having no duty to forbear X" (M. Dalgarno, "Reid's Natural Jurisprudence: The Language of Rights and Duties" [1984], p. 21). I have shown elsewhere that this rests on an anachronistic reading of Reid's concept of rights: in the Pufendorfian tradition, in which Reid stands, liberty-rights are, indeed, reflex claim-rights, which imply a duty on the part of others not to interfere. This is what is appointed by natural law. See Haakonssen, "Reid's Politics: A Natural Law Theory" (1986), pp. 10–12. See also Dalgarno, "Reid and the Rights of Man" (1985).

[62] See below, pp. 147, 199, 201.

[63] See below, pp. 147, 199–200, 201, 206, 208.

inal theory by means of the idea of the impartial spectator.[64] On this basis, though without using Smith's theory, Reid lists six rights:

> A man may be injured, *first*, in his person, by wounding, maiming, or killing him; *secondly*, in his family, by robbing him of his children, or any way injuring those he is bound to protect; *thirdly*, in his liberty, by confinement; *fourthly*, in his reputation; *fifthly*, in his goods, or property; and *lastly*, in the violation of contracts or engagements made with him. This enumeration, whether complete or not, is sufficient for the present purpose.[65]

Reid's purpose then was to criticize Hume for his neglect of the first four rights, the "natural rights," in his theory of justice—just as Smith's spectator theory of justice is obviously meant to correct Hume on exactly this point.[66]

At any rate, the basis for the distinction between innate or natural rights and adventitious or acquired rights is that the former do not presuppose any human action, whereas adventitious rights do. Innate rights are thus typically life, liberty, and free personal judgment. Original adventitious rights are principally the right to property, which arises from mere occupation and derives in a way from innate rights insofar as its justification is that it helps us to preserve the latter (sustaining life, etc.). Here it should be mentioned that, according to Reid, the whole world is given to mankind from the hand of nature (or the creator) in negative community—that is, everything is equally open to occupation by everyone.[67] Derived rights presuppose the prior existence of original adventitious rights, which can be transferred or otherwise transformed through succession, contracts, testaments, and the like. Reid confusingly, and inconsistently with his general terminology, talks of adventitious rights as rights that exist between people in an adventitious state—that is, in a state other than the natural one, such as the family or civil society—which rest upon contractual relationships.[68] Finally he also divides rights according to their "mutability," into alienable and inalienable rights—real rights, personal rights, and "some parts of our Liberty" being alienable.[69]

The most important division is, in some ways, that between perfect rights and imperfect rights.[70] Reid rejects the most common grounds

---

[64] See Haakonssen, *Science of a Legislator* (1981), pp. 99ff.

[65] A.P., p. 656.

[66] See Haakonssen, *Science of a Legislator*, pp. 102–103.

[67] See pp. 204–205 and 210; A.P., p. 658.

[68] See p. 209.   [69] See p. 201.

[70] Although Reid occasionally talks of the distinction between perfect and imperfect rights as a general division of the field, his more considered view was that the distinc-

for this distinction: that perfect rights can be legally enforced, while imperfect rights cannot, and that perfect rights alone are absolutely necessary to the very existence of society.[71] Instead, he relies on a more general reason: he takes perfect rights to be rights matched by negatively defined duties—for example, duties not to injure—while imperfect rights are matched by positive duties to render some good.[72] Though adopting this traditional distinction for conceptual clarification, Reid does not think that it has the moral and political significance often ascribed to it. First, he never gives the two kinds of rights and their matching duties different epistemological status. The moral qualities that people show in exercising them are equally objective and equally open to appreciation by our moral powers. Second, he does not think that they are so very different in moral urgency; in this regard the line between them will often be uncertain.[73] Third, because of this he does not think that a society can exist merely on the basis of the protection of perfect rights. Fourth, he consequently sees it as the task of government to protect both perfect and imperfect rights by legally enforcing their corresponding duties.[74]

Reid does not name his adversaries in this argument, but it should be noted that these four points collide head-on with ideas central to both David Hume and Adam Smith.[75] Hume and especially Smith had argued that some basic features of justice, conceived negatively as a matter of the protection of perfect rights (terms that Hume did not employ), are much more universally recognizable than other parts of morality. The uncertainty of the latter, the "positive" virtues, in itself makes them less morally urgent and makes it both difficult and dangerous to enforce them as legal duties. This does not, however, mean that the positive virtues on their view are irrelevant to the well-being of society; indeed, in some form or other they are indis-

---

tion was really only relevant to personal rights (see p. 198). I take his point to be that liberty-rights and real rights are all obviously perfect. It should also be noticed that Reid, in accordance with the jurisprudential tradition, distinguishes a third category, external rights (202, 209; A.P., p. 644). These are in fact a mere *fictio juris* created to match duties arising from ignorance, as in the case where one person innocently borrows from another, who has in fact stolen it. The law of nature here imposes an obligation on the former, in his ignorance, to restore the thing borrowed, and while the latter actually has no matching right, he has a semblance of right which is called external.

[71] See p. 197; A.P., p. 645b.   [72] See pp. 193–194; A.P., p. 643b–644a.

[73] See pp. 202–203; A.P., p. 645b.

[74] I return to this below in connection with political jurisprudence; in the meantime, see A.P., p. 645b.

[75] This interpretation of Hume and Smith is developed in Haakonssen, *Science of a Legislator*.

pensable to its stability, and in many historical situations it may be necessary for governments to further them by educational and cultural policies if for any reason they are endangered. For Hume and Smith the pursuit of some of the positive virtues is thus a matter of policy, for Reid it is a matter of legal enforcement. It is important to be aware of this contrast, for it makes clear the far-reaching political implications of the form of the doctrine of rights.

Property

Although Reid's discussion of the fundamental issues concerning natural law, rights, and duties is somewhat fragmentary in the manuscripts published here, there is much subtlety in this material and it adds considerably to the brief discussion in the published work. The same applies to the treatment of property, a topic already encountered in the general discussion of rights but to which some pages are directly devoted. We have seen how original and derived property rights are placed within the system of rights and how they serve in a way to realize natural rights. Here some further explanation is required, for as it stands it sounds far too individualistic.

As we saw above, the world is given to mankind in negative community from the hand of the creator—that is, everything is equally open to occupation by everyone. The justification for this is that it is a means to secure our innate or natural rights, such as life and liberty, but this conventionally individualist argument is combined with views of a different tendency. In occupying the world, man not only must discharge his obligation to look after his own natural rights but also is under a constant obligation to look after the rights of others. Reid illustrates this by a splendid allegory, taken from Epictetus and Simplicius, in which human life is depicted as a party, and the natural world as the refreshments provided by the host (the Lord).[76] While looking after himself, every guest must still be constantly concerned for the satisfaction of his neighbor, the general happiness of the party, and the honoring of his host. In short, individual claims are legitimate rights only when they do not conflict with the common good but as far as possible contribute to it.

When Reid says that the law of nature gives us all an equal right to occupy and use the nonhuman creation, he is not implying that this had been so arranged in order that we may realize our natural rights. The point is that we should do so in order to realize the common good, for only those requirements—of liberty, of goods, and of ser-

---

[76] See pp. 204–205.

vices—whose satisfaction contributes to the common good are in fact
rights at all. This is the real significance of maintaining that all rights
are matched by duties. Because all duty is pointed out by natural law,
whose ultimate objective is the realization of the common good, the
assurance that there are no free-floating rights unengaged by duties
shows that all genuine rights-claims are in harmony with the common
good.

I am aware that this use of the concept of the common good (or
public good) may lead to a charge of inconsistency, in view of Reid's
well-known criticism of Hume for using "public utility" as the justifying ground for the artificial virtues, especially justice. This issue is
connected with his problematic use of natural law, and the two problems can in fact be resolved together when we know more about
Reid's concept of the common good. Meanwhile, we may take the
common good to mean the fullest possible honoring of duties and
hence protection of rights.[77]

All this is simply to say that the right to property is heavily circumscribed.[78] We may occupy only such parts of nature as are necessary
for the satisfaction of the needs and wants of ourselves and those
dependent upon us, and we may do so provided only that we do not
injure others in their similar rights (the basic sufficiency of nature is
an unstated premise here; it was a common one). Further, such
things as air, water, and the ocean, which can benefit us without becoming private property, may not be occupied by individuals (or societies). This leads Reid to the interesting Lockean suggestion that
perhaps only what is actually consumed may become private property, while things of a "permanent Nature" may "be left in the Community of Nature or at least remain in a State of positive Communion."[79] Although Reid does not use it as an example of such durable
things, he undoubtedly meant to include all real estate, especially
land, and this view is very close to that recently ascribed to Locke in
a major reinterpretation.[80] Reid's own references are to Plato, "Utopia" (undoubtedly More's) and "Paraguay," by which he means the
Jesuit social experiments, to which also he refers elsewhere. In his
lectures, as in *Active Powers*, Reid rejects this idea, and it would indeed
have been extraordinary if the professor had lectured his young
charges on the illegitimacy of private property in land. In his final
political statement, however, he did toy with the idea in its most radical, utopian form, as we shall see.

[77] See pp. 79–80.   [78] See pp. 206–208; A.P., pp. 658b–659a.
[79] See p. 210; A.P., p. 658a.
[80] J. Tully, *A Discourse on Property: John Locke and His Adversaries* (1980).

The reasons Reid gives in the lectures for the legitimacy of private property, in durable as well as consumable things, are such that it is not a long step to arguing for the abolition of private property. Prominent among the reasons is the idea that the acquisition of such property is a means to make us realize our moral potential, partly by making us more diligent and thus socially useful, partly by enabling us to show generosity. In fact, the overriding justification for all private property is that it is a means to create a common good; once civil society has been instituted as the guardian of the common good, it has a complete prerogative over private property:

> In General as Property is introduced among Men for the Common Good it ought to be secure where it does not interfere with that end but when that is the Case private Property ought to yield to the Publick Good when there is a repugnancy between them. Individuals may be compelled in such cases to part with their Property if they are unwilling, but ought to be indemnified as far as possible.[81]

In fact, "A Man or a Nation may be hindred from acquiring such an extent of Property as endangers the Safety and Liberty of others," which Reid takes to imply the abolition of private monopolies and the legitimacy of restricting "the disposal of Property by will or by Entails." Further, "A Proprietor has no Right to destroy his Property when the common Good requires that should be preserved, not to keep up Mercatable Commodities when the common Good requires that they should be brought to Market."[82] Finally, the state may secure its own political stability by setting "Bounds to the Acquisition of Property by Agrarian Laws or other Means of that kind" and may secure itself militarily by confiscating necessary property.[83] Reid's ju-

---

[81] See p. 208.

[82] Reid was always suspicious of the emerging market-society and its alleged acquisitiveness. The most extreme expression of this occurs in his utopian scheme, discussed below, but note his reaction to Bentham's *Defence of Usury*. Writing to James Gregory on 5 September 1788, Reid says: "I am much pleased with the tract you sent me on usury. I think the reasoning unanswerable, and have long been of the author's opinion, though I suspect that the general principle, that bargains ought to be left to the judgement of the parties, may admit of some exceptions, when the buyers are the many, the poor, and the simple—the sellers few, rich, and cunning; the former may need the aid of the magistrate to prevent their being oppressed by the latter. It seems to be upon this principle that portage, freight, the hire of chairs and coaches, and the price of bread, are regulated in most great towns. But with regard to the loan of money in a commercial state, the exception can have no place—the borrowers and lenders are upon an equal footing, and each may be left to take care of his own interest" (*Works*, p. 73a).

[83] See p. 207.

ristic justification of the classical republican idea of an agrarian law and his whole treatment of property emphasizes the very direct political implications of his jurisprudential system.

The discussion of succession to property is disappointingly fragmentary, as only a few brief manuscripts seem to have survived, but two points deserve notice even in this survey. In keeping with the long-standing interest in feudal institutions and their influence on contemporary society in Britain, Reid is tempted into a more historical consideration than usual of one issue, that of entail, and a brief aside indicates that he has done the same with testamentary succession. Moreover, he condemns entail on natural law grounds as contrary to the moral good of both the individual and society, as we might expect from his justification of property in general, and thus adds his voice to the chorus of Scots philosophers who campaigned against this institution during the eighteenth century.

Contract

From "real" rights—rights in things—Reid's lectures turn to "personal" rights: rights to some prestation from particular people. Following the natural lawyers, Reid here considers not only the paradigm of contract but also the wider question, whether the use of language as such gives rise to rights and obligations. This leads to some of his most original ideas in combining his theory of language with moral and political themes as in the chapter on contract in the *Active Powers*[84] and the paper on implied contract given to the Glasgow Literary Society and printed below in Section XV.

Behind Reid's idea of language lies his important distinction between "solitary" and "social" acts of mind.[85] The central point here is that the second, unlike the first, presupposes the existence and (in some sense) presence of another mind or other minds. Social acts are necessarily communicative and thus a matter of signs, while solitary acts may or may not be expressed. Examples of the latter are seeing, hearing, remembering, judging, reasoning, deliberating, deciding, while the former include questioning, testifying, commanding, promising, contracting, and the like. For mental acts to be social, there must therefore be a community of signs so that mutual understanding is possible, and nature has in fact provided such a community of signs. It is, however, not only language in the conventional sense that functions as a set of signs. Any behavior directed by a will and judg-

[84] A.P., pp. 663ff.
[85] I.P., pp. 244a–245b; A.P., pp. 663b–666b.

ment and perceived to be so is a sign, or part of language. Consequently verbal promises and contracts are only special cases of the wider question concerning the moral implications of communicative behavior. Because this is a large part of voluntary behavior, it is subject to ordinary moral judgment in terms of the principles of duty. Veracity in our use of signs must thus be a First Principle of morals, and as such Reid maintains it. Veracity is an *undeniable* principle in the use of signs, for were it not assumed as the prima facie duty of all sign-users, no communication would be possible and to attempt it would involve a contradiction. The reflexivity argument encountered earlier is obviously not far off: How can Hume hope to argue that fidelity to promises is an artificial virtue without presupposing that the general virtue of veracity is being naturally imputed to him by the readers of this argument?

The voluntary undertaking of obligations and consequent creation of rights in others is, in traditional subjective rights theories, the fundamental operation upon which morality rests.[86] The fact that Reid reduces such obligations and rights to the operation of the principles of duty and thus to natural law merely strengthens the thesis with which we began. This is reinforced when we see how he extends the argument to contractual obligations. Because any voluntary behavior may function as a sign and thus "engage" the agent to some obligation, well-known patterns of behavior or common roles must invariably do so, and they are then, in the proper Ciceronian sense, the offices of human life. These offices will be known in their general character to any competent moral agent and, while all the moral facts making up the role may not be foreseen by the agent, the office is prima facie binding once the latter has signaled its beginning by his behavior. Once the agent has initiated a role, the reliance of others upon his fulfillment of it shows that his behavior has been taken as a sign and puts him under an obligation to complete the role, as if he had promised or contracted to do so. Failure in this would be to deny that the preceding behavior was what it pretended to be.

In other words, by broadening the concept of signs (or language) Reid relativizes the distinction between explicit and implicit promises and contracts and reduces the moral status of both to that of voluntary behavior in general. He almost certainly arrived at this idea by generalization from natural law ideas of quasi-contract, probably by following up a brief hint in Hutcheson to the effect that continuing obligation to government "is an obligation *quasi ex contractu*."[87] It was

---

[86] See R. Tuck, *Natural Rights Theories* (1979).

[87] Hutcheson, *Short Introduction*, p. 287. "Implied contract" and "quasi-contract" are

undoubtedly with the aim of reinterpreting the idea of a contractual
basis for government that Reid developed the theory.

Oeconomical Jurisprudence

Having dealt with the duties and rights of individuals, Reid turns to
the topic of oeconomical jurisprudence. Oeconomical jurisprudence
deals with the rights and duties of three relationships: between husband and wife, between parents and children, and between master
and servants. In the manuscripts as preserved,[88] he considers the first
two at considerable length, in a discussion that well illustrates his argument that we can read the intentions of the Creator from nonmoral facts of nature and thus derive the precepts of natural law that
apply in this area. From such facts and alleged facts as the natural
passion of love between men and women, its tendency to concentrate
on one person and to exclude third parties through the passion of
jealousy, from the natural modesty of women in sexual relations, the
roughly equal numbers of men and women in the world and their
parity in parental affection, and the protracted infancy of human offspring and their consequent need of parental care over many years—
from all these we can easily see that nature has prescribed lifelong
marriage between one man and one woman for mutual love and care
and with the aims of procreation and the rearing of children. On the
negative side this means that other forms of sexual relations, including homosexuality and polygamy,[89] and sexual relations with other
aims are proscribed.

As far as the parental relationship is concerned, distinctions must
be drawn between minors, adult children living in the parental home,
and adult children living outside the home.[90] While the children are

---

complex topics in modern natural law. Some details are supplied in the Commentary
below at pp. 355–358 nn. 122–127, pp. 402–403 n. 4 and 405–407 n. 9, but see principally
Peter Birks and Grant McLeod, "The Implied Contract Theory of Quasi-Contract"
(1986).

[88] See pp. 170–172 and 217–236. For a general discussion, see J. C. Stewart-Robertson, " 'Horse-Bogey Bites Little Boys'; or, Reid's Oeconomicks of the Family" (1986).

[89] Note, however, Reid's caution concerning polygamy: "Polygamy I conceive cannot
be said to be absolutely forbid in all cases by the Laws of Nature, otherwise it would
not have been permitted among the Jews by God himself. Yet on the other hand it
appears evidently more for the common good of human Society, that monogamy
should be established. And where it is established by the civil authority there Polygamy
may be forbid under the severest penalty. The Laws of Christianity absolutely forbid
polygamy" (p. 230). See also Smith's position in Haakonssen, *Science of a Legislator*, pp.
124–125 and 145.

[90] See pp. 232–233.

minors, the parents' moral guardianship is complete, with all the rights and duties this implies—especially to bring them up to be full moral agents. As long as adult children are living at home, they owe obedience to the parents "as the heads of the Family"; they must have their parents' consent to marry and must help them when in need. Like minors they can own property, but the parents are no longer guardians of such property. The mutual obligations when children have left the parental home are not specified, but apparently obedience is then reduced to respect. All these duties are of course the duties imposed by natural law, but Reid indicates that the role of positive law here is great.[91]

The relationship between master and servants is contractual;[92] it is based on an "onerous" contract in which there ought to be equivalence between the value of the service and its remuneration. Nevertheless, the master will normally have a social and moral authority that it is his duty to employ for the protection and edification of his servants' morals. In addition to our special offices, we always carry the overriding duty of promoting the common moral good according to our means. Reid here draws a parallel between the family (in the extended sense) and the state, which is equally revealing of his views on both:

> Every Family is a little political Society wherein the Master of the Family is the Supreme Magistrate, & is in some degree accountable for the conduct of those under his Authority, & therefore that Authority ought to be employed to make them understand their duty and to engage them to the practice of it. The Supreme Magistrate in a State cannot with innocence be unconcerned or negligent with regard to the Morals of his Subjects neither can the Master of a Family with regard to the Morals of his Family.[93]

While a person may contract for lifelong service, one cannot validly contract for posterity, nor can one's inalienable rights be relinquished. Reid mentions that servitude may also be based "on Delict, on Captivity, or on Incapacity,"[94] but he does not explain whether this is justified under natural law. In his political testament he maintains that incurable criminals and the morally incapacitated—which come to much the same thing—may justifiably be enslaved by the public.

[91] See p. 233.
[92] See pp. 233–236.
[93] See p. 235. See also Thomas More, *Utopia*, p. 149.
[94] See pp. 235 and 236.

Political Jurisprudence: The Contract of Government

Many of the preceding parts of the jurisprudential system have clear political implications that are of importance in interpreting the manuscripts concerned with political jurisprudence proper. These lectures must also be supplemented by Reid's political testament, a twenty-seven-page paper read to the Glasgow Literary Society in 1794 and here printed in Section XVIII.

Reid distinguishes sharply between the actual historical origins of political society and the question of "The Reasons that ought to induce men Sufficiently enlightened to prefer the Political State to that of Natural Liberty."[95] As was common at the time, he sought the origins of government in the need for leadership in tribal warfare and collective expeditions and ventures, subsequently reinforced by the need for arbitrators in internal disputes. The rational man's motivation for living in civil society is partly prudential, partly moral: he will gain protection and better living conditions, and he will be enabled to develop morally as an active member of the moral community that the creator obviously intended for mankind.[96]

This rational foundation for political society must be understood in what appear to be contractual terms, but instead of operating with the conventional ideas of explicit and tacit contract and consent, Reid adopts an ingenious argument around the difficulties of contract theory by which he largely deprives "contract" of its usual meaning and role. In the paper on contract (Section XV below) the central idea of implicit contract is probably inspired by Carmichael's and Hutcheson's speculations on the concept of obligations *quasi ex contractu*, which Grotius and Pufendorf, among others, had originally constructed from Roman law materials.[97] More particularly, Reid appears to be seeking to support the idea of a contractual basis for political authority by developing Hutcheson's suggestion, already noted, that continuing obligation to government "is an obligation *quasi ex contractu*."[98]

Reid's strategy here is to argue that there is no moral difference between an explicitly stated contractual obligation, a tacitly implied

---

[95] See p. 248.   [96] See pp. 174ff. and 247ff.

[97] Carmichael, supplementum IV, "De Quasi Contractibus," in Pufendorf, *De officio*; Hutcheson, *Short Introduction*, pp. 223–227; and idem, *System*, II.77–86. See pp. 67–68 and n. 87 above, and see also Birks and McLeod, "The Implied Contract Theory of Quasi-Contract," for the wider context. In ibid., pp. 50–51, Birks and McLeod draw attention to the connection that Blackstone saw between the original contract and quasi-contractual obligation, but there is no evidence that this weighed with Reid; they do not discuss Carmichael or Hutcheson.

[98] Hutcheson, *Short Introduction*, p. 287.

contractual obligation, and an obligation implied *as if* (*quasi*) there were a contract, when in fact there is none. That the obligation is not altered by these different situations is underlined by the fact that we are not always able to draw clear distinctions between them. The point is that contractual obligation does not really depend upon contract at all, but upon the assumption of an "office" as a position carrying specifiable obligations. In short, Reid's basic idea is that, whatever our walk in life or whatever social action we engage in, we assume an office or a set of duties pointed out to us by the common good and the law of nature, which are matched by corresponding rights and which our moral powers enable us to perceive immediately. This applies as much to the offices of magistrate and citizen as to any other offices. To hold the position of a magistrate carries with it certain obligations, and these point out the rights that the citizens hold against him. The same is true in reverse for the duties implied in being a citizen and the rights in being a ruler. These rights and duties are held together *as if* they had arisen from a contract, but they are in fact in the nature of things, to use the natural lawyers' idiom.

This interpretation of the relationship between rulers and the ruled means, for Reid, that the origins of government have nothing to do with its justification. Just as a marriage originating in rape is legitimate, according to Reid, if the offices of husband and wife are subsequently discharged properly, so a government begun in violence, conquest, or the like is legitimate if the governors proceed to carry out the duties of their office. Its origins are entirely irrelevant. "A Government unjustly imposed may afterwards acquire Right by tacit consent,"[99] if we understand tacit consent in the wide sense of implied contract as characterized by the mutual offices and rights of rulers and ruled, which are matched by the law of nature so as to promote the common good. Accordingly we find Reid repeatedly emphasizing the classical principle that "The Sole End of Government is the Good of the Society," that "The Publick Safety ⟨is⟩ the Supreme Law to Prince & People."[100]

This argument is explicitly directed against Hume's criticism of contract theory and I believe it is also implicitly against his rejection of the providential justification of government. It may therefore be useful briefly to develop this view as a supplement to what is said in the Commentary below. Put very simply, we may say that Hume conflated the various theories justifying the postrevolutionary settlement of British government into two main categories that often functioned as one—namely, contract and consent, and what may be called "prov-

[99] See pp. 242–243 and 177.   [100] See p. 252.

idential de factoism."[101] In the former I include the many attempts to rest the new settlement upon one or more contractual arrangements, such as the Convention Parliament's call to William and Mary, the oath of allegiance and the coronation oath, and/or the supposed consent of the people as shown, for example, in their acceptance of the benefits—the provision of protection and law and order—offered by the government. Hume's rejection of these ideas is too well known to need repetition here. "Providential de factoism" is the general idea that Providence has appointed government to secure the common good of society and that any government that does so is ipso facto legitimate.

Hume rejects the notion of providentially appointed aims of government while retaining the idea that a government that serves the common good, understood as the interests of the governed, is legitimate as long as it is seen to do so. This brings Hume close to one aspect of de facto theory in the stricter sense: the argument that the Stuarts remained kings de jure but that because by historical accident the line settled by the revolution was the only government that could function it was therefore owed allegiance de facto. While denying that the de jure question could be settled by history, he accepted the second part of this argument, virtually reducing the de jure question to a de facto one.

Reid agreed that the legitimacy of government did not depend on its origins, and to that extent he was predisposed toward some form of "de factoism," but he could not accept in Hume the idea that opinion of interest was the basis for de facto government, since this would make it an amoral institution. For Reid, government was a moral institution resting upon moral judgment, but because such moral judgment could not properly be held to be expressed in an original contract and because tacit consent, as commonly understood, seemed to be empirically meaningless, he had to reinterpret it as a matter of Common Sense perception of the implications of the respective offices of ruler and ruled. Finally, because the offices of life were divinely instituted in natural law, Reid's theory may be seen as a refinement of "providential de factoism." Civil society was ultimately legitimated by its end, which was the common good elevated by natural law, and the offices of rulers and ruled were instituted accordingly.

[101] For the postrevolution debates, see, e.g., H. T. Dickinson, *Liberty and Property* (1979), parts I–II; J. P. Kenyon, *Revolution Principles* (1977); Reed Browning, *Political and Constitutional Ideas of the Court Whigs* (1982); and J. G. A. Pocock, *Virtue, Commerce, and History* (1985), pp. 215–253, which presents a comprehensive discussion of the relevant literature. I am indebted to Conal Condren for a discussion of these matters.

Rulers and the Ruled

As indicated earlier, the relationship between rulers and the ruled may be considered either from the point of view of the rights of the individual and the duties of the government or from that of the rights of the government and the duties of the governed. When Reid takes the former line, he sounds at first almost libertarian: the task of the government is to protect the rights of its citizens, who may legitimately hold it to its task, because government rests on consent and is limited in its authority by the law of nature. Although this is the impression eager eyes may get from the manuscripts referred to here, there are a number of difficulties. First, it is disquieting that Reid indicates neither which rights are to be protected nor to what extent. This problem will be solved when we look at it from the point of view of the government's rights; we shall then find that all rights, even those one might have thought inalienable, may on occasion be overruled by concern for the common good. Let us deal first, however, with the question of resistance.

Reid is quite clear that the authority of government is bounded by what is in accordance with the law of nature and that rulers "are not to ⟨be⟩ obeyed in things unlawful."[102] This is further explained in brief form: "Active Obedience due onely in things lawfull . . . Passive Obedience . . . Due in many cases where our Rights are violated. Due wherever the publick good requires it. The Example of Socrates."[103] The legitimacy of a government's action is one thing, the right of resistance to such action quite another, for the right of the governed that the governors fulfill their duty to act according to natural law is obviously not identical with a right of resistance. The latter is a separate natural law question—whether the exercise of such a right of resistance contributes to the common good—and this will normally be doubtful: "Changes in a form of Goverment that hath been established & acquiesced in ought not to be made without very weighty Reasons."[104] Indeed, "The great mischief arising from violent changes of Government shew that they ought not to be attempted without urgent Necessity."[105] The right of resistance is certainly there in cases of dire necessity, but so it was for everyone who employed natural law modes of thinking, including Hobbes and the various

[102] See p. 251.   [103] See p. 252.   [104] See p. 253.

[105] See p. 177. See also the first pages of Reid's paper on the utopian system, esp. p. 279 in the manuscript below: "violent & sudden Changes of the Form of Government . . . are so dangerous in the Attempt, so uncertain in the Issue, and so dismal and destructive in the means by which they are brought about, that it must be a very bad form of Government indeed, with circumstances very favourable to a Change concurring that will justify a Wise and good Man in putting a hand to them."

German natural lawyers who were concerned with legitimating absolutist forms of government. The fact is that for the mainstream of
natural lawyers until late in the eighteenth century the right of resistance was heavily circumscribed, and Reid plainly agreed with them.

The true character of Reid's politics is revealed in the relationship
between rulers and ruled, seen as a matter of the former's right over
the latter. He here elaborates a point implicit in natural law architectonics, that the rights of the political society over its members derive
from its duties under natural law. First he argues that the state consists of moral individuals who

> unite in one incorporate Body . . . so as to have in a manner one
> Understanding one will one Active power, & thereby resemble
> one person, and consequently this political Person must be a
> moral Person and partake of the Nature of the individuals of
> which it is made up. . . . Political Bodies therefore or States are
> under the Same Obligation to regard . . . each others Rights as
> individuals. And hence it follows that the Law of Nations is in
> reality a very exact Copy of the Law of Nature. . . . As therefore
> we Divided the Duty of Individuals into that which they Owe to
> God to themselves and to others we might divide in the same
> Manner the duty of Nations or States.[106]

Usually the analogy between individuals and states led only to the
third category mentioned here, that of the rights and duties contained in the law of nations, but Reid develops it more fully.

Nations are as dependent as individuals upon the deity, and like
them cannot well live without the four cardinal virtues, for which
"the most powerfull motive" is religion. "It necessarily follows that a
State neglects one of its most essential Interests if it neglects Religion
and leaves that altogether out of its Consideration."[107] The state must
by law provide for the religious education of the citizens by establishing an official religion, which if it is to serve its moral function cannot
be a mere form of worship but must have a doctrinal content. Because not even "good and pious men" can agree on such matters, "it
is necessary in every State, that there be a Tolleration for those whose
sentiments do not allow them to joyn in the National Religion, while
at the same time they may have no notions of Religion that are inconsistent with their being good Subjects and good members of the Society."[108] Reid does not make it clear how wide a religious toleration
he would accept. This comes under the general principles of the

---

[106] See pp. 254–255. Cf. p. 181.
[107] See p. 256. For the following, see pp. 257–259.   [108] See p. 258.

state's duty to itself, which are that "A State may lay restraints upon Actions of Men that are hurtfull though not criminal" and that it may not only restrain, but also punish as a crime, actions that spring from a "malus animus," such as immorality, even when not injurious to other individuals.

> Whatever impairs the Morals, enervates the mindes, or bodies of the Members of a State is hurtfull to the State and as every individual so every political Body has right and is obliged to use its endeavours to preserve all its Members in that Sound State which fits them for being most usefull to the Society.[109]

In this way the four cardinal virtues very appropriately find a place in the jurisprudential system at the collective, political level, becoming in effect civic virtues. Indeed, when we remember Cicero's broadly practical interpretation of them, the following sample of the state's duties appears much less heterogeneous than it otherwise might:

> The duty of a State to promote Industry Agriculture Arts and Science. To provide for the Necessities of the Poor. to Punish idleness Riot and Dissipation. To manage the Publick Revenue to provide Ships & Harbours and all the Implements of forreign Trade to drain Marches make highways Bridges Canals Fortresses. To polish the Manners as well as preserve the Morals of its Subjects. To maintain the Respect due to Magistrates Parents Seniors persons of Superior Rank. . . . To attend carefully to the Glory of the Nation. The Dominium Eminens of the State over the Lives & Property of the Subjects.

Reid's elaboration of this last right of the state over its citizens (or duty under natural law) not only spells out the full extent of the authority of civil society, but also shows the structure of the general argument:

> The State not onely ought to defend the property of its Subjects against all who invade it, but has also a Right to Use it in as far as the publick Good Requires. When a Mans personal Service and even his life itself is . . . due to his country when its Safety demands it, it would be very odd to imagine that his Country should not have right to demand a farthing of his Money without his Consent. In a State the good and Safety of the whole is the very End of the Political Union . . . and therefore must be the

---

[109] See p. 258.

supreme Law to which both the Life and the property of Individuals must submit as far as the Publick good Requires.

One part of this *dominium eminens* is the right of taxation. This is, naturally, restricted to what is necessary for the public good, and taxes must be "frugally managed" and "made as equal as possible."

> But there does not appear to me a Shadow of Reason why the Consent of a Subject should be necessary to his bearing an equal Share of the publick burdthen which the service of the State demands. An Error of Mr. Locke on this Subject Second Treatise concerning Government § 138.[110]

The pivot of his argument is clearly the natural law idea of the common (or public) good. It is this that allows such rights as individuals have and that imposes the duty on civil society to exercise a range of rights over its members, a duty limited only by the requirements of the common good. The rights of individuals are by no means open-ended claims to satisfaction, subject to the vicissitudes of fortune, the bargaining of life. Consequently it is quite erroneous to think with Locke that the state's *dominium eminens* over the property of individuals is a matter of negotiation, to be settled by consent. The common good settles this and all similar questions. The rights of individuals are not claims against others, including the state, beyond what the law of nature and the common good allow, and the same applies to the rights of the state against citizens. While the principle is symmetrical, the outcome is far from being so.

Utopia

In view of this, it is hardly surprising that Reid in his final political statement[111] argues that maybe private property ought not to be recognized as a right at all but should be abolished in favor of communal

---

[110] See pp. 258–260. On *dominum eminens*, see A.P., p. 659. Reid's view of taxation and consent is the exact opposite of that put forward by Americans and their British supporters in the Stamp Act crisis and the debates leading up to the American Revolution. See p. 260 and the Commentary below at pp. 425–426 n. 24. There is scant evidence from Reid's own hand about his attitude toward the American conflict, though his interest is clear from a letter written during the Stamp Act crisis (*Works*, p. 43b) and Jack's notes from the lectures in 1776 (lecture xx, pp. 667ff.) confirm his hostility to the American cause and its Lockean principle. For a brief discussion, see J. C. Stewart-Robertson, "Sancte Socrates" (1982).

[111] AUL MS. 3061/6, the address to the Glasgow Literary Society in 1794 on "Some Thoughts on the Utopian System," already referred to and printed in Section XVIII below.

ownership. The first premise for Reid's argument is that, apart from the desire for self-preservation,

> the Desire of Distinction and Preeminence among his fellowmen is one of the strongest Desires of Man; And when his whole Activity is not necessarily employed in providing the means of Subsistence, is the strongest, the most general, & lasting spring of Activity and Exertion. Now Riches, in all civilized Societies, seem to have advantages above all other Qualifications for gratifying this Desire.[112]

The second premise is that acquisitiveness totally corrupts the morals of both poor and rich, mainly because it divides people into poor and rich.[113] Third, Reid suggests that when all but the most basic exertions of men are concerned with the acquisition of private property, a sharp division will occur, both between the interests of individuals and between those and the public or common interest of society. The result will be a strife-ridden society in which public spirit and all concern for the public good is lost.[114]

The remedy is "the Utopian system," largely inspired by Thomas More,[115] which has as its basic principle that moral exertion should replace economic exertion. Property arises out of labor, so if we abolish private property in favor of communal ownership we shall all be working for the state, and that is a much more direct and effective manifestation of the benevolent side of our moral character than anything made possible by private property.[116] As for the acquisition of property as a spur to activity, this can readily be replaced by a system of public honors for moral exertion and merit that will also provide a much better social stratification than one based directly or indirectly on riches. Further, moral merit may be reinforced and its influence enhanced by state allowances of "Servants, Horses, Chariots, Houses and Furniture," though it must be stressed that servants remain in the employment of the state, whoever they serve, and presumably the rest remains the property of the state, whoever benefits from it from time to time.[117]

For such a system to work, the people must be properly educated. This does not mean simply literacy, numeracy, higher scholastic education, and vocational training:

> to form the Character to good Habits and good Dispositions, & to check those that are vicious; this is the Soul and Spirit of right

[112] See p. 285.
[113] See pp. 286–287.
[114] See p. 287.
[115] See p. 283.
[116] See pp. 284–285.
[117] See pp. 291–292.

Education. To accomplish this as far as can be done by human Means, requires great Knowledge of human Nature, constant Attention, great Temper, Patience and Assiduity. The diseases of the Mind while it is pliable and docile as well as those of the Body may, by prudent Means, be cured or alleviated.[118]

Such moral training must be given to all the people, because "Nature has not made the Talents of Body or Mind that are usefull in Society, hereditary, or peculiar to any Rank." But equality of opportunity does not mean equality in the result, and "in such a State there will be a much greater variety of Ranks than in any other."[119] In order to establish the membership of these ranks, it is necessary that a constant supervision and record is kept of each individual's contribution to the common good in all its aspects:

As the Labour in every Employment is for the Publick, it must be overseen by Officers appointed by the Publick, who shall at stated times make a Report to superior Officers of the Industry, Skill and moral behaviour of every Individual under their Charge.[120]

According to how people fare in this assessment, they will be given "Distinctive ba⟨d⟩ges or habits, by which every Mans Rank & the Respect due to him may be known"; similarly "a Man may be made to carry about him the Marks" of "Dishonour & Disgrace." If this system of incentives and disincentives is not sufficient for some "to make them act their part in Society," Utopia has recourse to punishment. Indeed, "Such Persons have the Temper of Slaves and ought to be degraded into that state, being altogether unworthy and incapable of being Citizens of Utopia."[121] The task with which the Utopian state is burdened is thus extensive:

The Education of all the Youth of both Sexes. The Oversight of all the labouring hands. The collecting, storing and dispersing the Produce of their Labour. The publick Registers that must be kept of the Merits and Demerits of every Individual, & of every Step of his advancement in Honour and Rank. The Regulations for confering Degrees with Justice and Impartiality, and the Management of the trading Stock of the Nation.[122]

Reid argues at some length that the legislative and judiciary branches of government in Utopia will be relieved of so much work as will easily compensate for the increased executive load.

---

[118] See p. 289.   [119] See pp. 289–291.   [120] See p. 290.
[121] See pp. 290, 292.   [122] See p. 293.

It is now abundantly clear that the overriding element in Reid's notion of the common good is moral perfection. The striving for all-round moral perfection is the basic precept of natural law that justifies the imposition of all necessary duties. Against this individual rights have no force; there are simply no other rights than those whose enforcement is in keeping with this common good.

This enables us to consider the two central problems, noted briefly above, concerning the role of natural law and the common good. We may unite them and describe Reid's suspected dilemma as follows. As we have seen, he was a moral realist in the sense that he held that the basic moral category is an objective relation—namely, duty—between a person and an action; the relation is objective in the sense that it is established by moral First Principles, which cannot in any sense be reduced to subjective states, whether cognitive or emotive, of the agent or the spectator. At the same time, he held that human actions are sorted into rights and duties by the law of nature, which God prescribes for man in order to create the common good. Are these views not mutually exclusive?

Reid does not, of course, suggest that natural law *makes* actions good or bad; it points out which actions *are* in fact good or bad, by being internalized as each person's conscience or moral faculty. Further, the actions that are good and that natural law therefore prescribes do indeed contribute to the common good. This is moral in character, which means that it is realized when the doing of one's duty—that is, the carrying out of morally right actions—is optimal. We can therefore take it as a sign that an action is not morally right if it conflicts with the common good, and if an individual claims a right to perform such an action we can be certain that he has no right in the matter, for there cannot be any duty to respect his claim.

We may also understand Reid's position by contrasting it with the theory of the artificial virtues, particularly justice, which he found in Hume.[123] As Reid saw it, Hume maintained that acts of justice have no inherent or natural moral quality but are lent a certain moral coloring by their connection with public utility; they are morally justified because in general they contribute to the public good. By contrast, Reid maintains that the common good is made up of actions that are in themselves or inherently morally good. Moreover, although not the ground justifying the moral goodness of actions, it may obviously be the criterion by which we can discern morally right actions in situations where their direct contemplation is not sufficient, such as sit-

[123] A.P., v.v, and ibid., pp. 667–670. On Hume's and Smith's concept of public utility, see Haakonssen, *Science of a Legislator*, pp. 40–41, 87–88, 120–123.

uations with competing rights-claims or situations where people's moral sense is warped by selfishness, criminal inclinations, and so on. This is why the concept of the common good plays a key role in Reid's system of *practical* ethics and hence in his utopian polity. The idea of the common good as a sign or criterion of recognition, rather than a ground of justification, should also make it clear that Reid is not a consequentialist in his political theory, save in the trivial sense that political institutions serve an end; but that end is moral rightness.

When Reid's version of Pufendorf's system of natural law is combined with the idea that all morality can be certainly taught, his utopian vision follows readily:

> if ever civil government shall be brought to perfection, it must be the principal care of the state to make good citizens by proper education, and proper instruction and discipline. . . . The end of government is to make the society happy, which can only be done by making it good and virtuous. That men in general will be good or bad members of society, according to the education and discipline by which they have been trained, experience may convince us. The present age has made great advances in the art of training men to military duty. . . . And I know not why it should be thought impossible to train men to equal perfection in the other duties of good citizens. What an immense difference is there, for the purposes of war, between an army properly trained, and a militia hastily drawn out of the multitude? What should hinder us from thinking that, for every purpose of civil government, there may be a like difference between a civil society properly trained to virtue, good habits, and right sentiments, and those civil societies which we now behold?[124]

Revolution or Reform

Reid's political theory is at one level an unusually explicit synthesis of one brand of natural jurisprudence with humanist utopianism. The former undoubtedly developed during his tenure of the Glasgow

---

[124] A.P., pp. 577b–578a. There is in Reid a never-resolved tension between this kind of moral perfectibilism, which points toward a "perfect moral commonwealth," and an acceptance of man's inherent moral imperfectibility, which points to institutional arrangements that will make up for this—i.e., a Utopia proper. For this general distinction, see J. C. Davis, *Utopia and the Ideal Society* (1981), ch. 1. While this cannot be adequately discussed here, it should be kept in mind in the following section. The former line leads readily to Dugald Stewart's historicism (see this Introduction, below, p. 86), while the latter is more amenable to the possibility of institutional reform, to which Reid is attracted for reasons set out in the next section.

chair with its jurisprudential tradition; the latter probably dated from
his early introduction to the republicanism of the Commonwealth
tradition and its sources and certainly remained of central concern
throughout his life. Not only do republican and utopian authors figure prominently in his Aberdeen *Orations* and in the Glasgow lectures
on political jurisprudence, but the lectures on politics, following on
pneumatology and practical ethics in his Glasgow course, are strongly
influenced by James Harrington. When William Ogilvie, his successor
at King's College and subsequently professor of humanity, published
his utopian scheme for agrarian reform, Reid approved of it.[125]

Yet Reid was far from being a Harringtonian republican. While an
agrarian law might improve on existing social conditions, it still
founded civic virtue and political authority on property, and "It may
be doubted whether there is in this Model sufficient provision for
preserving that degree of Morals and publick Virtue which is necessary in a Commonwealth."[126] Nor would agrarian redistribution affect any of the other forms of property that had emerged in modern
society and that seemed much more difficult to control.[127] Political
reform could thus not be guaranteed by a change in property relations, but had to rely on moral reform of the sort outlined above.

This brought Reid into conflict not only with the Harringtonians
but also with the theory, favored by Hume, Smith, and Millar, of a
necessary though not exclusive link between forms of property and
forms of government. It is not implausible to see Reid's utopian
moral commonwealth as yet another criticism of Hume, in this instance of his adaptation of Harrington to a more advanced "Idea of
a perfect commonwealth."[128] It would be a sobering study of the com-
plexities of the reaction to the French Revolution and of the concept
of Whiggism to contrast Reid's scheme with the reform program of
his colleague, John Millar, in the latter's *Letters of Sidney* two years
later.[129]

[125] See Reid's letter to Ogilvie of 7 April 1789 in MacDonald's edition of Ogilvie's
Birthright in Land (1891), pp. 151–152. Ogilvie's *Essay on the Right of Property in Land*
was published anonymously in 1781 or 1782 (see *Birthright*, p. 186). On Ogilvie's usefulness in the nineteenth century, see J. Morrison Davidson's quaint Georgist tract *Concerning Four Precursors of Henry George* (1890).

[126] 4/III/6,4v. This is part of his lectures on politics.

[127] Ibid., 4r.

[128] See Hume, *Essays* (1898), pp. 480–493. On Smith, see Haakonssen, *Science of a
Legislator*, pp. 181–188. In this regard, Reid was preceded by Robert Wallace's *Various
Prospects of Mankind* (1761), which may well have inspired him.

[129] (John Millar), *Letters of Sidney, on Inequality of Property* (1796), and Haakonssen,
"John Millar and the Science of a Legislator" (1985). The *Letters* cannot certainly be
ascribed to Millar himself, but they clearly derive from him; see Haakonssen, "John
Millar," p. 42 n. 6.

Further light on Reid's views on the French Revolution may be gained indirectly. William Ogilvie thought that his agrarian scheme might be useful in India, and in a letter written in 1805 to Sir James Mackintosh, his former student and then recorder at Bombay, he tried to engage the latter's interest:

> I do not suppose that you, any more than myself, have embraced the philosophy of common sense, as it has been called, in all its latitude; but surely Dr. Reid's eminence in various sciences, and his successful endeavours to throw light on that which he cultivated, cannot have escaped your notice, any more than the merits of the 'Vindiciae Gallicae' escaped him. Mrs. Carmichael, his surviving daughter, at whose request I take the liberty of giving you this trouble, informs me that he was struck with admiration on reading that Essay, and used frequently to speak of it as one of the most ingenious works of the kind he had ever met with.[130]

This leads one to wonder whether Mrs. Carmichael's "request" perhaps echoes a wish of her father. It certainly indicates that Reid's esteem for Mackintosh's youthful radicalism survived the reaction against the French Revolution after 1791, lasting until his death in 1796. Why else would the daughter who cared for him in his last years be so concerned with it nearly ten years later?

Seen against this background, it is hardly surprising that Reid supported the early, hopeful phase of the French Revolution, when it was still possible for British sympathizers to see it as a delayed "English" revolution. It is thus of more than symbolic significance that when the Glasgow Friends of Liberty in 1791 called a Bastille Day celebration, at which Reid officiated as a steward, the public announcement echoed the language that Britons had been using for a century about their own revolution of 1688:

> The 14 of July being the anniversary of the late glorious revolution in France, by which so many millions have been restored to their rights as men and citizens, the Friends of Liberty in Glasgow and neighbourhood are invited to celebrate the second anniversary of that revolution.[131]

This liberal-Whig constitutionalist perspective, combined with Reid's moral progressivism, nonnecessitarian Calvinism, and republican

---

[130] Ogilvie to Mackintosh (received in June 1805), in R. J. Mackintosh, ed., *Memoirs of . . . Sir James Mackintosh* (1836), 1:380. For Mackintosh's answer and his appreciation of Ogilvie, see ibid., pp. 17 and 381–386. On Mackintosh's thought and its relationship to the themes discussed here, see Haakonssen, "The Science of a Legislator in James Mackintosh's Moral Philosophy."

[131] *Glasgow Mercury*, 5 July 1791. See also Wood, "Thomas Reid," pp. 181ff.

leanings, explains his enthusiasm for the revolution as a renewed attempt to implement moral freedom and in that sense the "rights of man," but to see Reid as the protagonist of some modern ideology of subjective rights of man is a misunderstanding of both his morals and his politics.[132] Reid himself brought together a number of these traditionalist elements in his account to an anonymous correspondent of the Glasgow celebration and its aftermath:

> Dear Sir   I have been in your Debt as a Correspondent since Christmas. You then rejoiced in the Return of that Anniversary, & in the great Events which had happened in our Neighbouring Kingdom both Civil & Ecclesiastical. In all this I think you did what might become a good Praefectorian, & I give you the right hand of Fellowship. Among the other Wonders of our Day, let the pure Wine of Rome & Geneva mix, leaving the Dregs behind! . . .
>
> I have been very long persuaded, that a Nation, to be free, needs onely to know the Rights of Man. I have lived to see this Knowledge spread far beyond my most sanguine hopes, and produce glorious Effects. God grant it may spread more & more & that those who taste the Sweets of Liberty may not turn giddy but make a wise and sober Use of it.
>
> Some few here think or affect to think, that to be a Friend to the Revolution of France is to be an Enemy to the Constitution of . . . Britain, or at least to its present Administration. I know the contrary to be true in my self, & verily believe that most of my Acquaintance who rejoice in that Revolution agree with me in this.
>
> In this belief, upon the sollicitation of some friends in the College & others, I permitted my Name to be used, for a meeting of Friends to the French Revolution on the 14 of July, upon the Condition & promise of my fellow Stewarts that no unfavourable Reflection direct or oblique either on the Constitution or present Administration of Great Britain was to be heard. I meant nothing more than to own myself not ashamed to be thought a friend to the French Revolution, & thought no Mortal needed to take offence at this. But I have within this four and twenty hours received an Anonymous letter in a feigned hand professing friend-

---

[132] Seen in this light, neither Reid's recommendation of Mary Wollstonecraft's *Vindication of the Rights of Woman* (1792), nor his qualification of it, is surprising: "Have you ⟨Dugald Stewart⟩ read a *Vindication of the Rights of Woman?* I think a Professor of Morals may find some things worthy of his attention, mixed, perhaps, with other things which he may not approve" (Letter to Stewart, 21 January 1793, in Veitch, "Memoir of Dugald Stewart," p. cxlviii).

ship, and great Surprize *that my Name should appear at the bottom of an Advertisement calling together a set of political Madmen and Black- guards; and acquainting me that the time is fast approaching when I and some of my brethren will repent the steps we have taken.*

Whether you do think it more odd that an old deaf Dotard should be announced a Stewart of such a Meeting, or that it should give any Man such offence.[133]

Reid caused further offense when in the following year, with many others, he gave money to the French National Assembly.[134] After that he could no longer approve of the course of the revolution, and by 1794 he was prepared to indicate this publicly, in his Utopia paper. It is, however, a misunderstanding to see this as a political *volte-face*.[135] It was the political situation that had changed, not Reid's position. His defense of the British constitution in that paper is entirely in line with his "rights-of-man" letter quoted above and with everything he had previously said on the topic.

By way of his esteem for Mackintosh and the sort of token support for the beginnings of the French Revolution that many liberal and radical Whigs gave, we have let Reid slide away from utopianism to- ward the third element in his political thought, which tempers this and brings us back to natural law. Reid was apprehensive of the uto- pian implications of his moral thought. In the course of unraveling these implications,[136] he breaks off in alarm: "But I fear I shall be thought to digress from my subject into Utopian speculation." Six years later he again indulged in utopian speculation in his lengthy paper to the Glasgow Literary Society, but he prefaced that passage with a caution against the dangers of sudden wholesale political in- novation and praised the British constitution as a vehicle for gradual peaceful change. The paper as a whole is entitled "Some Thoughts on the Utopian System," but only the prefatory remarks were pub- lished in a local newspaper, under the title "Observations on the Dan- gers of Political Innovation."[137]

---

[133] 3/III/8. The draft letter is neither addressed nor dated; it was presumably written soon after 14 July 1791 and clearly to someone close to Reid.

[134] See M. Forbes, *Beattie and His Friends* (1904), p. 273.

[135] See Meikle, *Scotland and the French Revolution* (1969), pp. 155–156.

[136] See n. 124 above.

[137] *Glasgow Courier*, 18 December 1794. We do not know whether Reid himself initi- ated its publication or chose the title. The newspaper article is, oddly enough, re- printed in the *Discourses on Theological and Literary Subjects* (1803) of Reid's successor, Archibald Arthur, and the editor, William Richardson, says that it was "published with his ⟨Reid's⟩ consent in the Glasgow Courier" ("An account of some particulars in the life and character of the Rev. Mr. Archibald Arthur, late Professor of Moral Philoso- phy in the University of Glasgow," in Arthur, *Discourses*, p. 514 n.; see also ibid., p.

By the British constitution Reid undoubtedly meant the 1688–89 principles of government, interpreted on liberal Whig lines, though it is difficult to determine exactly which lines. What is important is that this respect for constitutional principles in Reid demonstrates a more general constitutionalist bent—that is, a tendency to see politics as a rule-governed system. It is significant that, with Harrington, Montesquieu is the dominant influence on his lectures on politics. In the lectures on Harrington, Reid is obsessively concerned with the labyrinthine regulations of the Commonwealth of Oceana, and it is easy to imagine his fascination with the mechanical politics of other utopias. To such a mind the idea of organizing all morality into neat jurisprudential categories of duties and rights governed by natural law must have had strong appeal, especially as an extension of a moral philosophy that showed there were objective, universally valid principles of moral knowledge. Consequently the moral uncertainty, historical chance, and mere political probability inherent in radical political change appalled him. Indeed his dislike, even fear, of these often seems to amount to a mistrust of politics as such, and it is not surprising that in his utopia politics are replaced by moral accountancy. The constitutionalist element in his thought is thus the natural result of his dread of a life governed by political chance, which Hume and Smith had accepted as the inevitable lot of mankind but which he felt it his moral and philosophical duty to oppose.

Reid's desire for a different society and his fear of change as a means of achieving it constitute the traditional utopian dilemma, and he had not yet succumbed to the temptation of seeking refuge in the future. It was left to his self-appointed disciple, Dugald Stewart, to find a way out of the dilemma in the historicist idea of the inevitable and unpolitical march of the mind toward the moral commonwealth of the future.[138] If this was a fitting response to the political ambiguity of postrevolutionary Europe, the reader may be left to consider whether Reid was too simple or too honest to adopt it, or whether he was spared by living too soon.

518). Richardson, however, is so determined to lump Reid and Arthur together as upright, consistent opponents of the French Revolution that both his judgment and his intentions are suspect.

[138] For further development of this, see Haakonssen, "From Moral Philosophy to Political Economy: The Contribution of Dugald Stewart" (1984). In his last years, Reid was close not only to Stewart but also to the intellectually minded artists around him, one of whom, Raeburn, made Reid the subject of an outstanding portrait painted in the year of the Utopia paper and dramatically echoing Ramsay's portrait of Rousseau. Another painter, Alexander Nasmyth, also probably influenced by Reid's and Stewart's theory of perception, apparently found in Reid support for his own utopian leanings. See Macmillan, *Painting in Scotland*, pp. 145–146.

4. Reid's Manuscripts

and the Editor's Commentary

Organization of the Text

ALL THE MANUSCRIPTS printed in this volume, except for that in Section XVIII, are in the Birkwood Collection held by Aberdeen University Library in Scotland. This extensive collection includes well over five hundred manuscripts, which encompass the full range of Reid's intellectual concerns as well as some more private papers. There are a few manuscripts from the years before Reid became a regent at King's College, Aberdeen, in 1751, and some from his time in Aberdeen from 1751 to 1764, but the bulk of the material dates from his years in Glasgow, from 1764 to his death in 1796.

The papers on practical ethics all appear to have been written in Glasgow. The paper printed in this book in Section XV was undoubtedly presented in this or a similar form to the Glasgow Literary Society, as was the paper printed here in Section XVIII. Apart from these and the reading notes in Sections X and XVII, all the papers in this volume, directly or indirectly, were notes for Reid's lectures to the "public" class prescribed for the arts degree and perhaps for his examination session, which supplemented it.[1] A large number of the manuscripts are admittedly undated, but most of these elaborate on themes dealt with in Reid's first winter of lecturing in Glasgow. I suspect that nearly all were written during the first four or five years of the Glasgow period, with occasional small additions dated 1770 and 1771. It is safe to say that Reid gave substantially the same lectures on practical ethics throughout his years in Glasgow, for the notes taken by Robert Jack in 1776 (preserved only in part) and by George Baird in 1779–80 agree with Reid's own notes from the 1760s.

The order in which the manuscripts, including those on practical ethics, have been preserved and cataloged bears little relationship to the intellectual order from which they sprang and which it has been the editor's first task to reconstruct. As far as the core of the lectures

---

[1] See p. 26 above.

on practical ethics is concerned—namely the sections on Duties to Others—this task was greatly aided by the lucky circumstance that it was possible to find *dated* material for this group of lectures on natural jurisprudence as presented in the spring of 1765, Reid's first academic year at Glasgow.[2] This provided the basic structure for the major part of Reid's course, which, as we see from the students' notes, he retained thereafter. These 1765 notes are printed without interruption in Sections IV, V, VI, VII, and VIII, while all material that systematically belongs with this portion but is dated later than 1765, or not dated, is presented in Sections X–XVI (elements of Section XVII belong here as well).

The lectures on "Duties to Others," did not exhaust the field of practical ethics. At the opening of his second Glasgow session on 5 November 1765, Reid's notes suggested that "The End of Ethicks or Morals is to shew what is right and what is wrong in human Action. The Duty of a Man in all the different circumstances and Relations in which he may be placed is the Object of this Branch of Philosophy."[3] Later in that session (see Sections II and III below) he elaborated this in accordance with the Pufendorfian tripartite scheme by lecturing on duties to God and to ourselves before dealing with duties to others. We have no equivalent material from the 1764–65 academic session, and there is clear evidence that Reid, presumably pressed for time, passed from pneumatology, as the foundation of practical ethics and politics, to "duties to others," as the dominant branch of practical ethics, by way of some very brief remarks on the other duties.[4] The first two parts of Reid's Practical Ethics, Sections II and III below, thus do not date from Reid's first year in Glasgow, but from 1765–66 and 1768–69, and to these is added some undated material in Section IX.

Conventionally, modern natural lawyers dealt with rights and obligations between states as part of natural jurisprudence, and Reid

---

[2] A few days are not explicitly noted but can be accounted for as follows. Friday 8 March: It seems obvious that Reid covered the separate topic of "Adventitious Rights" (p. 148); Friday 15 March: Here Reid must have dealt with "Pledges. Morgages. Servitudes" (p. 153); Monday 18 March: Transfer of property must have taken up this lecture (pp. 153–154); Friday 29 March: This is only apparently missing; in fact, Reid made an error in his dating, as explained in the Textual Notes at 162/40; 5 and 8 April were Good Friday and Easter Monday; finally, there is no lecture dated 16 April but, as explained in the Commentary, pp. 368–369 n. 9, Reid probably finished Practical Ethics at the end of his lecture on 15 April or the beginning of 16 April with some brief comments on international law and then started directly on Politics, for by 17 April he was already well advanced into Politics. Reid's general lecturing calendar is explained above, p. 26.

[3] 4/II/1,1r.   [4] See the Commentary, p. 316 n. 1.

plainly intended to follow convention,[5] though it is not entirely clear whether he managed to do so in his first year at Glasgow. The brief, undated manuscript printed below in Section VIII seems either to have been delivered in that session or to have been written later in 1765 as part of the preparation for the 1765–66 session.[6] On this topic there are, however, very ample materials, undated or from later years, and these are collected in Section XVII.

Finally I print at the head of Reid's course in practical ethics an Introductory Lecture. Before embarking on his survey of pneumatology, ethics, and politics, Reid gave a general introduction to his course. In 1765–66 the notes for this ran to a mere three pages; over the next few years this material increased, until at some time after 1769, probably in 1770 or 1771, it had become a substantial seventeen-page lecture, which I print as Section I.

Some manuscripts have been excluded, although they deal with topics falling within the range of this volume; these are 2/II/14, 4/III/18, 7/VII/2–6, and 6/I/9. The last of these is probably an early draft of part of *Active Powers*, essay V, chapter 5, and indeed is headed "Ch 5." The other manuscripts taken together constitute an almost complete draft of chapter 6 and provide valuable material for a critical edition of *Active Powers*, but in view of their closeness to the published text it is pointless to print them here.

It should be noted that in the Commentary, as in the Introduction, when I refer to the manuscripts of the Birkwood Collection I drop the first four digits (2131), which are common to all the manuscripts. Thus 2131/8/IV/9 becomes 8/IV/9.

The Principles of the Commentary

In commenting on Reid's text I have been guided by four related principles.

1. I have seen it as a primary task to identify the questions Reid was addressing. This has been a major undertaking, partly because the tradition in which his course stands is no longer well-known, partly because his text sometimes consists of mere keywords and briefly indicated points to assist him in his lecturing.

2. I have also tried to identify Reid's sources, but because he is rarely explicit about these I have in most cases only been able to make probable suggestions.

3. In order to identify Reid's topics and justify the probability of

[5] See the Commentary, p. 317 n. 7.
[6] See pp. 368–369 n. 9.

his sources, I have attempted to reconstruct the wider context in which Reid's discussions must be viewed. This is, however, a virtually endless task, so it was necessary to be selective, and I have in general restricted myself to providing pointers, leaving the remaining work to the reader.

4. In identifying Reid's topics, sources, and contexts, I have generally sought to avoid interpretation of what Reid himself had to say on these topics and sources and thus of what he contributed to the contexts. This goal may appear to be unattainable. The very organization of the manuscripts rests on an interpretation—the selection of some points rather than others for commentary or further reference implies some interpretation, and so do the contents of such commentaries and references. The fact that the distinction between identifying topics, sources, and contexts and interpreting Reid's contributions to these is an elusive one is, however, exactly what makes the maintenance of this distinction an important restraint on editorial interference. If it were a sharp criterion, rather than merely a guiding ideal, its discipline would not be so necessary.

In view of the difficulties in identifying Reid's sources, a few general remarks are called for here. At one point Reid recommends to his students a list of "Authors upon this Subject ⟨Natural Jurisprudence⟩: Grotius, Hobbes Selden Puffendorf. Barbyrack upon Grotius & Puffendorf. Carmichael upon Puffendorf. Locke. Hoadly. Hutcheson Burlamaqui Vattel. Cocceij."[7] It is clear that he himself did not make use of all these in his lectures, while there are several others that he did use. Reid's most immediate sources for long parts of his course were evidently Hutcheson's *Short Introduction* (or its Latin original) and *System*. Its general outline was Pufendorfian, and in his reading of Pufendorf he was undoubtedly aided by Barbeyrac's and Carmichael's annotations and commentaries, though it is difficult to gauge to what extent—in the case of Carmichael partly because so much of Hutcheson is borrowed from Carmichael. It is interesting that Reid does not mention any of the numerous other commentators on Pufendorf, perhaps especially Titius, who is discussed frequently by Barbeyrac and Carmichael and to whom Reid refers in *Active Powers*.[8] I have therefore used Titius only occasionally.

Reid certainly studied Grotius closely, apparently in a Latin edition with Barbeyrac's notes, though it is likely that he was also acquainted with Barbeyrac's edition in either English or French. The only reference to the vast array of commentaries on Grotius, apart from Barbeyrac, is to Cocceius, and here Reid does not make it clear whether

---

[7] See p. 197.   [8] A.P., p. 663a.

he means Heinrich Cocceius's enormous four-volume commentary or his son Samuel's five-hundred page introduction to the latter. There is no decisive evidence that Reid used either, and I have accordingly compromised as follows. Because every reference to Grotius can be used as a reference to the commentary, which follows the *De iure* point for point, I have not provided references to Heinrich Cocceius. I have, however, given references to Samuel Cocceius for most of the topics central to the discipline, namely, private jurisprudence—partly because Reid may have used the work here and others may be able to take the matter further than I have, partly because the organization of the younger Cocceius's work is a good deal more opaque than that of his father.

Returning to the rest of Reid's list, Hobbes, Locke, and Hoadly are mainly used in political jurisprudence, while Vattel completely dominates Reid's discussion of the rights and obligations of states. As for Selden, there can be little doubt that Reid has some acquaintance with his *Mare clausum* and must at least have known of Selden's other main work of relevance for natural jurisprudence, *De jure naturali et gentium juxta disciplinam Ebraeorum*, from the frequent discussions of it in his main jurisprudential reading. I do not find any evidence that Reid used Selden for his lectures and have therefore not used him in the Commentary. The same applies to Burlamaqui, whose main work, *The Principles of Natural and Politic Law*, was translated into English in 1748, with a second edition in 1763. While Reid knew of and may have read the book, there are no discernible traces of it in his lectures.

There are two works to which I have referred systematically in the Commentary although Reid himself does not do so in the text. The first is Heineccius's *System of Universal Law*, the other is David Fordyce's *Elements of Moral Philosophy*. Heineccius's work was translated by Reid's teacher, George Turnbull, and Reid could not have avoided it. In Turnbull's supplements we find an explicit attempt to draw together the teachings of modern natural law and of Harrington, and this alone requires the presence of the work in our context. Furthermore, Heineccius's text is a particularly systematic exposition of natural law that had some influence on Scottish legal thought—for example, on Erskine. References to Fordyce's intellectually feeble *Elements* are provided mainly because the work represents the moralizing-educative function of practical ethics which was important in Reid's environment and in his own work.[9]

[9] Reid's familiarity with Fordyce's work is hardly in doubt in view of their friendship; see p. 10 above.

Of all the natural lawyers who play little or no role in the Commentary, four should be mentioned. Leibniz's metaphysics was certainly known to Reid, but Reid's acquaintance with Leibniz's practical philosophy probably derived largely from Barbeyrac and Carmichael. Thomasius seems to have been as unknown, or as uninteresting, to Reid as to nearly everybody else in Britain. As for Wolff, Reid knew his *Psychologia empirica* (though not the *Psychologia rationalis*) and the *Ontologia*,[10] but the works on jurisprudence seem to have been known to him only through Vattel. Because Wolff had little influence on British moral thought, I have hardly made use of him. The same applies to Richard Cumberland. Reid knew Cumberland's work, but he simply bracketed it with that of Pufendorf and Hutcheson in a rather broad category. In some notes he says that "Cumberland, Puffendorf and Dr. Hutcheson build their moral Reasoning Chiefly upon" the following axiom, "That course of conduct which conduces to the happiness and perfection of human Society is Right & the contrary wrong."[11] Beyond this I have not been able to trace more specific influences on Reid's scheme of practical ethics.

Reid had no legal training, and his reading of Roman law seems to have been sporadic and mainly though not entirely guided by Grotius and Pufendorf. More remarkable is the lack of evidence that Reid made use of any of the great Dutch civilians, such as Vinnius, Voet, Huber, and Bynkershoek. As for Scots law, Reid's knowledge appears patchy; he had certainly informed himself on particular topics, such as entails, with his friend Lord Kames as the apparent chief source, but it is not possible to determine his use of such authorities as Mackenzie, Stair, or Erskine.

With regard to ancient and modern historians and moralists, the Commentary should be self-explanatory both in what it includes and in what it omits, but special mention of Adam Smith must be made. Reid had succeeded Smith in the Glasgow chair, and in what seems to have been his inaugural lecture he asked his audience for notes of Smith's lectures.[12] We do not know the results of this request, but

[10] See A.P., pp. 220, 307, and 377.

[11] 7/v/5,1r. Cumberland's *De legibus naturae* was published in 1672, and there are English translations of 1727 and 1750 and an important French translation with annotations by Barbeyrac of 1744. The latter is the most satisfactory and the one with which I have generally checked Reid's manuscripts. The only satisfactory study of Cumberland is Kirk, *Richard Cumberland and Natural Law. Secularisation of Thought in Seventeenth-Century England* (1987).

[12] 4/II/9,2r: "I am . . . much a stranger to his ⟨Smith's⟩ System unless so far as he hath published it to the world. But ⟨as⟩ . . . a man of so great Genius and penetration must have struck new light into the Subjects which he treated, as well as have handled them in an excellent and instructive manner, I shall be much obliged to any of you Gentle-

because the tracing of direct influences is at best speculative and because comparison of Smith's and Reid's lectures, thanks to the analytical table provided by the former's editors,[13] is easy, the present and Smith-inclined editor has restrained himself in this regard.

I have not tried to draw parallels between Reid's teaching and that of such of his contemporaries at the other Scottish universities of whom we have manuscript records. As far as moral philosophy is concerned, this is currently so unexplored that it would be courting disaster to attempt it here. It is hoped that the publication of Reid's record will be of assistance to those undertaking such a task.

Finally I should point out that, in view of the many repetitions of themes in the manuscripts and the difficulty of deciding which is the most significant, I have *in general* provided the main annotation and discussion of a theme on its *first* occurrence. This, together with the often very abbreviated form of the notes from Reid's first Glasgow session, explains why the Commentary for Sections IV–VIII is so extensive.

The Printing of the Manuscripts

My aim has been to maintain as accurate a representation of the manuscripts as is compatible with the creation of a readable text. Because most of the manuscripts contain a good many deletions, insertions, corrections, and the like, this has been difficult. The main body of the text presents what I consider to be the final version of each manuscript. Everything else of significance on the manuscript pages is printed or explained in the Textual Notes following the Commentary, according to principles explained below.

EDITORIAL INTERVENTIONS IN THE MAIN TEXT. I have occasionally inserted in Reid's text a word or a few letters when it is quite clear that their absence is a slip of the pen and that the insertion facilitates the reading. Such insertions are contained in ⟨angle brackets⟩. Much more infrequently, I have tried to assist readability by enclosing the reverse kind of slips of the pen—that is, material that should not be in the text—in [square brackets]. It should be stressed, however, that one type of editorial deletion has been made silently—without square brackets and without remark in the Textual Notes. These are repetitions of phrases, some of which are simply errors; others are the con-

---

men or to any other, who can furnish me with Notes of his Prelections whether in Morals, Jurisprudence, Police or in Rhetorick." See p. 32 above.

[13] Smith, *Lectures on Jurisprudence*, Introduction, pp. 24–27.

ventional catchwords at the bottom of a page. On two occasions (p.
146 l. 6 and p. 199 ll. 37–38) I have enclosed superscribed additions
in (parentheses) in order to make the passage readable, as explained
in the Textual Notes to those places. Within these guidelines and with
these exceptions, Reid's spelling and grammar have been left un-
touched, and the reader will simply have to trust my proofreading.

PUNCTUATION. With the exception of three deletions (at p. 166 l. 31,
p. 209 l. 17, and p. 277 l. 13, as noted in the Textual Notes), I have
preserved Reid's punctuation, however much it varies from present
conventions and from his own conventions in published work. Often
Reid signals a period by an otherwise unexpected capitalization but
without using a period point. On such occasions I have *silently* inserted the period point. Otherwise, no punctuation has been editorially added. The reader should be aware that Reid often used a period point where we would expect a comma. It is my impression that
he often inserted much of his punctuation after completing a paragraph or more, and this would certainly explain many peculiarities.
Something similar applies to the consecutive dates in the notes from
1765. In my opinion, most if not all of the dates were inserted after
the writing and probably also after the delivery of the lectures.

PAGE BREAKS. Page breaks in the manuscripts are indicated by a
slanted bar: /. In the page margin at the line with which Reid began
a new manuscript page the conventionally abbreviated manuscript
number is printed and followed, after a comma, by an indication of
the page number in the original manuscript. In the case of the fully
paginated manuscripts—the Introductory Lecture that is Section I
and the paper on the utopian system in Section XVIII—the manuscript *page* is given. Thus, in the margin of page 105, line 25, I indicate that the text turns to MS. 2131/7/v/4, page 3, by printing "7/v/
4,3." In the case of unpaginated or incompletely paginated manuscripts, I give the folio number and the side—recto (r) or verso (v)—
of the folio. Thus on page 139, line 11, I indicate that the text turns
to the verso side of folio number 4 of MS. 2131/8/IV/3 by printing "8/
IV/3,4v" in the margin. This should allow the reader to follow the way
I have arranged the manuscripts. Reid often used the same pad of
paper for different purposes, so it has been necessary to divide a
number of manuscripts. Similarly, the rejoining of manuscripts that
cohered originally has meant that their pages are printed here in an
order different from that in which they happen to have been preserved.

THE TEXTUAL NOTES. In the Textual Notes, which follow the Commentary, Reid's wording is printed in roman and everything supplied by the editor is in *italics*. The notes first of all record text variants, according to the following principle. Deletions that never formed an autonomous part of the text—false starts—are *not* recorded. Variants that conceivably may be considered complete are printed. Because the text often takes the form of notes, a number of doubtful cases are left for the editor's judgment; I have been generous in my recording of such cases. Text variants are indicated by the page and line number(s), followed by the first and the last word in the final text to which a variant exists, followed by the sign], followed by the variant. For example, on page 158, lines 40–41, Reid had at first written "thinks himself highly dishonoured" but changed it to the final version: "is affronted in the highest degree." This is recorded thus:

158/40–41 is . . . degree] thinks himself highly dishonoured.

In some cases there are variants of the variants; these are recorded according to the same principle. Frequently there is nothing in the final text that corresponds to a deletion. Thus on page 206, line 7, Reid mentions rights that are "original," but in an earlier version of the manuscript he had written "original which are either Real or personal," subsequently deleting "which . . . personal." In such cases it is necessary to have the notes maintain an overlap in the wording of the final text and the variant, in this case the word "original," in order to "anchor" the deletion to the appropriate place in the final text. The note for this example therefore reads:

206/7 original] original which are either Real or personal.

In other words, where a word from the final text reappears at the beginning of the variant, this word is not itself part of the variant. (In a few cases Reid actually does repeat words in such situations, but these would be silently passed over, as mentioned above.) In addition to recording text variants, the Textual Notes explain a wide variety of features in the appearance of the text and note the few deviations from the general principles explained here. Finally, the Textual Notes for the beginning of each section list the manuscript(s) printed in that section and give an indication of the length and the amount of text in each.

NOTE INDICATORS. All note indicators in the text are to the Commentary. The notes are consecutive within each section. The Textual Notes are not referred to in the text.

5. Index of Manuscripts

Below are indexed all the Thomas Reid manuscripts printed in whole or in part in this book. This includes manuscripts quoted in the editor's Introduction and Commentary but not those merely referred to. Details of the collections from which these manuscripts stem are given above, p. 86. It is important to note that for all the manuscripts from the Birkwood Collection—that is, all the manuscripts indexed except the last one—the manuscript numbers printed below and elsewhere in this book drop the first four digits (namely, 2131), which they have in common. The page numbers in italics refer to Reid's text, the remainder to the Introduction and the Commentary.

Birkwood Collection Manuscripts

MS. NUMBER	PAGES IN THIS VOLUME	MS. NUMBER	PAGES IN THIS VOLUME
2/II/10	*237–244*	7/V/5,5r–v	*185–187*
3/II/4,1v	*377–378* (n. 2)	7/VII/1	*190–192*
3/II/5	*269–270, 272–276*	7/VII/1a	*193–197*
3/III/8	*83–84*	7/VII/1b	*201–203*
4/I/27	*103–104*	7/VII/1c,1r–2r	*204–205*
4/I/31,1r	29	7/VII/1c,1v	442 (n. 158)
4/II/3	*303–304* (n. 4)	7/VII/1c,2r–2v	*197–201*
4/II/9,2r	*91–92* (n. 12)	7/VII/6,1r	348–349 (n.
4/III/4	*158–162, 165–166*		105)
4/III/6,4v	81	7/VII/6,2r	350 (n. 108)
4/III/17	*162–165*	7/VII/8	*184–185*
4/III/23c	*270–272*	7/VII/11,1r–v	*205–208*
6/I/17,1r	306 (n. 5)	7/VII/11,2v	*208–209*
6/V/34,1v	394–395 (n. 13)	7/VII/12	*213–214*
7/V/1,14r	56 (n. 52)	7/VII/13	208, *209–212*
7/V/3	*188–189*	7/VII/14	342 (n. 79)
7/V/4	*103–116*	7/VII/15	*217–219*
7/V/5,1r	91	7/VII/17	*219—222*
		7/VII/18	*222–226*

MS. NUMBER	PAGES IN THIS VOLUME	MS. NUMBER	PAGES IN THIS VOLUME
7/VII/19	226–229	8/IV/3	133–139
7/VII/20	229–236	8/IV/4	192–193
7/VII/21	182–183	8/IV/5,2r–v	149–152
7/VII/22	268–269	8/IV/6	380 (n. 11)
7/VII/23	257–264	8/IV/7	154–158, 166–172
7/VII/25	215–216		
8/III/2,2r–v	152–154	8/IV/8	264–268
8/III/10,1r	56 (n. 52)	8/IV/9	245–257
8/IV/1	140–149	8/IV/10	173–181
8/IV/2	117–132	8/V/1	18–19

Aberdeen University Library Manuscript

3061/6	277–299

6. Diagrams of Reid's System

DIAGRAM I represents Reid's general view of philosophy as he sets it out in his Introductory Lecture (Section I below). Diagram II begins with the structure of Reid's basic course in philosophy in Glasgow and proceeds to set out in some detail the portion on practical ethics, which is reconstructed in this volume. This diagram gives only a general orientation, but combined with the General Index it provides a detailed guide to the system.

DIAGRAM I

Thomas Reid's general view of philosophy as set out in his Introductory Lecture.

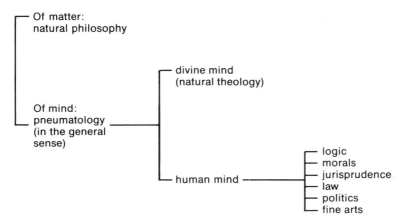

DIAGRAM II

The structure of Thomas Reid's basic course in philosophy, with the portion on practical ethics in detail.

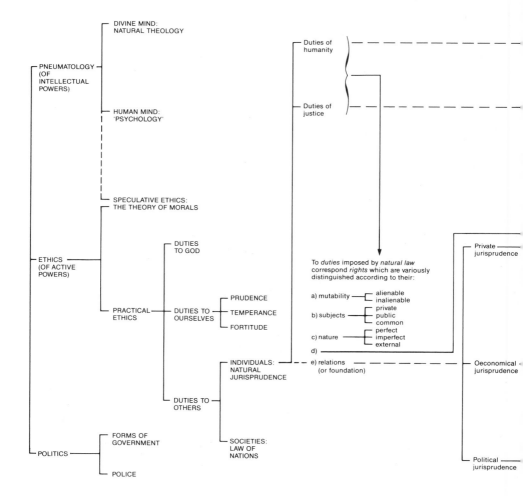

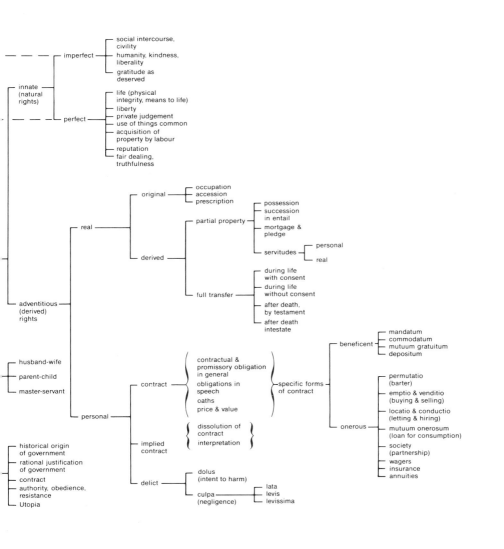

- innate (natural rights)
  - imperfect
    - social intercourse, civility
    - humanity, kindness, liberality
    - gratitude as deserved
  - perfect
    - life (physical integrity, means to life)
    - liberty
    - private judgement
    - use of things common
    - acquisition of property by labour
    - reputation
    - fair dealing, truthfulness
- adventitious (derived) rights
  - real
    - original
      - occupation
      - accession
      - prescription
    - derived
      - partial property
        - possession
        - succession in entail
        - mortgage & pledge
        - servitudes
          - personal
          - real
      - full transfer
        - during life with consent
        - during life without consent
        - after death, by testament
        - after death intestate
  - personal
    - contract
      - { contractual & promissory obligation in general, obligations in speech, oaths, price & value }
      - specific forms of contract
        - beneficent
          - mandatum
          - commodatum
          - mutuum gratuitum
          - depositum
        - onerous
          - permutatio (barter)
          - emptio & venditio (buying & selling)
          - locatio & conductio (letting & hiring)
          - mutuum onerosum (loan for consumption)
          - society (partnership)
          - wagers
          - insurance
          - annuities
    - implied contract
      - { dissolution of contract, interpretation }
    - delict
      - dolus (intent to harm)
      - culpa (negligence)
        - lata
        - levis
        - levissima

- husband-wife
- parent-child
- master-servant

- historical origin of government
- rational justification of government
- contract
- authority, obedience, resistance
- Utopia

Thomas Reid
Lectures and Papers on
Practical Ethics

7/v/4,1   My Course consists of these three Branches, Pneumatology, Ethicks and Politicks.[1] I shall in the beginning of it give
some general View of these three Parts of this Course & of
the dependance they have one upon another, for although
5   they are distinct Branches of Philosophy and have always
been considered as such, yet their Connection and Dependance is greater than has commonly been thought. The two
last in particular depend so much upon the first, that they
can not be understood nor treated scientifically unless they
10   are built upon Sound Principles drawn from Pneumatology.
    1   To begin with Pneumatology then, we may observe
4/1/27v   that / All Human Knowledge is employed either about Body
or Mind about things Material or things Intellectual. The
whole System of Bodies in the Universe, of which we know
15   but a very little part, may be called the Material World; And
the whole System of Minds or thinking Beings in the Universe from the Infinite Creator to the meanest Creature endued with thought may be called the Intellectual World.
About the one or the other of these or something pertaining
20   to them all Sciences treat, & all Arts are occupied. Those are
the two great Kingdoms of Nature to which human thought
is limited. Nor can the boldest flight of Imagination carry us
beyond their limits. Whether there be in the Universe any
other kinds of being, which are neither Extended Solid and
25   inert like Body, nor thinking & intelligent like Mind is beyond the Reach of our Knowledge; and therefore it would
be rash to determine. There is indeed a vast interval between Body & Mind; whether there may be some intermediate Substance that connects them together we know not.
30   We have no Reason to ascribe Intelligence, or even Sensation to Plants, yet there is an active Force and Energy in
them which cannot be the result ⟨of⟩ any arrangement or
combination of inert Matter. The same thing may be said of
those active Powers by which animals grow & by which Mat-

ter gravitates, by which Electrical & Magnetical Bodies attract and repell each other, & by which the parts of Solid Bodies cohere. Some have conjectured that the Phenomena of the Material World which require active Force are produced by the continual operation of intelligent Beings. Others have conjectured that there may be in the Universe Beings that are active without Intelligence, which as a kind of incorporeal Machinery contrived by the supreme Wisdom perform their destined task without any Knowledge or Intention. But laying aside conjecture & all pretence to form Determinations in things beyond the reach of the human faculties we must rest in this that Body and Mind are the only kinds of Being of which we have any Knowledge or can form any Conception. If there are other kinds they are not discoverable by the faculties which God hath given us, & with regard to us are as if they were not. /

7/v/4,1   As therefore all our Knowledge is confined to these two Objects of Bodies & Minds, or things belonging to one or other of these, so there are two great Branches of Philosophy; one of which relates to Bodies another to Minds. The general Properties of Bodies and the Laws that obtain in the Material World are the Object of Natural Philosophy or Physicks as that word is now used. The Nature & Operations of Minds is the Object of Pneumatology./

4/1/27,v   What variety there may be of Minds or Thinking Beings Throughout this vast Universe, we cannot pretend to say. We dwell in a little Corner of Gods Dominion, disjoined from the rest. The Globe which we inhabit is but one of six Planets which encircle our Sun. What various Orders of Beings and with what Powers endowed, may inhabit the other five, their Secondarys, & the Comets belonging to our System; & how many other Suns may be encircled with like Systems, are things altogether hid from us. Although human Ingenuity and Industry have discovered with great Accuracy the Order & Distances of the Planets & the Laws of their Motion, we have no means of corresponding with them. That they may be the habitation of animated Beings, we probably conjecture; But of the Nature or Powers of their Inhabitants we cannot even form a conjecture. It may therefore be asked, What are the thinking Beings of which we may attain any Knowledge? I answer Our own Minds.[2] /

7/v/4,2   Every Man is conscious that he thinks, & therefore concludes the Existence of a Mind or thinking Principle in himself. And we have sufficient Evidence of such a Principle in other Men. Even the Actions of Brutes show that they have some thinking Principle, though of a Nature far inferior to the human Mind. Every thing we see about us may convince us of the Existence of a Supreme Mind the Maker and Governour of the Universe. The Supreme Mind therefore, the Minds of Men, and those of the brute Animals that inhabit this Earth, are all the Minds that Reason discovers to us. Although Revelation teaches us the Existence of Angels and Archangels of various Orders some of whom fell from their first Estate of Purity and Happiness and others continued in it as this is a Doctrine of Revelation it does not belong to Philosophy but to theology.

I Divide Pneumatology therefore into two Branches; the first treats of the human Mind, To which Wolfius has given the name of Psychologie[3] the other treats of the Supreme Mind, and commonly goes by the name of Natural Theology. As the human Mind seems to be possessed of all the Faculties which we observe in Brutes, besides some of a Superior Nature of which there is no appearance in the most sagacious Brutes; there is no Necessity for treating separately of the Minds of Brutes. The agreements and Differences between their Faculties and those of Men may be noted in treating of the human Mind. /

We are therefore First to treat of the human Mind which is one constituent part of Man & the noblest part; & here we shall endeavour first to explain as distinctly as we are able the various powers and Faculties of the human Mind, & then shew what Reason discovers of its nature & duration whether it be material or immaterial Whether we have reason to think that it shall perish with the Body or continue to live in some future State.

The Mind of Man is the noblest Work of God that our Reason discovers to us, and therefore on account of its dignity deserves to ⟨be⟩ known.

It is justly reckoned a valuable branch of human knowledge to know the Structure of the human Body, the Uses of its various parts external & internal, the disorders and diseases to which they are liable & the Proper Remedies. There is a Structure of the Mind as well as of the Body. which is not less worthy to be known. Its various Powers & Faculties are the Workmanship of God no less than the various Parts of the Body and no less wisely adapted to their several Ends.

See Burke on the Sublime pag 35.[4] The knowledge of it is
indeed attended with many and great difficulties as I shall
afterwards shew. And there is no part of Philosophy in
which Speculative Men have run into so many and so great
Errors and even absurdities. This has raised a Prejudice
against this Branch of Knowledge with the Ignorant and superficial. Because ingenious Men in different ages have
given different and contradictory accounts of the powers of
the Mind they conclude that all that can be said upon this
Subject must be chimerical and visionary. But such general
Prejudices whatever Effect they may have upon superficial
thinkers, will, by the judicious and discerning, be easily perceived to be built upon very weak grounds. About 150 years
ago, nay much later, the opinions of men in natural Philosophy were as various and contradictory as they are at present with regard to Pneumatology. Galileo, Torricelli / Kep-
ler Bacon and Newton had the same Discouragements in
their attempts to find the Truth in natural Philosophy as we
have in the Philosophy of Mind. If they had been deterred
by such General Prejudices as that we have implied we
should never have enjoyed the benefit of their noble Discoveries, which do Honour to Human Nature and will render
their Names Immortal. Those elevated Spirits that have a
true relish for Science, are roused by difficulties, & the
Motto of a Philosopher is *Inveniam viam aut faciam*.[5]

There is a natural Order in the Progress of the Sciences,
as well as of the Arts: and good Reasons can be assigned
why the Philosophy of Body should both be elder Sister to
the Philosophy of Mind, and of a quicker Grouth. But the
last hath the *stamina vitae* no less than the first, & will,
though perhaps slowly grow up to Maturity. Des Cartes was
the first that pointed out the right road in this Branch of
Philosophy. Malebranch, Arnaud Locke Berkely, Shaftsbury. Hutcheson Butler Hume & others have laboured in it,
nor have they lavoured in vain;[6] for however different and
contrary their conclusions in many things are, & however
sceptical some of them they have all given new light to the
Subject; & have cleared the way in many respects to those
that shall follow them. Nor ought we at all to despair of human Genius and Industry; but rather to hope that in time it
may produce a System of the powers and operations of the
human Mind built upon principles no less certain than those
of Opticks or Astronomy.

This is the more devoutly to be wished, that it is certain, a distinct knowledge of the Powers of the human Mind would give great Light to many other branches of Philosophy. Mr Hume hath very justly observed that all the Sciences have a Reference to the human Mind & however far they may seem to go off from it, they still return by one channel or another.[7] This is the main fortress of Science & if we can once become Masters of it we shall extend our Conquest far and wide. The first Principles of all the Sciences are to be found in the Science of human Nature. This is a just & important Observation. I shall add that as Mr Humes sceptical System is all built upon a wrong & mistaken Account of the intellectual Powers of Man, so it can onely be refuted by giving a true Account of them. /

It is evident that the faculties of the human Mind are the Engines and Tools with which we work in every branch of Science and therefore it must be of great Importance to the advancement of every Science to understand well the Nature and Force of the Tools we use. Locke gives this Account of the occasion of his entring upon his Essay concerning human Understanding Pref. Pag 2d: "Five or six Friends, says he, meeting at my Chamber and discoursing on a Subject very remote from this, found themselves quickly at a stand by the difficulties that rose on every side. After we had for a while puzzled our selves without coming any nearer to a Resolution of those Doubts which perplexed us; it came into my Thoughts that we took a wrong Course; and that before we set our selves upon Enquiries of that Nature, it was necessary to examine our own abilities, & see what Objects our Understandings were fitted, or were not fitted to deal with. This I proposed to the Company who all readily assented. And thereupon it was agreed that this should be our first Enquiry."[8]

We shall find this indeed to be generally the case; when we are puzzled and perplexed in any scientifick Enquiry, and can neither see our way clearly nor discover whether it is possible to be seen or not. The Cause of this perplexity commonly is the want of a Right understanding of the powers of our own Minds. If this is the Case even in those Sciences which have the least relation to the human Mind, as the most Judicious Philosophers have acknowledged, it must be much more so, in those Sciences that have a very close & immediate connection with it.

As all the objects of our Knowledge are reducible ⟨to⟩
these two Heads of Body and Mind, or what belongs to one
7/v/4,6   or / other, so the Sciences may be distinguished into two
Classes; They are either such as relate to Body, or such as
5   relate to Mind. Medicine Chemistry Agriculture & all the
Mechanical Arts are employed about Bodies: But Logic,
Natural Theology, Morals Jurisprudence Law Politicks and
the fine Arts are employed about Mind and what belongs to
it. And therefore the Knowledge of the Mind and of its
10   Powers must be in a more particular Manner subservient to
these Sciences.

Whether therefore we consider the Dignity of the Object
of Pneumatology, or its subserviency to Science in General,
& to the noblest branches of Science in particular; it cer-
15   tainly deserves our closest study and attention. It is indeed
the ground work and foundation of all that follows in my
Course, And I cannot expect that those who are inattentive
to this part of it, can attain any just and accurate Notions in
the subsequent Parts which are built upon it. And as there
20   are many things that are New in what I shall deliver upon
this Subject, which are not to be found in the Authors who
have treated of it I expect that those who desire to improve
will give the closer attention.

The second part of Pneumatology is Natural Theology,
25   by which is meant what Reason discovers of the Nature &
Operations of the Supreme Mind. I need not use many
words to convince you of the dignity and importance of this
branch of Philosophy. It is the prerogative of Man among
all the inhabitants of this Earth, to be capable of knowing
30   his maker, of worshiping him, and imitating his Perfections.
There is no Knowledge that tends so much to elevate and
to purify the Mind as the Knowledge of God. Piety towards
God is an essential part of the Duty incumbent upon us as
Men. It is the strongest Support of every other Virtue & the
35   onely rational Foundation of tranquility & peace of Mind,
7/v/4,7   of / hope and Comfort and Magnanimity of Fortitude in all
the adverse Circumstances of Life. And there can be no rational Piety but what is founded upon just Notions of the
Perfections and Providence of God.

40   It is true that Revelation teaches the Truths of natural
Religion, as well as *other Truths*, which Reason could not discover. But it is no less true that Reason as well as Revelation
comes from God. Both are lights afforded us by the Father

of Light, and we ought to make the best use of both, and
not to put out one that we may use the other. Revelation has
indeed been of great Use to enlighten men even with regard
to the truths of Natural Religion. As one Man may enlighten another in things that can be discovered by Reason,
it is easy to conceive how a Revelation from Heaven may
give men new Light in things which Reason can discover.
And that it has actually done so is sufficiently evident to
those who compare the System of Natural Religion that is to
be found in Christian Writers, with that which we find in
the most enlightned Heathens. We acknowledge therefore
that Men have been much indebted to Revelation even in
Matters of Natural Religion. But this is no Reason why we
should not make the best Use we can of our Reason in these
Matters. Revelation is given to us as reasonable Creatures,
not to hinder the Use of Reason, but to aid and encourage
it. It is by Reason that we must Judge whether that which
claims to be a Revelation be really such. It is by Reason that
we must judge of the meaning of what is revealed, and
guard against such interpretations of it, as are absurd or /
impious or inconsistent. As the best things may be abused,
so Revelation itself when men lay aside the Use of Reason,
may be made the tool of low Superstition or wild Fanaticism.
And that Man is surely best prepared for the study of revealed Religion, who has just and Rational Sentiments of
natural Religion.

The best Notions we can Form of the Divine Nature are
extreamly imperfect and inadequate. But such as they are,
they must be drawn from what we know of our own Minds.
We cannot form the least Idea of any Attribute intellectual
or Moral of which there is not some Image or Resemblance
in the Human Mind. And therefore our Knowledge of the
Deity must be grounded upon the Knowledge of the human
Mind.

When we have acquired just Notions of ourselves and of
the Supreme Being, we may more easily discover the Duty
we owe to God and to one another, this is the Business of
Ethicks the Second branch of my Course.

It is mentioned by many Ancient writers, to the honour
of Socrates the greatest & wisest of all the Greek Philosophers, that he called off mens Attention from vain Enquiries Into the Origin and Generation of the Heavens and the
Earth, to the study of their Duty as Men, and as Citizens.

The Philosophy of Socrates was entirely of the moral Kind,
adapted to make Men wiser and better; and for this Reason,
as we may presume, he obtained from the Oracle, the Ap-
pellation of the wisest of the Greeks.[9] He has allways been
reckoned the Father of Moral Philosophy, as Hipocrates has
been of Medicine. The several Sects among the Greek Philosophers who derived themselves from the Socratick
School ever accounted Ethicks or morals as the most important Branch of Philosophy. Haec quidem Quaestio communis est omnium Philosophorum: quis est enim qui nullis of-
ficii praeceptis tradendis, philosophum se audeat dicere Cic
Off Lib 1.[10] /

There are two capital Powers or faculties of the human
Mind to which all the rest have been referred, to wit the
contemplative and the Active. The first is employed in the
Discovery of Truth; the second in directing our Conduct in
Life. The contemplative power is intended to be subservient
to the active, and this is its main purpose. As therefore the
End is allways to be accounted more noble than the Means,
so the right application of our Active power, is a matter of
higher moment than the Right application of our Speculative power. The Dignity the Glory and Perfection of a Man
consists in doing his duty and acting the Part that is Proper
for him. Ethicks therefore or Moral Philosophy which treats
of human Duty and of the conduct that men ought to hold
in the various Stations in which they may be placed in Society, has allways on account of its Dignity and importance
been considered as a chief branch of Philosophy.

There is in Ethicks as in most Sciences a Speculative and
a practical Part, the first is subservient to the last. This Division of Ethicks is very Ancient. It must have occurred to
Men as soon as they began to study this branch of science.
Cicero mentions it in the beginning of his Offices[11] and his
three books of Offices are a System of practical Ethicks as
his five books De Finibus explain the several speculative Systems of the Greek Philosophers on this Subject.

The practical Part of Ethicks is for the most part easy and
level to all capacities. There is hardly any moral Duty which
when properly explained and delineated, does not / recommend itself to the heart of every candid and unbiased Man.
For every Man has within him a touchstone of Morals, the
dictates of his own Conscience which approves of what is

Right and condemns what is wrong, when it is fairly represented and considered without prejudice.

There is therefore no branch of Science wherein Men
would be more harmonious in their opinions than in Morals
were they free from all Biass and Prejudice. But this is
hardly the case with any Man. Mens private Interests, their
Passions, and vicious inclinations & habits, do often blind
their understandings, and biass their Judgments. And as
Men are much disposed to take the Rules of Conduct from
Fashion rather than from the Dictates of Reason, so with
Regard to Vices which are authorized by Fashion the Judgments of Men are apt to be blinded by the Authority of the
Multitude especially when Interest or Appetite leads the
same Way. It is therefore of great consequence to those who
would judge right in matters relating to their own Conduct
or that of others, to have the Rules of Morals fixed & settled
in their Minds, before they have occasion to apply them to
cases wherein they may be interested. It must also be observed that although the Rules of Morals are in most cases
very plain, yet there are intricate and perplexed cases even
in Morals wherin it is no easy matter to form a determinate
Judgement.

With Regard to the Theory of Morals, its chief Use as we
have already observed is to be subservient to the practical
part of this Science, and to furnish those principles from
which we reason with regard to duty. The practical part of
Morals is not more plain & level to all capacities, than the
Theory is intricate, subtile, and abstract. The proper object
of the Theory of Morals is to explain the Constitution of the
human Mind so far as regards Morals, that is to explain the
Moral and active Powers of the human Mind. In this Men
have gone into very different Systems both in ancient and
modern times. And the disputes upon this Subject are / as
intricate and subtile as any in Philosophy. These disputes
are owing to the small Progress men have made in Pneumatology. For the Theory of Morals must be founded upon
the knowledge of Pneumatology or rather makes a part of
it. The duty of a Man must be grounded upon the human
Constitution. If we had not the powers and faculties of Man,
the duty of a Man would not be incumbent upon us. Therefore if ever we come to an end in the Disputes that have
been raised about the Theory of Morals, it must be by a

clearer insight into the Principles of Pneumatology. This is one Reason why I think it necessary in my Course to spend so much Time as I have usually done on Pneumatology.

If any one should imagine that because the Theory of Morals is so intricate and disputable, the practical Rules of Morals must therefore be built upon a slippery Foundation; I say if any Person thinks thus he deceives himself greatly. I shall have occasion to show this more fully hereafter; at present let it suffice to observe that the same conclusions may be drawn from very different principles. It is so in the present case. The various Theorists differ not about what is to be accounted virtuous Conduct but why it is so to be accounted. They agree for instance that Justice and Humanity are Virtues. But according to one they are to be accounted Virtues because they tend to promote our private Interest according to another System because they promote the publick good to another because they are agreable to our moral Sense to another because they agree with the Relations of things. But although it is true and ought to be / understood that very different Theories in Morals do in most instances lead to the same practical Conclusions yet it must also be owned that there have been Licentious Theories advanced on this Subject that tend to overturn all good Morals, and that even of those Theories that do not deserve the Name of Licencious, some have a happier influence upon morals than others, and there is no false Theory whatsoever which may not in some cases at least mislead a Man in Practice. We shall therefore consider the different Theories concerning Morals that have been advanced; and hope that those who are capable of entring in to such abstract Speculations will find this intricate Subject set in a clearer light than it has hitherto been by the Authors that have Wrote upon it.

The practical Part of Ethicks is a very wide Field.[12] For there are certain duties which we owe to the Supreme Being and under this Head we comprehend all the Duties of Piety or of Natural Religion and their Counterfeits or Opposites there are in the Second Place certain Duties which are incumbent upon us considered meerly as Reasonable Creatures without any Relation to society, These Duties we are commonly said to owe to ourselves, & under them we explain the Virtues of Prudence Temperance and Fortitude. There are Thirdly certain duties which as social Creatures we owe to other Men. And these all comprehended under two General Heads of Justice & Humanity. The Claim which one Man has upon another in point of Justice is called a Perfect Right, and the claim which he has upon another in point of Humanity is called an imperfect Right. And

7/v/4,13 these Rights of Mankind perfect and imperfect / are various according to the different Relations which men bear to each other. There is a general Relation which every Man bears to every Man, as a reasonable & social Creature of the same Nature and origin with himself. And the Rights arising

10   from this Relation are called the natural Rights of Mankind. There are more Special Relations which we bear to others of the same family and the Rights arising from family Relations are called Oeconomical Rights. There are other Special Relations which we bear to persons that belong to the

15   same State or political Society, and the Rights arising from these Relations are called Political Rights. The Oeconomical & Political Rights of Mankind are properly natural as well as those which have that special Designation for all these Rights are founded upon Natural Reason and Equity, and

20   not barely upon positive institution and Compact, and therefore all of them taken together are called the Law of Nature.

I need not use many words to show the utility and Importance of Jurisprudence.

25   The end of all Constitutions of Government of all Civil Laws and of all Civil Judicatories is to preserve & support the Rights of Mankind. And this is the proper Test or Touchstone by which Forms of Government & of Civil Judicatories and Systems of civil Laws are to be tried and

30   Judged, Namely, if such Forms or such Systems are agreeable to the Rights of Mankind and conducive to the preservation of them, that is if they are founded upon the Law of Nature, they are good, otherwise they are bad and ought to be corrected.

35   Moreover all Civil Laws require Interpretation, & Application to Particular Cases, and the chief Rule in all Interpretation or Application of Civil Laws is to make it as agreable as possible to the Laws of Nature. /

7/v/4,14 From these general Hints I conceive it is sufficiently evi-
40   dent of what great Importance it is to Men to be well acquainted with the Rights of Mankind or with the Law ⟨of⟩ Nature, not onely for the direction of their private conduct that they may deal with every man according to the Rules of

Justice and Humanity, but also for the direction of their
publick conduct when they act in the Capacity of Legislators
of Judges or Council, and in general in every instance
wherein they have any Concern, in the framing or amend-
ing, in the Interpretation or application of Civil Laws.

There is yet another branch of practical Ethicks, For besides the Rights competent to Individuals, as Men, as Members of a Family, as Members of a State; There are also
Rights competent to Communities of Men and particularly
to States, that is to Communities which have no superior on
Earth. One independent State may have a just Claim upon
another either in point of Justice or Humanity, and that
either in peace or in War. The Sum of these Rights of Nations is called the Law of Nations, or the Law of Peace &
War the Jus Belli & Pacis. This is a Law to which Sovereigns
are most Sacredly bound, in all their transactions with other
Sovereigns or Independent States whether in Peace or in
War as well as with individuals who are not their Subjects.
All Sovereigns profess to act according to this Law otherwise
they would justly be deemed the common Enemies of Mankind. And the more this Law is understood and practised
the more will the peace & Happiness of Mankind be promoted. If wars and devastations of Enemies are less frequent in Europe at this day than in former Ages, if when
Wars happen they are carried on with less cruelty / and
more humanity we may justly attribute so happy an Event
to this that the Laws of Peace and War are more distinctly
and more generally understood than they were in former
Ages.

Thus you see that Practical Morality or Ethicks comprehends these four Branches all of them of vast importance to
the well being of Mankind. Namely The duties of Natural
Religion, The Duties of self Government, The Law of Nature or natural Jurisprudence and the Law of Nations.

The last General Branch of my Course is Politicks.[13] This
word Politicks is sometimes used to signify the knowledge of
the Political Rights of Mankind, or of political Jurisprudence, and in this sense it is a part of Ethicks as has been
already mentioned. But I consider Politicks as a Science
quite distinct from every part of Ethicks; and, it may be defined to be the Knowledge of the Causes Connexions and
Effects of Political Events. By Political Events I understand
those Events, which are produced by the joint force and

council of Numbers joyned in Society. Every individual of
the human Kind has a certain Sphere of Power and may
produce Effects that are not Inconsiderable. But the grandest Effects of human Power are these that are produced by
the concurrence of many joyned in Society. I call these Political Events. Such are the Establishment of Empires or
Commonwealths, their Growth Progress and Decline, &
their various Revolutions & Changes Their Wars Conquests
and Colonies, their Laws & Judicatures their Establishments
for Regulating police, for promoting Religion and Virtue,
Arts and Sciences, Agriculture Trade / Manufactures.
These are the grand Effects of human Powers, and of all
Events that concern this Life the most important, because
the happiness and Improvement of Mankind or their Misery and degeneracy depend upon them. We see these great
Political Events produced, improved, impaired, destroyed,
& again revived variously in various parts of the Globe. We
see some Nations Barbarous and some civilized. Among
these we see different Forms of Government, different
Laws Customs and Manners. We see some Nations, who for
Ages nay for thousands of years continue in the same State
and cannot be said to have improved declined or changed
in a long tract of ages. Their Government their Laws their
Manners and their national Character is still the same. We
see other Nations in a perpetual Flux in regard to all these
things, still going from worse to better, or from better to
worse, from poverty to Riches, from laziness to industry,
from Ignorance to Barbarity to Knowledge and politeness;
from simplicity to Luxury; from a high Degree of Publick
Spirit and Contempt of Riches & pleasure to Venality Avarice and Voluptuousness.

These great Events whether they be good or Evil proceed
from human Operation, they are the Effects of human Reason and human Passions operating variously according to
the Characters of the Agents and the Circumstances in
which they are placed, and by their cooperation in multitudes producing, very often without Design, one great
Event.

Now it is the design of Political Knowledge, to discover
the causes of Such great Events whether good or evil in the
tempers Characters and Circumstances of those / Societies
in which they are produced, and to point out the Means by
which political Events that are good may be brought about

and the bad prevented. I divide Politicks into two Parts the first treats of the various Forms of Government their Causes & Effects the Second of Police. The Form of a Government depends chiefly upon the hands in which the Soverign Power in a State is placed. And the Sovereign Power may be placed either in the hands of One, of a few or of Many which make the Simple forms of Government or Some parts of the Supreme power may be placed in one of these ways others in others, which makes the mixed forms of Government.

By Police I understand those Regulations which are common to Different forms of Government for Promoting Religion Virtue Education, Arts & Sciences Agriculture Trade Manufactures & for Regulating the Arms and Finances of the State and other Objects of that kind which are not essential to the being of a State or Government but conducive to its well being and Security.

Thus I have given you a General Notion of my Course. And because I know not any one or even a few Authors who have treated these Subjects in that Order & Method which to me seems most Natural. I shall not confine my self by any Text Book. But under the different branches shall direct you to such Authors as I think have wrote best on these Subjects. /

⟨II. Duties to God⟩

Of the Duty we owe to the Supreme Being[1]

MAR 7 1766

5   As all that Duty we owe to God must be grounded upon
just sentiments of him, Our first Duty must be to endeavour
by the best use of our Reason to attain just Notions of him,
his perfections and Universal Government. But having already in the Lectures on Natural Theology endeavoured to
10   point out what Reason teaches us concerning his Nature his
Attributes and his Government[2] we shall not resume what
was then Delivered but suppose it as the proper Ground ⟨of⟩
all that Piety and devout Affection which is due to him.

2[3] The Duty to the Supreme Being consists in a Devout
15   and Loyal Affection of the heart towards him corresponding to his Nature & the relations we stand in to him. Love
Esteem Veneration Gratitude Submission Obedience. External Religion.[4]

2 Supposing then that we have just Sentiments of the Su-
20   preme Being. It is our Duty to maintain upon our Minds
constant and lively impression of our Dependance upon
⟨him⟩ as we are his Creatures. It is the saying of a heathen
poet, adopted by one of the Sacred writers, that we are his
ofspring.[5] We are so in a much stricker sense than we are
25   the offspring of our Natural Parents. He is the Universal
Mind and Soul that pervades all Nature that upholds its
whole frame and directs all its movements. From his infinite
Intelligence all created intelligence is derived.

In what Sense God may be said to be the Soul of the
30   World. All the life & light that is found in finite beings are
emanations from him the father of Lights the fountain of
Life. The curious texture of our Bodies the more curious
and wonderfull structure of our Minds, with all their several
intelligent and Active powers are his workmanship. Our no-
35   blest powers, our Rational & Moral Powers, which are the
Glory of the human Nature, are a faint Image of the Deity,

and by them it is that we are capable of resembling him in
some degree as well as of knowing him. The inanimate and
brute creation are his property and his Servants, for he is
Lord of all. But the Human kind by their Rational & moral
Natures are so far exalted as to be dignified with the tittle
of his children, his offspring. And as he has given to man
some resemblance of his intellectuall and moral Perfections,
in the constitution of the human Nature he has likewise
given him some Image of his Dominion in this World. The
extent of human Power is so very considerable when it is
properly Exerted, especially in the higher Stations of Life;
That such Persons are justly represented as Gods Vicegerents on Earth.[6] /

Now it is evidently most Just and reasonable that our
Minds should be constantly impressed with a lively sense
and Conviction that we derive our being and all the Privileges & Prerogatives of it from our father in heaven. That
every blessing we taste is his gift that every degree of power
we are possessed of is derived from him that all the tender
Charities of Relations friends Benefactors Country are Rays
of his Benignity and Goodness. That all human Excellence,
even the most exalted and most heroick virtues which every
heart admires, and every tongue celebrates; are onely faint
images & copies of that Perfection of moral Excellence
which is in the Supreme Being. It is just and reasonable that
we should see the Supreme Beauty in all the Beauties of
Nature, the Supreme Wisdom in the admirable contrivance
of all his Works, the Supreme Goodness in everything that
is agreable to us or to our fellow creatures.

2 It is just and reasonable that we have a constant and
lively Conviction of his Presence with us, and of his Perfect
Knowledge of all our Actions and even of our most secret
thoughts; So that no secret wickedness can escape his Eye
nor any good intention fail of his gracious notice & approbation. Men see not our Intentions, they onely guess at
them by their outward signs, and these Signs are sometimes
ambiguous, and often misinterpreted from prejudice Envy
or Malignity. These considerations ought to moderate our
desire of the praise & applauses of Men especially of the
foolish and ignorant Rabble, and make their Censure more
tollerable when we are conscious that it is unjust. It is no
small Comfort to a good man in such circumstances that he
has a witness in his own breast that cannot be bribed. But it

is still a much greater Comfort that he has a higher Witness
whose Judgment is infallible as his Knowledge is perfect,
and whose Approbation is of more avail than that of all the
World besides.[7] He can discern Integrity of heart where it is
the prevailing principle under every disadvantage that may
cloud or disfigure it in the eyes of the World. He onely can
make the proper Allowances for the frailty of our Nature,
for our involuntary errors, and for the strength of temptations, for he knows our frame & remembers our frailty and
pities us as a father pities his Children. It is therefore most
reasonable that our desire of the Approbation of our Supreme Judge & the Supreme Judge of Men & Angels
should in a great measure Swallow up our desire of the Approbation of our fellow Men. This the true the proper and
Natural Direction of that thirst of Honour which God himself hath planted in the human Breast. That as the Gravitation of the Planets bends chiefly towards the / Sun the Center of the System & in a much inferior degree towards one
another; So this desire of Honour should lean chiefly toward that Honour that is from God the fountain of true
Honour & the sole infallible Judge of Worth, and more
weakly towards the honour that is from Men.

3 It is just and reasonable that we consider the Supreme
Being not onely as the Witness and the Judge of our whole
Conduct, but as our compassionate Father and faithfull
Guardian, whose goodness sympathizes with us even in the
afflictions and trials which his wisdom sees necessary for our
discipline and culture, who does not afflict willingly, but
onely for the best purposes, as a father may sometimes chas-
tise, & sometimes prescribe severe tasks to his dear children.
Reason and Revelation concur in representing the Deity as
the Refuge of the Distressed and those who have none to
help them. We are led by a kind of Instinct to implore his
mercy when all help of Man fails. Nor will he who gave us
this instinct be deaf to its voice. Reason and Revelation concur in representing him to us as a faithfull Guardian ready
to afford divine Aid to every Soul that makes any virtuous
Effort and pants after true Glory & Honour. The Wisdom
of God for ends which perhaps it is impossible now fully to
comprehend, has placed us in such a State that the path of
Virtue is not always smooth and easy. It is sometimes beset
with briars & thorns, sometimes steep & difficult. Reason
can discover some causes of this and there may be others

5

10

15

8/IV/2,2r

20

25

30

35

40

which our Reason cannot discover. Our Appetites and Passions are of quicker Growth than Reason & Conscience and ripen more early. They are strengthened by habits of Indulgence before the Governing powers can exercise their

5   Authority. And although there is no natural appetite affection or passion which is not usefull & necessary as a subordinate part of the human Constitutions, yet however usefull they may be as servants they are hurtfull as masters and give often a violent impulse to courses which are contrary both

10   to our real happiness and our duty. If we add to this the influence of bad example and of bad education; it is easy to see that a steady Course of Virtue requires a continued Effort. It is a conflict between the flesh and the Spirit, between the inferior principles of our Nature and those which ought

15   to bear Sway. In this conflict a man who has good purposes in the main, finds many reasons to be diffident of himself. /

8/IV/2,2v He can recollect many instances wherein his purposes have failed him and have been baffled by a strong temptation. As between Winter & summer there is a Season wherein these

20   two seem to struggle against each other and sometimes one seems to gain the Ascendant and sometimes the other. it happens so in this Strugle in the human Mind between Virtue and Vice especially while good habits have not been long confirmed or bad ones retain a considerable degree of their

25   power. In this dubious Conflict as in every other circumstance of distress or danger, a Mind impressed with just sentiments of the supreme Being, naturally looks up to him for divine Aid to strengthen his weakness, to fortify his good purposes to guard him in the Course of his Providence

30   from such temptations as might be too strong for him. Nor will the hearer of Prayer be deaf to these requests. Virtue is his Care. Its votaries are under his protection & guardianship. He will cherish the Divine Principle as his own offspring, till it grows up to maturity.

35   Lastly it is just and Reasonable to consider what befalls us whether in it self agreable or disagreable as a part of the Divine administration as what seems meet to the Supreme Governour to do or permit, as a part of that Culture & Discipline which he sees meet for us. In Distress and Affliction,

40   to which all Men are equally liable from the Accidents of Life, the firm perswasion that nothing befalls us but by the appointment or permission of our Father in Heaven, is the truest Source of Consolation to a pious Mind. He pretends

not to a Stoical insensibility to pain and Grief. But he is per-
swaded that the Evils that befal him are a part of that Discipline which a wise and compassionate Father sees necessary for his good. He takes them therefore as he does a
harsh but salutary Medicine. The Cup which my Father
hath given me shall I not drink.[8] To bear our Afflictions in
this way, as it is an essential Part of true Piety so it is the
most soveraign Cordial to the Afflicted. Resignation to God
is the softest Pillow upon which a man can lay his Head in
Distress. That perfect indifference with regard to pain Sickness poverty loss of Friends, which the Stoicks pretended to,
grounded on the perswasion that there are no Evils, I say
this Indifference were it really attainable by human Nature,
would be so far from adding to the Worth of the Virtues of
Patience under these Evils & perfect Resignation to the Will
of God, that it would diminish it, or rather totally annihilate
⟨it⟩. For where lies the Merit of bearing patiently what is no
Evil or the loss of what is no God.

An indifference with regard to what happens to us,
whether health or sickness, poverty or Riches, the favour of
great Men or their Neglect, a publick Employment or a private Station, was much inculcated by the Stoicks they taught
Men to employ their whole concern not about what should
happen to them but about what they should do and how
they should behave themselves in that station and in those
circumstances in which they were placed what ever they
were. This was surely a very Noble lesson and does great
honour to that Ancient System of Morals. Yet Zeno[9] and the
more ancient Stoicks seem to have built this elevated System
upon too weak a foundation, when they left out of their System the consideration of the Providence of the Deity. and
maintained that health Riches Honour were not at all goods
nor the contrary, Evils. That the former were not objects of
Desire but of Election, the latter were not objects of Aversion but of Rejection, that Virtue was the onely good and
therefore the onely object that ought to be desired, and Vice
the onely Evil that ought ⟨to be⟩ shunned. The Solidity and
firmness of the Foundation does not Answer to the Grandeur and Sublimity of the Superstructure. And a Man must
already be possessed of a very high love and Admiration of
Virtue who can Enter into the reasonings of the Ancient
Stoical School and feel the force of them so strongly as to
influence his conduct. They have too much the appearance

of Rant and Enthusiasm rather than of Sober Reason. But
when we consider a good Man as under the Paternal Care
of a Supreme Being so that Nothing can befall him but by
the Order and direction of Infinite Wisdom and Goodness,
his Conduct may be justified to the Soberest Reason, when
he leaves the care of his happiness to him that made him,
being perfectly assured that he can never suffer in that Respect While he is carefull to do his duty and to act properly. /

But tho Zeno and some of the More Ancient Stoicks left
out the Consideration of the Providence of God of their System yet we find even some of the heathen Philosophers
Urging this as an Argument to moderate our Concern
about external goods or evils that happen to us. Plato in his
Alcibiades represents Socrates as urging this doctrine in a
most beautiful manner and with great Strength of Reason
the later Stoicks Epictetus Arrian and M.A. Antoninus frequently use the Same Argument.[10] None of them in a more
beautiful and Striking Manner than Juvenal in his 10 Satyre

> Nil ergo optabunt homines? Si consilium vis,
> Permittes ipsis expendere Numinibus, quid
> Conveniat nobis rebusque sit utile nostris.
> Nam pro Jucundis aptissima quaeque dabunt Dii
> Carior est illis homo quam sibi. Nos animorum
> Inpulsu, et caeca magnaque cupidine ducti
> Conjugium petimus, partumque Uxoris; at illis
> Notum, qui pueri, qualisque futura sit uxor. . . .
> Orandum est, ut sit mens sana in corpore sano
> Fortem posce animum et mortis terrore carentem
> Qui spatium vitae extremum inter munera ponat
> Naturae; qui ferre queat quoscumque labores;
> Nesciat irasci, cupiat Nihil, et potiores
> Herculis aerumnas Credat, saevosque labores
> Et venere, et cenis et plumes Sardanapalli.[11]

These Oracles of Right Reason correspond exactly with
the Oracles of Divine Wisdom in the Christian Religion. Not
my Will but thine be done. says our divine teacher. — Take
no thought what you shall eat or what you shall drink or
where withall ye shall be cloathed. Your heavenly Father
knoweth that ye have need of these things. But seek ye first
the Kingdom of God and his Righteousness and all these

things shall be added unto you.¹² The passage I have quoted
from Juvenal looks as if it had been intended for a paraphrase upon these Precepts of our Divine Teacher.

5   I must not Omit as a part of the Duty we owe to the supreme Being Obedience to his commands.

Every act of Virtue becomes an Act of Piety towards God
when it is done from a Regard to his Authority, a desire to
imitate his perfection and obtain his approbation. /

8/IV/2,3v   The vices contrary to Piety come under the Denomination
10   of Impiety. The neglect or contempt of those duties of true
Piety. Dishonourable Sentiments of the Supreme Being lead
to those Corruptions of true Piety. Superstition. a Persecut-
ing Spirit, Enthusiasm Fanaticism. Irreverence to the Deity
in common Swearing. Contempt of Publick Worship. Attrib-
15   uting to Chanc Fortune Luck, the Events that befall us. Discontent with our Condition. Undue Anxiety about Events.
Every Vice is in some Sense Impiety.

Reflexions. 1 Piety an essential Part of Virtue and one of
the Strongest Inducements to every other part of it. A
20   Sourdce of Joy. 2 Too little considered by heathen Philosophers in this view.

3 The Christian System more Rational in this Respect. /

25
8/IV/2,4r   MARCH 8 1768

There are some persons who pretend to high Notions of
Virtue and Honour, who seem to entertain a very mean
Opinion of Piety & Devotion as something that may be fit
30   for the Entertainment of Monks and Old Women, but is
rather an unnecessary incumbrance to a Man in Active Life;
and that one may be a Man of Virtue and Honour without
minding Religion at all.¹³ /

8/IV/2,4v   Nothing in human Character is more surprising or unac-
35   countable than the manner in which some Men impose
upon themselves by empty forms of Virtue and Honour,
others by no less empty forms of Religion. No Man can bear
the thought of being perfectly worthless this would make a
man detestable to himself and to account his existence a
40   Curse. Therefore a Man to preserve a Character with himself as well as with the rest of Mankind will cultivate some
good Quality which may cover all his faults with himself and

perhaps with others. His good Qualities however must be dignified with the sacred Names of Virtue, Honour or Religion. /

But I cannot help thinking that such Virtue as disdains any aid of Religion stands upon a very slippery foundation, & will hardly be able to endure any severe trial. For how can we conceive a man to believe himself under an obligation to reverence his parents and at the same time to owe no Reverence or filial Affection to his Maker and father in heaven, Whose Offspring he is in a stricter sense than of his earthly parents. Is a Man bound to be gratefull to his benefactors and under no obligation of Gratitude to his greatest and best benefactor. A Man who vainly imagines that he has no need of the Aid the protection and Guardianship of the Almighty, must be extreamly arrogant and ignorant of himself. And he who has a just sense of his own weakness and frailty, but thinks it useless and unprofitable to implore divine Aid and Direction must have very wrong notions of the Deity & be deaf to the voice of his own Conscience.

The exercises of a rational Piety and Devotion have a manifest & powerfull tendency in their very Nature to strengthen every virtuous principle to confirm every good purpose, to fortify the Mind against every temptation, to raise it in adversity, to temper the giddiness of prosperity and to enlarge our hearts in Sentiments of humanity & kind affection towards the whole creation of God.

Besides The exercises of Piety towards God, as they have the most salutary effects for cherishing and strengthning every virtuous Disposition, so they have afforded to the worthiest and best Men in every Age the most rational and most elevated Joy and Consolation, especially in circumstances of the greatest distress when men stand most in need of Consolation. The Testimony of Christians Jews and Heathens who have experienced this leaves no Room to doubt of the Fact. For these reasons I conceive that those who profess to be friends to Virtue while they hold in contempt Piety towards God, must either be hypocrites or very grossly deluded. Shaftsbury Enquiry End of the first Book

'Hence we may determine justly the Relation which Virtue has to Piety, the first being not compleat but in the later: Since where the later is wanting, there can neither be the same benignity firmness nor constancy; the same good com-

posure of the Affections or uniformity of Mind. And thus
the perfection and height of Virtue, must be owing to the
Belief of a God.⟨'⟩[14] /

8/ɪv/2,4v   The Same Noble Author elsewhere Observes ⟨'⟩That the
5   Notion of a Real Divinity is not dry and Barren, but such
consequences are Necessarly drawn from it as must set us in
Action and find Employment for our Strongest Affections.
All the Duties of Religion evidently flow hence and no Exception remains against any of those great Maxims which
10   Revelation has established.'[15] These are the Sentiments of
my Lord Shaftsbury whose freedom of thinking in Matters
that concern Religion will not be questioned. Let me add to
this the Opinion of a free thinking Heathen. The Person I
mean is the great Roman Orator & Philosopher Tully in his
15   second Book de Legibus. The passage I am to recite is the
Preface to his Code of Laws, the passage is rather long for
a quotation, but on account of its sublimity and Elegance, as
well as justness of Sentiment it deserves to be got by heart.
       Cicero de Legibus 2.7 Sit igitur hoc ⟨iam⟩ a principio per-
20   swasum civibus, Dominos esse omnium rerum ac Modera-
tores Deos, eaque quae gerantur, eorum geri, vi͵ ditione,[16]
ac numine eosdemque optime de genere hominum mereri,
et qualis quisque sit, quid agat, quid in se admittat, qua
mente, qua pietate colat religiones, intueri : piorumque et
25   impiorum habere rationem. His enim rebus imbutae
mentes, haud sane abhorrebunt ab utile et a vere sententia.
Quid est enim verius, quam neminem esse oportere tam
stulte arrogantem, ut in se, rationem, et mentem putet
inesse, in caelo, mundoque non putet? aut ⟨ut⟩ ea, quae vix
30   summa ingenij ratione comprehendat, nulla ratione moveri
putet? Quem vero, astrorum ordines, quem dierum nocti-
umque vicissitudines, quem mensium temperatio, quemque
ea, quae gignuntur nobis ad fruendum, non gratum esse co-
gant ⟨cogunt⟩, hunc hominem omnino numerare ⟨-rari⟩ qui
35   decet? cumque omnia quae rationem habent praestent iis
quae sint rationis expertia, nefasque sit dicere, ullam rem
praestare naturae omnium rerum, rationem inesse in ea
confitendum est. Utilis esse autem opiniones has ⟨has op.⟩,
quis neget cum intellegat, quam multa firmantur ⟨firmen-
40   tur⟩ iure iurando, quantae Salutis ⟨-ti⟩ sint foederum religiones, quam multos divini supplicij ⟨-ci⟩ metus a Scelere re-
vocarit, quamque sancta sit societas civium inter ipsos diis

immortalibus interpositis, tum judicibus, tum testibus.[17] To
this I shall add an Authority which I respect as much as Any
human Authority whatsoever.

Sir I. Newton in the Queries subjoyned to his Opticks Q
31 at the End Observes that this is the first Precept of the
Moral Law given to all Nations.[18] Unum esse agnoscendum
summum Dominum Deum ejusque cultum non esse in alios
transferendum, to which he subjoyns this Remark of his
own, Etenim sine hoc Principio, nihil esset Virtus aliud nisi
merum Nomen.[19]

⟨III. Duties to Ourselves⟩

⟨*Prudence, Temperance, Fortitude*⟩

8/ɪᴠ/2,4ᴠ   Justice in the division of the Ancients comprehends all the duty we owe to our Fellow Creatures. This like most other words regarding Morals is taken sometimes in a larger Sense & sometimes in a more restrained one.[1] /

8/ɪᴠ/2,5ʳ   Three of the Cardinal Virtues so celebrated among the Ancients To wit Prudence Temperance & Fortitude relate to the duties of Self Government. I shall endeavour to give some brief View of these duties under these three heads beginning first with Prudence which here we must take in a

10   like most enlarge sense of the word[2] so as to Signify the proposing to our selves worthy ends in our Conduct and prosecuting these ends by the most proper Means. The first of these may perhaps more properly ⟨be⟩ called Wisdom, the Second Prudence in the strict Sense of the Word.[3]

15   1 As to the former It is evident that Nature intended us for action and that we can neither answer the end of our being nor enjoy any degree of happiness in a lazy inactive slouthfull life. This our Divine teacher has very properly taught us in one of his Parables wherein Mankind are rep-

20   resented as the Servants of one Master who gives to each of them so many talents to be laid out in the most profitable way till he come to call them to an account.[4] All the powers & abilities of body & mind fortune or Station which a man is possessed of by Nature, or may acquire by his industry are

25   the talents which God has given him. We cannot indeed profit our maker by the right use of these talents but we may please him and deserve his approbation, and may greatly profit our selves and our fellow creatures, by using our talents in a right manner this God requires of us as our Duty,

30   and we must be accountable to him for the proper Discharge of it. And if we had no Account to make to God, our own Conscience must condemn us if we do not employ the

powers and Abilities that Nature has given us to the best
and worthiest Purposes. This ⟨is⟩ the proper Notion of Wisdom which excells folly as far as light excells darkness.

5　　The Ends which Men may pursue are as various as the
Active principles of their Natures, nay they are much more
various for the same Original Principle may lead different
men different ways in pursuit of its Gratifications. Thus the
desire of Power may lead one man to accumulate Riches,
and to starve every other desire in order to have the means
10　of gratifying it. The same Desire of Power leads another
man to lay out all his fortune in courting the favour of those
by whose means he expects advancement. The same desire
of Knowledge leads one man to wander over the Surface of
the Globe from pole to pole to discover & arrange the Pro-
15　ductions of Nature. Another to wear himself out in retire-
ment with study and application to some of the Abstruse
Sciences. Of the infinite Variety of Ends which men may &
do pursue, it is impossible for us not to prefer some to
others in point of Dignity. Some we cannot help judging to
8/IV/2,5v　be mean, trifling, / and useless and on that account altogether unworthy of a Man. Who for instance can approve
of a Roman Emperor employing himself in catching flies
consuming that time which ought to have been employed in
the important business of that vast Empire.[5] Supposing a
25　man could employ his life in an exercise of this kind with
pleasure, as perhaps any kind of Exercise may by habit be
made agreable. Yet whatever pleasure the man enjoyed in
this his favourite Exercise all the world must look upon him
as a mean, contemptible, useless animal, unworthy of the
30　name of a man, because he is a disgrace to his kind. If he is
capable of Reflexion he will think thus of himself.

There are other employments that are low & humble but
usefull and necessary. Thus a man that threshes his corn or
beats hemp has a humble employment but such employ-
35　ments are usefull and necessary in human Society. We have
reason to admire the wisdom of Divine Providence who has
given such various talents to different individuals of the
same Species, that one is fit onely to forge hob nails while
another is fit to fabricate or to govern a Commonwealth.
40　Therefore we do not, we ought not to despise a man placed
in the lowest usefull station of life, if his talents his fortune
& circumstances render him unfit for a higher or set it out
of his reach. He is usefully employed though in a humble
Station, and may be a good man and a good Citizen. Tho'

the employment of a great part of his Life be meer bodily
labour perhaps little above what a brute might be employed
in; yet his End in being this employed may be honourable
and good and far beyond what a brute is capable of. He
intends by his honest Industry to provide for his family to
educate his children to virtue and Industry, to be injurious
or burdensome to no man to be just to all and usefull to his
country according to his power. A man therefore even in
the lowest Station in Society may act from honourable and
worthy motives and have good Ends. But there are ends of
mens Actions that on account of their meanness are unworthy of a man others that are base. The improvement of our
Minds in usefull Knowledge and Wisdom is a more worthy
end than the enjoyment of any bodily pleasure. The relief
of the miserable the promoting the happiness of our fellow
Creatures is a more worthy end than the attainment of
Knowledge.[6] Every Station in life is more honourable according as it gives an Opportunity to being more extensively
usefull to Mankind, and as it requires the Exertion of the
noblest powers and faculties of the human Mind.

True Wisdom therefore will direct a Man, in the Conduct
of his Life to pursue the best and the Noblest Ends. And it
is evident beyond all / doubt that the noblest ends we can
propose in the conduct of Life are to obtain the Approbation of Almighty God, to be usefull to Mankind & to behave
suitable to the Dignity of our Nature.

Mar 10 1766

These are ends which every man in the lowest Station of
Life is capable of pursuing and they are the Noblest that can
be pursued by men in the highest Station. The Man who has
these ends in view and Steadily pursues them has the most
essential Part of true Wisdom as well as of true worth and
real Magnanimity. And as these are the Worthiest & Noblest
Ends a Man can pursue so they are most in our Power.
Every man may obtain by right conduct the Approbation of
his maker; Every man may live suitably to the dignity of a
Man; Every man may be usefull to mankind in Some degree, tho indeed persons possessed of greater natural Abilities or whom fortune has placed in more eminent Stations
may be more usefull to Mankind than Others.

Inferior Ends may be pursued for their own Sake in subordination to those we have Mentioned. Health Life Riches

Honour Knowledge. Wisdom requires that we make a just
Estimate of the Value of these, & that our Zeal and Ardor
in pursuit of them be onely in proportion to their real Value
& that they be never pursued by means inconsistent with
5   what ought to be our main Ends.

2 Prudence

2 Prudence strictly so called consists in the choice of
10   proper means for the attainment of our Ends. Deliberation
Impartiality.

It is no small point of Wisdom for a Man to Know himself
and to make a right judgment of his own Talents that he
may not put on a Person which Nature has not qualified him
15   to act Nor attempt things beyond his Force. Here the contrary extremes are to be avoided of Presumption & Arro-
gance on the one hand & of Pusilanimity on the other.
Every Man should endeavour to know his weak side and his
Strong.

20   As Speech is one of the Main Instruments of transacting
Matters with our fellow Creatures a Capital Part of Prudence consists in the Right Government of Speech. Ex-
treams of being too open or too close Speaking too much or
too little. An habit of circumspection. Obstinacy & facility.
25   Moroseness and Flattery.

How far Prudence is to be accounted a Moral Virtue?
How far a Quality of the Understanding?[7]

Knowledge of Men wherein there are two Extremes. Excessive Suspicion & excessive Credulity & Trust. Firmness
30   in our Purposes.

Vices opposite to Wisdom & Prudence. Sloath. To have
no end in Life. Inconstancy. Putting an undue Value upon
things. Ignorance of our Selves. & all the ridiculous follies
that arise from it. Rashness Irresolution & Procrastination.
35   Prudence to be distinguished from Cunning Craft &
Dissimulation[8] on one hand and from Simplicity and folly
on the Other. /

8/IV/2,6v MAR 11 1766

In Order to have a Just Idea of the Virtue of Temperance
taken in its most extensive meaning, we may observe that
our appetites and Passions and Affections, have their partic-

ular Objects. The attainment of the Object is all they aim at.
They give an impulse to the Mind towards the object, more
or less forcible according to their Strength. The Mind carried on be these impulses without restraint would be like a
ship that drives before the Wind without any person at the
helm in which case she would soon be over set or dashed to
pieces upon Rocks or Shouls it is the business of him that
sits at the helm to temper & direct her Motion so that she
may not go wherever the wind would drive her, but that she
may steadily keep the Course and at last arrive at the port
he intends. Our Passions and Appetites if indulged without
restraint, would be as far from carrying us on in that course
of life we ought to pursue or bringing us to the port we have
in view as the winds without any government of the ship
would be from carrying her safely to her desired ports. In
order therefore to carry us on in a Right Course Our Passions and Appetites may indeed be of great Use, as the
winds in carrying the ship in her voyage. But there must be
some Gouverning Principle in the Mind as well as in the
ship otherwise all would soon go to wreck. We are conscious
that we have power to restrain our Appetites ⟨and⟩ to bridle
our passions, or we can give them the Rein and be carried
away wherever they lead us. Temperance is that Noble and
manly Effort of the Mind whereby we temper restrain and
check those inferior principles when they would lead us out
of our destined Course of Life & dash us upon dangerous
Rocks and inhospitable Shores.9 No Man can steadily pursue any end in Life who has not the command of himself.
The Passions and Appetites are not to be extinguished as
the stoicks maintained.

General Rules of Temperance. Some Indulgences of our
Inclinations are directly contrary to Virtue. Some to health,
Some too Expensive Some unfit or disable us for doing our
Duty. Some are indecent and unmanly, when they betray
want of self command. or a Superiority of passion or Ap-
petite to the calm dictates of Reason or Conscience. Some
Passions may be indulged to a degree of Enthousiasm.

Enthousiasm in friendship, in Love, in Patriotism, in Virtue, in Religion. Different Objects of Temperance. Bodily
Appetites. Desires of every subordinate Good. Temperance
in our Behaviour and Speech in every thing wherein there
is an Excess and Defect.

It is easy to see the End of every Appetite and Passion

God has implanted in us. And this End should be made
the Measure of them beyond which they are not to be indulged. /

5
8/IV/2,3v   *Fortitude*

MARCH 10 1767

Of all the Virtues there is none that leads so directly to
the temple of Honour as Fortitude. The Admiration of this
Virtue is equal in the Savage and in the civilized. The word
Virtus in Latin & αρητη in Greek[10] in their original and most
proper Signification denoted Valour or Fortitude. Justice
and Humanity excite our Love, Prudence and Temperance
our Esteem, but Fortitude commands our Admiration.[11]
Time, which is said to be the devourer of things soon buries
in oblivion the Memory of Men of their Councils & Projects.
But Heroes and Heroick Deeds resist its forc longest. The
Labours of Hercules, the Conquests of Sesostris of Gengiskan of Tamerlane[12] transmitted to us through the wreck of
Time are a proof of this. The most admired & elevated Species of Poetry has Heroick Virtue for its Subject. There is
something therefore in Fortitude more than in any other
Virtue which raises the admiration of Mankind. and gives
immortal Fame to those who are possessed of it. The only
Charm of a Military Life is that it gives so frequent oppor-
tunites of displaying this Virtue. The Ardor that a Brave
man feels in the day of Battle in encountering danger &
Death gives him more real Happiness than the soft and en-
ervating Pleasures of Wine and Love and all the Luxury of
high Living. Those who have been well acquainted with
both have born witness to this. There is indeed in Mankind
a strange Partiality in favour of Military Glory in the Estimation of most Men it covers a multitude of imperfections
and even of great Vices. We are more apt to admire the her-
oism & magnanimity of Alexander and Caesar than to de-
test their ambition & thirst of Power to which they sacrificed
the lives and liberties of so many thousands. The proper
Use of Fortitude is to arm us against all the Evils of Life
which we either feel or fear, and to prevent our being deterred or dispirited by difficulties that occur in the course
of our Duty. Fals Sham. /

10

15

20

25

30

35

40

8/IV/3,1r MARCH 7 1769

We have considered the Duty which we are taught by Reason to pay to the Author of our Being: This is the first part of Practical Ethicks. We have likewise considered the Duties of Self Government under these three heads of Prudence Temperance & Fortitude. Prudence teaches us to weigh in an even Ballance both the Ends we pursue & the Means of attaining them.

It is the prerogative of Man in his adult state to be able to propose to himself and to prosecute one great End in Life & by this to reduce the whole of his Life to a connected System making every part of it subservient to his main End and regulating the whole of his conduct with a view to that. The brutes are incapable of this: They are necessarly carried away by the appetite or Instinct which ⟨is⟩ strongest at the time without any view more distant than its Gratification. We have a Superior Principle given us by the Author of our Being, by which we can, from an Eminence as it were, take a view of the whole Course of human Life; and consider the different Roads that men take & the Ends to which they lead.

When we thus take a general View of human Life we cannot but perceive that some Roads we may take lead to Ruin and infamy, others are mean and below the dignity of our Natures; Prudence will direct us to chuse that which is most excellent in itself & which has the most desireable Issue. Nor can any Man who uses his Reason be in doubt which is the best. The noblest End we can pursue is to Act Suitably to the Dignity of that Nature which God hath given us. And to acquire his Approbation who is the best Judge of Real worth & will infallibly Reward it. This End every man in the lowest Station of Life may pursue and may Attain. But as men have various Talents bestowed upon them, which fit them for different Provinces in Life wherein they may Act their Part with honour to themselves and advantage to Society. Prudence will lead us to study to know our selves and what we are fit to undertake and to know mankind among whom we live, that we may avoid the fatal Extremes of unreasonable distrust and suspicion of every man on the one hand, and of exposing our selves to the Arts of the crafty, by too great trust and security on the other. /

8/IV/3,1v   He who makes a right choice of the main and Ultimate

End of his Life hath the most essential Part of true Wisdom and he who has that Knowledge of himself and of Mankind which a man of ordinary talents may by Experience & Study acquire will rarely be at a loss to know the proper Means of prosecuting his Main End or to Judge of those subordinate ends that conspire with it. Integrity of heart & uprightness of intention enlighten the understanding. & often give better direction in the Path of Wisdom & true Prudence than greater intellectuall Abilities that are clouded & distorted by malignant passions.

Temperance the bridle of the Passions the appetites and all the inferior principles of Action. It is in vain for a Man to propose any end in Life whether good or bad who has not the command of himself. As a ship without hands to guide her motion, driven wherever the winds or the tides carry her, cannot be said to be bound to any port, nor will probably ever arive at any port as little can a man be said to have any End in Life who is the Dupe of his passions and his appetites. It is not the business of Temperance to eradicate our passions or appetites, if it were in our power; this would onely be to make our selves other Creatures than God has made us. Every passion every Appetite that God has implanted in us has a good End and makes a proper part of our Constitution: as every Muscle nerve and artery in the body has its use, so has every part in the constitution of the Mind. And the Ends for which our Several Passions and Appetites are intended by the Author of our Nature are no less apparent than the Ends of the several parts of our bodies. While we regulate them according to those Ends we live temperately. The restraint of our passions in our power.

Fortitude is that Virtue which enables us to face dangers and strugle with difficulties that occur in the way of our Duty with a Noble Ardour of Soul. To bear up in Adversity with Magnanimity. & to acquire a Superiority over the fear of Death over Pain over Poverty over unjust Reproach & in a word over every Evil that is incident to a good Man. When this Virtue is called forth in great and Arduous Attempts and / properly exerted, every heart admires it and every tongue celebrates its praises. Justice & Benevolence procure our Love, Prudence and Temperance our Esteem, but Fortitude & Magnanimity raise our admiration. Hence we ac-

count that the highest Species of Poetry which has heroick
Virtue for its Subject.

Nor is this Virtue above the Reach of any Rank of Men
or even of the weaker sex. History Profane & Sa⟨c⟩red as
5 well as Experience furnish many Instances of true Fortitude
and Magnanimity in every station of Life, & among the Savage as well as the civilized. Indeed the Polish of Life often
enervates the Mind and we see among Canadians & Eski-
maux Examples of a Superiority to Death and torment and
10 to all the Evils of Life which civilized Nations would ⟨have⟩
been apt to conceive to be beyond the pitch of human nature, if Experience had not taught us that every savage is
capable of acquiring it.[13]

As Dishonour, to every generous Mind, is more terrible
15 than Death, the greatest Effort of Magnanimity is to adhere
to what ⟨is⟩ right even when it may bring upon us the contempt or Scorn of the multitude whose judgment is not always according to truth. Such Cases may sometimes happen
in Life where false honour or false Shame draw one way,
20 while the Duty we owe to God and to Mankind draw the
Contrary, So that a man must make a Sacrifice either of his
Reputation or of his Conscience. In such a case as this True
fortitude and Magnanimity will make a man glory in the
Opportunity of offering so costly a Sacrifice to the inviolable
25 Law of his own Mind. And why should a Man who fears not
Death, fear the Opinion of an unthinking and deluded multitude, while he is secure of the Approbation of his own
Conscience & the Approbation of his Supreme Judge. /

8/IV/3,3v The Virtue of Fortitude lays a Man under no obligation
30 to expose himself to danger or to any Evil without Just
Cause. It is the duty of every Man to preserve his life & his
limbs when by lawfull & honourable means he can do it. If
a Man exposes his Life to imminent danger without any reasonable call to do so, this is Temerity and folly but it is not
35 fortitude nor ought it to be honoured with that Name. But
when he is called to expose his Life in defence of his Country of his Friend or family or in his own just Defence. Fortitude requires that the fear of Death should not induce him
to desert his Duty or to betray his Trust. In like Manner it
40 is a Mans Duty to gain & to preserve the good Opinion of
others by all fair and Laudable means, and to avoid what
may lessen his Reputation with them. But when a Mans

Duty calls him to do what may lessen his Reputation with others, through their ignorance or prejudice, though it ought not; then fortitude requires of him that he prefer a good Conscience to a good Name, & do not desert his Duty through the fear of Unjust Reproach.

There are many Arguments that Justify true Fortitude & Magnanimity in every instance wherein we are called to exercise it. The passion of Fear when excessive defeats its own end. It magnifies the Evil which we dread, and the fear is often a greater Evil than the thing feared. It depresses the Mind, & deprives us of the free Use of our Reason: which might often discover a way of avoiding the Danger, if our faculties were not benummed by fear. It is the common Effect of a Panick, to make a Man run headlong into the very danger he dreads, because the Mans Mind is disorded & he knows not what he does. While the Man of Fortitude who can look danger in the face with a Composed Mind, & retains the Use of all his faculties, has a much better chance of escaping the danger. A Man of true fortitude not onely retains the Use of his Reason in Danger. but is elevated above himself. That Magnanimity of which he is conscious not onely makes his Countenance to shine but brightens all his faculties. /

From what I have said it appears evident that in Evils or Dangers that may be avoided honourably, Fortitude puts us in a more probable way than Fear of avoiding the Evil.

And as to those Evils which cannot be avoided at all or not in a consistency with our Duty. The timorous and weak-minded Man anticipates the Evil by his dread of it, like one who dies for fear of Death. Pain sickness and Disease are often unavoidable. Yet we see these evils born by some Men, even in the highest Degree, with such Fortitude & Magnanimity, that they cannot be said to be unhappy. A Man never is so till his Spirit is sunk & his courage fails. Then indeed the slightest Evils are a burthen too heavy to be born.

Death is an evil which we must all undergo. And while a Man fears Death it is impossible he can be happy. This enemy lurks in every corner of his Body. It is carried about by every Element. And he is liable to its attack every Moment. No Man therefore can enjoy real tranquillity of Mind untill he has overcome the fear of Death. /

There are Cases respecting each of thes Virtues of Pru-

dence Temperance and Fortitude in which it ⟨is⟩ difficult to
discern the precise line which divides the Right from the
wrong. But these cases rarely occur in practice, & where
they do a man of an upright heart is in no danger from
them, he will avoid going too near the dubious limit. And
while he follows the best Light of his Mind after making due
Enquiry; his Error, if he is in any, will not be imputed by his
righteous judge.

But the excellence and the Obligation of these virtues in
the general, cannot be hid from any man who calmly and
impartially considers them. They are / intended as a Rule of
Life to all Mankind and therefore their Obligation is obvious to all nor does it require any deep or refined Reasoning to discover it. They tend equally to the happiness and
perfection of our own Nature and to the benefite of human
Society. The constitution of our Nature considered as a System made up ⟨of⟩ various principles some of which are subordinate & others intended to lead and Govern, immediately points them out to us as the course intended for us by
the author of our being. And they have an intrinsick worth
and dignity which every human heart acknowledges and re-
veres, even those who have not the resolution to practise
them. /

⟨IV. Duties to Others: Justice⟩

8/IV/3,4r   The third general Branch of our Duty is that which
we owe to our Fellow Creatures. The Latin Word Iustitia, as
well as the greek Word δικαιοσυνη were sometimes taken in
so large a Sense as to includ the whole of our Social duty,
but in English the Word Justice has a more restrained Signification. We account him a Just Man who does no Injury
to any Man. Justice & Humanity may however include the
whole of Social Duty. The first implying the abstaining from
all Injury, the second that we do all the good in our Power.[1]

Justice has been distinguished into two kinds Commutative & distributive.[2] Commutative Justice is employed in the
Ordinary affairs between Man & Man considered as on a
footing of equality. It implys that we invade no Mans property nor violate his Right. That we do not injure him in his
person in his family, in his good Name or in his friends.
That we pay our just Debts. make Reparation to the best of
our Power for any damage we have done or offence we have
given to others. That we fullfill our contracts and be faithfull to our promises. That we use no fraudulent dealing nor
take advantage of the weakness Ignorance or Necessity of
those with whom we deal. And in a word that we be fair
honest and without guile in our Speech and Behaviour.
These things and others of like Nature constitute what we
call fair dealing, honesty, integrity, Justice. It is opposed
both to Violence and to Deceipt. So Necessary is this Commutative Justice to the very being of human Society, that
without it there could ⟨be⟩ no Society at all. And it has been
very justly observed that even Gangs of Robbers and Pirates
who pay no Regard to the Rights of other Men must observe
the Rules of Justice and fidelity to one another otherwise
they could not possibly keep together.[3] It would be more
safe as well as more comfortable for a Man to renounce all
human Society & to live as a hermit in the wilderness, or to
dwell with the beasts of the field than with Men who had no

regard to Justice. It is chiefly with a view to defend themselves from Injury that men Associate & form human Societies. The first end of all Government & the chief Object of
human Laws is to secure Men from unjust violations of their
5   Rights that may be attempted either by Violence or fraud;
and to deter men by punishments from all such violations
of the Rights of others.

Distributive Justice in its strict and proper Sense is the
Justice of a Judge in executing the Laws and distributing
10 Rewards or Punishments. /

8/IV/3,4v   Humanity is another branch of the Duty we owe to our
fellow Men. He is a just Man who does no Injury to any
Man, though he should at the same time do no good. Such
a Man may be very useless very insignificant fruges consu-
15 mere Natus;[4] and therefore may be very far from discharging the duty incumbent upon him as a Member of Human
Society. As a withered Arm or hand is to the natural Body
an Useless incumbrance, so that the body would be as well
or better without it: In like Manner a Person who is in no
20 way subservient to the good of the Political Body, is onely a
dead weight upon it. it receives no benefite from him, it
would be at no loss if he were extinct.

It is I think to the honour of the British Nation that in
our Language all the Amiable and Benevolent Virtues
25 which prompt us to do good to our fellow Creatures are
summed up in the Word Humanity, which implys their
being the proper Characteristicks of a Man. Homo sum &
nihil humanum a me alienum puto.[5] This noble Sentiment
is interwoven into our Language. And indeed as man is by
30 his very Constitution a Social Animal, & is not born for himself alone but for his friends his family his Country;[6] he who
has no social and benevolent Dispositions is surely Defective
in one of the Noblest and best Parts of human Nature, as
really Deficient in what belongs to the Nature of Man as if
35 he were without hands and feet, or without the sense & Understanding of a Man.

8/ɪᴠ/1,1r   In That common and ancient Division of Virtue into
Four heads Prudence Temperance Fortitude and Justice.
The former three comprehend the duties of Self Government of which we have Spoke, in General.[1] nor do I intend
to lay down any particular rules concerning them and it is
indeed impossible to lay down such Rules with regard to
these as will distinguish the right from the wrong in every
particular case. And although there is no doubt a line that
separates them our faculties are not so nice and acute as to
be able to see with the utmost precision what lyes on this
Side of the line and what on the other. And although in
most cases we can very easily determine that this is the prudent Course that the Imprudent. This is temperance that
Intemperance. This is fortitude that pusillanimity. yet there
are some particular cases where the right and the wrong are
as it were contiguous to each other and it is hard to determine precisely where one ends and the other begins. What
seems prudent to one wise and good man, may to another
equally wise and good in the same circumstances seem
rather to be crafty and to imply a faulty dissimulation. What
to one man may seem a lawfull indulgence may to another
seem to be some degree of intemperance. But in such cases
a man may often prescribe Rules to himself, which he ought
not to prescribe nor has any tittle to prescribe to another.

    This vicinity of good to ill in many cases of Prudence
Temperance and Fortitude in men who do not heartily love
virtue but want to satisfy themselves with a certain Medioc-
rity in it leaves great Room for self deceit and leads them by
degrees to extend the limits of what is lawfull into the territory of Vice. But to men of thorrough integrity it is no-
ways hurtfull.

    The best general coarse in such Cases is to be strict in the

rules we prescribe to our selves and not to venture too near
the disputed limit but to be large in our Charity when we
pass Judgement on others. Instance in the Rules of Temperance with regard to eating and drinking & fasting. In-
5   stance with regard to Economy & Expence. /

8/IV/1,1V   *Jurisprudence*

MARCH 1
10

We come now to the 4th of these called Cardinal Virtues.
to wit Justice which in this Division is taken in so large a
Sense as to comprehend under it all that duty which we owe
to our fellow creatures and that part of Morals which treats
15   of Justice in this large Sense is called Natural Jurisprudence.
In order to give a more distinct notion of this part of Morals, It is proper to attend to consider the origin of the Name
that is commonly given to it *Natural Jurisprudence* and to give
some account how it came to be considered as a particular
20   Science in modern times and how it is distinguished from
politicks. Jurisprudentia among the Romans signified the
knowledge of their Civil Laws. Those who were Skilled in
the knowledge of the roman Law were called Juris pru-
dentes and Juris consulti in Ciceros time.[2] and afterwards in
25   Justinians time we find them called Jurisprudentes from
whence the Word Jurisprudentia, which signified with them
nothing else than Skill and knowledge in the Roman Law.

The words Jus and Fas in the latin tongue originally signify what the law commands or allows and are derived from
30   Jubere & Fari.[3] As all words are apt in course of time to
undergo some change of their original Signification and to
be transferred to things similar to or connected with that
which they originally signified. The word Jus among the
Romans came to signify the body or System of the Roman
35   Law. And those who were skilled in this System of the Roman Laws were called &c.

MAR 4

40

Jus came afterwards to signify what we would call a legal
right, or what a man had a tittle by law to do or possess or
enjoy.[4] All Laws circumscribe a Mans actions and confine
him within a certain Sphere within which he may exercise

his power and act according to his pleasure but he cannot
go beyond this Sphere without transgressing the laws and
thereby becoming obnoxious to punishment. And this
sphere of Action within which if a man confined himself, he
was no way obnoxious was called his Right. The Law not
onely circumscribes my Actions and fixes certain limits to
them, but it likewise directs & prescribes certain actions to
be done by others that respect me & tend to my benefite.
Thus it obliges those who owe me to pay their just debts, &
those who have contrated with me to perform their Engagements. It obliges my tutors or Curators to the faithfull management of what belongs to me while I am under age. Now
what the Lawiers call my right includes not onely what I
may lawfully do or possess but likewise what others are
bound by Law to do towards me every prestation for which
I have a legal demand upon them. It appears from what has
been said that this later Sense of the Word Jus must have
taken place onely after Law became a formal Study and
Profession. The Latin Writers use the Words Facultas and
Potestas in the same Sense.[5] The Word Jus is taken in the
former / of these Senses when it is joyned with the Name of
any Particular Country or State As Jus Romanum. As Jus
Romanum signifies the Body or System of the Roman or
Civil Law. But when the word Jus is joyned with a particular
person Office or Relation it is taken in the later Sense as Jus
mariti Jus-meum or Jus tuum, and signifies the Same thing
as the later Words facultas or potestas. So the Jus patria and
the Patria potestas mean one and the same thing. These two
meanings of the latin Word Jus are better distinguished in
our Language for we call the one Law the other Right. Jus
Civile would be improperly translated the Civil Right but
the proper English for it is the Civil Law. Again Jus Mariti
would be improperly translated the Law of a husband and
the English for it is the Rights of a husband. Jus Dominii
the Right of Property. Jus therefore in this later Sense, includes not onely all that a man can do enjoy or possess without breaking the Law, but likewise all that his fellow citizens
one or all are bound by law to do or perform for his benefit.
The including all these things under one word of Jus or
Right shews a considerable degree of Refinement in Speculations with regard to law. And therefore this Sense of the
Word is later than the others I have mentioned, & answers
precisely to what we call a mans Right.

Another meaning of the word Right equivalent to Rectum Honestum.

Jurisprudentia signifies the Knowledge both of the Laws and of the rights of men which are founded upon the Laws.

Having shewn the original Meanings of the Latin Words Jus and Jurisprudentia. It is easy to see how men those especially who made the Laws their Study would be led to form a Notion of a Natural Law and Natural Rights of Men which were not grounded upon the Code or Pandects[6] but in the human Nature and in that faculty by which we discern Right from Wrong.

The best System of Civil Laws cannot provide against every wrong suppose then that the Laws of the State of which I am a Member do not admit an Action for the implementing of a promise or bargain made privately between the parties without witnesses without writ & without the Interposition of a Judge. If a man refuses to fulfill his promise made to me in such Circumstances. I find I am wronged I cannot but think him under an obligation, altho the law does not oblige him, I am sensible that he wrongs me altho he withholds nothing from me which the law obliges him to give nor is deficient in any prestation which the law requires of him. I am therefore very naturally led to conceive of some more extensive law which is more adequate to my notions of right and wrong.

The Law of Nations.[7] /

When men have thus formed the Conception of a Law of Nature and a Law of Nations. They are apt to Consider it in the same light as they were wont to consider the Civil Law to borrow both their Notions of one from the other, and to apply the words that belong to one, in explaining the other and even to treat of the Laws of nature in the Same order and under the same divisions which have been commonly used in treating of the Civil Law.

As Civilians have comprehended, all that a man may do, all that he may possess or enjoy, according to Law, and all that the Law obliges others to do towards him or for his benefite;[8] under the Name of the mans Right so writers on natural Jurisprudence in like manner comprehend all that a man may do possess or enjoy according to the Law of Nature and all likewise that others ought to do for his benefit; as the mans Right by the Law of Nature. A Mans legal Rights therefore have the Same Relation to the Civil Laws

8/IV/1,2v

under which he lives as these Rights which writers on Jurisprudence ascribe to him have to the Law of Nature.

To every Right there is an Obligation which Corresponds.
And a Right in me implys an Obligation upon some other
person or persons.[9] The onely exceptions to this Rule are
either. Where [there] the right is unknown to the person
who would be under the obligation if he knew it. Or where
a Right is believed where there is none.[10] But where there is
neither ignorance of the Right nor a wrong Notion of it. It
is impossible that any Right can belong to me, but it must
imply some obligation upon another one or more.

In order to make these two Notions of Right tally with
each other Civilians as well as writers on Jurisprudence have

Mar 5 1765

In treating of the Principles of Morals in General we endeavoured to shew that by our Moral Faculty we have an
immediate perception of Right and wrong of Moral Rectitude & Depravity in moral Agents in like Manner as we have
a perception of black and white in visible Objects by the
Eyes of harmony and Discord by a Musical Ear and of other
qualities in objects by means of the several faculties of our
Nature which are adapted so by the Author of our Nature
as to give us not onely the Ideas of such Qualities but an
immediate perception of their Existence in certain Subjects.[11] This Moral Rectitude or Depravity is the immediate
Object of our Approbation & Disapprobation. This Right or
wrong this moral Rectitude or pravity is a real Quality in
Moral agents but as it is onely on Account of some Action
of an Agent or some determination of his will that we either
approve or disapprove / of him, hence by a figure of Speech
we say the Action is right or wrong and deserves to be approved or disapproved, although in reality and in strict propriety the Rectitude or pravity is in the Agent and it is the
Agent that is the proper object of approbation or disapprobation. This is the most proper and direct Sense of the
Word Right in Morals and it answers to what the Ancients
called the Honestum as its contrary answers to the turpe.[12]
In this Sense we say its right for a Man to honour his parents to obey his Maker to love his neighbour.

In Natural Jurisprudence the word Right is taken in a
very different Sense when I say I have a Right to such a
house or have no right to it.[13] When we speak of the rights

of Men and divide them into perfect unperfect & external.[14]
In order therefore to have a clear and distinct Notion of
these Rights of Men which are the Objects of Natural Jurisprudence, it is necessary to observe that such Rights have
the Same Relation to our moral faculty as the legal or civil
Rights of men have to the law of the Land. Every mans Conscience is a law to him. It enjoyns certain actions & forbids
others it prescribes to him a certain rule of conduct and as
far as he deviates from this Rule, so far is he guitly in his
own Judgment and in the Judgment of others. He deserves
punishment for every such transgression of the Law of his
mind. And the conscience of guilt and dread of punishment, is indeed a real punishment for his transgression.
Moreover the dictates of our Conscience or Moral faculty
ought to be considered as the Law of the supreme Legislator who has given us this faculty to be the guide of our
Lives, and made us so that we cannot transgress its laws
without an inward conviction that we do what is displeasing
to him and are obnoxious[15] to his just punishment. Juven
Sat 13 V 393 & seq

> Cur tamen hos tu
> Evasisse putes quos diri conscia facti
> Mens habet attonitos, & surdo verbere caedit;
> Occultum quatiente animo tortore flagellum
> Poena autem vehemens ac multo saevior illis
> Quas et Caeditius gravis invenit & Radamanthus
> Nocte dieque suum gestare in pectore testem[16]

Since therefore the dictates of our Moral faculty are a law
to which we are Subjected by the constitution of our Nature,
even without considering our Relation to the deity;[17] Since
when we reflect upon our Relation to the Deity, this law of
our Nature appears also the Law of God, and a plain indication of his will, it is undoubtedly very natural and Just to

8/ɪᴠ/1,3v   conceive of Mankind / as Subject to a Law by means of their
moral Nature; a Law which is antecedent to all civil Laws,
and of higher obligation, as being both the Law of our Nature and the law of God. Hence it is that writers on Natural
Jurisprudence have with great propriety given the Name of
the Law of Nature to the Whole System of Conduct which
our moral faculty shews to be right & honest.

Justinians Def. of the Law of Nature. Quod Natura omnia
animanlia docuit.

Jus Gentium quod Naturalis Ratio inter omnes homines

Constituit. Grotio Jus Gentium. Quod Gentium omnium aut
multarum Voluntate vim obligandi accepit.

Eidem Jus Naturae Dictatum Rectae Rationes indicans
Actui alicui inesse M. turpitudinem aut Nec M.[18]

Of this Law of Nature that duty which we owe to our fellow
men (see all the different relations we may stand to ⟨them⟩)
is an essential part and is by writers on Natural Jurisprudence called by the name of Justice. But it is evident that
Justice taken in this large Sense so as to comprehend all the
Duty we owe to our fellow men is onely a technical Word,
and that the meaning of the word Justice in common conversation is very different. We conceive of Justice as onely a
negative kind of Virtue and implying rather the doing no
hurt than the doing good to our fellow creatures. We call a
man just if he neither injures another in his person nor in
his just fame and estimation nor in his property nor in his
family nor in any of his Relations. But such a just man may
yet have no social Virtue no kind Affection, no Generosity
or publick Spirit no concern for the good of his fellow creatures. As writers on natural Jurisprudence therefore extend
the meaning of the word Justice so as to extend it to all Social Virtues. They find it necessary to Divide it in to various
branches so as to make it comprehend all the duty we owe
to our fellow Creatures.[19] Those Writers have also given a
technical meaning to the Word Right corresponding to that
which they give to the word Justice.[20] For these two words
are relative to each other and ought to have equal Extent.

What a Right to any thing implys.

It is not a Quality of the thing or of the Person having
right. Nor is it any Real Relation between the thing and the
Person. Nor is it any connexion or association between the
thing and Person in our Imagination.[21]

When we say that a man has a Right to such a house or to
such a prestation from an other, This is no more but a short
technical way of expressing what would require many words
to express it in the most direct and natural way. It is an artificial way of signifying that certain actions of the person
who is said to have the right are within the limits of his duty,
and at the same time it signifies certain actions of others towards him to be their duty. Upon the whole therefore Mans
Civil Right is a figure of Speech by which we understand all
that the Law of the State allows him to do possess and enjoy
and all which the Law obliges others to do for his benefit. /

MAR 6

5

10

15

20

25

so the Rights of Men which are the Objects of Natural
Jurisprudence signify by a like figure of Speech what the
Law of Nature allows a man to do possess or enjoy and what
that Law requires others to do towards him.

Obligation and Right are Relative and Reciprocal, unless
where upon account of some Error in Judgment they are
unnaturally Separated. Perfect Imperfect & external Rights.

Wherein the Right of the Deity to govern his Creatures is
founded. Acknowledged Superiority in Wisdom and Goodness gives Authority. What he commands must be right.[22]

Whether the Law of Nature is Perfect, & immutable. Does
it admit of any Dispensation.[23]

Another Division of Rights 1 Private 2 Publick 3 Common.[24]

The Rights of Men Correspond to their different States.[25]

1 The State of Natural Liberty, not a chimerical one.
Whether a State of War. Perfect Rights competent to this
State. 1 Life & the Integrity of our Members & the neces-
sary means of Life. Of a Mans Power over his own Life of
Suicide.[26]

2. Liberty 3 Private Judgment 4 The Use of things Common and the Acquisition of Property by our Labour 5 Estimation of Probity Character 6 To fair dealing and Truth in
those that converse with them.

MAR 7

30

35

40

The Natural Equality of Men in these Rights. None naturally born to be Slaves.

Imperfect Rights competent to this State. 1 To Social Intercourse and civil Treatment. 2 To such offices of humanity from others as cost them little or no trouble. 3 Even to
offices of some Expense in cases of Distress. 4 To all offices
of humanity & Kindness & Liberality which are suited to
their worth and uniqueness and our abilities. 5 To the Gratitude of those who have been benefited by us.

In General It cannot be said that in a perfect Conformity
to the Imperfect Rights of Mankind[27] but following that admirable rule of our Divine Teacher of doing to others whatsoever we would and think reasonable that they should do
to us in like Circumstances. It seems impossible to fall upon
a more happy expedient to divest ourselves of that bias

which inordinate selflove and other private affections give
us than to apply this Rule.

Cautions about Liberality. 1 Worth 2 Indigence 3 Natural
4 Affection 5 Gratitude 6 usefull Offices rather than Pleasing.

See Cicero Offic Lib 1 c 14..18

Ne obsit benignitas iis quibus beneficere velle videamur.
Ne major sit benignitas quam facultates. Ut pro dignitate cuique tribuatur[28]

Adventitious Rights[29]

Distinguished into Real and Personal.
1   To the fruits of the Earth for food
2   To the Service of the inferior Animals. Gen 1 29, 30[30]
3   To Use them ⟨for⟩ food. Gen 9. 2, 3
4   The Right of private Property. Original Derived.

Of Things in the State of Negative Communion Res Nullius &c, of Positive Com⟨munion⟩.[31]

Of Occupation. 1 Of things for present Use 2 Of
permanent Property[32]

1 Of Moveables 2 Of Immoveables

Of Dereliction[33] /

8/IV/1,4v MAR 11

The foundation of Property. D Humes Notion of it.[34] Extension of Property in Different Periods of Society. Wills
Land Property. What things are incapable of Occupation.[35]

MAR 12

We have endeavoured to shew that Although permanent
Original Rights may be obtained by Occupation yet there
are some things to which either Private Men or States cannot obtain an exclusive Right in this Way. And all Right of
Occupation as it is founded upon the common good of human Society, so it must be limited and restrained as the common good requires. By the Law of Nature & Right Reason
occupation then onely founds a valid Right when it is made

without any injurious intention towards our fellow men and
when in reality it neither hurts them nor deprives them of
any advantage ease or Security which they formerly enjoyed. Our moral faculty here approves of the Occupier, it
disapproves of the person or State by whom he is molested
or disturbed in an acquisition which hurts no body. But if
this occupation is of Such a Nature as to threaten the Safety
of others who are not subject to the Occupant. The occupation gives no right. it[36] Why? because every candid Spectator must disapprove of such occupation ⟨as⟩ an encroach-
ment upon the peace the Security of those who are exposed
to danger by it, and must approve of their using their best
endeavours to guard against such a danger.

Example. Suppose an Island discovered by the French or
English in the Atalantick.

Ex 2 The Encroachments of Europeans upon the hunting
Grounds of the Americans.

Ex 3 A Deserted City occupied at the Same time by two
neighbouring States.[37]

Rights by the Law of Nature may depend even upon the
intentions of Men civil Rights must therefore often be different and determined by different Rules.[38]

Accessions.[39] Fructus, Alluvio, Insula Nata in flumine,
Adjunctio, Inaedificatio. Scriptura. Specificatio. Commixtio
Confusio Plantatio and Satio. What full property implys.[40]

13 MAR.

The Right of Occupation by private Persons limited by
the Laws and Customs of States. Land. New Discoveries.
Large accessions. Royal Mines. Royal Fishes. Excheats.
Hunting Game.[41]

Prescription a Kind of Intermediate Right between the
Original and Derived.[42] /

8/iv/5,2r   Derived Rights Either Real or Personal. This Distinction
is grounded in Reason and has considerable Effects even by
the Law of Nature.[43]

Real Derived Rights are either the full Property or some
part of it. There are several Real Rights which include not
the full property of the Subject but only some part of the
full Right detached from the Rest.[44] These are here to be
explained and they are.

1 The Right of Possession. Rules regarding it.[45]

MAR 14 1765

2 The Right of Succession in Entails.[46]

Enails a Modern Invention. State of the Great Barons in
the Feudal Times they either did not contract debt or if they
did it was either to Merchants or Jews neither of whom were
in those days considered as being in a condition of evicting
their Just Debts from a great Lord. So that Estates without
any aid of Entails often continued in one family for many
Generations.

The Natural Respect payed to the Representative of a
very ancient family who can count among his Ancestors
many illustrious Heroes and Statesmen that have been remarkably usefull to their Country and whose Actions make
a figure in the History of Mankind.

This is a great part of the Natural Reward of heroic virtue
that it reflects Honour not onely upon the hero or Patriot
himself while History preserves the Memory of his Actions,
but it also reflects Honour upon his descendants and even
upon his Ancestors.

How by the gradual Change of Manners the great Land
holders began to lose their Estates and to have their families
sunk in Oblivion. It was very reasonable and lawfull for
them to remedy this Evil if it could be done by fair Means,
and Entails seem to afford a Remedy for it.

To pledge of the Equity and Reasonableness of Entails it
would be necessary to weigh in an even Ballance the good
and the bad Effects of them 1 with regard to the Family
itself 2 with regard to the Publick. 3 How far they correspond with the general Laws of Nature & Providence. 1
With Regard to the Family. All the advantage that can be
procured by them to the family is to perpetuate the Estate
in it. If this could be effected it is doubtfull whether it be
any great Benefit. Every man would wish his Son to have an
Estate providing he can make a proper use of it. But it does
not appear that it would be a real good to one half of
Mankind that they had Estates. If we take an equal Number
of those who have been properly educated without the Ex-
pectation of any Fortune but what they may acquire by industry / and Virtue, with such as have been educated in the
hopes of enjoying a plentifull fortune we shall not find the
latter to have any great advantage over the former in point
of real Happiness or of Virtue.

On the contrary the sure prospect of an ample Fortune
very often weakens those incitements to Industry and Virtue which the Wisdom of Providence has provided in the
natural Course of things. And a young Heir has less inducement to Industry and Virtue than one who has his fortune
to make.

Every human Institution is unfavourable to Virtue & Industry which provides other Roads to Riches and honour
than this which Nature has appointed. Entails, therefore
seem to have a natural Influence to take away the incitements to Virtue and Industry in a family, in the same degree as they secure Riches to every Heir of Entail without
those Qualities which onely can enable a man to make a
proper use of them.

2 Entails seem to lessen too much the Paternal Authority
which Nature has ordained for the benefite of Children and
for the Punishment of those who are incorrigibly vicious.

3 They prove a great hardship upon the younger Children, whose right naturally is equal by straitning them in
their Education and provision after they have been brought
up in Opulence. Hinder them from marrying and so families often become extinct or the estate and honours go to
distant collaterals ⟨in⟩ Entails.[47]

Effects of Entails with regard to the Publick.

1 They are an unreasonable Extension of Property, beyond what can be justified by the Law of Nature. A man is
capable of acquiring property because Nature has endowed
him with such a measure of Judgment and Understanding
as that he may make a good use of it. And if he had not
such a measure of Reason and Understanding there is nothing in the Law of Nature that could justify the Acquisition
of Permanent Property. Now tho a Man may make a good
use of a very extensive Property in his lifetime, although
perhaps he may act reasonably in leaving it at his Death to
persons then in being who as he may have grounds to think
will make a proper Use of it. Yet Nature has not given to
him such a measure of Understanding as that he can fore-
see how his Estate ought to be disposed of to the end of the
World. When he substitutes heirs of Entail who have yet no
Existence, this can be justified by no other principle but that
fond partiality Which leads a man to conceive that his heirs
of entail to the end of the world shall be such Persons as

ought to enjoy his Estate, that they shall be endowed with
such Qualities that it is for their own Good the Good of the
Family and the publick Good that they should hold this Estate.

5   If I have an Estate I am capable of Judging which of my
8/III/2,2r   Children or / relations is like to make a good Use of it for
themselves for the family or for the publick. As I may therefore make a rational Choice there may be some Reason why
I should have the power of making this Choice. But with
10   regard to persons yet unborn it is impossible I can make a
rational Choice and therefore no Law of Nature can entitle
me to make such a Choice.

2 It is for the Publick good that Riches and that Power
which is consequent upon them should as much as possible
15   be the reward of Virtue and Industry, and in the Natural
Course of things, they are so in a great degree. Entails counteract this order of Nature By Securing Riches to a Succession of Men, who have no greater probability of being men
of Industry and Virtue than Others; Nay who have the
20   greatest temptations by this very institution to Vice and
Sloth.

3 The Ambition of great Men to perpetuate their family,
which is both a Natural and laudable Ambition, would perhaps take a turn more favourable to the good of Society as
25   well as more proper for answering its end if the hopes of
accomplishing this end by entails were cut off. The onely
mean then left for a man to perpetuate his family would be
to take all possible care to train all his children to those qualities which make men truly great and to put each of them in
30   this way of raising families of their own whom they might
train in like Manner. The great families in Rome kept up in
this way not by Entails.

4 Entails are a great Discouragement to trade 1 As they
lessen Credit. 2 As they exclude Entailed Estates from being
35   Subjects of Commerce, Preclude those who have made fortunes by their Industry from the great end they have in
View in all their Labours, And tend to lead us back to that
Gothick Constitution wherein Merchants Manufacturers &
Farmers were the Slaves of the Land holders. Prosperous
40   traders will desert a Country where they can find no land to
purchase.[48]

5 They discourage the improvement of Estates.
Whether a hereditary Nobility may not be allowed un-

alienable Estates. This seems not disagreeable to our Constitution. /

8/III/2,2v
5

If we consider in the last place how far perpetual Entails are agreable to the laws of Nature and the Course of the Divine Providence.

Every Extension of the Right of Property which is hurtfull to human Society must be contrary to the Law of Nature which Justifies & guards Property onely as far as it conduces to publick Utility. If perpetual Entails therefore be contrary to common Utility especially in a commercial State as I conceive they are for the Reasons already Mentioned, they cannot be justified by the Laws of Nature.

10

By the Course of Nature appointed for the wisest Purpose by the Divine Providence Prodigality Luxury & Idleness & Vices bring Men & Families to Poverty and Want. This is the Appointment of God for the Discouragement of those vices and for a Constant Warning to Mankind. Perpetual Entails are a vain & impotent Attempt to counteract this Order of the Divine Providence; and to secure Greatness and Riches for ever to a family without any Regard to Merit. Which if it could be effected would be a most dangerous temptation to Vice to those who represent that family and a most pernicious Example to Mankind in General. The Heirs of the Caesars the Alexanders the Gengiskhans and the Sesostris's are now mixed with the common herd of Mankind unknown and undistinguished As the Ashes of those Mighty Conquerors are mixed with the Common Dust. Not onely great Estates but mighty Kingdoms and Empires are crumbled into dust by all devouring Time. And could the Secret be found (which is as hopless ⟨as⟩ finding the Philosophers Stone or the Universal Medicine) of embalming and preserving them to all future Generations like so many Egyptian Mummies they would be as useless an encumbrance to the Earth as those Monuments of Ancient Vanity are.[49] /

15

20

25

30

35

8/III/2,2r

Pledges. Morgages.[50]

Servitudes. Personal. The Use of any thing for a time or for Life. Life rent.

Real Urban. tigne immittendi, Altius non tollendi, luminum prospectus. Stillicidii.

40

Rural Iter, Actus, Via, /

8/III/2,2v

Compleat property May be transferred either during the Proprietors life or in the Event of his Death.[51]

1 During the Proprietors Life 1 With his Consent by Gift or Sale which will be treated of Afterwards under the head of Contracts 2 Without the proprietors Consent when it is necessary to satisfy any Just Claim against him this will be

5 afterwards considered under the head of the Rights arising from the injuries done by others.

2 In the Event of the Proprietors Death the Property he enjoyed may be conveyed two Ways. 1 By his Will or Testament 2 By Succession to the intestate.

10 1 Wills Grot. Testamentum est alienatio in Mortis Eventum, ante eam revocabilis, retento interim Jure possidendi ac fruendi.[52] The Objections of Puffendorf against this Definition.[53] /

8/IV/7,1r   *Of Succession to the Intestate*[54]

MAR 19 1765

The most early Custom in most Nations seems to have

20 been that Children who were not foris familiate[55] Succeeded to their fathers and that rather as continuing in the possession of the Goods of the family than by any other Right.[56] And if ther were no Children in the family even Servants Succeeded to their masters in the Same way as continuing

25 the possession of the goods belonging to the family. If a man intended to convey his Succession to one who was not of his family the method of doing this in the most early ages seems to have been not by any Testamentary deed but by adopting him into his family.[57]

30 In the Gradual Improvement of Society the connection between parents and Children becomes more Strong and even between more distant Relations, Men come to have more property and are able not onely to leave the necessary means of Subsistence to the survivors of the family but to

35 better the Situation of their Children who are foris familiate and of other near Relations. In a Rude and Savage State men hardly consider any connexions beyond their own family. They have no dependance upon others and very little intercourse with them especially if settled at any distance

40 from them. But as Society improves mens connexions enlarge their wants their dependance their power are increased and the most natural of these is the association of Near Relations who have been once in the Same family and

thereby contracted friendship as an additional tie to natural Affection, and thereby come to have an interest in one another.

Much is left to the civil Laws in the Matter of Succession. Yet every thing determined by civil laws in this matter is not just as for instance that Shipwrecks should belong to the proprietor of the Coast.[58] /

8/iv/7,1v *Contracts and Covenants*

The definition of a Contract not easy.[59]

In a Contract or promise the Will or intention does not bind unless it be expressed Nor 2 The expressing an intention without actually contracting Nor 3 Words without intention, Nor 4 Does the want of an intention to perform hinder the Obligation. Not even when the person with whom the Contract is made perceives that it is made without the intention of performance.

We must here distinguish between the intention of performing and the intention of binding or contracting. The second is absolutely necessary the first is not. This intention signified and accepted of constitutes a contract or Covenant. The Effect of such a Covenant is that by the immediate judgment of our Moral faculty the person contracting is under a moral obligation to perform what he has lawfully contracted to do or perform & the person with whom he has contracted has a right to the performance of what is contracted.[60] Bargains between the Negroes and the Bartering people.

A Contract[ed] supposes a moral faculty. Therefore no definition can express the Nature of it which does not include the notion of obligation. Hence likewise Brutes cannot make contracts nor Children before they are capable of understanding moral obligation. Contracts of Pupils Minors. Men Drunk or Disordered.[61]

How far Error makes a Contract Void.[62]

When the Contract is founded upon the presumption of something which is not found to hold.[63]

The necessity of Signs. The baseness of Equivocation mental Reservation &c.[64]

How far a Contract extorted by fear binding.[65]

Faith to be kept with Hereticks Rebells & the worst of Men.[66]

MAR 20

Contracts to do an unlawful thing not binding.[67]

Contracts may be binding although rash and hurtfull to the party contracting.[68] The duty of the other party in such a case.

Candor and open dealing in Contracts indispensibly obligatory.[69]

Fundamentum autem Justitiae Fides i.e. dictorum pactorumq constantia & veritas.[70]

It is very justly observed by Cicero and many other Ancient Authors, that Justice and Fidelity towards those who live in Society is so Necessary, that it is found even in the dens of Robbers & Crews of Pirates. Altho' they have no regards to the Rights of other Men that are not of the Gang, yet they find a Necessity of observing strict justice towards one another. Their Associates in Iniquity must be prescried by Justice and fair dealing to each other.[71] Pudor & Justitiae Soror incorrupta Fides nudaque Veritas.[72]

Acceptation how far Necessary.[73]

The consideration of Contracts alone sufficient to convince us of the Existence of a Moral Faculty. Because without such a faculty we could not have the very Idea of a Contract. And because all Mankind not onely have the Idea but a Conviction of the Obligation of Contracts this shews that the Moral faculty is common to all Mankind.[74]

From this also we may infer that Justice is a Natural Not an Artificial Virtue. The justice of keeping contracts if grounded upon an immediate perception.[75]

Without fidelity in Contracts there could be no Society among Mankind,[76] and if according to the Ancient Fable Astraea should quite abandon the Earth human Society must disband & Men keep at as great distance from each other as possible.[77] /

8/IV/7,2r MAR 21

We come now to speak of the Obligations whether perfect or imperfect which we are under in the Use of Speech.[78] And these may be deduced without much Labour from the manifest intention of the supreme being in endowing us with this noble faculty of Speech from the immediate Judgment of our Moral Powers from the common good of Soci-

ety and from the honour and advantage acruing to our
selves & the benefit to human Society arising from a proper
Use of this excellent Gift of God.[79]

By Speech I understand not onely those artificial Signs
whether of Sound or Writing by which men are wont to
communicate their minds to one another, but under the
Name of Speech I comprehend every Sign whether natural
or Artificial by which men can affirm or deny accept or refuse, promise or contract, threaten or Supplicate, praise or
blame, encourage or discourage, and in a word by which we
can communicate to others our thoughts our Sentiments
our purposes our passions and afflictions.[80]

When we treat of Speech in Morals and of our obligations
in the use of it we ought to take it in this extensive sense;
because as a Contract or promise has the same force and
obligation whether made in french or English whether by
word or writing so it has the same force whether made by
means of artificial or of Natural Signs and the same thing
may be affirmed of every obligation arising from the use of
Speech.[81] We gave an instance of A traffick carried on between nations who never saw one another nor employed
any agent or factor to go between them. Yet these nations
tho extreamly rude and unimproved are conscious of their
obligation to deal fairly & honestly by one another and act
accordingly.[82]

Now having explained what we mean by Speech it will
easily be allowed that it is one of the best gifts that God has
given to men that without it human Life would be a most
dismal state of being. Even the brute animals have something that may be called speech in the sense we now use this
word.[83] They can express their love or hatred, their hostile
or amicable disposition, their shame or pride, their submission or Authority. But they are incapable of entring into
contracts of promising or bearing testimony the old cannot
communicate their Experience to the Young or inform
them of what they have seen or heard or learned. Thus they
are incapable of any improvement and to the end of the
World can neither be wiser nor more foolish better nor
worse than they were at the beginning. Man by being endowed with the gift of Speech is put on a very different
footing. A young man may learn more of things of real Importance to his happiness in one Month than he would have
been able to discover by his / own natural and unimproved

powers in a long life. What would man be without any kind of instruction? We may learn to answer this Question by the Accounts we have of Some of the Species who having been early exposed or left in woods have grown up to mans Es-
tate without any Instruction, without conversing with any of their kind. Such was a young man found in the woods in Hanover 20 or thirty years ago. and some others.[84] All of them as far as appears seemed in nothing to differ from brutes but in their outward form. All the improvement which Mankind have attained beyond the pitch of these wild Men we owe to the use of Speech. By means of which the knowledge and Experience of one Generation can be conveyed down ⟨to⟩ the next. And Mankind as if animated by one Soul may be still in a progressive state with regard to knowledge and improvement. This is evidently the inten-
tion of the faculty of Speech and it is admirably fitted for this end. The various parts of our frame both of body and mind by which we are fitted for this communication of our Sentiments by Speech shew that the Author of Nature had this end in view but has been Sollicitous about it. For this purpose the Features of the Face the Motions and Attitudes of the body the modulations of the Voice are made to be naturally signs of our thoughts purposes and affections we are taught by Nature without any human Instruction or Experience to interpret those Signs.[85] The human Organs are fitted for a Vast Variety not onely of tones and Modulations, but of Articulate Sounds which are the most proper mate-
rials for artificial Signs of our thoughts. Children learn very early to understand & to imitate the Language of those about them and by particular Instincts are led to believe what is told them and to express their own Sentiments with Candor. This point ought to be treated more fully.[86]

2 When they grow up to years of Understanding they perceive themselves to be under the most perfect moral Ob-
ligation to that candor and truth in their declarations which in infancy they practiced from mere instinct.[87] There are Some Vices which men may have the effrontery to own and to glory in. But lying and falsehood never was nor will be justified by the worst men. The turpitude of those Actions is so manifest as to admit of no disguise. Every man is affronted in the highest degree by the imputation of them and is conscious of his being abused and injured by those

4/III/4,1r   who impose upon him by means / of this Kind. And if giving

the Lye be the most heighnous affront as it is in the judgment of all mankind, then making a Lye must be one of the
basest and most dishonourable actions. Every man hates
lying and falsehood in others and therefore must be self-
condemned if he practices it himself. Every man desires to
be trusted in his declarations and therefore ought to deserve it.

MAR 22

3 The influence of Faith and Truth on the good of Society. Want of regard to Truth a Sign of the utmost depravity.
4 The Effect of Faith on a mans own happiness as it needs
no Art fears no discovery, procures Credit and Trust which
⟨is⟩ one of the chief engines of business.
Two Kinds of Deception.[88] When we give occasion to a
mans making a false Judgment. 2 When by testifying or affirming what is false we abuse the trust which others have
in our veracity. All lawfull Stratagems of War reducible to
the former head. The latter in no case lawfull.[89] The former
onely to be used with those whom we are at liberty to use
either as enemies or as weak headstrong unreasonable men.
To conceal our sentiments artfully sometimes allowable, but
the less it is used the better. The character of an artfull man
to be avoided. An open undisguised behaviour amiable,
easy to ourselves & to others. The character of Nathaniel.[90]
In a witness it may be a great crime to conceal the truth.[91]
Reproof. Witnessbearing. Selfdefence. Caution to a third
person. What is publick.[92] Duties of Conversation. Candor
kind affection good Manners. Vices. Calumny. Slander. De-
traction. Defamation. Sowing seeds of Discord. Invective
Ranting & Backbiting. Obscenity. Most things have three
kinds of Names in Language 1 Such as barely denote the
Object without any affection of the speaker 2 Such as denote Esteem Approbation or Liking in the Speaker 3 Such
as denote Dislike Contempt or abhorrence in the Speaker.[93]
Of Oaths and Vows. Definition. Act of Religion.[94] Est Ius-
jurandum affirmatio religiosa, quod autem affirmate quasi
Deo teste promiseris id tenendum est. Cic.[95] Nullum vinculum ad adstringendam Fidem majoris nostri jurejurando artius esse voluerunt. Idem.[96] Lawfully only on weighty occasions. Quakers. Common swearing. Imposing of oaths
unnecessarily or where there is temptation to perjury.[97] By

whom we should Swear.[98] The form of an Oath.[99] The end
of an Oath, to give security. The kinds of Oaths.[100] The
Strict obligation of an Oath, & guilt of Perjury.[101] An Oath
brings no new obligation but strengthens what we confirm
5   by it.[102] Cannot oblige to what is unlawfull.[103] /

4/III/4,1v   *Of the Price of Things.*[104]

MAR 25

      That men may be enabled to make exchanges with one
another in traffick it is necessary that some price or value
should be put upon things which are the subjects of traffick.
Traffick and Commerce when carried to a considerable
15   pitch produces a wonderfull Change in many of our Notions, but in none of them does it produce a greater Change
than in our notions of the Value of things which may be the
Subjects of Traffick. If we suppose a man cut off from all
traffick and exchange with other men. The several things
20   which he accounts his property would return to their original Value pretty nearly, and be estimated by him pretty
much in the same manner as they would be before traffick
was begun. In this case a man will value everything according to the benefit advantage or pleasure he receives by it.
25   Land can be of no use to him but as far as he tills and plants
it or feeds his cattle on it or hunts on it. If he is not straitned
in these Articles anybody may take the rest that pleases he
does not think it worth occupation. If he had a forrest of
the finest Wood a very small part of it serves all the purposes
30   he can have for wood. If he had full granaries he can consume but a very small part before the grain is corrupted and
all that is over is of no more value to him than the clods of
the field. If he had Gold and Jewels in aboundance they
would probably be of no more value in his eye than a bud
35   of tulips. He would not even find that pleasure in his riches
which they borrow from the vanity of a man who enjoys
them in civil Society because they could procure him no
courtship or flattery.
      Yet even in this unsocial State the man would put some
40   comparative estimation upon the things that were usefull or
agreeable in proportion to their Use or agreableness. Thus
if we should suppose his habitation to take fire and that it is
not in his power to save every thing: he would endeavour to
save in the first place what he valued highest and other

things in proportion to the value he put upon them. However the comparative value he puts upon things in this State
is measured onely by his own wants & Desires.

If we now shift the Scene and suppose him to have access
to exchange his property with other men for what he had
occasion for, his notion of the Value of things will by degrees be altered will become more complete and be subjected to a different Measure. For although he will at first
be disposed to consider onely his own wants and desires in
rating things, he will soon learn to take in the desires and
wants of other men into the Account. Thus we shall suppose
him / very dextrous above others at making bows and ar-
rows and that he has a store of this kind by him of which he
uses onely a few of the best. The rest are of no use to him
and he could without any loss give them for a song. Others
however who have not the skill to make so good for themselves will desire to have them and find great benefit from
what is altogether useless to him. They will therefore be
willing to give him for one of them something which he values. And now his superfluous bows acquire a value in his
own Eye, for every thing is worth what it brings. So that we
see this value or Estimation is produced Solely by the wants
and desires of others not by his own. He will in like manner
learn to put a value upon all his Superfluities which may be
usefull to others. Nay he will learn to estimate his time his
Labour and his Skill upon which before he could never have
thought of putting a price now his labour for a day or a
week may be valued according to the value of what is produced by it. Indeed in his former State we may account
among his superfluities all the time which was not employed
in providing his conveniencies. But now this as well as other
superfluities can be turned to account.

The State of Society not onely gives a value to those things
which the proprietor put no value upon before Such as all
his superfluities that can be usefull to other people & even
his superfluous time his skill and ingenuity: but it likewise
greatly alters the value of things which men formerly put
some value upon. Every part of my property is more or less
valuable according to what I can have in exchange for it.
And what was highly valuable to me in a solitary state because usefull and Scarce, may perhaps in the Social State be
easily had from others who have more than they have use
for. So that their plenty diminishes the value of my small
pittance.

We may add that if there were no Exchanges among men
no man would ever think of putting any value upon what
was the property of another man because it is not attainable
by him and therefore can be of no use to him. There may
be fruitfull fields and rich materials on the Moon for what
we know but we never think of valuing the commodities of
that planet while we despair of having any traffick thither.
But we put a value upon the Lands and moveables of other
men as well as upon our own because they are in commerce
and are bought and Sold.[105] /

4/III/4,2v   We have seen how men estimate things in a solitary or
unsocial State and what a mighty change is made in the
value they put upon them in a social & commercial State.
But it may still be asked by what rule or measure must they
be estimated in this last State or can any such rule be discovered.

It is difficult in this question to separate the Provinces of
Morals and Politicks. Though I have given such Definitions
of these as make them very Distinct Sciences, & propose to
handle them distinctly yet; yet in this particular Inst⟨ance⟩
and in some others they meet as it were together. In Politicks we do not enquire what is Right or wrong, but what
are the Causes that produce such or such Events in Society;
or on the other hand what are the Effects and consequences
that follow from such or Such constitutions. But in Morals
of which Iurisprudence is a part we enquire what is right or
wrong in human Conduct, what conduct in us is consistent
with the rights of our fellow Men & what inconsistent.[106]
When therefore we here enquire into the natural Measure
of the Price of things in Society it is that we may be able to
determine more justly the limits of right and wrong in those
Contracts wherein a price or value is put upon things. It can
admit of no doubt that a Man taking advantage of the Ignorance or Necessity of another may take an unreasonable
or exorbitant Price and thereby Injure his Neighbour; even
the civil Laws of all Nations suppose this and allow redress
for such injuries. But it is impossible to determine when we
injure others in this way without knowing upon what principles the Natural and Reasonable Price depends & how it
is measured. /

4/III/17,1r   As the natural Use of Commodities which are the Object
of Commerce is to Supply Mens real or Imaginary Wants
and to gratify their desires; their greater or less subserviency to this End, must be the Natural Measure of their

Value. But this Value is by no means the measure of their
Price. It is onely the utmost limit beyond which the price
cannot go. A Man that sells his Birthright for a Mess of Pottage, shewes that in his present distress he values the one
more than the other.[107] Yet on ordinary occasions he would
pay no more for his pottage than the Market price. When
Bargains are made there is a kind of Conflict between the
desires of the buyer and those of the Seller. The buyer desires to have the Commodity as cheap as he can have it. The
Seller desires to have as good a price as he can get. These
contrary desires after some bidding and Edging like lines
that cross one another meet in a certain point, and there the
bargain is struck. Since therefore the price of things hath
such dependance upon the wants of individuals real or
imaginary their opinions whether wise or foolish, their desires whether reasonable or unreasonable; it may seem impossible to discover any fixed principles or Rules by which
it is governed. The Price of things in Commerce is an Event
that depends upon a vast Multitude of Contingencies which
may seem beyond the reach of Human Prudence and foresight. Indeed I apprehend it is so in some Measure and that
the most skillfull in Subjects of this Nature ought to be modest & even somewhat diffident in their Conclusions.

Yet as the Rules or Maxims that Regulate the price of
things are a subject of Curious Speculation to a Philosopher,
& as the knowledge of them, if they can be known, is of
great importance in a Commercial State Every Attempt to
discover and ascertain such Maxims is laudable. Nor ought
we to despair of being able to do something in this way that
may be of Use. Although the Many are made up of individuals, yet is it easier, in many cases relating both to Government & Commerce, to guess at the behaviour of the Many
than at that of individuals taken Separately. The jarring
passions interests & views of individuals when thrown together into one Body, make a compound whose nature is
more fixed and determined than that of the Ingredients of
which it is made up. Wisdom and Folly Reason and Passion
Virtue and Vice blended together make a pretty uniform
Character in the Multitude of all Nations and in all Ages. It
is from this Uniformity of Character in a Multitude of Men,
notwithstanding the diversity of the Individuals that all general Principles relating both to Government & Commerce
must be derived.

When a man brings his Goods to Market he deals with the

Multitude of which some indeed would easily be imposed upon but there are others as quicksighted as he is himself. & he must deall equally by all otherwise he will soon lose his character. He must likewise consider that if he fixes his price too high other dealers in the same commodity may undersell him and draw all the business. Prudence therefore will lead him to sell at what is, in his own Estimation, a moderate Profit.

If one Man had the sole Property of any of the Necessaries of Life, & power to defend that Property he might make all others / give him what he pleased to demand, that is he might make them his Servants. Thus Pharaoh by monopolizing the Corn of Egypt became proprietor of all Egypt.

But when the Necessaries or Conveniencies of Life are in many hands who have separate interests, & cannot combine or have not such Confidence in each other to fix a price upon their Commodities, every ones desire of a high price is tempered by his fear of having his good lie on his hands while others sell theirs, at a reasonable rate. As all goods that come to Market are produced by human Labour or Ingenuity, the price of them may be considered as the price of that Labour & skill which is employed in fitting them for the Market. This is the lowest price they can have for any considerable Time. However there is not such an equality among men even ⟨in⟩ the State of Nature, far less in political Society but that a days Labour of one Man may bear a much higher price than a days Labour of another man. One mans Labour may require a Stock of expensive Tools, a Stock of Materials, or of Money, it may require an expensive apprenticeship or education; Fashion regulates the manner in which persons of particular occupations & professions must live and that must in a great degree regulate the price of their Labour or the profits of their profession. Some Occupations require uncommon talents or such a degree of study and Thought as the bulk of Mankind are incapable of, and where such uncommon Endowments are turned to supply the Wants or gratify the desires of a few of the Rich or a great many of the Multitude they bear a high price. Such a Poet as John Milton might at this day make a Fortune in Brittain, tho an hundred years ago he could hardly make bread. I know no reason for this but that the productions of such Artists were much less in demand at that time than Now.

From these genneral Observations we may form some
Notion of what we may call the Natural or Reasonable Price
of a Commodity To Wit that it is such as enables those by
whose Labour the Commodity is produced to live in the
5   manner in which according to the Customs and Opinions of
the Country, they are entitled to live. I cannot fix any other
Standart of what is commonly called a Reasonable Price. Yet
this very Standart must vary as Customs and Opinions vary
in different Countrys or change in the Same country in
10   Succession of time.

It may seem to be a necessary consequence of the Definition we have given of the natural price of Commodities, that
when the Expence of living among all ranks even down to
the lowest is increased by the spread of Luxury the Price of
15   the Commodities produced by their Labour should be increased nearly in the same proportion. I think indeed this
must be the case & I apprehend will be found to be the case
where the Labourers are not more industrious, nor have
discovered any methods of producing the same quantity of
20   the Commodity in the same time by fewer hands, either by
the help of Machines or by the division of the work into
different professions or by some such Means. /

4/III/17,3r   I believe it will be found that the wages of a Journeyman
Taylor Weaver watchmaker or of a journeyman in any other
25   profession is risen within a hundred years much in the same
proportion as the expence of his living. yet the work produced by him may bear no greater price now than it would
have done then. This may be the case when by greater skill
& industry or by new Inventions or the division of Labour,
30   when I say by any or all of these means his work turns out
to as good account to the Master as it would have done in
former times when the wages was less.

But when human Wit is at a stand in the invention of better ways of making any particular commodity then the price
35   of it must rise as the expence of living of the people employed in it rises.[108] /

4/III/4,2v   Profits of those who sell may vary from other circumstances Such as that the commodity often lyes long on hand,
is perishable, got or kept with danger much subject to varia-
40   tion in the price. Combinations to raise prices wrong. Monopolies in order to raise the price to an unreasonable
height no less so. The Utility and Necessity of a common
Measure. The properties requisite in such a Measure. Universal Estimation & permanent Value. Durable easily con-

veyed. Divisible into Small parts. Silver & Gold fittest for
this Purpose. They may either ⟨be⟩ 1 weighed. Alloy to prevent wearing. or 2 Coined & Stamped. The intention of the
Stamp to ascertain their Value. Gives no value. The Practices of Princes and States in debasing the Coin or Raising
its Nominal Value Contrary to Equity. These practices injurious to individuals because Money is not barely a Measure
of the price of things but it is a commodity which has an
instrinsick value according to its weight and fineness. The
counterfiting coining clipping or washing the Coin highly
Criminal or uttering false coin knowingly. Melting it down
or exporting it made criminal in most nations.[109] /

8/ɪv/7,3r MAR 25

Contracts 1 Beneficent

1   Mandatum[110]
2   Commodatum & mutuum gratuitum.[111] In the first the
    real Right to the thing is not transferred, in the Mutuum
    it is, and the obligation on the borrower is onely per-
    sonal.
3   Depositum.[112]

MAR 26

2 Onerous Contracts.

Permutatio,[113] Emptio venditio. Delivery present or future.
Payment present or future,[114] Monopolies Engrossing.[115]
Locatio Conductio,[116] Mutuum onerosum.[117] Usury.[118] So-
ciety.[119] Wagers.[120] Games of Chance. Lotterys private and
Publick. Insurance. Purchase and Sale of Annuities and Re-
versions.[121] Purchase of Stocks on Time. Interpretation.[122]

MAR 27

Obligations quasi ex Contractu[123]

Negotium Utile Gestum. Possession bona fide. In absense.[124]
In Pupilarity or Minority in Passion Melancholy or disorder
of Mind.[125] In Parents acting for their Children. In purchase of Slaves or in Educating Children that are Destitute.[126] The Rhodean Law de jactu.[127]

MAR 28

Of Rights arising from the Delinquencies of others.[128]
Damnum datum sive ab inscio sive nostri commodi causa.[129]
Culpa lata, levis, levissima.[130] The imperfect Obligation to
pass over such faults when not very hurtfull, to put the best
construction upon the Actions of others no punishment
due. The obligation of the delinquent to indemnifie. Dolus.
The obligation of the delinquent to reparation to repentance & to Security.[131] The Right of punishment.

APR 1

We had considered the rights arising from the Injuries of
others. The person Injured has a right to demand just Reparation & future Security. In trifling injuries indeed which
are not like to be so often repeated as to become intollerable
it is the part of a great and generous Soul to forgive, to do
good for evil & if possible to overcome evil with good, to
make friends to enemies by patience forbearance, and len-
ity. This Conduct towards those who offend us is essential
to true greatness of Mind. It is an imitation of the benignity
and forgiving Disposition of the Supreme being which we
have must have recognition & ought to imitate. Where benevolence humanity and pity the noblest disposition that
can lodge in the human breast, I say where these take possession of the heart they will check that waspish pronness to
resent and revenge every little injury. The Romans reckoned it noble and a sign of true greatness of Mind *donare
inimicitias rei publicae*[132] to sacrifice their private quarrels to
the good of their country. And every man perceives that in
this they judge Right—The Same principle will lead us to
sacrifice private Resentment in slight injuries at least to the
peace of human Society and the common good of Mankind.
The proneness to revenge every Injury is always most remarkable in Savages with whom courage and ferocity is accounted the highest accomplishment of a Man. The reveng-
ing of Injuries and affronts gives frequent occasion to
display courage & is honoured upon this Account / and the
inclination to revenge is strengthned by indulgence as all
other inclinations are, & still more by being considered as
honourable.[133] Yet even Savages think it honourable to forgive injuries done by parents by children by brothers by

near relations or those to whom we ly under great obligations. The notions even of Savages therefore lead us to conceive that the more we are united with others in Society the more we ought to be disposed to a mild and forgiving disposition towards them. Now the most perfect virtue leads men to that gentleness and indulgence to others which the Savage sees he ought to exercise towards his Children, while he wants that noble enlargement of Soul which ought to extend his good affections beyond the narrow limits of his own family.

The Symbol which our Scotch Kings were wont to put upon their Coins of a Thistle with this Motto *Nemo me impune lacessit*,[134] suits well enough with the Notions of a barbarous age. And this is the best apology we can make for it. A Canadian chief at the head of his tribe might think himself honoured by such a motto. And our Kings were probably little better than Indian Chiefs when this Symbol was invented. If we consider the state of a Mind enflamed by resentment and meditating upon Revenge: It is surely of all states the most undesireable the most unlovely. A fever or Ague cannot be more opposite to the sound health of the body than this State is to the health and happiness of the Mind. From these considerations I think it appears that that gentle forbearing and forgiving disposition of mind which was so amiably examplified and so strongly inculcated by the divine Author of our Religion is so far from being contrary to reason, & good morals, that it appears even to Reason and to the Judgment of our moral faculty to be a magnanimous and heroical Virtue. As it is an imitation of that attribute of the divine Nature which we most admire and love and to which we are most indebted. It is the natural Issue of an enlarged and ardent affection to mankind. It is ⟨the⟩ noblest sacrifice we can make to the publick good, & the peace and happiness of Society. And one of the noblest exertions of Self government, in subjecting our strongest passions to the dominion of Reason and Conscience.[135] Juvenal last Pag

Juv At Vindicta bonum, vitâ jucundius ipsâ.
Nempe hoc indocti, quorum praecordia nullis
Interdum, aut laevibus, videas flagrantia causis:
Quantulacumque adeo est occasio, sufficit irae.
Chrysippus non dicet idem nec mite Thaletis

Ingenium dulcique Senex vicinus Hymetto
Qui partem acceptae, seva inter vincla cicutae
Accusatori nolet dare.
                    . . . quippe minuti
Semper et infirmi est animi exiguiqe voluptas
Ultio: continuo sic collige, quod vindicta
Nemo magis gaudet quam faemina.
Semper et infirmi e Satura 13 lin 180 &c[136]

But after all there may be injuries so atrocious in their
own Nature or so frequently repeated and persisted in that
a man of the best disposition for his own Sake, for the sake
of his family or friends, or for the sake of the publick may
think it his duty to seek redress of them. He has a perfect
right to do so for every injury, and if his Virtue and Generosity leads him to give up this right where the publick
good requires such a sacrifice the same disposition will lead
him to assert and maintain his right where the good of
others or of the publick requires that he should do so.

However in seeking redress of such Injuries a good man
will act consistently with his Character. He is not guided by
resentment / or Revenge but by nobler principles.

Resentment sometimes is used to signify a sudden impulse to resist whatever hurts us. This ⟨is⟩ an Instinct common to men and Brutes. Sumetimes a Sense of injury done
us this peculiar to man. But not intended to be a principle
of action.[137] It is however Lawfull to repell Atrocious injuries and defend our selves even by violence when all fair
Means have been Used in Vain.

The just Causes of War in the State of Nature.[138] The
means to prevent it and to terminate Differences. The
Rights of the Conqueror.

Of Duels.[139]

May 2 1771

Of the Right of Punishment of crimes that do not directly
injure us but are of bad Example & hurtfull to Human Society grounded upon this that every man ought to do his
utmost to promote the common Good of the human kind.

⟨VI. Duties to Others: Individuals in Oeconomical Jurisprudence⟩

Book 2 Of the Rights & Duties arising from the Domestick Relation.[1]

Apr 2

1 Of the Marriage Relation.

Account of the Oeconomy of Nature in the Continuance of the several species of Animals.[2]

5 The passion of Love between the Sexes in the human kind. — Lays a foundation for a lasting Union between one Male and one female and points out the Marriage alliance as the way in which Nature intended that the human Species should be continued. This passion gives an attachment 10 & preference to one object which it is impossible to have to more than one. It cannot be satisfied without a like reciprocal attachment and preference in the person beloved. Jealousy—The offspring of Love. Love always supposes some worth and dignity in the object. It is the most disinter- 15 ested passion and leads the lover to undergo any toil to run any hazaard that may make him agreable to the object of his love or may promote her happiness, without desire of any other reward than the good acceptance of his Service & a mutual Return of the like affection. This passion supposes 20 some equality between the persons and is not satisfied with a return that is the effect of force or fear. Nature has so contrived our make that the same Object does not equally attract this passion in all men. Variety of Faces proportions Graces and Manners in the Sex, suited to the various modi- 25 fications of this passion in Men. Every thing which excites the passion must appear amiable and must either be some

agreable quality in the person or the sign of some agreable Quality.

The different Modifications of this Passion in the different Sexes.

The Effects it produces in both. The qualifications in Men that are chiefly amiable to women & vice versa.

Polygamy.

Divorce.

Prohibided degrees of Consanguinity.[3] /

8/IV/7,4v OF THE PARENTAL RELATION[4]

APR 3

Parental Authority Founded in the Parental Affection and the indigence of the Children. Their need of Education and Instruction. Not upon Generation. as Hobbs grossly imagines.

Here we are first to consider the Grounds of the Authority of Parents, for that which is the foundation of it must likewise be the measure of it and set bounds to it. 2 How far it Extends and what are the mutual Obligations of Parents and Children. 3[ly] Make some observations upon the Civil Laws of different nations with respect to the parental Authority. Hobbes Notion Filmers.[5]

All Original Authority over Persons according to Grotius arises from one or other of these three Sources Generation, Consent Delict. To which we may add want of Reason on the part of the Person Governed and The Tuition of the person undertaken from a Benevolent Motive on the part of the Person Governing. The necessities of Children & the Parental Affection. 1 It is the intention of Nature that children should be reared & educated. 2 Nature points out the parents as the Persons to whom this b⟨l⟩essing is committed not onely by their being the instruments of the Childs being brought into the World but chiefly by the Natural Affection planted in their breasts.

The desire of offspring natural to those who enter into the relation of Marriage. The affection of husband and wife strengthned by it. Affection disinterested. The duties of Parents. How far their Authority reaches.[6] Relation Perpetual. Common to both Parents.[7] May be lost by esposing, selling. Cruelty. Duties of Children in the family in Marriage.

Foris familiate.[8] Adoption. Tutory. When children have a
separate Property.

5   OF THE RELATION OF MASTERS AND SERVANTS[9]

APR 4

The Notion of Servitude which prevailed among ancient
Nations That the Servant was the property of his Master,
10   inconsistent with the Natural Rights of Men, and their natural equality.[10]
How this Servitude was introduced. Its effects among the
Romans & Greeks.[11] The pretences by which it is justified.[12]
Domestick & farming Servants.[13] The former gradually dis-
15   used as Christianity prevailed. The latter still continue in
some parts of Europe. Adscriptitij Glebae.[14] The steps by
which their condition has been bettered.

8/iv/10,1r Apr 9 1765

We have considered the Rights and Duties arising from
the several Relations of the Domestick State. And it now remains that we consider the Rights and duties that arise from
5   the political State or that of Civil Government. There is
onely one Relation that is proper to this State, that of civil
Magistrates and Subjects. Before we enquire into the reciprocal Duties and rights of these it will be necessary to consider the Origin of Civil Government and the ends of it and
10   what principles in the human Constitution are adapted to it.

There can be no civil Government whatsoever which does
not in some degree abridge the liberty of those who live under it.[1] Now the Love of Liberty is so natural to mankind
that there must be some considerable inducement to engage
15   them to give up their Natural Liberty & to subject themselves to laws and taxes. And be bound to that submission
and allegiance which is due to the civil Powers. There is
nothing which men desire more earnestly than independence and it is not to be supposed that any man will subject
20   himself to the will of others and submit his actions to their
controul without some urgent cause.

If we should suppose a ships crew to lose their master &
mate upon a voyage. They will very naturally chuse a master
and submit themselves and their ship to his direction be-
25   cause it is absolutely necessary to their preservation that
they should be under some government. If they should be
cast away upon some unknown Island or coast, and found
it necessary for their common safety either against wild
beasts, or savage inhabitants, to keep united they would still

chuse a leader and submit to his command. But if they
should be cast upon some desart Island where every man
could provide for his own Subsistence independant of the
rest; their political union would probably cease, and every
man would chuse to live after his own way. Nor indeed does
there seem to be any need for a political Union in such a
case if all of them were wise and good, and had plenty of
Subsistance. Men may enjoy the pleasure of mutual conversation they may trafick with one another they may do mutual good offices or unite their strength and council upon
occasion in order to promote any common good without
being under any common political Government. And if they
are just & human and peaceable and wise they may live happily together without any common superior. Thus in all
ages many tribes have lived without laws and without Government. And thus most of the nations in North America
live at this day, unless when they make war upon any of
their Neighbours. But there are two / causes that require a
political union among people living in such an independant
way. First when they are invaded by any forreign power
which might easily subdue the individuals one after another
and yet may be resisted by the united force of the whole. In
this case necessity will lead them to unite and to chuse a
leader or commander to whom they will be subject in the
operations of the War. When such wars are rare and happen after long intervals, the power of the commander will
probably cease when peace is restored. And then men will
resume their natural liberty and independance. And this is
the State of the North Americans.

2 Another cause of Mens uniting into political Bodies is
for the redress of private injuries. When the wants of men
are multiplied and the innocence and simplicity of Life gives
way to Avarice Fraud and Rapacity, Men find themselves
under a necessity of having Laws and Magistrates for the
protection of their Rights and the punishment of Crimes.

The first regular Governments would probably be established among those who were very frequently engaged in
war, among whom that Government and Discipline which
they found necessary in War would continue in the short
intervals of peace untill the people being accustomed to it,
or conceiving themselves benefited by it came to acquiesc in
it. This probably is the reason why the most ancient Governments we know of Were kingly Governments.

APR 10

When kingly Governments consist of a small territory
such as one city and its dependant territory, so that the Subjects meet often together and inflame one another with their
resentiments they will not bear a kingly Government when
it degenerates into Tyranny. They commonly change into
an Aristocracy or Democracy as the Ancient states of Greece
and Italy for the most part did. But when a kingly Government spreads out far and includes a number of tribes which
differ in their customs and Manners, and have little communication with one another. Such large kingdoms affording great Revenues to support the Royal Dignity, it becomes
too strong for the people. They cannot unite together to
obtain a redress of their Grievances and therefore must
bear them however heavy. The Monarch enlarges his power
more and more supports it by a strong standing Army and
becomes master of the lives and properties of his Subjects
and transmits his power to his children after him. The people long inured to arbitrary Government grow tame and
think no more of / changing the form of their Government
than of changing the Elements or the course of Nature.
Such Governments we see established throughout Asia.
Where every Subject is taught an absolute submission to the
Sovereign as the most essential article of his Religion and
when an Executioner comes with orders from the Sovereign
or his Visier to Strangle him without a trial without so much
as telling him his crime, he receives the Order as devoutly
as if it came immediately from Heaven, spends his last
breath in praying for the life of the Emperor and extends
his neck to the bowstring. Under such Governments people
come in some Generations to lose all sense of the Rights and
privileges of human Nature & become incapable of Liberty.
The ignorance in which they are kept & the slavish doctrines of their Religion prevent any sentiments of liberty
from entring into their minds or if they can enter fear and
Superstion and that pusilanimity which are their natural Effect immediately stiffle every desire of asserting their Liberty. So wonderfull Effects does Education and Custom
produce in the minds of men a Tyger and a Lamb are not
more contrary in their natures than a Canadian and an
Asiatick. You would think it impossible that they could be of
the same Species. In The one country we see creatures each

of whom would die a thousand deaths rather than own any
son of Adam as a Superior. In the other Myriads who are
willing to stretch their necks to the sword of one Man and
adore him most devoutly when he gives orders to strike off
their head. Yet there can be no doubt but an Asiatick
brought up from infancy among the Canadians would be a
canadian in ferocity and the Spirit of independancy and on
the other hand a Canadian brought up from infancy in the
dominion of the great Mogul would be as tame as other
Asiaticks. So flexible is the human Disposition by Education
and Discipline that it may with regard to political Notions
be wound up to the highest Spirit of Liberty and Independance, or brought down to the lowest pitch of Servility even
to adore the chain that binds it. Nor do we see less flexibility
in mens Religious opinions which when formed entirely by
Authority and Education may be eith⟨er⟩ wound up to the
most extravagant heights of Enthusiasm or sunk into the
most abject Superstition.

It is impossible that any just Notions of Political Goverment can be found either among those who never were under any Government or who never had any Idea but of the
Worst. We must turn our eyes to the more mild and Equitable Goverments if we would form any / Notions of the
Ends that may be attained by Government from which we
must deduce both the rights of civil Governours and the duties of Subjects. And Europe is the happy Continent which
can afford us any Models from which we can form any just
notions of Political Government. Moderate Governments
give occasion to the noblest exercise of human Power. To
the most Enlarged Affections. They tend to make mankind
gentle without Servility They furnish occasion for the most
extensive plans for the improvement of Mankind in Knowledge in Virtue in Arts that are usefull to life.[2]

The ends first in view in voluntary Submission to Government would be protection from forreign enemies and the
preservation of private Rights.

A Government of Laws better than independence. To obtain redress of injuries by the Law better than by private
revenge. The burthen of taxes compensated by the advantage of defence by the Laws and arms of the State.

There are certain Instincts that lead men to submission
Respect to Age and Wisdom and Valour.

Respect to the Rich & powerfull & especially to those who

have had riches and power transmitted to them through a
long Race of Ancestors. These instincts ground a Natural
Subordination and men more easily submit to the Government of Such.[3]

APR 11

From the Account we have given of the Valuable Ends
that may be attained by a good plan of Government it is
evident that such a Plan is indeed the greatest Good that can
be bestowed upon a Nation. Why? Hence Legislators so
highly revered. Every Man ought in his Station to contribute
his best endeavours for the preservation and defence of
such a Government. And to be ready to sacrifice his Life
and all that is dear to him in so important a Cause. Every
man ought to pay that obedience to the Laws of his Country
which is necessary to the good estate of Government. No
state can subsist without a veneration for its laws. Also a Respect to those who have the administration of the Government.

As men may suffer hardships and injuries under the best
Government from iniquity of witnesses or of Judges these
ought to be patiently born. This / is a Sacrifice to the publick
weal. Socrates Conduct Noble and worthy of the Prince of
Philosophers.

Those who have power or have any share of the Legislature ought to be very watchfull to discover the diseases of
the body politick and to apply timely remedies.

A Political Society cannot be justly constitute but by consent express or tacit. How far it is binding upon the posterity of those who first consented to it. A Government unjustly
imposed may afterwards acquire Right by tacit consent.[4]

The great mischief arising from violent changes of Government shew that they ought not to be attempted without
urgent Necessity.[5] A Political Body once constituted may be
considered as one person.[6] Enter into Covenants & pledge
the publick faith which ought to be sacred both towards forreign States and Subjects.

Succession to Crowns or other Magistracys must be determined either by the Laws or Custom. Both which imply tacit
consent. Of the Active obedience due to the Supreme
Power. Of the Passive Obedience due to the Supreme Power
and the Doctrine of Non Resistance. The Opinion of Gro-

tius. Filmer & Leslie and Atterbury. Sidney Locke Milton
Hoadly.[7]

APR 12

APR 15

We have now considered the most important Rights of
Men and the Obligations corresponding to them.[8] Not onely
those that are competent to the State of Natural Liberty but
those also which arise from the Oeconomical and Political
State. And I think it appears from the whole that notwithstanding the different Systems which have been advanced
both in ancient and Modern times with regard to the Abstract Nature of Virtue and the Principles of moral Approbation, yet there has been very little difference among
thinking men with regard to that tenor of Life and Conduct
which Men ought to hold, and in which real Worth and virtue consist. The Great Virtues of Prudence Temperance
Fortitude and Justice are revered by Epicureans Platonists
Peripateticks & Stoicks. They not onely agree in paying
homage to those venerable Names but they agree also in the
Notions they affix to them. So that we may venture to affirm
that there is not any other Science wherein men of thought
and Reflexion in all Ages have so universally agreed as in
what is right and laudable and what on the other hand is
wrong & blamable / in human Conduct. In mens Notions of
Justice in particular we may see such a correspondence in
the laws of Different Nations and in the Sentiments of Poets
Historians Orators and Moralists as may satisfy us that the
rules of Justice & Equity have a real foundation in the nature of things as well as the laws of Nature which take place
in the spheres. and that the former are more obvious to our
Moral Faculty than the latter are to our Reason and Understanding. Ingenious and thinking Men have from the beginning of the World been inquisitive about the laws of the
planetary Motions and of the other Phaenomena of the Material System, as well as about the dutys of men in their different Stations and relations yet after blundering about the
former and groping in the dark for thousands of Years, we
are at last in Europe within a century and a half to get in to
the right tract and to discover some light. But with regard
to the other, if we examine the wise and thinking of all ages

and in all parts of the Globe what is their notion of a just
and a good man a good father a good citizen a good prince
we shall find them all agreeing in one System. Confutius
and Zoroaster, Indian Bramens European Druids and the
5   Incas of Peru as well as the more refined Greek and Roman
Philosophers heathens Mahometans and Christians had the
same notions of Virtue and of Justice. The points wherein
men have differed in their opinions with regard to what is
good and what is ill in human conduct are both few and of
10   small moment when compared with those wherein they
agree. so universal a Consent of Mankind with regard to the
main points of right and wrong of virtue and vice ought to
satisfy the most sceptical not onely of the reality of the distinction between the one and the other, but also that the
15   Almighty has taken care of the constitution of our Nature,
to make this distinction so apparent and obvious that it requires no deep enquiry or laborious reasoning to discover
it. That moral Faculty or Conscience which God hath
planted in every mans breast distinguishes right conduct
20   from wrong in most instances no less immediately, no less
clearly and certainly than the taste discerns sweet from bitter. If you consult this inward Monitor in your calm and
serious moments, you can hardly judge wrong in any important point of Duty. In all the fair train of Virtues there
25   is ⟨not⟩ one which is not immediately approved by our
Moral faculty when it has been a little strengthned by exercise, and when the noise of our passions is hushed and its
calm voice attended to. Can any of you hesitate a moment /
8/ɪᴠ/10,4r   whether he ought to approve the love of truth the love of
30   Virtue and the love of Mankind? Whether he ought to approve a plan of life and conduct dictated by these noble
principles and pursued with manly prudence and firmness.
Whether he ought to approve of that Magnanimity and Elevation of Mind which sets a man above the fear of death,
35   the scorn or the flattery of fools the allurements ⟨of⟩ sensual
pleasure and the pursuits of avarice and ambition. & determines him to pursue the paths of Wisdom and Virtue; trust-
ing to God the care of his happiness, while he concerns himself about what is his duty. Does not every man immediately
40   approve of Justice and Veracity and fidelity? Nay does not
every man perceive that these virtues which regard what we
call the perfect Rights of Mankind constitute but a very imperfect Character? they make a man innocent & harmless

and that is all. an attention to what we commonly call the imperfect rights of Mankind constitutes the perfection of Virtue. Generosity Compassion readiness to bear with the infirmities of others to forgive injuries to stiffle resentment
5   and to overcome evil with good. This is true goodness, which every man approves as a more noble & elevated pitch of virtue than meer Justice.

I shall onely further observe before I have done with this Subject that there are many minute points both of Jurispru-
10   dence and of Casuistry which deserve not the attention of a wise and a good man. There is a minute Philosophy in this as well as in other Subjects of enquiry. The territories of Virtue and vice are often divided by a line which is not easily discerned. But why should any man be anxious to discern it
15   in this case, unless it be that he wants to go as near to the borders of vice as possible without passing the forbidden limit. This is not the temper of a good man he will keep at such a distance as makes it unnecessary to for him to define this limit very nicely when it is not obvious. When intricate
20   and difficult cases occur which can seldom happen, after us-ing the best help in his power, endeavouring to purge his mind of prejudices partiality and passion, imploring sin-cerely the divine Aid. And then he may safely follow his best judgment, confident that as his own heart condemns him
25   not he shall not be condemned by the righteous & equitable Judge of all. If he errs it is an invincible error which will not be imputed to him. The best of Men may err, nor is it the will of God that we should be altogether exempted from Er-ror. But he who takes pains to be rightly informed and acts
30   according to the light of his Conscience shall never be con-demned. /

8/IV/10,4v   It has been shewn that in the State of Natural Liberty every Man has a certain Freedom & Independance, a Right to direct his own Actions so as not to injure others, and that
35   he cannot justly be deprived of this his Natural Liberty with-out his consent or Fault. Now a Political Body is made up of such Men naturally free; but who have by consent given up a part of their Natural Liberty to the State for the sake of common Utility. They have submitted to be governed by the
40   Laws of their Country. To have their Rights judged & their controversies with their fellow Subjects determined in a le-gal Manner and not by violence or private Revenge. They have likewise engaged to bear their Share in the defence of

the Publick. And to tender its interest as they do their own. These are the Obligations naturally implied in a Mans being a Member of a State, & by coming under these Obligations, he is in return entitled to that protection in all his Rights and Privileges which the Laws afford, to defence against forreign enemies & a just redress by Law for injuries done to him, in his Person his goods his family or his good Name.

From this it appears that the Subjects of a State have not all the Liberty which Men in the State of Nature have they having given up a Part of their natural Liberty to the State for a valuable consideration. But as that which they have parted with is given to the State, it is evident that the whole Political Body considered as one Moral Person, has all that Liberty and independance upon other States, which Men in the State of Nature have upon one Another.

As Men by becoming Citizens or Members of a State do not cease to be Men; so the Obligations of the Law of Nature which bound them as Men continue to bind them as Citizens. The Will of the State being the Result of the United Wills of the Citizens, is subject to the Laws of Nature & Bound to conform to them. And as there is all ways a Right corresponding to every obligation it will follow that States have Rights belonging to the Community of a Similar Nature with those which belong to individuals.[9]

⟨VIII. Duties to Others: States⟩

Of the Law of Nations

Justinians Def. Quod communis Ratio inter omnes homines constituit. Lex Naturae quod Natura omnia Animanlia Docuit.[1]

5 The Law of Nations is that by which the Conduct of States or Independent Political Societies ought to be governed.

A State Defined.[2] May justly be considered as a Moral Agent Having an Understanding, A Will, Active Power. A Conscience of Right and Wrong. Capable of Possessing
10 Property of Contracting, plighting its Faith keeping or violating its engagements. Doing good to its Neighbours or injuring them. States would be the most dangerous and unjust Combinations if they were not under Law.

The Notion of some Minute Politicians that however men
15 in private life are bound by the Laws of Justice and Equity yet it is impossible to govern States properly without sometimes transgressing the Rules of Justice. But as in private Life nothing is more contrary to true Wisdom than cunning and Deceits and the crafty man is often taken in his own
20 Snare and falls into the pit which he dug for others. The same thing holds no less with regard to political Wisdom. The Reputation of Justice and integrity in the Administration of a Nation is of the highest Moment in its transactions with other Nations. On the contrary dark and crooked Pol-
25 iticks, always sink the credit of a Nation and make it suspected and hated.

Cic de Leg. Nihil est quod adhuc de Republica dictum putem, et quo possim longius progredi, nisi sit confirmatum, non modo falsum esse illud, sine injuria non posse, sed hoc
30 verissimum, sine summa Justitia Rempublicam regi non posse.[3]

Cic de Leg Lib 2 § 8. Ad Divos adeunto caste. Pietatem abhibento. Opes amovento. Qui secus faxit Deus ipse Vindex erit. Separatim nemo habessit Deos neve novos: Sedne advenas, nisi publice adscitos privatim colunto.4 /

7/VII/21,1v Every one who has any Idea of War; every one who reflects on its terrible Effects and the fatal Consequences it draws after it; will easily ⟨see⟩ that it ought not to be undertaken but upon the strongest Motives. Humanity is shocked when the Soverign of a State, lavishes the blood of his most faithfull and bravest subjects, without the most pressing Necessity and exposes a Nation to the calamities of War when it might enjoy peace in honour and safety. And if to this inhuman disregard to the peace & happiness of his own People he adds injustice to those whom he attacks; what a complication of Guilt does he draw down upon his own head? He is answerable before God & his own Conscience for all the Evils he draws upon his people, & all the Evils he brings upon his enemies The blood Spilt the Cities pillaged the provinces ruined. The Widows & Fatherless his sword has made cry to heaven for vengeance, and will one day stand up in Judgment against him. He is accountable, as the first Cause, for all the disorders the Violence and the Crimes, which are the natural Consequences of the tumult and License of War. And must answer for these things before the tribunal of the Righteous Judge of all the Earth. Every State therefore in Order to preserve Peace & prevent War ought to deal justly by other States.5 /

⟨IX. Supplement to Duties to Ourselves⟩

The Duty we owe to ourselves or the Duty of Selfgovernment may be not improperly comprehended under three of the Cardinal Virtues of the Ancients, to wit those of Prudence Temperance and Fortitude. It might no doubt admit of other Divisions and has by most authors been otherwise divided; but this Division seems to be as little liable to Objection as any other, & Antiquity has stamped an Authority upon those names, which intitles them to Respect.

Of Prudence

From the Poverty of Language or from some other Cause it happens, that many of the Names we give to the Virtues have some ambiguity & particularly that they are sometimes used to signify a Quality of the Understanding or Contemplative Powers of the Mind, sometimes to signify a Quality of the Heart or of the Active Powers. Indeed it is hardly possible from the Nature of the thing that it should not be so; because, although Virtue is properly seated in the Heart; yet it necessarly supposes some Degree of Understanding and cannot possibly exist without it. And although there may be a great Degree of Understanding without virtue, yet there can be no Virtue without some Degree of human Understanding. Hence it happens that the Names of Particular Virtues are often given to that degree or that Quality of the Understanding which they include & without which they cannot Exist. This Observation is more applicable to the Name of Prudence than to that of almost any other Virtue, because it seems to borrow more from the Understanding than other Virtues do.

Another general Observation it is proper to make with regard to the Division of the Virtues. To wit. That we are

not to expect such a Division of them as answers precisely
to the Logical Rules of Division. Logicians reckon a Division
faulty, when that which is contained in one branch of the
Division, may also fall under another so as to belong to both.
Therefore they lay it down as on⟨e⟩ of the general Rules of
Division that the Parts into which a thing is Divided should
be so distinct that everything belonging to the whole should
belong to one of those Parts and to no other. / And this is,
no doubt, a good Rule when it can be observed, but it may
happen in some Cases that Divisions may be very proper
and usefull in which this Rule is transgressed. As every Man
has two Parents and may justly be said to belong to the families both of Father & Mother so Virtuous Actions have
often many Parents, so to speak, to whom they may properly be said to belong, & to which they may be referred. The
Noble Behaviour of Scipio to his fair Captive was an Act of
Justice, without doubt; but it was not the less an Act of Magnanimity, of Temperance & even of Prudence.[1] This connexion and Alliance of the Virtues, by which they often
mingle so sweetly together in producing one and the same
Action has been Observed by Cicero. Offic. Lib 1.[2]

We must not think it strange if in every Division of the
Virtues we can frame, we find them encroaching as it were
upon the Provinces of each other & mingling together in
the production of one and the same Virtuous Action. This
must often happen from the very Nature of things, nor is it
to be accounted a Sign of an improper Division. In that
Triumvirate of the Virtues of selfgovernment we have
named, it may be truly said that Temperance is Prudence
that Magnanimity & Fortitude is Prudence they are Sister
Virtues of the same Blood, differing in Form but yet having
a great Resemblance. Facies non omnibus una, nec diversa
tamen, qualem decet esse Sororum.[3]

To return to the Virtue of Prudence I understand by it
the Habit of determining properly what ends we ought to
pursue and by what means they are to be pursued. Wisdom
and Prudence are sometimes used as Words of the same Signification, & sometimes they are distinguished. When we
distinguish them. Wisdom may be more properly applied to
the choice of our Ends & Prudence to that of the Means of
Attaining them. /

Fortitude is a Virtue that supports the Mind under calamities and misfortunes, enables it to encounter Difficulties

and fortifys it against all undue impressions of Fear. The
Effect of Misfortunes and Calamities in those who want this
Virtue. The Effect of Fear. This Virtue may be acquired
even by Savages.

5   A Good Conscience & the hope of future happiness the
best foundation of Fortitude. This Virtue always had in the
highest Esteem among Mankind. The Brave and the Magnanimous have always the highest Seat in the Temple of
Honour. The Admiration we have of it is apt to Sanctify in
10   our Esteem even bad actions that are attended with it.
Hence the Glory of Conquest and the Rights it is supposed
to give over the Conquered. Hence the point of honour in
Men is accounted Courage. The passion for warlike Glory.
The practice of Duelling.

15   We ought to beware that the admiration of brave Actions
do not blind our judgements & hinder us from perceiving
what is amiss in them.

Temperance and Fortitude both included in Self command. Necessary to every Man that pursues any End in
20   Life. /

7/v/5,5v   From the General Account we have given of Temperance
it is evident that i⟨t⟩s Nature in General consists in Restraint.
It is the bridle of the Mind by which whatever is excessive
and too impetuous in our Motions is checked and tempered.
25   There is no Natural Appetite or Passion of the Mind that is
useless, far less noxious when properly regulated. As every
part of the human body has its use and there is not a bone
or a Muscle a gland or a ligament which does not contribe
more or less to the perfection of the whole. The same thing
30   may be said of the natural constitution and structure of the
Mind. Every natural Appetite every Natural Affection and
Passion has its use in the human Frame and the want of it
would be a defect and of bad consequences in such Creatures as we are. The Virtue of Temperance does not there-
35   fore consist in eradicating our Appetites and Passions. This
were it in our Power would onely be an effort to make ourselves other Creatures than God has seen fit to Make us.
Our appetites and passions as far as they are a part of our
Constitution are good and it is the bussiness of Temperance
40   to indulge or restrain them according to the Rules which
Reason prescribes, and so as that they may answer the intention for which they were given us by Nature. The Rules of

Restraint or of Temperance are in general so obvious that we can seldom be in any doubt with regard to them.

The Appetites of hunger and thirst require such qualification as is necessary for the health & vigour of the body. Plain and simple fare is in general best adapted to this purpose. When the body is in a sound State & properly exercised the periodical returns of Natural Appetites, are sufficient to direct us when and in what measure we ought to eat and drink. The natural appetite when neither vitiated by bad habits, nor provoked by the refinements of Luxury, I conceive to be a better rule than either the prescriptions of Physicians or of Casuists. For as men have various habits of body the Rules that suite one May be very unsuitable to another. That is to be accounted intemperance in eating or drinking which is injurious to health, which clouds the Understanding, or inflames the passions, which is too expensive for a mans fortune, consumes too much time or makes him less fit for any of the duties of Life than a stricter Regimen would. It is intemperance to hunt after refinements and delicacies in eating and drinking, these vitiate the Natural Taste, produce false and unnatural Appetites, which are never to be satisfied.

Temperance with regard to the amorous Appetite.

The desires of Knowledge Power Riches Honour.

Passions of Resentment Party Zeal Emulation Revenge.

Mortification. a voluntary Restraint in things Lawfull may be approved or disapproved according to the end and Measure of it.

Jurisprudentia Naturalis[1]

Feb. 17

Lex vel latius vel Strictius Sumitur. Lex latius Sumpta est
Norma secundum quam Operationes Entis cujusvis dirigun-
5 tur vel dirigi debent.

Omnia Entia seu animata seu inanimata. Bruta pariter atq
Rationalia habent suas Leges. Legum Entium Inanimato-
rum & Brutorum Exempla. Lex Physica seu Naturalis est
norma Secundum quam Operationes Naturae Irrationalis
10 actu diriguntur. Lex Moralis Norma secundum quam Actiones Entium Ratione praeditorum & perceptione Recti &
honesti dirigi debent. Uti omnes Naturae Irrationales habent Leges suas Physicas ita omnis Natura Rationalis habet
Leges Suas Morales ex Constitutione Naturae ejusdem de-
15 rivatas.

Naturae Divinae leges. Angeliae. Humanae.

Leges Physicae locum habent non Solum in Naturis Irra-
tionalibus verum etiam in Rationalibus. Exempla in Corporibus nostris in Anima Associatio Idearum & Passionum In-
20 stinctus Appetitus. Leges Morales solum in Entibus Ratione
& perspicientia honesti & turpis preditis.

Leges Physicae semper Servantur nec unquam transgre-
diunt⟨ur⟩ Leges Morales non item.

Omnis Scientia est vel Relationum Abstractarum quae
25 eaedem sunt sive Res Relatae existant sive non Existant atq
haec Scientia Mathesis dici potest generalius sumpto Voca-
bulo, vel est rerum phenomenoon id est Qualitatum vel Op-
erationum Actu Existentium; & dici potest Historia quae
rursus est vel Naturalis vel Civilis. vel tertio versatur Scientia
30 de Legibus ex Phaenomenis Eruendis. Ex Phaenomenis in-
notescunt Leges tum Physicae tum Morales. Scientiae Arti-

bus Subjiciuntur Artes vero praecipuae Mechanica quae
versatur circa operationes a proprietatibus omni Corpori
communibus pendentes Materiam quatenus est Mobilis
Iners impenetrabilis. Chemiam quae versatur Corpora inorganizata quidem sed virtutibus certis predita circa operationes quae pendent a proprietatibus quibusdam corporibus
inorganizatis competentibus. Qualia Sunt Metalla Sales Aer
Aqua Terra Oleum Sulphur lumen &c Spiritus Essentiales
seu rectores. 3 Vegetantium Cultura. 4 Animalium Brutorum Cultura. 5 Gymnastiae Medicina Cultura Animi. 6 Mu-
sica. 7 Poetica cujus partes sunt artes Plasticae. 8 Logica. 9
Rhetorica. 10 Economica. 11 Politica. /

Sicut Galenus Philosophus pariter atq Medicus Summus
Humani Corporis partes in Similares & dissimilares Distri-
buit ita Naturae omnis Corporis Nobis Notae partes sunt vel
Similares vel Dissimilares. Prioris generis Sunt Elementa et
alia Corpora maxime Simplicia. Dissimilares sunt Coniecta
ex his quae sunt vel Organizata vel Inorganizata.

Actiones lege Dirigendae sunt qui nobis volentibus fiunt
Nolentibus non fiunt.

⟨*Natural Jurisprudence*

⟨FEB. 17

⟨Law is understood in either a wider or a narrower sense.
Law understood in the wider sense is a norm in accordance
with which the workings of any entity are directed or ought
to be directed.

⟨All entities both animate and inanimate, brutes and rational beings alike have their laws. Examples of the laws for
inanimate entities and animals. The physical or natural law
is a norm in accordance with which the workings of a nature
which is irrational in its activity are directed. The moral law
is a norm in accordance with which the actions of entities
endowed with reason and the idea of right and virtue ought
to be directed. Just as all irrational natures have their physical laws, so every rational nature has its moral laws, which
are derived from the constitution of that same nature.

⟨Laws of divine, angelic, human nature.

⟨Physical laws apply not only to irrational natures, but also
to rational ones. Examples in our bodies and, in the mind,
the association of ideas and passions; instincts; appetites.

Moral laws apply only to entities endowed with reason and full understanding of virtue and vice.

⟨Physical laws are always observed and never broken; moral laws not so.

⟨Every science is either about abstract relations, which remain the same whether the things related exist or do not exist, and this science can be called mathematics, if the word is taken more generally; or it is about the qualities of things—i.e. about phenomena—or about the workings of existing things in action; and this can be called history which again is either natural or political. Or in the third place the science concerned with laws to be elicited from the phenomena. From the phenomena laws become known, which are either physical or moral. The sciences are comprehended under the arts; the particular arts are: Mechanics which is concerned with matter in so far as it is mobile, inert and impenetrable, that is with operations which are dependent upon the properties which are common to every body. Chemistry which is also concerned with bodies which are inorganic but endowed with certain qualities, i.e. with operations which depend upon properties belonging to certain inorganic bodies. Such are metals, salts, air, water, soil, oil, sulfur, light, etc. Essential or governing spirits. 3 Culture of plants. 4 Breeding of brute beasts. 5 Gymnastics; medicine; culture of the mind. 6 Music. 7 Poetics which includes the plastic arts. 8 Logic. 9 Rhetoric. 10 Economics. 11 Politics.

⟨As Galen, philosopher as well as excellent medical man, divided the parts of the human body into similar and dissimilar, so the parts of nature known to us in all bodies are either similar or dissimilar. Of the former sort are the elements and other most simple bodies. The dissimilar parts are put together of those which are either organic or inorganic.

⟨Actions to be directed by law are those which are done when we will and not done when we decline.⟩

7/VII/1,1r   *Jurisprudence²*

The chief Inducements that lead Men at first to Unite under one Government or Political Society, are either their Defence against common Enemies, who might be superior in Strength to individuals; but may be resisted & overcome by a great Number united under one Government; or secondly their protection against injuries from one another, which is most effectually provided for when all agree to refer their Differences to common Judges or Magistrates, who are impowered by the whole body to Judge between Man and Man; & who can enforce their sentences by the publick Authority to which every Man must submit.

In the first Periods of Civil Government Judges are chosen of those who have the highest Reputation for Wisdom & Integrity and they are left to determine causes between Man according to Equity without being tied down by laws. An Upright Judge although he had laws prescribed for him for regulating his Decisions, would be at no less ⟨Pains⟩ to discern in most cases what justice required. He would by degrees be led by his Reason & Conscience to frame to himself a body of Rules which would render his Decisions uniform in like cases and agreably to the general Rules of Justice.

But as Judges may through the Corruption of human Nature be swayed by Interest or Favour or Enmity where their Power is unlimited. Therefore in all improved and well regulated Governments Laws have been enacted by those to whom the Supreme Power in the Society is committed. By such Laws the mutual Claims which the subjects may have one upon another are ascertained, the Crimes which ⟨have⟩ been most commonly committed are defined, a method of trying Men for such Crimes, is prescribed, & the punishment due to them, or the Reparation to the person injured, is determined. When such a body of Laws are framed in a Government, much less Power is left to the Judge, because he is bound to judge according to the Law, & every Man may before hand know what actions are contrary to Law that he may avoid them; and what Reparation he may expect from the Judge for injuries done to him by others.

Laws that are thus made for the direction of Judges, will be framed according to the Notions of Justice & Equity, which the Lawgivers have had. They will allways be few & imperfect at first and gradually enlarged and explained / according as bad men invent new ways of being injurious to their Neighbours, or of eluding the laws already made.

If we compare the Laws that have been made by different Civilized Nations in different Ages & in Different Parts of the Globe, for protecting the Subjects from mutual Injuries and preserving their Rights we find a wonderful Agreement and Harmony. which demonstrates that all Men have the same Notions of Equity and Justice for the preservation of which Laws have been contrived.

It cannot be expected that the Laws of any Nation should at first be digested into a Systematical Order and Method. The Laws of a Nation are commonly the work of Ages, made as occasions call for them. and when they are multiplied to such a degree as to make the knowledge of them very difficult, it is then onely that men find it necessary to reduce them under certain Heads & Divisions into a regular Body and System. The Laws of the Jews given by God himself were not ranged in any nice Systematical Order nor indeed were they so bulky as to require it. Neither were the Laws of the twelve Tables very systematically digested. The first methodical System of Laws I know of was that which by Justinians Order was compiled from the Body of the Roman Laws after they were grown to an Immense Bulk, too great for the whole Study of a mans life. /

8/IV/4,1r MARCH 19 1766[3]

The Rights and obligations of men grounded upon the laws of Nature do not require deep or subtile reasoning to discover them. Nor indeed to they admit of it. The principles of Justice and Humanity are intended by the Author of Nature to be the Rule of every mans Conduct towards his fellow man. And if they were not very obvious to mens Reason or Conscience in Ordinary cases they would not be fit to be a rule to all mankind. A man who has a real regard to Justice and humanity and has had his faculties moderately exercised in judging what they require, although he has never studied a system of Jurisprudence will in most cases see at one glance what is the right and what is the wrong in conduct. If in some cases he is at a loss to determine they are cases that rarely occur and comparatively of less importance in conduct. For who can possibly doubt whether it is an unjust thing to murther to maim or wound an innocent person that has done us no injury, to deprive him of this Liberty when he used it inoffensively, not to allow him to judge for himself in matters that concern his own opinion or practice, to hinder him the free & innocent use of things which are no mans property, to rob him of the fruit of his honest labour and industry, to hurt his reputation by slan-

der and calumny, or to impose upon him by lying and
fraud. Does it require any reasoning to prove that those
things are unjust? that they are gross violations of right? No
surely. Yet this is all that is meant by writers on Natural Jurisprudence when they enumerate the natural rights of men
& reduce them to these heads that have been mentioned of
a Right & to the integrity of our Limbs, to Liberty, the Use
of our private Judgement, to the Use of things common &
to the good use of our Labour, to Character, & to fair dealing. Instead therefore of offering Reasons to support truths
that are self-evident when considered in general I shall
mention some Cases which may illustrate what is the right
& the wrong proof with regard to the preservation of our
lives in circumstances that are more difficult. /

8/ıv/4,1v   The Case of Mr. Burnet in the East Indies.

Of two Exkimaux Savages on the coast of North America
from Ellis voyage.[4]

Where there is a great inequality of the Persons and one
must die for a good man one would dare to die.[5]

The two friends at Syracuse. Damon & Phintias. Pythag-
oreans.[6]

The Conduct of a General must of the two Extremes
rather lean to temerity than excessive caution against personal Danger.[7]

Cases wherein a man may not beat the utmost pains or
expense in his power to save his Life.[8]

Case of the Primitive Christians under persecution.[9]

Slight injuries to be generously passed over in many
cases.[10] /

7/vıı/1a,1r   Of the different states of Men according to which their
Rights are divided viz the State of Natural Liberty the Oeconomical State & the Political State.[11]

As the duty we owe to the Supreme Being results from
the Natures of God & of Man, and from the Relation we
stand in to him as our Creator Benefactor and Moral Governour and Judge, So all the Duties we owe to Men result
from the common Nature of Men and the Relations they
stand in to one another, and the same thing may be said of
the Rights; For whereever there is Duty and Obligation on
one hand, there must be a corresponding Right perfect or
imperfect on the other.[12] When we say that a Man ought to
do such an Action, that it is his Duty, that he is under a
Moral Obligation to do it these are all Phrases of the same

Import, & the meaning of them is precisely the Same. Every
Action which is my Duty towards another Man or which I
am under a Moral Obligation to perform towards him is
either an Act of Justice strictly so called, and in that Case he
has a perfect Right to demand the prestation of that Action,
or it is an Act of Probity and Beneficence, & in that case he
has an imperfect Right to expect it of me. So that in every
Case where there is duty or moral Obligation on one hand
to any Action respecting our fellow Creatures there is on
the other hand a Right perfect or imperfect in the person
or persons for whose benefits the Action is done. Now the
Relations between Man and Man are some of them transient
and of short Duration and often varying, others are more
permanent and durable.[13] Of the first kind are the Relations
between the Debtor & Creditor, between the Person that ex-
ecutes a Commission or trust & the person who employed
him or gave him the commission, between the Speaker and
the hearers, and many others. But these Relations being
transient, & the Rights and Duties resulting from each of
them being few, they are on that Ground less proper to be
made the foundation of a General Division of the Rights of
Mankind. It is a General Rule in Division that the Members
of the Division ought not to be so many, but that the Mind
may be able to comprehend them all as it were at one View.
For this Reason Writers in Jurisprudence have chosen to divide[s] the Rights of Mankind according to the more permanent Relations which men may stand in to one another.
And these Relations are general or Special.[14] The General
Relations are these which every Man bears to every Man as
an intelligent Moral Agent of the same Nature and Species
with himself. The Special Relations are those which a Man
bears to one or more individuals of Mankind but not to the
whole Species. And the most remarkable & permanent relations of this kind are either Oeconomical or Political. The
Oeconomical or Family Relations[15] are those that subsist between the different Members of the same Family, and they
are three unequal to wit the Relation between husband &
Wife, between Parent and Child & between Master & Servant. & two equal between children of the same family &
between the Servants of the same Family. The Political
Relations[16] are those which Members of the Same Kingdom
or Commonwealth have to each other, which are either that

of fellow Subjects and Citizens or the Relation of Magistrate
& Subject. /

7/vii/1a,1v   Hitherto we have mentioned onely the Rights of Individuals, but there are Rights also Competent to Communities
or Political Bodies.[17] When a Number of Men Unite in one
Body under one Government in order to carry on some
common Interest or End, by their Joynt Understanding Will
and Power. Such a Confederacy or Association is called a
Community, & such a Community in many Respects resem-
ples a Person so much that it may very properly be considered as a Person. It has its Right and Obligations as a Community. For as a Community it has an Understanding a Will
and Active Power. As a Community it may do good Offices
or Ill to other communities or to individuals. It may be hurt
or injured as a communitie. It may enter into Engagements,
& may either keep faith or break it. It may be said to have a
publick Conscience as well as a publick Understanding Will
and Power. Those who are entrusted with the Government
of such a Community are under an obligation to act fairly
and conscienciously in their publick Capacity as well as in
their private. And the Community having agreed to be
guided by the Judgment and Conscience of their Rulers in
their publick Affairs must take the disadvantages along with
the advantages of this confederacy. What is well done by the
Governing part brings Honour & Advantage to the Whole
Community. And on the contrary if the Governing part
does injustice or injury the whole community must bear the
Disgrace and be bound to make reparation. The Injury was
perhaps in reality the deed onely of a few who act for the
Community & are entrusted with the Government of it, but
as this Injury is defended by the Power of the Whole, so the
reparation may be taken of the whole or any part; by those
that are injured. The injured cannot distinguish the Guilty
parts from the innocent when all is united in one body. And
when those who are not the Authors of the Injury submit to
be made the instruments of it they must take the consequences, and be liable to reparation when the principal authors cannot be discovered or cannot be reached.[18]

   The most considerable communities of Men are Nations,
that is Kingdoms or Commonwealths who are united under
one Government & who have no Superior on Earth. These
are commonly called States, or Political Bodies. The Rela-

tion which different States who have no Common Superior
have to each other is very Similar to that of different Individuals who have no Common Superior. And therefore
there must be a very great Analogy between the Rights of
States with respect ⟨to⟩ each other, & the Rights of individuals who have no common Superior. Yet there are several
good Reasons why the Rights of States or of Nations should
be considered by themselves as a Particular Branch of Natural Jurisprudence.[19] For first. Although we have observed
that a State may be considered as a Moral Person in many /
Respects, yet the Nature of a State and of an individual
Moral Agent is in other Respects different, and this difference of nature must be the foundation of some difference
with regard to the Rights that result from the Nature and
Constitution of the Person. 2. The Political Person is a Human Work. The Political Union of a Community is framed
by Men and may be dissolved by Men. The individuals of
which it consists may be disjoyned from it and lose their Relation to the Body politick others may acquire this Relation
who had it not before. Hence there are many Questions of
Right relating to the Formation and Dissolution of Political
Bodies or States, many Questions relating to the Adopting
new Members into the Political Union or excluding those
that are members which cannot be considered in treating of
the Rights of Individuals. 3. The Rights of a State with regard to the Persons and fortunes of its own Members; and
Matters that belong peculiarly to this part of Jurisprudence
and fall not properly under consideration when we consider
onely the Rights of Individuals. 4. The Grandest Operations
of States, in Legislation in Judicature in Revenue in Police
in taking care of the Morals the Manners and Religion of its
Members. As well as the great Operations of War of Treaties of Peace & Commerce & Alliance with other States, cannot be set in a just light while we consider onely the Rights
of Individuals. For these Reasons the Public Rights Competent to political Bodies or Nations as such have justly been
considered as a distinct and most important Branch of Natural Juris Prudence.

Having given this general View of the capital Branches of
Natural Juris Prudence. I shall divide it into four Parts. In
the first we treat of Rights and obligations of individuals &
secondly of Communities or Nations. The Rights of individuals shall be divided into three heads first Those that result

5

10

7/VII/1a,2r

15

20

25

30

35

40

from the Nature of Men and the common Relations which all mankind bear to each other as Men. 2 The Rights & obligations resulting from the relation a Man bears to a family of which he is a Member. & 3 The Rights and Obligations arising from his relation to that particular State of which he is a Member. That part of Natural Jurisprudence which treats of the first May be called Private Jurisprudence. That which treats of the second Oeconomical Jurisprudence and that which treats of the Third Political Jurisprudence. /

7/vii/1a,2v

Natural Jurisprudence

The Duty which we owe to other Men, and which is all included under the Virtues of Justice and Humanity, has been within 180 years past Handled at great Length and in a Systematical Form by many Eminent Authors. And has commonly obtained the Name of Natural Jurisprudence.

Authors upon this Subject: Grotius, Hobbes Selden Puffendorf. Barbyrack upon Grotius & Puffendorf. Carmichael upon Puffendorf. Locke. Hoadly. Hutcheson Burlamaqui Vattel. Cocceij.[20]

Reasons for treating of the Imperfect Rights of Man in Jurisprudence.[21] Wherein the difference of these properly Consists. Not in this that the Perfect Rights are such whose observation is necessary to the being of Society. Nor 2 In this that the Perfect Rights may be vindicated by force. According to the first Perfect & imperfect Rights would differ in Degree not in Kind. /

7/vii/1c,2r It ought to be shewn how each of the three kinds of rights mentioned below is related to the moral faculty & how grounded upon it. Our Rights either respect things as their Object or they respect the Actions of others or our Own Actions.[22] Right⟨s⟩ that Respect things as their Object are called Real Rights. A full Right in a thing implys[23] 1 That I may without transgression of the Law possess the thing and exclude others from the possession of it 2 That I may take any Use of it I please that is not contrary to the law of Nature nor hurtfull to my fellow creatures 3 That I may give it away or sell it upon any condition that is not contrary to the law of Nature or hurtfull to my fellow creatures. 4 That no other person without injury can interrupt or hinder me from this Exercise of my Right. A Partial Right to a thing implys some one branch or part of the full right in it.

2 Where a Right respects the Actions of Others, it implies an Obligation upon the Other person to some Prestation or Action for my Benefite or to forbear all such Actions as are to my Detriment. A Man is never said to have a Right to any thing that he thinks hurtfull to him. because a Right is always conceived to be some thing beneficial & not hurtfull. We do not say that a Thief has a right to be hanged, because it is not supposed that any man would chuse to be hanged. So that the Act or Prestation of another which I have a Right to must be something that tends to my benefite or which I conceive tends to my benefite. Rights of this Kind are called Personal Rights. It is onely our Personal Rights that are divided into Perfect and imperfect. When another person is oblidged in Justice to a certain Action or Prestation for my Benefit so as that he injures me if he withholds it I have a perfect Right to that Action or Prestation. But when his Obligation is not that of Justice but Charity humanity Probity my Right is said to be imperfect.

3 The 3 Kind of Rights are those that respect my own Actions. My Right to do such an Action implies that I may do it without transgressing the Law or being obnoxious to censure And this Right extends 1 To all Actions that I am obliged to do. 2 To the forebearing all unlawfull actions but 3 Most properly to all actions that are indifferent, which I may either do or omit without a trespass. We may call this the Right of Liberty. The Rights of Liberty and Property are all Perfect Rights becos the violation of them is an Injury. As all Personal Right implys an obligation upon others That obligation is either to do something for my Benefit or Not to do something that tends to my Hurt. May not the first Kind be called Special as the Obligation terminates on some particular person or Persons. And the last General. May not Jurisprudence be referred to the two Heads of Rights and Obligations. Under the first are included Liberty & Property. & Obligations. to do or not to do. A Part of a mans Liberty is to resent and Redress injuries or even to shew a due Resentment of unkindness & disrespect. It is one of a Mans Obligations to pay a due Regard to the Liberty & property of Others.

A Mans Liberty and Property include what he may and may not do His Obligations what he ought and ought Not to do.

Obligations that are indispensible Liberty that cannot be

given up make what are called inalienable Rights of Man.[24]

The Knowledge of a Mans Rights makes him sensible of his Dignity, but it is the Knowledge of his obligations that makes him sensible of his Duty. Our Rights shew what we may do but our Obligations point out what we ought to do.

It seems to be a good Reason for treating of Jurisprudence as consisting of Rights and Obligations rather than consisting of Rights onely or of Obligations onely because though it be in reality the same Science in all these three different ways of treating it, yet there are some cases where the Obligation is the Consequence of the Right not the Right of the Obligation. Thus the Obligation not to take away my Liberty or my Property is grounded upon my having a Right to such Liberty or such Property but it cannot here be said that my Right to such Liberty or Property is grounded upon the Obligations of others not to take it away. Therefore it is most proper to treat of Liberty or property as Rights; And when we consider them in this View The divisions and subdivisions of them will be most simple Natural & intelligible and it is enough to bring them in general and at the head of obligations.

On the other hand my Right to certain Prestations from others is grounded upon their Obligation to perform those prestations. But it cannot be said on the Contrary that a mans obligation to pay this debt or to keep his promise is grounded upon my Right to those prestations. The obligation is immediate and is easily understood without having recourse to the others Rights. Therefore all Acts and prestations which I am bound to are most naturally treated under the head of Obligations. /

7/VII/1C,2V 1770 March[25]

1 Rights may be Distinguished according to their Nature into Perfect Imperfect & External.

7 Private rights are div⟨id⟩ed According to their Foundation into Natural (General Absolute) Oeconomical & Political (Special Hypothetical).

6 According to their Subjects into Private Common and Publick.

3 According to their Objects into Real & Personal.

4 According to their Source into Natural Innate and Adventitious or acquired.

5   The Last according to the Manner of Acquisition into
     original and derived.
2   According to their Mutability as they are separable from
     the person into alienable and unalienable.

These Distinctions of Rights are necessary to be understood 1 Because they frequently Occur in Writers & Secondly Because the Divisions and Subdivisions of this Science
are grounded upon them.

MARCH 12

The Rights of individuals are either such as belong to
them as Men, or such as belong to them as Members of a
Family, or 3^{ly} Such as belong to them as Citizens that is
Members of a particular State. Writers on Jurisprudence
conceive 3 Different States of Men corresponding to this Division of their Rights. The State of Natural Liberty or the
State of Nature by some called Status Solutus.[26] 2 The Oeconomical or Family State 3 The Political State. Puffendorf
calls the Rights belonging to the first of these States Absolute Rights & those belonging to the two last Hypothetical.[27]
The former do not suppose any thing but that the Person
who is the Subject of them is ⟨of⟩ human Nature. The later
Suppose moreover that he is a Member of a family or a
Member of a Commonwealth. The three States I have mentioned must not be conceived to be exclusive of each other
so as that a Man by being in one of these states is excluded
from the Rights belonging to the others. It is evident that a
Man by being subject to Government or a Member of the
commonwealth does not cease to be a Member of a family,
he may be both at the same time and enjoy the Rights competent to both, although some of his Oeconomical Rights
may be limited by the laws of the State yet they are not an-
nulled and the greater part of his Oeconomical Rights are
not at all affected by his being a Member of the State. In
like Manner, when a Man becomes a Member of a Family or
of a State he continues to be a Man and the Rights competent to him as a Man continue with him unless in so far as
they are limited by his Family or Political State has given
them up to the Family Relation or to the Community.
Cic pro Milone cap 4 Lex non scripta sed nata, quod non
didicimus, accepimus, legimus, verum e natura ipsa arripui-

mus, hausimus, expressimus; ad quod non docti, sed facti, non instituti sed imbuti sumus.[28]

Having painted the Causes that led Authors in Modern times to reduce in to a large & complex System the Duty we owe to our fellow Men, under the Name of the Law of Nature or Natural Jurisprudence It is proper to point out the Utility of such a System. That it has been generally conceived of great Utility is very evident from the high Reputation which the firstrate Authors on this Subject have acquired the encouragement they have met with from princes & States and the Establishments of the Profession of the Laws of Nature & Nations in most of the States & Universities of Europe.[29] Its Utility appears 1 As it directs a Man in his Private Conduct. 2 As it may direct Legislators. 3 Judges & Interpreters of the Laws. 4 As it directs the Conduct of Independent Nations towards each other. /

7/vii/1b,1r   As the Writers on Natural Juris Prudence have treated of the Duty we owe to our fellow Creatures by delineating in a Systematic Manner the Rights competent to Men by the Law of Nature, I have endeavoured to explain what is meant by the Law of Nature and what is meant by mens Rights grounded upon this Law. I have explained the most common Distinctions of Rights. Which with regard to their Nature are of three Kinds Liberty Property. or Real Rights and Personal Rights. The Personal are distinguished into perfect and imperfect to which some add External.

According to their Subject Rights are Private common or Publick. According ⟨to⟩ their Source into innate & adventitious, the Adventitious into Original and derived.

Our Property and Personal Rights are alienable, And some Parts of our Liberty, but there are other Parts inalienable.

Lastly Rights are divided according to the Relations on which they are grounded into Natural, oeconomical & Political. The first are called by Puffendorf Absolute the two last Hypothetical.

To Every Right in one Person there is an Obligation corresponding in some other person. So that the Right in one
7/vii/1b,1v party and the Obligation upon the other / really mean one and the same thing.

Although there is a real Obligation on one party corresponding to every right in another yet it cannot be said that there is a real Right corresponding to every Obligation. 1

For not to speak of our Obligation to the duties of Self Government Obligations to Generosity Beneficence have not rights corresponding to them. 2 There are other Obligations grounded upon some Error or wrong Judgment in our selves or in others. As when a Man is believed to be the lawfull proprietor of something which he has really stolen When a Debt really payed is believed by the debtor to be still owing. 3 There are Cases where we are obliged to yield to an unreasonable claim to avoid a greater evil when a Judge gives an unjust Sentence, When a Nation unjustly attacked by war and unsuccessfull is obliged to give up its just right to prevent worse consequences. In these Cases there is an Obligation on one Side which does not constitute a corresponding right on the Other.

From this it follows that the more compleat Knowledge of the Rights of Men, may not imply a Compleat Knowledge of their Obligations, and consequently that a perfect Delineation of Mens Rights is not a perfect Delineation of the duty we owe to our fellow Creatures. But to obviate this objection against treating of the duty we owe to our fellow Creatures by dilinating the Rights of Men the Writers of Jurisprudence have by a kind of Fictu Juris (as the Lawiers call it) conceived a kind of Right or rather a shaddow of Right answering to the Obligations we have now Mentioned. These they have called imperfect Rights where the Obligation is not an Obligation of Justice but of Benevolence & where the obligation on one part is grounded upon Error, or upon the necessity of yielding to an unreasonable claim to avoid a greater Evil. They have feigned a Shaddow of Right in the other party which they call a external Right. by these fictions of imperfect Rights and external Rights Right & Obligation are made to correspond perfectly so as that there is not onely a real Obligation corresponding to every Right, but there is a Right perfect imperfect or external corresponding to every Obligation. And a compleat delineation of Mens Rights perfect imperfect and external is in reality a compleat Delineation of the Obligations of Men or of the duty they owe to their fellow creatures.

Some Writers of Natural Jurisprudence have been of the Opinion that this Science ought to be confined to the perfect Rights of Mankind & that the imperfect Rights should be alltogether left out. But the authors of greatest Reputation Grotius Puffendorf Barbeyrac Hutcheson have in their

Systems comprehended both.[30] And I apprehend with good Reason 1 Because it is very difficult to ascertain the precise limit between the two. 2 Because a Man does not fullfill his duty by paying a regard to the perfect Rights of Mankind if he neglects the imperfect. /

7/VII/1b,2r But it may perhaps be more proper to treat of the imperfect Rights of Men & indeed of all their Personal Rights under the Notion of Obligations Because 1 In Personal Rights, the Right on one hand is grounded on the Obligation & cannot be conceived without, whereas in the Rights of Liberty and Property the corresponding obligation is rather grounded on the Right. 2 Because mens Rights point more immediately to their Dignity & their priviledges, but their Obligations point more immediately to their Duty. Our Rights shew what we May do but our Obligations shew what we ought to do.

⟨XI. Property⟩

Of Property. 1 Original[1]

We have shewn how the Property of things is acquired
originally. To illustrate this Matter, We may conceive the
goods and Accommodations wherewith the Globe of this
Earth is stored by the bounty of heaven as an Entertainment
provided by the Author of Nature for his Creatures who are
the Guests. The Sea the Air and Earth The Hills and valies
the rivers and Streams the Woods & Caves & corn the Bow-
els of the Earth Make one great Table furnished with plenty
and variety not onely for Man the Noblest Guest but for all
his fellow Animals that are created by the bounty of heaven
to partake of the Entertainment but on account of the In-
feriority of their Nature may be considered as Servants to
Man and to be served after Man. Every man takes his place
and is made welcome by the Master of the Feast to take what
pleases him. Hitherto every thing is common. It cannot be
said that this man has a right to be served out of this dish
that Man out of that. Every man may be Served where he
likes best, and is guilty of No ill manners by being so, provided he be not troublesom to others. It may well be presumed that it is the Will of the Entertainer that everyone of
his Guests should be served according to their taste and
Choise: But that no one should incommode another. When
therefore I help my self out of the common Store This is
occupation. If any man should pretend to take from me
what I have thus helped my self to he injures me and is
guilty of a lowness against me against the Master of the feast
and against the Company. This is the invasion of My property.

Those who not onely serve themselves with discretion and
good Manners but as far as they can accommodate those
about them. And who even take more pleasure in serving
others and making all about them cheerfull and happy than
in Serving themselves. These surely shew the finest Spirit
These must be the most acceptable Guests to the Master of

the Entertainment and to the Company. And these undoubtedly have more real Enjoyment then they who mind
nothing but the gratifying of themselves.

5   Let every Man therefore in the Occupation of those
things which God has given to the Children of Men, behave
to every other Man as well bred men would behave to one
another at such Entertainment. Then they may be assured
that their Occupation is just ⟨as⟩ agreeable to the Will of
God, as it will be approved by their own Conscience and the
10   judgment of wise and Impartial Men.[2] /

7/VII/1c,2r   But even the brute Animals who serve us at this entertainment must not be neglected. They must have their Entertainment and their Wages for the Service they do us. If the
Almighty takes pleasure in communicating happiness to us
15   who are infinitely below him Let us imitate his Benignity in
communicating Happiness as far as we can to one another
and even to those Animals that are below us.[3] /

7/VII/1c,1v   Property Fatultas possedendi, Utendi, alios arcendi, alien-
andi.[4] The steps by which property is introduced. Hoarding
20   of necessaries. providing Shelter, Arms, Cattle, Water
Land.[5]
        Naming an Heir. A Succession of Heirs.[6]
        Justifying Reasons of Property.[7] 1 Man a provident and
Sagacious Animal 2 The Will of God the Supreme Proprie-
25   tor has given him this disposition and therefore the Deity
must approve the exercise of it according to Reason. 3 Property put it in a Mans Power to do good to others as well as
himself and may reasonably be sought for this End. By
means of it we may be enabled to provide for those who are
30   especially committed to our Care, to make proper Returns
for good offices, to supply the innocent to reward Merit to
encourage industry. And to promote the happiness of human Society.
        4 The power of acquiring Property is a proper Encour-
35   agement to Industry.
        Corol As Property is intended onely for the good and
Convenience of the Proprietor or of others it cannot be justified any farther than it has this Tendency.[8]
        Property is no Physical Quality in the thing nor any asso-
40   ciation between it and the Proprietor in the Imagination but
a relation between the thing and the Actions of the Proprietor and of other moral Agents.[9] /

7/VII/11,1r   Q Should we thank a Man for being just and honest.[10]
        It were desireable that Justice and Honesty were so com-

mon as like Air and Water to bear no price. But when the
Commodity is scarce the Value must rise in proportion.

The Rights may be divided according to their Nature into
Perfect Imperfect & External. According to their Founda-
tion they are Divided into Natural and Adventitious. The
Adventitious are divided into Original & Derived.

Of the Adventitious Rights of Mankind which are original
the most considerable is original Property. Of which we
have already discoursed in several Lectures.[11]

On this Subject we have endeavoured to explain that State
of Communion in which things necessary or convenient for
the Life of Man are left by the Supreme Lord and proprietor of all. 2[12] I have endeavoured to Shew that it is agreable
to the will of God and to Reason that every Man should be
supplied out of the Common Store house of Nature in such
a Manner as most for the common Good. From this it follows that every man has a Right to appropriate to his own
use from the common Store what is necessary to his present
Subsistence and comfort and hurts no other person, & no
man without injury can hinder him to do so. 3 Reason directs us not onely to supply present Wants but to provide
against the future.[13] I have pointed out the various Reasons
that justify the acquisition of permanent property by occupation. And to shew the limitations and Restrictions which
Nature Points out in the Acquisition of Permanent Property.[14] Such Acquisitions as are subject to those limitations
which the safety of others and the common good of Society
require. 4 We have considered whether things once appro-
priated to a Sacred Use can ever afterwards be put to civil
Use.[15] 5 We have considered in what ways things once occupied & appropriate may afterwards be devaluated & return to the Communion of Nature,[16] & how property may
be acquired by prescription.[17] 6 We come in the last place to
consider these things that are called accessions to Property.[18]

Limitations of the Right of Property

1   As God has given the Earth to the Children of Men in
Common & the Acquisition of Property in any thing that
God has made is justified onely by Utility, and as the Utility
of individuals ought to yield to common Utility or to the
Necessity even of individuals hence it is evident.

1 [19] That there can be no property in that which common Utility requires to remain common. If a Man could occupy the Light of the Sun or the Air we breath. or the water we must drink such Occupation if possible would be invalid and Null. Because it is inconsistent with the common and Natural Rights of Mankind. The Ocean can never be the Property of any Man or of any Nation Because it is intended by Nature to facilitate the intercourse of Nations, & is sufficient for all nor can any good End be answered by its being appropriate it ought therefore to remain in the Communion of Nature.

2 There are some Cases where that which was Property may become Common.[20] 1 A Ship at Sea in the Scarcity of Provision, may divide what is aboard. May through over board a mans property to save the Ship.[21] 2 A City in a Siege or Famine May divide the Store of provision.[22] /

3 A Ship in Want of provision Meeting with another that has plenty and to spare.[23]

4 A Man in danger of perishing for hunger may take it even by force where he can. Proviso. In these cases as much Regard should be had to property as is consistent with the common Good.[24]

5 An Army Marching commands Provision and Carriages Grownd to Encamp &c.[25]

6 A Town in danger of a Siege clears the Surrounding Ground destroys the Suburbs &c & deprives the Enemy of every Advantage.[26]

7 Monopolies that are oppressive ought to be prevented or punished.[27]

8 A Man or a Nation may be hindred from acquiring such an extent of Property as endangers the Safety and Liberty of others.[28]

9 Restraints may be laid upon the disposal of Property by will or by Entails.[29]

10 A Proprietor has no Right to destroy his Property when the common Good requires that should be preserved, not to keep up Mercatable Commodities when the common Good requires that they should be brought to Market.[30]

11 The State for its own Security and to preserve the Constitution may set Bounds to the Acquisition of Property by Agrarian Laws or other Means of that kind.[31]

Things Sacred. called by the Civilians Res nullius by the Canonists reckoned inalienable.[32]

12 In General as Property is introduced among Men for the Common Good it ought to be secure where it does not interfere with that end but when that is the Case private Property ought to yield to the Publick Good when there is a repugnancy between them. Individuals may be compelled in such cases to part with their Property if they are unwilling. but ought to be indemnified as far is possible.[33] The Equity of the British Legislature in passing private Bills for Roads Canals and others of that Kind.[34] In hearing those who think themselves aggrieved against the Bill. Spains Claim of all America by Occupation.[35]

Obligation corresponding to the Right of Property[36]

D Humes Notion of Property. That the Notion of it is artificial.[37]

Sr Robert Filmer.

Grotius and Puffendorf ground it upon a Tacit Compact.[38] /

7/VII/13,1r The Duty we owe to our Fellow Creatures is comprehended under one General Name Justice, which is defined to be the rendering to every one what is his due, or what is his Right.[39] Every Right of another infers an obligation upon us to act agreably to it and not to violate it so that to know the Rights of others is the same thing as knowing our duty towards them.

Division of Rights into Perfect & imperfect Justice into commutative & Distributive. & the Obligations Corresponding. /

7/VII/11,2v The Perfect Rights of Men may be all sumed up in this that they have a perfect Right not to be injured by their fellow Creatures. Their Imperfect Rights. in this that they ought to ⟨be⟩ benefited by their fellow Creatures when it is in their power. A Perfect Right is that which it is no favour to yield but an Injury to withhold. An Imperfect Right is that which it is either a favour to bestow or at least no Injury to withhold.

Rights may be divided 3 Ways. According to their Origin Natural 2 Acquired 3 Adventitious. 2 According to their Nature Perfect. Imperfect External. 3 According to their Objects Real Personal. Acquired Rights are Original or derived.

Acquired Original Real Rights are got by Occupation. Acquired Rights are those which are consequent upon some deed of ours. Adventitious those that are consequent upon some Adventitious State as of a Master.

There is another Division of Rights into external & Internal for understanding which it is proper to observe. 1 That Every Right is either 1 To do something or exert some faculty in our power. Ex Gr to march through such a territory to turn the course of such a Rivulet to eat drink beget Children &c. 2 to possess and use such a thing. 3 To demand some Action or prestation of another.

To the first Kind corresponds an Obligation upon all other persons not to hind disturb or molest us in doing those actions which we have a Right to do. To the Second an Obligation not to hinder or interrupt our Use or possession of what we have a Right in. To the third an Obligation to perform the Action or Prestation we have Right to Demand.⁴⁰

But altho' these several Rights always constitute the corresponding Obligations, so that the Right being supposed the corresponding Obligation must necessarly follow yet the Obligation may be real where there is onely a Shaddow or appearance of the Right without Reality. Thus one who has Stole a horse & is in possession of him where the theft is not known and it is believed he came lawfully by him he has no Right in Reality to the Horse yet he has such an Appearance of Right as obliges others not to disposses him. In like Manner An unjust Sentence of A Judge or Arbiter Or an Unjust Law may give ⟨one⟩ an External Right to what he has in reality no Right unto. A State unjustly invades another & being Successfull in the War obtains a Part of the Territory of the Injured State by a Peace which the Injured State is forced to make to avoid greater Evils. The Right here Acquired by such a Treaty is onely an External Right.⁴¹ /

Rights of Mankind must correspond to their Different States. of Man citizen father Husband &c.

The State of Man as a Man comprehends his being a Reasonable Creature endued with those powers and Faculties of Body & Mind that all Men have. The Rights Competent to him as such are called Natural Rights by authors. And this State abstracted from all others is called a State of Nature those Other States of Men as they are grounded upon some Act or deed of Men that adds some new Relation to their Natural State are called adventitious States & the Rights flowing from them Adventitious Rights.

The Natural Perfect[s] Rights of Men are either Personal or Real, perfect or imperfect. ⟨1⟩ A Right to life Members ⟨2⟩ A Right to dispose of their Actions called Liberty 3 A

right to judge for themselves in Matters of opinion & practice 4 A Right to use or to occupy these things that are common by Nature and capable of being occupied. 5 A right to
Commerce traffick & Marriage & all other Contracts & engagements that do not violate any Right. 6 to our good
Name. 6 A Right to fair dealing Candour and Truth in
others that converse with us or communicate their Sentiments in the way of Testimony. Imperfect Right.

Description of that State of Community in which things
are left by Nature called Negative Communion. Occupation
of these gives property. The things we may occupy are
either such 1 as are for present Use & Consumption or 2
such as are of a permanent Nature & are used without being
consumed. The first must be occupied; but it may be Disputed whether the second may not be left in the Community of Nature or at least remain in a State of positive Communion see Plato. Utopia. Paraguay.⁴² /

Our Right 1 to these fruits or other inanimate things for
meat drink or Cloathing which the Earth produces voluntarly. 2 To the labour & service of the inferior animals. 3 To
use them for food.

Property in permanent things may be lawfully acquired.
1 Because Reason directs us not onely to supply present[s]
wants but to provide against future. 2 Property serves to
give exercise to many of the Noblest Social Virtues. Liberality friendship Natural Affection. As then we may reasonably desire the means of gratifying generous & noble Dispositions we may as reasonably desire Property. 3 Property
makes us less dependent upon the good offices of our fellow
creatures. which we all naturally desire to be. & less exposed
to danger or Mischief by their ill offices. 4 As Reasonable
Creatures we are capaple of a wise & beneficent Administration of that Power which Property gives & this is one of the
Noblest employments we are capable of. must Men be alwise
Minors.⁴³ 5 The State of things requires Universal Diligence
in Mankind in Order to their well being. And the Acquisition of Property seems to be the most powerfull spur to Dil-
ligence & patience.

Requisites in things in capable of becoming property by
Occupation 1 That the Subject be inexhaustible, incapable
of Culture, need no Expence to preserve or Secure it. 2
That its becoming property hurts or endangers the Rights
of others.

Whether things Sacred are incapable of becoming Property? Neg.[44]

Disputes about Occupation or about the first Occupation can hardly be determined by general Rules. What is for the common benefit of Mankind is the last Rule in these cases, next to that what has been commonly practiced & allowed among the wisest Nations.[45]

Of Dereliction & Prescription.[46]

Of Accessions. Nativitas alluvio Specificatio Commixtio Confusio Edificatio.[47] The entire Right of Property includes a Right to the fullest Use & To exclude others from any Use of the Goods in Property 3 A Right of alienating & transferring to others in Whole or in part.

Of Derived Rights.[48]

Divided into Personal & Real. It is fit that there should be some outward Symbol of the transference of Real Rights. such as Delivery. Infeftment Registration or the like.[49] Wherein they differ from Personal Rights.[50] Real. Derived Real Rights are either partial or full Property. 1 Partial The Species of Partial Property. Possession. Succession. in Entaille. Morgage or Pledge. & Servitudes.[51] 1 The Right of devising by Testaments[52]

2 of Succession to the intestate.[53] /

7/vii/13,2r 3 Donations[54]

4 Contracts.[55] Obligation to fair & upright Conduct in Contracts

  1 from the immediate Perception of our moral Faculty
  2 from the Necessity of Trust in human Society
  3

5 The Obligations in the Use of Speech[56]

  Oaths
  Vows

6 Obligations quasi ex Contractu[57]

7 Obligations ex Delicto[58]

8   Obligations & Rights in Cases of Necessity. that is
     where one principle of Morals seems to Clash with
     another:59

5

Adventitious Rights in the State of Marriage

Parents & Children

Masters & Servants

10

Political Society

Of the Rights of War

⟨XII. Succession⟩

The Right of Succession by Entail[1]

The second Kind of partial Property we mentioned is that of Succession.[2] Here it is evident that as far as a Man hath right to devise his estate after his Death to a series of Heirs, so far every Heir hath a Right to succeed in his turn and a Prior Heir or Successor although he has the possession and fruits of the Estate during his time has no right to alienate it to the prejudice of those who are appointed to Succeed him. On the other hand if the full property of an Estate does not imply a Right to convey it for ever to a Series of Successors named by the Proprietor it is evident that their Right of Succession can extend no farther than his right to devise his Estate to such a train of Successors.

The onely Question therefore that occurs upon this Right of Succession is how far by the Law of Nature a Man hath Right, not onely to name his immediate heir, but who is to be heir to the first heir, who to the second and so on to the end of the world, or at least untill all the persons whom he pleases to name to his Succession and all their lineal heirs fail? and How far he may limit the heirs named by him so as that none of them shall have the power to sell or alienate any part of the Estate or to encumber it with debt beyond such an Extent as he thinks fit to allow? It is proper to observe that an Estate settled in this Manner upon a Succession of Heirs, who have no power to sell or alienate but are bare live renters,[3] is called an entailed Estate the Deed by which such a Settlement of an Estate is made is called an Entail, and the several persons named to succeed in a certain Order are called Heirs of Entail. I borrow these terms from the Scotch Law because Scotland is now the onely part of the british Dominions where a Man can effectually entail his Estate in this Manner.[4] Having explained these terms It will be proper to give a brief view of the Origin and History

of Entails before we consider the foundation of them in Equity and the Law of Nature.

In the infancy of Civil Society Men have few wants but
those of Nature which are easily supplyed, and therefore in
this period few think of hoarding Property and Riches to an
immoderate Degree. But after the use of Money is introduced, and the wants of Luxury and fancy are multiplyed.
After Riches come to give Men a superior rank and consideration among their fellow Citizens, the desire of Riches /
grows to an immoderate Degree and becomes the ruling
Passion with a great part of Mankind. Men not onely desire
to accumulate all the wealth they can in their Life time, but
to raise a family after them that shall be distinguished
among their fellow citizens for their wealth and Opulence,
for many Generations; and to provide as far as possible
against the Accidents that may defeat an Event they so
much desire.[5]

It is obvious that a dissipated or spendthrift heir who has
the full property may squander away the greatest Estate,
and sink into obscurity a family that has long made a great
figure. And the most obvious Method to prevent this is to
put it out of his power.

⟨XIII. On Dissolution of Obligations and On Interpretation⟩

In what ways obligations are loosed?[1]

1   By the performance of what we are bound to do, payment of debt &c.[2]

2   By Compensation. Where equal & contrary obligations destroy one another like positive and negative Quantities in Algebra.[3]

3   By Remission, or acceptelation.[4]

4   By mutual Consent.[5]

5   By breach of Faith on one Side the other may be loosed.[6]

6   Assignation of our Right to another which the Civilians called Cessio, or transferring the obligation to another which the Civilians called delegatio. here the consent both of Debtor or Creditor must Concur.[7]

7   By Confusion of Debtor and Creditor.[8]

8   By Death.[9]

Of Interpretation[10]

There is often occasion for interpretation in Treaties & Covenants & in Laws as when after the first Punic War an Article of the treaty of peace was that Neither Party should invade the Allies of the Other. A little after the City of Saguntum made an alliance with the Romans. The Carthaginians besieged it. Quere whether this was a breach of the Treaty.[11]

The Latins made a League with Tarquinius Superbus the last King of Rome after his Expulsion they made war upon Rome.[12] Q 1 Rule. Words to be taken in their usual Signification unless there be a necessity of interpreting them otherwise.[13] The Turks in a Capitulation of a besieged town having capitulated that none of the Garison should be capitally punished. cut off their hands & feet.[14]

2   That interpretation is to be preferred which is most reasonable. The Reason & End of a Law is to be considered, & that Interpretation to be followed which is most agreable to these.[15] Our Saviours Example in Explaining the 4 Command.[16] The Sabbath was made for Man not Man for the Sabbath.[17] His interpretation of the Law of the Sabbath & of the Law of Tythes Restrictive, of the 6th Command Extensive.[18]

A Poor Man bequeathed to one of his Sons the Four Elements. A Book of that Title.[19] The Romans in A Peace with Antiochus agreed that he should give up to them the half of his Fleet. In the Execution they insisted that Every ship should be cut in two & they should have one half.[20]

The Laws of the 12 Tables made the Nearest relation of a Pupil his Tutor in Law, quia ubi Successionis Emolumentum est ibi et onus Tutelae esse debet, hence the Roman Lawiers conclud that where there was no Relation the Patron was to be Tutor.[21]

3   That interpretation which is most agreable to the end of the transaction.[22]

4   A Humane Interpretation to be preferred to a rigorous one. Of things favourable and Odious.[23]

Of the Collision of Laws

1   A permissive Law yields to a preceptive

2   An Imperfect obligation yields to a perfect

3   An Act of Beneficence ought to yield ⟨to⟩ an act of Gratitude much more of Justice.[24]

7/VII/15,1r Private Jurisprudence, that is, the Rights and Obligations of Individuals is divided according to the different States in which men may be considered.[1] First they may be considered barely as Men, & the Rights and Obligations competent to Men as such have been already considered. Secondly they may be considered as Members of a Family. The Rights and Obligations competent to them in this view are now to be considered, and make what is called Oeconomical Jurisprudence.

The Relations that arise from the Family state are chiefly three That of Husband and Wife, that of Parents and Children & that of Master and Servants. These we shall consider in Order.

First we are to consider what Reason and the Law of Nature dictates with Regard to Marriage or the Relation between Man and Wife. And this will appear more evidently if we attend to the Oeconomy of Nature in the procreation of Animals in General. The intention & will of the Author of Nature may in some instances appear more evident from the Actions of the brute Animals than even from those of Men; because brute Animals having no other Guide but their instincts & Appetites they invariably follow these, and therefore act according to the Nature which God has given them & by the Course of their Actions shew the intention of their Maker. But Man has Reason & Conscience given him to be the Guides of his Conduct, together with Appetites and Passions similar to those of the Brutes, which ought to be subordinate to Reason and to yield to its dictates. He may therefore pervert his Nature and act the Brute while he ought to act the Man, submitting his Reason which ought to bear Sway according to the will and intention of his Maker to his Passions and Appetes. For this Reason we may say of every tribe of brute Animals that they live as their Maker

intended they should live. But we cannot say so of Man. His
prerogative of Reason however valuable in itself is often
abused and applied to purposes very different from those
for which it was given.

Let us first therefore attend to the Oeconomy of Nature
in brute Animals and the Means which the Divine Providence has contrived for preserving the Species in every
Tribe while the individuals perish. It is evidently for this
End that he hath made Animals Male and Female & given
them the power and the Appetite of procreating their kind,
and with such a Care of their Young as is necessary to their
preservation & Education. But as the kinds of Animals are
many and their manner of living various, / so they are no
less various in their manner of procreating and educating
their young.

Some Animals are Oviparous some are Viviparous. Of
those that are Oviparous some there are whose eggs require
no Incubation but are hatched meerly by the heat of the Air
in a certain Season of the Year & when placed in a convenient Situation. Nor do the young of such need any other
Care but to have their natural food within their Reach. This
particularly is the case of all the butterfly kind of which the
Species are almost innumerable. The progeny of all is first
an egg, from which a caterpillar is hatched, which feeds on
the leaves of some one plant or tree, & by successive trans-
mutations becomes an Aurelia and at last a butterfly. Here
we may observe that what Nature requires to the preservation of this kind of animals is that the eggs be laid in a
proper Season of the Year, when the Warmth of the Air is
sufficient to hatch them, & when Nature brings forth the
leaves which serve for their Subsistence, that they be so
placed as to be sheltered both from cold piercing winds and
from the scorching Rays of the Sun; and the Parent is by
instinct directed to deposit her eggs so as to answer all these
purposes.

In other tribes of the Oviparous Kind the Eggs must be
hatched by incubation. This is the Case of almost all Birds.
And we see the Parents are directed to build a Nest of the
most convenient form, in the most proper place and in a
Certain Season of the Year, when the proper food of the
Young is supplied by Nature in Plenty. But the Young when
hatched are naked & unfledged, must have their food
brought to them & put in their Mouth. All this is performed
with the greatest industry & skill by the parents, untill the

Young are able to shift for themselves: Then the Parents
take no farther their Care of them & seem not to distinguish
their own Offspring from others of the ⟨species⟩. The Conjunction of the Male & Female lasts while the Young have
need of their Assistance & commonly no longer.

In all Quadrupeds where the raising of the Offspring requires the Care & labour of both Parents, Nature has given
5   the στοργη² or parental Affection to both, & they continue
to live together untill the offspring is reared.

In some Quadrupeds indeed particularly in the Cattle we
tame the Care of the Mother alone seems sufficient. And
there we so no care or Affection in the other Parent, nor
10   any continued cohabitation of the Male & Female.

To all animals which are Male and Female Nature has
given the Appetite of conjunction for procreation. And we
may see from the few observations we have made, to which
a great Number of the same kind might be added, that Na-
15   ture has made proper provision for the preservation of
every Species, by giving to the Parents those instincts & Affections and Arts that are necessary for that Purpose. The
7/VII/15,2r Marriage or Cohabitation of the Parents / continues for a
longer or a shorter time, just as the rearing & education of
20   the Offspring requires. The Wisdom of Nature appears
conspicuous in giving to every species the instincts necessary
for the continuation of the species nothing is wanting to this
purpose Nothing is superfluous. And as this is the case with
regard to the very lowest Orders of Animals, we may be as-
25   sured that the Author of Nature has been no less carefull
to provide proper means for the continuance of the human
Species the noblest that inhabits the Earth. For this purpose
Man has Instincts and Appetites given him similar to those
of other Animals; and adapted to his particular manner of
30   Life.

But besides these Animal Principles, he is endowed with
Reason, by which he is capable of perceiving the Intention
of his Maker in the several Principles he feels within him &
of regulating his Conduct accordingly. We may therefore
35   best discover what the Law of Nature dictates with regard
to that Family Relation we are now considering by observing
the Intention of Nature with regard to the Manner in which
the Human Species is to be reared & educated. /
7/VII/17,1r First. That it is the intention of Nature that the care of both
40   parents should be employed in maintaining their ofspring.
This is evident from the necessities of Children and their

wants which it would be impossible for the mother alone to
supply. In the ordinary course of generation it is evident
that women moderately fruitfull would have more children
than their own labour would be able to maintain. We cannot
therefore conceive that Nature has imposed a task upon
them altogether disproportioned to their abilities, the con-
5   sequences of which must be that the greater part of the human race must perish in their infancy for want of Subsistence. 2 Man of all Animals has the longest infancy, & his
Education is a long Work. 3 We see that in many other Species of animals the male as well as the Female is employed
10   in rearing the common ofspring. To this the brute animals
are directed by instinct where it is necessary. Mankind have
reason to discern the Necessity of it in the human Species,
& the necessity of it for the preservation and wellbeing of
the offspring lays them under an Obligation to this duty. 4
15   The στοργη[3] or parental Affection is common to both parents, in the human kind as well as in many other Species of
Animals. And this is a certain and indisputable argument
that nature intended that both parents should contribute
their care for the maintenance and Education of their com-
20   mon offspring. If the Author of Nature had intended that
the care of Children should be left altogether upon the
Mother, to what purpose has the father this parental affection planted in his nature and interwoven into his constitution. There is no part of the human constitution superflu-
25   ous and without any end. We may therefore certainly
conclude on the one hand that if the maintenance and education of children had not been imposed by the Author of
Nature upon fathers as well as mothers, that the father
would naturally have been as indifferent about his own chil-
30   dren as about the children of another. And on the Other
hand from the parental Affection being common to both
parents we may as certainly conclude that Nature intended
that both Parents should exert this Natural Affection in the
care of the common ofspring. Now from this principle we
35   may deduce this corollary that the propagation of Mankind
ought to be under such an Oeconomy and Regulation, that
Fathers may know whom they are to care for as their Ofspring.
7/vii/17,1v Without this the Parental /Affection on the fathers part
would be altogether frustrated and have no Exercise.
40   A Second corollary which Necessarly follows from the
principle that we have laid down and demonstrated is that
Women are under a strong natural Obligation to chastity so

far as to ascertain the father of their offspring. It is impossible if this was not the case that Fathers could have any way wherby to distinguish their own Children from those of other men, consequently there would be no Exercise of the Parental Affection on the Part of the Father.[4]

2 That Nature has aided this Obligation to Chastity in the fair Sex by a Sense of Honour, a Natural Modesty, and consciousness of Worth, which serves as a guard to their Virtue even where a sense of duty would be insufficient for that purpose. We might here appeal to the most profligate of our own Sex, who find in their Experience what assiduity and Courtship what professions of pure love and friendship, what vows of everlasting attachment and fidelity are necessary to seduce even the more credulous and unwary innocents of the Sex. How cruelly they conceive themselves injured and robbed of all their worth Value and Honour when they find themselves abandoned by the Man whom they considered as attached to them for life, and to whose Sollicitations no other consideration would have induced them to yield. Chastity has in all ages been considered as the point of honour with the fair Sex, and Experience shew that when they are able to overcome the Natural Modesty of the Sex they become abandoned to every vice. How can this be accounted for, since it must be acknowledged that the temptations to indulgences of this kind are as strong as any whatsoever? The onely reasonable account that can be given of it is this that to restrain the violence of Natural Appetite Nature has given the sex in general Such a powerfull Sense of Honour Decency & Modesty that when this barrier of their Virtue is broke down the whole Moral Character is laid open to the inroads of every vice. All Nations of the World have had a particular regard to this Virtue in the Sex and ever have annexed dishonour and infamy to the opposite Vice. All Nations says Montesquieu Liv 16 ch 12 have with one accord agreed, to annex Infamy to Incontinence in Women. This is the Voice of Nature to all Nations.[5] There was a Law among the Greeks that no whore should borrow her Name from any of their Sacred Games.[6] Infamy indeed seems to be so essential to this Vice in the Sex, that we will scarce allow the bitterest repentance to wipe it off. We are told by Valerius Maximus that among the Ancient Romans there was not an instance of a Divorce for 500 years yet the Romans in those Ages were a rude and Barbarous people remarkable onely for their military Virtues their love of

their Country & the Simplicity of their Manners.[7] Chastity
indeed makes a Most remarkable figure in the Roman
History and gave Occasion to the most Considerable Revolutions of that State. The Romans Submitted with incred-
ible Patience to the / Tyrranical Government of the Tarquins; untill a resentment of violated Chastity roused all at
once that Spirit which a thousand other Acts of oppression
could not awaken, and the Vengeance provoked by the
Dishonour done to Lucretia, laid the foundation of that
Glorious Commonwealth. When the Romans again fell under the oppression of the Decemvirs, and their Cruelty became insupportable; all their Sufferings could not force
them to use the means of Redress, untill an attempt made
upon the honour of a plebeian Maid, roused that noble in-
dignation which a second time gave liberty to Rome. If this
had been a common Injury Appius might have accomplished it with impunity as he had a thousand others. But
that injury must surely have wounded the quickest and most
sensible parts of the human frame which could make a fond
father plunge his dager in the bosom of his innocent and
lovely young daughter, and could make all Rome take part
in a quarrel in which their own grievances and oppressions
could not engage them.[8]

   These are sufficient documents of the natural Sentiments
of Mankind with regard to the dignity and Importance of
this Virtue of Chastity in the fair Sex.

   3 It is agreeable to the Oeconomy of Nature that mankind
should be propagated in Consequence of a lasting Attachment and League of Love and Fidelity between the Parents.

   There is no part of the human constitution that appears
more admirably contrived for very noble ends than the natural passion of Love between the Sexes. It may appear a
light and trivial Subject to those who have never been accustomed to think of it as Philosophers. But is really a very noble Subject of Philosophical and moral Speculation.[9] It is evidently the nature of this passion to take its rise from some
amiable qualities or of some worth merit and dignity that
are conceived to be in the object of the Passion and of which
we see as we suppose manifest indications in the features,
mien and behaviour of the person. It is therefore invariably
accompanied with a high degree of respect and Esteem,
with a genuine & disinterested concern for the happiness of
the person loved, an ardent desire of mutual Love a partic-

ular attachment. Every kind of Labour and peril is courted
that demonstrates this attachment and merit a reciprocal
Regard and attachment. It is no less evident that it is impossible that two persons can at the same time be the objects of
this passion nor can it be satisfied with a return that is common to others with itself. As it gives a preference to the beloved object above all others so it cannot be satisfied without
a reciprocal Preference of the same Kind. In this / love
between the Sexes is an affection of a quite distinct Nature
from Friendship, which may be among three or more persons, whichout Jealousy or Rivalship. This Union of hearts
and interests and affections which goes by the sacred Name
of Friendship, is indeed included in Love but it includes
something more. There is nothing in the nature of friendship to exclude a third party. But in Love from the very
Nature of it there cannot possibly be more than two. A Preference or even an equal Regard in either party to a third
person immediately and by the very constitution of human
Nature excites another natural Passion that of Jealousy. A
Passion which is indeed the offspring of Love but as tor-
menting as the other is agreable. And it is evident that the
torment of Jealousy arises from an apprehension of the
highest injury from the person most highly respected &
loved. Those who conceive that the sensual Appetite is the
chief ingredient in this natural Passion between the Sexes,
know nothing of its Nature nor ever felt its influence. This
appetite is rather restrained and bridled by a Passion of a
more Serious Nature, which fills and occupies the Mind with
tender delicate and refined Sentiments. Love is indeed not
a single and unmixed principle; it is compounded and made
up of various ingredients. Esteem Sympathy Benevolence,
in their highest degree enter into the Composition. But all
of them modified in a peculiar manner; and what distinguishes it from all other Passions is the attachment & the
Preference which is given to its Object beyond all others and
the Ardent Desire of being the Object of a like Attachment
and Preference in the person Beloved. Without this it cannot be Satisfied. It finds or conceives in its Object some Superlative Worth merit and Beauty; that engrosses the whole
Mind, and the more it dwells upon this object the more it is
moved to an Enthousiastick Admiration. The very language
of Love, Like that of the more rapturous flights of poetry,
shews a high degree of Enthousiasm, a kind of Inspiration.

The mind is elevated above itself by being constantly filled
with the Idea of an Object which is, or at least is conceived
to be, of Superlative dignity and Beauty. The Natural Effect
of this Passion in both Sexes is to produce an Elevation of
Mind a quickness of Discernment, a vigor of Resolution
Generosity Courage and tenderness. It unites the Virtues of
both Sexes, while each Sex cultivates the virtues that are
most attractive of the Love of the other & imitates those virtues which it admires in the other. There is no greater
Charm in the fair Sex than tenderness of affection Delicacy
and Sensibility. And we shall find every thing in the colours
features proportions voice and Motions of the Sex which we
call beautifull to be natural Signs and Indications ⟨of⟩ these
Qualities of Mind. A Man in Love naturally & insensibly
falls into the Imitation ⟨of⟩ the Qualities he loves. On the
other hand Manly Sense and Wisdom, firmness and Constancy of Resolution vigor of Mind, Courage Fortitude and
Magnanimity. And the Qualities in Men which are most apt
to attract the Love of the fair, and while they admire these
Qualities in the Object of their Affection, they are inspired
with a degree of them beyond what is commonly possessed
by the Sex on other Occasions.

It is evidently the intention of Nature that Men should be
directed by this natural Passion in the choice of a Mate[10] / not
indeed blindly directed, but under the guidance of Prudence and Discretion. The blindness ascribed to Love is not
peculiar to that Passion but common to it with many others.
And in the Noblest Minds Reason has shewn its superiority
over this Passion as well as over others. But as the intention
of Nature is manifest in every other Passion which belongs
to the human frame, it is no less so in this. Its tendency
being evidently to unite one pair in an indissoluble friendship and Society for raising up an offspring. Which common offspring by the constitution of human Nature par-
takes a greater Share of the affection of both Parents in
proportion as they have a greater affection and attachment
to each other.

All intercourse between the Sexes, whether authorised by
the Laws or not, which has nothing of this passion for its
foundation, can hardly deserve any other Name than Mercenary prostitution, or mere Sensuality. But where the
union between the Sexes is grounded upon the Natural Passion accompanied by Discretion and Virtue on both sides, it

is thereby dignified & sanctified, it cherishes every virtue & tends equally to the felicity of the parties and of the off-spring. Every duty and every obligation arising from the connubial State, is the natural issue of a mutual attachment of hearts.

It deserves our attention when we consider this passion in a philosophical light, that notwithstanding the general Agreement of Mankind with regard to those qualities of Body and Mind which are in themselves most amiable and most beautifull, yet the passion of Love is not excited solely by those qualities which in the general Estimation of Mankind are best entitled to it. There are but few in comparison who have not charms and attractions to find a lover. The unthinking may attribute this to the caprice and blindness of this passion without seeking any other Cause. But as this diversity of Taste in Love in different persons is plainly natural, although we cannot assign a physical Cause of it, it plainly appears to have a very happy effect. Without it both sexes behoved to be unhappy, and therefore it may justly be conceived to be the intention of Nature for wise and excellent purposes.

Upon the whole when we consider that by the Constitution of Nature the care of both Parents is necessary to rear and train up the human ofspring, That both are endowed by Nature with the parental Affection, That the fair Sex is by Nature fortified by a peculiar Modesty and Reserve which teaches them to yield onely to an attachment of Love which they believe to be equally sincere and inviolable on both sides & to admit of no Rival. When we consider more-over the Nature of the Passion of Love between the Sexes, which can onely be between one Man and one Woman. All these things plainly point out that it is [not] the intention of Nature that the propagation of Mankind should be carried on not by a promiscuous intercourse of the Sexes, without any Order or Rule as in some Brute animals, Nor by pairing for a short time / as it is with other Animals whose offspring can receive all the training & Education they need or are capable off in a Season; but by a lasting Contract of mutual love friendship and aid between one Man & one Woman. The Natural Affection of Parents never ceases while their Children are in Life it descends to the third & fourth Generation, & to all the Subsequent Generations a Man can see.

The equality in Numbers between the Sexes strongly con-

firms this. In all the Places in Europe where Registers of
Births have been Regularly kept it has been found that the
numbers born of each Sex are nearly equal. The proportion
observed in the course of Nature being that of 13 females
to 14 males nearly. See Derham P.Th Book 4 ch 10.[11] This
proportion so regularly observed has very justly been urged
as a mark of Design in the Government of the Universe. For
chance never could produce any such Regularity in things
that are under its influence. And as we have from this fact
a plain intimation that it is the intention of Nature that the
Number of Females should not be much less or greater than
that of Males; the obvious consequence is that it is the intention of Nature, that one man should not have a Number of
Wives. If there had been many Women produced in the ordinary Course of Nature for one man, this would undoubtedly have been an argument that Polygamy is according to
the Intention of Nature. And the Argument is equally
Strong for Monogamy when we find the Number of Each
Sex allways kept so near equality. As this Fact is confirmed
by all the Bills of Births that have been kept in every European Nation of Europe. So there appears nothing contrary
in other Parts of the Globe that has any considerable Authority. The vast Reading of President Montesquieu furnishes him onely with two facts of this Kind. A Voyager to
Bantam says that in that place there are ten Women to one
Man. But this Montesquieu himself seems to think a travel-
ler's story. The onely other Instance he gives is from Kemp-
fers Acct of Japan who says that in a Numberment of the
inhabitants of Mecao there were found 18 000 Males & 22
000 Females.[12] It is plain that this is very consistent with
what we find in Europe where though the Number of Males
Born rather exceeds that of Females, yet in Most great
towns there will be found more Females than Males. There
are many obvious causes that may occasion (in great towns
especially) such a small Superiority in the Number of Females, as was found in Mecao, although the number born
of Males should rather exceed that of Femals. Traffick Wars
Intemperance migrations or of Strangers, & many other
Causes may occasion such an inconsiderable variation of this
Ballance between the Sexes as Kempfer Observes. / From all
this it appears that in all Places of Europe where observations have been ⟨made⟩ with care, the Number of Males
born in every Country is so nearly equal to the Number of

Females that Nature appears to intend an equality of both Sexes which could never be the case if it were agreable to the intention of Nature that one Man should have several wives or one woman several Husbands at the same time. And this proportion between Males and Females does not appear from any well attested account, to be broke through in other parts of the Globe.

These observations prove sufficiently that a lasting contract of Love & fidelity between one Man & one Woman; is the method of Propagating the human Race that is most agreable to the Intentions of the Author of Nature and most conducive to the happiness of human Society. The Supreme Being shewed in a very remarkable Manner what was most aggreable to his will in this Matter, when at the first formation of the human Race he made one woman onely for one Man to be the parents of the Human Race.[13]

Polygamy however has been permitted among many Nations ancient and Modern among others even heathen Nations it has been forbid. Among the Romans Polygamy was never authorised. Plutarch tells us that Antony was the first among the Romans who had two wives at the same time. But this was afterwards expressly forbid by the Imperial Laws under the pain of Death. The Ancient Germans down to the time of Tacitus had onely one wife. So it was at first among the Athenians by the Laws of Cecrops, but afterwards their Laws allowed Polygamy.[14]

The Natural Consequence of Polygamy is Jealousy & Quarrels of Wives and of the children of different wives which tends to make the family State unhappy. and frequently produces the most dismal tragedies in families. To prevent these the Eastern Nations among whom Polygamy has been most prevalent, find it necessary to shut up their wives in a Seraglio under the care of Eunuchs, and to exercise the most despotick Government over them. By this barbarous and inhuman treatment of their Wives, all that beautifull Order / and Oeconomy which Nature points out for the family Society is entirely overturned.

The Idea of a happy Family, which Nature exhibits and which the Poets and orators have painted from Nature is that of one Husband & one Wife first united by the tender bond of Love which by degrees mellows into mutual Friendship and Confidence, and forms in a Manner one Person of two, continued in their common ofspring.

Hail wedded Love! Mysterious law, true source
Of human Offspring, sole Propriety
In Paradise, of all things common else
          *   *

5   By thee
(Founded in Reason, loyal, just, and pure)
Relations dear, and all the Charities
Of Father, Son, and Brother, first were known
Perpetual fountain of domestick Sweets
10   *   *

Here Love his golden shafts employes, here lights
His constant Lamp; and waves his purple wings
Reigns here & Revels, not in the bought Smile
Of harlots, loveless, joyless, unendeared.[15]

15   Xenophon in the fifth book of his Memorabilia commonly
called his Oeconomicks has given us an Account of a long
conversation of the Divine Socrates upon the Administration of a Family. That truly wise Philosopher saw and admired the Wisdom of the Author of Nature in adapting the
20   tempers and talents of the Male and Female Sex to the different departments of the family Society. He has assigned
them their different Provinces in the Management of a
happy family & in the Education of the common offspring,
with great Judgment and Beauty. I recommend to your pe-
25   rusal this 5th book of the Memorabilia as a precious Piece
of Socratick Morals and Wisdom. Cicero thought it worth
his while to translate it into Latin and we have some large
fragments of his translation still remaining which deser⟨v⟩e
30   to be perused.[16] /

7/VII/19,2r   How far Marriages within the forbidden degrees are forbid by the Law of Nature & whence their turpitude arises is
a Question of some Difficulty. And may be looked upon as
one of the few points of Jurisprudence, which is not obvious
35   to the common Reason of Mankind. It is a matter of Less
consequence to us as these Marriages are plainly forbid by
the Christian Law to all Christians. They are forbid by our
Municipal Law in England Scotland & Ireland, and they
were allways prohibited by the Civil & Canon Law. & by the
40   Municipal Laws of all Christian Countries. I shall offer very
briefly the reasons that have been urged to shew that those
prohi[hi]bitions are not meerly positive divine Institutions,
grounded only upon the Authority of Revelation but that

the Marriages prohibited on Account of Consanguinity or affinity have some natural Inherent Turpitude on Account of which they ought to be condemned.[17] /

7/VII/20,1r   Apr 24 1768. The Domestick or Family Relations, from
5   which the Rights and Obligations belonging to the family State do arise are three. That of Husband and Wife, That of Parent and Children & That of Master and Servants. The rights competent to these several Relations are discovered by a wise and Judicious observation of the State and Frame
10   of human Nature, and the indications we may take from thence of the Intention of the Author of our Being.

With regard to the Relation of Marriage the long infancy of the human Race, the Education and training it requires, The Parental Affection being common to both Parents. The
15   Natural Modesty found even in Savages. The Natural Passion of Love between the Sexes, with all the delicate feelings & Sentiments it produces. The passion of Jeaulosy itself. The equality of Males & Females, do all point out the Intention of Nature with regard to the manner in which the hu-
20   man Race ought to be continued and reared, and that a Contract for Life of Love & Fidelity, for the purpose of rearing a family is most suitable to the Law of Nature. A great many things regarding Marriage & Divorce as well as
7/VII/20,1v the respective Rights of husbands and wives must be / left
25   to be determined by the Laws of every particular State. Nature has for the most part put a Difference between the two Sexes with Regard both to the Strength of their Bodies and the Dispositions of their Minds. The female part of the Species is commonly more delicate in their frame both of body
30   and mind; they have a greater degree of Softness and Sensibility a greater inclination to Dress elegance & cleanliness & more, of Anxiousness & timidity to the males Nature has given greater strength of limbs, and hardness of Constitution, more courage to encounter dangers, and greater mag-
35   nanimity & constancy of Resolution. These different Characters which Nature has imprinted upon the Sexes, though not without Exception, point out the different offices in the family Society which most naturally fall under the department of each. And the laws of all civilized Nations pay a
40   regard to this difference of Character in the different Sexes. Nature certainly intended them as proper Counterparts to each other. And although the Virtues that belong to us as reasonable Creatures & moral Agents are in substance the

same in both Sexes, yet they have in each Sex as it were a
different Form. So that the most amiable female Character,
would appear contemptible and ridiculous in a Man; even
to the fair Sex themselves; and on the other hand the most
5   perfect male Character would in a Woman be unamiable &
disgustfull. With such a wonderfull Propriety and Delicacy
has Nature adjusted the Graces and Ornaments proper to
each Sex, as if each were made onely for the sake of the
other. Indeed the whole Family Society of Husband Wife
10   and Children, is so admirably fitted for human Nature, and
Human Nature uncorrupted by vicious habits so adapted
for such a Society, that both must appear venerable to a wise
7/vii/20,2r and impartial observer, as contrived by the / Wisdom of the
Supreme being to promote the Felicity & improvement of
15   the human kind. Although as the Corruption of the best
things is commonly worst, it needs not seem strange that
these relations should often through the folly and corruption of men prove a Sourse of Vexation and trouble.

Marriage may be defined to be a Contract of Love & Fi-
20   delity between one Man & one woman, in order to promote
each others Felicity and to rear up their common Offspring.

Polygamy I conceive cannot be said to be absolutely forbid
in all cases by the Laws of Nature, otherwise it would not
have been permitted among the Jews by God himself. Yet
25   on the other hand it appears evidently more for the common good of human Society, that monogamy should be established. And where it is established by the civil authority
there Polygamy may be forbid under the severest penalty.
The Laws of Christianity absolutely forbid polygamy.[18]

30   The wiser heathens have condemned it. Euripides in Andromache ex Persona Hermiones.

Non etenim decet
Unum imperare feminis geminis virum
Contentus uno conjugis vivat toro
35   Quicunque cupiet rite curatam domum[19]

Plautus in Mercatore

Nam Uxor contenta est, quae bona est, uno viro
Qui minus vir una uxore contentus siet.[20]
40
Faecunda culpae secula, nuptias
Primum inquinavere & genus, & domos;
Hoc fonte derivata clades
In Patriam Populumque fluxit. Hor Lib 3. od 6 ver 17.[21]

1   of Fornication. Unnatural Passions.[22]

2   Of the Causes that render a Marriage Null.[23]

4   Incestuous Mixtures.[24]

The Passion of Love between the Sexes is a part of the Human Constitution, & is of chief consideration in Marriage which is really a kind of Prostitution where this Passion does not lead to it. In those who have been properly educated this passion is never found between Near Relations. Whether it is that there ⟨is⟩ some nateral incompatibility between it and the natural Affections between Parents and Children and other near Relations, or whether by our Constitution the Passion of Love has another direction given it by the Author of our being. Why may not the Passion of Love have its natural Objects as well as the Parental & filial Affection? May not by our Constitution near Relations be no Natural Objects of this Passion as Males are not. Nor the Old & Decrepit of the other sex. If this is so may it not account for a Natural Abhorrence of Incest as of other unnatural Lusts.

Is there not with regard to incestuous Mixtures a Moral Sense implanted in Man by the Author of his being which when Mankind extended to one family was not unfolded, but gradually sprang up as the race multiplied, & perhaps would vanish if the race was again reduced to one family. Perhaps this Moral Sense may be justly said to be implanted and arbitrary.

5   Divorce

6   Left Hand Marriages[25]

10   Duties and Rights of Husbands and Wives[26]

3   How far Consent of Parents is necessary in Marriage[27]

7   Much must be left to the Laws of each Country

8   The Christian Laws on this Subject agreable to Reason

9   The Respect payed to Celibacy as a more Perfect kind of Life.[28]

See a fine fragment upon the Subject of the Natural Laws concerning Marriage from Cicero's Oeconomicts of Xenophon Lib 1.[29] /

2³⁰ *The Relation of Parents and children.*

The στοϱυη³¹ points out the Duties on the Parents Side.
Not founded in Generation any more than in Nursing.³²
Three periods in the Life of Children to be distin-
guished.³³

1   While they are unfit to govern themselves.

They must then by guided by Parents as their Guardians
appointed by Nature. The Parents right the same as that of
the Guardian. May be transferred when important Ends are
to be served by it. Duty of Parents in Provision and Education. Rights belong to both Parents. Children in this Age
may have a Property, of which the parents are not the proprietors but the Guardians. Right to the Discipline and correction that is profitable for the Children and for the family.
In this Period the Parent is considered as a Parent & as a
Guardian, the child as a Child and as a Pupil.

2   When of Mature Age but not Foris familiate.³⁴

The Respect due to them as Parents particularly in Marrying by their Consent. The Right of Parents to their Service when they are poor. Right to Sell what? The Parent can
give no more right than he has Right to punish. In this State
the Parents are considered as Parents, & as heads of the
family the children as children, and members of the family,
& as indebted to the parents for the care trouble & Expence
laid out upon them. The Parents are considered as Seniors
grave & experienced, the children as young unexperienced
& giddy.

3   When Foris familiate

Here the Relation & children continues, & the debt upon
the children. In all these different States we may easily discover the Parents duty by putting ourselves in the Situation
of the Child, & that of the child by putting ourselves in the
state of the Parent. The patria Potestas among the Ro-
mans.³⁵

Antiquae Romanorum Leges, respicientes tum ad eam
quae a Natura est eminentiam, tum ad labores quos pro li-
beris parentes Sustinent, volentes praeterea liberos parenti-
bus sine exceptione subjectos esse, credo etiam confisi naturali parentum amore et venundandi, si vellent liberos, et
impune interficiendi ⟨parentibus⟩ jus dederunt. Epictet.³⁶

Jus autem potestatis quod in Liberos habemus proprium est civium Romanorum nulli enim alij sunt homines, qui talem in liberos habeant potestatem. Institut Lib 1 Tit 9 § 2.[37]

Apr 11 1770

The Political Compact in the first Stages of Civil Government is onely among Masters of Families. They are properly the onely Citizens; their Wives Children & Servants, are rather the Goods and Chattels of the Head of the family than the Subjects of the State. The Master of the Family is answerable for their Conduct towards the State & towards the other Citizens. They are not under the Government of the State, but of the Head of the familly. If he is guilty of injustice or Cruelty towards them. The State is not to blame. as when a Man uses his beast cruelly or Scolds his wife or Disciplines his children with too much Severity the State does not mind this. This seems to be the best Account of the Origin of the Patria Potestas & of Servitude in Ancient States. The Political Compact is gradually extended to Wives Children & Servants & then they become more the Subjects of the State & less the Subjects of the Pater familias[38] /

7/vii/20,3r   *Of Masters & Servants*[39]

The third family Relation is that of Masters and Servants. The natural Equality of Mankind as rational Beings & moral Agents of the same kind, endowed with like powers of body and mind, equally accountable for their actions to God the common parent of all, & equally bound to mutual good will and good offices. This natural Equality I say of which we have before spoke & shewn to be the foundation of certain common Rights and obligations which belong to them as Men, is not so perfect in all Respects but that it admits of certain preeminencies & advantages which some men may have over others. Men are not equal in bodily Strength, nor in quickness of understanding, nor in wisdom prudence and courage. Far less are they equal in temperance industry Justice and good Conduct. Besides the difference in mens talents which is the work of Nature, the difference in their Virtues and good Conduct which is owing to themselves,

when Property is introduced Fortune or the Providence of
God often makes a great difference in mens Riches Power
and Influence. One Man either by Industry, Skill in the
management of his affairs or by good Fortune becomes
5   Rich and Opulent. Another man, by his own fault or perhaps without any fault by cross accidents to which all human
things are Subject is reduced to want. Of all Animals Man is
most capable of being usefull to Man. The Rich will find
many occasions for the Service of the poor, and the poor
10   will find their advantage in serving the Rich. Such Service
therefore as is beneficial to both parties & injurious to neither must be perfectly agreable to the laws of Nature.

A man who has a Natural Right to dispose of his own Actions and employ his Labour in providing for himself the
15   conveniencies and Necessaries of Life without injury to
others, may agree to labour for another, & under his direction on conditions that are reasonable and equitable. /

7/VII/20,3v   A Contract of this kind by which a Man agrees to serve
another upon reasonable terms for a longer or Shorter time
20   or even for life, must be regulated by the same laws of Nature and of Equity as other Contracts are. This Contract
unites the interests of Master and Servant. And neither of
them can consistently with the nature of this Relation be indifferent to the concerns of the other. A just and humane
25   Master will think himself bound not onely not to do any injury to his Servant himself but to protect him from the injuries of others, to exact no task or Service of him that is
unreasonable or cruel, to allow him not onely the necessaries of Life but such comforts and conveniences as are
30   suited to his Station and do not tend to corrupt his manners
or render him unfit for the duties of his Employment. And
to make all reasonable allowances for the common infirmities of human Nature, which do not permit us to expect perfection in any Man, of any Station whatsoever.

35   The Authority of a Master intitles him to an inspection of
the morals of his Servants. Their Virtue and integrity is the
best Security he can have of their discharging faithfully the
duty of their Station. Their ill Example may be hurtfull in
many respects to the family and reflect dishonour upon it.
40   The Master who is bound to protect them from the injuries
of others has the same tie to hinder them as far as lies in
him from injuring and hurting themselves by bad conduct.
Servants often stand in need of moral & religious instruc-

tion & counsell, & may be greatly benefited by it in their most important interests. The Authority of a Master intitles him to do this good office to his Servants, & even lays an obligation upon him to do it according to his Ability. Every Family is a little political Society wherein the Master of the Family is the Supreme Magistrate, & is in some degree accountable for the conduct of those under his Authority, & therefore that Authority ought to be employed to make them understand their duty and to engage them to the practice of it. The Supreme Magistrate in a State cannot with innocence be unconcerned or negligent with regard to the Morals of his Subjects neither can the Master of a Family with regard to the Morals of his Family. /

Although the Divine Author of our Religion hath appointed a particular Order of Men for this very purpose of instructing others in their moral & religious Duties & stirring them up to the practice of them, and hath given them the Authority necessary for this purpose; it is not at all the intention of this institution to supersede the obligation of Parents and Masters to oversee the Morals of those under their Charge, but rather to supply their defects & to cooperate with them.

As Masters ought to use their best endeavours to promote real Worth and Probity among their Servants; so they ought to shew a just Esteem of these Qualities where they are to be found. In Moral Qualities the Servant may be equal to his Master or perhaps his Superior. And these are the Qualities that merit our Esteem in every Station of Life. Those who know how to Esteem them in Servants & to encourage them will be best Served & their Servants will be most happy.

In all cases Masters ought to exercise their Power over Servants with Humanity. A good man will be mercifull to his Beast. Much more to his Servant who is by Nature his equal & in the vicissitudes of Fortune may become his Master.

As all men are by Nature free Every just Servitude must be grounded either upon consent & Contract or Quasi Contract or Delict.[40] The two first Grounds of Servitude suppose that there is to be an equality preserved as in all onerous Contracts, so that the Service done to the Master be compensated by the Benefites received by the Servant as the price of his Service. In order therefore to Judge how far

Servitude grounded upon these foundations is just and agreeable to the Law of Nature. The value of a Servants Labour ought to be estimated & compared with the advantages he receives by it. If there be a manifest inequality between the two, the bargain is injurious to one party and the injured Party has a Right in this case as in all onerous Contracts to a Compensation.

The Labour of a Servant for Life is more than equivalent for his Maintenance.[41]

Though a Man should contract to serve another for Life upon equitable Conditions, he cannot validly make such a Contract for his Posterity.[42] /

Servants whether for Life or for a Term of Years must retain the unalienable Rights of men and of Reasonable Creatures.

Of the Right of Servitude founded on Delict, on Captivity. or Incapacity.[43] Notions of the Jews Romans and Greeks respecting Servitude. Domestick and Rural Slaves.[44]

The condition of Slaves more tollerable among rude Nations than the civilized.

⟨XV. Social Contract as Implied Contract⟩

2/11/10,1r The common definition of a Contract is That it is the Consent of two or more parties in some one thing, given with a view to constitute or to dissolve some obligation; this Definition seems to include all that is meant by a Contract
5 when the word is taken in its utmost latitude.[1] But it is to be observed that the Consent which is essential in all Contracts may be expressed many different ways; either by a formal writing Signed sealed and delivered; or by the verbal declaration of the several parties; or by the actions of the par-
10 ties; or even sometimes by their Silence, or by their doing nothing, when it may reasonably be presumed that they would not be silent or inactive if they did not consent. The meaning of Actions is in many cases as well understood as that of words or writing, and is no less binding upon honest
15 Men. And the same thing may be said of Silence or of doing nothing.[2] When I hear a Sermon my Silence signifies nothing, it neither implys my assent to what the preacher affirms nor my consent to what he requires me to do. But on the other hand If I am called to a meeting of Electors of a Mem-
20 ber of Parliament, where a Candidate is proposed by one and agreed to by others. Should it be at last moved that if any man has any Objection to the candidate mentioned he should speak, & that silence would be held for a Consent, here every honest man would conceive himself no less
25 bound by his Silence than by his Consent expressed by words. A Dumb Man who can neither speak nor write may yet Contract or bring himself under Obligation either by natural Signs or by such artificial signs as he commonly uses to express his Consent. Thus I conceive it is evident that the
30 consent of Parties which is essential to every real Contract may be expressed in a great variety of ways. By writing by words, by signs artificial or natural, by Silence or even by

doing nothing; it is sufficient if the meaning of the sign
2/II/10,1v   whatever it be is under / stood by the parties.

The terms of a Contract are sometimes most minutely expressed so as to remove every doubt as far as is possible with
5   regard to the obligations brought upon the several parties
by it; But the nature of human affairs will not always admit
of this caution & precision. A treaty of Peace or Commerce
often makes a Volume, while the Capitulation of a town
consists onely of a few lines. Nay in most contracts there is
10   no necessity to mention the terms, They are implyed in the
very nature of the Transaction. Thus I send for a Taylor, I
desire him to make me a suit of Cloaths of superiore Cloath
of such a Colour; he takes my Measure makes a bow and
walks off, under the same obligation as if by an Indenture
15   stamped paper we had been mutually bound to each other,
he to chuse the cloath according to his best skill to cut it
according to the fashion and the rules of his Art to fit it to
my size and shape to furnish and make it up workman like
& to charge a reasonable price, & I on the other hand to
20   take it off his hands & to pay him for it. This is all implyed
in the order I gave him though not a tittle of it be expressed. A Farmer asks of his Neighbur farmer the Use of
an Ox for a week which is readily granted. If he feeds the
beast properly and works him moderately & returns him at
25   the time appointed, he fullfills his obligation, for this was
the Use implyed in the transaction. But if he slays the Ox,
makes a feast and eats him, he is guilty of a breach of contract no less than if it had been extended in the most formal
manner. I apply to a man who professes the healing Art. I
30   tell him that I labour under such an ailment, & desire his
advice. He prescribes for me without any more ado. It is
evident that he comes under an obligation to prescribe for
me according to the best of his skill & I to pay him a reasonable fee though no such thing was expressed on the one
35   hand or the other. The consent to this reciprocal obligation
is implyed in the Nature of his Profession my application to
him & his prescription for my health. It is not solely The
Physicians Oath taken at his inauguration that binds him to
the faithfull discharge of the duty of a Physician; his taking
40   upon him the Character virtually & implicitly binds him to
this without Oath or Promise. He violates the contract implied in his profession, when he does not prescribe faith-
2/II/10,2r   fully / and honestly. The same thing may be said of every

profession and of every office in human Society; with this
difference onely that the more important the office is to the
well being and happiness of the human kind, so much the
more sa⟨c⟩red are the Obligations to the duties of it. But
every office & every character has its obligations and every
man who takes that office or character upon him takes upon
him its obligations at the same time. He who claims the character of a man binds himself to the duty of a Man, he who
enlists in the Army binds himself to the duty of a Soldier, &
he who takes the office of a General binds himself to do the
duty of a General. It is so in every office in Society from the
lowest to the highest. If in some offices it is the Custom, or
enjoyned by Law to take an Oath de fidele administratione
officij[3] this custom, as common in Sovereigns as in any other
office, brings a man under no new obligation. It is onely
intended, as oaths usually are, to strengthen an obligation
already contracted. The taking the office implys the contract to do the duty of it, no less than borrowing implys a
contract to restore or repay at the time appointed.

I conceive therefore that a King or Supreme Magistrate
by taking that Office upon him voluntarly (and no man is
forced into it) engages or contracts to do the duty of a king,
that is to rule justly and equitably & to preserve the rights &
promote the good and happiness of his people as far as lies
in his power. where the Laws have set limits to his power he
is bound not to transgress those limits. If the Commonwealth has committed to him the whole Power Legislative
executive & Judicial; he is not the less, but rather the more
sacredly bound to the right Excercise of it. As a General or
Admiral who is not limited by instructions but left to act according to his Discretion is not by that discretionary Power
under the less obligation to use his best Skill & Diligence to
answer the End of his Commission.[4]

In the Simple and primitive Periods of Society when a
Number of families unite for common Protection and common Justice they commonly chuse one Man of distinguished
Virtue and Wisdom. They trust him with the whole care of
the Government. / Their giving him this Power and his accepting it, is a Contract perfectly understood on both sides.
While he uses his Power according to the true meaning and
intention of this Contract; they fight his battles, they revere
his Laws, they acquiesce in his Decisions; they reverence
him as the Father of his People and think his Glory his

Splendor & Renown to be their own. He is the most absolute
Monarch upon Earth, and his people at the same time the
freest & the happiest people. For this I will venture to affirm
that a people may be free under the most absolute Government. They are free while they understand their Rights and
have the power & the Will to vindicate them when atro-
ciocesly violated. This was the case of the earliest kingly
Governments, Kings were trusted with unlimited Power,
and when they abused it, it was taken from them without
Ceremony. This was the case of the Roman people under
the Decemvirs. They were intrusted with unlimited Power
for a certain purpose. The nature of their Institution implyed that they were to govern the Roman people justly untill they had framed and established a body of Laws and
then to resign.

This was the Original Contract implied in their Institution. The undue prorogation of their Power, & every act of
Oppression and Tyrany they committed were violations of
this Contract the Rape of Virginia crowned all & roused the
Vengeance of that brave people.[5] They never had given up
their Liberty, they had onely committed it to the keeping of
Persons whom they esteemed worthy of that Trust. And
when they proved unworthy the Roman people wanted neither judgement to understand nor the Power and Spirit to
vindicate their just Rights. A People have lost their liberty
onely when they are either brought to believe that they have
no Right to resist oppression, or when they have not power
to resist it. While they do not believe in the Divine Right of
Kings to Govern wrong while they believe that their lives
and Fortunes are onely deposited in the hands of the Magistrate for Safe Custody, not given away to serve his pleasure and Ambition, they are free whatever / the form of the
Government may be; nothing but superior force can make
them slaves. The Subjects of the great Mogul want nothing
to make them free but to have their Minds enlightened and
their Courrage raised. The Mogul would then, notwithstanding the Absolute Nature of the Government, find himself bound by the Nature of his office and the Rights of his
Subjects, and if he disregarded their Rights and Ruled tyr-
ranically & oppressively he might justly be charged with
breaking the Original Contract between him and his people.
The Sum is this That every Supreme Magistrate, by taking
that office, voluntarily becomes bound to certain prestations

to his people; but this includes all that is essential to a Contract.

I know onely one way in which a Sovereign can plead freedom from this Contract, & that is if he has taken a protestation at his entering upon this office that in his administration he is to have no Regard to Justice or Mercy any farther than he finds them answer his own Ends. If his people submit to him upon these terms, I think he may be said to be under no Contract, nor can he be charged with breaking the Contract however tyrranical his Government may be. Rehoboam the Son of Solomon & Richard the second of England thought proper to make professions of this kind; but the event that followed in both their cases has discouraged other Kings from protestations of this kind.[6] On the contrary we shall find few instances in History of a King speaking to his people or to any Representative body of them without confirming in express words and in the most Sollemn Manner the Engagements which are implied in the Nature of his Office. K Jas who was no enemy to the prerogative of Kings, & who loved to instruct his People in sound principles in his speech to his Parliament Ao 1609 tells them That the King binds himself by a double Oath, to the Observation of the fundamental laws of his Kingdom: Tacitly by being a King and so bound to protect the People and the laws; & expressly / by his oath at his Coronation; so as every just King is bound to observe that Paction made to his People &c.[7] In our Constitution the Contract between King and People is not onely solemnly made at his Coronation but Solemnly renewed upon every Adress made to him by either Branch of the Legislature. As in every such address they promise to support his Kingly Power & Rights so he in his Answer allways promises to make the Laws the Rule of his Government.

This is a clear explication of the Original Contract between King and People and in this Sense I conceive it has always been understood. The Convention of Estates at the Revolution found by a Vote of both houses that King James had broke the Original Contract between King and People.[8] This was one of the most sollemn and important transactions that ever passed in the British Senate. And we may reasonably think that every word used in a Vote that was to draw such Consequences after it would be weighed. Mr Hume however in an Essay upon the Original Contract, has

employed his Learning and Eloquence to shew that there is
no such thing as a Contract between King and People in
these Ages, although he acknowledges that there was such a
Contract at the first Institution of kingly Government.[9] The
Sentiments which Mr Hume has on many occasions expressed of the claims of the house of Stuart, & of the Conduct of those who opposed their pretensions; make it less
supprizing that he should oppose a principle upon which
those who brough about the revolution justified their Conduct. If the Lords & Commons who found the throne to be
vacant upon this ground among others that King James had
broke the Original Contract between King and People acted
upon chimerical Principles they are not to be justifyed and
we ought either to condemn the Revolution altogether, or
justify it upon different Principles. But if on the other hand
this Notion of a Contract between King and People has a
Meaning, and a meaning consistent with the Principles of
Justice and Equity why should it be traduced as chimerical
& Visionary by those who have no intention to throw a Reproach upon the Revolution.

When we speak of the Contract between King and People
the Relation is supposed to subsist. It is supposed that he is
really the King of such a People & that they are the People
of such a King. I onely beg this as a postulation that no man
is under a Necessity of being a King, that he takes this Character upon / himself voluntarly and may lay it down when
he will. It is of no consequence in the present Question in
what way he acquired his Kingly Authority whether by Conquest or Hereditary Succession or Election, whether by
force or fraud or fair Means, whether his people obey him
willingly & freely or through Necessity; still this Relation
implys in the very nature of it an obligation to those prestations towards his people which belong to the kingly office.
And as the Relation must be voluntary upon his part he is
obliged by entering into this Relation to those prestations.
If therefore every obligation a Man voluntarly enters into is
a Contract there must be a Contract between King & People. It is no less evident that this Contract may be broken or
violated. The Relation between a King and People has been
often compared to that between a husband and Wife & in
this Respect they resemble each other that there is a contract necessarly implyed in both. It is of no consequence
how the Match was made up whether from mutual liking

and inclination or by the authority of Parents, or even if it was begun by a Rape, as soon as the Relation is constituted the obligations necessarily follow. and the parties are bound by contract to each other.

5   If it should be asked when this Contract was made, the Answer was obvious, The Political Contract which Constitutes a State was made when the State began to exist, & continues untill the State be dissolved, & this contract may continue firm under various Revolutions & Forms of
10   Government. The contract between a Particular King or civil Magistrate & his People began when he began to be King or Magistrate & continues while he excercises that office. When he violates the essential Obligations of a King which he came under by taking that Office he breaks the
15   Contract.

Although the Obligation of a King to do the Duty of a King must necessarily commence from the time of his taking that Character upon him; so the Obligation of the people to
2/II/10,4v subjection must commence from the time of their / taking
20   the Character of his Subjects. But there are different degrees of Subjection to a Prince. A Stranger that lives in Brittain is Subject in a certain Degree to the King of Brittain & to the British Laws which regard aliens. But a native Britton is subject in a Different Degree. Even of British People on⟨e⟩
25   Man may be under very different Obligations from another. A Privy counsellor or a Man who has taken the Oath of Allegiance may have different Obligations from a Man who barely acquiesces in the Government submitting to the Laws and paying his taxes without binding himself to defend the
30   King & to Support his Tittle.

The Case of Subjects under a Usurped Government or conquered. A Title begun by Usurpation or Force may become valid as a Marriage begun by a Rape may be. Or a Treaty of Peace to which a People submit onely to avoid a
35   greater Evil.

Remarks on D Humes Essay on the Original Contract.

The Divine Right the Same in Borgia or in Angria as in Elizabeth. Hume.[10] Strange that an Act of Mind supposed
40   to be formed by every Man should be unknown to all.[11]

The Allegiance of a Man in a forreign Country still claimed by his Native Prince.[12] Moral Duties are either such as Men are impelled to by some natural propensity Or are

performed from a Sense of Obligation when we consider
the Necessities of Human Society. Justice & fidelity to promises as well as Allegiance belong to the last Class and it is in
Vain to found Allegiance upon Promise.[13] No other Standard of Morals but General Opinion.[14]

In an Absolute Monarchy where the Throne is vacant it
belongs to the first Occupant.[15]

Mr. Hume acknowledges that our Obligation to allegiance
has the same foundation as our obligation to be faithfull to
our promises. Why are we bound to observe a Promise? Because their would be no living in Society without fidelity to
promises. For the same Reason we are bound to submit to
Government.[16] Mr. Hume affirms that in all Questions that
respect Morals as well as in those that respect Criticism
there is no other Standard but general opinion.

QUIBUS MODIS CONTRAHITUR OBLIGATIO.[17]

Ex Contractu, Quasi ex Contractu Ex Maleficio vel quasi
ex Maleficio. Hence it appears that every Obligation which
a man Contracts voluntarly is a Contract. Contract all obligations arising from Voluntary Actions

The Origin of Government
Quasi Contract the same with tacit Contract[18]
Government older than Contract
The force of Contracts smal in rude Ages
The Question How one comes to be King
A Tacit Contract Revokeable
Contracts do not bind posterity
Kingly Government not the first
Some men formed to be Rulers some to be Slaves.

Jurisprudence Part 3

1766 APR 24

We come now to the third and last part of Natural Jurisprudence which treats of the Rights and Obligations arising
from the Political State, or the State of Civil Government.
By a Civil Government we understand the Uunion of a Nation or of 〈a〉 Great Number of Men under the same Laws
and Government for the Sake of Common Utility. To the
Body thus united the Romans gave the Name of Civitas or
Res publica. Before we enter upon particulars in this part
of Jurisprudence it is proper to distinguish it from the Science of Politicks, and this is the more necessary because
most writers on Jurisprudence have confounded this part of
Jurisprudence with the Science of Politicks. This is particularly the case with Dr Hutchison who employs some of the
Chapters that follow entirely on Questions that belong to
politicks and not to Morals. These therefore we shall entirely pass over leaving the Subjects treated in them to be
considered in their proper place in Our System of Politicks.[1]
All Questions belonging to Jurisprudence are Questions
concerning Right and wrong. In the last part of Jurisprudence particularly we enquire: What the duties of the Citizens are towards the State in general, towards the Magistrate or towards their fellow citizens. In this part of
Jurisprudence therefore as well as in all the rest, the Rules
of Right and wrong are determined by the Judgment of our
Moral Faculty. And those Moral Axioms which we spoke of
in the General part of Ethicks are the foundation of all our
Reasoning. Politicks is a quite different Science and built
upon a different foundation. The intention of this Science
is to shew from what Causes the Different Kinds of Civil
Government Whether Despotick Monarchical Aristocratical
Democratical take their Rise how they are preserved or De-

stroyed, What Effects they produce with Regard to Liberty
National Riches Commerc Learning Morals & Religion. War
Conquest and what Constitution of them is best adapted to
produce those Effects whether Good or Bad. We do not
therefore in Politicks any more than in Mathematicks or in
Physicks Enquire what is right or what is wrong either in the
Conducts of States or in that of Individuals. We enquire
from what causes Political Events do arise. And what Political Constitutions are most adapted to produce certain Effects or promote certain Ends. And in this Science we Reason not from Moral Axioms but from Axioms of a quite
Different Nature which we shall afterwards Explain.[2] /

8/IV/9,1v   Having thus distinguished that part of Jurisprudence
which treats of the Rights and Obligations belonging to the
Political State from the Science of Politicks, we proceed to
the consideration of the former. It is usual with those who
have treated of this part of Jurisprudence to begin it with
pointing out the causes that induced men at first not onely
to unite in families, but to form those larger Unions which
we call States or Civil Governments.[3] Distinction between
Society & Political Union. Men in a State of Natural Liberty
have no Superior upon Earth. They are accountable for
their Conduct onely to God and their Own Consciences.
They have the Absolute disposal of their own Property as
well as their Actions, and are bound by no Law but by the
Laws of Nature. Whereas every Citizen or Member of a
State is bound by the laws of that State as well as by the Laws
of Nature he subjects himself, his Property, his Family, his
Life itself to the Laws and to the Judicatures of the State. /

8/IV/10,1r   There can be no civil Government whatsoever which does
not in some degree abridge the liberty of those who live under it. Now the Love of Liberty is so natural to mankind that
there must be some considerable inducement to engage
them to give up their Natural Liberty & to subject themselves to laws and taxes. and be bound to that submission
and allegiance which is due to the civil Powers. There is
nothing which men desire more earnestly than independance and it is not to be supposed that any man will subject
himself to the will of others and submit his actions to their
8/IV/9,1v   controul without some urgent cause. / Now as the Love of
Liberty is, and justly ought to be very powerfull in the human kind, there ought to be very powerfull Inducements to
engage Men to give up their natural Liberty and to submit

to the yoke of Laws and civil Policy. What these inducements were or might have been is now to be examined.

But here two very different Questions present themselves
which have not been sufficiently distinguished by writers on
this Subject. The first is 1 What really and in Fact was and
must have been the Origin of the Various States and Civil
Governments that have been established. Or what reasons
did actually induce those who first framed them to enter
into this political Union. The second Question is What
Might justly induce men sufficiently enlightened, and acquainted with the Effects that may be produced by Civil
Government to enter into this State. We shall consider these
Questions separately.[4]

To the first question. 1 Not necessity. / If we should suppose a ships crew to lose their master & mate upon a voyage.
They will very naturally chuse a master and submit themselves and their ship to his direction because it is absolutely
necessary to their preservation that they should be under
some government. If they should be cast away upon some
unknown Island or coast, and found it necessary for their
common safety either against wild beasts, or savage inhabitants, to keep united they would still chuse a leader and
submit to his command. But if they should be cast upon
some desart Island where every man could provide for his
own Subsistence independant of the rest; their political
union would probably cease, and every man would chuse to
live after his own way. Nor indeed does there seem to be
any need for a political Union in such a case if all of them
were wise and good and had plenty of Subsistance. Men
may enjoy the pleasure of mutual conversation they may
trafick with one another they may do mutual good offices
or unite their strength and council upon occasion in order
to promote any common good without being under any
common political Government. And if they are just & human and peaceable and wise they may live happily together
without any common superior. Thus in all ages many tribes
have lived without laws and without Government. And thus
most of the nations in North America live at this day, unless
when they make war upon any of their Neighbours. /

Nor can it be justly said that the worst political Government is preferable to the best state of Natural Liberty.[5] But
The advantages of mens uniting their Strengths & Council
in any common End obvious. When a Number are engaged

in some design there must be some Union in War there must be some Government and Subordination.

When a number of Men have any common Interest to pursue which requires the United Operation and force of all. Some one of them of distinguished Wisdom and Authority proposes some Scheme or System by which the common Interest may be served. The rest will easily be led into a Scheme that tends to the benefit of the whole.

In carrying on such a Design to propose there must be some Order and Subordination. Some to Direct & superintend others to execute. When the Business is urgent and the Interest of all Concerned they will readily settle some plan for the Execution of it. Instances a Ships Crew that have lost their officers. at Sea. Wrecked. A Tribe of independent families pasturing their Cattle in Common. Invaded by powerfull Neighbours. / Hunters Joyning in pursuit of their Game. Such Associations would last as long as the causes of them lasted.

Men finding the benefite of them and accustomed to the Subordination which they occasioned would more easily submit to it and continue this Union beyond the duration of those Events that Caused it. Those who were leaders in such associations would endeavour to find reasons and furnish Causes for its continuance spurred by the love of Honour and Power as well as that of Publick Good.

It is the Interest of those who Govern Societys to preserve Peace and to support Justice among the Members.

The Same Persons who conducted Societies in their grand Project at first made Judges of their Controversies and private Rights.

Why and in what cases Kingly Governments were abolished and Aristocratical or Democratical Substituted in their Place.

The beginning of Government resembles that of the human Body as it is described by Anatomists. The most essential & important parts appear first the others gradually and in course of time are brought to light.

2 The Reasons that ought to induce men Sufficiently enlightened to prefer the Political State to that of Natural Liberty.

1 The advantages that may be derived from it. Compare an American Savage with a European 1 As to Accommodations of the Body, by the division of Labour. 2 The advance-

ment of Knowledge. 3 In the Redress of private Injuries and the Security of Property. 4 Defence from forreign Ennemies. 5 As it furnishes occasion for employing the most exalted powers & Capacities of the Mind. 5 For the Exercise of the most Enlarged Affections and Noblest Virtues.

Rousseau is a professed admirer of Robison Crusoe. Yet he prefers the Savage State to the civilized. There is not a book I know that paints more strongly or more justly the Advantage of the Civilized above the Savage. Robison owed all the Advantages he had over his Man Friday to this that he had the civilization of a common English Sailor, Friday was next to a Savage. From this Difference, the one not onely retains his superiority as a Master but is revered almost as a God by the other.[6]

2 That Men should live in Political Society seems to be the intention of Nature. 1 Because it is most advantageous 2 Because Some Parts of the human constitution point that way.

1 We are fitted to live under Government. Foxes & Lions are not so. Sheep and Cattle & Some Species of Dogs.

1[7] The different Capacities of men, fit them to be parts of one great Whole.

2 The Bulk of Men tame and naturally disposed to follow a leader.

3 The qualities which produce this Submission and Respect in the Generality of men are to be found in a few & are Wisdom Valour Power, especially if transmitted through a long Race of Ancestors. The Stubborn Spirit of Independency of the Canadians, as well as the Servility of the Asiaticks the Effect of Custom and Education.

4 The Love of ones Country a Natural Affection & can have no Exercise without a Political Union.

Corollaries

1 We may see in what Sense Political Government is a Divine & in what Respects it is a human Institution a κτισισ ανθρωπινη.[8]/

Cor 2 A good Form of Political Government is the greatest of all temporal Blessings to a Nation, & ought to be valued Accordingly. It is a very false Sentiment that Mr Pope expresses in these lines

> For forms of Government let fools Contest
> Whatee'r is best administred is best.[9]

A Bad form of Government will corrupt those who have the Administration of it, & make them bad when otherwise they might have been good. On the contrary a good form of Government is one of the most effectual means of making both Governors and the Governance good, or at least of making them act a good part, & restraining them from actions that would be detrimental to the publick.

Cor 3 The End of all Political Government is to preserve the Rights and to promote the felicity of the Governed. The Prince who considers his Subjects as the tools of his Ambition, and who conceives that their Rights and their happiness may be Sacrificed to his Glory is a Tyrant. These onely have the true Spirit of Government who conceive of their exalted Station as a Publick Trust, in the Execution whereof the common felicity of their Subjects ought to be their first care. Cor 4 The Political Union between Governours and Subjects, in what manner soever it might have begun or been continued must have the Nature and force of an Onerous Contract.[10] The Obligations are mutual. And as the Subjects are bound to Respect and honour those who are set over them to obey the Laws and to contribute their utmost endeavours to support the government: So on the other hand those who are in the Government whether Kings or Senators Representatives of the people or Magistrates are under no less strict obligation in their several Stations to make the best laws they can devise for the preservation of Justice and for promoting the publick good, to execute those laws strictly and impartially, & to take the most prudent and Effectuall means to defend their people from foreign Ennemies.

Cor 5 That is the best Form of Government which is best adapted to answer the end of Government. Cor 5 That which is the End of Government, to wit the Good of the Body politick, must be the measure of those Rights & obligations which arise from the political Union. All human Actions that are morally good or morally ill, and which of consequence we are obliged to do or to avoid, may be reduced to two classes. 1 They are either such as are intrinsically and essentially good or bad without regard to any end or any circumstance beyond the Action itself, Thus to love God to love mankind to be fair and honest in our dealings are things in their own nature good and approvable and there-

fore in their own nature obligatory on the other hand, Malice Envy falsehood Calumny, are in their own nature Evil &
8/IV/9,3r   have a moral Turpitude inseparably adhering to them / nor
can any End whatsoever Justify them. Or 2 Morally good or
5   ill Actions are such as are indifferent in themselves ⟨and⟩
have not any morall goodness or turpitude essentiall to
them but are good or ill according to the End which they
promote and for which they are performed. Thus to occupy
and to use in property those things which God has given to
10   Men in common is an action indifferent in its self, and so
far as it injures no man, nor tends to the hurt of human
Society we may lawfully and rightfully do it. But when the
appropriating things is hurtfull to society they must be common and occupation cannot give a right to them. The end
15   of Property being the common Good that must be the Measure of the Rights and Obligations that concern it. In eating
or drinking or in the Gratification of any natural appetite,
the End for which such Appetite was given us by Nature
must be the Measure of what is Right or wrong. The Rights
20   and obligations of the several Oeconomical Relations of
Husbands & Wives of Parents and Children of Masters and
Servants must be deduced from the ends for which those
Several Relations are appointed by Nature or voluntarly enterd into by Men. And as the Ends of those Relations are
25   the foundation of the Rights and Obligations arising from
them so they must be the Measure of those Rights and Obligations.

In like Manner Political Government & Administration
being in itself neither intrinsically good nor Evil. The Good
30   or Evil of it the Rights and obligations relating to it are to
be deduced from the End of it and to be measured by that
End.

The Right of Sovereigns to Respect & to Obedience in
things that are lawfull and are not contrary to the Publick
35   Good or to the Constitution. They are not to ⟨be⟩ obeyed in
things unlawfull. The Behaviour of Orte Governour of Bayonne when he received the orders of Cha 9 at the Parisian
Massacre, & of the Count de Tende, Charney & others.[11]
Where the Supreme Power is not limited by the Constitu-
40   tion it is still limited to things that may lawfully be done or
that have no inherent turpitude in them & to things that are
not destructive to the Society. The deeds of a Monarch con-

trary to the constitution are void and null. The Rights of the
Subjects to be governed according to the Constitution to defend their Rights against a general & violent Oppression.

5 When Shadrach Meshach & Abed-nego whom Nebu-
chadnezzar had set over the affairs of the Province of Babylon were reprehended by that proud Monarch for not
serving his Gods nor worshiping the Golden image he had
set up & peremptarly ordered to do so for the future under
the penalty of being cast into a burning fiery furnace. They
10 nobly Answered Be it known unto thee o King We will not
serve thy Gods nor worship the Golden Image thou hast set
up.[12]

When the Rulers of the Jews strictly forbad the Apostles
Peter & John to speak or teach any more in the Name of
15 Jesus. The Apostles made this answer. Whether it be right
to obey you rather than God Judge ye.[13] /

8/IV/9,3v The importance of Stating truly the Submission due to
the Sovereign Power. To Princes and to the People, to mankind in General.

20 The Opinion of Ancient Nations upon this Subject,
Greeks, Romans. How the Controversy came to be raised
and carried on in England. The Opinion of Grotius & Puffendorf & Hobbes. Of the high flyers in England of Hooker
Algernon Sidney Locke Hoadly. Contra Barclay Hobbes Fil-
25 mer Leslie Atterbury.[14]

The Sole End of Government the Good of the Society.

The Supreme power in doing Hurt to the Society Acts
without Authority, from God, Reason, or human Laws.

See Extracts from Vattel p.25 & c.[15] Active Obedience due
30 onely in things lawfull.

Passive Obedience What? Due in many cases where our
Rights are violated. Due wherever the publick good requires
it. The Example of Socrates.

Where Resistance is necessary to save a Nation from tyr-
35 rany it is not onely Lawfull but laudable & glorious.[16]

The Publick Safety the Supreme Law to Prince & People.

The Precepts of Scripture enjoyning Obedience are General Precepts which therefore admit of Exceptions.

They enjoyn Active Obedience no less than Passive
40 Forbid Resistance to Private Injuries no less than to those
of Princes. The Qualification of this Doctrine. The Causes
of Resistance ought to be great and Evident &c. All the certain and probable Consequences of it duly weighed. The

Evils arising from Resistance greater than those that arise from Suffering.

The Parental Authority not irresistible.[17]

This Doctrine does not encourage Rebelion, nor tend to disturb Government.

The Respect due to Government in speaking and writing. Abuse of the Liberty of the Press.

Grotius acknowledges that there are cases of extreme Necessity wherein it may be lawfull to resist the supreme Power. The case of David towards Saul and of the Maccabees he conceives as of this Nature.[18] And although he conceives that the Christian Institution binds its votaries more strongly to Submission to Government than the Law of Nature, yet he mentions seven Cases wherein he thinks resistance Lawfull even to Christians. And even Barclay the most strenuous assertor of the divine power of Kings agrees with him in several of these.[19] Puffendorf of the same Opinion.[20] Both seem to Give with one hand & give with the other. The Notion of kings deriving their Power immediately from God was says Bp Burnet at first advanced among protestants in opposition to the Popish Doctrine of Kings deriving their Power from the Pope or the Church, because it was commonly the Office of the Bishops to set the Crown upon their heads and to anoint them.[21]

No form of Government of Divine Authority. In what sense Kings derive their Power immediately from God.

The Safety Peace & Happiness of the Political Body the Supreme Law both to Rulers and Ruled.

Changes in a form of Government that hath been established & acquiesced in ought not to be made without very weighty Reasons.[22]

Every Good Man respects the Laws and Government of his Country, and this is one of the chief Securities of Government. /

8/IV/9,4r   Political Jurisprudence Regards first The Mutual Rights and Obligations of the Supreme Power and the Subject. These are grounded upon the Nature and end of the Political Union. Secondly. The Rights of a Political Body or
5   State both in Relation to other States and in Relation to individuals. This Second Part of Political Jurisprudence is that which ⟨is⟩ Properly called the Law of Nations as distinguished from the Law of Nature.[1]

See Addit Extracts from Vatel[2]
10   A Nation incorporated and united into one Political Body becomes by this Union and Incorporation a Moral Person. It has a publick Interest and good which it ought to pursue as every private man pursues his own private good. It has an Understanding and Will; it has Power even the United
15   force of the whole Society under the direction of its Magistrates which force as it may produce great Effects either good or bad ought to be governd by Reason and Right & be subject to Law, for the same Reason as the power and force of Individuals. Nations may do the like Moral Actions as in-
20   dividuals; they may enter into contracts Covenants or treaties they may plight the Publick faith and Come under various moral Obligations. They may possess & enjoy Rights real and Personal and may transfer Rights to others.[3]

The Nation is made up of individuals each of whom is
25   indispensibly obliged to regulate all his actions whether of a publick or private Nature according to the Laws of Nature. And therefore when thes individuals unite in one incorporate Body so as to have in a manner one Understanding one will one Active power, & thereby resemble one person this
30   political Person must be a moral Person and partake of the Nature of the individuals of which it is made up. If it were not so, every Political Society would be indeed a Leviathan or Wild Beast under no Law or obligation and it would be for the common Interest of mankind to destroy all such Po-

litical Unions as leagues in Iniquity. Political Bodies therefore or States are under the Same Obligation to regard [the]
each others Rights as individuals. And hence it follows that
the Law of Nations is in reality a very exact Copy of the Law
5   of Nature.[4] /
7/VII/21,1r   The Notion of some Minute Politicians that however men
in private life are bound by the Laws of Justice and Equity
yet it is impossible to govern States properly without sometimes transgressing the Rules of Justice. But as in private
10   Life nothing is more contrary to true Wisdom than cunning
and Deceits and the crafty man is often taken in his own
Snare and falls into the pit which he dug for others. The
same thing holds no less with regard to political Wisdom.
The Reputation of Justice and integrity in the Administra-
15   tion of a Nation is of the highest Moment in its transactions
with other Nations. On the contrary dark and crooked Politicks, always sink the credit of a Nation and make it suspected and hated.
        Cic de Leg. Nihil est quod adhuc de Republica dictum pu-
20   tem, et quo possim longius progredi, nisi sit confirmatum,
non modo falsum esse illud, sine injuria non posse, sed hoc
verissimum, sine summa Justitia Rempublicam regi non
posse.[5] /
8/IV/9,4r   As therefore we Divided the Duty of Individuals into that
25   which they Owe to God to themselves and to others we
might divide in the same Manner the duty of Nations or
States.[6] A State depends upon God no less than an individual and can prosper onely by his blessing and favour. National Blessings and National Calamities are dispensed by
30   the Providence of God, as we have Reason to believe with a
strict regard to their merit and demerit as a Nation. This is
agreable to all that we can judge of the moral Administration of the Supreme Being, it is confirmed by all that we
know of the History of Nations and it is agreable to the dec-
35   larations of the Sacred Writings.
        Therefore that Nations as Such Should Honour God, by
stated Acts of Devotion & Piety should implore his Blessing
upon their Councils, his aid and Succour in publick Dangers
and that they should humble themselves under his mighty
40   hand by Supplications Repentance & Reformation when
they are punished by publick Calamities. This is the voice of
8/IV/9,4v   Reason and Common Sense, And / has been so in all Ages
among Jews and Christians Heathens and Mahometans.

Nor can any man doubt of the Propriety of it who believes the World to be under the Administration of a Sovereign moral Governour. Good Morals in a Nation are the foundation of its Strength Courage Industry and publick Felicity. Virtue gives Power in an Individual it does so much more in an incorporate Body, For the Prudence temperance Fortitude Justice and humanity of the whole Body must be as it were the Sum or aggregate of those Virtue⟨s⟩ in individuals. Therefore as I have had occasion before to shew that a Rational Piety and Devotion towards God is the most powerfull motive to Virtue.[7] It necessarily follows that a State neglects one of its most essential Interests if it neglects Religion and leaves that altogether out of its Consideration.

It is a part of the Religious duty of a Nation to make such provisions as are proper for the Instruction of their People in Just and Rational Sentiments of God and of Virtue, and for their having Persons qualified for thes purposes and Times and Places appointed by publick Authority for the ends of Publick Instruction and Publick Worship.

The way in Which all Nations and States almost without Exception have discharged this Part of their Duty is by establishing some publick form of Religion by Law. with proper provisions for its Ministers and Service.

Whether there ought to be an established Religion, or if a State may be well Governed without it of Pensilvania.[8] On[e] the one hand there are many things in Religion in which people are easily misled.[9]

There can be no form of Religion that has not its proper Articles of Belief as well as its Rites. If we should with the Athenians erect an Altar to the Unknown God,[10] the Rites by which we honour him and the Worship we pay to him must suppose some belief some Opinions concerning him. He that worships Jupiter or Bacchus must believe that there are Deities to whom those Names Belong. A Religion therefore without any Articles of Belief is a meer Chimera or rather a contradiction in Terms. There must necessarily be some belief or another either expressed or manifestly employed in the nature of its institutions. This ought the rather to be observed because some ingenious Authors have represented it as a piece of profound Wisdom in heathen Lawgivers, that though they established a form of Religion in their several Commonwealths yet this Religion consisted wholly of Rites and Observations it had no Credenda or Ar-

ticles of Faith so that any man whatever his opinion was
might conform to it.[11] This is a vain Imagination equally
contrary to Reason and to Fact. A Man who believed concerning Jupiter what the Priests and the Poets taught and
what was employed in the established form of the Worship
of that Deity might be a sincere and devout Worshiper. But
the man who performed this worship while he believed all
that was taught about Jupiter to be fable and Fiction must
certainly be guilty of the grossest Hypocrisy or the most impious profanation of all Religion. The onely Reason why
Christians could not joyn in heathen Worship was that
they held such Opinions as were inconsistent with that
Worship. /

As it is evident therefore that there must be Articles of
Belief in an established Religion either expressed or implyed as well as Modes of Worship.

The Articles of Belief in an Established Religion ought
not to be matters of doubtfull disputation about which the
best & wisest of the Subjects differ nor ought they to be matters of small importance to real Virtue and Piety. And all
the Institutions of an established religion ought, as far as
possible in a consistence with the End of that Establishment
to be adapted ⟨to⟩ the main body of the Nation, even those
who may differ in opinion from one another in many
points. Were it possible to frame a Model of established Religion in which every good & pious Man in the Nation could
joyn it were desireable. But this seems to be impossible. A
Christian and a Heathen may joyn in some Acts of Religion.
Thus Peter the Great Czar of Muscovy & the Emperor of
China when they settled the boundaries of their Respective
Empires & entered into a League they mutually Swore to
the observation of it by The God that Made Heaven and
Earth.[12] It appears plainly impossible however in consistence with the End of an established Religion that it should
contain nothing wherein some even good and pious men
may differ. The established Religion ought to undergo such
alterations as may make it to correspond with the alterations
of Opinion in the Generality of the Nation. Although such
alterations ought not to be made rashly nor without mature
deliberation, and discussion of the reasons upon which they
are grounded.[13] So various, nay so absurd and capricious
are often the opinions of Men, especially in more enlightened ages that a Legislator might almost as soon hope to

7/VII/23,1r

make one coat fit all his Subjects as one Religion. Therefore
it is necessary in every State, that there be a Tolleration for
those whose sentiments do not allow them to joyn in the National Religion, while at the same time they may have no
notions of Religion that are inconsistent with their being
good Subjects and good members of the Society.

The History of Tolleration

There may be Sects that are not tollerated: Suppose a Sect
whose Religion obliged them to offer human Sacrifices.[14]
Whether a state may punish impiety and disrespect to the
established Religion. Whether it may inflict penalties for
maintaining pernicious doctrines and Opinions? /

Instances that Dominion is founded in Grace. That no
obedience is due to Magistrates that are not of our Sect or
Religion. Suicide. History of Persecution for Religious
Opinions.

For resolving these Questions the following Principles
may be of use. 1 A State may lay restraints upon Actions of
Men that are hurtfull though not criminal. As upon Madmen persons infected with the Plague Fanaticks. History of
the Flagellantes.[15]

2 A Crime implies a malus animus and nothing ought to
be punished as a Crime where there is no Reason to conclude a malus animus.[16]

Whether the civil Power may punish Men for immorali-
ties in Selfgovernment where no injury is done to our
neighbour. Whatever impairs the Morals, enervates the
mindes, or bodies of the Members of a State is hurtfull to
the State and as every individual so every political Body has
right and is obliged to use its endeavours to preserve all its
Members in that Sound State which fits them for being most
usefull to the Society.[17] The duty of a State to promote Industry Agriculture Arts and Science. To provide for the Necessities of the Poor. to Punish idleness Riot and Dissipation.
To manage the Publick Revenue to provide Ships & Har-
bours and all the Implements of forreign Trade to drain
Marches make highways Bridges Canals Fortresses. To polish the Manners as well as preserve the Morals of its Subjects. To maintain the Respect due to Magistrates Parents
Seniors persons of Superior Rank.[18] Self Government in a
State, relates either 1 to the Constitution which it ought to
preserve & improve or 2 To the Subjects whom it ought to
train and Govern, to provide for and to protect. For these

5

10

7/VII/23,1v

15

20

25

30

35

40

ends a State ought to know itself. its advantages and disadvantages, & to know its neighbour States.

To attend carefully to the Glory of the Nation.

The Dominium Eminens of the State over the Lives & Property of the Subjects.[19] /

5

7/VII/23,2r This belongs to the Self Government of states.

It may be proper however to observe more particularly
10 the Nature of that Interest which the State has in the private
Property of its Subjects whether moveable or immoveable.
The State not onely ought to defend the property of its Subjects against all who invade it, but has also a Right to Use it
in as far as the publick Good Requires. When a Mans per-
15 sonal Service and even his life itself is [at the] due to his
country when its Safety demands it, it would be very odd to
imagine that his Country should not have right to demand
a farthing of his Money without his Consent. In a State the
good and Safety of the whole is the very End of the Political
20 Union as we have often said, and therefore must be the supreme Law to which both the Life and the property of In-
7/VII/23,2v dividuals must submit / as far as the Publick good Requires.
This Power which the State has over the property of Individuals is called by Writers on the Law of Nations Domi-
25 nium Eminens. It is by virtue of this eminent Dominion that
a State may take the Estate of a Subject for some Use, as to
build a fortress for the defence of the Country. Or may lay
it under water to hinder the Approach of an Enemy. It is by
virtue of this Eminent Dominion that when a town is like to
30 be besiged by the enemy the Suburbs are burnt or levelled
that they may not favour the enemys approach. By this
same Right an Army demands the Use of horses and Wag-
ons of the Subjects and their necessary Subsistence. By virtue of this Power the Parliament of great Britain lately au-
35 thorized a Canal for an inland Navigation betwixt the forth
and Clyde, which must take away part of the Property of
many individuals nor is their consent required to this measure. The Same Parliament impowered the City of Glasgow
to enlarge the new Church Yard & to build an Exchange
40 behind the town house.[20]

There are two things necessary to justify such Exercise of
the Dominium eminens over the Property of an Individual
1 That the publik good require it 2 That the individual be

indemnified for whatever property is taken from him to
serve the Publick. Another Exercise of the Dominium Eminens is when the State Imposes taxes upon the Subject for
the Service of the Publick.²¹ The necessary Expences of the
Government must be raised one way or other and if there is
not a fixed Revenue appropriate for that purpose the Subjects must raise what is necessary for the service of the State
in War and Peace.

The Publick Service is a Negotium utile gestum²² for
every Subject. Justice here Requires that the Subjects have
no unnecessary burthens laid upon them. That the publick
Money be frugally managed and that taxes be made as equal
as possible. But there does not appear to me a Shaddow of
Reason why the Consent of a Subject should be necessary to
his bearing an equal Share of the publick burdthen which
the service of the State demands.

An Error of Mr Locke on this Subject Second Treatise
concerning Government § 138.²³ Adopted by the Americans
& Ld Chatam²⁴

Taxes how far Benevolences in England.

The Right of private property in cases of Necessity yields
to common Utility even in the State of Nature, much more
in political Society.²⁵/ As the Right of Property was gradually
extended when men were more enlightned, & might justly
be extended as far as is consistent with publick good. So the
right of Civil Government has been graduall extended. At
first reaching onely to heads of families, afterwards to all
the members of the family. Laws of Succession of Wills, of
Prescription. Extension of the Rights of Empire agreable to
the law of Nations as far as consistent with the good of Mankind

Whether Territory acquired by occupation by the colonies
of a State comes under the Eminent Dominion of that State.

A.²⁶ The Laws of Colonization in ancient and in Modern
times very Different. In Ancient Times a Colony commonly
became a new State and resembled a Child that is foris fa-
miliate.²⁷ So that no other Connection remained between
them but that of alliance and Friendship, grounded upon
the Relation that was between them. The Colonies conceived themselves obliged to regard the Honour & Interest
of the State from which they sprung next to their own. to
Respect it as their Parent & to take its part in Wars wherein
it was engaged. The Mother Country on the Other hand

owed a reciprocal Aid and Protection to its Colonies, but the Colony was not subject to the Mother Country. It established a Form of Government for itself. & was to all intents an Independent State. In modern Times the manner of planting Colonies is quite different. A Colony planted abroad is still subject to the Mother Country they still enjoy all the Rights of Subjects of the State & therefore of course are Subject to the Legislature of the Mother Country. Those who reside in our Colonies in America are not Aliens as a french Man or a Duch Man is: They are intitled to all the Rights and privileges of British subjects. They may succeed to land in great Britain by Inheritance by Disposition or Sale or Testament as any Subject of Britain may. And in consequence of any Succession in Land may vote for members of Parliament or be members of Parliament as any other British Subject may be. The Necessary Consequence of this is that they should be subject to the Legislature of Great Brittain. /

7/VII/23,1v   Constitution Protection Training Improvement of Arts & Sciences & in Virtue Riches Trade Defence.[28] /

7/VII/23,3v   *Self Government in a State*

As every individual Person desires & ought to desire his own happiness and Perfection and Honour so likewise a State ought to take care of its own interest & Honour and to desire that its Condition may be the best the happiest & most honourable it can attain. Nay I think it may be fairly allowed that the Duty of self Preservation and Self Love in a State ought to ⟨be⟩ cherished more and indulged to a higher Degree than Self love in an individual. A Good Man loves his Neighbour as himself & can hardly be placed in any Situation of Life wherein he does not employ more of his time and thought and Labour for the benefit of others than for his own. Yet we cannot but acknowledge that a State ought to have more concern for its own happiness and improvement and bestow its Labour more for that End, than for the good of any other State whatsoever. A Man may Love his Friend as much as he loves himself. But we must allow that the first concern of every State ought to be for itself, that is for the happiness of its Subjects. It is right and Laudable that it should prefer the happy Condition of its own Subjects to the good of any other State. As every

British Man would and ought to prefer the Interest and
Glory of G Britain to that of France Spain or Germany so
this Patriotick Spirit which is commendable in every individual is no less so when it appears in the publick Councils and
5   Government of the Nation, & we might very Justly blame
those who are at the helm of publick affairs if they did not
make the interest and Honour of the Nation their first and
chief Object.[29]
     States are less dependant on each other & less connected
10   than individuals.[30] /

7/VII/23,1v   *Behaviour of States to other States*

     This as well as the Duties of individuals to each other may
15   be Reduced to two heads Humanity & Justice.
     The Duties of Humanity more Necessary in individuals
than in States & therefore more practiced. Enlarge. But
they are no less amiable and Honourable in States than in
individuals. May be expressed by benefactions to the Dis-
20   tressed. Preserving peace and composing Differences
among other States. Aiding the injured and oppressed. Q
Elizabeth aided the Dutch & Henry 4.[31] Treating well the
Subjects of forreign States granting Protection to the Per-
secuted. Hugonots in England. In Holland. Honouring and
25   Rewarding Merit in Forreigners. Being forward to promote
discoveries and improvements that may be usefull to Mankind in General. Q Eliz. Aiding the Dutch against the Span-
iards, & Henry 4 against the League. The French Mensu-
ration of the Earth. Europe concurring in observing the
30   Transit of Venus.[32] /
7/VII/23,2r   The Parl. of England voting 100,000 for relief of the Sufferers by the Earthquake at Lisbon.[33] The project of a Perpetual Peace by Henry 4 and Q Eliz.[34] The protection given
by O Cromwel to forreign Protestants. his Project of Uniting
35   them in a Protestant League.[35] Premiums for Discovery of
the Longitude.[36]
     There may be a Generosity and Magnanimity in States
that would give them a Distinction among other States no
less Honourable & Glorious than those Virtues give to In-
40   dividuals. Justice. If States ought to behave to each other
with humanity & Generosity they are under a much Stricter
Obligation to behave with Justice. The Rights of States as of
Individuals are either Real or Personal. Real Rights are the
Right they have to what belongs to them in Property. Their

Land Territory with the Lakes Rivers bays and Seas belonging to it. Their Ships Fortresses and the Goods of their Subjects. It is here to be observed that immoveable property in
one State may be the property of the Subject of another
State. Thus an English man may have an Estate in France.
In this Case he must hold the Land of the Crown of France
as it belongs to the Domain of France. It must be subject to
the Laws of France nor can it be said to belong to the British
State though it belongs to a British Subject. And the onely
Right the British Government has is to see that its Subject
be not wronged. But with regard to goods which the Subjects may have in forreign Countrys these the State as well
as the private proprietor have a real right in.[37] Property in
a State as well as in an individual may be original, that is it
may be got by occupation or produced by the Labour and
skill of the Subjects. Or it may be derived from a former
proprietor by donation, Purchase, Testament or Succession.
Equality of Nations.[38]

The Law of Nations regarding the Property of States
whether original or derived is so much the Same with the
Laws of Nature respecting the Property of Individuals that
it is unnecessary to repeat what has been already said, in
treating of the Laws of Nature.[39] /

7/vii/23,4v   War Defined Certatio per Vim.[40]

Distinguished into Private & Publick. The Publick 1 into
Solemn & less Solemn 2 Into civil and forreign.[41]

Private War 1 in the State of Natural Liberty. 2 In the
Political State how far allowable 1 In Defence of ones Life
when unjustly assaulted. 2 In Defence of ones House when
thieves attack it in the Night. Si nox furtum faxit, si im ali-
quis occisit, jure caesus esto 12 Tab.[42] Duels unjustifiable.
Their Origin Progress. Attempts to discourage them unsuc-
cessful In order to this Provision for a redress of those Injuries which are called affronts or insults. The Challenger
to be degraded from the rank of a Gentleman. and rendered incable of publick office.[43]

Publick War made onely by those haveing soveraign
Power, in the british Government by the King.[44]

OF THE IMPLEMENTS OF WAR[45]

The levy of Troops. The ancient way of enlisting Troops.
Modern Way by enlisting volunteers. By pressing Men. Can
Eclesiasticks plead Exemption?[46] Pay of Troops Lodging.

Hospitals Barracks & Encampments. Hospitals for invalids
Hire of Forreign Troops. Is it lawfull for a Man to engage
as a Soldier in forreign Service? Yes. Enlisting in a forreign
State, must require the consent of the State, & moreover
that none be enlisted but volunteers. Military Oath & Mu-
tiny Laws. Military Discipline introduced by the Swiss says
Matchiavel. Improved by the King of Prussia.[47] The Power
of a General or Commander in Chief. His Engagements ultimate in the Operations of the War. in Capitulations giving
Hostages &c But he has not tittle to end the War by a peace.
Instance of the Roman Defeat at Caudae.[48]
       Causes of War. Reasons. Motives. Pretexts[49]
       War is Offensive or Defensive
       Two things Required to justify the Agressor in a War.
That it be just, & that it be Prudent.[50] When the injurious
party offers just Reparation, & it is refused, the injured becomes an unjust agressor.[51] The Prudential Motives to War
belong to Politicks rather than Jurisprudence.[52] /

8/iv/8,1r   May 2 1766

       We have considered the Rights which the different Parts
of a Political body or State have with regard to one another,
and began to enter upon the Rights that are competent to
different States in their Intercourse with each other. These
we observed are very much the same with the Rights which
different individuals have with regard to each other in natural Liberty. A State once incorporated resembles a Moral
Agent, is capable of entering into Engagements and Contracts, and is under a Sacred obligation of fullfilling its Engagements and of behaving justly fairly and honestly with
other States. It ought in the first place to attend to its own
Safety and felicity, and as far as is consistent with that to act
with humanity and benevolence to other States to relieve the
indigent to assist the weak to take part with the injured, and
to be ready to reconcile differences and preserve peace and
tranquillity among its neighbouring States.
       States as well as individuals ought to be actuated not
merely by Selfish principles but also by benevolent ones towards other States, especially with those that are more near
to it or more connected with it in trade and Commerce.
       The Parliament of Great B acted a Noble part in voting
100,000 for the Sufferers in Lisbon when that Capital was
reduced to rubish by an Earthquake.[53]

There is a common interest of mankind that ought to be regarded by every State as well as the particular interest of its own Body. It were to be wished indeed that this disinterested regard to the common good of Mankind were more common in States, and that they had more enlarged views which might lead them to the noble ambition of being benefactors to the human kind. Some publick designs of this head that are imputed to Henry 4 of France and to Oliver Cromwell, will with impartial posterity raise the Glory of those heroes to a higher pitch than all their Victories. Vattel page 125.[54]

Plans and Prospects for the advancement of arts & Sciences very honourable to a State.

When one State receives injuries from another they are thought intollerable and of which no redress can be obtained by amicable disceptation or by the interposition of Mediators as such states have no common Superior these must in single cases have recourse to War. And every State has Right to defend it self from atrocious injuries and to seek the redress of them by force when all other methods fail.

1 Not to hurt other States by Encroaching upon their Territory. Obstructing their traffick injuring their Subjects. or Ambassadors. Exciting Seditions. Aiding their Enemies. Protecting Rebells or Attrocious Criminals

    2 Keeping faith.[55]

    3 Making Reparation for injuries done by the State or its Subjects.[56]

    4 Removing just ground of Suspicion. when Given Means of terminating Differ.[57]

    1 Amicable Disceptation.

    2 Mediation of a third party.

    3 Arbitration of a Judge.

Means of redressing injuries.[58]

    1 Lex Talionis commended by some; often unjust and Barbarous.

    2 Retortion.

    3 Reprisals. Last war with France begun by Reprisals.[59]

Public Funds not Subject to Reprisals nor private debts. Ships at Sea the chief Subject. Permitted only to the State or Letters of Marque given by the State.[60]

A declaration of War sometimes lawfull when Reprisals would be unjust, before declaration.[61]

A war between two independent States is by Writers on Jurisprudence called Bellum Solemne & Bellum publi-cum.[62]

A State of War is far from dissolving all the obligations of States to one another. Tho they are Enemies they are Still human Creatures, and there is a right and a wrong in conduct towards ennemies. The End of war is to defend our Rights to redress our wrongs. And War can give no license to any thing that is not conducive to the End of it. In Sollemn War both parties pretend to have Right on their Side, and although it is impossible that both can be in the Right, yet both may think themselves in the Right, and therefore each while it defends its own Right against its Enemy ought to treat that Enemy not as one who has laid aside all regard to Right but as one who injures them from prejudice and false Opinions of his Right. See Add. Extracts from Vattel B.[63]

The just Causes of War we have considered under private Jurisprudence for they are the same between individuals in natural Liberty & between States.[64] We have likewise considered the rules that ought to be observed in carrying on War.[65] The violation of faith given to an Enemy poisoned Weapons, cruelty to Captives.[66] The Duke of Cumberland's behaviour to a french Officer when wounded at Detingen.[67] Behaviour of a French advanced party t⟨o⟩ some English a hunting.[68] Of the English to the French Prisoners in England in the last war.[69] /

In a war between two States, a third State may where the injustice evidently appears on one Side espouse the Cause of the injured, as a third person may & ought to assist an innocent man when unjustly attacked. But when it does not appear in which Side the right lies, other States ought to observe a neutrality if they do not they make themselves parties in the war and may be accounted his Ennemies against whom they act.[70] It is not a breach of Neutrality to furnish troops to a State in consequence of treaties formerly made without any view to the War in which it is now engaged.[71] It is no breach of Neutrality to carry on commerce with one of the parties at war.[72] The Case of Contraband Goods.[73] Moveables taken from an Enemy in War may be Bought by a Neutral state but Territory ought not untill it is ceded by a treaty of peace.[74]

Capture of the trading Ships of a hostile Nation allowed. and making prisoners of the Crew. Striping or plundering the Men dishonourable. Captives not to be considered as Criminals but as men fighting in Defence ⟨of⟩ their Country.[75] Making inroads into an Enemies Country and laying it under Contribution, as well as Seizing every thing belonging to the State allowed.[76] Pillage not allowed.[77] Acts of hostility in a Neutral State not allowed. Nor marching armies thro' it without Leave.[78]

Ransoming of Captives. Cartel. Release upon Oath.[79]

Real Rights and Servitudes of a Neutral State upon a conquered territory not to be violated by the conqueror.[80] Precedency of Nations.[81] Honour of the Flag.

How far a State may give protection to the refugees of another State?[82]

Leagues & treaties not to be broke on the pretence of fear or force.[83]

The Rights of Ambassadours. A State is not obliged to permit an ambassador to reside with them, tho' it is commonly allowed. Their immunities & those of their Retinue.[84]

Of the dissolution of the political Union of a part of a State with the whole of the dissolution of a State.[85]

Laws of War with regard to the enemy while in Arms. To be killed or taken prisoners or put to flight.

Treatment of Prisoners, of the wounded.

Ships of the Enemy lawfull prize & the crew Captives.

An army in an Enemies Country.

Behaviour to those who are not in Arms.

Women and Children.[86]

What Money or Magazines belong to the publick lawfull prize.[87]

Contributions sometimes raised. Hostages taken for their payment.

Passage through a Neutral territory.

Hostilities in a Neutral territory.

Whether we may Use the Means of Poison or Assasination for taking away the life of our enemy.

Laws of War with regard to the Goods of the Enemy moveable and immoveable. Treaties between hostile Nations Made before the War. During the War.[88]

In a Conquered Province the Conquereor acquires onely the Rights of the conquered.[89]

Real Rights belonging to a third State as well as the estates
of individuals remain active.[90]

Civil War

5   a Tumult
       a Sedition
       an Insurrection.[91] /

7/VII/22,1r Def. of War. Private & Publick Its Lawfullness

Private 1 in the State of Nat Liberty
             2 in Political Society unlawfull Except in Self Def-
                ence
15   Duels Their History Origin. Reasons against them.

Public Wars Less Solemn against Pirates Robers Rebellious
Subjects

Solemn. Between Sovereign States onely.
20

Implements of War

       Levy of Troops. Hire of Ships or Troops. Lawfull to en-
       gage in forreign Service in a Just War.[92] Volunteers pressed
25   Land Sea Men.[93] None Exempted by the Law of Nations in
       Cases of Necessity.[94]

Enlisting in a forreign Country.

30   Power of a General or Governour of a fort.

Causes of War. Who are entitled to carry Arms.

A Ship or a Town may defend itself against a privateer.

35   Obligations of Allies. Neutral States.

Quibus modis solvitur Obligatio.[95]

       1 Performance
       2 Compensation
40   3 Remission or Acceptilation
       4 Mutual Consent
       5 Breach of Faith on one Side
       6 Assignation

7   Confusion
8   Death /

Septr 1766 Read The Laws of Nations; or Principles of
5   the Law of Nature applied to the Conduct and affairs of
       Nations and Sovereigns by M de Vattel Translated from the
       French Lond 1760 Newbery & c 2 Vol 4° 1 Vol 254 pages 2^d
       170.[96]
       In the Preface he endeavours to shew that the Law of Na-
10   ture as it[s] respects the conduct of Independent States &
       Sovereigns to each other ought to be treated as a distinct
       Science from that Law of Nature which respects the conduct
       of Individuals to each other. That the Baron de Wolfius was
       the first who had treated of the Law of Nations as a distinct
15   Science. But his treatise on this Subject is dependent on all
       those which the Same Author has wrote on the law of Na-
       ture. In order to read and Understand it it is necessary to
       have studied sixteen or seventeen volumes in 4to which pre-
       ceeded it.[97] Besides the Baron has wrote in a Geometrical
20   form and Method which gives a dryness to his work. Our
       Author therefore has drawn from him what he thought
       best, & followed his own plan, & in several things differs
       from Wolfius in his Opinions.

25   PRELIMINARIES

       A Nation is a body politick, united to gether to procure
       mutual safety and advantage by its Union. Such a Body by
       this Union becomes a Moral Person has its proper affairs
30   and interests, its Understanding and Will its Rights and ob-
       ligations. Before the establishment of Political Societies men
       lived together in the state of Nature, free and independent
       of one another. This blessing of natural freedom men could
       not lose without their consent (or fault). But Citizens sur-
35   render a part of their priviledges to the state or Sovereign
       in consideration of the Security and advantages they reap
       from the political Union. A state being made up of individ-
       uals who are subject to the Laws of Nature, their Union can-
       not free them from the obligation of observing those laws.
40   The common will being the result of the Wills of the Citi-
       zens remains subject to the Laws of Nature and is obliged to
       respect them in all its proceedings. But as a state or civil
       Society is a subject very different from an individual of the

human Race, in many cases it will have different obligations
and rights. This makes it proper to consider the law of Nature respecting individuals, and the Law of Nations as distinct Sciences.[98]

5   There is a necessary Law of Nations to which all are necessarily subject which is grounded upon the principles of
Right and wrong. By which lawfull Conventions & treaties
between Nations are distinguished from those that are unlawful & innocent Customs from those that are barbarous
10   and unjust. There is also a voluntary Law of Nations
grounded upon Consent express or tacit between Nations,
which binds onely those that have consented.[99] /

4/III/23c,2r   All states are by Nature free and independent of one another. Yet there may be several degrees of dependance
15   which leave to a State its Sovereignty. It may engage in an
unequal Alliance with a more powerfull State for protection
it may pay tribute it may be feudatory. without losing its
Sovereignty. Two states may have the same Prince & yet be
each of them sovereign within itself. The king of Naples
20   pays Homage to the Pope for his Kingdom.[100]

p 20

A king of France does not revenge the injuries of the
Duke of Orleans. a wise Saying of Lewis 12.[101]

25
        25

The kings of Danemark have formerly condescended by
solemn treaties to refer to those of Sweden, the differences
that might arise between them and their Senate. This the
30   Kings of Sweden have also done with regard to those of
Danemark. The Princes of Neufchatel established in 1406
the Canton of Bern the Judge and perpetual Arbitrator of
their Disputes. Thus also according to the Spirit of the Hel-
vetick Confederacy, the entire body takes Cognisance of the
35   troubles that arise in any of the confederated States, though
each of them is truly sovereign and independent.[102]

Those Governours of places who refused to execute the
barbarous orders of Cha 9 at the famous St Bartholomew
Massacre have been universally praised and the Court did
40   not dare to punish them at least openly. "Sire,⟨"⟩ said the
brave Orte, Governour of Bayonne, in his letter, ⟨"⟩I have
communicated your Majestys command to your faithfull inhabitants and warriors in the Garrison, and I have found

there onely good citizens and brave Soldiers but not one
hangman: Therefore both they and I most humbly beseech
your Majesty to be pleased to employ our Arms & lives in
things that are possible, however hazardous they may be,
5   and we will exert our selves to the last drop of our blood.⟨"⟩
The Count de Tende Charney and others replied to those
who brought them the Orders of the Court, that they had
too great a Respect for the King to believe that such Barbarous Orders came from him.[103]

10

33

No patrimonial States. All Sovereignty unalienable but by
the consent of the people.[104]

15   125

Pope Benedict 14 being informed that several Dutch
ships being at Civita Vecchia, dared not to put to sea for fear
of some Algerine Corsairs cruising in those parts, immediately issued Orders that the frigates of the Ecclesiastical
20   State should convey those ships out of danger; and his Nun-
cio at Brussels received instructions to signify to the Minister of the States General, that his holiness made it a law to
himself to protect Commerce and perform the duties of humanity without minding any Difference of Religion.[105]
25

127

It is said that some Sarcastick Medals and dull Jests of the
dutch against Lewis 14 were the chief cause of his Expedi-
30   tion in 1672 by which that Republick was brought to the
brink of Ruin.[106] /

4/III/23c,2v   The Dutch by a treaty with the King of Ceylon have en-
grossed the Cinnamon trade yet whilst they keep their profits within just limits no nation has any cause of complaint.[107]

35   132

The States General of the United Provinces, when their
Consul had been affronted and put under arrest by the
Governour of Cadiz, complained of it to the Court of
40   Madrid as a breach of the Law of Nations. And in the Year
1624 the Republick of Venice was near coming to a Rupture
with Pope Urban 8th on account of an Insult done to the
venetian Consul by the Governour of Ancona.[108]

133

At present Kings claim a Superiority of Rank over Republicks, but this pretension has no other Support but the Superiority of their Strength. Formerly the Roman Republick
considered all Kings as far beneath them, but the Monar-
chies of Europe having onely weak Republicks among them,
have distained to admit them to an equality. The Republick
of Venice and that of the United Provinces have obtained
the honours of Crowned heads, but their ambassadours give
place to those of Kings.[109] When England had driven out
her king, Cromwell would not suffer any abatement of the
honours that had been paid to the crown or to the Nation,
& maintained the English Ambassadours in the rank they
had always possessed.[110]

In the partition of the Empire in the house of Charle-
magne the eldest branch retaining the title of Emperor, the
younger who had the Kingdom of France yielded to him in
rank, the more easily as the Idea of the Majesty of the Roman empire was not Recent. His Successors followed what
they found established and were imitated by the other kings
of Europe.[111] Most of the other Kings of Europe have not
agreed among themselves about their rank. The Popes by
virtue of their Supremacy and the Emperors after the example of the Ancient Roman Emperors have both claimed
the Power of creating Kings.[112]

The Czar Peter I complained in his manifesto against
Sweden, for their not firing Canon on his Passage to Riga.
He might have complained of this as a mark of the want of
Respect; but to make it the cause of a War, was being ex-
tremely prodigal of human Blood.[113]

This performance is wrote with much spirit and good
Sense & breaths a warm concern for the good of Mankind,
a generous sense of Liberty and disdain of Slavish principles. The principles illustrated with many good Examples
most of them taken from Modern times. /

3/II/5,2r   ADDITIONS TO THE EXTRACTS FROM VATTELS LAW
            OF NATIONS

The translation I take to be a booksellers work and to be
very indifferent. Take this instance in a passage of Hobbes
de Cive wherein he gives as the Author thinks the first

proper Definition of the Law of Nations. These words of
Hobbes "Sed quia civitates semel institutae, induunt pro-
prietates hominum personales⟨"⟩ are thus rendred "But as
States in some measure acquire personal Property.⟨"⟩[114]

Though Justinian and his Institutiones gives a very indistinct and faulty definition of the Law of Nature; and makes
that to be the Jus Gentium which we call the Law of Nature.
Institut Lib 1 Tit 2. § 1, 2. Quod naturalis Ratio inter omnes
homines constituit, —id vocatur Ius Gentium. Yet the Romans had their Fecial Law which was that part of the Law
of Nations which Related to War & Treaties.[115]

Grotius founds the Law of Nations on the common consent of Nations, and has not distinguished the Natural or
necessary Law of Nations from the conventional or voluntary.[116]

The Law of Nations is chiefly the Law of Sovereigns of
whom the most powerfull and despotick are not exempted
from the Obligation of this Law. The maxim of some minute Politicians That a State cannot be governed happily
without injustice is as contrary to true Wisdom as to Equity
and Truth. The Authority of Cicero may ballance that of a
thousand such little Politicians. "Nihil est quod adhuc de
Republica putem dictum, et quo possim longius progredi,
nisi sit confirmatum, non modo falsum esse istud, sine injuria non posse, sed hoc verissimum, sine summa Justitia
Rem publicam regi non posse."[117]

32

In All Christian States except Portugal, no Descendant of
the Sovereign can succeed to the Throne unless he be born
in Lawfull Marriage.[118]

Book 2 Chap 17 of the Interpretation of treaties to be
read at leisure.[119]

Book 3 of War. It belongs onely to the Sovereign to Make
War. All the Subjects bound to the defence of the Country.
A Man may with the consent of his Sovereign engage in the
Service of a forreign Prince as a Mercenary Soldier.[120]

Report made to the King of G. Britain by Sir G. Lee Dr
Paul Sir Dudley Ryder & Mr Murray on occasion of the
Prussian Vessels seized and declared good Prizes during the
last War quoted as an excellent Piece on the Law of Nations.[121]

When Satisfaction for an Injury is offered by the Inju-

rious party and the other refuses to accept it he becomes an
unjust Aggressor, The Samnites had ravaged the Lands of
the allies of Rome; when they became Sensible of their Error they offered full Reparation but all their Submissions
could not appease the Romans on which Caius Pontius General of the Samnites observes justum est Bellum quibus ne-
cessarium, et pia Arma quibus nulla nisi in armis relinquitur
Spes.[122]

Politeness in declarations of War, in the expressions used.
Homers Heroes blamed.[123] In clauses annexed. In the Declaration of war against France 1744. are these Words. "And
whereas there are remaining in our kingdom divers of the
Subjects of the french King, we do hereby declare our Royal
Intention to be, that all the french Subjects who shall de-
mean themselves dutifully toward us shall be safe in their
persons & Effects."[124] Distinction of Externall Lawfull and
unlawfull War. The first is where causes may be and are
pretended, & where each Party ought to be supposed to act
bona Fide.[125]

Alliances Defensive, Offensive, Society in War, Subsidy.
Auxiliary Troops.[126] What a Neutrality allows or requires.[127]
Contraband Goods passage of Troops.[128]

THE RIGHTS OF WAR

The taking away the Life of an enemy after he has laid
down his arms always unjust. Prisoners may be detained untill they be ransomed, or their parole taken not to fight /
against the Captor during the War. Admiral Ansons behaviour to his prisoners when he took the Accapulco Ship.[129]

Poisoning and Assassinating unlawfull.[130]

D. of Cumberlands Behaviour at Dettingen to a French
wounded Officer.[131]

Not firing at a General or Princes Tent. Sending Provisions to the Governour of a Beseiged Town.

Of Right to the Goods of the Enemy. Cartell between
Louis 14 & the Confedrates with regard to Contributions.
Partie Bleu.[132]

Ravaging a Country hardly ever excusable. Destroying
Vines & Olives base and unmanly. Destroying Temples
Tombs and Publick Buildings Savage.[133]

In Solemn War both Parties consider themselves and are
commonly to be considered by neutral States as engaged in

Lawfull War. Hence Conquest gives an external Right even to the injurious.[134] Moveables belong to the conqueror so that another person may purchase them from him as soon as they are safe in his possession. Immoveables onely by the treaty of peace.[135] A State is not to meddle with the internal Government of another State and therefore may after a Revolution receive Ambassadours from or send them to the reigning Prince. Nor ought ⟨it⟩ any longer to own the expelled Prince as the Head of a State from which he is expelled.[136]

Ambassadours Envoys Residents Ministers.[137]

The Privileges and Immunities of Ambassadours[138] their Wives Domesticks, Houses and Goods.[139] The Judge of Ambassadours.[140]

Just Causes of War.

An Act of the Superior Power. Offensive Defensive.[141]
1 The Defence of the State, of its Subjects, Allies, of the oppressed, of Mankind.
2 The obtaining what is due by a Just and perfect Right.
3 The Reparation of Injuries done.
4 The Safety of the State where there is just Reason to apprehend a hostile Disposition, & no Security can be other ways obtained.[142]

Unjust Reasons Avarice Ambition Desire of Conquest.[143]

Means to be Used to prevent War.[144]

Denounciation how far Necessary before War, or soon after, for Reputation. for warning to Neutrals.[145]

Those onely entitled to commit Acts of hostility who are commissioned by the State. either expressly or by their Office. Subjects, Allies, Friends to Justice, Soldiers of Fortune.[146]

War cannot be just on both sides. The Party who had justice at first on his Side may become the unjust Party by refusing just Reparation for wrongs done. Treatys of Neutrality.[147] Both parties may conceive that they are in the Right and Charity should lead us to think so as far as we can. The Consequences of this presumption in the Parties; in others. External Right.[148]

What is Lawfull in carrying on the War. Force & Stratagem. Poisoned Arms, Waters, Contraband Goods. Of the Behavior of an Army in an Enemies Country. Passage through a Neutral Country.

Of Contracts and other Social Intercourse during the War. Of the treatment of Captives. Of the Seizure of Ships belonging to a hostile Nation. Of Conquest. of Civil War. Of Treaties of Peace.

Of Ambassadours. Envoys Ministers Residents Consuls & their Priviledges & Precedency.[149] Should their Houses be an Asylum. Should they be allowed to traffick.[150] Voluntary Law of Nations on this Subject or Custom.[151]

Who have Rights to send Ambambassadours. Of the Right of Punishment of forreigners.[152] Of the Right of Sepulture.[153]

Alienating a Part of the Body Politick.[154] And naturalizing.[155]

3 MAY 1770

When a State is dissolved. of Banishment.[156] When one ceases to be a Member of a State. When Ambassadours are discovered in conspiracies or plots against the State.[157] Where they reside.[158]

⟨XVIII. Some Thoughts on the Utopian System⟩

3061/6,1 *Some Thoughts on the Utopian System.*[1]

There are two Questions in Politicks which are perfectly distinct, & which ought never to be confounded. The first is, What is that Form or Order of political Society which, abstractly considered, tends most to the Improvement and Happiness of Man?

The second Question is, How a Form of Government which actually exists and has been long established may be changed, and reduced to a Form which we think more eligible?

The second Question is difficult in Speculation and very dangerous in Practice; Dangerous, not onely to those who attempt it but to the Society in General.

Every Change of Government is either Sudden and Violent, or it ⟨is⟩ gradual peceable and legal.

A violent Change of Government, considering the Means that must be used to effect it, & the uncertainty of the Issue, must be an Object of Dread to every wise, & every humane Man.

It is to wrest Power from the hands of those who are possessed of it, in the uncertain hope of our being able, and the more uncertain hope that, after a violent Convulsion, it shall fall into hands more to our Mind.

The Means of effecting such a change are Plots, Conspiracies, Sedition, Rebellion, Civil War, Bloodshed & Massacre in which the innocent and the Guilty promiscuously suffer.

If we should even Suppose that a total & sudden Change of Government could be produced without those violent Means. That by a Miracle those in power and Office should 3061/6,2 voluntarily lay / down their Authority, and leave a Nation to chuse a new form of Government. Suppose also that, by another Miracle, foreign Enemies should not take the advantage of this State of Anarchy. What would be the Consequence?

A very small State, like an ancient Greek City, when they banished their Tyrant, might meet & consult for the common good. The issue of this Consultation commonly was, to chuse a Wise and disinterested Man, who was superior to themselves in political knowledge, & to give him Power to Model a Government for them. And this was perhaps the wisest Method they could take. For a good Model of Government can never, all at once, be invented by a Multitude, of which the greater part is ignorant, & of the knowing, the greater part is led by Interest or by Ambition.[2]

A great Nation however cannot meet together to consult. They must therefore have Deputies chosen by different Districts. But previous to this, the Number and Limits of the Districtes, the Qualifications of the Electors and Candidates, & the Form & Method of Election must be ascertained. How these preliminaries are to be fixed when all Authority is dissolved & the Nation in a State of Anarchy, is a Question I am not able to resolve.

Supposing however this difficult point to be happily settled, and the Electors of a District, met to chuse a Deputy. Is it to be supposed that all or the greater part of those Electors are to be determined by a pure and disinterested regard to the good of the Nation? He surely knows little of human Nature who would admit such a Supposition. We know from long Experience how such Elections proceed. The poor Electors must have their Bellies or their purses filled, their burthens lessened or their Superiors mollified. The Rich must have their private Attachments & Friendships gratified, or good Deeds done, or promised or expected. There may no doubt be Electors who are both knowing and perfectly disinterested, but the proportion they / bear to the whole, I am afraid is too small to be brought into Estimation.

Such being the Electors, who are to be Candidates? It were to be wished that they should be the wisest & the best Men of the District. But this is rather to be wished than expected. It is evident they must be Men who have it in their power and in their inclination to offer the Inducements by which a Majority may be gained. Without this their pretensions would be laughed at.

To pass over these things, Suppose an Assembly of Deputies met, & a Constitution of Government determined,
unanimously or by a majority. Whether this Constitution is
to be imposed upon the Nation by a Despotick Authority of
the Deputies, or to be again submitted to the choice of the
People, I cannot pretend to determine, nor shall I enumerate the Dangers that may arise from the one of these ways
or the other. After all the favourable Suppositions I have
made, it seems to me that to bring such a Government to a
firm and settled Condition must be the work of a Century.

For we may observe that the Stability of a Government, if
it be at all tollerable depends greatly upon its Antiquity.
Customs & Manners by which we & our Forefathers for
many Generations have been governed, acquire an Authority and a Sanctity independent upon their Reasonableness
or Utility. To this disposition of human Nature, I think it is
owing, rather than to Climate or to any peculiarity in the
Genius of the People, that very imperfect forms of Government, when by a mild Administration they have continued
for many Generations, & acquired the Authority of Antiquity, continue to subsist after they become very tyrannical.
When intollerable Grievances are felt that produce Sedition,
they are imputed, not to the Form of Government, but to
the fault of those who administer it. Thus in Turkey, a Sedition is quelled by the Sacrifice of a Vizier, a Mufti, or
sometimes of a Sultan, without any Attempt to alter the
form of Government.[3] / Into this Reverence for the Ancient
Form of Government I think we must likewise resolve that
Maxim, admitted by all Political Writers, That when an ancient Government is overturned, either by Conquest or by
internal Disorder, the safest way to establish a new one, is to
keep as much as possible to the old Forms of Procedure and
the old Names of Offices.

What I have said hitherto relates to violent & sudden
Changes of the Form of Government, and the Conclusion
from the whole is, That such Changes are so dangerous in
the Attempt, so uncertain in the Issue, and so dismal and
destructive in the means by which they are brought about,
that it must be a very bad form of Government indeed, with
circumstances very favourable to a Change concurring, that
will justify a Wise and good Man in putting a hand to them.
It is not with an Old Government as with an old House,
from which the Inhabitant, who desires a new one, may re-

move with his Family and Goods till it be pulled down and rebuilt. If we pull down the old Government, it must be pulled down about our Ears, and we must submit to the danger of having the New built over our Heads.

But there may be changes that are not sudden & violent, but gradual peaceable and legal. New Laws and Ordinances wisely contrived may remedy the Defects of a Constitution, remove grievances, and promote general happiness.

This must be granted; Yet so limited is the Wisdom of Man, so short his Foresight, that new Laws, even when made with the best intention, do not always produce the Effect intended and expected from them, or they bring unforseen inconveniences that do more than counterballance their good Effects. For this Reason even such Changes ought not to be rashly made, but with good Advice & for weighty Causes.

Surely every Man who has the skill and ability to mend the Constitution by such peaceable Means merits the Blessings of a Nation. And every Constitution, in proportion as it gives Scope / for such Amendments, by allowing due Liberty of printing and petitioning, & by giving the people a share in the Legislature, is in the way of having its defects supplied & its Errors corrected.

We have the Comfort to think that in this Respect as in many others the British Constitution excells all others we know.

The Change made at the Revolution in 1688 was violent indeed but necessary. It affected onely one branch of the Legislature, & by the good Providence of God was brought about with fewer of the Evils that commonly attend such Revolutions than could have reasonably been expected. Since that time, we have had no Revolution, but such gradual and peaceable changes, by new Laws, as have improved the Constitution and greatly promoted the Prosperity of the Nation; and it is to be hoped we may long continue to have such.

Having said so much with regard to changes in Governments which actually exist, whether violent or peaceable I proceed to what I chiefly intended in this Discourse; To consider abstractly that Form of political Society which seems to be best adapted to the Improvement and Happiness of Man.

This is a point merely Speculative. For it may be that the

5

10

15

3061/6,5

25

30

35

40

Form which in Speculation seems best fitted to the end proposed may be impracticable in a particular Nation or even
in any Nation that exists.

Man, who is the subject of all political Discussion whether
Speculative or Practical, may be considered in two Views. In
the first he is the Subject of Speculative Politicks in the second of Practical. First he may be considered *in juris natural-
ibus* as the Schoolmen speak, that is, such as Nature has
formed him; a Being who brings into the World with him
the Seeds of Reason and Conscience, along with various Appetites and Passions, by which he is often missled into Error,
and seduced into wrong Conduct by Temptations / that
arise from within, or from external circumstances: At the
same time capable of a high Degree of Improvement in
Knowledge & Virtue, by right Education and good Government; and on the other hand, of great Degeneracy, to Barbarity & even to Brutality, by the Want or the Corruption of
these Means. This is the Man of Nature, the Subject of Speculative Politicks, & the Subject of what is to be said in this
Discourse. The practical Politician, who is to Model or to
direct the Government of a Nation actually existing, has to
do with men who are not in the State of Nature, but who by
Education & by the State of Society in which they live have
acquired Habits & Dispositions, which it is not in his Power
to eradicate, and which may be called a second Nature. To
this second Nature as well as to the first his Principles of
Government must be adapted.[4]

If it be asked, to what purpose it is to turn our Attention
to points merely Speculative and visionary? I answer that
Speculative points ought not to be excluded from the Circle
of human Knowledge. They tend to enlarge our Concep-
tions & to strengthen our Faculties. Speculation has a like
Effect with regard to our intellectual powers as bodily Exercises have, with regard to the health strength and agility
of the Body. Besides, when political Discussions have come
to be so much in fashion among all Ranks, it may perhaps
be as profitable to most men, to employ their thoughts upon
what is merely speculative, as upon what may influence their
practice.[5]

It were to be wished that the Conduct of Men in Society
was directed uniformly by the Principles of Religion & Virtue; but this is not to be expected, & if it were, there would
be no need of civil Government. The materials of the Polit-

ical Fabrick are Men, not such as they ought to be, but such
as they are, made up of Reason & Passion of Virtue and
Vice. The state of human Nature is such that to produce
happiness and Comfort in human Society, the Principles of
5   Virtue & Religion need the Aid and Cooperation of other
Principles of an inferior Order, which shall have sufficient
3061/6,7 Influence to restrain Men from / wrong Conduct, & induce
them to do what is Right.

Wrong Conduct is always owing, either to Error or Judg-
10   ment, or some Temptation which leads Men to do what they
know to be wrong. If there be any so very corrupt as to do
mischief for mischief's sake, without any temptation, they
are not fit to be members of Society, and can onely be Objects of Restraint and Punishment.

15   From this it follows that in an enlightned Society, Crimes
will bear proportion to the Number and Greatness of
Temptations, and that the least of ill conduct will be found
in a Society in which the Minds of the Citizens are properly
enlightned in their Duty, and have at the same time the least
20   temptation to do ill.

But to the happiness of Society it is not sufficient that
Men do no ill; they must do good; and by their Industry and
Activity promote the common Stock of Happiness.

To aid the Principles of Virtue and Religion in exciting
25   Men to that Industry and Activity which the happiness of
Society requires, the Love of publick Esteem Honour &
Rank seems, of all the inferior principles of human Nature,
to be the best adapted. It is by far a more generous and
Noble Principle than the Love of Money or of private Inter-
30   est. It is also more allied to Virtue. A Man may acquire
Riches by means Honest or Dishonest, but to acquire Esteem his Conduct must be accounted Honest and Laudable.
Esteem is the natural Reward of Merit, and so strong is the
natural desire of it in all Men, that if every Mans Merit or
35   Demerit were publickly known, & if he were to carry about
with him through Life & to leave at his Death, a degree of
publick Estem or Contempt proportioned to it, we can
hardly conceive a Man so degenerate, as not to be moved to
Industry and Activity in his Station by so powerfull an in-
40   citement.

From what has been said I think we may in general conclude that the best Form of political Society is that in which
these three things concur. First that the most effectual

3061/6,8   Means be used / to strengthen in the Minds of the Citizens the Principles of Virtue and true Religion & to enlighten them in what is right & wrong, honourable and dishonourable. Secondly That the Temptations to wrong and criminal

5   Conduct be as few as possible, and Thirdly, That publick Esteem, Honour and Rank be proportioned as exactly as possible to real Merit.[6]

          If this be so, Political Knowledge as far as it is Speculative, must be the Knowledge of the means by which these three

10   Ends may be most effectually accomplished.

          As to the first, the Means of enlightening the people in what is right and wrong & strengthing in their Minds the Principles of true Religion and Virtue, though I conceive it to be a point of very high Importance with regard to politi-

15   cal Government, yet it has been so often treated of, with regard to a higher End, to wit the Happiness of Men in another World, that I shall pass over it altogether, lest I should seem to degrade Religion by considering it as an Engine of State.

20   I proceed therefore to consider in what State or Order of Society there is least temptation to ill Conduct, and I confess that to me the Utopian System of Sir Thomas More seems to have the advantage of all others in this respect.[7]

          In that System, it is well known there is no private Prop-

25   erty. All that which we call *Property* is under the Administration of the State for the common benefit of the whole political Family.[8]

          This Government indeed very much resembles that of a single Family, which is the onely Government that can be

30   said to be purely the Institution of Nature, all others that exist being artificial & the Contrivance of Men.[9]

          It is the appointment of Nature, that Man should subsist by Labour, and to the comfortable Subsistance of a Nation, a certain Quantity and Kind of Labour is necessary. By this

35   Labour, almost all that which we call Property is produced;[10] and there are two ways in which this Labour may

3061/6,9   be regulated. Either every Man / labours for himself & his Family, as his Necessity & Desire prompt him, & is proprietor of the produce of his own Labour; Or, every Man la-

40   bours for the whole Nation, the produce of his Labour being put to the common Stock from which every Citizen is supplied according to his Wants.

          The first we may call *the System of private Property*, which is

exemplified in all Nations. The second is *the Utopian System*,
which as far as we know has not been followed by any great
Nation. It has been practised in different ages by Societies
of Cenobites and Monks who have lived sequestered from
the World, by the labour of their own hands. It was practised by our Saviour and his twelve Apostles who had a common Purse during his Ministry on Earth; and after his As-
cension, the first Christians had all things in common, they
that had Lands or Houses sold them and laid the price at
the Apostles feet, and distribution was made to every Man
as he had need. After the Christians amounted to a Multitude consisting of several thousands, the seven Deacons
were chosen to manage and distribute this common Stock.
And it was probably, their dispersion into different Countries, by the persecution of the Jews, that put an end to this
Community of Property among Christians.[11]

This System was also established by some Jesuites, over a
large tract of Country in Paraquay, which by good Deeds &
without Force they brought from a savage State under their
Despotick Authority. The Jesuites who governed this Country with a mild but despotick Authority, carried on a large
Traffic to different parts of South America, & paid a piastre
to the king of Spain for each of their Subjects, amounting
about the middle of this Century as it is said to above four
hundred thousand. But the Subjects had neither Money nor
Property nor Traffick. This Government of the Jesuites in
Paraquay lasted about a hundred and fifty years, & ended
onely by the entire Destruction of the Society of Jesuites.[12]

In the Utopian System the People are fed, cloathed, &
have their Wants supplied by the Publick, the Labour of
the / People must therefore be directed by the Publick, in
such manner that the produce of it may be sufficient in
Kind & Quantity for this purpose. The Labourers in every
Profession must be trained, directed and overseen, and the
produce of their Labour received and stored by proper Officers.

The means by which this is to be done will be a Subsequent Consideration, but first we ought to consider,
whether the End be of importance to the Happiness of Society.

Suppose then a Nation of which the individuals have all
their wants supplied by the Publick, the Produce of their

Labour being to be put to a publick Stock for the common
benefit. I would endeavour to prove that in such a Nation
the Temptations to wrong or criminal Conduct would be
small, compared with those which must happen in any Sys-
5   tem of private Property.

It is a Proverb of the highest authority that the Love of
Money is the Root of all Evil.[13] Like other Proverbs it must
be understood to admit of Exceptions. But the truth of it,
(which no Christian will deny) requires, that the Exceptions
10   should be few compared with the instances in which it holds
good. There may, no doubt, be Crimes which have no Relation to the Love of Money. But by far the greater part of
those we find in human Society, spring either immediately
or more remotely from this Root. Nor will this appear
15   strange if we consider how this Root, when once admitted,
spreds & infects the whole Society. Let it be oberved, by the
way, that the Words, *Property, Money,* & *Riches,* may be used
in this Subject Promiscuously as equivalent Terms; because
Money is the Measure of all Property & all Property may
20   ⟨be⟩ bought or sold for its Value in Money. Riches signify
onely a superfluity of Property either in Money or in other
kinds.

Next to the Desire of Life and of the necessary means of
Life, the Desire of Distinction and Preeminence among his
25   fellowmen is one of the strongest natural Desires of Man;
3061/6,11 And when his / whole Activity is not necessarily employed
in providing the means of Subsistence, is the strongest, the
most general, & lasting spring of Activity and Exertion.[14]
Now Riches, in all civilized Societies, seem to have advan-
30   tages above all other Qualifications for gratifying this Desire. For, First, in all such Societies, Riches are more looked
up to than Wisdom or Virtue or Learning or Art, or any
other Qualification by which one Man excells another.

Secondly, Riches are the means of gratifying almost every
35   desire. They are a Species of Power, which is a Natural object of Desire to all Men. They may be equally subservient
to the best Purposes & to the worst, to the Happiness or
Misery of the Possessor & of many others. In bad Men they
feed Pride, Vanity, Luxury, and Voluptuousness; they invite
40   to Oppression & Revenge & furnish the Means of gratifying
every bad Passion. In Good Men they may be the Means of
doing much good.

Thirdly riches & Hereditary Rank which commonly arises from Riches and accompanies them are the onely Advantages which a Man can transmit to his Posterity or Family.

Fourthly we may observe that the Acquisition of Riches requires neither Talents nor Virtues, so that this Road to Distinction invites all Men, even those who may despair of attan⟨in⟩g it by other means.

I add in the last place, that though many of our Passions may be satiated by their Objects, & even surfeited; the Love of Money is never satiated. It grows in old Age when other Passions fade.

These particulars have been mentioned to shew the Reason why, when private Property is once admitted, the Desire and the pursuit of it, & consequently all the Evils that spring from that Root should be so universal, and so prevalent in Society.

Indeed when we take a general View of Society, What is it else but a Scramble for Money? In a few perhaps, who have inherited fortunes, it is a Competition who shall make the most brilliant Exhibition / of Riches by Shew and Magnificence. Such is become the serious business of Mankind, in consequence of the System of private Property![15]

The Utopian System may be figured, by a Sum of Money prudently distributed to a great Multitude according to their Wants and their Merits. The System of private Property, to a like Sum, thrown promiscuously among the same Multitude leaving them to scramble for it.

Private Property has always been, & must necessarily be very unequally divided. Time, & the Progress of Society, naturally tend to increase this inequality, till at last the greater part of a Nation, by their Poverty are depressed & dependent upon the few that are rich; They must Labour, like Beasts of Burthen, to feed the Pride & Luxury of the Rich, & to earn a small Pittance for their own necessary Subsistance. By this Means both are equally corrupted; the greater Part being debased into a State of Servility, which tends to stiffle every generous Sentiment, & to produce Envy & Discontent in all, Adulation and cunning in the more timorous, & in the more daring, Theft, Robbery, Murder, Sedition & Rebellion.

On the other hand the Rich, being as much elevated above the natural Condition of Man, as the poor are sunk

5

10

15

3061/6,12

25

30

35

40

below it, & that commonly without Regard to Virtue or Merit, are as much corrupted by their Riches as the poor by their poverty. It is unnecessary to ennumerate the Vices to which Riches tempt the unprincipled; they are obvious to Reason & well known by Experience.

Nor is it less evident that the Distinction attending upon Riches very much diminishes the Inducement which such Persons would otherwise feel to distinguish themselves by more valuable Qualities.

For, among the Evils which may justly be imputed to the System of private Property, this is not the least, That the strong Desire which all Men have of Distinction and Eminence, which naturally / excites them to honourable and usefull Conduct in Society, & is implanted in us by the Supreme Being for that purpose, is perverted to the Love of Money, as the easiest and surest road to Distinction.

In the System of private Property every Man has his private Interest, distinct, not onely from the publick Interest, but from the Interest of every Individual with whom he has any connection or intercourse. There is an Interest of every Individual & an Interest of·the whole political Body. These different Interests must in innumerable cases interfere, and cross one another. And the publick Interest crosses that of every individual, because the publick must be supported at the Expence of the Individuals.

From this opposition of Interests arise Disaffection to the publick, Discontent, Contentions, Parties, and Law Pleas, by which all the bad Passions of Men are stirred, and fed. And in the same propor⟨tion⟩ publick Spirit and all the natural benevolent Affections are checked opposed and born down.

In the Utopian System there are no private Interests opposed to that of the Publick. A regard to the Publick acts without an Antagonist; nor is there any clashing of private Interests to produce Quarrels and Lawsuits. The benevolent Affections have no interested Motives to obstruct their Operation.

I know of no Temptations to bad Conduct that are peculiar to the Utopian System; deducing therefore those that are common to both Systems the ballance against that of private Property consists of all the Temptations which occur in an enlightned & flourising Nation, in the acquisition of property, in guarding it from the incroachments of other

Men, & in spending & laying it out. The Temptations from poverty in the greater part, from the greedy desire of gain in some, and from Superfluity of Riches in others.

3061/6,14   I grant, that notwithstanding the Temptations mentioned / Men guided by the Principles of Virtue and Piety may acquire Property by fair and honest means, and without hurt to the Publick may guard it prudently & peaceably, & lay it out temperately and charitably. But in all political reasoning we must consider, not what Men may do, or what they ought
10   to do, but what it may be expected they will do in the present weak and corrupted State of human Nature. We see in our dayly Experience that Temptations of Interest overcome, not onely the Sense of Duty, but the natural good Affections to Neighbours, to Friends, to the nearest Rela-
15   tions & even to the Publick.

From what has been said I think it appears that the Utopian System is that in which there are fewest Temptations to bad Conduct. I proceed therefore to consider whether in this System, Men may not have sufficient Inducement to all
20   the Labour and Exertion necessary to the Subsistence and Happiness of the Society by degrees of publick Esteem, Honour & Rank proportioned to their Merit.

With a View to this, it is absolutely necessary, that the right Education of all the Subjects, should be attended to by
25   the State, as one of its principal Concerns; & should be under the Direction of Persons qualified for that Office, & having a Degree of Rank & publick Esteem, suited to the Dignity and Importance of their Charge.

It is Education generally that makes a Man to be what he
30   is; not onely knowing or ignorant, but good or bad. For this we have the Authority of another Proverb. Train up a Child in the way he should go, and when he is old he will not depart from it.[16]

What more can be desired in order to the greatest hap-
35   piness of Society, than that its Members, in their several Departments, should go on to old Age in the Way they ought to go? The proper mean to attain this End, in the Judgment
3061/6,15   of the wisest of Men / is to train them properly. Till this be done, it is in vain to expect from any System of Govern-
40   ment, that Perfection and Happiness of Society which every good Man desires. The Materials of the Political Fabrick must be formed to fit the places for which they are destined.

Without this there can neither be beauty nor Stability in the
Building.

It seems to be a natural Consequence of the System of
private property, that the Education of the Youth in all Nations (if we except what is said of one or two very ancient
ones) has been left to the Judgment and Affection of the
Parents. And as the far greatest part of Parents in every Nation is poor and ignorant, it is a necessary consequence, that
the Education of the far greatest part of the Citizens must
be very different from what it ought to be; and that this
most efficacious mean of their acting a proper part in Society has been wanting.

In a Utopian Government, as the Labour and Exertion of
the Citizens is all for the publick Emolument, it must be one
of the most important concerns of the Publick to train them
properly for that Purpose.[17]

So much has been wrote upon Education in ancient and
modern times, that I shall not touch on that Subject. I would
onely observe, that to teach Men to read & write, the use of
Numbers, & the various Exercises that contribute to the
health strength & agility of the Body, and even to Latin
Greek Mathematicks and the various branches of Philosophy, & to instruct them in the principles of any particular
Science or Art usefull in Society; all this, however skillfully
performed, is but the Body of right Education. These At-
tainments are all of an ambiguous Nature, and may be used
either to the Good or to the Hurt of Society, according to
the Character of him who possesses them. And therefore, to
form / the Character to good Habits and good Dispositions,
& to check those that are vicious; this is the Soul and Spirit
of right Education. To accomplish this as far as can be done
by human Means, requires great Knowledge of human Nature, constant Attention, great Temper, Patience and Assiduity. The Diseases of the Mind while it is pliable and docile
as well as those of the Body may, by prudent Means, be
cured or alleviated.

Those who superintend Education in a Utopian Society,
ought to be Men who by their Merit have attained publick
Respect and Honour; which may give Authority to their
Admonitions, & make them Examples worthy to be imitated
by those under their Care. And, as Nature has not made the
Talents of Body or Mind that are usefull in Society, heredi-

tary, or peculiar to any Rank; the Symptoms of such Talents in whatever Rank ought to be carefully observed & cultivated, that they may in due time be put to their proper Use.

There is an Education that ought to be common to all the Citizens; such as may enlighten their Minds in the duties of Life, & dispose them to the practice of them. Another Education must follow this, suited to the different Employments for which the young Citizens are destined, according to their various Talents of Body and Mind, and as the publick exigency requires.

As the labour in every Employment is for the Publick, it must be overseen by Officers appointed by the Publick, who shall at stated times make a Report to superior Officers of the Industry, Skill and moral behaviour of every Individual under their Charge.

It is a capital Defect in the System of private Property that the different Professions and Employments are not honoured & esteemed in proportion to their real Utility, & the Talents required for the discharge of them. The most usefull and necessary Employments are held in no Esteem. Nor indeed do they deserve it; because they are undertaken onely for the sake of private Interest. Their Utility to the publick is accidental, & not in the view of those who practise them. / It is otherwise in a Utopian State where every Man labours in his Calling, not for his own, but for the publick benefit. He is therefore justly intitled to publick Esteem in proportion to the Utility the public receives from his labour, and the Difficulty of performing it.

In such a Society, there must be a Scale of Honour, in which all the different Professions and Employments have a Rank assigned them, proportioned to their Utility and the Talents necessary for discharging them. There must likewis be Distinctive ba⟨d⟩ges or habits, by which every Mans Rank & the Respect due to him may be known and observed in all cases of Precedency.

And, as in every Profession and Employment there will be different degrees of Eminence & Proficiency, these ought, in a Utopian System, to be used as a Spur to Emulation and Exertion. If in the Literary Professions the Degrees of Undergraduate, Batchelor, Licentiat & Doctor be found usefull to excite to Industry in those Professions, why may not like Degrees for every Employment be appointed. In a Utopian Society this ought by no means to be omitted. As in that Form of Society, next to the Principle of Virtue, the Desire of publick Esteem and Honour is the grand Spring which gives Motion to the whole Machine of the Commonwealth, it is proper that there should ⟨be⟩ many Roads to publick Honours, that every Man in his Station may be prompted to exert himself for the publick Good.

For this cause besides the Kinds & Degres of publick Honours I have mentioned, there ought to be an Order of Merit for those who have remarkably benefited the Commonwealth in any way not comprehended in these I have mentioned, which also will have various Degrees. If we add to this the Honours & Dignities arising from Offices of Trust and Authority in the State, which must be many, and of different Degrees; it will appear, that in such a / State there will be a much greater variety of Ranks than in any other; and these distinguished, not by Riches or Hereditary Descent, which are Distinctions not founded in Nature but on human Institution; but distinguished in a more natural way, by their Talents natural & acquired, by their Exertions for the publick Good, and by the Authority & Trust they have merited of their fellow Citizens.

Luxury and Intemperance in eating and drinking are pernicious in every State, and in a System of private property can hardly if at all be prevented. How they are prevented in a Utopian State is so obvious that it need not be mentioned. The Subsistence of all ought to be such as leads to health & strength, & therefore most liberal to those whose Labour requires it. Nature seems to point to no other difference among Citizens in this Article.

But there is a Splendor and Magnificence, in having Servants, Horses, Chariots, Houses and Furniture, which does not appear to me to be incompatible with the Utopian State, though Sir Thomas More seems to be of another Mind.[18]

When such Splendor is bestowed by the State, as the Reward of Merit, either in a Mans Life or at his Death; it is the most Substantial Reward such a State can give, and proves an incentive to Merit in others, as well as creates Respect in the lower Orders.

On the other hand, when Splendor & Magnificence is produced merely by Riches without Regard to Merit, it feeds Pride & Insolence in the Possessor, inflames the Love of Money in those who can acquire it, & produces Envy and Malignity in those who cannot.

When I speak of *Servants* in the Utopian State, the word
seems to convey a degrading Idea of Dependance, unsuitable to the Dignity of a Citizen of Utopia, and therefore we
should rather call them Attendants or Retainers. When a
Utopian of Rank is allowed more or fewer Attendants either
for Honour or for usefull / Purposes, they are the Servants
of the State as he likewise is, though of a higher Rank. They
depend not upon the person whom they attend, but upon
the State & upon their own Merit for their Subsistence and
for their Reward, & he has the same Dependance. They
have all the Privileges that belong to Citizens of Utopia, and
therefore are not degraded by such Attendance.

What I have said is intended to shew, That every Citizen
of Utopia, being properly educated, may, without the Motive of private Interest, have sufficient Inducement to exert
himself in his Station for the publick good, by being secured
in liberal Subsistence, and in such degrees of publick Esteem Honour and Rank as are propotioned to his Merit.

But if after all some Persons should be found so degenerate, as that either their Laziness and Indolence, or other
vitious Inclinations, are not to be overcome by these Inducements; the Utopian State has a mean in reserve for such
Persons; and that is Dishonour & Disgrace; of which a Man
may be made to carry about with him the Marks, as others
do of their Dignity and Honour.[19]

Supposing the Nature of some so very bad, that neither
the Motives of Honour, nor of Disgrace, are sufficient to
make them act their part in Society, penal Laws and Punishment, as in other States, are still in reserve for them, and in
the Utopian State ought to be applied to them onely. Such
Persons have the Temper of Slaves, and ought to be degraded into that state; being altogether unworthy and incapable of being Citizens of Utopia.[20]

It is ob⟨v⟩ious that in a Utopian state the Subjects can have
no Traffick either with one another or with Foreigners; but
the State may be Commercial. It may be so with great advantage; having the whole Stock of the Nation in its disposal. And it ought to be so, that what, in the produce of
the Nations Industry is over and above its Consumption,
may be disposed of to other Nations / or Individuals for its
Value & that the Utopians may be supplied with such forreign Commodities as are necessary or convenient.[21]

A Utopian State ought, by frugal Management of the

publick Stock, and by proper Incitements to the Industry and Labour of the Subjects, to be always provided in ample Stores & a rich Treasury, by which not onely the annual Consumption of the Citizens may be supplied, but an Accumulating Fund may be reserved for foreign Traffic, for the Expence of defensive Wars, for accidental Losses by unfruitfull Seasons, Inundations, Earthquakes or Tempests, and by unforeseen Variations in Commercial Affairs.

When the loss of Property occasioned by such Evils falls onely upon a Publick Stock which is able to bear it, & affects no Individual, every Man may imagine what a Comfort it must be to a Nation, to be free from the fears & from the Sufferings produced in other Nations by such Calamities. A Utopian has every thing that pertains to his Subsistence, and to his Rank in the Society, insured upon the Stock and Credit of the Nation, against all Accidents, excepting that of his own Misbehaviour. He fears no loss of Fortune or of Consideration by Fire or Water or any other Element, by Insolvency of Debtors or of Tenants, or by Depredations of Enemies Foreign or Domestick.

It may seem, that in this System, the State is burthened with a load of Work, additional to the common cares of Government, too great to be well accomplished. The Education of all the Youth of both Sexes, The Oversight of all the labouring hands, The collecting, storing and dispensing the Produce of their Labour. The publick Registers that must be kept of the Merits & Demerits of every Individual, & of every Step of his advancement in Honour and Rank. The Regulations for confering Degrees with Justice & Impartiality, and the Management of the trading Stock of the Nation, these things, without doubt, / will reqire much Attention & Fidelity, and many hands.

To form an equitable Judgment of a Utopian Government in this Respect, it would be necessary to ballance these additional burthens that are laid upon it, with those of which it is relieved; and likewise with those of which the Subjects are relieved; For as Government and Subjects are one Whole, having one common interest, what is taken from one Part & laid upon another Part, does not increase the burthen of the Whole.

In this System, Government is relieved of all the Care and Trouble of imposing and levying Taxes of Customs Excise and all others, affecting either moveable or immoveable

Property, and of all the hands employed for that purpose,
& for preventing and discovering the Frauds which Citizens
are tempted to by private Interest and Avarice, in opposition to the publick Interest.

In a System of private Property Taxes of all Kinds though
necessary for the Support of Government, are attended
with this Inconvenience, that they set the Interest of the
Whole in Opposition to the Interest of the Individuals,
which is apt to produce Disaffection to the Publick, Sedition
& Rebellion, and will always be attended with Smugling,
Frauds, & Concealments which corrupt the Morals of the
Citizens & produce innumerable Law pleas.

To manage the whole Traffick of a Nation is, no doubt, a
business of great Labour, and must require the Employment of many hands in its various subordinate Departments. But it is to be considered whether one great Mercantile Stock may not be managed better, and more profitably
for the Nation, than when it is divided into thousands of
different Stocks, of Companies and Individuals, whose private Interests must in innumerable cases cross one another,
& that of the Publick. /

The right Education of the Youth is a matter of such high
Importance in a Utopian State, that if it should require
more or abler hands than are commonly employed in it, this
will be more than compensated by its Effects on the Manners and Morals of the Citizens.

The Regulations for conferring, with Justice & Impartiality, Degrees of Honour and Rank, fall within the Rules of
common Prudence, as Cases of this kind must happen more
or less in every Society. Onely it may be observed that in
Utopia interested Motives to Partiality have no Place. And
that the Character and Behaviour of Candidates, their Skill
Exertion and Merit, must be perfectly known, from the particular Inspection they are under.

The Registers kept in Utopia of the Reports of Overseers,
& of the Degrees of Honour and Advancement conferred
on every Citizen, furnish the Government with a Fund of
Statistical knowledge of great Importance, which could not
otherways be had. From these are known the Strength or
Weakness, the Defects and Redundancies of the whole political Body, and of every part of it. If there be a Deficiency
of any Article of Life in the whole, or in any part from unfruitfull Seasons or any other Accident; it will be k⟨n⟩own in

time to provide a Supply. If a Redundancy it will be stored or exported to a Market. A Defect or Redundance of Hands in any Employment may be corrected. Any usefull Invention or Improvement is not kept a Secret by the Inventer for his private Interest, or confined to the knowledge of a small Neighbourhood, but is immediately made known to the whole Nation. The Persons fit for offices of Trust & Government will be known, and such Offices filled, not by Intrigue or Connection with great Men, as is common, but according to the publick Judgment of their Capacity & Merit.

It may farther be observed that if a Utopian Government be burdened with much work in its Executive branch it is relieved of a / great deal in its Legislative and Judiciary branches.

1st The Laws relating to Customs Excise & other internal Taxes; the Judicatures Superior & Subordinate which are appointed to put those Laws in Execution, & all the Pleas between Government and Subjects to which they give occasion, have no place in Utopia.

2ly All the Laws and Judicatures for determining pleas of Interest between Subject and Sub⟨j⟩ect, or between the Subjects and Foreignors, are likewise excluded in this System.

How great a Body of Law is required to regulate the Acquisition, the Conveyance, and the Succession to Landed Property, its Limits, its priviledges, Servitudes, & variety of Holdings? And what a World of business does it occasion to Judicatures higher & lower? How many the Laws required to determine Disputes about moveable property?[22]

The variety of Transactions which Property gives rise to, is boundless and in an ancient and flourishing Nation, is still accumulating, by new Inventions, new Trades, & new Fashions, which give rise to new Frauds and Injuries, & require new Laws. Thus the Body of Laws, which the Regulation of Property, and the Redress of Wrongs in Matters of Property, require, is still accumulating, till it becomes too great a Study for a Life, and must be divided & subdivided into various Professions and Departments, & besides Judicatures and Judges, employs an Host of Counsellors, Advocates, Sergeants Sollicitors Conveyancers, Clerks, Registers, who are supported by what some of them have been pleased to call, the glorious Uncertainty of Law.[23]

3dly We may observe, that as Property is the chief bone of

Contention among Mankind, by which the Passions of Anger & illwill are stirred and by which Men are tempted to
hurt one another in their Person & Reputation as well as
Property; in the Utopian System, all contention about Property being removed, and the feuel that feeds evil & malev-
olent Passions being withdrawn; the Evils which they produce in Society will very rarely appear.

So that to compensate the Labour laid upon the Executive /
Branch of an Utopian Government & the Hands employed
for that purpose, we ought to put in the other Scale, the
Savings of Labour and of Hands in the Legislative and Judicative Branches.

In the Legislative Branch is saved the Labour of contriv-
ing and imposing the Taxes of every kind necessary for the
Support of Government, and the greater Labour of making
the Laws for the Regulation of Property Real & Personal in
the Infinite variety of Transactions civil & commercial that
take place in Society.

In the Judicative Branch is saved, the Labour of Judging
and determining in all claims and pleas to be decided by
those Laws.

The saving of Hands is likewise great in the Utopian System, first to the Government, of the Hands necessary for
the Labour above mentioned in Lawmaking & in Judging;
& secondly to the Subjects of Counsellors, Pleaders, Conveyancers, and all their Retainers whatsoever who are employed in the Execution of the laws about Property.

A third Saving to the Subjects, which is the greatest of all,
is, that they are relieved of all the bitter Fruits which Spring,
either immediately, or more remotely, from Contentions
and Lawsuits about Property.

One who considers these things can hardly forbear to
conclude, that in a Utopian State the Code of Law will be
reduced to such a diminutive Size, that it will hardly be
thought worthy to be made a distinct Profession. The Law
may be understood by common Men come to years of Discr-
tion, & perhaps may be all contained in the Almanack.

What I have said of the Utopian System may be summed
up in these three particulars First That the Temptations to
wrong and criminal Conduct are by this System greatly di-
minished beyond what they must be in every System of private Property.

Secondly that by proper Education, and by D[r]egrees of

3061/6,25 Honour / & Rank conferred according to Merit, the Citizens
of Utopia may have sufficient Inducement to all the Labour
and Industry which is necessary to the comfortable Subsistence of the Nation and Thirdly That the Labour required
5   in the Executive Branch of a Utopian Government, is compensated, by the Labour of which it is relieved in the Legislative and Judicative Branches; and much more by the Subjects being relieved of all the bad passions, Quarrels,
Contentions & Lawsuits arising from Differences about
10   Property.
The view I have hitherto taken of the Utopian System
presents its fairest side; To form an equitable Judgement of
it, it ought likewis to be contemplated on its darker Side.
First it may be observed that political Reasoning is not of
15   the Demonstrative but of the probable kind. The Heart of
Man is a Labrinth, too intricate to be fully traced by his Understanding and we often see, not onely Individuals, but
great Bodies of Men act a part very different from that
which by the common principles of human Nature we
20   would have expected. And therefore political Writers are
wont to borrow Aid to their reasoning from Examples of
what has been done or has happened in similar Cases. In
the present Subject, we are totally deprived of this Admini-
cle to our Reasoning; & therefore it must have the less
25   Force. We cannot borrow Examples from Utopian Governments, because no Nation was ever so governed.
Secondly As the present State of Man is a State of Trial
and Improvement; Temptation is necessarily implyed in it.
It is by Temptation that Virtue is tried, exercised, and
30   Strenghned. That Innocence, which is the Effect of having
never met with Temptation, is, no doubt, a very amiable
thing. But tried Virtue which has encountered strong
Temptations, and has come off Victorious, is an Object of
much higher Esteem, both with God and Man. Man even in
35   the State of Innocence was not exempted from Temptation.
Some have more or greater than others, but to what Degree
Temptation may be proper for the present State of Man, is
not for us to kno, it can onely be known by him who made
us, and who will judge us. /
3061/6,26 Thirdly it may be observed, That as the Utopian System
greatly lessens Temptations to bad Conduct, so it deprives
Men of the Opportunity of exercising some very eminent
Virtues, to which the different Conditions of Poverty and

Riches give occasion. The Man depressed by Poverty, who not onely resists the Temptations of that State and discharges the duties of it, but is contented, & thankfull for his Lot as that which his Father in Heaven sees to be best for him, who looks with indifference upon the Splendor of Riches without a covetous Eye, without Envy or Malignity; Such a Man under all his Depression carries a noble Soul. His Poverty exalts him, & makes his Virtue more Eminent. The Temptations that arise from Riches and high Estate, are perhaps more difficult to be overcome than those which spring from poverty this is granted; & therefore they require a greater degree of Virtue to conquer them. If such a Man thinks of himself no more highly than he ought to think, condescends to those of Low Degree, spreads Happiness and alleviates Misery as far as his power reaches, he is a kind of God upon Earth, his Riches are a Blessing to himself and to all around him.

The Utopian System leaves no room for these noble Virtues. The Utopian may have the Disposition but he wants the Opportunity of exercising them.

I add in the fourth place, That the Desire of publick Esteem Honour and Rank, which must be encouraged in the Utopian System, as the chief Aid to virtue for exciting Men to do their Duty in Society, may be carried too far; so as to supplant the Virtue which it ought onely to aid. When this is the Case the Utopian indeed does his Duty, but he does it, to be seen of Men, when he ought to have higher Motives. And perhaps the constent pursuit of Honour & of the Esteem of Men, may produce an undue Elation of Mind, unfriendly, & unsuitable to that Humility, and that Sense of our Dependence and Demerit, which Religion requires. /

To conclude, Since we neither live, nor does it seem to be the design of Providence that we shall ever live, in a Utopian Society, but among Men surrounded with Temptations, and whose Interests interfere & cross on another in innumerable Instances let us not expect Perfection, in Individuals, in Societies, or in Governments. We are conscious of many Imperfections in ourselves. Those who hold the Reins of Government are Men of like Passions, & have greater Temptations.

The Relation between a Government and its Subjects, like that of Marriage, or of Parent and Child, is strong & important. It is a Relation instituted by the Author of Nature, as

without Government, Men must be Savages. To preserve
and strengthen this sacred Tie, concerns the honour and
the Interest of both Parties. The Duties are reciprocal. Protection and the Benefite of Laws on one hand. Respect, Sub-
5   mission, & Defence in Time of Danger on the other. Whatever is excellent in the Constitution, ought to be the Boast
& the Glory of the Subject, as we Glory in the Virtues of our
near Relations. If we see, or think we see, Imperfections in
the Constitution or in the Government, we ought to con-
10   sider, that there never was a perfect human Government on
Earth; We ought to view such Defects, not with a Censorious
and Malignant Eye, but with that Candor and Indulgence
with which we perceive the Defects of our dearest Friends.
It is onely Atrocious Conduct that can dissolve the Sacred
15   tie. While that is not the Case, every prudent and gentle
mean should be used to strengthen and confirm it. As He is
a good Friend or Neighbour with whom we can live in
Peace, Amity and the Exchange of good Offices; so it is a
good Government under which we can lead quiet and
20   peaceable lives in all Godliness & Honesty.[24]

Commentary

BY KNUD HAAKONSSEN

I. INTRODUCTORY LECTURE

1. It must be emphasized that this manuscript does not belong specifically with the Lectures and Papers on Practical Ethics. It is an introduction to Reid's course as a whole and is included here because it gives a clear idea of the place of the course on practical ethics within Reid's scheme as a whole (see the Introduction above, p. 88). Reid's text here, pp. 103–108, is in substance reproduced in the preface to I.P. in his *Philosophical Works*, pp. 216–218.

2. There are traces of the numeral "1" in front of "Our." The list should have been completed with the mind of God and the minds of animals, as we see below.

3. Christian Wolff, *Psychologia empirica, methodo scientifica pertractata* and *Psychologia rationalis, methodo scientifica pertractata*. Reid is referring to the former; see *Philosophical Works*, p. 307a. Although unusual in the eighteenth century, the word "psychology" was certainly available in English (see, e.g., David Hartley, *Observations on Man*, p. 354), and it is interesting that Reid turned to Wolff for it—Wolff was not well-known in the English-speaking world.

4. Reid is referring to the first, and anonymous, edition of Edmund Burke's *Philosophical Enquiry into the Origin of our Ideas of the Sublime and Beautiful*. Reid was fond of the passage in question, as we see from a fragmentary manuscript, 4/11/3, where he says:

> I shall confirm what I have said of the Importance of an accurate Enquiry into the Human Mind by the Authority of an ingenious writer who is not a man of meer Speculation, but one who makes a shining figure in the Political World, and thunders in the British Senate with uncommon Eloquence. I mean the Author of the Philosophical Enquiry into the Origin of our Ideas of the Sublime and Beautifull Mr Burke. "The Variety of the Passions is great, and, in every branch of that Variety, worthy of an attentive Investigation. The more accurately we search into the Human Mind, the stronger traces we every where find of his Wisdom who made it. If a Discourse on the Use of the parts of the Body may be considered as an Hymn to the Creator; the Use of the Passions which are the Organs of the Mind,

cannot be barren of Praise to him nor unproductive to ourselves of that noble and uncommon Union of Science and
Admiration which a Contemplation of the Works of infinite
Wisdom alone can afford to a rational Mind; whilst referring to him whatever we find of Right, or Good, or Fair, in
ourselves, discovering his Strength and Wisdom even in our
Weakness and imperfection, honouring them where we discover them clearly, and adoring their profundity where we
are lost in our Search, we may be inquisitive without imper-
tinence, and elevated without Pride we may be admitted, if
I dare to say so, into the counsels of the Almighty, by a consideration of his Works. This Elevation of Mind ought to be
the principal end of all our Studies, which if they do not in
some measure effect, they are of very little service to us."

Reid quotes with a few minor inaccuracies from pp. 35–36, and
he repeats the passage in I.P., p. 218b. For Reid's notion of a
"Structure of the Mind," compare Butler's idea of the "constitution" of human nature in "The Nature of Virtue" in Butler,
Sermons, i–iii.

5. "I will find a way or make one." A similiar passage in the preface
to I.P., p. 217b, containing the same names, ends thus: "The
motto which Lord Bacon prefixed to some of his writings was
worthy of his genius, *Inveniam viam aut faciam.*" Bacon does in
fact not seem to use this tag on any of his works, but I am unable
to account for Reid's apparent confusion over a saying usually
ascribed to Hannibal.

6. In I.P., p. 217b, Shaftesbury is left out while Claude Buffier,
Richard Price, and Lord Kames are included.

7. Hume, *Treatise*, p. xv: " 'Tis evident, that all the sciences have a
relation, greater or less, to human nature; and that however
wide any of them may seem to run from it, they still return back
by one passage or another."

8. Locke, Epistle to the Reader, *Essay*, p. 7; quoted with near accuracy.

9. See Plato, *Apology*, 21 a ff.

10. Cicero, *De officiis*, I.ii (5): "The subject of this inquiry is the common property of all philosophers; for who would presume to
call himself a philosopher, if he did not inculcate any lessons of
duty?"

11. Cicero, *De officiis*, I.iii (7): "Every treatise on duty has two parts:
one, dealing with the doctrine of the supreme good; the other,
with the practical rules by which daily life in all its bearings may
be regulated."

12. In this and the following paragraphs, Reid outlines the field of study that is the subject of the present volume.

13. The lectures on politics fall outside the scope of this volume; see the Introduction above, p. 31.

II. DUTIES TO GOD

1. Concerning the adoption by natural jurisprudence of the three Christian duties—to God, to ourselves, and to others—see the Introduction above, pp. 58–59. Reid's discussion of the duty to God may be compared with Pufendorf, *Duty of Man*, 1.4, and *Law of Nature*, II.3.xv and xxiv and II.4.ii–iii (esp. Barbeyrac's notes); Hutcheson, *Short Introduction*, pp. 72–78, and *System*, I.168–220; Fordyce, *Elements*, pp. 332–341; Heineccius, *Universal Law*, I.86–95; and Turnbull's Remarks, in ibid., pp. 95–97; Turnbull, *Principles*, I.203–214; Clarke, *Discourse*, pp. 64–66; and Price, *Review*, pp. 138–148. The *topos* is in a sense natural religion's equivalent to the three traditional "theological" virtues of revealed religion—faith, hope, and charity—and indeed one can discern echoes of this tripartite structure. See also, and not least, Cicero's organization of the Stoic doctrine of the gods in *De natura deorum*, book II.

2. Reid's lectures on natural theology do not seem to have survived, but see Robert Jack's and George Baird's notes from Reid's lectures.

3. Reid presumably uses the numeral 2 to indicate that he is now talking of the second duty to God in contrast to the "first Duty" of the first sentence in the previous paragraph. Cf. Hutcheson's formulation: "Piety consists of these two essential parts, first in just opinions and sentiments concerning God, and then in affections and worship suited to them" (*Short Introduction*, p. 72; see also *System*, I.168). See also Pufendorf, *Duty of Man*, 1.4.i, and *Law of Nature*, II.4.ii–iii, esp. Barbeyrac's n. 5, where he refers to Cicero (*De legibus*, II.7), Epictetus (*Encheiridion*, ch. XXXVIII [Arrian's summary of Epictetus, *Discourses*; see n. 10 below]), and Wollaston, *Religion of Nature Delineated*, and quotes Seneca:

> The first way to worship the gods is to believe in the gods; the next to acknowledge their majesty, to acknowledge their goodness without which there is no majesty. Also, to know that they are supreme commanders in the universe, controlling all things by their power and acting as guardians of the human race, even though they are sometimes unmind-

ful of the individual. They neither give nor have evil; but they do chasten and restrain certain persons, and impose penalties, and sometimes punish by bestowing that which seems good outwardly. Would you win over the gods? Then be a good man. Whoever imitates them, is worshipping them sufficiently. *Epistulae Morales*, III.89–91.

4. See Hutcheson, *System*, I.210. "The worship suited to the Divine Attributes is either internal, or external: the former in the sentiments and affections of the soul; the later in the natural expressions of them." External worship again was commonly divided into private and public (cf. Hobbes, *De cive*, xv. xv ff., and *Leviathan*, ch. xxxi, esp. p. 401; Pufendorf, *Duty of Man*, I.4.vi–vii; Hutcheson, *Short Introduction*, pp. 77–78; Fordyce, *Elements*, pp. 340–341; and Heineccius, *Universal Law*, I.93–95).

5. Aratus of Soli (ca. 315–240/239 B.C.), *Phaenomena*, ll. 4–5: "we all have need of Zeus. For we are also his offspring," quoted by Saint Paul in the speech he supposedly made on Areopagus in Athens, in Acts 17:27–28: "Yet he is not far from each one of us, for, 'In him we live and move and have our being'; as even some of your poets have said, 'For we are indeed his offspring.'" These lines of Aratus and Paul were naturally popular; for two pertinent examples, see Cudworth, *True Intellectual System*, 2:194–197, and Cumberland, *Traité philosophique*, pp. 59–60.

In this context the brief minutes of Reid's early Aberdeen philosophical club (see the Introduction above, p. 9) are of interest. The first entry, for 12 January 1736, has the heading "What Things in the Course of Nature we may reasonably ascribe to the continual influence & Operation of God or other active powerfull and Invisible beings under him." It contains the following passage:

Concerning the Divine Government Whether the Creating of Moral Agents does not include a right to Govern them? They are Subject to a certain Law by their Natures. This is the Divine Law Which Must be Enforced by Rewards and Punishments. Every Being has a right to Exercise its faculties when none are harmed or prejudiced thereby. Exercise of the Moral Attributes of God Not hurtfull to Creatures but on the Contrary. Our Obligation to Obedience founded on our Natures and Dispositions. Difficulties in the Divine Government. Blessings of Some Kinds dispersed both to Good and Bad—other Kinds Not. Necessity and Usefullness of General Laws. (6/I/17,1r)

6. The image is a common one, but in view of the tone and matter of these paragraphs (cf. n. 7 below) it inevitably recalls Adam Smith: "the author of nature has made man the immediate judge of mankind, and has, in this respect, as in many others, created him after his own image, and appointed him his vicegerent upon earth to superintend the behaviour of his brethren" (*Theory of Moral Sentiments* [TMS], note to III.2.xxxi, which reproduces the wording of the first edition, the one Reid used; cf. 3/1/26–27).

7. See Smith, "This inmate of the breast, this abstract man, the representative of mankind, and substitute of the Deity, whom nature has constituted the supreme judge of all their actions . . ." (TMS, note to III.2.xxxi; cf. n. 6 above). By echoing Smith's language, Reid may be subtly protesting against Smith's attempt to explain conscience without reference to God.

8. John 18:11.

9. Zeno (335–263 B.C.), founder of the Stoic school in Athens. Reid's principal sources for Zeno were undoubtedly Cicero, *De finibus*, book III, and Diogenes Laertius, *Lives*, book VII (for the ethics, see secs. 84–131). As was common in the eighteenth century, Reid's understanding of Stoicism was influenced by his reading of later representatives of the school (see n. 10 below). His criticism of Stoicism in the present paragraph may be contrasted with that of Smith, TMS, VII.ii.1.15–47.

10. Though one hesitates to think that Reid would find anything of particular beauty, let alone "great Strength," in the spurious Platonic dialogue *Alcibiades II*, this must be his reference (there is nothing of direct relevance in *Alcibiades I*). The first half of the passage that Reid quotes immediately below from Juvenal's tenth *Satire* is an elegant expression of the main thought of this small, much later Platonic imitation—namely, that one should pray only for the good, leaving it to the wisdom of God to determine what that is. Furthermore, this idea, which has its most direct Socratic imprimatur from Xenophon, *Memorabilia*, 1.3.2, is taken up in one of the passages from Arrian (*Encheiridion*, sec. 32), which Reid must have had in mind a few lines below. Sir William Hamilton also lends his authority to this reference in a note to a parallel passage in Reid's A.P., p. 583. Epictetus (ca. A.D. 55–135) wrote nothing himself, but his disciple Flavius Arrianus (dates uncertain) wrote down his *Discourses* in eight books, of which four survive. In these, three chapters are devoted directly to Providence (I.vi, I.xvi, and III.xvii), but there are also many other passages that would suit Reid's purpose and that

make use of the Greek word usually translated as "providence" (*pronoia*) and its associated verb (*pronoeō*) and adjective (*pronoēti-kos*)—e.g., II.xiv.11: "the philosophers say that the first thing we must learn is this: That there is a God, and that He provides for the universe." Reid was probably acquainted not only with John Upton's important critical edition (London, 1739–41) but also with George Stanhope's and Elizabeth Carter's popular English translations, all testifying to the contemporary taste for Stoicism. Apart from preserving Epictetus's *Discourses* for posterity, Arrian wrote a summary of them, an *Encheiridion*. Reid must here be thinking especially of secs. 17 and 31–32 (cf. n. 3 above and the Commentary below at p. 377 n. 2. The emperor Marcus Aurelius (A.D. 121–180) refers extensively to *pronoia* in his *Meditations* (e.g., II.3, IV.3(2), VI.10, VI.44, IX.28, XII.14).

The problems of a providential order in the universe pervade not only the classical Stoic texts but also the eighteenth-century treatment of them. A pertinent example is Hutcheson's extensive notes to his and his colleague James Moor's translation of Marcus Aurelius, which may well have been the text Reid used. Hutcheson and Moor also appended a translation of the "Summary of the Chief Maxims of the Stoic Philosophy," which had been provided by Thomas Gataker in the standard seventeenth-century edition of the *Meditations*. The first section of this summary is entitled "Of God, Providence, and the Love of God" and begins: "The Divine Providence takes care of human affairs; and not of the universe only, in general, but of each single man, and each single matter" (*The Meditations of . . . Marcus Aurelius* [1742], pp. 296–297). In a number of places in the *Meditations* there are similar formulations that in the eighteenth century would be seen as interesting approaches to the distinction between a general providence and a special providence, the relationship between which so preoccupied the period and which is echoed in Reid's discussion. Reid would of course have been familiar with Hume's onslaught on the former in "Of a Particular Providence and of a Future State" and on the latter in "Of Miracles," secs. XI and X in the first *Enquiry*.

11. Juvenal, *Satire X*, ll. 346–353 and 356–362 (also quoted in A.P., p. 583a). Compared with the text we use today, Reid's quotation shows a few variations in punctuation; in l. 4, *Dii* should be *di*; in l. 10 there should be no *et*; and in the final line, *plumes* should be *pluma*. In English the sense is: "Is there nothing then for which men shall pray? If you ask my counsel, you will leave it to the gods themselves to provide what is good for us, and what

will be serviceable for one state; for, in place of what is pleasing, they will give us what is best. Man is dearer to them than he is to himself. Impelled by strong and blind desire, we ask for wife and offspring; but the gods know of what sort the sons, of what sort the wife, will be . . . you should pray for a sound mind in a sound body; for a stout heart that has no fear of death, and deems length of days the least of Nature's gifts; that can endure any kind of toil; that knows neither wrath nor desire, and thinks that the woes and hard labours of Hercules are better than the loves and the banquets and the down cushions of Sardanapalus."

12. See Luke 22:44 (cf. Matt. 26:39) and Matt. 6:25, 32–33 (cf. Luke 12:22, 30–31).

13. Reid may be referring to Hume's swipe at "the whole train of monkish virtues" in *Enquiry*, p. 270, and to Smith's elaboration of this in TMS, III.2.35.

14. Shaftesbury, *An Inquiry concerning Virtue or Merit* (first in an unauthorized edition by John Toland 1699, subsequently as Treatise IV in Shaftesbury's *Characteristics* [1711]); here *Characteristics*, I.279–280. Price quotes the same words in a similar context in *Review of Morals*, p. 145n.

15. Shaftesbury, *The Moralists: A Philosophical Rhapsody* (first published in 1709, subsequently as Treatise V in *Characteristics*); here *Characteristics*, II.54. Reid does not begin the quotation exactly; he uses the contemporary convention of giving quotation marks at the end of each quoted line and rearranging the first few words for grammatical reasons. The quotation is verbatim from "is not."

16. The words "vi, ditione" indicate that Reid himself had got the passage "by heart," and in quoting from memory failed a little. It should be simply "indicio" instead of these two words.

17. Cicero, *De legibus*, II.7. Ignoring variations in spelling and punctuation, I indicate Reid's deviations from Cicero's text by insertions in angle brackets. The sense is:

> So in the very beginning we must persuade our citizens that the gods are the lords and rulers of all things, and that what is done, is done by their will and authority; that they are likewise great benefactors of man, observing the character of every individual, what he does, of what wrong he is guilty, and with what intentions and with what piety he fulfils his religious duties; and that they take note of the pious and the impious. For surely minds which are imbued with such ideas will not fail to form true and useful opinions.

Indeed, what is more true than that no one ought to be so foolishly proud as to think that, though reason and intellect exist in himself, they do not exist in the heavens and the universe. . . . In truth, the man that is not driven to gratitude by the orderly courses of the stars, the regular alternation of day and night, the gentle progress of the seasons, and the produce of the earth brought forth for our sustenance—how can such an one be accounted a man at all? And since all things that possess reason stand above those things which are without reason, and since it would be sacrilege to say that anything stands above universal Nature, we must admit that reason is inherent in Nature. Who will deny that such beliefs are useful when he remembers how often oaths are used to confirm agreements, how important to our well-being is the sanctity of treaties, how many persons are deterred from crime by the fear of divine punishment, and how sacred an association of citizens becomes when the immortal gods are made members of it, either as judges or as witnesses?

18. Reid is referring to the last few lines of Clarke's second Latin edition of Newton's *Opticks*, the only edition in which they occur. The full passage is as follows: "Lex enim moralis ab origine gentibus universis erant septem illa Noachidarum praecepta: quorum praeceptorum primum erat, unum esse agnoscendum summum Dominum Deum, ejusque cultum non esse in alios transferendum. Etenim sine hoc principio nihil esset virtus aliud nisi merum nomen" (Newton, *Optice*, p. 415). This may be rendered as: "For from the beginning the moral law for all people consisted of the seven precepts of Noah's sons. The first of these precepts was that one God is to be acknowledged as the supreme Lord and the worship of him is not to be transferred to others. For without this principle virtue would be nothing but a mere name." The seven precepts of the Noachides are the commandments that the Talmud built upon God's universal covenant with Noah at the beginning of Genesis 9: "Seven precepts were the sons of Noah commanded: social laws; to refrain from blasphemy; idolatry; adultery; bloodshed; robbery; and eating flesh cut from a living animal" (Babylonian Talmud. *Seder Nezikin*, vol. 3, Sanhedrin 56a [pp. 381–382]). The most famous invocation of the *ius Noachidarum* as the essence of justice and the law of nature is John Selden's *De jure naturali et gentium*, which is organized according to the seven precepts (see Praefatio, p. 69, and I.x).

19. This is the end of the treatment of duties to God. The manuscript continues immediately with the next major topic, duties to ourselves.

III. DUTIES TO OURSELVES:
PRUDENCE, TEMPERANCE, FORTITUDE

1. This paragraph is either a false start or, more probably, serves the following three purposes. First, it marks the transition from our duty to God to our duties to ourselves; second, it reminds Reid to introduce the distinction between the four cardinal virtues so that, third, he can explain that he will deal here with only three of these—prudence, temperance, and fortitude—because they constitute our duties to ourselves, while the fourth, justice, belongs to duties to others, that is, jurisprudence proper.

Concerning the combination of the concepts of virtue and duty and the significant consequences this had for the traditional use of the distinction between the four cardinal virtues, see the Introduction above, pp. 49ff. The distinction did, however, survive the transformation of the concept of virtue. In whatever way we are to understand the invocation in *Alcibiades I* (121E–122A) of a Zarathustran ancestry, it is clear that the distinction makes its effective entry into Western ethical thought with Socrates's repeated challenge to Protagoras in *Protagoras*, 329c ff. and 349b ff. The *loci classici* are *Republic*, IV.427e ff. and 441c ff., where the "piety" of the *Protagoras* is finally excluded, as well as in *Laws*, I.631c ff. and XII.963a ff. Although Aristotle uses the fourfold division in his early works and in passing references (e.g., *Politics*, VII.i.1323^{a}28–30 and 1323^{b}33–36; and VII.xv.1334^{a}18–34, which may, however, be early parts of the work), he goes well outside it in the *Nichomachean Ethics* (as well as in the *Rhetoric*, esp. 1.9.1166^{a}23 ff.), partly by adding a number of other virtues in book IV and partly by distinguishing between moral and intellectual virtue and thus giving wisdom a special and complicated role (in book VI). Undoubtedly of much more importance to Reid were his Roman sources, especially Cicero's *De officiis* (I.v ff.). Cf. *Tusculan Disputations*, II.xiii (31–32), III.viii (16–18), and III.xvii (36–37); *De finibus*, I.xiii–xvi (42–54) with II.xiv (45–48), xvi (51), and xix (60); v.xxi (58) and xxiii (65–67); *De inventione*, II.liii–liv (159–65); and the influential *Rhetorica ad Herennium*, III. ii–iii (3–6), which was generally though not universally believed to be by Cicero. Reid would have known about the early Stoic division of virtue from Diogenes Laertius, *Lives*, VII.87ff. (here esp. 92).

Although Reid saw the tetrad of virtues as Greco-Roman and the triad of duties as Christian (see A.P., p. 642b), he was undoubtedly aware of the former's presence in the Christian tradition. Apart from the interpretation of various passages of Scripture in the light of one or another of the four virtues, the basis for the Christian adaptation of the cardinal virtues is in fact apocryphal (Wis. of Sol. 8:7), while the use of the label is due to Ambrose, *De sacramentis*, III.2.9. Much more important, however, are Augustine's *De moribus ecclesiae catholicae*, II.15–16, and *City of God*, XIX.4; and the great systematization by Thomas Aquinas, *Summa theologiae*, Ia 2ae 61 and IIa 2ae 47ff.

For the distinction between the four virtues in Reid's immediate context, see Hutcheson, *Short Introduction*, pp. 65–68, 103–105; *System*, I.222–224 (cf. *Inquiry*, p. 126); and Smith, TMS, VII.ii.1.6–9. First, however, the whole of the following discussion should be compared with Reid, A.P., pp. 580a–586a.

2. That is, like justice in the previous paragraph.

3. The immediate background to Reid's distinction between wisdom and prudence is probably Cicero's distinction between *sapientia* and *prudentia*, which he sees as the proper translation of the Greek *sophia* and *phronesis*; *De officiis*, I.xliii (153). See also Smith's distinction between "superior" and "inferior" prudence, TMS, VI.i.14 (this was added in the 6th ed. [1790] but is implicit in the earlier editions, e.g., VII.ii.2.12–13).

4. Matt. 25:14–30; cf. Luke 19:12–27.

5. The emperor in question was Domitian (A.D. 51–96, reigned 81–96), of whom Suetonius wrote: "At the beginning of his reign he used to spend hours in seclusion every day, doing nothing but catch flies and stab them with a keenly-sharpened stylus. Consequently when someone once asked whether anyone was in there with Caesar, Vibius Crisbus made the witty reply: 'Not even a fly'" (*Lives of the Caesars*, XII.3).

6. See Reid's more extensive argument to the same effect at the beginning of his lectures on pneumatology (4/II/9).

7. For the contemporary debate about whether prudence is a *moral* virtue (or a duty) at all, see esp. Hutcheson, *Inquiry*, p. 126; *Short Introduction*, p. 65; and Smith's discussion, TMS, VII.ii.3 (cf. VII.ii.4.3–4) of Hutcheson, *Inquiry*, pp. 187–190, and *Illustrations*, pp. 299–300. Further, see Butler, "Of the Nature of Virtue," in *Analogy of Religion*, pp. 333–334; and Price, *Review of Morals*, pp. 148–151, 193–195, and 283. Of special importance is Hume, *Treatise*, pp. 609–610, and *Enquiry*, pp. 318–320, because the

context there is the question of the viability of a general distinction between moral virtues and "natural abilities." For Reid's later treatment of the specific problem here, see A.P., pp. 584b–586a.

8. See Cicero, *De officiis*, II.iii (10).

9. For the preceding paragraph, see A.P., p. 586b.

10. Reid should have written ἀρετή. Cf. Hume, *Enquiry*, pp. 254–255: "The martial temper of the Romans . . . had raised their esteem of courage so high, that, in their language, it was called *virtue*, by way of excellence and of distinction from all other moral qualities."

11. Reid may be reflecting and refining upon Hume, *Treatise*, pp. 607–608: "The characters of Caesar and Cato, as drawn by Sallust, are both of them virtuous . . . but in a different way: Nor are the sentiments entirely the same which arise from them. The one produces love; the other esteem: The one is amiable; the other awful" (cf. *Enquiry*, p. 316). He may also be reflecting upon Smith's similar distinction in TMS, I.i.5.1, III.3.34ff., and VII.ii.4.2–4 (cf. the later additions, VI.i.14–15 and VI.iii.12–13).

12. Sesostris (alias Rameses II) was a mythical Egyptian king (fourteenth century B.C.) credited by Herodotus (*History*, II.102ff.) with conquering, inter alia, the Scythians and Thracians. Tamerlane or Tamburlaine are the usual anglicized versions of Timur-i-Lenk, Timur the Lame, the great Tatar conqueror (1336–1405) and the subject of Marlowe's play and Handel's opera. The eighteenth century saw in him—along with Genghis Khan, Sesostris, Attila, and the like—the typical oriental despot; cf. Montesquieu, *Spirit of Laws*, XXIV.3; Smith, TMS, VI.iii.30, and LJ(A), iii.44–45, iv.40 and 52ff.; Gibbon, *Decline and Fall*, ch. LXV.

13. See Smith, TMS, V.2.9–16, VII.ii.1.28 and 34. Reid's description of the virtue of fortitude in the previous manuscript, and even more so in this one, makes one suspect that he had fresh in his memory Ferguson's extolling of it in the *Essay on the History of Civil Society* (e.g., pp. 44–48, 61, 146–147, 256–257, but here esp. pp. 81–96). See also part I of Rousseau, *Discours sur l'origine de l'inégalité*.

IV. DUTIES TO OTHERS: JUSTICE

1. The idea that justice is somehow superior to the rest of virtue is particularly well known from the fourth book of Plato's *Republic*, but Reid is undoubtedly thinking more immediately of Aris-

totle's famous distinction in the first two chapters of book v of *Nicomachean Ethics*, between general and particular justice, of which the former "is complete excellence in its fullest sense" (1129^b30–31), while the latter concerns equality between individuals (1131^a10ff.). As for the Latin *iustitia* Reid may well have had in mind Cicero's exposition in *De finibus*, v.xxiii (65–66), as well as his suggestion in *De officiis*, iii.vi (28), that justice "is the sovereign mistress and queen of all the virtues," which is explained at length in ibid., i.xliii–xlv (152–160). It is difficult to tell to what extent Reid was acquainted with Leibniz's speculations about a general concept of justice, though we know that he was acquainted with Leibniz's metaphysics of law (especially the concept of the "city of God") from his reading of the brief *Système nouveau de la nature* and *Principes de la nature et de la grace*, which he refers to in I.P., p. 308. The extent of his discussions of Leibniz (e.g., I.P., pp. 306b–309b and 382; A.P., pp. 624–626; *Essay on Quantity*, pp. 718b–719a) leads one to think that he had a wider knowledge of the Leibnizian oeuvre. Reid certainly knew the modern jurists' occasional use of "justice" in the loose sense in which it is identical with that which is right (*rectum*); see Grotius, *War and Peace*, I.l.ix, and Cocceius's extensive discussion of *ius laxius* in *Introductio*, ii.

The Ciceronian background to the division of the whole of social duty into justice and humanity is *De officiis*, i.vii (20) and xiv (42) (*iustitia* vs. *beneficentia* or *benignitas* or *liberalitas*). This distinction pervades the moral philosophical context in which Reid is writing; see esp. Clarke, *Discourse*, pp. 67–76; Kames, *Essays*, pp. 71–75; Hume, *Treatise*, iii.ii.1, and *Enquiry*, sec. iii and appendix iii; Smith, TMS, ii.ii.1 (compare also Cumberland, *Laws of Nature*, p. 316). Cf. A.P., pp. 643b–644a, and the Commentary below at p. 319 n. 19. It should, however, be pointed out that there is a tendency to identify this distinction with the one Reid mentions in the following sentence between commutative and distributive justice (e.g., Smith, TMS, vii.ii.1.10) and an even more pervasive tendency to identify the distinctions between general and particular justice and between justice and benevolence with Grotius's division of justice into *iustitia attributix* and *iustitia expletrix* (*War and Peace*, i.l.viii; cf. Cocceius, *Introductio*, 1.13.15), of which the latter is concerned with perfect rights and the former with imperfect rights. Grotius's conversion of the classical language of virtues into the language of rights is again converted into the language of duties by Pufendorf, first in the *Elementa*, 1.8.ii and v, subsequently in *Law of*

Nature, 1.7.vi–xvii (cf. *Duty of Man*, 1.2.xiv), where his discussion of Grotius, *War and Peace*, 1.l.viii, and Hobbes, *De cive*, III.5–6 (cf. *Leviathan*, ch. 15, esp. pp. 206–208) together with Barbeyrac's notes (*Law of Nature*, 1.7.vi–xvii and 1.2.xii–xvi) were of seminal importance. In these converted forms the distinction was spread even further; see the Commentary below at pp. 320–321 n. 25. See also the Introduction, above, pp. 61–62.

2. This distinction goes back to Aristotle's division of particular justice (see n.1 just above) into distributive and corrective (or rectifying or equalizing) justice (*Nicomachean Ethics*, 1130^{b}31–1131^{a}1), though the currency of the two labels is due to Aquinas's reformulation of the distinction (*Summa theologiae*, IIa IIae, q. 61). Grotius's reworking of the Aristotelian distinction in terms of expletive and attributive justice (*War and Peace*, 1.l.viii; cf. II.17.ii (2) and II.20.ii (1–2)) led to a flurry of reexaminations of Aristotle by the Grotius commentators and natural lawyers, and Reid would have had a fair knowledge of this from Pufendorf, *Law of Nature*, 1.7.vi–xiii, and from Barbeyrac's annotations to both of these. In addition, Reid may have used Heinrich Cocceius's commentary to Grotius, here *Grotius illustratus*, 1:84ff. See also the Commentary below at p. 319 n. 19. Reid's peculiarly narrow formulation of the concept of distributive justice here is due to the connotations of "a judge"; "a magistrate" in the eighteenth-century sense would probably be closer to his intention.

3. This has been observed by a good many authors—for example, Plato, *Republic*, 1.351c–352c; Cicero, *De officiis*, II. xi (40); Locke, *Essay*, p. 66; Pufendorf, *Law of Nature*, III.4.ii, and VIII.4.v; Heineccius, *Universal Law*, 1.301–302; and Hume, *Enquiry*, p. 205. Barbeyrac in his annotation to the latter place in Pufendorf refers us to a pertinent tale in Heliodorus's wonderful *Aethiopian History*, book v, ch. 15 (i.e., p. 150). Contrast Augustine, *City of God*, IV.4: "if justice is left out, what are kingdoms except great robber bands?" Cf. A.P., p. 666a, and the Commentary below, at p. 341 n. 71.

4. Horace, *Epistles*, 1.ii.27: "nos numerus sumus et fruges consumere nati" ("We are but ciphers, born to consume earth's fruits"). Reid's context forced him to change "nati" into the singular.

5. Terence, *The Self-Tormentor* (*Heauton timorumenos*), act 1, l. 77: "Homo sum: humani nil a me alienum puto" ("I am a man, I hold that what affects another man affects me," usually rendered "I hold nothing human foreign to me"). Quoted, e.g., in Cicero, *De legibus*, 1.xii (33), and Seneca, *Epistulae*, xcv.53; cf. the following note.

6. Plato, letter IX, to Archytas of Tarentum (358a): "You must . . . consider this fact too, that each of us is born not for himself alone. We are born partly for our country, partly for our parents, partly for our friends." This is quoted loosely in Cicero, *De officiis*, I.vii (22), and both are quoted in Pufendorf, *Law of Nature*, III.3.i, where Seneca's quotation from Terence (see n.5 above) is also quoted. Further, "Mankind we ought from the heart to love . . . and not believe, we are born, and to live for ourselves alone . . ." ("Maxims of the Stoics," translated from Gataker's "prefatory discourse to his excellent edition and commentary on Antoninus" in Hutcheson's and Moor's translation of Marcus Aurelius's *Meditations*, pp. 300–301).

V. DUTIES TO OTHERS: INDIVIDUALS IN PRIVATE JURISPRUDENCE

1. As explained in the Introduction, above, pp. 32 and 87, Reid did not in his first year at Glasgow begin "practical Ethicks" with lectures on our duties to God and to ourselves. This arrangement was achieved only during the following couple of years, and I have reconstructed it accordingly in the preceding two sections. In 1765 Reid ended the theoretical part of ethics on 28 February, as shown by the final few lines in MS. 8/IV/5,1v (not in this volume), and on the following day, 1 March, he began "Jurisprudence," as shown on fol. 1v of the present manuscript. This leaves the first page of this manuscript unaccounted for. We must presume that Reid used it on that Thursday 28 February as a brief transition to "practical Ethicks," and although it systematically constitutes a return to duties to ourselves, I print it here with the rest of the manuscript in which it occurs in order not to interfere with Reid's first Glasgow course in "practical Ethicks," which the reader can now follow without interruption to its concluding section on the law of nations (see Section VIII, "Duties to Others: States").

2. For Cicero's usage, see, e.g., *De oratore*, I.xlv (200); xlviii (212).

3. *Jubere*, inf. of *jubeo*, perhaps a contraction of *ius habere*, to consider right, whence to order, decree, etc. *Fari*, inf. of *for*, to speak or say; the noun *fas* may derive from *for*, and its original meaning was dictates of religion or divine law, as opposed to *ius*, human law. *Fas* was thus often represented as a divine force (e.g., Seneca, *Hercules furens*, l. 658) or deified righteousness (e.g., Valerius Flaccus, *Argonautica*, 1.790–794, and Livy, *From the*

Founding of the City, I.xxxii.6); and Livy, ibid., VIII.v.8, has the consul Titus Manlius exclaim, "Audi, Iuppiter, haec scelera . . . audite, Ius Fasque" ("Hear, Jupiter, these wicked words! Hear ye, Law and Right!"). It is a matter of dispute when such usage was employed to express a clear distinction between divine and human law, but it is quite clear in Isidorus's influential etymological work from the early seventh century: "Fas lex divina est, ius lex humana" (Isidorus, *Etymologiarum*, v.ii). This is quoted by, e.g., Aquinas, *Summa theologiae*, IIa IIae.57.i (3).

4. See n. 8 below.

5. See, e.g., Grotius, *War and Peace*, I.l.iv–v, and Pufendorf, *Law of Nature*, I.l.xix–xx, 1.6.iii, and III.5.i.

6. *Pandectae* is the Latinization of the Greek word for "digest." The two words are used interchangeably as the title of the great collection of Roman civil law made by order of the emperor Justinian in A.D. 530 and codified in 533.

7. Conventionally, natural lawyers drew parallels between the juridical status of individuals and that of states, or between the law of nature and the law of nations. This is undoubtedly what Reid was doing here, as he did in 7/VII/1,1v (see Section X of this book) and in A.P., p. 645. See also Grotius, *War and Peace*, I.l.xiv; Hobbes, *De cive*, XIV.4, and *Leviathan*, p. 394; Pufendorf, *Law of Nature*, II.3.xxiii; Cocceius, *Introductio*, IV.23 and 33–36; Heineccius, *Universal Law*, 1.14–16, and Turnbull's quotation (ibid., p. 18) from Montesquieu's *Persian Letters*, nos. 94 and 95 (pp. 176–177); and Vattel, *Law of Nations*, esp. preface and preliminaries.

8. Reid is referring to the classical division of law: "All the law that we observe pertains to persons, to things or to actions" (Justinian, *Institutes*, 1.ii.12). This was generally followed by the natural lawyers: Grotius, *War and Peace*, I.l.v; Pufendorf, *Law of Nature*, I.l.xix; Cocceius, *Introductio*, XII.51 and 104; Hutcheson, *Short Introduction*, p. 120, and *System*, 1.253.

9. This is a central and difficult point in modern natural law, especially after Pufendorf. Reid takes it up again in A.P., pp. 642a–644a and below, pp. 198ff. (Section X). See Pufendorf, *Law of Nature*, III.5.i; Hutcheson, *Short Introduction*, pp. 121 and 139, and *System*, 1.264: "To each right there corresponds an obligation, perfect or imperfect, as the right is." See also the Introduction, above, pp. 59–60.

10. These are the so-called "external rights." See the Commentary below at p. 384 n. 41.

11. Reid had dealt with these topics in his ethics lectures in late January and early February, as we can see from 8/III/3, esp. fol. 4r

(not in this volume). Out of this grew the fully developed treatment in A.P., pp. 586–599 (cf. pp. 670–679).

12. Reid had lectured on this topic only on 19 February (see 8/III/ 3,8v), quoting in support Cicero, *De finibus*, II.xiv (45); see 8/III/ 2,1r. For *honestas* as the general concept of moral rightness, and *turpitudo* as its opposite, see also Cicero, *De inventione*, II.lii–liii (157–159) and *De officiis*, I.ii (4) and I.v (15). Cf. Reid's expansion on this in A.P., pp. 587–589 and 651.

13. For the relationship between *ius* and *rectum*, see also Hutcheson, *Short Introduction*, pp. 118–120, and *System*, I.252–253. The following discussion eventually led to that in A.P., pp. 643ff.

14. See below, n. 25.

15. "Obnoxious" in the sense of being liable or exposed to injury or punishment.

16. The lines from Juvenal's thirteenth Satire are in fact ll. 192–198 (p. 260) and their sense is: "But why should you suppose that a man escapes punishment whose mind is ever kept in terror by the consciousness of an evil deed which lashes him with unheard blows, his own soul ever shaking over him the unseen whip of torture? It is a grievous punishment, more cruel far than any devised by the stern Caedicius or by Rhadamanthus, to carry in one's breast by night and by day one's own accusing witness" (Juvenal, *Satires*, p. 261). Apart from variations in punctuation and spelling of names, the quotation is accurate. Caedicius is unknown, and Rhadamanthus, son of Zeus and Europa, was rewarded for an exemplary life with not dying—instead he went to Elysium as a judge (Plato, *Apology*, 41ᵃ; *Gorgias*, 523ᵉ; Virgil, *Aeneid*, VI.566, etc.).

17. See Grotius's famous dictum in *War and Peace*, Prolegomena, sec.11, that the laws of nature would apply "though we should even grant, what without the greatest Wickedness cannot be granted, that there is no God, or that he takes no Care of human Affairs." This became one of the most fundamental disputes in modern natural law, especially after Pufendorf's denial of it; see *Law of Nature*, II.3.xix, and the references in n. 22 below.

18. See Justinian, *Institutes*, I.ii, pr. and 1: "Jus naturale est, quod natura omnia animalia docuit"; and "quod vero naturalis ratio inter omnes homines constituit, id apud omnes populos peraeque custoditur vocaturque jus gentium, quasi quo jure omnes gentes utuntur" ("Natural law is that which nature instils in all animals"; and "but what natural reason has established among all men is observed equally by all nations and is designated *ius gentium* or the law of nations, being that which all nations obey").

Grotius, *War and Peace*, 1.l.xiv (1): "Latius autem patens est jus gentium; id est quod gentium omnium aut multarum voluntate vim obligandi accepit" ("But the more extensive Right, is the Right of Nations, which derives its Authority from the Will of all, or at least of many, Nations"). Further, *War and Peace*, 1.l.x (1): "Jus naturale est dictatum rectae rationis, indicans actui alicui, ex ejus convenientia aut disconvenientia cum ipsa natura rationali ac sociali, inesse moralem turpitudinem, aut necessitatem moralem" ("Natural Right is the Rule and Dictate of Right Reason, shewing the Moral Deformity or Moral Necessity there is in any Act, according to its Suitableness or Unsuitableness to a reasonable Nature").

19. The too wide concept of justice against which Reid here protests is not that of general righteousness or goodness, which we find in the subtitle to Plato's *Republic* or in Aristotle's idea of "general justice" (*Nicomachean Ethics*, v.ii.10), but it does have some affinity with the Aristotelian concept of "particular justice"—namely, the goodness-as-fairness one shows others (see the Commentary above at p. 314 n. 1). For further clarification we refer to the discussion of perfect and imperfect rights and duties below (see n. 25). It should, however, be stressed that the line Reid takes here—that the concept of justice should be taken in the narrow sense—easily misleads, for his considered view was clearly that there were no *sharp* distinctions on moral and epistemological grounds within the concepts of justice, right, and duty (see Section X, p. 203, as well as A.P., pp. 643b–644a). In this he contrasts sharply with Hume and Smith (see Hume, *Treatise*, III.2.i–ii, and *Enquiry*, secs. II–III, but esp. app. III; Smith, TMS, II.ii.1–3. Cf. Reid in A.P., p. 657, and 6/I/9, fol. 2v. For examples of the effect of the debate about the concept of justice, see also Hutcheson, *Short Introduction*, I, ch. 3, and his subsequent organization of the material in I, chs. 4–6, and II, chs. 2 and 4.

20. See the references in nn. 13 and 19.

21. The two first points probably echo Hume's discussion of property (*Treatise*, p. 527), though Reid adds the rejection of the idea that rights are qualities of persons. This undoubtedly refers to Grotius's definition of *ius* in *War and Peace*, 1.l.iv–v, and to its repercussions in much subsequent natural law thought. See Pufendorf, *Law of Nature*, 1.l.xix–xx (cf. his *Elementorum jurisprudentiae universalis*, I, def. 8); Hutcheson, *Short Introduction*, pp. 119–120, and *System*, 1.253. Reid's third point refers to his rejection of Hume's theory of property.

22. Reid is here again (see n. 17 above) touching upon one of the

most central questions in modern moral philosophy, which Grotius had ensured prominence in natural jurisprudence; see *War and Peace*, Prolegomena, sec. 11; I.l.x, with Barbeyrac's notes, esp. n. 3, pp. 9–11; Barbeyrac, "Historical and Critical Account of the Science of Morality," secs. 6–11; Hobbes, *De cive*, III.33, IV, 1, and xv.4–8; *Leviathan*, pp. 216–217 and 397–399; Pufendorf, *Law of Nature*, I.6, esp. x, and II.4, esp. iii–vii; *Duty of Man*, I.3.x–xi and I.4; Leibniz, "Opinion on the Principles of Pufendorf," secs. iv–v; Carmichael's supplementum I, secs. 10 and 19–20, and supplementum II, secs. 1, 3, and 5, in his edition of Pufendorf, *De officio*; Locke, *Essay*, II.288 (cf. II.21.49), with *Treatise*, I.52–54, and *Treatise*, II.6; Cocceius, *Introductio*, pp. 3, 11ff. and 240; Heineccius, *Universal Law*, I.6–12, 41–44, 60, and Turnbull's Remarks, ibid., pp. 16–18 and 62–65; Hutcheson, *Short Introduction*, II, ch. 1, esp. p. 111, and *System*, I.264–267; Fordyce, *Elements*, pp. 263–267. In general, Reid's perception of the issue will also have been influenced by Cudworth's onslaught on Hobbes, that "late pretender to politics," on "divers modern theologers" (namely, Calvinists), and on Descartes—"but an hypocritical Theist, or personated and disguised Atheist" (*True Intellectual System*, 2:532ff., 577, and 3:498–516; *Eternal and Immutable Morality*, p. 528, and, in general vol. 1, chs. 2–3). Further, see the development of similar arguments in Clarke, Wollaston, Balguy, and Price. See also the Commentary above at p. 306 n. 5.

23. These issues are closely connected with the previous one; see esp. Grotius, *War and Peace*, I.l, esp. x and xv; Pufendorf, *Law of Nature*, I.6.xvii–xviii (with Barbeyrac's nn. 5 and 6 on p. 73) and II.3.iv–v (cf. *Duty of Man*, I.2.ix); Cocceius, *Introductio*, pp. 241ff.; Hutcheson, *Short Introduction*, pp. 115–117, and *System*, I.271–280.

24. Private rights pertain to individuals, public rights to any social grouping, common rights to mankind as a whole. See Section X, pp. 199 and 201. See also Hutcheson, *Short Introduction*, p. 141, and *System*, 1,284.

25. The following discussion of the perfect and imperfect rights that pertain to all people equally in the state of nature is very close to Hutcheson, *Short Introduction*, pp. 139–146, and *System*, I.257–259 and 280–284. The "different States" are the moral states man can be considered in—namely, the state of "natural liberty" or one of the adventitious states, such as the family and civil society. These concepts of the moral states derive from Pufendorf, *Law of Nature*, II.2.i (cf. II.3.xxiv), and *Duty of Man*,

II.l.ii. Reid deals at length with all three states in subsequent manuscripts (for the actual distinction, see Section X, pp. 199–201 and Section XI, p. 209). In the margin just below the date, "Mar. 7," is added another topic that Reid has dealt with extemporaneously: "What Rights are alienable." This cuts right across the natural rights, as the references to it in Section X (pp. 199, 200, and 201) show. I have removed it from the text because wherever it is put it would break the continuity. For the distinction between alienable and inalienable rights, see Hutcheson, *Inquiry*, pp. 261–262, *Short Introduction*, p. 124, and *System* 1.261–262. The distinction between perfect and imperfect rights and perfect and imperfect duties was of central importance to modern natural law. Reid discusses it in A.P., pp. 643b–645b, and in Section X, pp. 197 and 202–203. While this has a terminological precursor in Cicero's idea of *officium perfectum* (*De officiis*, I.iii (8); cf. *De finibus*, III.xviii (59)), the determining influence was Grotius's division of *ius* as a moral quality of persons into perfect and less perfect rights, of which the former is a "faculty," the latter an "aptitude," and to which correspond two different kinds of justice; see n. 22, above, and *War and Peace*, I.l.iv–viii. This is later supplemented by Pufendorf's corresponding distinction between perfect and imperfect duties; see the references in n. 19 above, and see Hutcheson, *Inquiry*, pp. 256–259, *Short Introduction*, pp. 122–123 and 141–145 and *System*, 1.257–259 and 293–308; Heineccius, *Universal Law*, I, chs. 7–8, esp. pp. 123–24 and 154–55, with Turnbull's Remarks, pp. 164–168. In summary, there were by Reid's time three common grounds for the distinction between perfect and imperfect rights and duties: (1) The infringement of perfect rights was injury and a breach of perfect duty, while the infringement of imperfect rights was merely the withholding of some good and the neglect of imperfect duty. (2) It was morally justifiable to enforce perfect rights and duties—in the state of nature through war, in civil society through the legal system—but not so the imperfect ones. (3) The observance of perfect rights and duties was necessary for the very existence of society, while the imperfect ones were an embellishment of society (cf. Aristotle's distinction between *merely living* and *living well: Politics*, I.2.1252^{b}30 and III.6.1278^{b}20–30).

A few lines earlier in the present text and again in Sections X and XI, pp. 201–202 and 209, and in A.P., p. 644, Reid adds a third category: external rights. See the Commentary below at p. 384 n. 41 for an explanation of this topic.

26. Both the word for self–homicide and the debate about the act were renewed in early modern Europe (see Montaigne, *Essays*, II, ch. 3; Montesquieu, *Persian Letters*, nos. 76–77 (pp. 152–154); Voltaire, *Prix de la justice et de l'humanité*, art. v, "Du suicide"). The role of natural law theory in this debate is particularly interesting because, while it was constrained by the Christian insistence that suicide is a breach of the sixth commandment, it nevertheless conveyed to Protestant Europe the much more lenient attitude of Roman law and of Roman Stoicism. In Pufendorf, suicide is dealt with under "duties to ourselves," namely as a question of whether we have a right to take our own life (*Law of Nature*, II.4.xvi–xix, and *Duty of Man*, 1.5.xi; cf. Heineccius, *Universal Law*, I.100–102). Yet it clearly provides a transition to treating of our duties to others when it is asked whether any such duties imply a duty (or a right) to self-murder (Pufendorf, *Law of Nature* II.5–6 and 1.5.xii ff., respectively). It is presumably because of this ambiguity and perhaps under the influence of Locke (see, e.g., *Treatise*, II.23 and 135) that Hutcheson and Reid deal with the topic in connection with the fundamental right to life (cf. Hutcheson, *Short Introduction*, p. 142, and *System*, I.296–298). See also Hume's essay "Of Suicide" (1777) and Smith, TMS, VII.ii.1.24–37 (added in 1790). Reid returns to the issue at greater length in 8/IV/4 (printed here in section X, p. 193.

27. Reid presumably meant to say that "that admirable rule of our Divine Teacher" amounts to a "perfect Conformity to the Imperfect Rights of Man."

28. See Hutcheson, *System*, I.306–307: "When many claim relief or support from us at once, and we are not capable of affording it to them all; we should be determined by these four circumstances chiefly, . . . the dignity or moral worth of the objects; the degrees of indigence; the bonds of affection, whether from tyes of blood, or prior friendship; and the prior good offices we have received from them." Like Reid, he then goes on to gratitude (pp. 307–308) and, like Reid, he refers to Cicero, *De officiis*, I.xiv–xviii (42–61). All of this is matched by *Short Introduction*, pp. 145–146 and indeed by Pufendorf, *Law of Nature*, III.3.15, and *Duty of Man*, 1.8.v. Reid quotes loosely from *De officiis*, I.xiv.42: "Videndum est enim, primum ne obsit benignitas et iis ipsis, quibus benigne videbitur fieri et ceteris, deinde ne maior benignitas sit quam facultates, tum ut pro dignitate cuique tribuatur." Cicero is listing the caution with which beneficence and liberality must be exercised: "We must, in the first place, see to it that our act of kindness shall not prove an injury either to the

object of our beneficence or to others; in the second place, that it shall not be beyond our means; and finally, that it shall be proportioned to the worthiness of the recipient."

29. In addition to the distinction between natural and adventitious states (see above, n. 25) it was common to distinguish between natural and adventitious duties and rights: Some of "those Duties which are to be practis'd by one Man towards another . . . proceed from that common Obligation which it hath pleas'd the Creator to lay upon all Men in general; others take their Original from some certain Human Institutions, or some peculiar, adventitious or accidental State of Men. The first of these are always to be practis'd by every Man towards all Men; the latter obtain only among those who are in such peculiar Condition or State. Hence those may be called Absolute, and these Conditional duties" (Pufendorf, *Duty of Man*, 1.6.i; cf. *Law of Nature*, 1.l.vii and 11.3.xxiv with Barbeyrac's notes). In Hutcheson this is translated into rights-language (*Short Introduction*, p. 141, and *System*, 1.293; cf. Heineccius, *Universal Law*, 1.124–125). The distinction has its ancestry in Grotius, *War and Peace*, 1.l.x, sec. 4.

Following Pufendorf, *Law of Nature*, 111.5.iv, and Hutcheson, *Short Introduction*, p. 147, and *System*, 1.309, Reid adopts the traditional division of adventitious rights into real and personal (see Gaius, *Institutiones*, 1.8; Justinian, *Institutes*, 1.ii.12; *Digest*, 1.v.1). In the *System*, Hutcheson says: "Adventitious rights . . . are either real, 'when the right terminates upon some certain goods'; or personal, when 'the right terminates upon a person, without any more special claim upon one part of his goods than another.' In personal rights our claim is to some prestation, or some value, leaving it to the person obliged to make up this value out of any part of his goods he pleases. Of real rights the chief is property." It is to the latter that Reid then turns.

The first three points that follow refer to the earliest period when men were few and used the things of the natural world as they needed them and without cultivating or improving upon them. There was thus no division of labor, no scarcity, and consequently no need for claiming as a right the things used. This and the changes that necessitated the institution of private property (Reid's point no. 4) are portrayed by Grotius, *War and Peace*, 11.2.ii (who refers to the same passages of Genesis); Pufendorf, *Law of Nature*, iv.3 and iv.4.i–iv, and *Duty of Man*, 1.12.i–ii. Cf. Hutcheson, *Short Introduction*, pp. 139–140 and 147–148, and *System*, 1.280–284 and 309–316.

Following both Grotius, *War and Peace*, 11.2.ii (5), and Pufendorf, *Law of Nature*, IV.4.iv, and *Duty of Man*, I.12.ii, most natural lawyers insisted that a contract was necessary to turn the original "indefinite Right" or "indefinite Dominion" (Pufendorf) into exclusive property rights. Following Locke, as he alleges, Barbeyrac strongly denies the necessity or possibility of such a contract and maintains that the institution and spread of property rights can be understood in terms of the gradual occupation of the natural world and that such occupation consists in labor, as Locke understood it in the *Second Treatise*, ch. v (an idea that is not without ancestry in Pufendorf himself; see *Law of Nature*, IV.4.vi). See Barbeyrac's n. 2, pp. 366–367, and n. 2, p. 373, in Pufendorf, *Law of Nature*, and his note on p. 136 in *Duty of Man*. The combination of Pufendorf's concept of negative community with Locke's concept of labor to account for private property was taken over by Carmichael (n. 1 to Pufendorf, *De officio*, I.12.ii), and he is again followed closely by Hutcheson (*Short Introduction*, pp. 149–151 and 153–154, and *System*, I.319–329), who is led to conclude: "Thus we need not have recourse to any old conventions or compacts, with Grotius and Pufendorf, in explaining the original of property" (*System*, I.331; likewise *Short Introduction*, p. 159). This dispute became particularly important with Hume's discussion of property (*Treatise*, III.2.ii–iv, and *Enquiry*, sec. III and app. III), and we learn about Reid's ideas on it in A.P., v.5, esp. pp. 657–659, and in 7/VII/11, 7/VII/13, 7/VII/1b (all printed in this book in Section XI).

The division of real adventitious rights into original and derived also comes from Pufendorf, *Law of Nature*, III.5.iv, which is followed by Hutcheson, *Short Introduction*, p. 152, and *System*, I.324. In the former place, Hutcheson explains: "Property is either original or derived. The original property arises from the first occupation of things formerly common. The derived is that which is transferred from the first Proprietors." Cf. Heineccius, *Universal Law*, I.176.

30. Gen. 1:29–30: "And God said, Behold, I have given you every herb bearing seed, which is upon the face of all the earth, and every tree, in which is the fruit of a tree yielding seed; to you it shall be for meat. And to every beast of the earth, and to every fowl of the air, and to every thing that creepeth upon the earth, wherein there is life, I have given every green herb for meat: and it was so." The following reference is: Gen. 9:2–3: "And the fear of you and the dread of you shall be upon every beast of the earth, and upon every fowl of the air, upon all that moveth upon the earth, and upon all the fishes of the sea; into your

hand are they delivered. Every moving thing that liveth shall be meat for you; even as the green herb have I given you all things."

31. In modern natural law, negative communion (or community) was the (original, natural) state in which things did not belong to anyone but were open for division and occupation by anyone (see above, n. 29). In the Pufendorfian tradition, positive communion is exclusive, collective ownership by several people of things hitherto in negative communion (Pufendorf, *Law of Nature*, iv.4.ii–iii, and *Duty of Man*, 1.12.iii; cf. Hutcheson, *Short Introduction*, p. 159, and *System*, 1.330–331). In more theologically inspired natural law, like that of Richard Cumberland and (according to some scholars) John Locke, positive communion was the condition in which the whole world was given to mankind, so that occupation could never give rise to exclusive rights in things but only to more or less temporary use-rights determined by a concern for the common good (Cumberland, *Laws of Nature*, pp. 64ff.). Most of Locke's *First Treatise* is relevant, but see ch. iv, secs. 21ff., and *Second Treatise*, ch. v, sec. 25; cf. also J. Tully, *A Discourse on Property*. These issues are dealt with at much greater length below in 7/vii/11, 7/vii/13, and 7/vii/1b (printed in Section XI).

Res nullius (lit. nobody's thing) is a concept derived from Roman law, which in general had a significant influence on the theory of property in modern natural law. In the first title in book ii of the *Institutes*, Justinian divides the things of the world into those that are or can be held in individual property and those that are not or cannot be so held. The latter may be outside property either by divine law or by human law, and there are *res nullius* in both categories. The former are especially "sacred things" (churches) and "religious things" (graves) (ibid., secs. 7–10). This topic acquired some jurisprudential (and confessional) significance when Grotius maintained that such things derive their special qualities only from positive law and that they therefore may be legitimate targets of conquest and destruction in war (*War and Peace*, iii.5.ii), subject to the limitations of "moderation" (iii.12.vi–vii). The topic turns up in the manuscripts printed here in Section XI, pp. 207 and 211. In the latter place, Reid denies that "sacred things" are incapable of becoming property, thus indicating his agreement with Hutcheson, that the opposite would be tantamount to subscribing to "the mystery of consecration" within "the Popish religion" (*System*, 1.335; cf. ibid., pp. 331–335, and *Short Introduction*, p. 159). *Res nullius* by human law are the things of the natural world before they are occupied by men (*Institutes*, II.i.11–18), and this concept could therefore be used in natural law to describe both the original negative community and what was subsequently left unoccupied.

32. Central to the dispute between the two traditions referred to in the previous note was the issue indicated here—whether exclusive property rights to things lasting beyond present use were defensible. The color of Locke's answer in the crucial ch. v of the *Second Treatise* is controversial but was traditionally taken to be affirmative; Carmichael (n. 1 to Pufendorf, *De officio*, 1.12.ii) and Hutcheson (*Short Introduction*, p. 156, and *System*, I. 324–325 and 328–329) followed the same line, and Reid followed them, as we see from the extensive treatment of this topic in A.P., p. 658, and the papers printed here in Section XI. In his late "Some Thoughts on the Utopian System" (Section XVIII, below), Reid did, however, subject the whole matter to more searching discussion.

33. Presumably Reid has here discussed how previously owned things could be abandoned and return to negative community and thus be open for reoccupation by others. Usually this was dealt with as a preliminary to property right from prescription (see Section XI, pp. 206 and 211; Grotius, *War and Peace*, II.3.xix and the following ch. 4; Pufendorf, *Law of Nature*, IV.6.xii and IV.12.viii, and *Duty of Man*, 1.12.vi and 1.12.xii; Hutcheson, *Short Introduction*, pp. 159–160, and *System*, I.335–336).

34. See Reid's extensive discussion of Hume's theory of property in A.P., pp. 657b ff. In the extreme left-hand margin Reid has written, vertically, the following note: "This Comunity of things prior to occupation gave occasion to the poetical Fiction of a Golden Age. See Abstract." There is no indication of where this belongs or any entirely obvious place for it. It does, however, seem likely that Reid in his lecture on 11 March recapitulated some of the earlier material by discussing Hume's theory of property and that he is here echoing Hume's well-known passage "This poetical fiction of the golden age is, in some respects, of a piece with the philosophical fiction of the state of nature" (*Enquiry*, p. 189, and cf. *Treatise*, p. 493). In that case the "Abstract," which we otherwise cannot identify, may be one of the drafts that eventually became ch. 5 of essay v in A.P. and of which we have a specimen in 6/I/9, where Reid on fol. 2v (see his point no. 7) clearly refers to the passage in the *Enquiry* quoted above.

35. As mentioned above in n. 31, this issue was raised in Roman law, whence it entered modern natural law and acquired the highest importance in the disputes of the sixteenth and seventeenth centuries as to whether the high seas could become the "private" (exclusive) property of nations (the most famous protagonist against being Grotius in *Mare liberum* [1609], and for this proposition, John Selden in *Mare clausum* [1636]). The problem did, however, concern many other things, especially waters other than the high seas (coastal waters, bays, lakes, rivers), the air (meaning also space), sunlight, the wind, the earth as a whole, wild animals in general, and so on. While it was relatively clear what it meant to claim exclusive property rights in particular parts, or individual specimens of some of these things, it was not clear how individuals or states could claim such rights in the whole or in the generality. The problem therefore forced natural lawyers to try to clarify the concept of property rights and especially to weigh the relative importance of "physical" or "natural criteria," such as controllability and limitability, and "moral" criteria, such as our own needs and the needs of others (which for the contractarian theorists involved interpretation of the original agreement's intentions). See Grotius, *War and Peace*, II.2.iii and II.3.vii ff.; Pufendorf, *Law of Nature*, IV.5, and *Duty of Man*, I.12.iv; Hutcheson, *Short Introduction*, p. 158, and *System*, I.329–330; and Hume, *Treatise*, p. 495, and *Enquiry*, p. 184. As is evident from the following sentence, Reid has given the topic an extemporaneous elaboration and he returns to it in Section XI, pp. 207 and 210.

36. Perhaps "to it," although the period before "it" is quite distinct.

37. I read the three examples as follows. The first case exemplifies the hitherto unoccupied, which is equally open for acquisition to all so that nobody is harmed when it is taken. Such concern with the rights of colonizers was common in the natural law literature. The second case illustrates the harmful occupation of what has already been taken by others. The third is a case of occupation of that which was once occupied but had been abandoned and is thus again available to the occupier who comes first. This case was in fact a famous one and played a wider role in natural law. The story is told by Plutarch in *Quaestiones Graecae*, question 30, of the two spies representing the allied peoples of Andros and Chalcis who see that the city of Acanthos is deserted. The Chalcidian spy runs in order to claim Acanthos for his people, while the slower Andrian spy throws his spear and plants it in the city gate, on the basis of which he claims first occupancy of

the deserted city for his people. The story is retold by both Grotius (*War and Peace*, II.8.vi) and Pufendorf (*Law of Nature*, IV.6.viii) when they discuss what counts as physical occupation of a thing, which for them is a necessary condition for first occupancy to establish a right. This indicates that Reid has used the examples as a transition to the following point in his lecture, where he makes it clear that he followed Barbeyrac and Hutcheson in denying this condition. Like Barbeyrac and Hutcheson, Reid thought that any clear demonstration of intention to occupy, not just the physical occupation, was enough to establish a property right through first occupation. See Barbeyrac's n. 2 to Pufendorf, *Law of Nature*, IV.6.viii, and see also Hutcheson, *Short Introduction*, pp. 152-153, and *System*, 1.318, 325-326, and 346. Grotius and Pufendorf did not mean to say that property right by first occupation was the same as physical occupation, but only that this was necessary to prove unequivocally the intention to occupy and who had it first. Nevertheless, Barbeyrac and Hutcheson take this opportunity to reject the "confused imagination that property is some physical quality or relation produced by some action of men" (Hutcheson, *System*, 1.318) and thus to stress the idea of property as a moral link, the solidity of which depends on the status of our moral ideas. In this they were followed by Reid; see Section XI in this book. p. 205. It is clear that this line of criticism also was aimed at Locke's famous theory in ch. v of the *Second Treatise* that "whatsoever" a man "hath mixed his Labour with" becomes his property (sec. 27). Also, Hume tells the story in his discussion of what counts as first occupancy (*Treatise*, pp. 507-508).

38. As mentioned in the previous note, property right by first occupation presupposes intention. However, property rights under positive ("civil") law may be conferred also on those incapable of having intentions, or relevant intentions, such as "Infants and delirious Persons") (Pufendorf, *Law of Nature*, IV.4.xv; cf. Grotius, *War and Peace*, II.3.vi).

39. After property rights by first occupancy, people may come into further property rights when the occupied things are somehow added to. The jurisprudential problem is to find criteria for what should count as such accessions. In Roman law, *accessio* was a broad category containing a variety of cases (*Institutes*, II.i.19–38). Most of this became stable fare in modern natural law's treatment of property (Grotius, *War and Peace*, II.8.viii–xxi; Pufendorf, *Law of Nature*, IV.7, and *Duty of Man*, 1.12.vii; S. Cocceius, *Introductio*, pp. 311–321; Hutcheson, *Short Introduction*,

pp. 160–162, and *System*, 1.337–338; Heineccius, *Universal Law*, 1.183–196; Hume, *Treatise*, p. 509 and the note pp. 509–513, and *Enquiry*, p. 310).

Fructus: Although one could say that there is an implicit distinction in Justinian between *accessio* (II.i.20–34) and *fructus* (II.i.19 and 35–38), this is never made clear, and in natural law *fructus*, fruit, becomes more or less synonymous with accession: "The Increments, Multiplication, and Profits of any kind of things are usually stiled Fruits" (Pufendorf, *Law of Nature*, IV.7.iii; similarly, Stair, *Institutions*, II.i.34).

Alluvio: the gradual deposit of soil by a river (Justinian, *Institutes*, II.i.20–24). These brief paragraphs provided a rich material on which natural lawyers could test how much was fixed by natural law principles of property and how much had to be left for positive law. Relevant considerations included the following: Whether the river was the border between two states and, if so, on what principles the border had been fixed. Whether a river within a state was public or private property or outside the original division of land. If it was public, as was commonly held in natural law, how much the river encompassed—the flowing water or also the riverbed? In the latter case, an island formed in the river (*insula nata in flumine*) by deposit would be public. But what about floating islands? Did the banks and thus deposits on them form part of the riverbed? What difference did a sudden rather than a gradual, less perceptible transportation of soil from A to B make? Who should own deposits by a river when it left its usual channel—for example, through flooding? See Grotius, *War and Peace*, II.8.viii–xvii; Pufendorf, *Law of Nature*, IV.7.xi–xii; Hume, *Treatise*, p. 511n., and *Enquiry*, p. 310n. The following cases listed by Reid raise the questions of what is the principal thing and what is the accessory thing, and how do we distinguish one from the other?

Adiunctio, like most of these labels, is not used in Roman law but stems from the commentators. In natural law it is a vague concept that is not clearly distinguished from the other forms of accession. Thus in Heineccius, *Universal Law*, 1.191, it is described as "when something belonging to another is added to our goods by inclusion, by soldering with lead, by nailing or iron-work, by writing, painting, &c." It is, however, likely that Reid is using the concept in a narrow sense for that which is separable from the principal thing without the destruction of either, but not without destroying the thing they make up together. The classical example (Justinian, *Institutes*, II.i.26) is the garment in which one man's purple thread is woven into another's coarser yarn (or one's purple cloth is sewn up with another's coarser cloth; Pufendorf, *Law of Nature*, IV.4.ix): is the coarse material accessory because of its lower value, or the purple because of its smaller volume? Cf. Grotius, *War and Peace*, II.8.xix.

Inaedificatio, building in or upon. Stemming from Justinian, *Institutes*, II.i.29–30, this label covers two clusters of cases: (1) A builds a house with B's materials (a) in bad faith; (b) in good faith; (c) in good faith, but the materials have been delivered by C who stole them from B; (d) A is in de facto possession of the house. (2) A builds a house with own materials on B's land, with subdivisions similar to the preceding. See Grotius, *War and Peace*, II.8.xxii; Pufendorf, *Law of Nature*, IV.7.vi; Heineccius, *Universal Law*, I.192–193.

Scriptura, a writing: If one man writes on another's paper, does the writing accede to the paper or the other way around? Justinian, *Institutes*, II.i.33, takes the former view; Pufendorf, *Law of Nature*, IV.7.vii, takes the latter. Cf. Grotius, *War and Peace*, II.8.xxi; Heineccius, *Universal Law*, I.193.

Specificatio, "Under accession may be included specification, by which is understood a person's making a new species or subject, from materials belonging to another" (Erskine, *Institute of the Law of Scotland*, II.i.16). When A makes jewelery of B's gold, or bread of his corn, or a ship of his wood, does the form of the final product accede to the materials or the other way around? Does this depend on whether form and material can again be separated and the material returned to its original condition? Or on the relative value of the material and the thing formed? Or on the amount of work expended in forming the thing? Or will different cases require different principles? It is, of course, presupposed that joint ownership by A and B is excluded. See Justinian, *Institutes*, II.i.25; Grotius, *War and Peace*, II.8.xix; Pufendorf, *Law of Nature*, IV.7.x; Heineccius, *Universal Law*, I. 190–191.

Similar questions arise from cases where substances belonging to different owners are mixed but are readily separable, though the individual elements are not identifiable and assignable, such as heaps of corn or flocks of unmarked sheep of the same breed (*commixtio*), or where the mixed substances cannot be separated, such as two lots of wine (*confusio*). See Justinian, *Institutes*, II.i.27–28; Grotius, *War and Peace*, II.8.xix; Pufendorf, *Law of Nations*, IV.7.x; Heineccius, *Universal Law*, I.194.

The cases of *plantatio*, planting, and *satio*, sowing, by one man in another's field again raise similar questions, a crucial factor in planting being whether the plant has taken root. Justinian, *Institutes*, II.i.31–32; Grotius, *War and Peace*, II.8.xxii; Pufendorf, *Law of Nature*, IV.7.v; Heineccius, *Universal Law*, 1.195.

In both Roman and natural law (as well as in Scots law) consideration of the agents' good or bad faith plays an important role in the treatment of all the cases falling under accession because this was crucial for the forms of legal action that could be taken in cases of conflict.

40. See Hutcheson, *System*, 1.338–339, and *Short Introduction*, p. 162: "Full property originally contains these several rights: first, that of retaining possession, 2. and next, that of taking all manner of use. 3. that also of excluding others from any use; 4. and lastly, that of transferring to others as the proprietor pleases, either in whole or in part, absolutely, or under any lawful condition, or upon any event or contingency, and of granting any particular lawful use to others. But property is frequently limited by civil laws, and frequently by the deeds of some former proprietors."

41. In this paragraph Reid refers to the standpoint, common to Grotius and Pufendorf, that once people live in civil society their right of occupancy is subject to regulation by positive law. Therefore, vacant land (including large accessions to land, as from rivers in flood), treasures in the ground, and wild life may in various degrees be made public property. See, e.g., Grotius, *War and Peace*, II.2.iv–v; Pufendorf, *Law of Nature*, IV.6.iii–vii; Hutcheson, *Short Introduction*, p. 162, and *System*, 1.339. This point should not be confused with the sovereign's *dominium eminens*, as the discussion of the distinction between *regalia maiora* and *regalia minora* shows. The former are the essential parts of sovereignty, and the latter are the less essential elements, which may be delegated and which traditionally included such things as those mentioned above; see Grotius, *War and Peace*, II.4.xiii, and esp. Barbeyrac's note to this. Grotius (II.3.xix) also makes the point that as far as land is concerned this will often be held in a sort of positive community by the society because it has commonly been taken possession of by a people as a whole, so that private property is derivative from and dependent upon this. It is undoubtedly this point that led Reid to talk about the feudal law on excheat (today escheat) which was the lapsing of land to the Crown (or to the feudal lord) when the owner died intestate and without heirs (in Scotland sometimes in the wider sense including confiscation and forfeiture of real or personal prop-

erty). The whole topic of the paragraph would have been closely tied to the final one, because what was barred from becoming private property through occupation could not be prescribed.

42. Prescription in its negative aspect is the extinction of a right through nonassertion of that right for some period of time. In its positive aspect it is the creation of a new right through de facto occupancy, use and so on, for some period, of things to which somebody else's right has been (or was being) extinguished in the former way. Deriving from Roman law's notion of *usucapio* (Justinian, *Institutes*, II.vi), it was stock-in-trade in natural law: Grotius, *War and Peace*, II.4; Pufendorf, *Law of Nature*, IV.12, and *Duty of Man*, I.12.xii; Hutcheson, *Short Introduction*, pp. 159–160 and *System*, I.335–336; Hume, *Treatise*, pp. 507–509.

43. See Hutcheson, *Short Introduction*, pp. 163–165, and *System*, I.340–343.

44. See Hutcheson, *System*, I.343–344: "Derived real rights are either some parts of the right of property transferred to another, and separate from the rest, or compleat property derived from the original proprietor. The parts of property frequently transferred separately from the rest of it are chiefly of these four classes. 1. Right of possession, thus one may have a right to possess the goods he knows belong to others, until the true proprietor shews his title. This right is valid against all others, and often may be turned into compleat property. 2. The right of succession, which one may have to goods, while another retains all the other parts of property except that of alienating. 3. The rights of a mortgage or pledge. 4. Rights to some small uses of the goods of others, called servitudes." Cf. *Short Introduction*, p. 165. Reid mentions the two first rights immediately below and the two last in 8/III/2,2r (below, p. 153). It should be pointed out that the Hutchesonian systematics, which Reid follows, here deviates somewhat from Pufendorf's. In *Law of Nature*, IV.8, Pufendorf treats rights of possession (v) and servitudes (vi–xii) between original and derived rights (cf. *Duty of Man*, I.12.viii), while pledge and mortgage are dealt with under the law of contract (v.10.xiii–xvi; cf. *Duty of Man*, I.15.xv), where it also makes a token reappearance in Hutcheson (*Short Introduction*, pp. 221–222, and *System*, II.77). For the general distinction between complete and partial property, see Grotius, *War and Peace*, I.l.v and II.3.ii; Pufendorf, *Law of Nature*, IV.4.ii, and *Duty of Man*, I.12.ix.

45. In *Short Introduction*, pp. 166–168, Hutcheson gives six such rules; in *System*, I.344–349, the discussion is more elaborate.

Hutcheson's discussion derives from Pufendorf, *Law of Nature*, IV.8.v; cf. Grotius, *War and Peace*, II.10. The natural lawyers' discussions of the legal effects of the de facto possession of another person's property was a direct extension of Roman law's treatment of it (Justinian, *Institutes*, II.vi; *Digest*, XLI.2). It was closely connected with the issue of prescription and the obligations arising from property (see Pufendorf, *Law of Nature*, IV.12–13, and *Duty of Man*, I.12.xii).

46. Hutcheson, *Short Introduction*, p. 168, and *System*, I.349–350. In view of his general interest in an agrarian law, Reid's criticism of the law of entails in the following pages is hardly surprising. It is also not surprising that he here goes far beyond Hutcheson's brief discussions, for the problem was very topical in the 1760s (and undoubtedly of relevance for a fair number of Reid's young listeners). From 1764 the Faculty of Advocates in Edinburgh led a campaign against the Act Concerning Entails from 1685 (Acts of the Parliament of Scotland, viii, 477 (26); cf. N. T. Phillipson, "Lawyers, landowners, and the civic leadership of post-Union Scotland," pp. 113–119). Reid was undoubtedly aware of this and of some of the literature surrounding it, such as Sir John Dalrymple's *Considerations on the Polity of Entails in a Nation* and *An Essay towards a General History of Feudal Property in Great Britain* (ch. 4); more important, however, is Lord Kames's *Historical Law-Tracts* (tract III, "Property") and his well-publicized "Considerations upon the State of Scotland with Respect to Entails," which he addressed to the Lord Chancellor in 1759. Reid and Kames were friends from 1762, they corresponded, Reid paid visits to Kames's country seat at Blair Drummond, and Reid read and commented on Kames's manuscripts. It is therefore impossible to imagine that Reid should have been unaware of Kames's criticism of entails, and it is worth noticing that of the tripartite criticism of entails which Reid presents below, the first two points—effects on the family and on the public—are identical with Kames's two general points in appendix 1, "Scotch Entails Considered in Moral and Political Views," in his *Sketches of the History of Man*. Reid's third point, that entailing is a breach of the law of nature, is clearly stated by Kames too, though not as a third point. Although this work was not published until 1774, Kames had obviously been thinking about and working on it long before (see I. S. Ross, *Lord Kames and the Scotland of His Day*, pp. 333ff.), and Reid was certainly privy to the genesis of the work, for he contributed a minor piece to it (an appendix on Aristotle's logic in book III, sketch 1), which he may

already have begun in 1767 (see Reid, *Works*, 1:49b). Similarly, Reid has hardly been unaware of the critical attitude toward entails taken by his predecessor Adam Smith (see LJ(A), i.160–ii.1 LJ(B), 166–169; cf. WN, III.ii.5–7) and by his young colleague, John Millar (see notes from Millar's "Lectures on the Institutions of the Civil Law," dated Glasgow 1794, Edinburgh University Library MS. Dc. 2. 45–46 [2 vols.], 2:45–53). On this topic Millar would hardly have changed his tune in the intervening thirty years; cf. *Origin of Ranks*, pp. 232–235. Also, the recent work of historians would have impressed upon Reid the importance of entails: Robertson, *History of Scotland*, 1:20–21, and Hume, *History of England*, 3:302.

47. See the same point in Kames, "Considerations," pp. 328–329. For some of the subsequent points concerning the public effects of entails, see ibid., pp. 329–330.

48. See Kames, *Sketches*, 4:457: "every prosperous trader will desert a country where he can find no land to purchase."

49. Reid has rearranged his text (see the Textual Notes) so that it follows the same order as Hutcheson's *Short Introduction*, pp. 168–171, and *System*, 1.350–352.

50. See Hutcheson, *Short Introduction*, pp. 168–169: "For further security to creditors pledges and mortgages were introduced, or goods so subjected to the power of the creditor that, if the debt is not discharged at the time prefixed, the goods should become the property of the creditor." Generally speaking, one could pledge moveables and mortgage real estate, as Hutcheson explains in *Institutio*, p. 173, and in *System*, 1.350–351. He here follows Pufendorf, *Law of Nature*, v.10.xvi, and *Duty of Man*, 1.15.xv. Pufendorf's discussion is again built around the Roman law's treatment of *pignus* (approx. pledge) and *hypotheca* (approx. mortgage) in Justinian, *Institutes*, III.xiv.4 and IV.vi.7; *Digest*, xx. The following points should be read in the light of the following references (Hutcheson, *Short Introduction*, pp. 169–170): "The last class of real rights are servitudes that is 'rights to some small use of the property of others'; which generally arise from contracts; or from this that in the transferring of property they have been reserved by the granter; or sometimes from civil laws. All servitudes are real rights, terminating upon some definite tenement. And yet with regard to the subject they belong to, and not the object they terminate upon, they are divided into real and personal. The personal are constituted in favour of some person, and expire along with him: the real are consti-

tuted for the advantage of some tenement, and belong to whatever person possesses it. An instance of the former is tenantry
for life impeachable for waste" (cf. *System*, 1.351). The distinction
between personal and real servitudes is built upon Pufendorf
(*Law of Nature*, iv.8.vi, and *Duty of Man*, 1.12.viii), who again derives it from Roman law's distinction between predial and personal servitudes (*Institutes*, ii.iii–iv, and *Digest*, viii.1.i). In the final sentence quoted, Hutcheson in fact seems to amalgamate
Roman law's *usufructus* and *usus*, which he mentions in his Latin
text (*Institutio*, p. 174), where he also mentions the third of the
classical personal servitudes, *habitatio* (*Institutes*, ii.5.v), the right
to the *usus* of a house for life. Reid obviously used the Latin
version of Hutcheson's textbook, as he, in contrast to the *Short
Introduction*, goes on to specify "Life rent." For the personal servitudes, see Pufendorf, *Law of Nature*, iv.8.vii–x, and *Duty of
Man*, 1.12.viii. Reid's mention of the real servitudes is a précis of
Hutcheson's Latin version (*Institutio*, p. 174): "Reales sunt vel urbanae, vel rusticae. Urbanae sunt oneris ferendi, tigni immittendi, altius tollendi, aut non tollendi, luminum, prospectus, &c.
Rustica, contra, spectant praedia, iter, actus, via, &c." This is not
fully rendered in *Short Introduction*, but its sense is: "The real
⟨servitudes⟩ are either urban or rural. The urban ones are to
support the burden ⟨of the neighbour's wall when two houses
are attached⟩, to insert beams ⟨into a neighbouring wall⟩, to
build higher or, rather, not to build ⟨above a certain height⟩, ⟨to
have unhindered⟩ light ⟨i.e. windows⟩ ⟨and⟩ view." To this Reid
adds "stillicidii" ⟨recipiendi⟩—that is, the servitude to receive
dripping rain water from another's house. He has undoubtedly
taken this from Pufendorf, *De officio*, 1.12.viii. The rest of Reid's
formulation does, however, agree with Hutcheson much more
than with Pufendorf, let alone the *Institutes*, which deals with the
same urban servitudes in ii.iii.1–2. For a more extensive treatment, see Pufendorf, *Law of Nature*, iv.8.xi, where detailed references to the *Digest* are also given. As to the rural servitudes,
Hutcheson is saying: "Rural lands, on the other hand, concern
iter ⟨the right of *way* to walk⟩, *actus* ⟨the right of way to drive
animals or vehicles⟩, *via* ⟨the general right of *passage* including
both *iter* and *actus*⟩." The explanations in angle brackets derive
from the *Institutes'* treatment of rural servitudes in ii.iii., pr.; cf.
Hutcheson, *Short Introduction*, p. 170, and *System*, 1.351; Pufendorf, *Law of Nature*, iv.8.xii, and *Duty of Man*, 1.12.viii. *Usufructus*, *usus*, and *habitatio* are dealt with in *Digest*, book vii; real

servitudes are in book VIII. See also Grotius, *War and Peace*, III.2.ii; Cocceius, *Introductio*, pp. 93 and 333–335; Heineccius, *Universal Law*, 1.213–214.

51. The following fourfold division is identical with that of Hutcheson, *Short Introduction*, p. 171, and *System*, 1.352, and of Pufendorf, *Law of Nature*, IV.10.i, and implicitly *Duty of Man*, 1.12.x and xiii–xv. Donation is not dealt with by Reid, while delict is discussed below, pp. 167–169.

52. Grotius, *De iure*, II.6.xiv: "Alienatio autem in mortis eventum, ante eam revocabilis, retento interim jure possidendi ac fruendi, est testamentum," which in the English translation is rendered: "For a Will is the making over one's Effects in Case of Death, 'till then to be reversed or altered at Pleasure; and in the mean Time reserving the whole Right of Possession and Enjoyment" (*War and Peace*, II.6.xiv).

53. Pufendorf's objection, which he expresses in *Law of Nature*, IV.10.ii (quoting the same passage from Grotius), but not in *Duty of Man*, is that a testament cannot be called an alienation. An alienation presupposes an alienator and a willing receiver, but after the death that brings a testament into force there is no alienator, and before this death there is often no willing receiver, for intended heirs may be unaware of the testator's intention and their willingness is anyway irrelevant until after the testator's death. Further, in obvious contrast to an alienation, a testament has no effect on the property right of the testator as long as he is alive, as is shown by his right to alienate his property to others and to change his testament as he pleases. Accordingly, says Pufendorf, "We shall express the Nature of a Testament more plainly and more agreeably to the sense of the Roman Lawyers, if we call it, A Declaration of our Will touching the Successors to our Goods, after our Decease, yet such as is mutable and revocable at our pleasure whilst we live, and which creates a Right in others to take place only when we are gone" (*Law of Nature*, IV.10.iii; cf. *Duty of Man*, 1.12.xiii). The Roman lawyers' sense was expressed in the *Institutes*, I.x., pr., and the *Digest*, XXVIII.i.1. Quoting part of Pufendorf's definition with approval (*System*, 1.354), Hutcheson protests against "the metaphysical subtilities" of these very common disputes; see *Short Introduction*, p. 172, and *System*, 1.354n., where he refers to Pufendorf, *Law of Nature*, IV.10.iii, and Barbeyrac's protest there, p. 419, n.2.

54. As in the case of entails, Reid, in the following brief discussion of intestate succession, adopts the kind of historical approach

that is so well-known from such contemporaries as Kames, Smith, and Millar, and there is in fact broad similarity between the following two paragraphs and Kames, *Historical Law-Tracts*, pp. 100ff. At the same time the topic did have its firm place in the systematics of natural jurisprudence (see above, n.51): Grotius, *War and Peace*, II.7.ii–xi; Pufendorf, *Law of Nature*, IV.11, and *Duty of Man*, I.12.x–xi; Hutcheson, *Short Introduction*, pp. 173–175, and *System*, I.355–357; Cocceius, *Introductio ad Grotium illustratum*, pp. 313–328; Heineccius, *Universal Law*, I.222–230; cf. Justinian, *Institutes*, III.i (and following titles). Reid would here have found the general points that in natural law the basis for intestate succession was a presumption about the deceased's natural intention concerning his estate, that is, what this ought to be. It would be natural that the deceased's offspring should have the benefit of his property, otherwise those nearest to him in the family, at least to the level of basic maintenance and that beyond this positive law had to determine. Further, he also would have found that positive law actually did much more, and often in contravention of natural law. Some, like Grotius and Heineccius, take the obligation to maintain offspring to be merely imperfect, and the right to intestate succession is for them accordingly imperfect. Pufendorf takes the same rights and obligations to be perfect as far as children who are "unable to maintain themselves" are concerned (Pufendorf, *Law of Nature*, IV.11.iv). This brings in a distinction between the ages of children, which Barbeyrac emphasizes in making the same point (see n. 1 to Grotius, *War and Peace*, II.7.iv) and which was of great importance in Reid's later discussion of the jurisprudential status of the family. Hutcheson, finally, takes the middle line that "God and nature, by making these tyes of blood bonds also of love and good-will, seems to have given our children and kinsmen if not a perfect claim or right, yet at least one very near to perfect" to the property of their parents or relatives (*Short Introduction*, p. 173). Hutcheson's denial of a sharp distinction between perfect and imperfect rights should be kept in mind here.

55. Foris familiate: outside the family—that is, who has left the family (traditionally lawyers used the old ablative in this connection, thus perhaps facilitating the anglicization "to forisfamiliate" of the medieval "forisfamiliare"). See the Commentary below at p. 365 n. 8.

56. See *Digest*, XXVIII.ii.11, and perhaps of more direct relevance, Cocceius, *Introductio ad Grotium illustratum*, pp. 322–323, and

Kames, *Historical Law-Tracts*, pp. 109–110: "originally there was not such a thing as succession in the sense we now give that term. Children came in place of their parents: But this was not properly a succession; it was a continuation of possession, founded upon their own title of property. And while the relation of property continued so slight as it was originally, it was perhaps thought sufficient that children *in familia* only should enjoy this privilege." Similarly, ibid., pp. 100–101.

57. See Grotius, *War and Peace*, II.7.viii.

58. See Grotius, *War and Peace*, II.7.i: "There are some of the Civil Laws ⟨concerning 'derivative Acquisition, or Alienation'⟩ that are plainly unjust; as those by which all shipwrecked Goods are confiscated." The same point is made with the same example by Pufendorf in *Law of Nature*, IV.13.iv. Reid's use of "succession" in the present context is obviously very wide, and like Pufendorf he has undoubtedly been addressing the general problem of when it is not legitimate according to the law of nature to take over another's property right, whatever the positive law says. Cf. Pufendorf, *Duty of Man*, I.13.

59. See A.P., p. 663, and below, Section XV, p. 237. The topic for the second half of Reid's lecture on Tuesday 19 March 1765 was exceptionally fertile for him. The end-product was his considerations "Of the Nature and Obligation of a Contract" (A.P., v.6), which form a cornerstone in his criticism of Hume's theory of justice. En route to this we have some significant drafts (2/II/ 14 and 7/VII/2–6 in part, not in this volume). Furthermore, Reid used his thoughts about the nature of contracts to interpret the foundation for civil society in an important paper (2/II/10), which I print in Section XV. Folios 1r–2r of that manuscript throw much light on the present manuscript. The soil had been well prepared for Reid, because contract had been of central concern to all the natural lawyers, who again drew on a rich classical material. Reid himself does not indicate any direct concern with Roman law on this topic, and the reader is therefore referred to the detailed citations in the passages of Grotius, Pufendorf, and Cocceius referred to below. However, it should be pointed out that Reid does not take up the classical distinction between pacts and contracts, thus apparently accepting Hutcheson's point in *Short Introduction*, pp. 177–178, that according to the law of nature there is no such distinction, a point also made by Barbeyrac (n. 2, p. 473 of Pufendorf, *Law of Nature*). But for Pufendorf's discussion of the distinction both in Hobbes (*De cive*, II.9) and in Roman law, see *Law of Nature*, v.2.i–iv.

60. The distinctions in the two first paragraphs should be seen against the background of Grotius's distinction between (1) "a bare Assertion, signifying what we intend hereafter, in the Mind we are now in" (*War and Peace*, ii.11.ii); (2) "The second Manner, when the Will determines itself for the Time to come, is by giving some positive Token, that sufficiently declares the Necessity of its Perseverance. And this may be called an imperfect Promise, which . . . obliges either absolutely or conditionally; but yet gives no Right, properly so called, to him to whom it is made" (ibid., ii.11.iii); (3) "A third Degree is, when to this Determination we add a sufficient Declaration of our Will to confer on another a real Right of demanding the Performance of our Promise. And this is a compleat Promise" (ibid., ii.11.iv). Reid may have been aware of the entry into Scottish legal thought of these distinctions in Stair, *Institutions*, 1.10.i–vi, and would certainly have been influenced by their substantial repetition in Pufendorf, *Law of Nature*, iii.5.v–vii (cf. *Duty of Man*, 1.9.vi–vii), Hutcheson, *Short Introduction*, pp. 179–180, and *System*, ii.5–6 (cf. Cocceius, *Introductio*, p. 102). Heineccius denies the distinction between perfect and imperfect (or incomplete) promises, *Universal Law*, 1.302–303. See further Hume, *Treatise*, iii.2.v, and *Enquiry*, pp. 199–200, and Reid's criticism in A.P., pp. 666a–670b.

61. See A.P., p. 665b; Grotius, *War and Peace*, ii.11.v; Pufendorf, *Law of Nature*, iii.6.iii–v, and *Duty of Man*, 1.9.x–xi; Hutcheson, *Short Introduction*, pp. 180–182, and *System*, ii.8–12; Cocceius, *Introductio*, p. 370; Heineccius, *Universal Law*, 1.305.

62. See Grotius, *War and Peace*, ii.11.vi; Pufendorf, *Law of Nature*, iii.6.vi (cf. v.3.ix), and *Duty of Man*, 1.9.xii; Hutcheson, *Short Introduction*, pp. 182–183, and *System*, ii.14–15; Cocceius, *Introductio*, pp. 103 and 367; Heineccius, *Universal Law*, 1.306.

63. See Pufendorf, *Law of Nature*, iii.6.vii (and v.3.ii–iii); Hutcheson, *Short Introduction*, p. 183, and *System*, ii.15; Coccceius, *Introductio*, p. 367.

64. See Grotius, *War and Peace*, ii.4.iii, ii.11.xi, and ii.16.i; Pufendorf, *Law of Nature*, iii.6.ii and xvi, and *Duty of Man*, 1.9.ix; Hutcheson, *Short Introduction*, pp. 184–185, and *System*, ii.6; Heineccius, *Universal Law*, 1.304–305; Cocceius, *Introductio*, p. 361. Concerning this and the following point, see also the next lecture on obligations in the use of speech and, concerning "mental Reservation," see further Pufendorf, *Law of Nature*, iv.l.xiv, and *Duty of Man*, 1.10.x; Hutcheson, *System*, ii.37–38 ("The crime of equivocation and mental reservations").

65. See Grotius, *War and Peace*, II.11.vii and xx; Pufendorf, *Law of Nature*, III.6.ix–xiii, and *Duty of Man*, I.9.xv; Hutcheson, *Short Introduction*, pp. 187–191, and *System*, II.16–23; Heineccius, *Universal Law*, I.307–308; Cocceius, *Introductio*, pp. 103 and 368. The topic was generally divided into two: the fear that the other party to a contract will not fulfill his part, and the fear of unpleasant repercussions if one does not enter into some contract. The problem is, does either kind of fear invalidate the contract? Reid's formulation indicates that he has concentrated on the second kind of fear.

66. See Grotius, *War and Peace*, II.13.xiv–xvi, III.19, and III.23.ii; Pufendorf, *Law of Nature*, III.6.ix–xiii; Hutcheson, *Short Introduction*, p. 188, and *System*, II.17–18: "No tenet can be of more horrid consequence than this, that 'bad men have no valid rights, or that good men are under no obligations to them,' whether they are deemed bad on account of practices, or of opinions we may call heresies. The laws of God and nature bind us to consult the happiness even of the worst of men as far as it consists with that of the more useful members of the great system. . . . Again, how dangerous must this tenet be while it is so hard to judge of the moral goodness of others, and men are so frequently led by prejudice and party-zeal into the most unfavourable opinions of the best of men. . . . And how shall we fix that degree of vice which forfeits the common rights of men, or makes them incapable of acquiring any. This tenet cannot take place even against such as avowedly disregard all laws of God and nature." Cf. *Short Introduction*, p. 188. Further, Cocceius, *Introductio*, p. 371.

67. See Grotius, *War and Peace*, II.11.viii–ix; Pufendorf, *Law of Nature*, III.7.vi–xi, and *Duty of Man*, I.9.xviii; Hutcheson, *Short Introduction*, pp. 191–193, and *System*, II.24–26; Heineccius, *Universal Law*, I.308–311; Cocceius, *Introductio*, pp. 371–372. The basic point is this: "To make a Promise or Pact truly Obligatory, it is . . . Requisite, that we have a Moral Power of performing the thing agreed upon. And if the thing be unlawful, and we consequently want this Power, we cannot tie ourselves by any such Engagement" (Pufendorf, *Law of Nature*, III.7.vi).

68. See Grotius, *War and Peace*, II.11.i; Pufendorf, *Law of Nature*, III.5.x; Hutcheson, *Short Introduction*, p. 192.

69. Echoing Hutcheson, *System*, II.15, Reid here probably recapitulated some of the points made the previous day.

70. Cicero, *De officiis*, I.23: "Fundamentum autem est iustitiae fides, id est dictorum conventorumque constantia et veritas" ("The foundation of justice, moreover, is good faith—that is, truth and

fidelity to promises and agreements"). The word I have tran-
scribed as "pactorumq" is nearly impossible to decipher and
might be "factoring," which in Scotland referred to the appointment by a landholder or proprietor of an agent or steward to
manage an estate (see below p. 157, for its use). However, apart
from the unlikelihood that Reid would mix an English word into
a standard Latin quotation, this would seem to be far too special
and indeed parochial a concept to weave into such a general
thought, whereas "pactorum" would be a very obvious near syn-
onym for a lecturer quoting in a hurry and maybe from memory; certainly "pactum" was constantly used in Reid's sources.
The Cicero passage is quoted by Grotius, *War and Peace*, II.11.i
(5); Pufendorf, *Law of Nature*, III.5.ix; and Cocceius, *Introductio*,
p. 360.

71. See Cicero, *De officiis*, II.xi (40); Plato, *Republic*, I.351c ff.; Heliodorus, *An Aethiopian History*, p. 150. The passage in Cicero is
quoted by Pufendorf, *Law of Nature*, III.4.ii, and by Heineccius,
Universal Law, 1.301–302, while Heliodorus is referred to by
Barbeyrac in Pufendorf, *Law of Nature*, VIII.4.v, where there is
an extensive discussion of the point. See the Commentary above
at p. 315 n. 3.

72. Horace, *Odes*, I.xxiv: "cui Pudor et Justitiae soror, incorrupta
Fides, nudaque Veritas, quando ullum invenient parem?"
("When shall Honour, and Justice's sister, Loyalty unshaken,
and candid Truth e'er find a peer to him?"). The passage is
quoted, in part, in the present context by Grotius, *War and
Peace*, II.11.i (5) and by Cocceius, *Introductio*, p. 360.

73. See Grotius, *War and Peace*, II.11.xiv–xv; Pufendorf, *Law of Nature*, III.6.xv, and *Duty of Man*, I.9.xvi; Hutcheson, *Short Introduction*, p. 185, and *System*, II.12–13: "To the validity of contracts
mutual consent is necessary; and that even in donations, as well
as other translations of rights . . . The proprietors can suspend
their conveyances upon any lawful conditions or contingencies
they please. Present acceptation is not always necessary; as in
legacies to persons absent; and in all conveyances to infants. No
man indeed acquires property against his will, or until he consents to it, but the granter may order the property to remain in
suspense till it can be accepted by the grantee; or may commit
the goods to trustees till the grantee shews his will to accept
them. . . . All this is very intelligible if we remember that property is not a physical quality. . . . If property were a physical
quality, it must indeed have a present subject." See further, Heineccius, *Universal Law*, 1.308, and Cocceius, *Introductio*, p. 104.

74. Reid is here giving the kernel of his argument for an irreducible active power in man, and the present passage is clearly an antecedent of the final version in A.P., p. 517b.

75. This passage shows that Reid already in 1765 had Hume's theory of justice firmly in view when developing his own. See above, p. 338 n. 59.

76. See A.P., p. 666b; Hutcheson, *Short Introduction*, pp. 177–179, and *System*, II.1–3.

77. In the Golden Age the goddess of justice, Astraea, daughter of Zeus and Themis, lived among men, but when humanity had slumped through the silver age to the "age of hard iron," "all evil burst forth into this age of baser vein": "Piety lay vanquished, and the maiden Astraea, last of the immortals, abandoned the blood-soaked earth" (Ovid, *Metamorphoses*, I.127–128 and 149–150). Reid would also have known the similar passages in Juvenal, *Satire* VI, 19–20, and (pseudo) Seneca, *Octavia*, 423–425, and Seneca, *Thyestes*, 857.

78. This was a standard topic in Reid's natural law sources, but in Reid it assumes a much more central role by its connection with his general theory of language, which must be seen in the light of contemporary discussions of language, not least that of Condillac, *An Essay on the Origin of Human Knowledge*, rather than in the light of the natural lawyers' simple contractualist views. As indicated in subsequent notes, the following two lectures are closely linked to the signal contribution to language-theory that we find scattered through Reid's published works. At the end of the two lectures (see below, n. 88) Reid does, however, take up parts of the traditional natural law treatment of the duties in speech.

79. See Hutcheson, *Illustrations*, pp. 253–274. In a brief undated note, Reid made a different beginning on the present topic. It is on fol. 1r of four otherwise blank quarto pages in 7/VII/14:

> In treating of Speech we shall first consider the Obligations to Veracity. 2 The other Duties and Obligations that relate to Speech. 1 Veracity what? There is the same Difficulty in defining accurately a Declaration testimony or affirmation as in defining a Promise or Contract. It is a social Act of the Mind and Supposes a Social Intercourse with intelligent & moral Agents.

80. On natural and artificial language, see Reid's discussions in *Inquiry into the Human Mind* (H.M.), pp. 117–119 (121–122), 194–201, and in A.P., pp. 664–665; cf. also 4/II/5,2v and 7/V/1,12r.

81. See the theory of the "social operations of the mind" developed in I.P., pp. 244–245, and A.P., pp. 663–665, and the theory of contract in 2/II/10, Section XV below.

82. See H.M., p. 118a.

83. Concerning the comparison of human and animal language, see further H.M., p. 118a, and A.P., p. 665b.

84. Wild Peter from Hanover (Hameln) was one of the most famous cases of a human being supposed to have grown up in isolation from other humans. The story was that he had been abandoned in the Hanoverian forests and was found at the presumed age of thirteen in 1724, living like an animal. He became particularly well-known in Britain, as Swift relates: "This night I saw the wild Boy, whose arrivall here hath been the subject of half our Talk this fortnight. He is in the Keeping of Dr. Arthbuthnot ⟨sic⟩, but the King and Court were so entertained with him, that the Princess could not get him till now" (Swift to Thomas Tickell, London, 16 April 1726, in Swift, *Correspondence*, 3:128; cf. *Gentleman's Magazine*, 21 [1751]: 522). Reid is likely to have known of this case from Rousseau, *Discours sur l'origine de l'inegalité*, p. 94, and from Linné *Systema naturae*, 1.20. As for other cases, Rousseau (*Discours*, pp. 94–96; cf. p. 110) would have provided him with four, and Linné (*Systema naturae*) with six, some of them the same and one of them also likely to have been known to Reid from Condillac, *Essay*, p. 131. There were further contemporary (esp. French) discussions of such cases.

85. See H.M., pp. 118a and 195a; I.P., pp. 449–450; A.P., p. 664b.

86. Reid had in fact treated the last point more fully in H.M., pp. 196–197 (cf. A.P., pp. 665a and 666a, and letter to James Gregory, *Works*, p. 71a). The numeral, 2, presumably indicates that Reid now goes on to the second of the four sources of our obligations in speech mentioned at the beginning of the lecture, "The immediate Judgment of our Moral Powers."

87. See, e.g., A.P., pp. 666a–b.

88. Reid here returns to the beaten track of the jurisprudential system. His distinction between two kinds of deception corresponds to Grotius's distinction between negative and positive fraud (*War and Peace*, III.l.vii–viii), which is adopted and to some extent adapted by Hutcheson, *Short Introduction*, pp. 196–198, and *System*, II.29–32. Pufendorf prefers to put the distinction as one between an "Untruth" (falsiloquium) and a "Lye" (mendacium); see *Law of Nature*, IV.l.ix. Reid's discussion should be related to the extensive treatment of deception in Grotius, *War and Peace*, III.l.vi–xx; Pufendorf, *Law and Nature*, IV.l.vii–xxi,

and *Duty of Man*, 1.10.iv–ix; Hutcheson, *Short Introduction*, pp. 198–201, and *System*, 11.32–38. As Sissela Bok (*Lying*, p. 39) explains in her stimulating discussion of the problem:

> The final way ⟨after mental reservation⟩ to avoid Augustine's across-the-board prohibition of all lies seeks to argue that not all intentionally false statements ought to count as lies from a moral point of view. This view found powerful expression in Grotius. He argued that a falsehood is a lie in the strict sense of the word only if it conflicts with a right of the person to whom it is addressed. A robber, for instance, has no right to the information he tries to extort; to speak falsely to him is therefore not to lie in the strict sense of the word. The right in question is that of liberty of judgement, which is implied in all speech; but it can be lost if the listener has evil intentions; or not yet acquired, as in the case of children; or else freely given up, as when two persons agree to deceive one another. . . . Grotius helped to bring back into the discourse on lying the notion, common in antiquity but so nearly snuffed out by St. Augustine, that falsehood is at times justifiable.

This perspective should be kept in mind in the following.

89. See Grotius, *War and Peace*, III.l.xvii–xix; Pufendorf, *Law of Nature*, IV.l.xix, and *Duty of Man*, 1.10.ix; Hutcheson, *Short Introduction*, p. 199, and *System*, 11.33–34.

90. John 1:45–51.

91. See Pufendorf, *Law of Nature*, IV.2.xx and V.13.ix; Hutcheson, *System*, 11.37.

92. I venture the following hypothetical identification of the questions of which Reid reminded himself with these five marginal points. "Reproof" is to be taken in the now obsolete sense of "disproof" or "refutation," and Reid has here taken up the problem raised by Pufendorf (*Law of Nature*, IV.l.xx) whether a guilty person can legitimately deny his guilt in a (human) court of law. Thence he goes on to consider the use of the testimony of the accused and, more generally, the moral status of judicial self-defense (e.g., Pufendorf, ibid.). "Caution to a third person" may refer to the deterrent effect of punishment, which Pufendorf mentions in passing, but it may also belong to "What is publick," which again is to be related to the following few lines of the main text. Here Reid in general terms follows Hutcheson, *System*, 11.38–40, in giving a list of duties and vices in conversation, and "What is publick" refers to the following point raised

by Hutcheson (ibid., pp. 40–41)—namely, that we must carefully consider whether the faults of others are such that the maximum moral gain will be derived from making them public or from keeping them secret and instead of telling the magistrate give private "caution to a third person."

93. See Hutcheson, *System*, II.42–43: "Under this head of the use of speech comes likewise in the old logical and moral debate between the Cynicks and the other sects of antient philosophy, about obscenity. The Cynicks allege that 'there is no work of God, no natural action, which may not be matter of inquiry and conversation to good men, and we must use their names; hence, they conclude there is no obscenity.' The answer to this is obvious. Many words in every language, beside their primary signification of some object or action, carry along additional ideas of some affections in the speaker; other words of the same primary meaning may have the additional signification of contrary affections; and a third set of words may barely denote the object or action, without intimating any affection of the speaker. . . . Few objects want these three sorts of names, one barely denoting it, another sort denoting also our joy or approbation, or our relish for it, and a third denoting our aversion or contempt of it. . . . An anatomist, or any modest man, can find words denoting any parts of the body, or any natural actions, or inclinations, without expressing any lewd dispositions, or any relish for vicious pleasures. In such words there is no obscenity. Other words may import an immoderate keenness for such pleasures, a dissoluteness of mind. . . . These are the obscenities of conversation."

94. All Reid's main natural law sources devoted a separate chapter to oaths and vows: Grotius, *War and Peace*, II.13; Pufendorf, *Law of Nature*, IV.2, and *Duty of Man*, I.11; Hutcheson, *Short Introduction*, II, ch. 11, and *System*, II, ch. 11; Cocceius, *Introductio*, pp. 108–109 and 388–391. The principal Roman law background is *Digest*, XII. 2, but much more important is Cicero's discussion of oaths in *De officiis* book III. Grotius (II.13.i(3)) quotes Cicero's definition of an oath, and Reid follows him. The definitions in all the other sources clearly echo this passage: Pufendorf, *Law of Nature*, IV.2.ii, and *Duty of Man*, I.11.i; Hutcheson, *Short Introduction*, p. 203: "an oath is 'a religious act in which for confirmation of something doubtful, we invoke God as witness and avenger, if we swerve from truth' " (a virtual quotation of Pufendorf). Cf. *System*, II. 44, and Cocceius, *Introductio*, pp. 108 and 388.

Reid says nothing about vows in these notes, but we may take a clue from Hutcheson's definition: "A vow is an oath in which men are not confirming any conveyance of right properly and immediately to their fellows, or any contract with them; but 'tis 'a promise made to God, binding us to some performance, and an invocation of divine punishment if we omit it' " (*System*, II.50; cf. *Short Introduction*, pp. 207–208). This derives from Pufendorf, *Law of Nature*, III.6.xv and IV.2.viii; cf. Grotius, *War and Peace*, II.13.xv (2).

95. Cicero, *De officiis*, III.xxix (104): "an oath is an assurance backed by religious sanctity; and a solemn promise given, as before God as one's witness, is to be sacredly kept."

96. Cicero, *De officiis*, III.xxxi (111): "Nullum enim vinculum ad astringendam fidem iure iurando maiores artius esse voluerunt" ("For our ancestors were of the opinion that no bond was more effective in guaranteeing good faith than an oath"). This quotation is also brought by Grotius, *War and Peace*, II.13.i (1). It should be noted that in Grotius's Latin text Cicero's word order is changed in exactly the same way as here by Reid, while in Barbeyrac's French translation, where the quotation is preserved in Latin, Barbeyrac corrected it.

97. See Hutcheson, *Short Introduction*, p. 204: "To swear about trifling matters, or without any cause, is very impious; as it plainly tends to abate that awful reverence which all good men should constantly maintain toward God; and is a plain indication of contempt. Where perjuries in serious matters grow frequent in any state, the magistrates or legislators are generally chargeable with much of the guilt, if they either frequently exact oaths without necessity in smaller matters, or when the oaths give no security in the point in view; when the engagement designed may either be impracticable, or appear to the persons concerned to be unlawful; or if oaths are required where there are great temptations to perjury, with hopes of impunity from men." Hutcheson's illustration of oaths that give no security is "engagements by oath to adhere to certain schemes of religion . . . or to a government" (cf. *System*, II.44–46). Above "lawfully onely" Reid has written "Quakers" and thus reminded himself to point out that the Quakers rejected oaths altogether because they took Matt. 5:33–37, strictly. See Grotius, *War and Peace*, II.13.xxi, and Cocceius, *Introductio*, p. 389.

98. The natural lawyers insisted that the core of an oath was the invocation of divine vengeance even when the oath did not mention God directly. Further, they saw sufficient common ground between all religions on this point to allow that the swearing of

an oath was binding irrespective of the person's religion. Grotius, *War and Peace*, II.13.x–xii; Pufendorf, *Law of Nature*, IV.2.iii–iv, and *Duty of Man*, I.11.iii–iv; Hutcheson, *Short Introduction*, pp. 204–205, and *System*, II.46; Cocceius, *Introductio*, p. 389. See Reid's manuscript printed in this book at p. 257. It should be pointed out that English law had recently been changed along the general lines of the natural lawyers. In the important case of *Omichund v. Barker* (1744), 1 Atkyns 21, Lord Hardwicke accepted the argument of the solicitor-general, Sir William Murray (later Lord Mansfield), that an oath could be taken by and evidence thus admitted from anyone who believed in divine retribution in some form, even a non-Christian (Omichund was a Hindu).

99. See Hutcheson, *Short Introduction*, p. 205: "As in covenants, so in oaths, he is justly deemed to have sworn . . . who professing an intention of swearing makes such signs as ordinarily signify to others that one swears. Altho' an oath and a promise, or an assertion, may often be expressed by one and the same grammatical sentence; yet the act of swearing is plainly a distinct one from that of promising or asserting; as it consists in the invocation of God to avenge if we violate our faith." See also *System*, II.46–47; Pufendorf, *Law of Nature*, IV.2.v; Grotius, *War and Peace*, II.13.iii; Cocceius, *Introductio*, p. 108.

100. The general division of oaths was into those regarding the past or the present, called assertory (or affirmative), and those regarding the future, the promissory (or obligatory) oaths. See Grotius, *War and Peace*, II.13.xxi; Pufendorf, *Law of Nature*, IV.2.xviii, and *Duty of Man*, I.11.x; Hutcheson, *Short Introduction*, pp. 206–207, and *System*, II.48; Cocceius, *Introductio*, p. 389. "Beside the general division of oaths into promissary and assertory, there are several sub-divisions. Assertory oaths demanded from witnesses under a penalty, are called necessary. When one of the contending parties, with consent of the judge, leaves the cause to the oath of the other, 'tis called a judicial oath. When the same is done without order of a judge, by mutual consent, 'tis called a voluntary oath. When it is enjoined on the party accused in a criminal action, in which he is to be absolved upon swearing his innocence, 'tis called a purgatory oath. When the oath is demanded only that the person accused may discover his crime, or be deemed guilty upon his declining to swear, it is called expletory, as it compleats an imperfect proof" (Hutcheson, *System*, II.48–49; cf. *Short Introduction*, pp. 206–207). Hutcheson builds on Pufendorf (*Law of Nature*, IV.2.xviii–xxii, and *Duty of Man*,

1.11.x, and Pufendorf's starting-point is *Digest*, XII.2 (cf. *Institutes*, IV.xiii.4). See also Cocceius, *Introductio*, p. 453.

101. See Pufendorf, *Law of Nature*, IV.2.xxiii; Hutcheson, *Short Introduction*, p. 207, and *System*, II.49–50.

102. This was the opinion of Pufendorf, *Law of Nature*, IV.2.vi, and *Duty of Man*, 1.11.vi; and Hutcheson, *Short Introduction*, p. 205, and *System*, II.47 (who asserts the same about vows; see *Short Introduction*, p. 208, and *System*, II.52). Grotius had, however, been of another opinion; in Barbeyrac's summary: "Grotius ... supposes on the contrary, that every Oath by which we engage our selves to do or not to do any thing to another, contains a double Promise; the one respecting the person that took the Oath, and the other the God by whom we swear; and that one of these Promises may oblige, though the other does not" (n. 2, p. 341, in Pufendorf, *Law of Nature*). The reference is to Grotius, *War and Peace*, II.13.xiv. This gave rise to an interesting dispute, the essence of which is in Barbeyrac's notes to these two passages in Grotius and Pufendorf.

103. Grotius, *War and Peace*, II.13.vi; Pufendorf, *Law of Nature*, IV.2.ix, and *Duty of Man*, 1.11.vi; Hutcheson, *Short Introduction*, p. 206, and *System*, II.47–48; Cocceius, *Introductio*, pp. 108 and 390.

104. Both in respect to the systematic location of this topic within the law of contract and in respect to its tripartite division (the nature of value, the measure of value, and the nature of money), Reid follows Hutcheson (*Short Introduction*, pp. 209–213; *System*, II.53–64), who again follows Pufendorf (*Law of Nature*, v.l; *Duty of Man*, 1.14) and Carmichael's notes to Pufendorf (*De officio*, pp. 247–254), while Pufendorf's own discussion has reference to Grotius's rudimentary treatment of value and money in *War and Peace*, II.12.xiv and xvii. Heineccius, *Universal Law*, 1.252–259, also follows this pattern.

105. The distinction between value in use and value in exchange was repeatedly stated in ancient and medieval authors, but Reid seems to be mainly in line with Pufendorf, *Law of Nature*, v.l.vi and esp. Hutcheson, *Short Introduction*, pp. 209–210, and *System*, II.53–55.

This topic is elaborated in a brief note in another manuscript (7/VII/6,1r), which I print here:

1769 Mar 26 Exchanges have always been and must be where there is Society. To make Exchanges Equitably Things must be valued & estimated. In a Solitary State things may have a greater or less Value but have not properly a price for a price supposes Exchange. In a Solitary State we value things which we have in property according as they are necessary usefull or agreable to ourselves. In Society we consider how far they may be usefull or agreable to others, with whom we may Exchange them. Things that cannot be appreciate 1 Such Ether Sun Moon as come not into property nor can be subjects of Commerce 1 Things Common 2 Things Sacred. 2 Things for which there can be no Competition either first because of no Value to any man or Secondly because they are inexhaustible and in every mans power to obtain. Or thirdly Where they are onely conveyed as appendages to other things. Such as a Wholesom Air fine prospect.

The manuscript as a whole consists of two folios, of which fol. 1r and fol. 2r carry text in the form of scattered notes apparently written at different times. The first note is printed here, above. Beneath a horizontal line follow two notes in two of Reid's different styles of handwriting, the first referring mainly to Hume's theory of justice, the second referring to Reid's distinction between solitary and social acts of the mind. Both are closely related to the now disjointed manuscript made up of 7/VII/2,3 and 5, which together with 2/II/14 constitute a draft of the chapter on contract in A.P. (pp. 663–670). These manuscripts are not in this volume. The final note in the present manuscript is printed below in n.109.

The threefold distinction that Reid makes in the manuscript (7/III/6,1r) just quoted in this note—the distinction between "necessary usefull or agreable," which is so important for the development of the idea of marginal utility—is also formulated in the English translation of Pufendorf (*Law of Nature*, v.l.iii); it is less clear in the Latin original. In the same manuscript, the following points ("Things that cannot be appreciate," including the examples and the spelling "Wholesom") derive from Pufendorf, *Law of Nature*, v.l.v, and *Duty of Man*, 1.14.iii, where "Things Common" are "the Air, the Sky, the heavenly Bodies, and the vast Ocean" and "Things Sacred" are religious places and offices. By things "of no Value to any man" are meant things of no value to any *other* man because they are not transferable, Pufendorf's example being personal freedom. Things inexhaustible are light and shade, wind and air, etc. But though these things are not subject to price, they can yet be associated with things that are subject to price so that they influence the latter's price (a block of land with "Wholesom Air" and a "fine prospect").

106. Reid's general dissatisfaction with what he saw as the traditional lack of a clear distinction between normative and technico-explanatory concerns (see above, pp. 114–116, in his Introductory Lecture) leads him to a partial break with the systematic position that modern natural law, following Roman law, allocated to economics within the law of contract. See also the Textual Notes at 162/40.

107. See Gen. 25:29–34.

108. Reid's attempt to combine a traditional subjective analysis of the concept of value with a labor concept of the measure of value should be compared with Adam Smith's famous and controversial attempt in the same direction: WN, I.iv.13 and I.v–vii; contrast LJ(A), vi.7–16 and 58–126; LJ(B), 205–209 and 223–244.

109. Before going on to the notes on contracts, it should be mentioned that in the 1765 course a small item is missing here from the general Pufendorfian agenda. After dealing with "Price" and with "Contracts in General, that presuppose the Price of Things" (*Law of Nature*, v.1–2; cf. *Duty of Man*, 1.14 and 15.i–ii), Pufendorf devoted a chapter (in *Duty of Man* a couple of sections: 1.15.vi–vii) to "the Equality that ought to be observed in Chargeable ⟨onerous⟩ Contracts" before going on to the detailed chapters on beneficent and onerous contracts (topics that Reid deals with immediately below). Among Reid's undated manuscripts there is a brief note (7/vii/6,2r) that shows that at some stage he paid attention to this topic, and I print the note here:

> In all onerous Contracts there is an equality to be observed. And where this equality is violated the Suffering party is in justice entitled to redress. We must determine this equality according to the natural or reasonable price of things. When a Man taking advantage of my ignorance Simplicity or Necessity takes 10£ from me for what is not worth above 1£ Altho' I consented to the bargain yet I am really injured, and he is under an obligation to redress the Injury. My consent was given from the perswasion that the bargain was equitable, and as soon as I know that I have been imposed upon, I am immediately conscious of the injury done me.

The note has a clear resemblance to *Law of Nature*, v.3.i, and *Duty of Man*, 1.15.vi. For a description of the full manuscript in which the note appears, see above, n.105.

110. Having dealt with contracts in general and with the theoretical

issues arising out of this, Reid turns in the following three lectures to the specific forms of contract. In this he follows Hutcheson and Pufendorf very closely, as we shall see. The division between the first two lectures follows the basic distinction between beneficent and onerous contracts: "Contracts are either beneficent, where a gratuitous favour is professedly done on one side; or onerous, where men profess to give mutually equal values" (Hutcheson, *System*, II.64; cf. *Short Introduction*, p. 214). This is based on Pufendorf, *Law of Nature*, v.2.viii, and *Duty of Man*, 1.15.ii; and on Grotius, *War and Peace*, II.12.ii. Grotius, ibid., sec. v, and Pufendorf, *Law of Nature*, v.2.x, added a group of contracts that are "mixed." The modern natural lawyers thus classified contracts according to the people on whom they imposed an obligation. By contrast, the Roman law classified contracts according to the way in which they arose: "there are real, verbal, literal and consensual contracts" (*Institutes*, III.xiii.2). This leads to significant differences in presentation. To take just one example, *mandatum* as a consensual contract is presented together with contracts of sale, letting, and hiring and partnership; while the natural lawyers grouped it with what for Roman law were real contracts—*mutuum*, *commodatum*, and *depositum*. Despite this, the natural law treatment of each of the contracts owes a great deal to Roman law.

"The mandatum is when 'one contracts to manage the business of another without reward' " (Hutcheson, *System*, II.64). See also Hutcheson, *Short Introduction*, p. 214; Pufendorf, *Law of Nature*, v.4.i–v, and *Duty of Man*, 1.15.iii; Grotius, *War and Peace*, II.12.ii; Cocceius, *Introductio*, pp. 383–384; Heineccius, *Universal Law*, 1.267–269; *Digest*, XVII.1; *Institutes*, III.xxvi.

111. "*Commodation* is 'the loan for use without any price or hire, where the same individual goods are to be returned.' . . . When the same individual is not to be returned, but equal quantities or measures, and this without price or interest, the contract is much of the same moral nature, but the Civilians call it *mutuum gratuitum*, or the gratuitous loan for consumption" (Hutcheson, *System*, II.65–66). See also *Short Introduction*, p. 215; Pufendorf, *Law of Nature*, v.4.vi, and *Duty of Man*, 1.15.iv; Grotius, *War and Peace*, II.12.ii; Cocceius, *Introductio*, pp. 377–378; Heineccius, *Universal Law*, 1.265; *Digest*, XII.1, and *Institutes*, III.xiv, pr. (*mutuum*) and *Digest*, XIII.6, and *Institutes*, III.xiv.2 (*commodatum*). These references refer to the respective authors' discussions of *mutuum* in general—that is, both *mutuum gratuitum* and *onerosum*. True to the basic distinction between beneficent and onerous

contracts, Reid deals with *mutuum onerosum* in the following lecture. Both kinds of *mutua* are loans for use of consumable goods, including money; the difference between them is that *mutuum onerosum* is a loan carrying interest.

112. "The *depositum* is a branch of the *mandatum*, where 'the business committed and undertaken is the safe custody of goods' " (Hutcheson, *System*, II.68). See also *Short Introduction*, p. 216; Pufendorf, *Law of Nature*, v.4.vii, and *Duty of Man*, I.15.v; Grotius, *War and Peace*, II.12.ii; Cocceius, *Introductio*, p. 378; Heineccius, *Universal Law*, I.265–266; *Digest*, XVI.3, and *Institutes*, III.xiv.3.

113. *Permutatio* is "Barter, or the exchanging goods of equal values; which differs from mutual donation in this, that in donations there is no obligation to equality" (Hutcheson, *System*, II.69). See also *Short Introduction*, p. 217; Pufendorf, *Law of Nature*, v.5.i, and *Duty of Man*, I.15.viii; Grotius, *War and Peace*, II.12.iii (3–4); Cocceius, *Introductio*, pp. 386–388; Heineccius, *Universal Law*, I.260–263; *Digest*, XIX.4 (and *Institutes*, III.xxiii.2). In Roman law this belonged to the innominate contracts—contracts falling outside the classical categories of verbal, written, real, and consensual contracts.

114. *Emptio* and *venditio* are "Buying and selling; the simplest manner of which is when the buyer at once pays the price, and receives the goods. If the price be paid . . . and the goods delivered, as the property is compleatly transferred, no subsequent sale . . . can elude the buyer's right. If the goods are to be delivered on a future day, but the bargain compleated about them; if they perish before the day, the loss falls on the seller. If they perish after that day, and the seller was ready to deliver them upon it, he is deemed after that day only as the depositary. . . . Where an agreement is made about certain quantities of goods which cannot be now delivered, such as about a future crop; and the seller afterwards contracts with a third person not apprized of the prior contract, and delivers the goods upon receipt of the price; the civil law favours the latter, as a fair purchaser, and deems all sales imperfect without delivery" (Hutcheson, *System*, II.69; cf. *Short Introduction*, pp. 217–218). For a fuller discussion, see Pufendorf, *Law of Nature*, v.5.ii–vi, and cf. *Duty of Man*, I.15.ix. See also, Grotius, *War and Peace*, II.12.iii (4–5), xv, and xxvi; Cocceius, *Introductio*, pp. 379–382; Heineccius, *Universal Law*, I.270–278; *Digest*, XVIII.1–7 and XIX.1; *Institutes*, III.xxiii.

115. Apparently at a later date Reid wrote "Monopolies Engrossing" above the whole paragraph. He is undoubtedly following Pufen-

dorf, who in *Law of Nature*, v.5.vii, completes his treatment of buying and selling by dealing with monopolies, making, inter alia, the following point: "Monopolies, as such, imply that others too would sell the same did not one Man ingross the whole Trade to himself. And therefore, he who alone brings a Commodity from a Foreign Country, cannot be said to set up a Monopoly, provided he does not hinder others from importing the same." The word "ingross" is used in a similar way to characterize true monopolies in the English translation of Grotius, *War and Peace*, II.12.xvi; cf. p. 207 above.

116. *Locatio* and *conductio*: "Setting and hiring includes all these contracts wherein 'one agrees for a certain price to do any work, or to grant the use of any goods, moveable or immoveable'" (Hutcheson, *System*, II.70). "Setting" is Scots for "letting." Cf. *Short Introduction*, pp. 218–219; Pufendorf, *Law of Nature*, v.6, and *Duty of Man*, 1.15.x; Grotius, *War and Peace*, II.12.iii (4–5) and xviii–xix; Cocceius, *Introductio*, pp. 382–383; Heineccius, *Universal Law*, 1.278–280; *Digest*, XIX.2; *Institutes*, III.xxiv.

117. *Mutuum onerosum*: "In loan for consumption at a set price or interest, the lender claims not the same individual ⟨goods⟩, but equal quantities, and the price for the loan" (Hutcheson, *System*, II.71; cf. *Short Introduction*, pp. 219–220). For the rest of the sources for *mutuum* and the distinction between *mutuum gratuitum* and *onerosum*, see above, n.111.

118. In Reid's day "usury," like the Latin *usura*, still did not necessarily connote more than either the loan of money on interest or the interest thus gained. All Reid's natural law sources discussed the justifiability of this practice, agreeing that it was not against the law of nature and that God's prohibition of it (e.g., Exod. 22:25; Lev. 25:36–37; Deut. 23:19–20) was meant as a positive law for the Jews only. (Grotius, however, wavered on this—see n. 10 on pp. 307–308, of *War and Peace*—and Luke 6:34–35 required some special pleading: see Barbeyrac's n. 1 on p. 515 of Pufendorf, *Law of Nature*). Cf. Hutcheson, *Short Introduction*, pp. 219–220, and *System*, II.71–74; Pufendorf, *Law of Nature*, v.7.viii–xii, and *Duty of Man*, 1.15.xi; Grotius, *War and Peace*, II.12.xx; Cocceius, *Introductio*, pp. 351–352; Heineccius, *Universal Law*, 1.283–285.

119. Society here means partnership: "In the contracts of partnership, which are of very different sorts, the terms of agreement determine the rights and obligations of the partners" (Hutcheson, *System*, II.74; cf. *Short Introduction*, p. 220; Pufendorf, *Law of Nature*, v.8, and *Duty of Man*, 1.15.xii; Grotius, *War and Peace*,

II.12.iv and xxiv–xxvi; Cocceius, *Introductio*, pp. 107–108 and 384; Heineccius, *Universal Law*, 1.291–294; *Digest*, XVII.2; *Institutes*, III.xxv).

120. "In some contracts a certain price is paid for an uncertain prospect of gain, as in the purchase of annuities for life, or of tickets in lotteries. . . . Private lotteries, wagering, and contracts of gaming, produce no good to the publick. . . . Upon some publick exigence no doubt money may be prudently raised by this way of lottery" (Hutcheson, *System*, II.74–75; cf. ibid., pp. 76–77, and *Short Introduction*, pp. 220–221; Pufendorf, *Law of Nature*, v.9.i–vii, and *Duty of Man*, 1.15.xiii; Cocceius, *Introductio*, p. 371).

Insurance: "There are other contracts of hazard where a small price is paid to obtain security against a great uncertain danger; or to have such losses made up when they happen. Such are the insurances against the dangers at sea, or those from fire" (Hutcheson, *System*, II.75; cf. Pufendorf, *Law of Nature*, v.9.viii, and *Duty of Man*, 1.15.xiii).

121. By annuities in this context Reid undoubtedly meant the same as Hutcheson (see the first quotation in the previous note) and Pufendorf, *Law of Nature*, v.10.v: "I receive Money upon Condition to pay such a certain Man, so much Interest as long as he lives, provided that after his Death, the Principal be my own." Pufendorf reckons this among the so-called accessory or additional contracts, which do not concern us here, and in connection with these Barbeyrac refers us back to an associated phenomenon which explains what Reid meant by "reversions" (see Barbeyrac's note at ibid.). Pufendorf: "Sometimes . . . either the Laws of the Land, or the Parties themselves grant one another the Liberty of breaking off the Bargain, which is done several ways; for sometimes a Clause is added, that upon Tender of the Price at any time, or by such a certain Day, the Buyer shall be obliged to restore the Goods to the Seller, or his Heirs" (*Law of Nature*, v.5.iv). This is further explained by Barbeyrac in a note to this passage: "*Retractus, seu pactum de Retrovendendo*, as the Lawyers speak, and our Author says, *Retractus* comes of the Word *retrahere*, which according to the Roman Lawyers signifies, to resume, what has been alienated ⟨*Digest*, L.8.ix.1⟩. The Custom of Redeeming a Thing sold, allowed by the Law, is called a Legal Retracting, but that which is done by the Agreement of Parties is a Conventional Retracting." The actual term "reversion" would have been known to Reid from Scots law: "An heritable right is said to be redeemable when it contains a right of reversion, or return, in favour of the person from whom the

right flows. Reversions are either legal, which arise from the law itself, as in adjudications, which law declares to be redeemable within a certain term after their date; or conventional, which are constituted by the agreement of parties, as in wadsets, rights of annual rent, and rights in security" (Erskine, *Principles of the Law of Scotland*, II.viii.1; cf. Stair, *Institutions of the Law of Scotland*, II.x.1–4, and Kames, *Historical Law-Tracts*, pp. 46ff.). It should be noticed that Stair also treats of reversions in the same general context as Reid here—namely, in *Institutions*, I, title xiv: "Permutation and Sale, or Emption and Vendition" (sec. 4).

122. After discussing the various forms of contract, Pufendorf devoted a chapter to the ways in which obligations are dissolved and one to interpretation (*Law of Nature*, v.11–12, and *Duty of Man*, I.16–17). The latter topic is similarly placed in Grotius (*War and Peace*, II.16), while elements of the former are in ibid., III.19.xiv–xix. In Hutcheson, *Short Introduction*, the two topics are huddled together in a brief chapter right at the end of "private jurisprudence" and immediately before "Oeconomicks" (II.17, pp. 248–253), while the corresponding chapter in the *System* (II.18, pp. 141–147) is devoted to the nature and necessity of judicial arbitration and relegates interpretation to "the art of criticism" (p. 147)—an interesting reflection of the fact that the natural lawyers in dealing with this topic drew heavily on the rhetorical tradition. In Reid's notes dated 1765 there is nothing on the dissolution of obligation, and interpretation is mentioned here only before quasi-contract. We do, however, have a brief treatment of the former topic and a more substantial one of the latter in an undated manuscript, 7/VII/25, which is printed below in Section XIII.

If we attend to Pufendorf's introductory remarks about interpretation and remember Reid's discussion of the obligation to promises and contracts (see above, pp. 155ff.), we will immediately see how Pufendorf's treatment of interpretation could lead on to quasi-contract: "since in all Obligations certain Signs are made use of, to express the Minds of the Parties, and the Laws and Heads of the Contract; and since these Signs may sometimes be taken in different Senses, 'tis highly necessary to have some Rule to find out that which is true and genuine. . . . If then we consider for what End Obligations are made, we shall find that every Man is bound to that which he intended, when he enter'd into the Obligation. It is here suppos'd that he enter'd into it freely and of his own accord . . . ; in this Sense is that of Cicero to be taken; 'In Obligations Regard is to be had not so much to the Expression as to the Intent of the Party' " (*Law of Nature*, V.12.i–ii, quoting *De officiis*, I.xiii (40)). The rest of *Law of Nature*, V.12 is devoted to a detailed discussion of the rules of interpretation that might achieve this goal, and some of these are discussed by Reid in 7/VII/25 (printed below in Section XIII). Cf. *Duty of Man*, I.17; Grotius, *War and Peace*, II.16; Hutcheson, *Short Introduction*, pp. 251–252, and *System*, II.147; Cocceius, *Introductio*, pp. 109–110 and 394–397; Vattel, *Law of Nations*, II.17.

123. A consequence of the interpretation in contractual terms of the central social institutions—language, property and money, domestic relations, civil society, and government—was an increased attention to the very concept of a contract, and one of the beneficiaries of this was the Roman law concept of quasi-contract. In Grotius and Pufendorf the terminology is not very firm, but the substance is there; see *War and Peace*, II.10 (cf. II.4.iv–v; III.1.viii and III.24.i), *Law of Nature*, IV.13, and *Duty of Man*, I.13. However, in Reid's later natural law sources we do see the need for a sharper delineation of the topic, including its label; see Carmichael, supplementum IV, "De Quasi Contractibus," in Pufendorf, *De officio*, pp. 264–268, which was the foundation for Hutcheson's discussion, (*Short Introduction*, pp. 223–227 and *System*, II.77–86; further Cocceius, *Introductio*, pp. 117–118, 343–344 and 417–422). (The topic of the quasi-contract was obviously in the air; see e.g. also C. Wolff, *Institutiones juris naturae et gentium*, II.14.) Most significant perhaps is that Hutcheson explicitly, though briefly, uses the concept of quasi-contract in connection with the relationship between parents and children and to interpret the continuing force of the political contract beyond the original contractors; see *Short Introduction*, pp. 270 and 287; *System*, II.197–198 and 231; and cf. Wolff, *Institutiones*, II.I.1.836. It was undoubtedly attention to this which made Reid's speculations about the relationship between contract, tacit contract, and implied contract so fertile, as we see in 2/II/10, printed below in Section XV. See the Commentary above at p. 338 n. 59.

Hutcheson (*System*, II.77–78) explains: "Some rights arise, not from any contract, but from some other action either of him who has the right, or of the person obliged. These actions founding rights are either lawful, or unlawful; when the actions are lawful, the Civilians to avoid multiplying the sources of obligation . . . call them *obligationes quasi ex contractu ortae*: feigning a contract obliging men in these cases to whatever could reasonably have been demanded by the one party, and wisely promised

by the other, had they been contracting about these matters. . . . When the action is unlawful, these are the rights arising
from injury, of which in the following chapter" (Reid's two following lectures parallel Hutcheson, ibid.). Hutcheson further
insists that obligations from quasi-contracts "are quite different
from those of tacit conventions, as in tacit conventions we truly
conclude consent from some action; but in those 'tis plainly
feigned, tho' we know there was no consent, as the matter itself
is equitable" (*Short Introduction*, p. 223). For the Roman law background to the division of the sources of obligation, see *Digest*,
XLIV.vii.1, pr, and *Institutes*, III.xiii.2; and for quasi-contract, *Institutes*, III.xxvii (for the *Digest*, see subsequent notes).

124. Obligations *quasi ex contractu* are so to speak symmetrical in that
they partly fall upon those who somehow benefit from what is
another's (whether goods or services), partly upon those who
benefit from the handling of what is theirs by others. Thus the
person who is bona fide (without fraud, etc.) in possession of
somebody else's property has certain obligations to the real
owner of this property, depending on the circumstances. Con-
trariwise, the owner of something may have a variety of obligations to him who has taken care of his property: *negotium utile
gestum* means "⟨somebody else's⟩ business usefully managed ⟨for
him⟩," for instance, in his absence. Reid's note "In absense" may
also have referred to the situation where the bona fide possessor
of another's property no longer holds this property. A host of
such obligations, including *negotium utile gestum*, are discussed in
all the sources mentioned in the previous note. See further *Digest*, III.v; "De negotiis gestis."

125. See Hutcheson, *System*, II.80: "one is obliged ⟨quasi ex contractu⟩
to indemnify his tutors and curators in all their prudent management of his affairs" (cf. *Short Introduction*, p. 224, and the earlier discussion, ibid., p. 182, and *System*, II.10–11). As for people
of a disturbed mind, Reid was probably following Pufendorf,
Law of Nature, III.6.iii in making the point that those who are
only temporarily without the full use of their reason will regain
their moral responsibilities, such as property, once they return
to normality. Similarly they may assume obligations incurred
quasi ex contractu during the leave of their reason—for example,
from the care by others of themselves and their property. The
point should thus be contrasted with the one made above, p.
155, concerning the need for full reasoning power in explicit
contracts. As for Reid's opinion of the permanently insane, we
can only guess; according to Pufendorf, "if the Madness be

judg'd Incurable the Person is in all Legal and Moral Consideration to be accounted Dead" (*Law of Nature*, III.6.iii). For the extensive Roman law background concerning guardianship of all kinds, see *Institutes*, I.xiii–xxvi, and *Digest*, XXVI.

126. In general, children were not considered by the natural lawyers to incur obligations *quasi ex contractu* through the benefit of their parents' support, education, and general guardianship, except "if a parent is in great straits, or if any child has some other way ⟨than from the parents⟩ obtained a plentiful fortune" (Hutcheson, *Short Introduction*, p. 225; cf. *System*, II.80). See also the lectures on oeconomical jurisprudence printed in Section VI and Section XIV below.

The situation was considered rather different if one undertook the upbringing of somebody else's child: if the child was destitute and no one else could or would pay, Hutcheson considered it legitimate to charge the child itself once it had reached maturity. At the same time, he was at pains to stress that slavery could not be justified this way. Reid's mention of the "purchase of Slaves" is a reference to Hutcheson's further point that, although in some cases the purchasers of slaves saved their lives, this could not be taken to establish a quasi-contractual obligation on the slaves to remain such in perpetuity but only to pay the purchaser's expenses with the accepted amount of interest— normally, of course, through their labor. See Hutcheson, *System*, II.81–85, and *Short Introduction*, pp. 225–226; see also Pufendorf, *Law of Nature*, VI.2.ix and VI.3.iv, and *Duty of Man*, II.3.x and xii, and II.4.ii–iii; Grotius, *War and Peace*, II.7.v (1) and II.5.xxx.

127. Like Grotius and Pufendorf, Reid took *Digest*, XIV.ii ("De lege Rhodia de jactu") into his explanation of obligations *quasi ex contractu*. The essence of the law "about throwing" (*de jactu*) items overboard from a ship in difficulties at sea in order to save the ship and any remaining goods is that losses thus incurred should be shared by all the consignors and the captain. In the absence of any evidence that this was ever made part of contracts about sea-freight, the natural lawyers interpreted it as a quasi-contractual obligation. See Grotius, *War and Peace*, II.10.ix (2), and Pufendorf, *Law of Nature*, IV.13.xiii. Reid also refers indirectly to the Rhodian law in 7/VI/11 (printed in Section XI below, p. 207).

128. Reid, like Hutcheson (*Short Introduction*, II, ch. xv; *System*, II, ch. xv) and Smith (LJ(A), ii.88ff.; LJ(B), 181ff.), follows Grotius (*War and Peace*, II, ch. xvii) and Justinian (*Institutes*, IV.i) in deal-

ing with delict in extension of contract—that is, as a question of the sources of rights, while Pufendorf deals with it as a question of the duties imposed by natural law and by positive law (*Law of Nature*, III.1 and VIII.3; *Duty of Man*, I.6 and II.13). Heineccius follows the Pufendorfian arrangement (*Universal Law*, I, ch. vii, and II, ch. viii). Reid's subsequent points should be read in the light of these references.

129. "Loss/harm caused either by ignorance or in order to serve our own advantage." It is difficult to be entirely certain about Reid's intentions here and hence about the proper translation of "damnum" in this untraced quotation (which may, of course, be from memory). "Damnum datum" puts in mind the Lex Aquilia (cf. Justinian, *Institutes*, IV.iii), which dealt with damage, as well intentional as negligent, to property, and "loss" would therefore seem the proper translation. However, while the Lex Aquilia undoubtedly is in the background, especially as it by early modern time had been developed into the civil law's general theory of civil wrongs, the context here seems to make it plain that Reid was not talking just about damage to property but also about harm or injury in general. Like Titius, Hutcheson, and Smith he divided this into *culpa*, negligence, and *dolus*, intent to harm, as we see in the following lines; cf. Titius, Observation 164, p. 230 in Pufendorf, *De officio*; Hutcheson, *Short Introduction*, p. 228, and *System*, II.86; Smith, LJ(A), i.23 and ii.88, and LJ(B), 181. While the elusive quotation thus may stem from a commentary on the Lex Aquilia, its language was (as so often) generalized when adopted into natural law (see the following note), and in the case of *damnum* this had excellent parentage: it was due to Grotius himself (*De Jure*, II.17.ii).

130. The neat division of *culpa* into three degrees of severity had become common by the late seventeenth century; see, e.g., Titius, Observation 164, p. 230, in Pufendorf, *De officio*; cf. Barbeyrac's n. 3 to Grotius, *War and Peace*, II.17.ii. It was mainly employed in the law of contract, as we see in Erskine, *Principles*, III.i.8, but it was being transferred to natural law for a much more general use. This process is particularly clear in Smith's lectures, where the tripartite division was first introduced when he considered the question "To what degree of diligence the contractors shall be bound" (LJ(A), ii.78), while only a few pages later he applies it to delict in general: "Negligence or culpa may . . . be considered . . . as being of 3 sorts. Either the negligence is so great as that no man could have been guilty of the like in his own affairs, tho this man has been in those of another, in which case the

delinquency is said to arise from culpa lata; or 2dly, it is called culpa levis, where the delinquent has been guilty of no greater negligence in the affairs of an other than he is in his own, being generally a man who was not very attentive to his affairs; or lastly, from culpa levissima, where the negligence or culpa is no more than the most attentive man might have been guilty of" (LJ(A), ii.88–89). It was in this general sense that Smith discussed the tripartite division of culpa in TMS, II.iii.2.8–10, which has undoubtedly been in Reid's mind in writing the present notes.

131. See Hutcheson, *Short Introduction*, p. 231, and *System*, II.90.

132. See Cicero, *Letters to His Friends*, v.iv.2: "Tu tuas inimicitias ut reipublicae donares, te vicisti" ("You have won a victory over yourself so far as to lay aside certain private enmities of your own in the interests of the state").

133. See Smith, TMS, v.2.9. The following modification of this picture of savages may well owe something to Reid's reading of Henry Ellis's *Voyage to Hudson Bay*, pp. 189ff., a passage that he uses in 8/IV/4 (see the Commentary below at p. 372 n. 4).

134. "Nobody harms ⟨or provokes⟩ me unpunished." This, the motto of the Order of the Thistle, first appeared in Scots coinage, together with a crowned thistle, on the "Thistle" dollar in 1579 and thereafter on a variety of coins during the reign of James VI and up until the Union of 1707 (private correspondence from Gordon Donaldson). Since Reid would hardly rate James VI on a par with an Indian chieftain (see below), we may hazard the guess that he transferred the (supposed) distant origins of the Order of the Thistle in "a barbarous age" to the coinage.

135. This and the subsequent discussion must be seen in the light of the treatment of resentment and anger in Shaftesbury, "An Inquiry Concerning Virtue and Merit" II.2.ii, *Characteristics*, 1.319–321; Butler, *Sermons*, VIII–IX, pp. 91–117; Smith, TMS, I.ii.3; II.i.1–5; II.ii.1.1–4; II.ii.2, and II.iii.1; Kames, *Historical Law-Tracts*, tract I, "Criminal Law," and *Elements of Criticism*, 1:83–87 and 186–190; as well as in Reid's later discussion in A.P., pp. 568a–570b, where he from a starting-point in Butler and Kames develops a sharp distinction between resentment as an impulse and as a rational principle of action.

136. Juvenal, *Satire* XIII, 180–187 and 189–192: " 'O! but vengeance is good, sweeter than life itself.' Yes; so say the ignorant, whose passionate hearts you may see ablaze at the slightest cause, sometimes for no cause at all; any occasion, indeed, however small it be, suffices for their wrath. But so will not Chrysippus

say, or the gentle Thales, or the old man who dwelt near sweet Hymettus, who would have given to his accuser no drop of the hemlock-draught which was administered to him in that cruel bondage. . . . For vengeance is always the delight of a little, weak, and petty mind; of which you may straightaway draw proof from this—that no one so rejoices in vengeance as a woman."

137. Contrast A.P., p. 568a.

138. The focus of Grotius's second book of *War and Peace* is the discussion of the causes of war, within which he places his chapter on delict. Hutcheson and Reid follow him (see above, n.128) to the extent that within their discussion of delict they deal with the causes of war (Hutcheson, *Short Introduction*, pp. 231–237, and *System*, II.92–97). The main treatment of this topic is, however, reserved for the lectures on the law of nations—in keeping with the basic Pufendorfian system which Reid, like Hutcheson, is following. See Section XVII, pp. 263ff.

139. Since the only justifiable use of violence (private or public war) is to redress the infringement of perfect rights when no other means is available, and because other means normally are available when duels are resorted to and duels are virtually never able to redress the wrongs they are aimed at anyway, "such duels as are often practised among us . . . cannot be justified either in natural liberty or civil society" (Hutcheson, *Short Introduction*, pp. 237–238; cf. *System*, II.97–101, and Pufendorf, *Law of Nature*, II.5.ix and xii, and *Duty of Man*, I.5.xx).

VI. DUTIES TO OTHERS:
INDIVIDUALS IN OECONOMICAL JURISPRUDENCE

1. These rights and duties ("oeconomical jurisprudence") are dealt with in "Book II" of the following: Grotius, *War and Peace* (ch. 5); Pufendorf, *Duty of Man* (chs. 2–4); Heineccius, *Universal Law* (chs. 2–5); and Fordyce, *Elements* (sec. iii, chs. 1–3).

2. Reid's "Account of the Oeconomy of Nature," which in general agrees with his natural law sources, is significantly expanded in the manuscripts printed below in Section XIV. His treatment of marriage should be seen against the background of Grotius, *War and Peace*, II.5.viii–xvi; Pufendorf, *Law of Nature*, VI.1, and *Duty of Man*, II.2; Carmichael's extensive notes in Pufendorf, *De officio*, pp. 323–336; Hutcheson, *Short Introduction*, pp. 255–266, and *System*, II.149–187; Heineccius, *Universal Law*, II.23–43;

Cocceius, *Introductio*, pp. 260–262 and 271–283; Fordyce, *Elements*, pp. 308–312; Montesquieu, *Spirit of Laws*, XXIII.1–10 and XXVI.13; Hume, "Of Polygamy and Divorce," "Of Love and Marriage," and cf. *Treatise*, p. 486, and *Enquiry*, pp. 206–208. The main Roman law background is *Institutes*, I.10, and *Digest*, XXIII.2. Reid returned to the "passion of Love between the Sexes in the human kind" (see the following paragraph in the text) in A.P., pp. 563b–564a.

3. Concerning polygamy, see below, pp. 226–227 and 230 in Section XIV. Cf. Grotius, *War and Peace*, II.5.ix; Pufendorf, *Law of Nature*, VI.1.xv–xviii, and *Duty of Man*, II.2.v; Hutcheson, *Short Introduction*, p. 260, and *System*, II.160–161; Heineccius, *Universal Law*, II.31–34; Cocceius, *Introductio*, pp. 48, 51, 74, and 275; Fordyce, *Elements*, p. 312; Montesquieu, *Spirit of Laws*, XVI.2–11; Hume, "Of Polygamy and Divorce," pp. 232–236.

   Concerning divorce, see Grotius, *War and Peace*, II.5.ix and I.l.17; Pufendorf, *Law of Nature*, VI.l.xx–xxiv, and *Duty of Man*, II.2.vi; Hutcheson, *Short Introduction*, pp. 261 and 265–266, and *System*, II.161–163 and 175–183; Heineccius, *Universal Law*, II.41–42; Cocceius, *Introductio*, pp. 48 and 282; Montesquieu, *Spirit of Laws*, XVI.15–16; Hume, "Of Polygamy and Divorce," pp. 236–239. According to the student Robert Jack, Reid in 1776 followed Pufendorf, *Law of Nature*, VI.l.xxiv, in drawing arguments from Milton's *Doctrine and Discipline of Divorces* to extend the legitimate grounds of divorce beyond mere adultery (Jack, "Reid's Lectures," p. 592). Concerning prohibited degrees, see below, p. 228; Grotius, *War and Peace*, II.5.xii–xiv; Pufendorf, *Law of Nature*, VI.1.xxvii, xxxii–xxxv, and *Duty of Man*, II.2.viii; Hutcheson, *Short Introduction*, pp. 264–265 and *System*, II.170–175; Heineccius, *Universal Law*, II.34–36; Cocceius, *Introductio*, pp. 276–282; Montesquieu, *Spirit of Laws*, XXVI.14.

4. The general background to this topic and its systematic position is found in Grotius, *War and Peace*, II.5.i–vii; Pufendorf, *Law of Nature*, VI.2, and *Duty of Man*, II.3; Hutcheson, *Short Introduction*, pp. 267–271, and *System*, II.187–199; Heineccius, *Universal Law*, II.44–62; Cocceius, *Introductio*, pp. 73–74, 262–269 and 270–271; Fordyce, *Elements*, pp. 306–308 and 312–315. See also the references to Hobbes, Filmer, and Locke in the next note. The present text should be read together with 7/VII/20,2v (below, pp. 232–233).

5. Like Pufendorf, Hutcheson, and Heineccius, Reid contrasts his position with that of Hobbes and Filmer and formulates it with reference to the conceptual framework of Grotius (see the fol-

lowing sentence). Grotius's bald statement "By Generation, Parents
... acquire a Right over their Children" (*War and Peace*, II.5.i),
was sorely in need of explanation, for the physical process of
"Generation" did not warrant Grotius's treatment of the relationship between parents and children as a moral one, as evi-
denced by his choice of vocabulary and in his theory of how this
relationship is subject to change as the moral faculty develops in
children (ibid., ii–vi). Cf. Filmer's criticism, *Patriarcha*, p. 72, and
Observations Concerning the Originall of Government, pp. 268–269;
also Carmichael's comment in Pufendorf, *De officio*, pp. 337–
338. Hobbes suggested (or was commonly taken to suggest) that
parental authority was a matter of power (*De cive*, ch. 9; *Leviathan*, ch. 20), but this scarcely seemed a properly moral notion
that could explain, for instance, the continuance of authority beyond a child's actual dependence upon its parents. By contrast,
Filmer maintained that "Every man that is born, is so far from
being free-born, that by his very birth he becomes a subject to
him that begets him" (*Directions for Obedience to Government*, p.
232). By this he meant, or was widely taken to mean (among
others, by Locke, *First Treatise*, 52), that the child belonged to
the father because it was the father's work and was thus a link
in a chain of workmanship and ownership instituted by God at
the creation. This raised a number of theological and philosophical problems, most of which were formulated by Locke in the
Two Treatises; these were then taken up by the natural lawyers
and form the direct background to Reid's lecture. First, if life,
and not just biological generation, was transferred from man to
man, the dependence of man on God seemed more remote (cf.
Locke, *First Treatise*, 52ff.). Second, such a doctrine smacked too
much of materialism and hence, at that time, of improper determinism (cf. Wollaston, *Religion of Nature*, pp. 88–91). Third, if
children were the work and property of their fathers, inequality
and paternalism were woven into the fabric of the world. See,
by contrast, Hutcheson, *Short Introduction*, p. 268: "Both the bodies and souls of children are formed by the divine power, that
they may, as they grow up, arrive at the same condition of life,
and an equality of right with ourselves, tho' for some time they
must be governed by the wisdom of others." If individual human life (generally, the soul: "the soul, the principal part, is
⟨God's⟩ own immediate workmanship"; Hutcheson, *System*,
II.191) comes directly from God, it is open not only to argue for
Calvinist necessitarianism but also to break with Calvinism by arguing for the divine institution of man's free moral power and

for man's equality in this endowment. Hence the notions of guidance by precepts (e.g., laws of nature), of error and of education. Accordingly, we find that Pufendorf (*Law of Nature*, VI.2.iv) sees generation as no more than a special "occasion" for exercising our basic natural law duty of sociability by morally educating children to become agents under the same natural law. This natural law duty to educate confers a right to the necessary means thereto—that is, a right to power (i.e. authority) over one's children. See Pufendorf, *Law of Nature*, VI.2.iv and vi, and *Duty of Man*, II.3.iv and xi; Hutcheson, *Short Introduction*, pp. 267–268, and *System*, II.187–189 and 191–193; Heineccius, *Universal Law*, II.44–46. See also Wollaston, *Religion of Nature*, pp. 159–162. It should also be pointed out that the idea of the child as a moral agent *in spe* leads to the suggestion that parental authority rests on the tacit consent of the children (Pufendorf, *Law of Nature*, VI.2.iv, and *Duty of Man*, II.3.ii; and cf. Hobbes, *Leviathan*, p. 253, and Heineccius, *Universal Law*, II.45–46) or on a quasi-contract (Hutcheson, *Short Introduction*, p. 270; *System*, II.197–198). While Reid does not take this up here, it provides a parallel of the first importance to his discussion of implied contract in 2/II/10 (printed in Section XV, below), for it presents *in nuce* the whole problem of the contractual versus the natural law foundation for social relations. Finally, it should be mentioned that, in his 1776 lectures, Reid said that "we should only consider Parents as the means appointed by God . . . to take care of their Children" (Jack, "Reid's Lectures," p. 596).

6. This was, first, a question of duration, as indicated by the following point, and it was dealt with in terms of the different periods in a child's life. This is detailed in 7/VII/20,2v (pp. 232–233, below). Second, it was a question of extent and method, especially whether the parents could impose death or use cruel punishment, whether they could dispose of the child by exposition or by sale into slavery, to what extent they were obliged to recognize the child as a moral agent under natural law (the equivalent of legal personality under positive law), especially whether a minor could have (though of course not exercise) property rights, and whether children needed parental consent to marry. Finally, there was the question whether parental authority and duty could wholly or in part be taken over by others, such as adoptive parents, guardians, and tutors. For discussion of some or all of these points, which are alluded to in the following lines and further dealt with in pp. 232–233, below, see Grotius, *War and Peace*, II.5.ii–vii and x, and II.20.vii; Pufendorf, *Law of Na-*

ture, VI.2.vi–xiv, and *Duty of Man*, II.3.iv–viii and x; Hutcheson, *Short Introduction*, pp. 267–268, and *System*, II.189–190, 192–194, and 196–198; Heineccius, *Universal Law*, II.47–50 and 62.

7. See Grotius, *War and Peace*, II.5.i; Pufendorf, *Law of Nature*, VI.2.ii–v, and *Duty of Man*, II.3.iii; Hutcheson, *Short Introduction*, p. 268, and *System*, II.190–191; Heineccius, *Universal Law*, II.46.

8. Forisfamiliate (from Latin, *foris*, outside, etc., and *familia*, family, household, etc.), to emancipate, common in Scots law. See Stair, *Institutes*, I.5.13: "As to the father's power to keep his children within his family, and to apply their work for his use . . . it is not to be doubted but that children may be compelled to remain with their parents, and to employ their service for their use, even after their majority; unless they be forisfamiliat by marriage, or by education in a distinct calling from their parents; or unless their parents deal unnaturally with them, either by atrocity, or unwillingness to provide them a competent marriage in due time, and with means suitable to their condition . . . or if the father countenance or allow the children to live by themselves, and to manage their own affairs apart; from whence his tacit consent to their emancipation may be inferred. In which cases . . . the consuetude of Germany is the same with our customs. . . . The English account children to be emancipate so soon as they pass their minority" (Cf. ibid., III.8.45, Erskine, *Principles*, 1.7.36, and above, p. 337 n. 55).

9. The context for Reid's treatment of this topic here and in 7/VII/20,3r–4v., printed below, pp. 233–236 (which should be read with the present manuscript), is provided by Grotius, *War and Peace*, II.5.xxvi–xxxii; Hobbes, *De cive*, ch. VIII, and *Leviathan*, ch. XX; Pufendorf, *Law of Nature*, VI.3, and *Duty of Man*, II.4; Locke, *Treatise*, II, ch. 4; Heineccius, *Universal Law*, II.63–73; Cocceius, *Introductio*, pp. 255–257; Fordyce, *Elements*, pp. 315–316; Hutcheson, *Short Introduction*, pp. 272–278, and *System*, II.199–212; and Montesquieu, *Spirit of Laws*, book XV. Cf. the slightly later (1771) discussion in Millar, *Ranks*, ch. 6. Further references are in n. 10, below, and in the Commentary below at pp. 399–400 nn. 39–42. Roman law discussions of this topic are numerous, and many of the references are in Grotius and Pufendorf; the starting-point, however, is the *Institutes*, 1.3, and the *Digest*, 1.5.iii ff.

10. This paragraph and its important elaboration in 7/VII/20,3r–4v (printed below in Section XIV) is to be seen not only in the light of, for example, Locke's or Montesquieu's well-known criticism of slavery (see references in n. 9), but is to be connected with

Carmichael's development of some Lockean ideas and Hutcheson's borrowing of these. The starting-point is that man is created in God's image. From the notion of creation follows (see Locke, *Treatise*, II.23) that man is God's property and that consequently no human being can own a man, whether himself or another, as property unless by special dispensation from God; consequently, not only is it morally impossible to hold someone in servitude (implying full property-right), but it is similarly impossible to give or sell oneself into such servitude. Presupposed in the notion of man as God's creation is further that all men are equal in this regard; the latest born is as much God's work as Adam. Being created in God's image, man is created to love God both directly and indirectly through love of his creation. The purpose of such love is the creation of happiness—for Carmichael this is restricted to human beings, for Hutcheson it goes further (see the Commentary below at pp. 378–379 n. 3)—which is the basic precept of natural law. As in all such "consequentialist" theories, efficiency is an important consideration, and because men in general are best at looking after their own happiness, the total happiness of creation is best served by each person having a natural right to take care of himself and a natural duty to respect the equal rights of others. Consequently, nobody is created without such equal rights. By the same token, people have the natural right to look after their happiness by putting themselves into any kind of service that does not imply an actual property-relationship—a point that Reid takes up below, p. 234. See Carmichael, supplementum I, secs. 1–10 and 19–20; supplementum II, secs. 6–17; and notes on pp. 354–358 in Pufendorf, *De officio*.

11. Nearly all the sources mentioned above in n. 9 deal with the introduction and subsequent development of slavery. Reid may here have been thinking more specifically of the effects of slavery on the size of the population, a point that was particularly hotly disputed after Hume's and Robert Wallace's discussion; see Hume, "Of the Populousness of Ancient Nations," *Essays*, 1:381–443, and Wallace, *A Dissertation on the Numbers of Mankind in Ancient and Modern Times*, Appendix.

12. Reid was probably referring to the most widely debated "pretence"—that prisoners of war could justifiably be enslaved in lieu of being killed; he did so in 1776 (Jack, "Reid's Lectures," pp. 605–607). Cf. Grotius, *War and Peace*, III.14 and 20; Hobbes, *De cive*, VIII.i–v, and *Leviathan*, pp. 251–257; Pufendorf, *Law of Nature*, VI.3.v–vii, and *Duty of Man*, II.4.i and iv; Locke, *Treatise*,

II.24 and 85; Hutcheson, *Short Introduction*, pp. 274–278, and *System*, II.203–209; Heineccius, *Universal Law*, II.65–66.

13. See Hume, *History of England*, 1:190: "There were two kinds of slaves among the Anglo-Saxons; household slaves, after the manner of the ancients, and praedial or rustic, after the manner of the Germans. These latter resembled the serfs, which are at present to be met with in Poland, Denmark, and some parts of Germany."

14. *Adscriptitii glebae* (those ascribed, i.e., joined to the land): "Husbandmen, who belonged to the Lands given them. . . . Men in that State went with the Lands which they cultivated; for the Proprietor might alienate them when he alienated his Lands. But their State was not so hard as that of Slaves." Barbeyrac, n.4 to Grotius, *War and Peace*, II.5.xxx. In Roman law these were a proper form of slaves; in medieval English law they eventually became identical with villeins; in Scotland a category very like them still existed: "Colliers, coal-bearers, and salters, and other persons necessary to the collieries and salt-works, as they are particularly described, 1661, c. 56, are, like the *adscriptitii glebae* of the Roman law, tied down to perpetual service at the works to which they had once entered. Upon a sale of the works the right of their service is transferred to the new proprietor" (Erskine, *Principles*, 1.7.39).

VII. DUTIES TO OTHERS: INDIVIDUALS IN POLITICAL JURISPRUDENCE

1. Reid's subsequent discussion of the origins of political society should be seen in the light of Hutcheson, *Short Introduction*, pp. 279–284, and *System*, II.212–225; cf. Pufendorf, *Duty of Man*, II.5, and *Law of Nature*, VII.1.

2. The preceding reflections on political government are closely connected with Reid's introductory lectures on politics proper, which he engaged on the following week. The ideas of despotic government, which are clearly inspired by his close study of Montesquieu, were elaborated on the following Wednesday, 17 April, as we see from 4/III/5 (not in this volume).

3. In this and the preceding paragraph, Reid encompassed what his predecessor Adam Smith had specified in his lectures as "the principle of authority" in government (as distinguished from "the principle of public or generall utility"): "Several things tend

to give one an authority over others. 1st, superiority of age and of wisdom which is generally its concomitant. 2dly, superior strength of body . . . 3d, superior fortune also gives a certain authority . . . , and 4thly, the effect is the same of superior antiquity when everything else is alike; an old family excites no such jealousy as an upstart does" (LJ(A), v.129; cf. LJ(B), 12, and TMS, I.iii.2). The idea reaches its final elaboration in WN, v.i.b.4–8. Very similar views were held by Reid's young colleague John Millar; see, e.g. his *Ranks*, ch. III. See also Montesquieu, *Spirit of Laws*, pp. 276–277: "Amongst such ⟨primitive⟩ nations . . . the old men, who remember things past, have great authority; they cannot there be distinguished by wealth, but by wisdom and valor."

4. The central issues mentioned in this paragraph are discussed at length in Sections XV and XVI in this volume.

5. For Reid's final reflections on this, see his "Some Thoughts on the Utopian System," printed here in Section XVIII.

6. This is one of the central points in the treatment of international law within the systems of natural jurisprudence; see the following section and Section XVII.

7. These topics are spelled out in 8/IV/9, where Reid on fol.3v (p. 252) gives a more extensive list of references that includes all the names here except Milton. See the Commentary at pp. 413ff. n. 14 for a discussion.

8. In the subsequent pages (up to p. 180, line 31), Reid rounds off his lectures on the jurisprudence of the individual, considered "privately," "oeconomically," and "politically," by developing the well-known theme of the universal obviousness of morals. See the Introductory Lecture, above, pp. 110–112.

9. The two final paragraphs of this manuscript seem to be intended to provide a transition from the jurisprudence of individuals to that of states. There is, however, no manuscript extant, dated 1765, which deals with the law of nations. Circumstantial evidence also makes it clear that Reid can have dealt only very briefly with this topic: the present lecture is dated 15 April, and the next surviving and dated lecture of 17 April makes it plain that Reid had meanwhile (i.e., on Tuesday 16 April) already made a good start to his course on politics (see 4/III/5,1r in the lectures on politics). Among the undated manuscripts there is, however, one that Reid could have added to the end of his lecture on Monday 15 April and that gives the kind of general survey to be expected of a lecturer pressed for time. There is, furthermore, some evidence that this manuscript

may well date from 1765. When Reid rewrote his lectures on political jurisprudence in the following year, he used material from 1765; see the Textual Notes, below, at 173/11. Therefore, when in the same manuscript (8/IV/9) he arrives at the topic of the law of nations and there makes an insertion sign followed by the words "The Notion of see N," and when in an undated manuscript (7/VII/21,1r), headed "Of the Law of Nations," we find a passage marked "N" in the margin, beginning "The Notion of" and fitting the context perfectly, it seems entirely possible that this represents what Reid had to say about international law at the end of his lecture on Monday morning, 15 April 1765. One circumstance tells against this suggestion, though not decisively. Manuscript 7/VII/21 shows fairly clear signs of being influenced by Reid's study of Vattel's *Law of Nations*, but his first reading-notes from Vattel (3/II/5), which I print in Section XVII, are dated "Septr 1766." While there is no reason to suppose that Reid had not looked at Vattel before then (the English edition in question was published in 1759), it does make the inclusion of 7/VII/21 here as part of Reid's 1765 course hypothetical: it may have been produced half a year later as a first draft for the following academic session. See the Textual Notes below at 182/14 and 255/6–23.

VIII. DUTIES TO OTHERS: STATES

1. The first sentence is a bowdlerized excerpt from Justinian's definition of the law of nations (*Institutes*, I.ii.1): "quod . . . naturalis ratio inter omnes homines constituit, id apud omnes populos peraeque custoditur vocaturque *ius gentium*" ("What natural reason has established among all men is observed equally by all nations and is designated *ius gentium* or the law of nations"). The second sentence is Justinian's (Gaius's) famous and troublesome wide definition of natural law, which properly reads: "Ius naturale est quod natura omnia animalia docuit" ("Natural law is that which nature instils in all animals"; *Institutes*, I.ii. pr.). Both are quoted by Vattel, *Law of Nations*, preface, p. iv, and there is little doubt that Reid used these two quotations as keywords for a brief instruction (after Vattel's preface) in one of the central disputes in modern natural law—namely, whether the law of nations is a matter of established conventions or whether it is or is derived from the law of nature. The former was seen as Grotius's standpoint (*War and Peace*, Prolegomena, 41, and I.l.xiv),

the latter as descended from Hobbes, *De cive,* xiv.4, via Pufendorf, *Law of Nature,* ii.3.xxiii, and Wolff, *Jus gentium,* praefatio and prolegomena, sec. 3, to Vattel. Within the latter line of argument fell the further problem of whether the law of nations was identical with the law of nature or whether the precepts of the latter needed fundamental change, since "A state or civil society is a subject very different from an individual of the human race" (Vattel, ibid., i. preliminaries, sec. 6). Vattel saw the latter as Wolff's great improvement over Pufendorf and Hobbes and as the object of his highly successful popularizing efforts. On this issue Reid did not express himself clearly.

2. The view of the state as a corporate moral personality, which is sketched in this paragraph, is obviously to be seen in the light of Hobbes, Locke, and Pufendorf, but it would seem that Vattel's preliminaries to *Law of Nations* is the most immediate inspiration.

3. This quotation is not from Cicero's *De legibus,* as Reid indicates. It is one of the few fragments of Cicero's *De re publica* that were known to the world—mainly through patristic quotations—prior to Cardinal Mai's find of a major fragment in 1819. The fragment quoted here is identical to Vattel's quotation in *Law of Nations,* p. xiv (except for two minor variations) and it corresponds to ii.xliv (70) of *De re publica* as we now know it; Reid quotes it again in his notes from Vattel, p. 273, below, and also p. 255. It translates: "I would hold for nothing what has been said about the state so far, as I cannot make any progress, unless it is established, not only that it is false that the state cannot be governed without injustice ⟨injuria⟩, but that it is quite certain that it cannot be governed without the strictest justice."

4. Cicero, *De legibus,* ii.viii (19): "They shall approach the gods in purity, bringing piety, and leaving riches behind. Whoever shall do otherwise, God Himself will deal out punishment to him. No one shall have gods to himself, either new gods or alien gods, unless recognized by the State. Privately they shall worship ⟨those gods whose worship they have duly received from their ancestors⟩." It is not clear why Reid breaks off the quotation in mid-sentence nor, indeed, why he quotes Cicero's first few laws for his commonwealth at all.

5. Concerning the morality of war, Reid has more to say in 7/vii/ 23,4v, 8/iv/8, and 7/vii/22 (printed below in Section XVII).

IX. SUPPLEMENT TO DUTIES TO OURSELVES

1. There is no end to the tales of Scipionic nobility, but the "fair Captive" would seem to identify Reid's reference as the following episode during the capture of New Carthage in Spain in 210 B.C. by the Romans under Publius Cornelius Scipio (234–183 B.C.), afterward Scipio Africanus (major): "It was at this time that some young Romans came across a girl of surpassing bloom and beauty, and being aware that Scipio was fond of women brought her to him and introduced her, saying that they wished to make a present of the damsel to him. He was overcome and astonished by her beauty, but he told them that had he been in a private position, no present would have been more welcome to him, but as he was the General it would be the least welcome of any, giving them to understand, I suppose, by this answer that sometimes, during seasons of repose and leisure in our life, such things afford young men most delightful enjoyment and entertainment, but that in times of activity they are most prejudicial to the body and the mind alike of those who indulge in them. So he expressed his gratitude to the young men, but called the girl's father and delivering her over to him at once bade him give her in marriage to whomever of the citizens he preferred. The self-restraint and moderation he displayed on this occasion secured him the warm approbation of his troops." (*The Histories of Polybius*, x.19.3–7).

2. *De officiis*, I.v (15): "Although these four ⟨virtues⟩ are connected and interwoven, still it is in each one considered singly that certain definite kinds of moral duties have their origin." At the end of the book (chs. xliii–xlv (152–161)) he argues that the duties arising from the four virtues may well be in conflict and that they can be ranked in importance. It was common Stoic teaching that the virtues are intertwined; cf. Cicero, *Tusculan Disputations*, II.xiv (32–33) and III.viii (17), and Diogenes Laertius, *Lives*, VII.125–126.

3. Ovid, *Metamorphoses*, II.13–15: "They have not all the same appearance, and yet not altogether different; as it should be with sisters."

X. NATURAL LAW AND NATURAL RIGHTS

1. This Latin manuscript presents a mystery. It has the appearance of being a précis of the beginning of a book, but neither the

editor nor any of the many learned colleagues approached for advice have been able to identify Reid's source. It is impossible to tell in which year it was written on "Feb. 17," though my intuitions about Reid's handwriting lead me to think that it is comparatively late. It should be mentioned that Reid used the same piece of paper to write a brief abstract of Archibald Campbell's *Enquiry into the Original of Moral Virtue* from 1733—which was first published in 1728 by Alexander Innes, who had "borrowed" the manuscript from Campbell—but this abstract is equally impossible to date. The ideas expressed in the present manuscript were exceedingly common, and in the absence of the crucial information about Reid's reference, any attempt at commentary would be so general that it would be of little use. Therefore, the manuscript is presented along with my fairly literal translation in the hope that someone else may be able to provide the decisive information. This may well give us an additional source for Reid's knowledge of natural jurisprudence.

2. The reflections in this manuscript are quite general and might belong to the beginning of the lectures on jurisprudence or to the beginning of the subsection of the course dealing with political jurisprudence. Only Reid's heading for the text points in the direction of the former and determines inclusion in this section.

3. In his second year at Glasgow, Reid apparently decided to go into more detail than in 1765 concerning the implications of perfect rights and especially the right to life (see the Commentary above at p. 322 n. 26). The manuscript should be read in the context of the natural lawyers' debate about an individual's rights over his own life in cases of self-defense and situations of need (Grotius, *War and Peace*, II.1; Pufendorf, *Law of Nature*, II.5–6, and *Duty of Man*, I.5; Heineccius, *Universal Law*, I.100–102 and 110–120, with Turnbull's Remarks, pp. 120–122). The topic also had importance for the relationship between natural law and God's revealed law—"The Christian Religion commands that we should lay down our Lives one for another; but who will pretend to say, that we are obliged to this by the Law of Nature" (Grotius, *War and Peace*, I.2.vi (2))—upon which Barbeyrac comments (n.2 at ibid.): "This Instance is not altogether just. The Law of Nature, rightly understood, requires us in certain Cases to sacrifice our Lives for others, when a considerable Advantage may result from such an Action to the Publick."

4. While the case of Mr. Burnet has not been traced, the reference here is Henry Ellis, *Voyage to Hudson's Bay*, pp. 189–191: "When ⟨the Esquimaux Indians⟩ are sober, they are very courteous, and

compassionate, and that as well to those who are absolute strangers, as their own Family; and their Affection for their Children is singularly great. An extraordinary Instance of this happened lately at York-Fort: Two small Canoes, passing Hayes's River, when they got to the middle of it, one of them ... sunk, in which was an Indian, his Wife and Child: The other Canoe being small, and incapable of receiving more than one of the Parents, and the Child, produced a very extraordinary Contest between the Man and his Wife, not but that both of them were willing to devote themselves to save the other, but the Difficulty lay in Determining which would be the greatest Loss to the Child. The Man used many Arguments to prove it more reasonable, that he should be drowned, than the Woman. But she alleged on the contrary, it was more for the Advantage of the Child, that she should perish, because he, as a Man, was better able to hunt; and, consequently, to provide for it. . . . ⟨T⟩hey took leave in the Water; the Woman quitting the Canoe was drowned, and the Man with the Child got safe a-shore."

5. See Pufendorf, *Duty of Man*, 1.5.xi: "the lawful Governour has Power to lay an Injunction on any private Man . . . not to decline by Flight such Danger of losing his Life. Nay further, he may of his own Accord provoke such Danger, provided . . . by thus Adventuring he has Hopes to save the Lives of others, and those others are such as are worthy so dear a Purchase. For it would be silly for any Man to engage his Life together with another to no purpose; or for a Person of Value to die for the Preservation of a guilty Rascal." See also Pufendorf, *Law of Nature*, II.5.xiv, and Grotius, *War and Peace*, II.1.viii–ix.

6. Cicero, *De officiis*, III.x (45): "They say that Damon and Phintias, of the Pythagorean school, enjoyed such ideally perfect friendship, that when the tyrant Dionysius had appointed a day for the execution of one of them, and the one who had been condemned to death requested a few days' respite for the purpose of putting his loved ones in the care of friends, the other became surety for his appearance, with the understanding that if his friend did not return, he himself should be put to death. And when the friend returned on the day appointed, the tyrant in admiration for their faithfulness begged that they would enrol him as a third partner in their friendship" (also in *Tusculan Disputations*, v.xii (63)).

7. See Grotius, *War and Peace*, II.1.v, n.1: "Phrynicus, General of the Athenians, said he ought not to be blamed, if, finding his Life in Danger, he did all in his Power to avoid being destroyed

by his Enemies. Thucydides, Lib. VIII"—to which Barbeyrac rightly objects, "That General's Case was not one of those mentioned by our Author; as appears from consulting the Historian, in the Place here quoted." Reid probably did so consult and found, more or less, the point he is making (Thucydides, *History of the Peloponnesian War*, VIII.27).

8. See Heineccius, *Universal Law*, 1.116: "it is a more difficult question . . . whether he does contrary to his duty, who being in the direful necessity above mentioned ⟨the need to have an amputation to survive⟩, chooses rather to die than to bear pain, to which he feels himself unequal; especially when it is not certain what may be the event of the amputation, seeing not fewer who have undergone the torment with great constancy have perished than have been saved." Cf. ibid., p. 101, and Pufendorf, *Law of Nature*, II.6.iii.

9. See Heineccius, *Universal Law*, 1.110: "The Martyrs were in the case of extreme necessity, being obliged to renounce Christ, or to undergo the most violent tortures." See also Barbeyrac's n.2 to Grotius, *War and Peace*, 1.2.vi (2) (the reference to the martyrs is made explicit in the Latin version).

10. See Pufendorf, *Law of Nature*, II.5.xii: " 'Tis another famous Question, Whether the Danger of receiving a Box of the Ear, or some such ignominious though slight Injury, will excuse the killing of a Man in our own Defence." The fame of the question may be gauged from Grotius, *War and Peace*, II.l.x; Pufendorf, *Duty of Man*, 1.5.xiv, and from Barbeyrac's notes in these three places. The question became famous because it illustrated a crucial feature of the Grotian notion of expletive justice—namely, that it did not involve any element of proportionality, especially equality (as here between the injury done and the protection or punishment sought)—and further because it showed the relationship between natural law and positive law, divine as well as human: the latter could narrow the scope of the former, for instance, as here by prescribing some particular relationship between injury and reaction. Common prudence points the same way (Pufendorf, *Law of Nature*, II.5.iii, and *Duty of Man*, 1.5.xiv), and this may have been Reid's point here.

11. See the Commentary above at pp. 320–321 n. 25.

12. See the Commentary above at p. 317 n. 9.

13. The latter is a defining characteristic of the moral states. In this formulation, Reid appears to be echoing Hutcheson, *System*, 1.280; cf. *Short Introduction*, p. 139.

14. See Pufendorf, *Law of Nature*, II.2.i.
15. See, in general, Grotius, *War and Peace*, II.5.i–xvi and xxvi–xxxii; Pufendorf, *Law of Nature*, book VI, and *Duty of Man*, II.2–4; Heineccius, *Universal Law*, II, chs. 2–5; Hutcheson, *Short Introduction*, book III, chs. 1–3, and *System*, book III, chs. 1–3. For Reid's extensive treatment of this topic, see Reid's MS. 8/IV/7,4r–4v ("Oeconomical Jurisprudence," printed above, pp. 170–172) and Reid's manuscripts in Section XIV of this book.
16. See, in general, Grotius, *War and Peace*, II.5.xvii–xxv; Pufendorf, *Law of Nature*, VII and VIII.1–5, and *Duty of Man*, II.5–15; Heineccius, *Universal Law*, II, chs. 6–10; Hutcheson, *Short Introduction*, book III, chs. 4–8, and *System*, book III, chs. 4–9. See Reid's MS 8/IV/10,1r–4v ("Political Jurisprudence," printed above, pp. 173–181), and Reid's manuscripts in Section XVI of this book.
17. See above, p. 317 n. 7 and Reid's MS. 7/VII/21,1r–1v (above, pp. 182–183). See also Reid's manuscripts in Section XVII of this book.
18. See Grotius, *War and Peace*, III.2 and III.20.viii (esp. n. 1); Pufendorf, *Law of Nature*, VIII.6.xiii and n.1, and *Duty of Man*, II.16.x.
19. Reid is here taking up a debate started by Grotius, *War and Peace*, I.1.xiv, and picked up by, among many, Pufendorf, *Law of Nature*, II.3.xxiii, Barbeyrac in his notes to those two, and (of special importance for Reid) Vattel's preface and preliminaries to *Law of Nations*.
20. Like most Protestant thinkers, Reid took Grotius to be the founder of modern natural law (see A.P., p. 645a) and the "180 years past" mentioned above was meant to indicate Grotius's birth in 1583. The work by Selden most commonly used by natural lawyers, apart from *Mare clausum*, was *De iure naturali et gentium iuxta disciplinam Ebraeorum* (1640). Barbeyrac "upon Grotius and Puffendorf" refers to Barbeyrac's annotated editions; the same applies to Carmichael. Concerning the remaining references, see the Bibliographic Index and the Introduction above, pp. 89ff.
21. In discussing the grounds for distinguishing between perfect and imperfect rights (see the references in the Commentary above at pp. 320–321 n. 25), the natural lawyers saw themselves as discussing the extent of the concept of justice and thus of the discipline of jurisprudence (see references in the Commentary above at p. 319 n. 19). The political implications are evident from the two central points Reid briefly makes here and elaborates on in 7/VII/1b below at n.30, and in A.P., p. 645b. He is

following Carmichael, notes to Pufendorf, *De officio* I.2.xiv–xv (pp. 47–50), and Hutcheson, *Short Introduction*, pp. 122–123, and *System*, I.262–263.

22. For this and the following sentence, see the Commentary above at p. 317 n. 8.

23. The following is a paraphrase of Hutcheson; see the Commentary above at p. 331 n. 40.

24. See the references in the Commentary above at pp. 320–321 n. 25.

25. The numbering of the following points has clearly been added later in order to indicate a revised order of presentation. All seven distinctions have been explained in the Commentary above at pp. 320–321 and 323–324 nn. 24, 25, and 29.

26. The free or unfettered state. See Hutcheson, *Institutio*, p. 144: "Status est . . . vel solutus et liber . . . vel adventitius."

27. Pufendorf, *Duty of Man*, I.6.i (cf. II.1.ii), and *Law of Nature* II.3.xxiv. Pufendorf does not, however, identify hypothetical duties, and hence rights, with those arising from familial and civil life. This tendency is due to such commentators as Barbeyrac (note on p. 89 in *Duty of Man*), whereas Pufendorf uses the general definition that hypothetical duties "take their Original from some certain Human Institutions, or some peculiar, adventitious or accidental State of Men" (*Duty of Man*, I.6.i).

28. Grammatical and quotational rigor would have led Reid to write "quam" instead of "quod" on both occasions. Otherwise he quotes accurately from Cicero, *Pro T. Annio Milone Oratio*, IV (10), the sense of which is in N. H. Watt's free translation: "a law which ⟨is⟩ a law not of the statute-book, but of nature; a law which we possess not by instruction, tradition, or reading, but which we have caught, imbibed, and sucked in at Nature's own breast; a law which comes to us not by education but by constitution, not by training but by intuition."

29. The first professorship in the law of nature and nations is commonly ascribed to Pufendorf and the University of Heidelberg (1660). It was in fact a personal chair in international law and philology that Pufendorf later remembered as being "Juris Naturalis & Gentium" (preface to *De jure*; see Krieger, *Politics of Discretion*, p. 19). At any rate, Reid is correct that the profession mushroomed very quickly in Protestant Europe. As for his assessment of the utility of the new discipline, see A.P., p. 645.

30. It is difficult to avoid the impression that Reid is here criticizing Adam Smith. Although Smith did not discuss perfect and imperfect rights in the *Theory of Moral Sentiments* (his only pub-

lished book at the time of Reid's lectures), he did explicitly confine natural jurisprudence to justice, and justice to commutative
justice, that negative virtue which we already know as particular
or expletive justice, the "justice strictly taken" which protects
perfect rights. See the Commentary above at p. 319 n. 19, and
TMS, VII.iv.7–15 and II.ii.1–2. In addition it is possible that Reid
had access to some account of his predecessor's lectures on jurisprudence, such as the ones we have from the hands of students, according to one of which Smith made the point very directly: "The common way in which we understand the word
right, is the same as what we have called a perfect right, and is
that which relates to commutative justice. Imperfect rights,
again, refer to distributive justice. The former are the rights
which we are to consider, the latter not belonging properly to
jurisprudence, but rather to a system of moralls as they do not
fall under the jurisdiction of the laws" (LJ(A), i.15). When Reid
says that Grotius, Pufendorf, Barbeyrac, and Hutcheson "in
their Systems comprehended both" perfect and imperfect
rights, he is therefore in effect saying that these writers did not
admit a sharp distinction between jurisprudence and "a system
of moralls" on the epistemological and moral grounds that led
Smith to this distinction. The two points that follow are then
meant to indicate Reid's rebuttal of exactly these grounds, the
first the epistemological point that there is no sharp distinction
between our perception of justice and of other parts of morality,
the second the moral point that man's duty comprehends both
rights of justice and imperfect rights. Concerning the four natural lawyers, see the Commentary above at pp. 319 and 320–
321 nn. 19 and 25.

XI. PROPERTY

1. Although no relevant section "2" is preserved, it is clear that it
   would concern "derived" property, which is dealt with in 7/VII/
   13 (p. 211 of this book); see also the titles of Hutcheson's chs. 6
   and 7 in book II of *Short Introduction* and chs. 7 and 8 in book II
   of *System*.
2. Reid has developed this analogy in the present context from the
   similar analogy in Epictetus's *Morals*, ch. 21, and especially Simplicius's commentary on this chapter. Many years earlier Reid
   had made an "Abstract of Epictetus Morals" chapter by chapter,
   the entry for ch. 21 being: "Behave yourself in the Affairs of
   Life as at an Entertainment dont Snatch at what is sent to an-

other but wait patiently till it comes to your turn to be served; what is given you receive with Modestie, & Refuse & Disdain Delicacies" (3/II/4,1v). See also Cicero, *De natura deorum*, II.xi–xiv (153–162). This abstract seems to have been made before September 1750, the date of a brief note on Xenophon, which follows (ibid., 2r) and the ink of which appears newer. I believe that Reid used George Stanhope's translation of Epictetus and Simplicius. Ch. 21 in this and other older editions corresponds to ch. 15 in the modern editions of Arrian's arrangement of Epictetus. Concerning the principles illustrated by the analogy, see Reid's manuscript 8/IV/1,4r–v (above, pp. 147–149) and A.P., pp. 657b–659a. Concerning Epictetus, see also the Commentary above at pp. 305 and 307–308 nn. 3 and 10.

3. The use of inanimate nature by animals, human and nonhuman, was in general not considered a moral problem by modern natural lawyers. Man's use of nonhuman animals for work, for produce such as milk, eggs, and wool, and especially for food, was an entirely different matter. The jurisprudents were well aware of the objections against this, which philosophers since antiquity and various religions had raised. They did not want to answer such objections by referring to God's gift to Adam (Gen. 1:28)—which was anyway inconclusive as far as the consumption of flesh was concerned (see Gen. 1:29)—or to God's dispensation to Noah (Gen. 9:3). For Pufendorf, as for most other natural lawyers, this would be tantamount to relying on revealed religion, and the overriding ambition of modern natural jurisprudence was precisely to be independent of revelation (as opposed to natural religion). Pufendorf's answer is that the nonhuman animals are not part of the sociability that is the basic injunction of natural law because they are incapable of being party to relations of obligation (*Law of Nature*, II.3.ii–iii; cf. Grotius, *War and Peace*, Prolegomena, secs. 6–7, and I.1.xi, and *The Truth of the Christian Religion*, I.7). The only moral (as opposed to prudential) limitations on the use of animals thus arise from respect for God as the Creator and from our relations with other humans (*Law of Nature*, IV.3). This is significantly changed in Hutcheson, who (following Carmichael) maintains that the basic command of natural law is the maximization of happiness in God's creation. From this he draws the conclusion, which Carmichael did not (n.1 to Pufendorf, *De officio*, I.12.i), that nonhuman animals also have rights—namely, rights to happiness. At the same time, however, Hutcheson does operate with the idea that there are qualitative differences between the happiness

of which humans and animals are capable and that the former in cases of direct conflict takes precedence over the latter. Nevertheless, the rights of animals must be a tempering reality, for although they are incapable of realizing that they have such rights and of pressing their claims, this does not absolve humans as moral agents from recognizing them; in this there is no difference between animals and human infants (Hutcheson, *System*, 1.309–316; cf. *Short Introduction*, pp. 147–149). Hutcheson is thus giving meaning to Ulpian's famous broad definition of natural law, so often criticized by natural lawyers: "Natural law is that which nature instals in all animals. For this law is not peculiar to humankind but is shared by all animals" (Justinian, *Institutes*, 1.ii., pr., and *Digest*, 1.1.i.3). At the same time he anticipates the well-known argument of Soame Jenyns, *Disquisitions on Several Subjects*, "On Cruelty to Inferior Animals," pp. 12–26. It is interesting to note that simultaneously with Hutcheson the Danish philosopher Friederik Christian Eilschov used the Wolffian version of hedonism to develop the most elaborate and original eighteenth-century argument for a moral community of man and animals under natural law; *Philosophiske Skrifter* and *Philosophiske Breve*.

4. I.e., "the ability to possess, to use, to exclude others, to alienate." See Hutcheson, *Institutio*, p. 167: "Plenum igitur Dominium continent haec quatuor. (1) Jus rei possidendae. (2) Jus omnem ejus usum capiendi. (3) Jus alios ab eo arcendi. (4) Jus, prout domino libuerit, eam transferendi."

5. This was probably Reid's clue to making the point that even in the absence of population pressure and the deepening of the division of labor that was its consequence, men became property-owners. See Hutcheson, *Short Introduction*, pp. 149–150, and *System*, 1.319–320.

6. Reid has apparently jumped the gun and foreshadowed the subject of succession, especially entail. See Reid's manuscripts printed here, pp. 150ff. and Section XII in this book.

7. On the following four points, see also Hutcheson, *Short Introduction*, pp. 149–151, and *System*, 1.317–324. See also Reid, p. 210 below, and A.P., pp. 658a–659a. For a questioning of this justification of property, see "Some Thoughts on the Utopian System," printed as Section XVIII of this book.

8. For an elaboration of the corollary, see below, pp. 206–208; cf. also Hutcheson, *Short Introduction*, pp. 156–158, and *System*, 1.326–328.

9. See the Commentary above, pp. 327–328 n. 37.

10. An opening question is often a sign that a manuscript was prepared as a paper for either the Aberdeen Philosophical Society
or the Glasgow Literary Society. In the present case, however,
Reid broke off after the following two sentences and used the
rest of the manuscript to sketch lecture material. This is evident
both from the content and from the change of pen and handwriting.

11. It may be a snippet from one of these lectures, which has come
down to us as MS. 8/ɪv/6, a single folio containing eight lines of
text, which I print here:

> March 20 1769
> Among the Adventitious Rights of Mankind, that of Prop-
> erty bears a very considerable Rank. And what Civilians call
> a Real Right as distinguished from a personal is nothing
> else but Property of one kind or another. We have therefore
> endeavered to show how the Property of things is originally
> acquired by Occupation. We have endeavered to explain
> that state of negative Communion in which things usefull to
> human Life are placed by the Author of Nature.

12. Reid has not indicated how much of the preceding counts as
point number 1. The material is in general known from the previous manuscripts; see also the following, 7/vɪɪ/13.

13. See A.P., p. 658, and the Commentary above at p. 326 n. 32.

14. The most substantial surviving treatment of this is immediately
below in the present manuscript.

15. See the Commentary above at pp. 325–326 n. 31.

16. See the Commentary above at p. 326 n. 33.

17. See the Commentary above at pp. 326 and 332 nn. 33 and
42.

18. Instead of following this intention, Reid apparently found it
necessary to elaborate on "Limitations to the Right of Property."
Concerning accession, see the Commentary above at pp. 328ff.
n. 39.

19. For this paragraph, see the Commentary above at p. 327 n. 35.

20. Reid is here taking up a contested point in modern natural law's
theory of property. Grotius (*War and Peace*, ɪɪ.2.vi) had maintained that the original contract about property (cf. the Commentary above at pp. 323ff. n. 29) had been entered into with
the proviso that in cases of extreme need the property rights of
individuals would be inoperative, because the original use-right
of all to the natural world in such situations would overrule private rights. Against this, Pufendorf (*Law of Nature*, ɪɪ.6.v–vi)

held that the original contract about property granted those in extreme need an imperfect right to assistance which they were justified in pressing against those who were able to relieve their distress, and indeed that in civil society this might well be backed by law. A third line is taken by Locke, according to whom natural law imposes a duty to preserve the creation of God (*Second Treatise*, ch. II.6) which implies a natural duty to charity (*First Treatise*, ch. IV.42). Hutcheson, finally, resolves the problem on purely utilitarian grounds (*Short Introduction*, pp. 241–246, and *System*, II.117–140). Reid may also have drawn on Vattel, *Law of Nations*, II.ix. See the Commentary below at pp. 423ff. nn. 19ff.

21. The first case stems from the *Digest*, XIV, title ii: "II De lege Rhodia de iactu, 2," and it occurs in Grotius, *War and Peace*, II.2.vi (3), and is referred to in Pufendorf, *Law of Nature*, II.6.vii. The second case is in the elder Seneca, *The Controversiae*, IV.4 (*Declamations*, 1:447), from which Grotius gets it (*War and Peace*, II.2.vi, n. 5). It occurs further in the *Digest*, XIV, title ii: "II De lege Rhodia de iactu, 1," and in Justinian, *Institutes*, II.i.48, from the former of which Pufendorf quotes it (*Law of Nature*, II.6.viii). It is alluded to by Hutcheson in *Short Introduction*, p. 244, and *System*, II.126. See also Cocceius, *Introductio*, p. 421, and the Commentary above at p. 358 n. 127.

22. See Pufendorf, *Law of Nature*, II.6.v, Barbeyrac's n.3, and VIII.5.vii; Hume, *Enquiry*, p. 186; Hutcheson, *System*, II.125.

23. Not traced.

24. See Pufendorf, *Law of Nature*, II.6.ii, v, and vii.

25. See Grotius, *War and Peace*, II.2.x and xiii, and III.17.iii (1).

26. See Pufendorf, *Law of Nature*, VIII.5.vii.

27. See Grotius, *War and Peace*, II.2. xxiv, and II.12.xvi; Pufendorf, *Law of Nature*, v.5.vii.

28. According to Pufendorf, the acquisition of property is always so limited by the law of nature that each one "only possesses himself out of the common Store of what is sufficient for his private Service, but not so as to destroy the whole Fund, and so prevent a Stock for future Uses" (*Duty of Man*, 1.12.ii; cf. *Law of Nature*, IV.4.v, and concerning individual and collective colonization, cf. 1.12.vi and IV.6.iii, respectively). The contract about property was meant to regulate and, as it were, codify this. When Barbeyrac, Carmichael, and Hutcheson rejected the idea of a property contract in favor of Locke's notion of labor, they also adopted the Lockean idea that property was limited to what one could use through one's labor, provided "there is enough, and as good left in common for others" (*Second Treatise*, v.27),

though their concept of community was negative. Reid is here echoing Hutcheson's formulation of this point in *Short Introduction*, pp. 156–158, and *System*, 1.326–328. On Barbeyrac, Carmichael, and the context of the present problem, see the Commentary above at pp. 323–324 and 327–328 nn. 29 and 37.

29. Concerning wills, see Grotius, *War and Peace*, II.6.xiv; Pufendorf, *Law of Nature*, IV.10.iv–vi and IV.11.xviii, and *Duty of Man*, I.12.xiii; Hutcheson, *Short Introduction*, pp. 172–173, and *System*, 1.352–353. Concerning entails, see Hutcheson, *Short Introduction*, p. 168, and *System*, 1.350. Entails are dealt with at length in Reid's manuscript above at pp. 150ff. (see also the Commentary at pp. 333–334 n. 46); the topic of testaments is touched upon, p. 154.

30. See Grotius, *War and Peace*, II.2.xi and xix; Pufendorf, *Law of Nature*, II.6.vii; Hutcheson, *Short Introduction*, pp. 246–247.

31. See Hutcheson, *System*, 1.327: "as . . . some publick interests of societies may justify such Agrarian Laws as put a stop to the immoderate acquisitions of private citizens which may prove dangerous to the state, tho' they be made without any particular injury; the same or like reasons may hold as to acquisitions made by private men in natural liberty, or by states and nations." The classical notion of an agrarian law, as adapted by James Harrington, played a significant role in Reid's political thought, as will be seen in his lectures on politics, where he rejects the idea in 4/ III/6.

32. See the Commentary above at pp. 325–326 n. 31. See also Grotius, *War and Peace*, III.12.vi–vii, and Pufendorf, *Law of Nature*, VIII.6.vii (esp. Barbeyrac's note) and VIII.6.xix.

33. Reid here follows Grotius, *War and Peace*, I.l.vi, I.3.vi, II.14.vii–viii, III.19.vii, and III.20.vii–viii; Pufendorf, *Law of Nature*, VIII.5.vii; and Hutcheson, *Short Introduction*, p. 290 (cf. ibid., p. 246), and *System*, II.236–237 (cf. ibid., pp. 124–125) in seeing the state's *dominium eminens* as a right to overrule private property. On compensation, see also *War and Peace*, II.2.ix, and n. 1; *Law of Nature*, II.6.vi; *Short Introduction*, pp. 245–246, and *System*, II.124. See also the Commentary at pp. 331–332 n. 41 and at pp. 423ff. nn. 19ff.

34. According to P. D. G. Thomas, *The House of Commons in the Eighteenth Century*, pp. 45–46, in the eighteenth century "the great mass of legislation was personal and local in scope, largely consisting of enclosure bills, turnpike and canal bills, and naturalization bills," but Parliament had reached "a clear procedural distinction between such private business and public legislation:

and the old rule that all legislation had to be initiated by petition still applied to private bills." Concerning petitions in general, see ibid., pp. 17–20 and 57–59. See also the Commentary below at p. 424 n. 20.

35. Smith makes the same point in WN, IV.vii.b.9. See also Vattel, *Law of Nations*, 1.18.208: "But it is questioned whether a nation may thus appropriate to itself, by merely taking possession of a country, which it does not really occupy, and in this manner reserve to itself much more than it is able to people or cultivate. It is not difficult to determine, that such a pretension would be absolutely contrary to the law of nature, and opposite to the views of nature, who appointing all the earth to supply the wants of man in general, gave to no nation the right of appropriating to itself a country but for the use it makes of it, and not to hinder others from improving it."

36. See the Commentary above at p. 317 n. 9 for the general point about the correlation between right and obligation. For the particular case of property, see Grotius, *War and Peace*, II.10; Pufendorf, *Law of Nature*, IV.13, and *Duty of Man*, 1.13; Hutcheson, *System*, 1.339.

37. See A.P., pp. 657b–662a.

38. Hutcheson, *System*, 1.331: "we need not have recourse to any old conventions or compacts, with Grotius and Pufendorf, in explaining the original of property: nor to any decree or grant of our first parents with Filmer." See also *Short Introduction*, p. 159, and, concerning Grotius and Pufendorf, see the Commentary above at pp. 323–324 n. 29 and at pp. 380 ad 381 nn. 20 and 28. Sir Robert Filmer rejected Grotius's theory of the original negative community and the consequent idea of a contractual basis for private property, for "if propriety be brought in by a human law (as Grotius teacheth), then the moral law depends upon the will of man. There could be no law against adultery or theft, if women and all things were common" (*Patriarcha*, p. 65). Further, such a doctrine implies that all people are equal moral judges who carry rights and this implication is the bane of civil society (ibid., ch. IX). The truth, as revealed in Genesis, however, is that there never was any negative community, because God granted the whole world as private, exclusive property to Adam and all private properties stem from this original one by way of inheritance or alienation. This is the doctrine that Locke savages in the *First Treatise*, here esp. ch. IV; cf. Barbeyrac's general agreement at n. 1 on p. 366 of Pufendorf, *Law of Nature*.

39. Reid is here echoing the classical formulations that everyone

dealing with justice has used. See Cicero, *De finibus*, v.xxiii (65); *De officiis*, i.v (15); and *De legibus*, i.vi (19), but first of all Ulpian as rendered in *Digest*, 1.1.10, pr. and in the *Institutes* 1.1, pr.

40. See the Commentary above at p. 317 n. 8, and A.P., p. 643b.

41. Here and on p. 202 and at A.P., p. 644, Reid extends the notion of external rights to include claims that are not only immoral but also without proper legal force. Behind this lies a shift in the criterion of externality best picked up by attending to the obligations. For Hutcheson the externality of an obligation is purely a matter of the obliged person's perception of the immorality of the right being claimed, and the foundation of the obligation is simply prudential (see *System*, 1.260). Consequently, illegal acts are excluded because they are not prudent. For Reid the externality of an obligation is a question not of perception but of the actual immorality of the corresponding rights-claim, and the basis for such obligation may be either prudential or a genuine though misguided sense of duty. Reid makes sure to obliterate the reminder of Hobbes's distinction between obligation in *foro externo* and in *foro interno* that Hutcheson inevitably provides. Cf. *De cive*, iii.27, and *Leviathan*, p. 215. The reader may also want to see this topic in the light of Pufendorf's distinction between intrinsic and extrinsic obligation (*Law of Nature*, 1.6.vi–xii, and the preface to *Duty of Man*; cf. Heineccius, *Universal Law*, 1.4–5).

42. This possibility occupied Reid a good deal; see the Commentary above at p. 326 n. 32. When he took it up again, in his late "Some Thoughts on the Utopian System" (printed as Section XVIII of this book), it was exactly in the context of a discussion of Sir Thomas More's *Utopia*. In the present context he is likely to be writing with Hutcheson, *System*, 1.323, in mind and perhaps in sight: "The inconveniences arising from property, which Plato and Sir Thomas More endeavour to avoid by the schemes of community, are not so great as those which must ensue upon community; and most of them may be prevented where property is allowed with all its innocent pleasure, by a censorial power, and proper laws about education, testaments, and succession." As for "Paraguay," it is a reference to the Jesuits' experiments with communes in that country. This obviously interested Reid, and we find him returning to it in his lectures on politics.

43. See Hutcheson, *System*, 1.323: "what plan of polity will ever satisfy men sufficiently as to the just treatment to be given themselves, and all who are peculiarly dear to them, out of the com-

mon stock, if all is to depend on the pleasure of magistrates, and no private person allowed any exercise of his own wisdom or discretion in some of the most honourable and delightful offices of life? Must all men in private stations ever be treated as children, or fools?" The preceding discussion (ibid., 317–323) covers the same ground as Reid's five points here and is followed immediately by the passage quoted just above in n. 42. Cf. *Short Introduction*, pp. 149–151, and the Commentary above at p. 379 n. 7.

44. See the Commentary above at pp. 325–326 n. 31.

45. See Hutcheson, *Short Introduction*, pp. 153–155, and *System*, I.325–326.

46. See the Commentary above at pp. 326 and 332 nn. 33 and 42.

47. *Nativitas*, birth, refers to the principle of accession that "the young born of animals which are subject to your power become yours" (Justinian, *Institutes*, II.i.19). This is discussed in Grotius, *War and Peace*, II.8.xviii; Pufendorf, *Law of Nature*, IV.7.iv; Heineccius, *Universal Law*, I.185; Cocceius, *Introductio*, p. 311; and is referred to in Hutcheson, *Short Introduction*, p. 160, and *System*, I. 337–338 (in a note on the latter page, Hutcheson gives exactly the same list as Reid does here). The rest of the list is explained in the Commentary above at pp. 328ff. n. 39.

48. See the Commentary above at p. 324 n. 29 and Hutcheson, *Short Introduction*, p. 163: "The derived rights are either real or personal. The materials whence all real rights arise is our property. Personal rights are founded on our natural liberty, or right of acting as we choose, and of managing our own affairs. When any part of these original rights is transferred to another, then a personal right is constituted." See also *System*, I.340.

49. This is a précis of Hutcheson, *System*, I.342–343, using the same keywords.

50. Hutcheson, *System*, I.341: "the advantage of the personal obligation to the debtor is this, that he is still master of all his goods, and retains it still in his own election, within the time limited, to discharge the claims upon him in the manner he likes best. And the advantage of the real right to the creditor consists in this, that from the goods specifically subjected to his claim he may be secure, notwithstanding of any subsequent debts incurred to others, or even prior personal debts which his debtor may be incapable of discharging." See also *Short Introduction*, pp. 164–165.

51. Concerning the distinction between partial and full property and the fourfold division of the former, see Reid's manuscript

at pp. 149ff.; cf. also Reid's manuscript printed here as Section XII concerning entails.

52. See Reid's manuscript above at p. 154.

53. See Reid's manuscript above at p. 154.

54. The topic of donation is present in natural law theory only for the sake of systematic completeness—namely, as a contrast to contractual transfer of property: "By the deed of the proprietor among the living, property is transferred either gratuitously in donations; or for valuable consideration in commerce" (Hutcheson, *Short Introduction*, p. 171; see also Hutcheson, *System*, 1.352; Pufendorf, *Law of Nature*, IV.9.i–ii (cf. IV.10.ix), and *Duty of Man*, I.12.xiv).

55. See Reid's manuscript above at pp. 155–156 and 166.

56. See Reid's manuscript above at pp. 157–159.

57. See Reid's manuscript above at p. 166 and the manuscript printed in this book as Section XV.

58. See Reid's manuscript above at pp. 167ff.

59. See Grotius, *War and Peace*, II.2.vi–vii (and ff.); Pufendorf, *Law of Nature*, II.6, and *Duty of Man*, I.5.xxv–xxxi; Hutcheson, *Short Introduction*, book II, ch. 16, and *System*, book II, ch. 17; Heineccius, *Universal Law*, I.110–120, and Turnbull's Remarks, ibid., pp. 120–122. Reid follows Hutcheson in placing this topic after delict.

XII. SUCCESSION

1. This manuscript should be read in conjunction with the discussion of entails in the 1765 course (printed above, pp. 150–153). See also the Commentary at pp. 333–334 n. 46.

2. By "succession" Reid here obviously means "succession in entail," because the other forms of succession give complete property. The reference is to the fourfold division of the partial real derived rights into (1) possession, (2) succession in entails, (3) pledge and mortgage, (4) servitudes. See the Commentary above at p. 332 n. 44 and p. 336 n. 51. Concerning the circumstances of and possible sources for Reid's discussion of entails, see above, pp. 333–334 n. 46.

3. According to Kames, a man who entails his estate does reduce his heirs "to the state of mere liferenters" (*Sketches*, 4:450–451).

4. Concerning the gradual undermining of entails in England, Reid would probably have been enlightened by Dalrymple, *Gen-*

eral History of Feudal Property in Great Britain, pp. 157–160 (cf. Kames, *Sketches*, 4:450). Concerning the introduction of entails into Scotland and its eventual entry into the statute book with the Act Concerning Entails of 1685, see Dalrymple, *General History*, pp. 161–167; Kames, *Essays upon Several Subjects concerning British Antiquities*, essay 1; *Historical Law-Tracts*, pp. 132ff., and *Sketches*, 4:450–451.

5. The points made in this paragraph agree substantially with Kames, *Sketches*, 4:447–449.

XIII. ON DISSOLUTION OF OBLIGATIONS AND ON INTERPRETATION

1. Concerning the systematic place of this topic, see the Commentary above at pp. 355–356 n. 122. Reid's eight points correspond closely to Pufendorf, *Law of Nature*, v.11, and *Duty of Man*, 1.16; to Hutcheson, *Short Introduction*, pp. 248–249; to Heineccius, *Universal Law*, 1.314–322; and to Cocceius, *Introductio*, pp. 345–350, although the final three points are in a slightly different order here and there are a few points more in Pufendorf, Heineccius, and Cocceius. The general Roman law basis is in *Institutes*, III.xxix; for the *Digest*, see the following notes. For the likely origin of Reid's discussion, see the Commentary below at p. 438 n. 95.

2. Pufendorf, *Law of Nature*, v.11.i–iv and *Duty of Man*, 1.16.i; Hutcheson, *Short Introduction*, p. 248; Heineccius, *Universal Law*, 1.315–316; Cocceius, *Introductio*, p. 345; *Digest*, XLVI.iii.

3. Grotius, *War and Peace*, III.19.xv–xvi; Pufendorf, *Law of Nature*, v.11.v–vi, and *Duty of Man*, 1.16.ii; Hutcheson, *Short Introduction*, pp. 248–249; Grotius, *War and Peace*, II.7.ii, and III.19.xv–xviii; Heineccius, *Universal Law*, 1.316–317; Cocceius, *Introductio*, pp. 348–349. The topic is dealt with in a variety of places in the *Digest*, and it is difficult to compare Roman law and natural law directly here; see, however, *Digest*, XVI.11.1, for a definition.

4. Pufendorf, *Law of Nature*, v.11.vii: "The Obligation ceases also when the Creditor, or he who has a Title to it, forgives it. . . . This Release is performed either expressly or tacitly; to the former belongs what the Roman Law calls Acceptilatio, an Acquittance or Discharge, by which the Person acknowledged himself to have receiv'd what indeed he had not." See also *Duty of Man*, 1.16.iii; Hutcheson, *Short Introduction*, p. 249; Heineccius, *Uni-*

versal Law, 1.317–318; Cocceius, *Introductio*, pp. 345–346. Pufendorf is referring to *Institutes*, III.xxix.1. Concerning *acceptilatio*, see also Grotius, *War and Peace*, II.4.iv (2), and *Digest*, XLVI.iv.

5. Pufendorf, *Duty of Man*, 1.16.iv: "Those Obligations are likewise sometimes dissolved, which imply some Performance on both Sides, by a mutual Breaking off before any Thing on either Side be done in the Contract." See also *Law of Nature*, v.11.viii; Hutcheson, *Short Introduction*, p. 249; Heineccius, *Universal Law*, 1.318–319; Cocceius, *Introductio*, p. 346; *Institutes*, III.xxix.4.

6. Pufendorf, *Law of Nature*, v.11.ix, and *Duty of Man*, 1.16.v; Hutcheson, *Short Introduction*, p. 249; Grotius, *War and Peace*, II.15.xv, and III.19.xiv; Heineccius, *Universal Law*, 1.319; Cocceius, *Introductio*, pp. 347–348.

7. Reid is here stretching the use of the words *cessio* (surrendering) and *delegatio* (delegation) to make a distinction that is indistinct in both Pufendorf and Hutcheson. Take the case where B owes money to A and C owes money to B, and either B himself or a court (acting perhaps at A's instigation) "substitutes" the latter debt to him for the debt he has to A. By this transaction B's right against C is renounced and C's obligation to B is thus dissolved: this Reid calls *cessio*. At the same time B's obligation to A is discharged by being delegated to C: this he calls *delegatio*. There does not seem to be any basis in Roman law for this technical use of *cessio*, though there is a good foundation for the substance of the matter (*Digest*, III.v.38, XLVI.iii.53 and 72 (3); and *Institutes*, III.xxix, pr.). In the *Institutio*, pp. 256 and 257, Hutcheson merely hints at such a distinction, and Reid's attention has probably been drawn to it either by Carmichael's somewhat clearer discussion in n. 1 to Pufendorf, *De officio*, 1.16.ix, or by Heineccius, who after explaining delegation basically as above says "There is a great difference between delegation and cession, by which a creditor transfers an action against his debtor to another, without his debtor's knowledge, and against his will" (*Universal Law*, 1.322). Pufendorf himself hints at the distinction but makes it one between two aspects of *delegatio*: "By Delegation a Man substitutes his Debtor to his Creditor to make Payment for him; or I make over to my Creditor the Debt another owes me: And here the Creditor's Consent is necessary, but not the Consent of the third Debtor, whom, in this Case, I can make over unknown to him, and against his Will: For 'tis the same thing to whom a Man pays, but not the same from whom he is to demand a Debt" (*Law of Nature*, v.11.xiii; cf. *Duty of Man*, 1.16.viii, [in the Latin text, 1.16.ix]; Hutcheson, *Short Introduction*, p. 249;

Cocceius, *Introductio*, p. 346). It is possible that Reid's adoption
of a technical use of *cessio* arises from confusion with—or perhaps association with—the concept of *cessio bonorum*, a debtor's
voluntary surrender of property for sale before a court in part
settlement of his debt (*Digest*, XLII.iii; cf. *Institutes*, III.xii). This,
however, did not constitute dissolution of the obligation as such,
and Cocceius, *Introductio*, p. 350, insists that this was in any case
a Roman law invention without hold in natural law.

8. Pufendorf, *Law of Nature*, V.11.xiv: "There is no need to say
   much of Confusion; for since the same Man cannot be his own
   Creditor and Debtor, it follows, if a Man becomes Heir to his
   Debtor, his Action ceases, not finding an Object to exert it self
   upon." See also Cocceius, *Introductio*, p. 348; *Digest*, XVIII.iv.2
   (18), and XLVI.iii.107.

9. Hutcheson, *Short Introduction*, p. 249: "death takes away such
   ⟨obligations⟩ as only respected the persons, and were not designed to subsist to the heirs of the creditor, or affect the heirs
   of the debtor" (cf. Pufendorf, *Law of Nature*, V.11.xii, and *Duty
   of Man*, 1.16.ix [in the Latin text, 1.16.viii]; Heineccius, *Universal
   Law*, 1.320). In the *Digest* the topic is dispersed on the various
   relevant obligations.

10. Concerning the systematic position and the general background
    to this topic, see the Commentary above at pp. 355–356 n. 122.

11. Grotius, *War and Peace*, II.16.xii (1): " 'Tis a remarkable Ques-
    tion, whether by Allies are meant those only who are so at the
    making of the League, or they also which come in afterwards;
    as in that League made between the Romans and Carthaginians
    after the Sicilian War ⟨i.e., the first Punic war 264–241 B.C.⟩,
    where it was agreed, 'That the Allies of the one should not be
    molested by the other.' " Grotius is quoting Polybius, *Histories*,
    III.27 (3); this and the following chapters in Polybius, plus Livy,
    From the Founding of the City, XXI.19, give the material for this
    example which is also used by Pufendorf, *Law of Nature*, VIII.9.x,
    and Vattel, *Law of Nations*, II.17.309.

12. Reid is here referring to the dramatic events recounted in Livy,
    From the Founding of the City, 1.52 and 60, and at the beginning
    of book II. Some related examples are referred to in Grotius,
    War and Peace, II.16.xvi–xvii. The point of the example must be
    gauged from a traditional distinction made in natural law: "An-
    other celebrated Distinction of Leagues is that which divides
    them into real and personal. The latter are such as are made
    with the Prince, purely with Relation to his Person, and expire
    with him. The former are such as are made with the Kingdom

and Commonwealth, rather than the Prince or Government; and these outlive the Ministry and the Government it self under which they were first made" (Pufendorf, *Law of Nature*, VIII.9.vi; similarly *Duty of Man*, II.17.vii, and Grotius, *War and Peace*, II.16.xvi). Both Pufendorf and Grotius claim some foundation in *Digest*, II.xiv.7 (8).

13. See Grotius, *War and Peace*, II.16.ii; Pufendorf, *Law of Nature*, V.12.iii; Vattel, *Law of Nations*, II.17.271. Further, *Digest*, L.xvii.34 and 114.

14. In Pufendorf, *Law of Nature*, V.12.iii, and Vattel, *Law of Nations*, II.17.273, the garrison of Sebastia is buried alive, while in other cases a man has his head saved only to be cut in two at the waist.

15. See Grotius, *War and Peace*, II.16.viii; Pufendorf, *Law of Nature*, V.12.x; *Duty of Man*, I.17.vii; Vattel, *Law of Nations*, II.17.287.

16. Matt. 12:1–13 and Mark 2:23–28 and 3:1–5.

17. Mark 2:27.

18. The distinction between restrictive and extensive interpretation is to be gathered from Grotius, *War and Peace*, II.16.ix; Pufendorf, *Law and Nature*, V.12.xi; *Duty of Man*, I.17.ix; and Vattel, *Law of Nations*, II.17.290: "When the sufficient and sole motive of a provision, whether of a law or of a promise, is perfectly certain and well understood, the provision is extended to cases to which the same motive is applicable, although they are not comprised in the meaning of the terms. This is what is called extensive interpretation." And "restrictive interpretation . . . is the contrary of extensive interpretation . . . if a case should arise which can not at all be brought under the motive of the law or promise, the case should be excepted from its application, although if the meaning of the terms be alone regarded, the case would fall under the provisions of the law or promise" (ibid., sec. 292). Thus, a literal interpretation of the concept of working on the Sabbath might exclude the care for human needs, but a restrictive interpretation in accordance with the intention of the fourth commandment (such as keeping the Sabbath holy for God) would not; see Matthew and Mark as referred to above in n. 16. For the "Law of Tythes," see Matt. 10:10 and 23:23 and Luke 11:42. For the extensive interpretation of the sixth commandment, see Matt. 5:21–26.

19. Reid's reference here is obscure. It could be John Rastell's *Four Elements*, but I find this unlikely, and anyway, it does not seem to assist in identifying the puzzling tale.

20. The story of Quintus Fabius Labeo's destruction of Antiochus the Great's fleet in 188 B.C. is told by Valerius Maximus, *Facto-*

rum et Dictorum Memorabilium, VII.3.iv, and (without the presently relevant finesse) in Livy, *From the Founding of the City*, XXXVIII.39; it is repeated in Grotius, *War and Peace*, II.16.v; Pufendorf, *Law of Nature*, v.12.vii; and Vattel, *Law of Nations*, II.15.233.

21. Reid's intention here is less than clear, but on the basis of the references, which are clear enough, the following interpretation may be tentatively offered. The central point is that the concept of "Nearest relation" or *cognatus* is ambiguous and in need of interpretation: "*Cognati* in the Roman Law is spoken generally of all the collateral Kindred, but more particularly *Cognati* are the collateral Kindred on the Mother's Side, and *Agnati* of the Father's Side. See ⟨Justinian's⟩ *Institut.*, Lib I. Tit. 15. *De Legitima Agnatorum tutela*, 1" (Barbeyrac, n.4 to Pufendorf, *Law of Nature*, v.12.xi; also briefly referred to in Grotius, *War and Peace*, II.16.ix). On this Reid must have elaborated as follows. According to the *Institutes*, I.15, pr., "Those for whom no tutor has been appointed by will have their agnates as tutor under the law of the XII Tables." The justifying clause, which Reid quotes in Latin, means "because, where there is the benefit of succession, there also . . . should be the burden of guardianship." Although this stems from *Institutes*, I.17, which deals with the guardianship by patrons over freedmen, it is not inappropriate because it really applied in general to *tutelae*. It is anyway to this topic in title 17 that Reid's final clause relates, his point being that Roman law stretched the concept of "Nearest relation" to cover even the relationship between a patron and his freedman's children: "For, by the very fact that the ⟨XII⟩ Tables ordained that, if freedmen or freedwomen should have died intestate, their estate should go to their patron or his children, the lawyers of old believed it to be the intention of the law that guardianship should also go to them, because it directs those agnates whom it would summon to succession also to be tutors and because, where there is the benefit of succession, there also, in general, should be the burden of guardianship" (*Institutes*, I.17; cf. Montesquieu, *Spirit of Laws*, XIX.24). (By "Pupil" was meant the person under guardianship—i.e., a ward.)

22. See above, n.15, and *Digest*, XLV.i.41, pr., and 80; L.xvii.67.

23. See Grotius, *War and Peace*, II.16.x: "We must also observe, that of Things promised some are favourable, others odious, and others of a mixt or middle Nature. The favourable are those that carry in them an Equality, and respect the common Advantage, which the farther it extends, the greater is the Favour of the Promise, as in those that make for Peace, the Favour is

greater than in them that make for War; and a defensive War has more Favour allowed than one undertaken upon any other Motive. Others are odious, such as those that lay the Charge and Burden on one Party only, or on one more than another." On this basis Grotius develops a number of rules of interpretation in the subsequent paragraphs. All this is rehearsed in Pufendorf, *Law of Nature*, v.12.xii ff., and *Duty of Man*, 1.17.ix ff. The distinction became controversial and was widely discussed. Among Reid's natural law sources, Barbeyrac flatly rejected it for its "Want of Solidity and Usefulness" (see his extensive notes to Grotius and Pufendorf, at the places cited above in this note), while Carmichael and Vattel defended it (notes to Pufendorf, *De officio*, 1.17.ix ff., esp. pp. 298–299, and *Law of Nations*, II.17.300ff.).

24. Grotius put forward six rules to dispel the collision of laws (*War and Peace*, II.16.xxix), Pufendorf put forth eleven and eight respectively (*Law of Nature*, v.12.xxiii, *Duty of Man*, 1.17.xiii), Vattel ten (*Law of Nations*, II.17.311–321). Reid's first rule, which is put first in all four sources referred to here, is justified by Pufendorf in these words: "For a Permission includes a Liberty, but a Command carries along with it a Necessity of Acting" (*Law of Nature*, v.12.xxiii [1]. Barbeyrac and Carmichael discussed whether the rule was valid without considering the generality or particularity of the permissive and preceptive laws in collision (Barbeyrac, n. 2 to Grotius, *War and Peace*, II.16.xxix; Carmichael, notes to Pufendorf, *De officio*, 1.17.xiii [pp. 304–305]). Reid's second rule corresponds to Pufendorf's seventh (in both books) and Vattel's seventh and more or less to Grotius's fourth. The final rule is the equivalent of Pufendorf's eighth (in both books). The references in Grotius and Pufendorf concerning these rules reveal an important connection with the rhetorical tradition.

XIV. OECONOMICAL JURISPRUDENCE

1. This and the subsequent manuscripts in Section XIV provide an elaboration of the treatment of "oeconomical jurisprudence" in the 1765 course and should be read in conjunction with MS. 8/IV/7,4r–v (printed above, pp. 170–172) and the Commentary thereto at p. 361ff.

2. A sporadically used term; see, e.g., Plutarch, *Moralia*, 1100d. It was used not only for parental love but also for children's love

of parents, as is curiously reflected in Cicero's invocation of it in *Letters to Atticus*, X.8.

3. See n. 2 just above.

4. This point and the concern with chastity (especially women's) were common; see the references in the Commentary above at p. 361 n. 2.

5. Reid seems to provide his own translation of the first sentence of *Spirit of Laws*, XVI.12.

6. Reid seems to have enjoyed one of the books of Athenaeus's *Deipnosophists*, which he would hardly have recommended to his students. At 587c we read: "Nemeas the flute-girl is mentioned by Hypereides in the Speech against Patrocles. Concerning her one may rightly wonder how the Athenians permitted the whore to be so called, since the name she had assumed was that of a highly-revered festival; for the adoption of such names as these had been forbidden, not only to women practising prostitution, but also to other women of the slave class, as Polemon declares in his work *On the Acropolis*."

7. The story of Carvilius Ruga's repudiation of his wife is told by, among others, Valerius Maximus, *Factorum et dictorum memorabilium*, II.1.iv, and retold by Grotius, *War and Peace*, II.5.ix; Pufendorf, *Law of Nature*, VI.1.xxi; and Montesquieu, *Spirit of Laws*, XVI.16. Cf. Montaigne, *Essays*, II.15 (p. 338).

8. According to tradition, when Sextus Tarquinius (Superbus), king of Rome, raped the chaste Lucretia, wife of Tarquinius Collatinus, the people of Rome led by Lucius Junius Brutus rose against him, drove him and his family into exile, and founded the Roman Republic, Brutus and Collatinus being the first two consuls (509 B.C.). The second episode Reid is referring to is the suspension of the constitution in 451 B.C., when ten men (*decem viri*) of the patricians were given absolute power in order to carry through a major codificatory-cum-legislative project, the result of which, after a renewal of the *decemviri* for 450 B.C., was the Twelve Tables. The *decemviri* were suspected of tyrannical intentions, some of the provisions of the new code were antiplebeian, and the political proposals of the *decemviri*, although perhaps originally intended as compromises between patricians and plebeians, were seen as hostile to the latter (esp. the proposal to abolish the *tribuni plebis*). Therefore, when one of the leading *decemviri*, Claudius Appius, tried to gain for himself the young Verginia, daughter of a plebeian centurion, through a fraudulent claim that she was really the slave of one of his clients, and

the father saw no other way to protect her honor than by stabbing her to death in the Forum, the people revolted against the *decemviri*, who resigned. The old constitution was restored, and the new consuls for 449 B.C. published the Twelve Tables.

Especially as told by Livy, *From the Founding of the City*, I.57–60 and III.44–49 (and ff.), these episodes in Roman history assumed the greatest symbolic importance not only for the Roman republican tradition but also for its renewal in modern political thought, and the idea that personal virtue, liberty, and proper (self-)government are intimately connected was crucial for Reid, as is seen in his lectures on politics. As milestones on their way to Reid, we may refer here to the deployment of these Roman stories in Machiavelli, *Discourses on the First Ten Books of Titus Livy*, I.3–4, 40ff. and 57 and III.2, 5, and 26; Harrington, *Oceana*, pp. 268–272 (etc.), and *A Discourse upon this Saying*, p. 741; Montesquieu, *Spirit of Laws*, VI.7, XI.12–15, XII.21 (etc.), and *Les Causes de la grandeur des Romains, et de leur décadence*, ch. 1.

9. See A.P., p. 563b.
10. See A.P., p. 563b.
11. See Pufendorf, *Law of Nature*, VI.1.xviii, p. 576, Barbeyrac's n. 2: "Mr. Derham, in his *Physico-Theologia*, Lib. IV, Ch. X. endeavours to prove Polygamy unlawful for this Reason; 'that there are more Males born than Females.'" Barbeyrac objects to the reasoning here, and it would seem that Reid has had this in mind in the following. The reference is William Derham, *Physico-Theology*, pp. 175–178; the specific figures and their application against polygamy are in Derham's n. 8. Reid's own robust proposal for a population policy is set out in 2/II/17 in the lectures on politics.
12. See *Spirit of Laws*, XVI.4; Montesquieu does not quite express the sort of skepticism mentioned by Reid. Montesquieu's reference is Engelbert Kaempfer, *Histoire*, 1:308. Kaempfer and Montesquieu were, however, not concerned with "Mecao" (maybe Reid was thinking of Macao), but with Meaco; and the numbers concerned were 182,070 and 223,572 (in Kaempfer). Reid may well have been directly acquainted with Kaempfer's well-known work, which had already received at least a couple of English translations, from one of which it was made French.
13. Reid elaborates on the divine institution of marriage in a fragmentary manuscript (6/v/34,1v) added here:

When God made Man and furnished this world with a variety of Creatures for his Use he thought it not good that he should be left alone, but made Woman as a help meet for him and commanded that a Man should leave his father and Mother and cleave unto his Wife. Marriage therefore being the institution of God himself and that in the State of innocence is justly declared by an inspired writer to be honourable in all.

The ends of this Institution being the mutual Comfort & happiness of both parties the regular propagation of the human Race & the right Education of Children it is abundantly evident that those who stand in this Relation ought to cultivate the most tender affection towards each other, to do their utmost to promote each other good both temporal & spiritual and if God bless them with Children to unite their Care and endeavours to train them up in the Nurture and admonition of the Lord & in such a Manner as may make them usefull members of Society. The different departments of Husband and Wife in this natural Society, are pointed out in the Constitution of the different Sexes. To the one Sex Nature has given more hardiness and Robustness of Constitution for toil & labour more Courage for Defence and greater steadines and constancy of Resolution for the Government of a Family. To the other more tenderness & delicacy fitted to domestick Oeconomy and Order, and for the nursing and training of children in their tender Years.

This manuscript consists of three folios. Folio 1, recto, is nearly full of notes on "Measures. 1 Space 2 Duration 3 Number," while the verso side carries the lines of text printed here. The rest of the manuscript is blank. At the end of the first paragraph, Reid indicated that "by an inspired writer" should be transposed from the end of the sentence to its present position. The "inspired writer" is probably the unknown author of the New Testament letter to the Hebrews (see Heb. 13:4); to Reid the author would be known from the Authorized Version as Paul.

14. These historical reflections are clearly under the influence of Grotius, *War and Peace*, II.5.ix, and Pufendorf, *Law of Nature*, VI.1.xvi–xviii. The reference in Plutarch is *Lives*, IX.iv (p. 339) ("Comparison of Demetrius and Antony"), Antony's two simultaneous wives being Octavia and Cleopatra (if he did marry the latter). The imperial law is *Codex*, V.5.ii (cf. *Digest*, III.2.i), and the penal clause is *Codex*, IX.9.xviii (it does not specify the death penalty, but the previous law concerning adultery does); these are

both referred to by Pufendorf, *Law of Nature*, VI.1.xvi. As for Tacitus, see *Germania*, 18, quoted by both Grotius (*War and Peace*, II.5.ix, and by Pufendorf, *Law of Nature*, VI.1.xvi). The point about the Athenians and Cecrops (according to legend, the first king of Athens) is out of Athenaeus, *The Deipnosophists*, XIII.555d, while the Athenians' supposed later polygamy is exemplified by Socrates as represented in Diogenes Laertius, *Lives*, II.26 (p. 157), and Gellius, *Attic Nights*, XV.20.6. Cf. Reid's MS. 7/VII/20,2r (printed here, p. 230).

15. Milton, *Paradise Lost*, IV, ll. 750–752, 754–757, 760, and 763–766.

16. Reid's fondness for the *Oeconomicus* was long-standing; he took notes from it in September 1750, as we see from 3/II/4,2r (see the Introduction above, pp. 11, 16, 17–18). Heineccius was equally keen on the Xenophontian work (see *Universal Law*, II.78 and 79). We do not know which edition of the fragments of Cicero's translation of the *Oeconomicus* Reid was using. They were included in various collections. In the 1653 edition used here there are eleven fragments, which take up four small octavo pages.

17. For the comprehensive discussion of these topics in Reid's sources, see the references in the Commentary above at p. 362 n. 3.

18. For the points in this paragraph, see the references in n. 14 above as well as above, p. 362 n. 3.

19. Euripides, *Andromache*, ll. 177–180:

> Bring not such things midst us! We count it shame
> That o'er two wives one man hold wedlock's reins;
> But to one lawful love men turn their eyes,
> Content—all such as look for peace in the home.

In his Latin text, Grotius quotes the same passage in the same Latin translation using the same introductory phrase ("Euripides . . . Hermiones"); see *De jure belli*, II.5.ix, note n.

20. Plautus, *Mercator*, IV.6, ll. 824–825:

> Now a wife, a good wife, is content with just
> her husband; why should a husband be less
> content with just his wife?

Quoted by Grotius, *De jure belli*, II.5.ix, note n., and by Barbeyrac, n. 4 to Pufendorf, *Law of Nature*, VI.l.xix.

21. Horace, *Odes*, III.6, ll. 17–20: "Teeming with sin, our times have sullied first the marriage-bed, our offspring, and our homes;

sprung from this source, disaster's stream has overflowed the folk and fatherland" (quoted by Pufendorf, *Law of Nature*, VI.l.v).

22. See Pufendorf, *Law of Nature*, VI.l.iv, and Hutcheson, *System*, II.155.

23. The "circumstances which may either make any contract of marriage null and void from the beginning, or free either party from the bond of a contract formerly valid" (Hutcheson, *System*, II.166–167), were traditionally divided into the "natural" (or "physical") and the "moral." The former were physical and mental illnesses and deficiencies, including too high or too low age. The latter were prior marital obligations or the "incestuous mixtures" Reid refers to below. When Reid in the following paragraphs suggests that the abhorrence at incest is natural, it may be seen against the background of this distinction between the moral and the natural and, more especially, against Hume's treatment of it. See Pufendorf, *Law of Nature*, VI.l.xxv, and *Duty of Man*, II.2.vii; Hutcheson, *Short Introduction*, pp. 262–263, and *System*, II.166–169. Furthermore, Reid's suggestion about the natural abhorrence at incest may refer to Hutcheson's (and others') idea that it may derive from "some *positive* divine law in the earlier ages of the world" (*Short Introduction*, p. 264, my emphasis; cf. *System*, II.170–172), an idea that must again be seen against the background of the discussion of what is prohibited by natural law and what by divine positive law in Grotius, *War and Peace*, II.5.xii–xiv, and Pufendorf, *Law of Nature*, VI.l.xxix–xxxv; cf. Reid's point no. 8 below.

24. See the Commentary above at p. 362 n. 3.

25. See Grotius, *War and Peace*, II.5.xv: "there is a Sort of Concubinage, which is indeed a real and valid Marriage, tho' it may not have some of those Effects that are peculiar to the Civil Right, or perhaps, may lose some natural Effects by an Obstruction from the Civil Law." It is presumably the latter that Reid is referring to in his subsequent point no. 7. Cf. Pufendorf, *Law of Nature*, VI.l.xxxvi; Hutcheson, *Short Introduction*, p. 262 n., and *System*, II.162–163; Heineccius, *Universal Law*, II.42–43, where Turnbull's note (p. 43) explains left-hand marriage in terms of "Morgengabe" (morning present) marriage. Robert Jack's report of Reid's definition in 1776 of left-hand marriage is very wide—namely, simply as a second marriage (Jack, "Reid's Lectures," p. 593).

26. See Grotius, *War and Peace*, II.5.viii; Pufendorf, *Law of Nature*, VI.l.x–xiii, and *Duty of Man*, II.2.x; Hutcheson, *Short Introduction*,

p. 266, and *System*, II.183–184; Heineccius, *Universal Law*, II.36–41.

27. See Grotius, *War and Peace*, II.5.x; Pufendorf, *Law of Nature*, VI.2.xiv, and *Duty of Man*, II.3.viii.

28. Here Reid was probably discussing the traditional topic— whether man has a natural *duty* to marry; see Pufendorf, *Law of Nature*, VI.l.iii, vi–vii, and *Duty of Man*, II.2.iii; Hutcheson, *Short Introduction*, p. 259, and *System*, II.156; Heineccius, *Universal Law*, II.29–30.

29. This fragment, which in fact appears to be only a paraphrase, stems from Columella's *De re rustica*, preface to book XII (Cicero's editors erroneously say book XII, ch. 1). Cicero, *Fragmenta*, pp. 34–35, and Columella, *On Agriculture*, XII, preface: "Xenophon . . . in the book . . . *Economicus*, declared that the married state was instituted by nature so that man might enter what was not only the most pleasant but also the most profitable partnership in life. For in the first place, as Cicero also says ⟨in his translation⟩, man and woman were associated to prevent the human race from perishing in the passage of time; and, secondly, in order that, as a result of the same association, mortals might be provided with help and likewise defense in their old age."

30. Although Reid has not given any "1" to precede this "2," it is clear that topic no. 1 in oeconomical jurisprudence is the marriage relation dealt with above. For the present topic, see the Commentary above at pp. 362ff. nn. 4–8.

31. See the Commentary above at p. 392 n. 2.

32. See the Commentary above at pp. 362ff. and 365–366 nn. 5 and 10, and below, p. 400 n. 42. "Nursing" may here be meant in the physical sense; cf. Hutcheson, *System*, II.191–192: "children cannot be deemed accessions or fruits going along with the property of their parents bodies. . . . Generation no more makes them a piece of property to their parents, than sucking makes them the property of their nurses, out of whose bodies more of the matter of a child's body is sometimes derived, than was from both parents."

33. For this tripartite division in natural law, see Grotius, *War and Peace*, II.5.ii, and Pufendorf, *Law of Nature*, VI.2.vii. It is presupposed in Pufendorf, *Duty of Man*, II.3.vi; Hutcheson, *System*, II.193–194; Heineccius, *Universal Law*, II.48.

34. See the Commentary above at p. 337 n. 55 and p. 365 n. 8.

35. See Grotius, *War and Peace*, II.5.vii; Pufendorf, *Law of Nature*, VI.2.xi; Hutcheson, *System*, II.192.

36. "The antient Roman Laws having a Regard both to that Supe-

riority which Nature gives to Parents, and to the Pains and Labour their Children cost them, and also willing that Children
should be altogether subject to them; at the same Time, I presume, depending upon that Affection which Nature inspires
Parents with, have indulged to Parents the Liberty ⟨*ius*⟩, if they
please, either of selling or killing their Children with Impunity"
(Simplicius, *Commentarius in Epicteti Enchiridion*, ch. XXXVII, p.
321; in the Schweighäuser–edition; Grotius was using the 1611
edition by D. Heinsius). This is quoted in the original Greek followed by a Latin translation in Grotius, *De jure belli*, II.5.vii, and
Reid follows the latter. The English translation here is that presented in Grotius, *War and Peace*. In Stanhope's translation it is
pp. 246–247.

37. Justinian, *Institutes*, I.ix.2: "The power that we have in respect of
our children is particular to Roman citizens: for there are no
other men who have such power over their issue." This well-
known passage is quoted in part in Grotius, *War and Peace*,
II.5.vii, and in Pufendorf, *Law of Nature*, VI.2.xi (and, inciden-
tally, in Stair, *Institutes*, 1.5.13; cf. the Commentary above at p.
365 n. 8).

38. Just as the family or household society was thought of as composed of the three "simple" societies (of husband and wife, of
parents and children, and of master and servant; see the detailed analysis in Heineccius, *Universal Law*, II.73–80), so civil society was held to be composed of several families. Like Pufendorf (*Law of Nature*, VI.2.x–xi, and *Duty of Man*, II.3.vii) and to a
lesser degree Grotius (*War and Peace*, II.6.xiii), Reid uses the
present context to draw up the relationship between familial
and civil societies. Behind this, of course, lies Aristotle's distinction between perfect and imperfect societies in book I, chs. 1–2,
of the *Politics*. See Grotius, *War and Peace*, I.l.xiv; and Pufendorf, *Law of Nature*, VII.2.xx; Locke, *Treatise*, II.2; and for a brisk
Harringtonian analysis, see Turnbull's Remarks in Heineccius,
Universal Law, II.80–84.

39. The general references for and background to this topic were
given in the Commentary above at pp. 365–366 nn. 9–10. Implicit in Reid's argument in the first paragraph below is a criticism of the general Aristotelian idea of natural inequality (cf.
Aristotle, *Politics*, 1.3, and Pufendorf's criticism thereof, *Law of
Nature*, III.2.viii and VI.3.ii).

40. See Grotius, *War and Peace*, II.5.i: "We have a Right, not only
over Things, but over Persons too, and this Right is originally

derived from Generation, from Consent, from some Crime."
Having rejected "Generation" and having followed Carmichael
and Hutcheson in refining "Consent" (cf. Section XV), Reid naturally comes to this scheme. The subsequent contractual interpretation of the service-relation is close to that of Hutcheson,
Short Introduction, p. 272, and *System*, ii.199–200.

41. In connection with his implicit denial of the Roman idea that the
child of a slave is by the law of nations (not so clearly by Roman
civil law) like an accession or an usufruct born to be a slave too,
Grotius raises the problem that such a child will nevertheless be
bound to serve its mother's owner in order to recompense him
for its maintenance, if it ever can (*War and Peace*, ii.5.xxix). Pufendorf maintains, however, that apart from being a legitimate
accession or usufruct, such a child will never be able to "much
exceed the Value of his Maintenance" (*Duty of Man*, ii.4.vi, and
Law of Nature, vi.3.ix). This argument for "natural" slavery is
strongly denied by Carmichael and, following him, Hutcheson
and here Reid (Carmichael, n. 3 in Pufendorf, *De officio*, p. 359,
cf. ibid., supplement iv.7; Hutcheson, *Short Introduction*, p. 272,
and *System*, ii.200). The theory of man's surplus productivity as
an argument for free labor thus enters Scottish thought as an
argument against slavery.

42. Reid here reflects the most crucial of Carmichael's arguments
against Pufendorf in the dispute about natural slavery. Pufendorf had justified the idea that the child of a slave is also a slave
"by this Maxim, That whosoever is Proprietor of the Body, is
also Proprietor of whatsoever is the Product thereof" (*Duty of
Man*, ii.4.vi). (For a similar argument, though based on the explicit idea of the child as an accession, see Heineccius, *Universal
Law*, ii.66.) Apart from exploiting Pufendorf's vagueness and
the complexity of the civil law in this question to deny that a
slave child *is* a usufruct (Justinian, *Institutes*, ii.i.37), Carmichael
makes this point: "I add that since the soul, the nobler part of
man, is not derived from the parents, it is reasonable ⟨aequum⟩
that it carries with it the less noble part" (Carmichael, n. 1 in Pufendorf, *De officio*, p. 358). As one might expect of a man from
a Calvinist background, Carmichael here suspects that, true to
his Lutheran origins, Pufendorf is basing his standpoint on a
traducianist view of the origins of individual human life. While
his suspicion may well be wrong, it highlights the importance to
Carmichael, and to Hutcheson and Reid, of the creationist line
of argument, which was sketched above in the Commentary at
pp. 362–364 and 365–366 nn. 5 and 10 (cf. also p. 398 n. 32),

according to which each individual is equally God's work. For
Hutcheson, see *Short Introduction*, p. 277, and *System*, II.210, and
for some uncharacteristically lame responses to Carmichael, see
Barbeyrac's nn. 2–4 to Pufendorf, *Law of Nature*, p. 617.

43. Concerning delict, see Grotius, *War and Peace*, II.5.xxxii;
Hutcheson, *Short Introduction*, pp. 273–274, and *System*, II.201–
202. Concerning captivity, see the Commentary above at p. 366
n. 12. "Incapacity" probably refers to moral incapacity. Like
Hutcheson, *System*, II.202, Reid thought that incurable immorality warranted public slavery (see Reid's manuscript "Some
Thoughts on the Utopian System," printed as Section XVIII of
this book.

44. See the Commentary above at p. 367 n. 13.

XV. SOCIAL CONTRACT AS IMPLIED CONTRACT

1. See A.P., p. 663a-b: "the definition of ⟨Pactum⟩ in the Civil Law,
and borrowed from Ulpian, is, *Duorum pluriumve in idem placitum
consensus*. Titius, a modern Civilian, has endeavoured to make
this definition more complete, by adding the words, *obligationis
licitè constituendae vel tollendae causa datus*. With this addition, the
definition is, that a Contract is the consent of two or more persons in the same thing, given with the intention of constituting
or dissolving lawfully some obligation." The references here are
Digest, II.xiv.1 (2) and Titius, Observation 198, pp. 261–262, in
Pufendorf, *De officio*. Titius is, however, apparently quoting Ulpian after the *Digest*, IV.xii.3, which excludes the words "in idem
placitum," while both Carmichael and Hutcheson quote the
fuller formulation and Carmichael renders Titius's addition as
well (Carmichael, n. 1, pp. 161–162, in his edition of Pufendorf,
De officio; and Hutcheson, *Philosophiae moralis institutio compendiaria*, p. 182). Cf. Pufendorf, *Law of Nature*, III.6.xv, and Barbeyrac's notes.

2. For the wide concept of signs used here, see Grotius, *War and
Peace*, II.4.iii–iv, III.1.viii, and III.24.i–ii (cf. also the distinction
between perfect and imperfect promises explained in the Commentary above at p. 339 n. 60); Pufendorf, *Law of Nature*,
III.6.xvi, and *Duty of Man*, I.9.ix. Concerning silence as a sign of
consent, see Grotius, *War and Peace*, II.4.v, and Pufendorf, *Law
of Nature*, III.6.ii. Reid's examples in the sequel are akin to those
of Pufendorf, *Law of Nature*, III.6.iii.

3. That is, "about the faithful discharge of the office."

4. In this manuscript, some of the most original elements of Reid's philosophy of mind meet with his theory of language and interpretation (see the Commentary above at pp. 342ff. nn. 78–93; and pp. 389ff. nn. 10ff.; and the Introduction, pp. 70ff.) with the general theory of contract (see above, pp. 355ff., nn. 59ff.) and, more especially, with his ideas on implied contract and social contract (see above, pp. 355ff. nn. 122–127; and pp. 409ff. nn. 4ff.). In order to unravel the context of Reid's discussion in the opening pages of the manuscript, it will be necessary to enter into interpretation of Reid himself further than is generally the case in this commentary.

Behind Reid's idea of language here and elsewhere lies his important distinction between "solitary" and "social" acts of mind (see I.P., pp. 244a–245b, and A.P., pp. 663b–666b). The central point is that, in contrast to the solitary, the social acts of the mind presuppose the existence and (in some sense) presence of another mind or other minds. Social acts are necessarily communicative and thus a matter of signs, while solitary acts may or may not be expressed. Examples of the latter are seeing, hearing, remembering, judging, reasoning, deliberating, deciding, while examples of the former are questioning, testifying, commanding, promising, contracting, and the like. For mental acts to be social, there must be a community of signs so that mutual understanding is possible, and nature has in fact provided such a community of signs. First, body language is highly communicative, not only among humans but also in rudimentary form among animals, and indeed between men and animals. "But there are two operations of the social kind, of which the brute-animals seem to be altogether incapable. They can neither plight their veracity by testimony, nor their fidelity by any engagement or promise" (A.P. p. 665b).

This parallel between veracity and fidelity is a good indication of the character of Reid's theory. Contrary to the impression one might at first form, Reid's idea of social acts of the mind is not a theory of language-game in the modern sense. Just as a descriptive account, whose veracity we may testify to, refers to some objective feature of the world, so "engagements," whose obligation we may pledge fidelity to, refer to something objective. Or rather, such engagements, though established by us through the use of some sign or other, have objective features, such as obligatoriness, which are immediately perceived by all—which is the same as saying that the signs that establish engagements constitute a language universally natural and objective to mankind. This is the point in the opening pages of the present manuscript, and it gives us the clue to some of Reid's background here—namely, Wollaston, Hutcheson, and Hume.

In his *Illustrations upon the Moral Sense*, Hutcheson has a lengthy discussion of Wollaston that begins thus: "Mr. Woolaston ⟨in his *Religion of Nature Delineated*⟩ has introduced a new Explication of moral Virtue, viz. Significancy of Truth in Actions, supposing that in every Action there is some Significancy, like to that which Moralists and Civilians speak of in their Tacit Conventions, and Quasi Contractus!" (p. 253). After a number of criticisms, many of which anticipate Hume (*Treatise*, III.i.1 and note therein on pp. 461–462), Hutcheson ends the section thus: "It may perhaps not seem improper on this occasion to observe, that in the Quasi Contractus, the Civilians do not imagine any Act of the Mind of the Person obliged to be really signified, but by a sort of *fictio juris* supposing it, order him to act as if he had contracted, even when they know that he had contrary Intension. In the Tacit Conventions, 'tis not a Judgment which is signified, but an Act of the Will transferring Right, in which there is no Relation to Truth or Falsehood of itself. The Non-performance of Covenants is made penal, not because of their signifying Falshoods, as if this were the Crime in them: But it is necessary, in order to preserve Commerce in any Society, to make effectual all Declarations of Consent to transfer Rights by any usual Signs, otherwise there could be no Certainty in Mens Transactions" (*Illustrations*, pp. 273–274). Leaving aside for the moment (see n.9 below) the distinction between implied contract and tacit contract, Hutcheson's discussion of Wollaston along with the well-known one by Hume (*Treatise* III.i.1 and note therein on pp. 461–462) should make it clear that what *Reid* wanted to avoid was the idea that the virtue of fidelity is (like) the truth-value of propositions (actions), but without making it dependent upon something that he saw as external to the action, such as utility. This was achieved by the idea that the action (of promising, etc.) immediately establishes a moral fact of universal validity that can be understood by our moral powers. In this sense the roles of human life or man's offices, as he calls them in this deeply Ciceronian discussion, are objective moral facts established *quasi ex contractu* through the nonreferential and nonrelativistic system of signs called the social acts of the mind.

5. See the explanation in the Commentary above at pp. 393–394 n. 8.

6. For Rehoboam, see 1 Kings 12:12–19. This was a commonly

cited case in Reid's favorite political writers (see Machiavelli, *Discourses*, I.19.2; Harrington, *Oceana*, p. 236; *Pian Piano*, pp. 379–380; *Prerogative of Popular Government*, pp. 450 and 476). Richard II was a similarly common *bête noire* in the historiography utilized in the ideology of the mid-eighteenth-century Country opposition. See, e.g., Bolingbroke, *Remarks on the History of England*, p. 329: "Richard the second . . . had a brutality and a good opinion of himself. . . . Hence came those famous and foolish sayings of this prince . . . which gave his people timely warning what they had to expect from him. Of his commons he said, 'that slaves they were, and slaves they should be.' "

7. King James I and VI, "A Speech to the Lords and Commons of the Parliament at White-Hall," *Workes*, pp. 530–531: "in the first originall of Kings, whereof some had their beginning by Conquest, and some by election of the people, their wills at that time served for Law; Yet how soone Kingdomes began to be setled in ciuiliti and policie, then did Kings set downe their minds by Lawes, which are properly made by the King onely; but at the rogation of the people, the Kings grant being obteined thereunto. And so the King became to be *Lex loquens*, after a sort, binding himselfe by a double oath to the obseruasion of the fundamentall Lawes of his kingdome: Tacitly, as by being a King, and so bound to protect aswell the people, as the Lawes of his Kingdome; And Expresly, by his oath at his Coronation: So as euery iust King in a setled Kingdome is bound to obserue that paction made to his people by his Lawes, in framing his gouernment agreeable thereunto, according to that paction which God made with Noe after the deluge."

8. We do not know whence Reid got his information about the proceedings of Parliament, but in this case he could have taken it from numerous sources since the implications of the wording of this resolution had been a central point in the political debate for decades after it was passed. A typical and likely source is an anonymous pamphlet, *The Revolution Vindicated* (probably by Bishop Burnet), printed in *State Tracts*, vol. 3: "On the 28th of January the Commons pass'd the following Vote: 'That King James II. having endeavour'd to subvert the Constitution of this Kingdom, by breaking the Original Contract between King and People; and by the Advice of Jesuits and other wicked Persons having violated the Fundamental Laws, and having withdrawn himself out of this Kingdom, hath abdicated the Government, and that the Throne is thereby vacant.' This Vote occasion'd several Conferences between the two Houses, which ended at last

in the Lords assenting on the 6th of February to the Vote as it is here" (p. 715).

9. Hume's concession is in "Of the Original Contract," *Essays*, 2:445. It should be remarked, however, that in the last, posthumous revision of his *Essays* Hume added a paragraph (ibid., 2:445–446) heavily qualifying the concession and that he had previously in the essay on the "Origin of Government" (1774) already avoided a contractarian account of the institution of government. This is relevant to any speculation about the likely date of Reid's composition of the present manuscript. Reid's use of the idea of an implied contract as basis for civil society is a late high point in the peculiar Scots debate about the original contract that Carmichael had started when he tried to use Locke's idea of consent to rebut Titius's and Barbeyrac's criticism of the historicity of this contract (see the Commentary below at pp. 409ff. n. 4). It was Carmichael's assertion (and Hutcheson's after him) that allegiance to government was derived from a historically real original contract, which gave Hume's well-known criticism a polemical point it would hardly have had if it had been aimed simply at Locke. The central point in Hume's argument was that the contractual origins of civil society, if it had such origins, were irrelevant to the question of what justifies subsequent allegiance. This did not, however, affect the argument that Hutcheson put briefly and in passing—that the continuation of allegiance beyond the original contract is to be understood as a quasi-contractual relationship (*Short Introduction*, pp. 286–287, and *System*, ii.228–231). It is precisely this argument that Reid is spelling out in the present manuscript, but at the same time he makes it perfectly clear, as appears below, that the question of historical origins is entirely irrelevant to the justification of government. The paternity of a given set of civil relations does not justify them; only the discharging of the offices they establish does—in any period of human history (see above).

While Hume did not explicitly attack Hutcheson's idea of quasi-contract as the foundation for continued allegiance, he did criticize something that was apparently very similar—namely, the more common idea of tacit consent: "Should it be said, that, by living under the dominion of a prince, which one might leave, every individual has given a tacit consent to his authority, and promised him obedience; it may be answered, that such an implied consent can only have place, where a man imagines, that the matter depends on his choice. But where he thinks (as all mankind do who are born under established governments) that by his birth he owes allegiance to a certain prince or certain form of government; it would be absurd to infer a consent or choice, which he expressly, in this case, renounces and disclaims. Can we seriously say, that a poor peasant or artizan has a free choice to leave his country, when he knows no foreign language or manners, and lives from day to day, by the small wages which he acquires? We may as well assert, that a man, by remaining in a vessel, freely consents to the dominion of the master; though he was carried on board while asleep, and must leap into the ocean, and perish, the moment he leaves her" ("Of the Original Contract," p. 451).

While this criticism may have force against tacit consent, it does not hit the notion of implied contract so well, and there can be hardly any doubt that one of Reid's primary targets in spelling out this notion was to show the inadequacy of Hume's criticism. First, Reid emphasizes that the relationship is symmetrical: there are duties and rights on both sides. Second, he neatly points out that at least one side in the political "contract"—the ruler—has a very high degree of freedom in the assumption of his office. Third, he maintains that *collectively* the governed have a high degree of freedom. Finally, he suggests below that allegiance is a matter of degree that depends on how much is contracted for in the "contract," so that while Hume's peasant has few rights he also has few duties.

If this interpretation of Reid is correct, it helps us to single out the wider context in which we must read him, for it seems to make it clear that implied contract as used here is essentially different from tacit consent. Hume's criticism of the latter presupposes that obligation arises when the will of the obligee is signaled, even if only tacitly. By contrast, in the tradition upon which Reid is drawing, the hallmark of an implied contract is that the will of the contracting parties is irrelevant to the establishment of an obligation. Based upon a fund of Roman law (see the Commentary above at pp. 356ff. nn. 123–127), this point was made by Titius, Observations 205 and 206, pp. 268–269, in his Pufendorf, *De officio*; by Barbeyrac, n. 1, p. 274, of Pufendorf, *Law of Nature* (and cf. n. 7, p. 454, and n. 1, p. 600); by Carmichael, supplement IV.2, pp. 278–279, in his Pufendorf, *De officio*; and by Hutcheson, *Short Introduction*, p. 287, and *System*, II.228 (cf. *Illustrations*, p. 273, quoted in n. 4 above). Barbeyrac puts it particularly well: "A tacit Consent properly arises from certain Things, which appear done, or omitted on Purpose; but yet, of themselves, do not imply directly an Approbation of the Thing that is doing. The Circumstances then may be reasonably supposed to explain the Will of him, who knowing them, also knows the Consequences which those concern'd may draw from them. But there is another Sort of Consent, which the Roman Lawyers, or their Interpreters, call'd sometimes tacit, or presumptive, tho' it be purely imaginary, as they own'd themselves. This is when a Person doth not think, nor, indeed, can think, of the Engagement he enters into, because he is ignorant on what it is founded; yet he is still supposed to acquiesce in it, because we presume, that if he knew the Thing, either he would, or should, consent to it, according to the Maxims of natural Equity; or, because the Laws, on Account of the publick Good, take it for granted, that every Man is bound to fulfil his Engagements" (Barbeyrac, n.1, p. 274, in Pufendorf, *Law of Nature*).

When this is transposed from the juridical to the political, we have Reid's idea of the relationship between rulers and ruled. This is not (or at least not commonly) a relationship established and justified by signaling a will to be bound in this particular way; it flows from our obligation to accept all the consequences, even unknown ones, that are implied by some of the various roles, or offices, that constitute our lives as moral beings. Consequently the relevant moral freedom is not that of consenting or not, *in isolation*, but rather that of choosing between alternative roles or offices with their more-or-less known but (as they arise) knowable duties (cf. n. 4 above).

10. See Hume, "Of the Original Contract," *Essays*, 2:444. As for Angria, see Defoe, *A General History of the Pyrates*, p. 124: "Angria is a famous Indian Pyrate, of considerable Strength and Territories, that gives continual Disturbance to the European (and especially the English) Trade: His chief Hold is Callaba, not many Leagues from Bombay, and has one Island in Sight of that Port, whereby he gains frequent Opportunities of annoying the Company. It would not be so insuperable a Difficulty to suppress him, if the Shallowness of the Water did not prevent Ships of War coming nigh: And a better Art he has, of bribing the Mogul's Ministers for Protection, when he finds an Enemy too powerful." This pirate dynasty thrived until Tulagee Angria was finally defeated in 1756.

11. Speaking of people's supposed consent to government, Hume says (*Essays*, 2:447): "It is strange, that an act of the mind, which every individual is supposed to have formed, and after he came to the use of reason too, otherwise it could have no authority;

that this act, I say, should be so much unknown to all of them, that, over the face of the whole earth, there scarcely remain any traces or memory of it."

12. Hume, *Essays*, 2:452.

13. Hume, *Essays*, 2:454–455.

14. Hume, *Essays*, 2:460.

15. Hume, *Essays*, 2:459.

16. Hume, *Essays*, 2:455–456.

17. It appears that some of the following points were issues for discussion rather than statements of Reid's opinion. The sense is: The ways in which obligation is contracted—from contract, from quasi-contract, from delict, or from quasi-delict. This is the fourfold division of obligations according to their origin found in Justinian, *Institutes*, III.xiii.2, and presupposed by the natural lawyers, who, however, hardly use the fourth. The first sentence appears to echo the "title" that immediately follows in the *Institutes*: "Quibus modis re contrahitur obligatio" ("The ways in which a real obligation is contracted"), real obligations being one of the four subdivisions of contractual obligations. Of the four *modi* mentioned by Reid, we have met with all except quasi-delict. This is dealt with in the *Institutes*, IV.v, and explained by Barbeyrac in n. 8 to Grotius, *War and Peace*, II.l.ii (1), where the four *modi* are also stated. Says Barbeyrac: "Roman Lawyers by ⟨quasi maleficio⟩ understood certain Trespasses, in Consequence of which the Person is obliged to Indemnification, tho' it was not committed with a bad Intention, or even was committed by another, without the least Concurrence of the Defendant."

18. If Reid had said "tacit consent" and if he had been stating his opinion and not, perhaps, points for discussion, this would contradict the interpretation offered in n.9 above.

XVI. POLITICAL JURISPRUDENCE

1. Presumably Reid found his brief treatment of political jurisprudence in 1765 unsatisfactory, which is understandable (see Section VII of this book), and decided to rewrite this part of the course for the following year. In the process his distinction between political jurisprudence and "the Science of Politicks" had firmed to a basic organizational principle that led him to his most significant deviation from the Pufendorfian-Hutchesonian systematics (but see also, on his rearrangement of the topic of price and value, the Commentary at p. 350 n. 106). In his lec-

tures in 1776, Reid explained how he had been led to this central distinction: "the only two who have distinguished them ⟨i.e., political jurisprudence and the science of politics⟩ have been Matchiavel & Harrington who seem to have understood it better than some ⟨any?⟩ other" (Jack, "Reid's Lectures," p. 611). It is therefore not surprising to see Reid associate himself with aspects of that distinctive mode of political thought which had developed in Britain since 1688 and which is now often referred to as classical republicanism.

2. See the lectures on politics, esp. 4/III/3.

3. See Grotius, *War and Peace*, 1.3.viii; Hobbes, *De cive*, ch. v, and *Leviathan*, ch. xvii; Pufendorf, *Law of Nature*, vii.1, and *Duty of Man*, ii.5; Locke, *Second Treatise*, ch. 8; Hutcheson, *Short Introduction*, pp. 279–284, and *System*, ii.212–225; Heineccius, *Universal Law*, ii.85–91, and Turnbull's Remarks, ibid., pp. 109–119, which include a Harringtonian analysis of the topic (pp. 112ff).

4. The distinction between the *quid facti* and the *quid iuris* of government was not exactly a novelty, and in Reid's immediate sources it was stated explicitly by, for example, Heineccius, *Universal Law*, ii.91, Turnbull's Remarks, ibid., pp. 110–111, and Hutcheson, *System*, ii.224–225: "we are inquiring into the just and wise motives to enter into civil polity, and the ways it can be justly constituted; and not into points of history about facts." The context for Reid's discussion of this issue is complicated, and only a few pointers can be offered here. While justification by history was still prevalent in the political debate in Britain, it would have been abundantly clear to a man of Reid's intellect and political inclination that this was at least a two-edged sword or, by the time of his lectures, a game at which two or more could play. Despite innumerable rescue attempts, the general idea of the immemorial and justifying antiquity of the British constitution, and especially of the Parliament, as a charter of liberty could well be seen by someone like Reid to have been significantly weakened or at least shaken by a succession of historical inquiries from, say, Robert Brady's *Introduction to the Old English History* (1684) and *Complete History of England*, vol. 1 (1685), to Hume's recent *History of England*. Similarly and of more direct importance, it was exactly the difficulty of finding a historical justification for the settlement of the crown on William III and for the Hanoverian succession that had made the post-1688 debate so extraordinarily vigorous, and Reid would have had fresh in his mind Hume's well-known argument that, while

the Revolution settlement was hardly justifiable in 1688–89, it had become so retrospectively, so to speak.

Hence it may well have concerned sympathetic Scottish spectators that the English Whigs often failed to distinguish between the idea of an ancient, free constitution and that of an original contract, using them more or less interchangeably. In consequence, the logic of the contractual argument seemed to be not fully appreciated—witness the fact that the English defense of the Revolution never found much use for Locke's abstract idea of the original contract. In Scotland, on the other hand, a much keener and continuing interest in natural law carried with it a preoccupation with the contractual ideas of Locke and others. This complicates Reid's situation for us in a most interesting way. Two of Pufendorf's editors—Titius and, following him, Barbeyrac—had questioned the historical realism of the original contracts as set out by Pufendorf (first a contract between the heads of families to establish a civil society, then a decree concerning the form of government to be instituted, followed by a contract between this government and the governed; *Law of Nature*, vii.2.vii–viii, and *Duty of Man*, ii.6.vii–ix). Against this they maintained that civil society was a slow growth from small beginnings and that it was entered into from a variety of motives (Titius, Observations 547 and 550, esp. pp. 530–532 and 534, in his edition of Pufendorf, *De officio*; Barbeyrac, n.2 to Pufendorf, *Law of Nature*, vii.1.vii, pp. 625–627). This criticism is rejected by Carmichael, who argues that Pufendorf's theory does not require that men actually entered civil society by means of a contract but only that once men are in civil society the basis for their membership is contractual, whatever the vicissitudes of history that brought them there. Further, the presupposition of a contract in this sense is necessary, albeit not inevitably in the precise form specified by Pufendorf. For one thing, the "historical" examples of adoption into a social combination by violence—alleged by Titius and Barbeyrac—presuppose an already existing combination of individuals (in view of the basic equality of power between individuals, a well-known Hobbesian problem). Much more important, however, is the moral necessity—namely, that God via the law of nature has commanded that contracts be entered into in order to realize the ends of natural law. This implies that any overlordship not based on contract is not over men as moral beings, beings under natural law. In short, if civil society is based upon contract, it is perpetual and unbreakable because it exists by divine authority. The alternative seems to be that civil society is dependent upon the continuity of government, especially an unbroken succession of monarchs, and that consequently if this continuity is broken, as it was in Britain in 1649 and 1688, it is not readily understandable on what basis a society could cohere and provide for its future government. This, says Carmichael, clearly referring to 1688, was the true function of Pufendorf's first and basic contract, and here Carmichael is reformulating one of the most radical of Locke's theses, that "when the Government is dissolved, the People are at liberty to provide for themselves, by erecting a new Legislative. . . . For the Society can never, by the fault of another, lose the Native and Original Right it has to preserve it self" (*Second Treatise*, sec. 220).

For Carmichael, Hutcheson, and Reid this line of argument is undoubtedly also a translation into contractual terms of the well-known (for them primarily Harringtonian) idea that while God has ordained government he has not specified any particular form of government (see, e.g., Harrington, *The Art of Lawgiving*, book II, esp. Conclusion, and Sidney, *Discourses concerning Government*, I.6); in other words it is an application of the distinction between God's general and particular providence, which the Scots also knew well in its original English form as the standard Anglican theory of church-government formulated by Richard Hooker and in its more recent use by such Whig Anglicans as Stillingfleet, Burnet, and Hoadly and neatly summed up by Thomas Long: "The Ordinance of Government is from God and Nature, but the species of it, whether by one or more, is from Men; and the Rule for Administration, is by mutual Agreement of the Governor, and those that are govern'd" (*A Resolution of Certain Queries concerning Submission to the Present Government*, p. 443; cf. Hoadly, *Original and Institution of Civil Government*, pp. 144–145). At the same time, the contractual translation of this ensured that the people as a body of moral agents under natural law was the continuing repository of authority from which any form of government had to be drawn.

Carmichael's argument was effective. In the fourth French edition of Pufendorf's *Law of Nature*, which was the basis for the English edition used here, Barbeyrac offered to "freely retract" the implications of his criticism of Pufendorf in view of Carmichael's points, and it is clear that he did so because he was beginning to see the possibility of retaining a contractual basis for society while yet engaging in a historically realistic investigation of its origins (Barbeyrac, n. 2, p. 637, and n. 2, p. 627, in Pufendorf, *Law of Nature*, VII.2.viii and VII.1.vii, see also Carmichael's notes to Pufendorf, *De officio*, II.5.vii and II.6.ix and xiv). The tendency of this argument was to make the question of origins irrelevant to justification, and this was precisely Reid's starting-point, but to make this effective he had to interpret the contractual basis for civil society in the quasi-contractual terms that we find in his important paper 2/II/10, printed in this book in Section XV. He was also driven in this direction by the need to counter a more recent theory critical of contract theories: Hume's attempt to found government on its sociopsychological "origins." This leads to the final feature of Reid's position to be mentioned here, a point that of necessity is interpretative of Reid. As a moral realist, for whom moral relations were objective features of the world exhibited in action, Reid could never have had any real use for historical justifications; whatever its origins, government was justified if it did the objectively right thing. This dictated the form his "contract" theory had to take, as we see in MS. 2/II/10.

5. See Hutcheson, *System*, II.218.

6. Reid is undoubtedly thinking of Rousseau's repeated use of Defoe's novel in *Émile*, esp. book III (see, e.g., pp. 455–460), but see also *Contrat Social*, I.2 (p. 354); the contrast is primarily with *L'Origine de l'inégalité*. Reid refers to the events that inspired Defoe in 4/I/30 (not in this volume).

7. The following four points are specifications of the previous "1 We are fitted. . . ."

8. κτισις: ordinance; ανθρωπινη: human. Reid's Greek hand is somewhat shaky, and the transcription rendered here would be conjectural if made in isolation. The context does, however, suggest a biblical reference, and this is confirmed by Robert Jack's notes from Reid's corresponding lecture in 1776: "we shall deduce some corrolaries first we may see whether ⟨government⟩ is a divine or human ordinance in the sacred scriptures it is called a κτισις ανθροπου & also κτισις θειου surely the particular government the particular form of government is a human Institution, but the Institution itself seems to be of divine origin" (Jack, "Reid's Lectures," p. 627). The Greek may be bad, but the passage makes it plain that Reid's point is in fact borrowed. Take Carmichael (n. 1, pp. 383–384, in Pufendorf, *De officio*): "Imperium Civile Auctori Deo recte tribuitur, etiam dum ab Hominibus immediate constituitur; estque simul, ut uni atque alteri Apostolo nuncupatur, τη του θεου διαταγη (Epist. ad Rom. XIII.2) & Ανθρωπινη κτισις (I. Pet. II.13)" ("Civil government is

rightly attributed to God as the author, even if it is immediately constituted by men; and it is, as ⟨is shown by what⟩ it is called by two apostles, at one and the same time 'the ordinance of God' (Romans, 13:2) & a 'human ordinance' (1 Pet. 2:13)"). The same point is made with the same biblical references in Grotius, *War and Peace*, I.4.vii (cf. Locke, *First Treatise*, sec. 6), and in this form it was constantly repeated in much of the English literature referred to in n. 14 below. Romans 13 was by far the most popular biblical justification for absolute submission, and consequently Whigs, republicans, and so forth had to counter it by citing other biblical texts and by reinterpreting Romans 13. Reid does the former in the two quotations below at nn. 12 and 13, and we get the tone of the latter from an interesting and typical anonymous Scots tract with which Carmichael, Hutcheson, and Reid were probably familiar because it was included in the well-known *Collection of State Tracts*: "But because the 13th of the *Romans* enjoining Obedience and Submission to the higher Powers, and forbidding Resistance, is so violently urg'd, I shall briefly consider it. And, 1. some, upon very good Grounds, think that the Apostle here by Power understands it in the Abstract, that Magistracy or Government is of Divine Appointment; but in the Concrete, as it relates to the Person or Persons vested with this Power, it is of Humane Extract, and therefore call'd by the Apostle Peter the Ordinance of Man, which implies the Consent of the People to be necessary in bestowing of it upon one or more; as the Consent of the Persons who enter into a married State is that which determines the Bargain, tho it is certain that Marriage is as well an Ordinance of God as Magistracy, and it is evident the Greek text warrants this Sense and Explanation" (*A Vindication of the Proceedings of the Convention of the Estates in Scotland*, p. 453).

9. Pope, *An Essay on Man*, epistle III, ll. 304–305.

10. This is the theme of 2/II/10 (Section XV of this book); see also n. 4 above. Concerning onerous contracts in general, see the Commentary at pp. 350ff. nn. 109ff.

11. These examples derive from Vattel; see Reid's notes on Vattel in the manuscript, pp. 270–271, and see the Commentary at p. 439 n. 103.

12. Dan. 3:18.

13. Acts 4:18–19.

14. The context of Reid's discussion in these pages of authority, submission, and resistance in political society is rich and complex, as indicated by the list of names given here, to which

should be added that of Milton, which was included in the corresponding list for the previous year (see Reid's manuscript above at p. 178). Judging from Robert Jack's notes of 1776, the "Opinion of the Ancient Nations" here simply provided some conventional wisdom out of Livy, especially: "the ancients have made this distinction between these two. Civil Liberty is according to them a government of laws, Tyranny a government of men" (Jack, "Reid's Lectures," p. 645). Disregarding the symbolic constant presence of Socrates (as immediately below), Reid begins the story with Grotius, Hobbes, and Pufendorf, as indicated in this text. The logic of a contractual basis for political authority implies that there are mutual rights and obligations between governors and governed and consequently that either party may be wronged or injured by the other. Grotius and Pufendorf sought to avoid the potentially radical applications of this in a variety of ways. First, it is emphasized, especially by Grotius, that the contract establishing political authority simply makes it unrightful to resist this authority; the content of the contract is exactly to this purpose. This is, however, a theoretically ambiguous standpoint, for while it takes away the right of the governed to exercise the rights established by the original contract, it does not take away these rights themselves, and especially not the right to be governed by a proper political authority. If the ruler therefore no longer plays his role but becomes an enemy, a tyrant, or the like, then there is an ultimate right to resist. This may, however, be whittled down by reference to the demands of Christian ethics (as we shall see below) and, as in Pufendorf, by the argument that because public affairs are so complex the governed commonly do not have sufficient knowledge to see whether they are being wronged under the terms of the contract, and that in any case the point of the contract is to establish a governor to exercise knowledge on their behalf. See Grotius, *War and Peace*, I.4; Pufendorf, *Law of Nature*, VII.8, and *Duty of Man*, II.9.iv.

Hobbes tried to avoid these problems by denying that the concept of injury had any application for a governor's actions toward his subjects, because while the foundation of government was contractual it did not involve the ruler as a party to the contract. Consequently, although there might be de facto resistance there could be no right of resistance (*De cive*, VII.7, 9, 12, and 14; *Leviathan*, ch. 18, pp. 228–232). The term "high flyer" has been put to many uses. Reid was hardly referring to loose women, but was he, as had been common, referring to "high church" men and Tories or, in view of the names immediately following, was he referring to the Puritans in the English revolution, thus helping turn the phrase into a (Scottish) label for evangelicals? In the latter case, the passage may have served the same function as Reid's reference to Milton in the previous year. For Reid, Milton had undoubtedly flown too high by defending the Puritans' execution of Charles I, an action hitherto unheard of in any age, as Carmichael said, and perpetrated by a *"furiosa Factio . . .* which had earlier used armed violence to subdue the state itself" (Carmichael, n. 1, p. 408, in Pufendorf, *De officio,* II.9.iv. The natural lawyers generally upheld a distinction between resisting the civil magistrate and killing his person.) That apart, Milton could undoubtedly be adapted to support Reid's political line as sketched in the following. We do not know to which of Milton's relevant works Reid was referring, but it is a safe guess that he would be well acquainted at least with *The Tenure of Kings and Magistrates, Eikonoklastes,* and *A Defence of the People of England.* Each of the two opposing groups that follow in the text constitutes a motley assembly that had been pressed into service together by the ideological debate in Britain since the Revolution. Richard Hooker was for Scottish thinkers closely associated with Locke because of the latter's frequent use of Hooker in the *Second Treatise,* a book that probably had more impact in Scotland than in England. Hooker did, however, have a much wider appeal because of his formulation of the central idea of the Anglican view of church government, which was subsequently transformed into a general idea of civil government (see n.4 above). For the present context, see especially Hooker, *Of the Laws of Ecclesiastical Polity,* book 1, pp. 185-198, and book VIII, pp. 390-405. Algernon Sidney, the republican martyr, inspired as he was by Machiavelli and espousing the view that the proper basis for civil government was in effect an aristocracy of virtue, must have been particularly congenial to Reid. The whole of book III of the *Discourses concerning Government,* following upon a close rebuttal of Filmer, must for Reid have been a classical text on the issues raised here (esp. secs. 1, 10, 12, 20, 36). While Locke's role in the English postrevolution debate seems to have been a limited one, he was always significant for Scottish thinkers because of their close adherence to the natural law framework and especially their concern with the exact requirements of a contractual basis for civil society (as indicated in

n. 4 above). In the present context, see especially *First Treatise*, secs. 104–105, 109–111, and 120ff., and *Second Treatise*, ch. XVIII.

Bishop Benjamin Hoadly was one of the most effective and influential Whig Anglican polemicists during the first two decades of the eighteenth century, and most of Reid's subsequent formulations have a Hoadlian tone. Amid a host of pamphlets and published sermons, Hoadly's main work was *The Original and Institution of Civil Government*, of which the first chapter is a fierce attack on Filmer and patriarchalism, while the second presents his theoretical basis as a Hooker-inspired contractualism. Hoadly's criticism of Filmer was savaged by the nonjuror Charles Leslie in *The Finishing Stroke*, which was one of the high points in a barrage of anti-Locke and anti-Whig Filmerian polemics, first published in Leslie's weekly the *Rehearsal* and subsequently as tracts. A different attack on Whig principles came from Bishop Francis Atterbury, a High Tory divine who published a large number of sermons and tracts setting out a theory of the providential appointment of every government and criticizing all forms of contract-based and rights-based resistance theory. In a famous sermon in 1709 he used Rom. 13:1 in a way that was typical of all those of his persuasion to press the idea of passive obedience; this was answered by Hoadly in a tract added to his *Original and Institution of Civil Government* (see Atterbury, "Omnis Anima Potestatibus sublimioribus subdita sit," *Sermons and Discourses*, 2:309–375). Reid probably also knew Atterbury's *Voice of the People No Voice of God*, an answer to the anonymous and popular *Vox Populi Vox Dei*.

"Barclay" is in fact written above "Hoadly," undoubtedly because there was no other space, "Leslie Atterbury" being written above "Hobbes Filmer," where Barclay's name properly belongs. William Barclay, a Scots jurist writing in France, was well-known for his defence of absolutism in his *De regno et regali potestate, adversus Buchananum, Brutum, Boucherium, et reliquos Monarchomachos* (1600) and for his attack on papal pretenses to authority over temporal government in the posthumous *De potestate Papae: an, et quatenus, in reges et principes seculares jus et imperium habeat* (1609); see n. 19 below.

15. These extracts are in Reid's MS. 4/III/23c,2r, printed below, pp. 270–271.

16. See one of Hoadly's early attempts to defuse Rom. 13:1 as a support for the doctrine of passive obedience: "tho' ⟨the ruler's⟩ Authority in carrying forward the End of his Power cannot be re-

sisted without the highest Guilt; yet his Authority in acting contrary to that End may be oppos'd without the shadow of a Crime; nay, with Honour and Glory" ("A Sermon Preached before the . . . Lord-Mayor," p. 15).

17. In criticizing patriarchalism, the usual argument was that civil government could not be assimilated with parental authority, but even if it could it would not serve the protagonists of absolute submission, because parental authority was not unlimited and irresistible. See, e.g., Hoadly, *Original and Institution of Civil Government*, pp. 15–35.

18. "A more difficult Question is, whether the Law of Non-resistance obliges us in the most extreme and inevitable Danger. For some of the Laws of God, however general they be, seem to admit of tacit Exceptions in Cases of extreme Necessity; for so it was determined by the Jewish Doctors concerning the Law of their Sabbath in the Time of the Maccabees; whence arose the famous Saying, 'The Danger of Life drives away the Sabbath.' . . .

I dare not condemn indifferently all private Persons, or a small Part of the People, who finding themselves reduced to the last Extremity, have made use of the only Remedy left them, in such a Manner as they have not neglected in the mean Time to take care, as far as they were able, of the publick Good. For David, who . . . was so famed for living exactly according to Law, did yet entertain about him, first four hundred, and afterwards more, armed Men; and to what End did he so, unless for the Defence of his own Person, in Case he should be attacked? But we must also observe, that David did not do this till he was assured by Jonathan, and many other infallible Proofs, that Saul really sought his Life" (Grotius, *War and Peace*, 1.4.vii, drawing on 1 Macc. 2:34–41 and 1 Sam. 22:2–23:18).

19. Having argued (*War and Peace*, 1.4.vii) that according to Christian ethics "those who are invested with the sovereign Power, cannot lawfully be resisted," Grotius goes on to state seven rules of exemption (ibid., viii–xiv): "First . . . Those Princes who depend on the People . . . if they offend against the Laws, and the State, may not only be resisted by Force; but if it be necessary, may be punished by Death . . . Secondly, If a King . . . has abdicated his Government, or manifestly abandoned it; after that Time, we may do the same to him, as to any private Man. . . . Thirdly, If a King alienates his Kingdom; or renders it dependent on any other Power, he forfeits the Crown, according to Barclay. ⟨Grotius qualifies this⟩ . . . Fourthly, The same Barclay

observes, that if a King shall, like an Enemy, design the utter Destruction of the whole Body of his People, he loses his Kingdom; which I grant. . . . Fifthly, If a Kingdom be forfeited, either for Felony against him of whom it is a Fief, or ⟨in breach of the conditions for conferring the sovereignty⟩, then also a King becomes a private Person. Sixthly, If a King should have but one Part of the sovereign Power, and the Senate or People the other, if such a King shall invade that Part which is not his own, he may justly be resisted, because he is not Sovereign in that Respect. . . . Seventhly, If in the conferring of the Crown, it be expressly stipulated, that in some certain Cases the King may be resisted; even though that Clause does not imply any Division of the Sovereignty, yet certainly some Part of natural Liberty is reserved to the People, and exempted from the Power of the King."

A little earlier (sec. viii) we find: "Barclay, the stoutest ⟨fortissimus⟩ Assertor of Regal Power, does thus far allow that the People, or a considerable part of them, have a Right to defend themselves against their King, when he becomes excessively cruel; tho' otherwise, that Author considers the King as above the whole Body of the People." The relevant passage in Barclay is quoted at length in Locke, *Second Treatise*, sec. 232, who frequently refers to Barclay, and as his editor says, between Grotius and Locke it has become conventional to see Barclay as the typical absolutist who makes concessions to the idea of resistance (Locke, *Two Treatises*, p. 443n.) The relevant references in Barclay are *De regno et regali potestate*, III.8 and 16.

20. Pufendorf, *Law of Nature*, VII.8.vii.

21. While the general idea is to be found repeatedly in Burnet's extensive oeuvre, especially the *History of the Reformation in England*, I have not found a formulation resembling the present one.

22. This is further developed in 1794 in the first five pages of Reid's paper on the Utopian system (printed in this book in Section XVIII), where Reid considers the situation of Britain in the aftermath of the French Revolution.

XVII. RIGHTS AND DUTIES OF STATES

1. Reid generally followed the Pufendorfian taxonomy and reserved the label "political jurisprudence" for the political relations of the individual, but here he makes it cover both individ-

ual and collective political relations. This is undoubtedly due to the influence of Vattel's pursuance of the analogy between the individual and the state. It is important to notice that the second part of what is here called political jurisprudence is made identical with the law of nations. The latter is thus a much wider concept than we might expect because it covers relations not only between states but also between the state and the individual. This too is in accordance with Vattel.

2. Reid is referring to 3/II/5,2r (printed in this volume, pp. 272ff.), the second, third, and fourth paragraphs of which are marked "A."

3. This paragraph is built upon Vattel, *Law of Nations*, preliminaries, secs. 1–5. Reid made an abstract of this; see his MS. 3/II/5,1v printed in this volume, pp. 269–270.

4. In the preceding paragraph, Reid combines points from the preface and sec. 6 of the preliminaries to Vattel's *Law of Nations*.

5. See the Commentary above at p. 370 n. 3, and Reid's manuscript at p. 273 ll. 22–26.

6. See the Introductory Lecture, printed in this book, pp. 112–113. In *Law of Nations*, I.2.xiii, Vattel divided a nation's duties into those to itself, which are detailed in book I, and those to others, which are dealt with in book II, while book III is more particularly devoted to war. Reid took the analogy with individuals a step further and began with a nation's duty to God, which Vattel included in book I, namely ch. 12's bland discussion "Of Piety and Religion" in political society.

7. See, e.g., Reid's manuscript printed in this book, pp. 123ff.

8. Although there is no direct evidence that William Penn had read Harrington, Reid was as certain as everyone else who has looked into the matter that the "Frame of Government" Penn tried to introduce in Pennsylvania in the 1680s was "perfectly Republican & Harringtonian" (4/III/19,1v). This in itself would have been enough to interest someone of Reid's political inclinations in Penn's work, and he was of course supported in this by Montesquieu's dictum that "Mr. Penn is a real Lycurgus" (*Spirit of Laws*, 1:35; there is an oblique reference to this in Robert Jack's notes of Reid's lectures in 1776, p. 650). The manuscript referred to above contains Reid's notes from "the Charter of Cha. 2d. to William Penn Proprietary & Governour of Pensilvania 4th March 1681" and from "The Frame of the Government of the Province of Pensilvania in America Together with certain Laws agreed upon in England by the Governour and divers freemen of the afforesaid Province; To be further ex-

plained and continued there by the first Provincial Council that shall be held if they see meet. 25 Aprile 1682." This manuscript does not mention the provisions for toleration. The famous fourth of Voltaire's *Letters on England* did much to keep this issue in people's minds, and this was reinforced not least for Scotsmen by the Jacobite rebellion in 1745. Penn had from 1686 supported the plans of James VII and II for a repeal of the Test Acts and the penal laws for Catholics and Dissenters, and it was therefore natural that the Jacobite insurrection should lead to an interest in Penn and a reprinting of some of his pamphlets (*Repentance, recommended to the inhabitants of Great Britain in general (Extracted from a book intituled An Address to Protestants . . .), and The free-born English man's unmasked battery . . . with some quotations from . . . William Penn . . .*).

9. In 1776 Reid declared that only experience could tell whether a state could do without an established religion. There was, however, only one example of this—Pennsylvania—and this was too little and too recent to provide much guidance. Instead Reid resorts to a telling analogy: just as those who treat the ills of the body must be trained professionals, so must those who attend to the maladies of the mind, otherwise "Individuals the most Impudent & the most Ignorant . . . might easily fill the people with Inthusiastic notions" (Jack, "Reid's Lectures," p. 651). According to these notes (ibid., p. 657), Reid also referred to Locke's *Letter concerning Toleration* as most sensible and politically effective despite attacks by "many very learned Divines in England."

10. Acts 17:22–23: "Then Paul stood in the midst of Mars' hill, and said, Ye men of Athens, I perceive that in all things ye are too superstitious. For as I passed by, and beheld your devotions, I found an altar with this inscription, TO THE UNKNOWN GOD. Whom therefore ye ignorantly worship, him declare I unto you." See also Cudworth, *True Intellectual System*, 2:192ff.

11. Reid is presumably thinking partly of Machiavelli's representation of religious rites as a tool of social and military control (*Discourses*, I.11–15), partly of Hobbes's distinction between public and private worship and his theory of the conventional, politically regulated character of the former (*De cive*, XV.12, 16–19, and cf. XVII.10–28; *Leviathan*, pp. 401, 405–406, 331–334; see also the Commentary above, at n. 4, p. 306), and partly of Rousseau's famous notion of a civil religion (*Contrat social*, IV.8, and the first of the *Lettres écrites de la montagne*, esp. pp. 703ff.), though the latter suggested a good deal more than mere rites. The idea of a more or less confessionless public religion was

often floated in the eighteenth century; two likely sources for Reid would be Hume, *History of England*, 4:25ff. and 273ff., 6:78ff., and Mandeville, *Letter to Dion*, p. 40: "Mix'd Multitudes of Good and Bad Men, high and low Quality, may join in outward Signs of Devotion, and perform together what is call'd Public Worship, but Religion it self can have no Place but in the Heart of Individuals."

Reid's discussion of public worship and an established church must also be seen in the light of William Warburton's influential contractualist defense of the Church of England, with which it has some similarities, *The Alliance between State and Church*, books I and II. See also Rousseau's criticism of Warburton, *Contrat social*, pp. 318, 384, and 464, and Warburton's reply in the fourth edition of *The Alliance*, pp. 175ff. of the edition used here. This issue must again be seen in the context of the general debate about the minimum of religion necessary for a cohesive society, a debate that repeatedly raised the question whether atheism was any worse or perhaps even better than idolatry and false religion. The issues were clearly set out by Bacon: "It were better to have no Opinion of God at all, than such an Opinion as is unworthy of him: For the one is Unbeleefe, the other is Contumely: And certainly Superstition is the Reproach of the Deity. . . . Atheisme leaves a Man to Sense, to Philosophy; to Naturall Piety; to Lawes; to Reputation; All which may be Guides to an outward Morall vertue, though Religion were not; But Superstition dismounts all these, and erecteth an absolute Monarchy in the Mindes of Men. Therefore Atheisme did never perturbe States; For it makes Men wary of themselves, as looking no further: And we see the times inclined to Atheisme (as the Time of Augustus Caesar) were civill times" ("Of Superstition," *Essayes*, pp. 96–97). These views and those ascribed to Hobbes were repeatedly rejected by natural lawyers and others who agreed with Locke's argument in the well-known passage from his *Letter concerning Toleration*, p. 93: "those are not at all to be tolerated who deny the being of a God. Promises, covenants, and oaths, which are the bonds of human society, can have no hold upon an atheist. The taking away of God, though but even in thought, dissolves all." The debate was particularly invigorated by Bayle's argument in the *Dictionary*, 5:811–814, and in the *Miscellaneous Reflections*, 1:234ff., that atheism was no worse a support for morality and society than religion, as commonly practiced, and that a society of atheists was eminently possible. This argument was carried on by Shaftesbury (e.g., *Characteristics*, II.196–215) and with typical forthrightness by Mandeville in the Third Dialogue of *An Enquiry into the Origins of Honour* (esp. pp. 154ff.). When Montesquieu attacked Bayle's version of it in *Spirit of Laws*, 2:24, the agenda for Hume's magisterial treatment of the whole issue was set, here especially his argument in the *Natural History of Religion* that polytheism is not inferior and is in some respects superior to monotheism as a social cohesive, and that polytheism may practically be identified with atheism.

12. Reid is referring to the treaty between China and Russia in 1689. See Voltaire, *Histoire de Russie*, pp. 121–122: "on jura une paix éternelle; et, après quelques contestations, les Russes et les Chinois la jurèrent au nom du même Dieu en ces termes: 'Si quelqu'un a jamais la pensée secrète de rallumer le feu de la guerre, nous prions le Seigneur souverain de toutes choses, qui connaît les coeurs, de punir ces traîtres par une mort précipitée.' Cette formule, commune à des Chinois et à des chrétiens, peut faire connaître deux choses importantes; la première, que le gouvernement chinois n'est ni athée ni idolâtre, comme on l'en a si souvent accusé par des imputations contradictoires; la seconde, que tous les peuples qui cultivent leur raison reconnaissent en effet le même Dieu, malgré tours les égaremens de cette raison mal instruite." See also Grotius, *War and Peace*, ii.15.ix–xii, and Heineccius, *Universal Law*, ii.206; and esp. the Commentary above at p. 346 n. 98.

13. This passage is close to Vattel, *Law of Nations*, xii.131 and 136.

14. A similar example is used by Locke, *Letter concerning Toleration*, p. 65; cf. Grotius, *War and Peace*, ii.20.xlvii (5). Apart from Locke and Vattel, the present discussion should be compared with Grotius, *War and Peace*, ii.20.xliv–li, and most important, with Hutcheson's discussion of the principles of toleration in *Short Introduction*, pp. 318–320, and *System*, ii.310–316, and with Warburton, *The Alliance*, book iii. As will be evident, Reid goes much more directly to the heart of the dilemma: how can the necessity of a public religion be combined with toleration?

15. Reid emphasizes even more strongly than, for instance, Hutcheson that aberrant religious practices, as opposed to opinions, may prove infectious and thus damaging to society if not restrained; cf. Hutcheson, *Short Introduction*, pp. 318–319, and *System* ii.315–316. The specific reference here is undoubtedly to Jacques Boileau's history of the flagellants and the considerable stir it caused. The *Historia flagellantium. De recto et perverso flagrorum* ⟨sic⟩ *usu apud Christianos*, was published anonymously in 1700 and immediately translated into French (1701); Reid may

have used the revised French edition of 1732. As late as 1777 de Lolme still found it worthwhile to issue an anonymous mockery of the work: *The History of the Flagellants, or the Advantages of discipline; being a paraphrase and commentary on the Historia Flagellantium of the Abbe Boileau, Doctor of the Sorbonne . . . By somebody who is not Doctor of the Sorbonne.* This was reissued in 1783 and 1784.

16. This is the end of the discussion of established religion. A *malus animus*, "evil intention" (Hutcheson, *Institutio*, p. 239), was the defining characteristic of *dolus* as opposed to *culpa*, negligence; see the Commentary above at p. 359 n. 129.

17. See Hutcheson, *Short Introduction*, pp. 310–311, and *System*, II.318–319, and Locke, *Letter concerning Toleration*, p. 71: "But idolatry (say some), is a sin, and therefore not to be tolerated. If they said it were therefore to be avoided, the inference were good. But it does not follow, that because it is a sin it ought therefore to be punished by the magistrate. For it does not belong unto the magistrate to make use of his sword in punishing everything, indifferently, that he takes to be a sin against God. Covetousness, uncharitableness, idleness, and many other things are sins, by the consent of men, which yet no man ever said were to be punished by the magistrate. The reason is, because they are not prejudicial to other men's rights, nor do they break the public peace of societies. Nay, even the sins of lying and perjury are nowhere punishable by laws; unless, in certain cases, in which the real turpitude of the thing and the offence against God are not considered, but only the injury done unto men's neighbours and to the commonwealth." Reid's discussion here should also be seen in the light of the distinction between perfect and imperfect rights and the debate about the enforceability of the latter, concerning which, see the Commentary above at pp. 320–321 n. 25, and at pp. 375 and 376–77 nn. 21 and 30. See also Warburton's standpoint, that the state via its alliance with the church may enforce the imperfect duties (*Alliance*, pp. 94–96 and 145; cf. pp. 29ff.).

18. This traditional agenda for government was, in Reid's view, more concerned with political means than with ends, and accordingly we find most of these topics dealt with at some length in the lectures on politics rather than here.

19. Concerning eminent domain, see Grotius, *War and Peace*, I.l.vi, II.14.vii–viii, III.19.vii, and III.20.vii–ix; Pufendorf, *Law of Nature*, VIII.5.vii, and *Duty of Man*, II.15.iv; Heineccius, *Universal Law*, II.166–170; Hutcheson, *Short Introduction*, pp. 289–290,

and *System*, II.236–237; Vattel, *Law of Nations*, I.20.244, and II.7.
See also the Commentary above at pp. 331–332 n. 41, and es-
pecially the discussion of the limitations on private property in
Section XI (above, pp. 206–208).

20. Concerning the four examples of the exercise of eminent do-
main for military purposes, see Pufendorf, *Law of Nature*,
VIII.5.vii (the first three examples), and Grotius, *War and Peace*,
III.17.iii (1); and see Reid's manuscript at pp. 207–208 above.
Concerning the Canal, see 8 Geo. III, cap. 63: "An Act for mak-
ing and maintaining a navigable Cut or Canal from the Firth or
River of Forth, at or near the Mouth of the River Carron, in the
County of Stirling, to the Firth or River of Clyde, at or near a
Place called Dalmuir Burnfoot, in the County of Dumbarton;
and also a collateral Cut from the same to the City of Glasgow;
and for making a navigable Cut or Canal of Communication
from the Port and Harbour of Borrowstounness, to join the said
Canal at or near the Place where it will fall into the Firth of
Forth." The canal act was passed in March 1768, but the project
was not completed until 1790.

See further 8 Geo. III, cap. 16: "An Act for making and wid-
ening a Passage or Street from The Salt Market Street, in the
City of Glasgow, to Saint Andrew's Church, in the said City; and
for enlarging and compleating the Church-yard of the said
Church; and for making and building a convenient Exchange
or Square in the said City." The details of the latter statute give
a perfect idea of the justification and operation of contemporary
expropriation (*Statutes at Large, 5 Geo. III–10 Geo. III*, vol. 10, pp.
454ff.). By "the town house" Reid meant the Tolbooth from
1626, of which only the steeple exists today. These references
provide some dating of the present manuscript.

21. It was unusual to subsume the right of taxation under eminent
domain; cf. Pufendorf, *Law of Nature*, VIII.5.iii–vii, and *Duty of
Man*, II.15.i–iv; Heineccius, *Universal Law*, II,166; Vattel, *Law of
Nations*, I.244.

22. *Negotium utile gestum* means, ⟨somebody else's⟩ business usefully
managed ⟨for him, on his behalf⟩; see the Commentary above at
p. 357 n. 124.

23. Locke, *Second Treatise*, 138: "The Supreain Power cannot take
from any Man any part of his Property without his own consent.
For the preservation of Property being the end of Government,
and that for which Men enter into Society, it necessarily supposes and requires, that the People should have Property, without which they must be suppos'd to lose that by entring into So-

ciety, which was the end for which they entered into it, too gross
an absurdity for any Man to own."

24. Reid would have known the relevant principles of the American
colonists from a host of source, such as the following pamphlets:
⟨Thomas Fitch, et al.⟩, *Reasons Why the British Colonies, in America,
Should Not be Charged with Internal Taxes* . . . ; ⟨James Otis⟩, *The
Rights of the British Colonies Asserted and Proved*; ⟨Stephen Hop-
kins⟩, *The Rights of Colonies Examined*; ⟨James Otis⟩, *A Vindication
of the British Colonies, against the Aspirations of the Halifax Gentleman* . . . ⟨Daniel Dulany⟩, *Considerations on the Propriety of Imposing
Taxes in the British Colonies for the Purpose of Raising a Revenue* . . . ;
all in B. Bailyn, ed., *Pamphlets of the American Revolution, 1750–
1776*. Principles such as those laid down in the postscript to
Otis's abovementioned *Vindication* were commonplace in the
pro-American literature on both sides of the Atlantic: "1. That
it is the incontestable right of the subject in Great Britain not to
be taxed out of Parliament; and every subject within the realm
is in fact or in law represented there. 2. The British colonists
being British subjects, are to all intents and purposes entitled to
the rights, liberties, and privileges of the subject within the
realm and ought to be represented in fact as well as in law in the
supreme or some subordinate legislature where they are taxed,
else they will be deprived of one of the most essential rights of a
British subject, namely that of being free from all taxes but such
as he shall by himself or representative grant and assess. 3. As
the colonies have been erected into subordinate dependent dominions with subordinate powers of legislation, particularly that
of levying taxes for the support of their respective subordinate
governments, and at their own expense have not only supported
the civil provincial administration but many of them have, to
their utmost ability, contributed both in men and money for the
common cause, as well as for their more immediate defense
against His Majesty's enemies, it should seem very hard that
they should be taxed also by Parliament, and that before they
are allowed a representation in fact and while they are quite unable to pay such additional taxes" (Bailyn, ed., *Pamphlets*, pp.
576–577). For the debate in Britain, see also the texts printed in
M. Beloff, ed., *The Debate on the American Revolution, 1761–1783*.
As for the elder William Pitt (since 1766 Earl of Chatham), Reid
is referring to his and his circle's (esp. Lord Camden) distinction
between legislation and taxation; the former is an exercise of
sovereignty, which in Britain belongs to the king in Parliament,
while the latter is a free grant—a benevolence, as Reid refers to

it in the following sentence—out of one's own property or the property of those one represents and it therefore is solely in the powers of the Commons who, however, do not represent the Americans. If legislation and taxation are not kept separate, rights of sovereignty and rights of property are in effect conflated: "Equally bound by its laws, and equally participating of the constitution of this free country, the Americans are the sons, not the bastards of England. Taxation is no part of the governing or legislative power. The taxes are a voluntary gift and grant of the Commons alone. In legislation the three estates of the realm are alike concerned; but the concurrency of the Peers and the Crown to a tax, is only necessary to close with the form of a law. The gift and grant is of the Commons alone. In ancient days, the Crown, the Barons, and the Clergy, possessed the lands. . . . At present . . . the Commons are become the proprietors of estates . . . and this House represents these Commons, the proprietors of the lands; and those proprietors virtually represent the rest of the inhabitants. When, therefore, in this house we give and grant, we give and grant what is our own. But in an American tax, what do we do? We, your majesty's commons of Great Britain, give and grant to your Majesty, what? our own, property? —No, we give and grant to your majesty the property of your Majesty's commons of America. It is an absurdity in terms. The distinction between legislation and taxation is essentially necessary to liberty. The Crown, the Peers, are equally legislative powers with the Commons. If taxation be part of simple legislation, the Crown, the Peers, have rights in taxation as well as yourselves; rights they will claim, which they will exercise, whenever the principle can be supported by power" (William Pitt, Speech in the Debate on the Address, House of Commons, 14 January 1766; in Beloff, ed., *Debate on the American Revolution*, pp. 94–95).

25. See Hutcheson, *System*, II.236–237: "as we shewed that some extraordinary cases of necessity give sometimes to private persons in natural liberty a right to recede from these laws which bind them in all ordinary cases: 'tis the same way with the governors of states, that in extraordinary cases they must have some extraordinary powers, beyond the common limits of the law, when these powers are necessary for the general safety, or for some very important advantage to the publick. ⟨Note: 'These powers some call *dominium eminens*; others more properly the *jus imperii eminens*, as they are not confined to the matters of property only.'⟩ Such powers are in every state, even in those where the

laws most rigidly secure to each subject his liberty and property, and extend over the labours and goods of the subjects in great exigences, especially in those of war. Thus the lands of any subject may justly be taken by the state when they are necessary for fortifying some important harbour, or city, or narrow pass. The ships of subjects may be taken for transporting of forces, so may their provisions too or military stores whether they agree to part with them or not. . . . Such extraordinary rights extend over life as well as property." Cf. *Short Introduction*, pp. 289–290, and the Commentary above at n. 19 and at p. 380 n. 20.

26. Reid does not explicitly pursue the list begun here. He probably had in mind the subsequent discussion of modern colonization as "B." Beginning opposite this line there is a marginal note that has been crossed out. It is not possible to find any clear place for it on this page and it belongs instead to the discussion of international relations. The note reads: "The Laws of Commerce with other Nations. Consuls & their privileges. Of Precedency and Titles of Honour among Sovereigns." Reid's contrast between ancient and modern principles of colonization, which were commonplace at the time, point to the need for a study of eighteenth-century concepts of colonies. For the natural law background to the distinction, see Grotius, *War and Peace*, I.3.xxi (3) and II.9.x–xi (2); Pufendorf, *Law of Nature*, VIII.11.vi and VIII.12.v (cf., for the analogy with the family, Hobbes, *De cive*, 9.viii); Heineccius, *Universal Law*, II.219–220; Vattel, *Law of Nations*, 1.18.208–210; and Hutcheson's important discussion in *Short Introduction*, pp. 316–317, and esp. *System*, II.306–309.

27. See the Commentary above at p. 365 n. 8 and at p. 357 n. 55.

28. See the Commentary above at p. 423 n. 18.

29. This paragraph should be compared with Vattel, *Law of Nations*, I.11.119–124.

30. This sentence gives a transition from the discussion of self-government to that of the relations between states. For the present point, see Vattel, *Law of Nations*, II.1.3: "Social bodies or sovereign states are much more capable of supporting themselves than individuals, and mutual assistance is not so necessary among them, nor of so frequent use. Now whatever a nation can do itself, no succour is there due to it from others." The general lines of the following discussion of international relations in peacetime should be seen in the light of Vattel, *Law of Nations*, II.1.

31. Concerning Elizabeth I's treaties of assistance with money and troops to the Dutch of 1578 and 1585, see Hume, *History*,

5:196ff. and 242ff. For her similar assistance in 1590 to Henry of Navarre, by then Henry IV of France, against the Catholic League, see ibid., pp. 318ff. See also Vattel, *Law of Nations*, II.1.4: "A powerful league was formed in favour of the United Provinces when threatened with the yoke of Lewis XIV. ⟨Note: 'In 1672.'⟩"

32. Reid is referring to two of the most important problems that occupied eighteenth-century scientists throughout Europe: the figure and measure of the earth, and the sun's mean distance from the earth, which could be used to measure the size of the solar system. Concerning the former, Reid is referring to the Parisian Académie Royale des Sciences' expeditions to Peru (conducted by Pierre Bouguer and La Condamine) and to Lapland (by Pierre Maupertuis) in 1735–36 with the aim of testing Newton's demonstration that the earth is flattened at the poles. He also celebrated this in the first of his *Philosophical Orations* in 1753 (p. 939). In January 1751, Reid made extensive reading notes from an account by Bouguer of the former expedition (3/I/7), and two other manuscripts (3/III/15 and 7/II/22) preserve his own computations. In the present context, it should be pointed out that in 3/I/7,1r he notes that the French expedition had Spanish participation.

Concerning the second problem, French scientists connected with the Académie had for years planned how best to exploit the transits of Venus across the face of the sun for measuring the distance between the earth and the sun. The transits occurred on 6 June 1761 and 3 June 1769, and on both occasions an extraordinary interest was generated all over Europe and its outposts. Nearly all European nations organized observations of the phenomenon, and both the French and the British sent expeditions around the world for the purpose. The usual tension between national rivalry and international cooperation in such matters was particularly intense in 1761, in the middle of the Seven Years' War, and it may be that Reid was well advised to use the ambiguous verb "concur." He himself had, within the Aberdeen Philosophical Society, been active in preparing for the transit since 1758, and on 14 July 1761 he read an account to the society of his own observations, which were partly frustrated by the weather conditions. He continued to follow the debate about the observations of the transit; see 2/I/7.

33. Vattel, *Law of Nations*, II.1.5: "The calamities of Portugal have given England an opportunity of fulfilling the duties of humanity with that generosity which distinguishes an opulent, power-

ful and magnanimous nation. On the first advice of the misfortune of Lisbon ⟨Note: 'the earthquake by which the greatest part of that city was destroyed'⟩, the parliament voted a hundred thousand pounds sterling for the relief of an unfortunate people."

34. See Hume, *History*, 5:385.

35. See Hume, *History*, 7:233.

36. See 12 Anne C. 15, "An Act for providing a Publick Reward for such Person or Persons as shall discover the Longitude at Sea." The Act provided for up to £2000 in subsidy for approved projects and up to £20,000 for an accurate determination of the longitude. The act was amended by 2 Geo. C. 18.

37. Concerning the status of foreigners, see especially Vattel, *Law of Nations*, 1.19.213 and II.8, and Grotius, *War and Peace*, II.2.v, II.11.v (2), and II.14.viii.

38. See Vattel, *Law of Nations*, preliminaries, 18, and II.3.36.

39. The discussion of peaceful relations between states ends here.

40. See Grotius, *De jure belli*, I.l.ii (1): "Cicero dixit Bellum certationem per vim" (English version: "Cicero defines War a dispute by force"). The reference is Cicero, *De officiis*, I.xi (34). Grotius goes on to say: "But Custom has so prevailed, that not the Act of Hostility, but the State and Situation of the contending Parties, now goes by that Name; so that War is the State or Situation of those . . . who dispute by Force of Arms." Hobbes obviously paid some attention to this point; *De cive*, I.12, and *Leviathan*, pp. 185–186. Cf. Hutcheson, *Philosophiae moralis institutio*, p. 239 (with a partial quotation of Grotius), and Heineccius, *Universal Law*, II.185.

41. See Hutcheson, *Short Introduction*, pp. 232–233: "Wars are divided into publick and private. The former are such as are undertaken by a state, or in the name of a body of people: private wars are those among private persons. The publick wars are divided into solemn, or these authorized on both sides by the supreme powers of states, upon some specious shews of rights; and those so authorized only on one side: such as the wars made upon bands of pyrates or robbers, or citizens making insurrections; or what are called civil wars, between different parties in the same state contending about some rights of the people, or of the government. We first treat of the private wars of men in natural liberty. And the same reasonings hold in publick wars; since sovereign states and princes are with respect to each other in the same condition of natural liberty." Cf. ibid., pp. 332–333. Similarly, in *System*, II.347–349 and cf. ibid., pp. 92–97. The ba-

sis is Grotius, *War and Peace*, 1.3.i–iv and III.3, followed by Pufendorf, *Law of Nature*, VIII.6.ix, and *Duty of Man*, II.16.vii; Carmichael, n. 1, pp. 482–487, in Pufendorf, *De officio*; Heineccius, *Universal Law*, II.188 and 192–193; Vattel, *Law of Nations*, IV.1.2.

42. The common position was that serious transgressions on perfect rights justified war; see Grotius, *War and Peace*, II.1; Pufendorf, *Law of Nature*, VIII.6.iii, and *Duty of Man*, II.16.i–ii; Heineccius, *Universal Law*, II.188–190; Hutcheson, *Short Introduction*, pp. 228–232, and *System*, II.92–94; Vattel, *Law of Nations*, III.3.26. Once men were living in civil society, the defense of their perfect rights was taken over by the state; nevertheless, in certain situations it would still be justifiable to exercise the original right to private war, and it is in this context that the distinction between a day-thief and a night-thief plays a role. When we confront a thief at night, we may wage private war and kill because it is hard to bring him to justice by court (because we cannot easily apprehend him or recognize him or find witnesses or be sure whether he is armed—the reasons vary and are disputed): ". . . that even since Tribunals of Justice were erected, every private War is not repugnant to the Law of Nature, may be gathered from the Law given to the Jews, where God thus speaks by Moses, 'If a Thief be found breaking up', (that is, by Night) 'and be smitten, that he dies, there shall no Blood be shed for him; but if the Sun be risen upon him, there shall be Blood shed for him.' . . . That of the Twelve Tables is well known, . . . 'If a Thief commit a Robbery in the Night, and if a Man kill him, he is killed lawfully' " (Grotius, *War and Peace*, 1.3.ii). Grotius's final quotation, from Macrobius, *Saturnalia*, 1.4, is the one Reid gives here from the Latin text. Cf. Grotius, *War and Peace*, II.l.xii (with Barbeyrac's notes); Pufendorf, *Law of Nature*, II.5.xvii–xviii, and *Duty of Man*, 1.5.xxiii; Hutcheson, *Short Introduction*, p. 235, and *System*, II.94.

43. Concerning duels, see the Commentary above at p. 36 n. 139. Grotius thought duels were justifiable under certain circumstances (*War and Peace*, II.l.xv); this is rejected by Pufendorf, *Law of Nature*, II.5.ix, and *Duty of Man*, 1.5.xiii; Hutcheson, *Short Introduction*, pp. 237–240, and *System*, II.97–101. For the remaining points, see also Grotius, *War and Peace*, II.20.viii (5), II.23.x, and III.20.xliii; Pufendorf, *Law of Nature*, II.5.xii, VIII.3.xxvi, and VIII.4.viii.

44. The starting-point for the natural law discussion of this topic was the great chapter in which Grotius develops his complicated theory of sovereignty in considering the question of who may

make war, *War and Peace*, 1.3. See Pufendorf, *Law of Nature*, VII.6.x–xi, and *Duty of Man*, II.16.viii; Heineccius, *Universal Law*, II, pp. 186–187; and Vattel, *Law of Nations*, III.1.4: "the sovereign power has alone authority to make war. But as the different rights which constitute this power, originally resident in the body of the nation, may be separated or limited according to the will of the nation . . . we are to seek the power of making war in the particular constitution of each state. The Kings of England, whose power is otherwise so limited, have the right of making war and peace."

45. The following paragraph is, point for point, a précis of Vattel, *Law of Nations*, III.2.

46. See Grotius, *War and Peace*, 1.2.x and 1.5.iv.

47. Vattel, *Law of Nations*, III.2.18: "The regulations, the particular end of which is to maintain order in the troops, and to render them capable of performing the best service, constitute what is called military discipline. This is of the last importance. The Switzers were the first among the modern nations that revived it. . . . Machiavel, in his discourse on Livy, says, That 'the Switzers are the masters of all Europe in the art of war.' The Prussians have very lately shewn what may be expected from a good discipline, and assiduous exercise: soldiers, collected from all quarters have, by the force of custom, and the influence of command, performed all that could be expected from the most zealous and affectionate subjects." The reference is Machiavelli, *Discourses*, II.16.6. As for Frederick the Great, Reid did of course not need Vattel to advise him about his importance. The alliance between Britain and Prussia during most of the Seven Years' War and Frederick's spectacular early successes had made him an extraordinarily popular hero in Britain and created a virtual craze for everything Prussian, which was an important ingredient in the notably increased preoccupation with things military in Britain from the 1750s onward. In the present context it should thus be mentioned that the Prussian military regulations were quickly translated into English and popularized: e.g., in *Regulations for the Prussian Infantry*, excerpted in *London Magazine* 23 (August and October 1754): pp. 356ff., and 46off.; *New Regulations for the Prussian Infantry; Regulations for the Prussian Cavalry*, excerpted in *London Magazine* 26 (June 1757): pp. 267–269; and *Military Instructions, written by the King of Prussia for the Generals of his Army*. Altogether more than two dozen official or semi-official Prussian works and works by Frederick were translated into English between 1741 and 1786, culminating with

Holcroft's translation of the *Posthumous Works of Frederic II* in thirteen volumes (1789). Prussian ways of exercising troops began to be introduced into the British army, and private "Prussian" exercise societies shot up all over the country, even in the Scottish Highlands (*Glasgow Evening Courant*, 30 January–6 February 1758). We may therefore safely assume that Reid's discussion of military matters, even though some years later, was listened to with considerable interest, especially considering its obvious relevance for the continuing debate about the relative merits of a standing army and a militia.

48. Vattel, *Law of Nations*, III.2.21: "if an inferior officer exceeds the authority of his post, his promise becomes no more than a private engagement. It is a *Sponsio* only. . . . This was the case of the Roman consuls at the Furcae Caudinae. They might agree to deliver hostages, and that their army should pass under the yoke, &c. but their power did not extend to their making peace, as they took care to signify to the Samnites." Vattel's reference is Livy, who gives the account of the Romans' disaster at the Caudine Forks in 321 B.C. in *From the Founding of the City*, IX.ii–vi; the specific reference for the *sponsio* is IX.v.1–6. Vattel uses the case for a detailed discussion of *sponsio* at II.14.209ff. This is directly derived from Grotius, *War and Peace*, II.15; Pufendorf, *Law of Nature*, VII.8.xii–xiii, and *Duty of Man*, II.17.viii; cf. Heineccius, *Universal Law*, II.205–206.

49. This line and the following paragraph select some of the main points in Vattel's chapter on "The Just Causes of War," *Law of Nations*, III.3. First the distinction between reasons and motives: "The reasons which may determine us to have recourse to ⟨war⟩ are of two kinds. The one manifest that we have a right to make war when we have a lawful cause for it. These are called justificatory reasons. The other taken from fitness and advantage. These shew whether it be expedient for the sovereign to undertake a war, and are called motives." This is built directly upon Grotius, *War and Peace*, II.l.i and II.22.i–ii. As for pretexts, see Vattel, *Law of Nations*, III.3.32: "there are just causes of war, real justificative reasons; and why should there not be sovereigns who sincerely consider them as their warrant, when they have besides reasonable motives for taking up arms. We shall therefore call pretences the reasons alledged as justificative, and which have only the appearance of such, and are absolutely void even of the least foundation. The name of pretences may likewise be given to reasons true in themselves, but which not being of sufficient importance for undertaking a war, are made use of

only to cover ambitious views, or some other faulty motive." Cf. Grotius, *War and Peace*, II.22.xvii.

As for offensive and defensive war, see Vattel, *Law of Nations*, III.1.5 and III.3.28: "we may set down this triple end as the distinguishing characteristic of lawful war. 1. To recover what belongs or is due to us. 2. To provide for our future safety by punishing the aggressor, or offender. 3. To defend ourselves from an injury by repelling an unjust violence. The two first are the objects of an offensive, the third that of a defensive war." Cf. Pufendorf, *Law of Nature*, VIII.6.iii, and *Duty of Man*, II.16.ii; Heineccius, *Universal Law*, II.189.

50. Vattel, *Law of Nations*, III.3.29: "As nations or leaders are not only to make justice the rule of their conduct, but also to regulate it for the good of the state. So decent and commendable motives must concur with the justificative reasons, that they should undertake a war." Concerning just war in general, see the Commentary above at p. 430 n. 42.

51. Vattel, *Law of Nations*, III.3.36.

52. This is one of the most explicit connections between Reid's distinction between jurisprudence and "the science of Politicks" and the distinction between ends and means, which is fundamental to modern natural law and provides the best clue to the true nature of Reid's distinction, especially the "scientific" nature of politics. See the Introductory Lecture, pp. 114–116 above.

53. See the Commentary above, at p. 428 n. 33.

54. The idea of a universal or general society of mankind is put forward by Vattel, *Law of Nations*, preliminaries, 10ff., and especially invoked in the present context in II.1. For Henry IV and Cromwell, see the Commentary above at p. 429 nn. 34 and 35. The reference to Vattel concerns a case that Reid quotes below, p. 271.

55. See the Commentary, at p. 435 n. 66.

56. See Vattel, *Law of Nations*, II.18.324.

57. For the following three points, see Vattel, *Law of Nations*, II.18.327–329 and cf. Grotius, *War and Peace*, II.23.viii; Pufendorf, *Law of Nature*, V.13, and *Duty of Man*, II.1.xi.

58. For the following three points, see Vattel, *Law of Nations*, II.18.334–338. Concerning retaliation, see also Grotius, *War and Peace*, III.4.xiii; Pufendorf, *Law of Nature*, VIII.3.xxvii. Concerning reprisals, see Grotius, *War and Peace*, III.2.iv ff.; Pufendorf, *Law of Nature*, VIII.6.xiii, and *Duty of Man*, II.16.x; Heineccius, *Universal Law*, II.198; Hutcheson, *Short Introduction*, pp. 335–337, and *System*, II.355–356.

59. Ever since the peace treaty of Aix-la-Chapelle, ending the War of the Austrian Succession in 1748, had failed to sort out the relations between the British and the French in North America, the conflict had intensified between the westward trade-push of the former and the grandiose plan of the latter for a French inland territory, a north-south corridor, from the Mississippi basin to that of the St. Lawrence, from Quebec to New Orleans. The focal point for the conflict was the Ohio Valley, where the French established a number of fortified positions during 1753 and 1754, imprisoning British traders. This was used by the British government to explain the capture of two French men-of-war with some troops on board off the coast of Newfoundland in June 1755 as a reprisal. The British tactic was basically to get the French to declare war as a consequence of this, so that they would be seen as the aggressor and so that Britain could invoke the provisions in the earlier peace treaty for assistance (from the Dutch, among others) in case of unjustified attack. They got the declaration of war in early 1756 but had difficulties having it seen in the desired light. See Gibbon, *Autobiography*, p. 86: "We were then ⟨Spring 1758⟩ in the midst of a war: the resentment of the French at our taking their ships without a declaration had rendered that polite nation somewhat peevish and difficult."

60. Vattel, *Law of Nations*, II.18.346: "in all civilized states, a subject who thinks himself injured by a foreign nation, has recourse to his sovereign in order to obtain the permission of making reprisals. This is what is called desiring letters of marque."

61. Vattel, *Law of Nations*, IV.18.354: "There are cases . . . in which reprisals would be justly condemned, even when a declaration of war would not be so, and these are precisely those in which nations may with justice take up arms."

62. See the Commentary above, at pp. 429–430 n.41.

63. As in the previous manuscript (and see the Commentary above at p. 432f. nn. 49ff.), Reid here clearly had recourse to Vattel, *Law of Nations*, III.3, esp. sec. 39, for the principle that both parties to a moral dispute cannot be right, which was so important to him. Concerning the extracts, see Reid's MS. 3/II/5 above, p. 253 l. 43.

64. See the Commentary above, at p. 361 n. 138.

65. This sentence confirms the point made in the Textual Notes for p. 254 that some of Reid's 1766 manuscript has been lost; the rules of war have not been dealt with in the previous manuscript.

66. Concerning untruthfulness in war, the common natural law position was that "deceiving our enemies, when we have a just cause of war, by any such signs as import no profession of communicating our sentiments to them are stratagems universally justified," but "as to all forms of contracts, truces, or treaties, the custom never was, nor ever can be received of deceiving an enemy by them; and such frauds ever will be deemed, as they truly are, highly criminal and perfidious" (Hutcheson, *System*, II.354–355; similarly *Short Introduction*, pp. 334–335. See further, Vattel, *Law of Nations*, III.10; Heineccius, *Universal Law*, II.194–196; Pufendorf, *Law of Nature*, VIII.6.vi and VIII.7.ii, and *Duty of Man*, II.16.v—all building upon Grotius, *War and Peace*, III.1 and III.19. It is tempting to speculate that Reid's reflections on the viability of the linguistic distinction employed here may have influenced his general theory of language and its application in the theory of contract; see the Commentary above at pp. 401ff. nn. 2 and 4.

Concerning poisoning, see Grotius, *War and Peace*, III.4.xv–xvi; Hutcheson, *Short Introduction*, p. 335, and *System*, II.352–353; Heineccius, *Universal Law*, II.194–195; Vattel, *Law of Nations*, III.8.155–157. Of these, only Heineccius asserts the legitimacy of poisoning.

As for the treatment of prisoners of war, see Grotius, *War and Peace*, III.7.iii, and Vattel, *Law of Nations*, III.8.149–151.

67. Vattel, *Law of Nations*, III.8.158: "The Duke of Cumberland, after the victory of Dettingen ⟨1743⟩, appears to me still greater then in the heat of battle. As he was under the surgeon's hands, a French officer, much more dangerously wounded than himself, being brought that way, the prince immediately directed his surgeon to leave him, and assist that officer." This is an illustration of the "Dispositions which should be maintained towards the enemy."

68. Not traced.

69. There are many testimonies to this. In a letter to the Comtesse de Boufflers in January 1763, Hume, regretting Rousseau's low opinion of the English, says, "He would have seen many instances of humanity very honourable to their character: besides the magnificent charities, which are supported by voluntary contributions, where superstition has little share, they practised, during the late war, a piece of humanity which was very commendable. We had sometimes near 30,000 French seamen prisoners, who were distributed into different prisons, and whom the Parliament maintained by a considerable sum allotted them.

They received food from the public, but it was thought that their own friends would supply them with clothes, which however was found, after some time, to be neglected. The cry arose, that the brave and gallant men, though enemies, were perishing with cold in prison: a subscription was set on foot; great sums were given by all ranks of people; and, notwithstanding the national foolish prejudices against the French, a remarkable zeal every where appeared for this charity" (*Letters of David Hume*, 1:373; cf. Smith, LJ(B), 346). The most significant of the charitable efforts to which Hume refers was organized in 1759 by Thomas Hollis, who printed the *Proceedings of the Committee appointed to manage the Contributions . . . for Cloathing French Prisoners of War* (1760), for which Dr. Johnson wrote a pithy introduction. Concerning the "zeal" for the French prisoners, see also Wesley's *Journal*, 4:237, 355–356 and 417, and 6:256. These efforts and the parallel ones in France drew much attention from the contemporary press. See also Vattel, *Law of Nations*, III.8.150.

70. Vattel, *Law of Nations*, III.7.106. See also Grotius, *War and Peace*, III.17.iii; Hutcheson, *System*, II.357.

71. Vattel, *Law of Nations*, III.7.110. See also Hutcheson, *Short Introduction*, p. 357, and *System*, II.360.

72. Vattel, *Law of Nations*, III.7.111. See also Grotius, *War and Peace*, III.1.v. On neutrality and trade, see also Barbeyrac's long n.1 on p. 842 of Pufendorf, *Law of Nature*. See also Hutcheson, *Short Introduction*, p. 339, and *System*, II.360–361; Heineccius, *Universal Law*, II.196–197. Reid has undoubtedly here referred to the problem that arose when France, in order to break the British navy's stranglehold on her colonial trade, relaxed the national monopoly on this trade and permitted Dutch merchant ships to carry it. The British captured a large number of these ships, and British courts treated them as fair prize, thus trying to establish the principle that subsequently came to be known as the rule of the war of 1756, that neutrals who during war carry out trade that is not open to them in peacetime, may be captured.

73. Vattel, *Law of Nations*, II.9.121 and III.7.112–116. See also Hutcheson, *Short Introduction*, pp. 338–339, and *System*, II.359–360. In addition to the incidents during the Seven Years' War, Reid is here likely to have made reference to the preceding War of the Austrian Succession, when Britain captured Prussian ships and confiscated, among other things, food supplies as contraband.

74. Vattel, *Law of Nations*, III.13.196–197. See also Grotius, *War and*

Peace, III.6.iii–iv; Hutcheson, *Short Introduction*, pp. 337–338, and *System*, II.357–358; Heineccius, *Universal Law*, II.197.

75. Vattel, *Law of Nations*, III.8.150.

76. Vattel, *Law of Nations*, III.9.165.

77. Contrast Grotius, *War and Peace*, III.5, and Vattel, *Law of Nations*, III.9.164.

78. Vattel, *Law of Nations*, III.7.119ff., and Grotius, *War and Peace*, III.4.viii. Concerning neutrality in general, cf. Grotius, *War and Peace*, III.17; Hutcheson, *Short Introduction*, pp. 337–340, and *System*, II.356–362.

79. Vattel, *Law of Nations*, III.8.153 and 150. Concerning ransom, see also Grotius, *War and Peace*, III.7.ix and III.14.ix. Cartels were among the relatively recent developments in international law that fascinated Reid's contemporaries: "In the same manner ⟨as humane treatment of prisoners of war⟩ cartel-treaties, by which soldiers and sailors are valued at so much and exchanged at the end of every campaign, the nation which has lost most prisoners paying the balance, is an evidence of our refinement in humanity. In the late war ⟨1756–63⟩ indeed, we refused to enter into any such treaty with France for sailors, and by this wise regulation soon unman'd their navy, as we took a great many more than they" (Smith, LJ(B), 346–347; cf. Hume, "Of the Populousness of Ancient Nations," *Essays*, 1:402, and Ferguson, *Essay*, pp. 199–200). An agreement about soldiers was, however, entered into in 1760, and in 1765 we see the newly appointed embassy secretary in Paris, David Hume, wrangling with the French over implementation (*New Letters of David Hume*, pp. 109, 113, and 129).

80. Vattel, *Law of Nations*, III.5.76–77.

81. Vattel, *Law of Nations*, II.3.37.

82. Hutcheson, *Short Introduction*, pp. 339–340, and *System*, II.362–363.

83. Hutcheson, *Short Introduction*, p. 341, and *System*, II.364.

84. Vattel, *Law of Nations*, IV.5.57 and 66; IV.7–9. See also Grotius, *War and Peace*, II.18; Heineccius, *Universal Law*, II.212–213; Hutcheson, *Short Introduction*, pp. 342–344, and *System*, II.366–371.

85. Pufendorf, *Law of Nature*, VII.12; Hutcheson, *Short Introduction*, pp. 344–347, and *System*, II.372–376. In the following a large number of points recur; they will generally not be noted.

86. See Grotius, *War and Peace*, III.4.ix and xix; III.11.ix (2).

87. See Grotius, *War and Peace*, III.6.xiv–xvi.

88. Vattel, *Law of Nations*, III.10.174–176 and III.16.

89. Vattel, *Law of Nations*, III.13.199 and 201.

90. Vattel, *Law of Nations*, III.13.200.

91. Vattel, *Law of Nations*, III.18.287ff.

92. Vattel, *Law of Nations*, III.2.13.

93. Reid may here have made reference to the personnel difficulties during the Seven Years' War.

94. Vattel, *Law of Nations*, III.2.10.

95. "The ways in which an obligation is dissolved." Pufendorf's chapter headings have this in the plural (*solvantur obligationes*), while Justinian has it in the singular but uses a different verb (*tollitur*, "is extinguished"); *Law of Nature*, v.11; *Duty of Man*, 1.16; *Institutes*, III.xxix. In the Pufendorfian systematics, this subject of course belongs elsewhere, as we have seen (above, pp. 355–356 n. 122, and p. 387 n. 1). The appearance here of these eight points, which are identical with those in 7/VII/25 (above, p. 215), is however, explainable by the fact that Grotius touches upon this topic (especially compensation) in his chapter "Concerning Faith between Enemies" (*War and Peace*, III.19.xv–xvi). See also the Commentary above at p. 387 n. 3.

96. This and the following manuscript, 4/III/23c (i.e., p. 269 l. 4 to p. 276 l. 20) are taken up by Reid's notes from his reading of Vattel's *Le Droit des gens ou principes de la loi naturelle*, which had been published in French in London in 1758. In the English translation, the first volume is dated 1760, while the second is dated 1759. Reid's notes consist of summaries, extracts, and paraphrases. In general, I have therefore not annotated them beyond identifying the relevant references in Vattel, and supplying the more important cross references.

97. The reference is to Christian Wolff, *Jus gentium*, which was preceded by his *Jus naturae* in eight volumes. For the rest, Vattel may have been thinking of the *Philosophia moralis* in five volumes, which is systematically prior though temporally subsequent to the *Jus gentium*. If we are to take Vattel's figure more literally, we may understand him to mean the whole of Wolff's practical philosophy, thus including also the *Philosophia practica universalis* in two volumes. Reference should then also be made to the compendium *Institutiones juris naturae et gentium* and the *Oeconomica*, both of which are, however, later than the *Jus gentium*. It is also possible that Vattel has been thinking of the somewhat earlier German works, and especially the *Deutsche Ethik* and the *Deutsche Politik*.

98. This paragraph summarizes secs. 1–6 of the preliminaries in Vattel, *Law of Nations*.

99. Vattel, preliminaries, secs. 7, 9, and 21.

100. The paragraph covers Vattel, *Law of Nations*, 1.1.4–8.

101. Vattel, 1.4.39: "⟨a wise king⟩ uses the public power only with a view to the public welfare. All this is comprehended in the fine saying of Lewis xii. 'A King of France does not revenge the injuries of a Duke of Orleans.' "

102. Vattel, 1.4.52.

103. Vattel, 1.4.54.

104. Vattel, 1.5.68.

105. Vattel, ii.1.15; cf. The Commentary above at p. 433 n. 54.

106. Vattel, ii.1.19.

107. Vattel, ii.2.33.

108. Vattel, ii.2.34.

109. Vattel, ii.3.38.

110. Vattel, ii.3.39.

111. Vattel, ii.3.40.

112. Vattel, ii.3.45.

113. Vattel, ii.3.48.

114. Vattel, preface, p. vi, note a. The reference is Hobbes, *De cive*, xiv.4. In the original English translation, the sentence is rendered, "but because Cities once instituted doe put on the personall proprieties of men."

115. Vattel, preface, p. iv. The passage from Justinian, which is quoted more fully by Vattel, is in the English translation of the *Law of Nations* rendered "that law, which natural reason has established among all mankind . . . is called the Law of Nations." The function of the priestly *collegium fetialium* is described repeatedly in Livy, *From the Founding of the City*. See also Cicero, *De legibus*, ii.ix (21), and *De officiis*, i.xi (36): "As for war, humane laws touching it are drawn up in the fetial code ⟨fetiali iure⟩ of the Roman People under all the guarantees of religion." Vattel himself gives a further explanation in *Law of Nations*, iii.4.51.

116. Vattel, preface, v. Vattel refers to Grotius, *War and Peace*, prolegomena, 41.

117. This is the fragment of Cicero, *De re publica*, already quoted in 7/vii/21 (printed above, p. 182), and again in 8/iv/9 (above, p. 255).

118. Vattel, 1.5.67.

119. As we know from 7/vii/25 (printed in Section XIII of this book), there is every indication that Reid did find the time for this task.

120. Vattel, III.1.4; III.2.8; III.2.15.

121. Vattel, II.7.84 and note a.

122. Vattel, III.3.36, quoting Livy, *From the Founding of the City*, IX.i (10): "Samnites, that war is just which is necessary, and righteous are their arms to whom, save only in arms, no hope is left."

123. Vattel, III.4.65.

124. Vattel, III.4.63.

125. Vattel, III.4.66–68 and III.12, to be read in the light of Vattel's preliminaries, 17: "the obligation, and the right correspondent to it, or flowing from it, is distinguished into external and internal. The obligation is internal, as it binds the conscience, and as it comprehends the rules of our duty: it is external, as it is considered relatively to other men, and as it produces some right between them. The internal obligation is always the same in nature, though it varies in degree: but the external obligation is divided into perfect and imperfect, and the right that results from it is also perfect and imperfect."

126. Vattel, III.6.78–82.

127. Vattel, III.7.103ff.

128. Vattel, III.7.112ff. and 119ff.

129. The heading refers to ch. 8 of book III in Vattel and the first paragraph to secs. 140 and 151 there. In the latter we find: "Admiral Anson, on taking the rich Acapulco Galleon near Manila, and finding his prisoners to out-number his whole ships company, he confined them in the hold, by which they suffered extremely."

130. Vattel, III.8.155; cf. the Commentary above at p. 435 n. 66.

131. Vattel, III.8.158; cf. the Commentary above at p. 435 n. 67. The following two points are from the same place.

132. The general reference is Vattel, III.9.165, where we find: "The instances of humanity and discretion cannot be too often cited. The long wars of France in the reign of Lewis XIV. furnish an instance which can never be too much commended. The sovereigns being respectively interested in the preservation of the country, used on the commencement of the war to enter into treaties, for regulating the contributions on a supportable footing: both the extent of the country in which each could demand contributions, the amount of them, and the manner in which the parties sent for levying them were to behave, were settled. In these treaties it was expressed, that no body of men under a certain number, should advance into the enemy's country beyond the bounds agreed on, under the penalty of being treated as *parti bleu* ⟨Note: 'Marauders, or robbers'⟩."

133. Vattel, III.9.166–168.
134. Vattel, III.12; cf. the Commentary above at n. 125.
135. Vattel, III.13.196–198; cf. the Commentary above at p. 436 n. 74.
136. Vattel, III.18.296 with II.4.54–56; II.12.196–197; and IV.5.68.
137. Vattel, IV.6.71–74.
138. Vattel, IV.7.80–85.
139. Vattel, IV.9.117–124.
140. I assume that Reid is here referring to Vattel's discussion of the jurisdiction over ambassadors in IV.8.
141. Vattel, III.1.4–5.
142. While Vattel does not use this arrangement in four points, they are all to be found in III.3.24–30.
143. Vattel, III.3.33–34 and 42.
144. Reid may be referring to Vattel's discussion of the benefits of a balance of power system, III.3.47–49.
145. Vattel, III.4.51 and 64.
146. Again Reid cuts across Vattel's organization to achieve his own. The most central references are III.2.19 and 8; III.6.78–80 and 83; III.2.13.
147. Vattel, III.7.107–108.
148. Vattel, III.3.40; for the consequences, see III.4.66–68 and III.12. See also the Commentary above at nn. 125 and 134.
149. Vattel, II.2.34 and IV.6.75.
150. Vattel, IV.8.114.
151. Vattel, IV.6.79 and IV.7.103.
152. Vattel, II.8.101–102.
153. This surprising arrangement may reflect Reid's remembering that in Grotius the right of burial arises from "the same arbitrary *Law of Nations*" as do "the Rights of Embassies"; see *War and Peace*, II.18 and 19.
154. Vattel, I.21.
155. Vattel, I.19.214.
156. Vattel, I.19.228.
157. Vattel, IV.7.95ff.
158. In one of the manuscripts containing disparate points in jurisprudence, we find a note in which Reid reminds himself of a number of disputed issues. Because these belong to or relate to political jurisprudence and have been encountered in the preceding, the note is added here below without further comment. The note is in 7/VII/1c,1v (which is described in the Textual Notes at 188):

Points of jurisprudence that have been disputed & in which Mankind have been gradually Enlightened. The Patria Posestas. Right of Conquest. Causes of War. Right over Captives. Dominion of the Sea. Popes Right to give Kingdoms and absolve Subjects from Allegiance. The Measures of Submission to the Civil Magistrate. The Rights of Conscience in Matters of Religion, & of Religious Liberty. Servitude.

XVIII. Some Thoughts on the Utopian System

1. For the circumstances of this paper and an interpretation of it, see the Introduction above, pp. 25 and 76ff. The paper should be read in the context of the lectures on political jurisprudence printed above in Sections VII and XVI.

2. In this and the following four paragraphs, Harringtonian-Machiavellian notions are particularly evident. Harrington and Montesquieu are the central figures in Reid's lectures on politics. For Harrington, see esp. 4/III/6–7.

3. The engagement in this paragraph of English constitutional wisdom with Montesquieu is pursued at some length in the lectures on politics (esp. 4/III/8), which clearly show that Reid was intimately acquainted with *The Spirit of Laws* (esp. 4/III/1, 4/III/5, and 4/III/14), so intimately that the Turkish example here is in the spirit rather than the letter of any of the numerous discussions in that work of despotic government.

4. On the distinction between "political jurisprudence" and "politics," see the Introduction above, p. 31, and pp. 114–116 of the Introductory Lecture (Section I).

5. See Hume, "Idea of a Perfect Commonwealth," pp. 480–481, and Smith, TMS, IV.1.11 and VI.ii.2.18.

6. To the extent that one emphasizes the first of these points—the perfectibility of moral character—as Reid does elsewhere (see the Introduction above, pp. 77–80), his scheme approaches what has been called the "perfect moral commonwealth." To the extent that the two latter points are seen as predominant, the model is properly utopian (see J. C. Davis, *Utopia and the Ideal Society*, ch. 1). In the preceding couple of pages the reader may also discern echoes of Rousseau's idea of natural man and his ability to master his second nature.

7. Sir Thomas More (1478–1535) coined the word "utopia" in the

title of his famous work from 1516, which marks the renewal of utopian speculation in Western thought. The reception of More in the eighteenth century is too complex to be indicated here (but see, for a start, Manuel and Manuel, *Utopian Thought in the Western World*, chs. 16, 17, 22, and 23), and we have no hard evidence about Reid's specific way to More, which would allow us any noninterpretative shortcuts. It should, however, be pointed out that there are a number of similarities between Reid's utopian sketch in this paper and "the model of a perfect government" constructed by the Scottish minister Robert Wallace in his *Various Prospects of Mankind, Nature, and Providence*, prospects II–IV, and that both have an implicit critical edge against Hume's "Idea of a Perfect Commonwealth," pitting adaptations of More against Hume's redeployment of Harrington. We do not know which edition of *Utopia* Reid used, but apart from numerous Latin editions, Ralph Robinson's (1551) and Gilbert Burnet's (1684) English translations were printed again and again throughout the eighteenth century, the latter also by the Foulis brothers in Glasgow in 1743 and 1762.

8. More, *Utopia*, pp. 103–105.
9. More, *Utopia*, p. 149.
10. See the Commentary above at pp. 323–324 n. 29, and Section XI.
11. See Acts 4:32–37 and 2:44–45. See More, *Utopia*, p. 219 (where Coenobites are referred to) and p. 243. In his famous chapter (ch. xxxvii) on the "Origin, Progress, and Effects of Monastic Life," Gibbon explains: "The monks were divided into two classes: the Coenobites, who lived under a common, and regular, discipline; and the Anachorets, who indulged their unsocial, independent fanaticism" (*Decline and Fall*, 2:362). For the seven deacons, see Acts 6:1–6.
12. In the third quarter of the eighteenth century, the Society of Jesus and (not least) its activities in South America provided exciting news for all of Europe. Founded by Loyola in 1534 and recognized by Pope Paul III in 1540, the society played a significant role in the Spanish settlements in America in the second half of the sixteenth century, Paraguay—a much more extensive area than the modern state—being established as a Jesuit province in 1604. By the middle of the eighteenth century, the Society of Jesus had become a hated and feared obstacle to the emerging enlightened absolutism in Spain and Portugal. Owing allegiance only to the general of the order and to the pope, the Jesuits enjoyed an independence that in the colonies enabled

them to be, or to run, a virtual state within the state. Thus, the independent trading activities of the Jesuits' Indian missions, especially with the British, flew in the face of the newfangled centralist mercantilism of the two Iberian crowns. In 1750 there was an attempt to solve the long-standing conflict over the Spanish-Portuguese borders in South America. A treaty that involved the clearance of seven Jesuit missions or "reductions," and the takeover of their land by the Portuguese was made. This led to armed uprisings by the Indians of the reductions, in which the exact role of the Jesuits is still a matter of dispute. By the mid-1750s, however, the sensational news in Europe was that Jesuits were in arms against monarchs, and even that they had made one of their own king of Paraguay, the spurious Nicolas I. In addition, Jesuits were accused of being behind an assassination attempt on Joseph I of Portugal and as a consequence expelled from all Portuguese territories (1759); in 1767 the order was banned from all of Spain for alleged subversive activity; in 1764 they were thrown out of France for alleged financial impropriety; and in 1773 the pope was prevailed upon by the Bourbon monarchs to dissolve the Society of Jesus. All this led to intense literary strife, and among the many Jesuit defenses is one of the century's most significant histories of Paraguay, Charlevoix's *Histoire du Paraguay* (1756). It is possible that Reid got his information from this work, but I am inclined to think that he got it indirectly, from Voltaire's *Essais sur les moeurs*, ch. CLIV, which is largely derivative from Charlevoix and contains the specific points mentioned by Reid here (*Oeuvres*, 23:186–187). Reid would presumably also have been aware of Voltaire's use of the Paraguayan Jesuits in *Candide*, chs. 14–15. Certainly Reid's attitude was influenced by his idol Montesquieu's enthusiastic description of the Paraguayan esperiment in *The Spirit of the Laws*, IV.6 (pp. 35–36), and only lightly tempered ("mild *but despotick*") by the controversy over the Jesuits that broke out a few years after Montesquieu wrote, and perhaps by the less than rosy account of the reductions in Bougainville's *Voyage Round the World*, ch. VII (this also mentions the payment of a piaster per Indian, p. 98, and provides an account of the eviction of the Jesuits). The actual influence of More's and other utopian writings has been a matter of much dispute; for a modern assessment, see Mörner, *The Political and Economic Activities of the Jesuits*. Useful contemporary summaries are to be found in *L'Encyclopédie*, "Jésuits" (8:512–516) and "Paraguay" (12:900–902), which Reid may or may not have consulted.

13. 1 Tim.6:10. On greed and riches, see also More, *Utopia*, pp. 139 and 241–243.

14. See More, *Utopia*, pp. 139 and 243–245.

15. Reid's criticism of existing property-relations is bound to have been influenced by that of his friend and successor at King's College, William Ogilvie, in *Right of Property in Land*, part I, sec. iii. See the Introduction above, at p. 81 n. 125. The appropriate scale on which to measure the degree of radicalism concerning property in Reid's utopian scheme is provided by, on the one hand, Thomas Spence's extreme redistributive plan in *The Rights of Man* and, on the other hand, the moderate proposals of Ogilvie, *Right of Property*, part II, or Paine in part II of *Rights of Man* and in *Agrarian Justice*.

16. Prov. 22:6.

17. See More, *Utopia*, pp. 125, 159, and 229.

18. E.g., More, *Utopia*, pp. 69–71 and 133–135.

19. See More, *Utopia*, p. 153.

20. See More, *Utopia*, p. 191.

21. See More, *Utopia*, pp. 147–151.

22. For the well-known utopian dislike of law, lawyers, and lawsuits, see More, *Utopia*, pp. 195 and 105. If Reid read Godwin's *Political Justice*, which was published two years before this paper was presented, he would have found much to agree with on this point; see esp. *Political Justice*, pp. 544–545 and book VII, ch. 8.

23. See Charles Macklin, "the law is a sort of hocus-pocus science, that smiles in yeer face while it pecks yeer pocket: and the glorious uncertainty of it is of mair use till the professors than the justice of it" (*Love à la Mode*, p. 72). For the Scottish attention paid to this interesting portrait of the Scotsman in London, see, e.g., the anonymous pamphlet, *A Scotsman's Remarks on the Farce of Love à la Mode*.

24. 1 Tim. 2:2.

Textual Notes

BY KNUD HAAKONSSEN

I. Introductory Lecture

103 *MS. 2131/7/V/4: Nine folios, paginated from p. 2 to p. 17; fol. 1 is unnumbered recto (r) and fol. 9 verso (v) is blank. MS. 2131/4/I/27: One folio, apparently detached from 7/V/4, carrying recto some canceled formulations of points belonging here and, verso, two marked insertions for 7/V/4.*

103/12– All human . . . not.] All the Objects of Human Knowledge
104/16 may be comprehended under two General Heads BODY & MIND, Things material & things intellectual. about one or other of these Objects or things pertaining to them all Sciences treat, all Arts are occupied all human Thoughts and designs are employed. The whole System of Bodies in the Universe of which we know but a very small Part is called the Material World & the whole System of Minds in the Universe from the infinite Creator of all things down to the meanest creature endowed with Thought may be called and has been called the Intellectual world. To determine positively that every Being in the Universe must belong to one or other of these Classes; that every thing that exists must either be extended solid and inert; or else that it must be thinking and intelligent, would perhaps be rash and presumptuous. There seems to be a vast interval between Body and Mind, and who can affirm that there can be nothing intermediate. We may indeed affirm that every thing which exists must be either material, or immaterial; for between these there can be no middle Nature. But it is not so evident that whatever is not material must be endowed with thought & intelligence. Is there not Reason to think that in Plants there is something more than inert Matter? Yet we have no Reason to ascribe to them Intelligence, thought or even Sensation. May there not possibly be in the Universe some immaterial Machinery (if we may Use that Expression) by which the Laws of Nature contrived by the Supreme Wisdom are put in Execution. It is highly probable that the Laws of Gravitation, Cohesion, Magnetism, & the other Laws of the Material System cannot possibly result from any Material Machinery whatsoever. Whether therefore those Laws of Nature having been at first contrived by the Supreme Wisdom, are now put in

Execution by the constant Energy of some Intellectual Being, or whether by some immaterial Machinery, if we may use that Expression, seems to be beyond the reach of our weak Comprehension. It becomes us ingenuously to confess our Ignorance in this Matter & to rest satisfied with this That although there may be for ought we know Beings which are neither Material, nor endowed with thought, yet if there be any such, they are Beings of which we have no knowledge nor can form any Conception. They are not discoverable by any of the Faculties God hath given to us, and therefore with Regard to us are as if they were not. We have no Means of acquiring any Knowledge or as much as of forming any Conjecture concerning them. (4/I/27, fol. 1r)] all the Beings or Substances in the Universe of which our Faculties give us any Intelligence may be reduced to these two classes, of Bodies, and Minds or Spirits. It would perhaps be too presumptuous to say that all Beings in the Universe belong to one or the other of these Classes. There may for any thing we know be in the Universe Beings of a different kind from both. If there be any such they are Beings of which we have no Knowledge nor can form any Conception. They are not discoverable by any of the Faculties which God hath given to us, and therefore with regard to us are as if they were not. We have no means of acquiring any Knowledge or so much as of forming any Conjecture concerning them. (7/V/ 4,1).

103/19– pertaining ... occupied.] belonging to them all Sciences
20   treat, all Arts are occupied, all human thoughts and designs are employed.

103/21– to which ... limited] and all that falls within our Knowl-
22   edge belongs to one or the other.

103/24   other ... being] things of an Intermediate Nature

103/25   is] is perhaps

103/27   is indeed] seems to be

103/31   in] employed in

103/34   &] & one word illegible.

104/3   conjectured] thought

104/5   intelligent] Intellectual

104/6   conjectured] thought

104/6–7 in ... Beings] unintelligent Natures in the Universe

104/25   What ... Minds] What a variety of thinking beings or Minds there are throughout this vast Universe we cannot pretend to say. We inhabit but a little Corner of God's Dominion. The Globe which we inhabit is onely one of six Planets that encircle our Sun. What various orders of Beings and with what faculties endowed may inhabit the other five, their Sattelites and the Comets belonging to our System? How many other Suns may be encircled with like Systems? These are things altogether hid from us and which we have no means of knowing.

105/6   therefore] *alternate* then
105/32   State.] State. Most Systems of Pneumatology begin with en-
         quiring Whether the mind be material or immaterial,
         whether mortal or immortal, and afterwards enter into an
         examination of its faculties. But this is certainly a prepos-
         terous order because all that our Reason can discover con-
         cerning the Nature and duration of the Mind must be de-
         duced from the Nature of its powers and Faculties. The
         operations of our Minds are known immediately because
         we are conscious of them. We reason from its operations
         and faculties to its nature and duration but not the con-
         trary way. The natural and scientific order in treating of
         the Mind therefore is to explain its Powers & Faculties.
106/20   General Prejudices] bugbears
106/28   Sister] Brother
107/9–   of . . . Sciences] upon which they must be built
10
107/10   in . . . Nature] there, if any where
107/12   wrong & mistaken] false
108/26   Mind] Being and the duty we owe to him
109/23   low] base
109/38   Second] Third
110/23– the . . . him] as he ought to act
24
111/5–   were . . . Man] were it not that
6
111/37   Pneumatology] the Powers of the human Mind
113/22   Nature. *A horizontal stroke divides the page after this line.*
116/11– are . . . of] may be framed in a
12

II. DUTIES TO GOD

117   *MS. 2131/8/IV/2: Six folios of varying sizes incompletely pagi-*
         nated 1 to 5, the sequence of the rest indicated in other ways.
117/21– our . . . Creatures] his being and his presence with us, and
22   in all parts of his Wide Extended Dominion

118/30 2. *There is no preceding No. 1 but No. 3 follows at 119/23.*

118/38 moderate] lessen

123/3   Teacher. *Reid here adds a reference to a marginal note on fol. 2v, printed above at 120/39–121/18,* In . . . God.

123/35 some Men] many

124/9   father . . . heaven] the father of his Spirit

III. DUTIES TO OURSELVES

127   *MS. 2131/8/IV/2: Those are the remaining passages of the manuscript described above at the textual notes for p. 117. MS. 2131/8/IV/3: Four folios incompletely paginated 1 to 5, the sequence of the rest indicated in other ways.*

127/19 taught us] represented

127/24 his industry] Culture

128/14– from . . . Nature] in quest of Shells and Butterflies
15

128/32 low & humble] mean

128/34 has . . . employment] is meanly employed

128/43– employed . . . Station] tho' meanly employed
44

129/11– on . . . man] are mean
12

129/29 Mar . . . 1766. *The date is in the upper left-hand corner and is probably a later addition.*

130/30 Purposes.] Purposes. Candor & Impartiality in Opinion.

130/32 Inconstancy.] Inconstancy. Excessive Desire

132/6   Fortitude. *The following brief discussion of fortitude occurs below a horizontal line on fol. 3v of the present manuscript; the preceding text on that page ended at 123/23 above. Reid has given no indication where the present section is to be placed. He does, however, invariably mention the three virtues that constitute the duty to ourselves, in the order, prudence, temperance, fortitude; and in the retrospect of the subject, at 133/1ff. below, this is also his order of presentation. There is thus good warrant for the arrangement chosen here.*

132/19 Sesostris of] Alexander of

132/20 Gengiskan of] Hannibal Scipio & Caesar of

132/23 therefore in] the Nature of

135/26 Opinion] breath

137/23 *The lower half of fol. 3r and fol. 3v are blank, thus separating the preceding discussion of duties to ourselves from the remaining one-and-a-half pages of text, which are printed in the following section.*

IV. DUTIES TO OTHERS: JUSTICE

138   *MS. 2131/8/IV/3: Those are the remaining passages of the manuscript described at the textual notes for p. 127.*

138/24 fair dealing] fairness

V. DUTIES TO OTHERS: INDIVIDUALS IN PRIVATE JURISPRUDENCE

140   *MS. 2131/8/IV/1: Four folios incompletely paginated 1 to 4. MS. 2131/8/IV/5: Two folios. MS. 2131/8/III/2: Two folios. MS. 2131/8/IV/7: Four folios. MS. 2131/4/III/4: Two folios. MS. 2131/4/III/17: Three folios of which fol. 2v is blank.*

142/22 Romanum.] Romanum. Or with Nature or Nations

142/24 Law.] Law. Jus Naturae the Law of Nature that is the Body or System

143/22 Honestum. *Reid instructs,* see A pages 4, 5, *thus referring forward to fol. 3v and fol. 4r (144/17 to 145/1,* In . . . external.)

143/15 implementing] *alternate* fullfilling

144/13 have. *The sentence breaks off here. There follows a canceled passage.* In treating of the principles of morals in General We have considered Right and wrong as qualities of Actions which make them the just object of approbation or disapprobation.

145/27 in] in corpore

145/42– Justinians . . . Nec M. *These definitions appear in the margin*
146/4   *and their position in the manuscript is conjectural.*

146/6   (see . . . ⟨them⟩). *This is a superscribed insertion and the brackets have been editorially added.*

146/38 signifying that] expressing

146/40 actions] duties

147/14– Another . . . Common. *Marginal note whose position is conjec-*
15   *tural.*

147/20– of . . . Suicide. *Marginal note whose position is conjectural.*
21

148/3– Cautions . . . tribuatur. *Marginal note whose position is conjec-*
10   *tural.*

149/10   ⟨as⟩] an

152/39–   Prosperous . . . purchase. *This line appears as a superscription*
41   *between* to *and* lead *in line 37. After* Land holders *in line 39,*
          Reid has instructed himself to turn over *to fol. 2v, where he*
          deals with the third general criticism of entailing—namely, that it
          is in conflict with the law of nature. This instruction was neces-
          sary because he already, at the bottom of fol. 2r, after leaving a
          small gap, had begun the next topic: pledges and mortgages. The
          situation is further complicated by his (probably later) insertion of
          a few lines between Land holders *and* Pledges, *and to these*
          lines he again added a marginal note and gave the whole addi-
          tion the number 5. This plainly means point no. 5 in his second
          general criticism of entails—namely, that they are harmful to the
          public.

153/35   are. *A horizontal line indicates the end of the third and final*
          criticism of entails. Before going on to the final paragraph on fol.
          2v, Reid must have turned over recto to the last two kinds of
          partial property.

155/16   with] to

155/26   with] to

155/36   Void. *A space of some three lines intervenes, and the next para-*
          graph appears to be a later addition.

158/22–   made . . . signs] naturally expressive
23

158/41–   man is . . . degree] man thinks himself highly dishonoured
42

158/42   is . . . and] grievously affronted and

159/32   Backbiting. *Reading is conjectural. The following word is illegi-*
          ble.

159/36   Speaker. *The transition to a new topic is indicated by a gap of*
          some three lines.

161/12   others] *alternate* his neighbours

162/3   was . . . of] belonged to

162/32–   It . . . of no] There can be no
33

162/40   measured. *Reid directs* Insert A. *There is no insertion marked*
          A in the present manuscript, but in view of the fact that Reid, as
          he has just pointed out, is moving on the borderline between juris-
          prudence and politics, it is not surprising to find this insertion as
          part of his economics lectures in the course on politics. It may
          well be that he not only used this passage from his economics lec-
          tures in his jurisprudence course but that he also used the present
          lecture on price in the economics lectures and that it is therefore

Reid himself who has lifted 4/III/4 from his original notebook (see textual note to p. 140 above). This gives a clue to another puzzle. The lecture Of the Price of Things *is dated 25 March; the same date is given for the following lecture on* Contracts *(p. 166 below). If Reid, as I think, entered some of the dates for his 1765 lectures after he had written (and presumably delivered) them, and if the lecture of Monday 25 March on price had already been removed by the time he dated the subsequent one, then it is readily understandable that this was given the same date and that, as we shall see (166/25), he was led to correct the subsequent dates.*

163/13   Since therefore] It might seem therefore that
163/28   such Maxims] them
164/2   quicksighted] sharp
164/32   particular] certain
164/32   professions] professions of Life
166/6–   These … fineness. *This marginal addition plainly belongs*
9   *here, although Reid in fact has placed the appropriate insertion sign after* Value *in l. 6.*

166/25   Mar 26. *The number 6 has been inscribed over 7 in the date, and similar emendations govern the two succeeding dates; hence* Mar 28 *becomes* Mar 27 *and* Mar 29 *becomes* Mar 28 *(ll. 35 and 167/1.) For the likely explanation of this, see the textual note to 162/40.*

166/26–   2 Onerous … Interpretation. *These lines consist in part of*
33   *dense superscriptions that, because of lack of space, present the points in an impossible order, if taken literally. I have reorganized the material in accordance with the standard order of presentation in Pufendorf and Hutcheson. In the process, one confusing comma in front of* Wagers *in l. 31 has had to be canceled.*

167/34   peace] good
168/24   gentle forbearing] gentleness forbearance
169/6–   continuo … faemina. *This has in fact been lined out.*
7
169/40   kind. *Below this line follows a blank space of some five lines.*

VI. Duties to Others: Individuals in Oeconomical Jurisprudence

170   *MS. 2131/8/IV/7: The remaining passages of the manuscript, described above at the textual notes for p. 140.*

171/19   Grounds] *alternate* Foundation] Original

VII. Duties to Others: Individuals in Political Jurisprudence

173   *MS. 2131/8/IV/10: Four folios.*
173/11   There. *This and the following paragraph (l. 22) are marked* A *and* B, *respectively, for insertion in the corresponding lecture in the following year, 1766. See below at 246/30 and 247/14.*
177/16   that] that respect and
178/4   Apr 12. *There is a gap of a few lines between this and the following marginal date. Apr 12 is in fact written opposite the preceding list of thinkers, whose ideas presumably were explained on that day.*
178/18   which . . . hold] which merits Approbation
178/37– Material] Planetary
38
179/7   notions] System

VIII. Duties to Others: States

182   *MS. 2131/7/VII/21: Two folios containing text on fol. 1r and one-third of fol. 1v.*
182/14   The. *A marginal* N *and a stroke of the pen single out the rest of this paragraph and the first Cicero quotation (l. 27–31) for use in the corresponding lecture in 1766. See pp. 368–369, n. 9, and the textual note at 255/6–23.*
183/2   colunto. *A gap of a few lines below this line indicate the transition to the topic of the morality of war.*
183/11   inhuman] criminal

IX. Supplement to Duties to Ourselves

184   *MS. 2131/7/VII/8: Four folios of which only fol. 1 carries text recto and verso. MS. 2131/7/V/5: Six folios; fol. 2v, most of fol. 3v, the lower half of 5r and fol. 6r and v are blank; fol. 1, fol. 2r and a couple of lines on fol. 3 deal with axioms in practical ethics (cf. A.P., pp. 637–640), while the text on fol. 4 appears under the heading* Estimate of the Goods and Evils of Life

and is a precursor of A.P., pp. 580a–586a, where Reid also touches upon the cardinal virtues (cf. p. 311 above, n. 1). The brief treatment of the virtues on fol. 5r and v is not, however, tied in with the rest of the discussion in this manuscript, but has the character of fragmentary notes that are best read in the light of the more substantial manuscripts printed in this section and in Section III above.

187/1   or] and

X. NATURAL LAW AND NATURAL RIGHTS

188   *MS. 2131/7/V/3: Two folios; only fol. 1r and the upper half of fol. 1v carry text. MS. 2131/7/VII/1: Three folios; only fol. 1r and the upper half of fol. 1v carry text. MS. 2131/8/IV/4: Two folios; only fol. 1r and the upper half of fol. 1v carry text. MS. 2131/7/VII/1a: Two folios; the text ends one-third down at fol. 2v. MS. 2131/7/VII/1c: Two folios evidently used at various times for five notes on and sketches of widely different points in jurisprudence: (1) fol. 1r and the first six lines of fol. 2r deal with property in terms of an analogy. (2) The rest of fol. 2r and the first sixteen lines of fol. 1v deal with the basic relationship between right and obligation. (3) The third note takes up the middle of fol. 1v and deals with various disputed points in jurisprudence concerning sovereignty and its exercise. (4) A short horizontal line separates the last note on fol. 1v, which gives some afterthoughts on property. (5) Finally fol. 2v, which is dated* 1770 *March and is likely to be later than any of the previous notes, presents yet another attempt to get a clear view of the various distinctions of rights. It would serve little purpose to print these notes together, but when they are put in their separate contexts they are of value. Notes 2 and 5 are placed here together with 7/VII/1a. Notes 1 and 4 are in Section XI, below, and note 3 is in Section XVII, n. 158, p. 441. MS. 2131/7/VII/1b: Two folios; the text ends one-third down fol. 2r. The first half of fol. 1r is closely related to the drafts of A.P., essay V, ch. 5 and is therefore not included here; see the Introduction above, p. 88.*

188/17   locum habent] obtinent
189/23–   *The English translation inserted here is the editor's.*
190/35
192/37   an . . . thing] a bad thing
194/16   the . . . who] him that
194/18   many] innumerable

194/38   Parent] Parents
194/38   Child] Children
194/35–   who . . . be] perhaps who are innocents are
36
195/36   it] the injured committed
196/41   treat of] treat of these
196/41–   of individuals . . . Nations] which result from the Nature
42   of Man and from the
197/22   Reasons. *A short horizontal stroke of the pen appears above this line.*
199/34   Distinguished] divided
199/37   (General Absolute). *This is a superscribed addition, and the brackets have been editorially added.*
199/38   (Special Hypothetical). *This is a superscribed addition, and the brackets have been editorially added.*
199/42   Source] Origin
200/24   human. *A short superscribed phrase in front of* human *is illegible. It may be* a Man
200/25   he] a man
200/40   they] he
200/40   are . . . State. *This is a superscribed correction or alternate to the following phrase,* has . . . Community. *Reid has failed either to delete the latter or to adjust it to the previous change from* he *to* they
202/17–   Delineation] knowledge
18

XI. PROPERTY

204   *MS. 2131/7/VII/1c: See the textual note at 188 above. MS. 2131/7/VII/11: Two folios; fol. 2r is blank, and the notes verso are more appropriately placed as insertions in 7/VII/13 (see 208/27 below). MS 2131/7/VII/13: Three folios; fol. 2v and fol. 3 are blank.*
205/22   Naming] Goods at his Death disposed by will Naming
206/5–6   Adventitious] Acquired] Adventitious *(On both occasions).*
206/7   Adventitious] Acquired] Adventitious
206/7   original] original which are either Real or personal
206/39   1. *This numbering is not followed up.*
208/25–   Division . . . Corresponding. *A cross-like marginal sign at the beginning and an asterisk at the end of this passage refer to two paragraphs similarly marked on 7/VII/11, fol. 2v. In my opinion,*
27

Reid first made the asterisked note, which takes up the first half of the insertion and concerns the distinction between external and internal rights, thus adding a new topic to the ones dealt with in 7/VII/13. He then apparently decided to expand upon the topic mentioned here in passing—namely, the distinction between perfect and imperfect rights—and this constitutes the cross-marked second half of the insertion. Only this assumption makes the arrangement of the insertion intelligible, and it conforms with the arrangement in Hutcheson, "Short Introduction," pp. 122–123, and "System," 1:257–260, as well as in Reid's text above at pp. 201ff. I here print the insertions in this presumed order (208/28–44 and 209/ 1–30) rather than according to the arrangement on the manuscript page.

208/34   bestow] yield

209/4   Ex Gr. *Presumably Reid was abbreviating* exempli gratia—*i.e., for instance.*

209/17   yet] yet. *The full stop may have been intended in front of* yet

209/42–   either . . . imperfect. *This passage is superscribed; in doing so,*
43   *Reid must have forgotten that he already had specified* perfect

210/6–   6 . . . Testimony. *This is a later addition, hence (presumably)*
8   *the inconsistent numbering.*

210/34   must . . . Minors. *This phrase is superscribed.*

211/35   3] 3 from the End of God in giving this Faculty

XII. SUCCESSION

213   *MS. 2131/7/VII/12: Three folios; only fol. 1r and part of fol.
          1v carry text.*

213/23   fit] proper

XIII. ON DISSOLUTION OF OBLIGATIONS
AND ON INTERPRETATION

215   *MS. 2131/7/VII/25: Four folios; only fol. 1r has a text that is
          divided into three sections by two inch-long horizontal lines, one
          above* Of Interpretation *(215/18) and one above* Of the Colli-
          sion of Laws *(216/24).*

216/28–   an . . . Justice] to Charity. *In canceling* Charity, *it appears*
29   *that* to *has been crossed out inadvertently; I have restored it.*

XIV. Oeconomical Jurisprudence

217 *MS. 2131/7/VII/15: Two folios; the lower half of fol. 2r and fol. 2v are blank. MS. 2131/7/VII/17–19: One folio plus two folios plus three folios, which form one continuous text. 7/VII/19, fol. 1v is only two-thirds full of text, fol. 2r is only half full, and fol. 3v and fol. 4 are blank. MS. 2131/7/VII/20: Four folios; the text ends seven lines down fol. 4v.*

219/9 *so. Undoubtedly see was intended.*

219/39 First. *This is followed by 2 (221/5) and 3 (222/27). These seem clearly to be later additions made to underline the structure of the material.*

219/39– First . . . Parental. *The following note is written vertically in the*
220/38 *extreme left-hand margin along the full length of 7/VII/17, fol. 1r.* To This Shedule ought to be prefixed some general Observations upon the Oeconomy of Nature in the propagation of Animals . *That Reid did make such observations is shown by the preceding manuscript, 7/VII/15.*

220/5 must] behoved to

220/6 must] behoved to

221/11– friendship] attachment
12

221/13 seduce] gain

221/29 broke down] overcome

221/33– All . . . Nations. *This is a marginal note written vertically over*
35 *the full length of the page. There is an insertion sign in the margin at 2 (221/5) above. But since the note does not fit with the first sentence of that paragraph, since the insertion sign may point to the paragraph as a whole, and since the note obviously fits the present place, I have ventured to print it here. Alongside this note there is another disconnected one* The Education of Men is a Long work . *Although this has not been canceled, I do not insert it in the text of fol. 1v, where it is well nigh impossible to find a sensible place for it. I believe that Reid mistook the verso for the recto side of the folio when he added this note; discovered his error, but did not cross out his false start, and turned to the recto side where he wanted to insert what is now 220/7–8* Man . . . Work.

221/38 this . . . Sex] the Idea annexed to this Word

222/38– of . . . in] which are indicated as we conceive by
39

222/42 concern . . . the] desire of

222/43 of . . . Love] to please and

223/1–2 Every . . . merit] and a strong ambition of meriting

223/10   among] between
223/30   principle] affection
224/25   guidance] direction
225/28   they believe] is believed
226/4   13] twelve
226/5   14] 13
226/38   or] *one word illegible after* or
227/20   authorised] permitted
227/20   authorised.] authorised. And by the Laws of Cecrops it ap-
          pears to have been prohibited among the Athenians
228/29   perused. *The transition to a new topic is signaled by leaving the
          last quarter of fol. 2v blank.*
229/11   Being] It is manifestly the Intention of the Supreme being
          that mankind should be propagated by Generation and he
          hath in the human Constitution made sufficient provision
          for the continuance of the Race to the End of the World.
          The long infancy and helpless State of Children requires
          the care of both parents to provide for and to rear them.
          And the Author of Nature hath implanted the Parental
          Affection in Parents for this very Purpose. That Modesty
          which is a part of the human frame, is intended by Na-
          ture to Bridle our animal appetites.
229/43   in substance] substantially
230/16   commonly] often
230/18   trouble. *A short horizontal stroke appears below the paragraph
          ending here.*
230/39   siet. *A short horizontal line separates the verse ending here from
          the following one.*
232/15   profitable] necessary
232/29   giddy. *A gap of some five lines follows.*
233/7   Apr . . . 1770. *This date appears in the upper right-hand corner
          immediately above the subsequent paragraph, which has been writ-
          ten along the right-hand margin. I presume that the dating per-
          tains to the note only, but it could be of the entire fol. 2v.*
233/41   good Conduct] other virtues
234/33   permit] allow

XV. SOCIAL CONTRACT
AS IMPLIED CONTRACT

237   *MS. 2131/2/III/10: Four folios.*
237/1   The . . . is That] The word Contract is like many others
          taken sometimes in a larger sometimes in a more con-

strained sense. The common definition That

237/2   given] entered into
237/21   moved] proposed
238/14   an Indenture] a deed upon
239/10— do . . . duty] the office
11
240/7   violated] invaded
240/18   committed] were guilty of
243/19   taking. *On turning to the last page of the manuscript, Reid apparently found that he had already scribbled some notes at the top of the page. He accordingly drew a line under them and continued the present text below it. I print the notes from the top of fol. 4v at the end of this section at 244/18–32 below.*
243/23   aliens] foreigners
244/20   Obligation] voluntary deed by
244/21   voluntarly] an obligation

XVI. POLITICAL JURISPRUDENCE

245   *MS. 2131/8/IV/9: Four folios.*
245/10   publica] publica. The Rights & obligations arising from this State are either Such as belong to the whole State as one Body or such as belong to the particular Parts of which the State is composed, which are chiefly Rulers and Subjects.
245/22   enquire:] enquire what ought to be the Conduct towards other States whether in peace or in War
246/12   which] as
246/30— There . . . cause. *See above at 173/11.*
40
247/14— If . . . Neighbours. *See above at 173/11.*
39
253/18   give. *Presumably "take" was intended.*

XVII. RIGHTS AND DUTIES OF STATES

254   *MS. 2131/8/IV/9, continued (see above at p. 245). MS. 2131/7/ VII/23: Four folios; fol. 4 is blank recto. The composition of this manuscript is complicated, and it is impossible to be entirely certain of the proper order of its elements. The manuscript begins in the middle of a discussion of established religion, the beginning of*

which is in the preceding manuscript, 8/IV/9, though it is impossible to say whether the two manuscripts originally were one. Following the few clues given by Reid and the sense of the material, I have organized the text as follows: (1) Established religion from 257/14 As to *258/24* animus *; (2) internal self-government from 258/25* Whether *to 262/70* individuals *; (3) relations between states from 262/13* Behaviour *to 263/23* Nature *; (4) war from 263/24* War *to 264/18* Jurisprudence. MS. *2131/8/ IV/8: Originally two folios; apparently two-thirds of one of them have been cut off vertically, the other third appearing as an extra wide margin of the remaining folio. This flap is full of marginal addenda. The main text ends verso in the middle. The manuscript is dated 2 May 1766; the previous date we have for that year is 24 April (245/2). While the latter contains so much material that it must have taken Reid most of the following week to get through it, there is clearly something missing between this and the present manuscript, as we see from the recapitulation in the opening lines (264/22ff.). This gap may originally have been filled by the brief, undated 7/VII/22 (268/10–43), while Reid a year later decided to expand this material and hence inserted 7/VII/23, just as I have done here (257/14–264/18). MS. 2131/7/VII/22: One folio inscribed only recto. MS. 2131/3/II/5: Two folios. Fol. 1 is recto dated* September 1766 *and taken up by notes from Reid's study of Herbert of Cherbury's "De veritate," which have no direct relevance to the present volume. MS. 2131/4/III/23c: Two folios; the text ends two-thirds down fol. 2v. This manuscript originally formed the middle part of the preceding manuscript, 3/II/5. This is obscured because the two leaves of the present manuscript, as preserved, have been folded over the wrong way. I have corrected this in the printing and numbering. Fol. 2 contains reading notes of no relevance here, and I have not printed it.*

255/3   each others Rights] Rights of other States as in. *In making this correction Reid apparently failed to cancel* the *in front of* each.

255/6–   The . . . posse. *See the textual notes above at 182/14; and the*
23   *Commentary at p. 368, n. 9, and p. 419, n. 2. See also the textual note at 273/5.*

256/30–   Rites . . . and] Service we pay to him and
31

257/36   differ] not agree

259/15   due to] Service of. *Reid appears to have overlooked* at the *in front of the cancellation.*

261/12   Inheritance] blood

262/17   Enlarge. *This is a superscribed self-instruction.*

273/5–   Though . . . posse. *These paragraphs are marked by an* A *and*
26   *a line in the margin for the cross-reference in 8/IV/9, fol. 4r; see*
         the textual note at 255/6-23 above.

273/43– When . . . Fide. *These paragraphs are marked by a* B *and a*
274/19   *line in the margin; see the Commentary at p. 434, n. 63.*

275/13– Ambassadours. *Under this line appears a short horizontal*
14   *stroke, marking the return to the third book of Vattel.*

275/20   obtaining . . . a] vindicating

275/20   Right] Right of the State

XVIII. SOME THOUGHTS ON
THE UTOPIAN SYSTEM

277   *AUL MS. 3061/6: Fourteen folios paginated recto and verso*
         from 1 to 27. The first pages, 277/2 to 280/35, and the final
         paragraph, 298/41 to 299/20, were published in the "Glasgow
         Courier" on 18 December 1794 under the title "Danger of Politi-
         cal Innovation" (henceforth referred to as GC), and reprinted in
         Appendix II to Arthur, "Discourses," pp. 518–523, under the
         heading "Observations on the Danger of Political Innovation,
         from a Discourse delivered on 28th November 1794, before the
         Literary Society in Glasgow College, by Dr. Reid, and published
         by his consent" (henceforth A). The manuscript has been collated
         with the two partial publications, except for spelling and punctua-
         tion.

277/7   Question. *Deleted in GC and A.*

277/13   attempt] attempt,

279/7   the one] one *in GC and A.*

279/12   upon] on *in GC and A.*

279/16   or] and *in GC and A.*

279/33   Offices] Officers *in A.*

280/12   intended and. *Deleted in GC and A.*

280/35   Nation;] Nation. *in GC and A, both of which then jump to*
         298/41, and both of which appear to indicate the exclusion of
         material by two lengthy dashes.

282/18   are] being

282/19   and] they

283/43   we . . . call] is

285/2   would . . . prove] assume

285/4   any] the

286/18   but] than

286/19   it . . . a] a
291/36   Substantial] proper
293/13   such] these
297/18–   that . . . Nature] what
19
298/18   leaves . . . for] gives no opportunity to the Exercise of
298/25–   When . . . Case] In this Case
26
298/26   does his] may do his
299/19–   lead . . . Honesty] "lead . . . Honesty" *in GC and A.*
20

Bibliographic Index

This Bibliographic Index lists the authorities cited in the Introduction, Reid's text, the Commentary, and the Textual Notes. In the entries for Reid's text, the page numbers are set in italics.

AMBROSE of Milan
De sacramentis. In his *Des sacremens*; *Des mystères*, nouv. éd. . . . par B. Botte. Sources chrétiennes 25. Paris, 1961.
312 n. 1

ANONYMOUS
A Scotchman's Remark on The Farce of Love à la Mode. London, 1760.
445 n. 23
Notes from the Lectures of Dr. Reid, 1766–1767. Aberdeen University Library, Birkwood Collection, MS. 8/VII.
Sketch of the Character of the Late Thomas Reid, D.D., Professor of Moral Philosophy in the University of Glasgow. Glasgow, 1796.
6 n. 1
A Vindication of the Proceedings of the Convention of the Estates in Scotland. Reprinted in *A Collection of State Tracts, Publish'd on Occasion of the Late Revolution in 1688 and during the Reign of King William III*, 3:441–465. London, 1705–7.
413 n. 8
Vox populi vox Dei: Being True Maxims of Government. . . . London, 1709.
416 n. 14

AQUINAS, Thomas. See THOMAS Aquinas.

ARATUS of Soli
Phaenomena. In *Callimachus and Lycophron*, with an English translation by A. W. Mair, and *Aratus*, with an English translation by G.R. Mair. Loeb Classical Library. New York and London, 1921.
306 n. 5

ARISTOTLE
Complete Works. Revised Oxford translation, edited by J. Barnes. 2 vols. Bollingen Series 71, 1–2. Princeton, 1984.
Nicomachean Ethics. Translated by W. D. Ross. Revised by J. O. Urmson. In *Complete Works*, vol. 2.
311 n. 1; 314–315 nn. 1–2; 319 n. 19
The Politics. Translated with an introduction, notes, and appendixes by Ernest Barker. Oxford, 1946.

311 n. 1; 321 n. 25; 399 nn. 38–39
Rhetoric. Translated by W. Rhys Roberts. In *Complete Works*, vol. 2.
311 n. 1

ARMYTAGE, W. H. G.
"David Fordyce: A Neglected Thinker." *Aberdeen University Review*
36 (1956): 289–291.
11 n. 19

ARRIANUS
"The *Encheiridion* of Epictetus." In Epictetus, *The Discourses, as Reported by Arrian, the Manual and Fragments*, with an English translation by W. A. Oldfather, 2:482–537. Loeb Classical Library. Cambridge, Mass., and London, 1926–28.
11–12 n. 23; 305 n. 3; 307–308 n. 10; 378 n. 2

ARTHUR, Archibald
Discourses on Theological and Literary Subjects. With an account of some particulars in [Arthur's] life and character by William Richardson. Glasgow, 1803.
33 n. 94; 84 n. 37; 464

ATHENAEUS of Naucratis
The Deipnosophists. With an English translation by C. B. Gulick. Vol. 6. Loeb Classical Library. Cambridge, Mass., and London, 1937.
393 n. 6; 396 n. 14

ATTERBURY, Francis
Sermons and Discourses on Several Subjects and Occasions. 2 vols. London, 1730.
416 n. 14

⟨ATTERBURY, Francis⟩
The Voice of the People No Voice of God. . . . London, 1740.
416 n. 14

AUGUSTINUS, Aurelius (Bishop of Hippo)
The City of God against the Pagans. With an English translation by W. C. Green, W. M. Green, P. Levine, G. E. McCracken, E. M. Sanford, and D. S. Wiesen. 7 vols. Loeb Classical Library. Cambridge, Mass., and London, 1957–72.
312 n. 1; 315 n. 3
On the Morals of the Christian Church. Translated by R. Stothert. In *Basic Writings*, 2 vols., edited with introduction and notes by W. J. Oates, Vol. 1. New York, 1948.
312 n. 1

AURELIUS, Marcus
The Meditations. . . . Edited with translation and commentary by A. S. L. Farquharson. 2 vols. Oxford, 1949.
308 n. 10
The Meditations. . . . Translation and notes by Francis Hutcheson and James Moor, books I–II. Glasgow, 1742.
308 n. 10; 316 n. 6

BACON, Francis (Viscount St. Albans)
The Essayes, or Counsells Civill and Morall. . . . Newly enlarged edition. London, 1639.
421 n. 11

BAIRD, George
Notes from the Lectures of Dr. Thomas Reid, 1779–1780. 8 vols. The Mitchell Library, Glasgow. MS. A104929.
33 n. 91; 38 n. 1; 86; 305 n. 2

BARBEYRAC, Jean
"Historical and Critical Account of the Science of Morality." In Samuel von Pufendorf, *Of the Law of Nature and Nations.* Fifth edition. London, 1749.
320 n. 22

BARCLAY, William
The Kingdom and the Regal Power. Translated by G. A. Moore. Chevy Chase, Md., 1954.
416 n. 14; 418 n. 19

BARFOOT, Michael
"James Gregory (1753–1821) and Scottish Scientific Metaphysics, 1750–1800," Ph.D. dissertation, University of Ediburgh, 1983.
23 n. 61; 33 n. 93; 44 n. 14

BARKER, S. F., and T. L. BEAUCHAMP (eds.)
Thomas Reid: Critical Interpretations. Philadelphia, 1976.
39 n. 3

BAYLE, Pierre
The Dictionary Historical and Critical. . . . Second edition by the author, revised, corrected, and enlarged by Mr. Des Maizeaux. Translated from the French. 5 vols. London, 1734–38.
421 n. 11
Miscellaneous Reflections Occasion'd by the Comet Which Appear'd in December 1680 . . . Chiefly Tending to Explode Popular Superstitions. Translated from the French. 2 vols. London, 1708.
421 n. 11

BEANBLOSSOM, Ronald
"Russell's Indebtedness to Reid." *The Monist* 61 (1978): 192–204.
35 n. 99

BELOFF, Max (ed.)
The Debate on the American Revolution, 1761–1783. Second edition. The British Political Tradition 1. London, 1960.
425–426 n. 24

BENTHAM, Jeremy
Defence of Usury. Third edition. London, 1816.
24; 65 n. 82

BIRKS, Peter, and Grant McLEOD.
"The Implied Contract Theory of Quasi-Contract: Civilian Opinion Current in the Century before Blackstone." *Oxford Journal of Legal Studies* 6 (1986): 46–85.
68 n. 87; 70 n. 97

⟨BOILEAU, Jacques⟩
Historia flagellantium. De recto et perverso flagrorum ⟨sic⟩ usu apud Christianos. . . . Paris, 1700.
422 n. 15

BOILEAU, Jacques
Histoire des Flagellans, ou l'on fait voir le bon et le mauvais usage des Flagellations parmi les Chrétiens. Amsterdam, 1732.
422 n. 15
The History of the Flagellants, or the Advantages of Discipline; being a paraphrase and commentary on the Historia Flagellantium of the Abbé Boileau, Doctor of the Sorbonne . . . By somebody who is not Doctor of the Sorbonne [J. L. de Lolme]. London, 1777.
423 n. 15

BOK, Sissela
Lying: Moral Choice in Public and Private Life. New York, 1979.
344 n. 88

BOLINGBROKE, Henry St. John (Viscount)
Remarks on the History of England. In *Works,* 5 vols., edited by D. Mallet, 1:271–534. London, 1754.
404 n. 6

BOUGAINVILLE, Lewis de
A Voyage Round the World. Performed by Order of His Most Christian Majesty, In the Years 1766, 1767, 1768, and 1769. Translated from the French by John Reinhold Forster. London, 1772.
444 n. 12

BOUTROUX, Emil
De l'influence de la philosophie écossaise. Edinburgh, 1897.
  35 n. 99

BROWNING, Reed
Political and Constitutional Ideas of the Court Whigs. Baton Rouge, La.,
  1982.
  72 n. 101

⟨BURKE, Edmund⟩
*A Philosophical Enquiry into the Origin of Our Ideas of the Sublime and
  Beautiful.* London, 1757.
  106; 303 n. 4

BURLAMAQUI, Jean Jacques
The Principles of Natural and Politic Law. Translated by T. Nugent.
  Second revised edition. 2 vols. London, 1763.
  90

BURNET, Gilbert
The History of the Reformation of the Church of England. 3 parts. Second edition (Parts 1 and 2). London, 1681–1715.
  418 n. 21

⟨BURNET, Gilbert?⟩
The Revolution Vindicated.... Reprinted in *A Collection of State
  Tracts, Publish'd on Occasion of the Late Revolution in 1688 and during the Reign of King William III*, 3:694–728. London, 1705–7.
  404 n. 8

BUTLER, Joseph
The Works.... 2 vols. Oxford, 1874:
  Vol. 1:
  *The Analogy of Religion, Natural and Revealed, to the Constitution and
  Course of Nature.*
  9–10; 17 n. 39; 42; 44; 52 n. 40
  Dissertation I. 'Of Personal Identity'
  10
  Dissertation II. 'Of the Nature of Virtue,'
  10 nn. 15, 17; 51 n. 33; 52 n. 41; 304 n. 4; 312 n. 7
  Vol. 2:
  Sermons.
  10 nn. 14–15; 369 n. 135

CAMPBELL, Archibald
An Enquiry into the Original of Moral Virtue.... Edinburgh, 1733.
  372 n. 1

CARMICHAEL, Gershom. *See* PUFENDORF, Samuel Freiherr von, *De officio.*

CHARLEVOIX, Pierre
Histoire du Paraguay. 3 vols. Paris, 1756.
444 n. 12

CHATHAM, William Pitt (1st earl of)
Speech in the Debate on the Address, House of Commons, 14 January 1766. In Max Beloff, *The Debate on the American Revolution, 1761–1783,* 2nd ed., pp. 92–96. London, 1960.
425–426 n. 24

⟨CICERO, Marcus Tullius (attributed to)⟩
Ad C. Herennium de ratione dicendi (Rhetorica ad Herennium). With an English translation by H. Caplan. Loeb Classical Library. Cambridge, Mass., and London, 1954.
311 n. 1

CICERO, Marcus Tullius
De finibus bonorum et malorum. With an English translation by H. Rackham. Loeb Classical Library. Cambridge, Mass., and London, 1971.
29; *110;* 307 n. 9; 311 n. 1; 314 n. 1; 318 n. 12; 321 n. 25; 384 n. 39
De inventione. De optimo genere oratorum. Topica. With an English translation by H. M. Hubbell. Loeb Classical Library. Cambridge, Mass., and London, 1949:
De inventione.
311 n. 1; 318 n. 12
De natura deorum. Academica. With an English translation by H. Rackham. Loeb Classical Library. Cambridge, Mass., and London, 1967:
De natura deorum.
305 n. 1; 378 n. 2
De officiis. With an English translation by W. Miller. Loeb Classical Library. Cambridge, Mass., and London, 1975.
17; *110; 148; 185;* 304 nn. 10–11; 311–316 nn. 1–6 passim; 318 n. 12; 321–322 nn. 25, 28; 340–341 nn. 70–71; 345–346 nn. 94–96; 371 n. 2; 373 n. 6; 384 n. 39; 429 n. 40; 439 n. 115
De oratore. With an English translation by E. W. Sutton. 2 vols. Loeb Classical Library. Cambridge, Mass., and London, 1979.
316 n. 2
De re publica. De legibus. With an English translation by W. Keyes.

Loeb Classical Library. Cambridge, Mass., and London, 1977: *De legibus.*
125–126; 182–183; 255; 305 n. 3; 309 n. 17; 315 n. 5; 370 nn. 3–4; 384 n. 39; 439 n. 115

Letters to Atticus. With an English translation by E. O. Winsledt. 3 vols. Loeb Classical Library. Cambridge, Mass., and London, 1913.
393 n. 2

. . . Letters to His Friends. With an English translation by W. G. Williams. 3 vols. Loeb Classical Library. Cambridge, Mass., and London, 1958.
360 n. 132

"Pro T. Annio Milone oratio." In *The Speeches.* With an English translation . . . by N. H. Watts. Loeb Classical Library. New York and London, 1931.
200–201; 376 n. 28

Scriptorum fragmenta, a Roberto Stephano, Carolo Sigonio, Andrea Patricio &c collecta . . . Leyden, 1653.
231; 396 n. 16; 398 n. 29

Tusculanae disputationes. With an English translation by J. E. King. Loeb Classical Library. Cambridge, Mass., and London, 1966.
311 n. 1; 371 n. 2; 373 n. 6

CLARKE, Samuel
A Collection of Papers, Which Passed between . . . Mr. Leibnitz, and Dr. Clarke in the Years 1715 and 1716 . . . To Which Are Added, Letters to Dr. Clarke Concerning Liberty and Necessity . . . with the Doctor's Answers . . . Also Remarks Upon . . . [Anthony Collins's] A Philosophical Inquiry Concerning Human Liberty. London, 1717.
9 n. 10

A Discourse concerning the Unchangeable Obligations of the Natural Religion, and the Truth and Certainty of the Christian Revelation. London, 1716.
305 n. 1; 314 n. 1

COCCEIUS, Heinrich von
. . . Grotius illustratus seu Commentarii ad Hugonis Grotii De jure belli ac pacis libros tres. . . . 4 vols. Bratislava, 1744.
315 n. 2

COCCEIUS, Samuel von
Introductio ad Henrici L. B. de Cocceji . . . Grotium illustratum, continens dissertationes proemiales XII in quibus principia Grotiana circa ius naturae . . . ad iustam methodum revocantur. . . . Halle, 1748.

Davie, George E.
The Social Significance of the Scottish Philosophy of Common Sense. Dow Lecture, University of Dundee. Dundee, 1973.
35 n. 99

Davis, J. C.
Utopia and the Ideal Society: A Study of English Utopian Writing, 1516–1700. Cambridge, 1981.
80 n. 124; 442 n. 6

Defoe, Daniel
A *General History of the Pyrates.* Edited by Manuel Schonhorn. London, 1972.
407 n. 10
The Life and Strange Surprizing Adventures of Robinson Crusoe, of York, Mariner . . . Written by Himself. London, 1719.
412 n. 6

Derham, William
Physico-Theology; or, A Demonstration of the Being and Attributes of God, from His Works of Creation. Boyle Lectures, 1711, 1712. London, 1713.
394 n. 11

Dickinson, H. T.
Liberty and Property: Political Ideology in Eighteenth-Century Britain. London, 1979.
72 n. 101

⟨Diderot, D., and J. le Rond d'Alembert⟩
Encyclopédie, ou dictionaire raisonné des sciences, des arts et des métiers, par une societé de gens de lettres. Vols. 8 and 12. Neufchâtel, 1765.
444 n. 12

Diogenes Laertius
Lives of Eminent Philosophers. With an English translation by W. D. Hicks. 2 vols. Loeb Classical Library. Cambridge, Mass., and London, 1925.
307 n. 9; 312 n. 1; 371 n. 2; 396 n. 14

⟨Dulany, Daniel⟩
Considerations on the Propriety of Imposing Taxes in the British Colonies for the Purpose of Raising a Revenue. . . . In *Pamphlets of the American Revolution, 1750–1776,* edited by Bernard Bailyn . . . and J. N. Ganett, vol. 1: *1750–1765.* John Harvard Library. Cambridge, Mass., 1965.
425 n. 24

⟨FORDYCE, David⟩

The Elements of Moral Philosophy. In *The Preceptor, containing a General Course of Education,* 2:241–379. London, 1748.

11 n. 19; 90; 305 n. 1; 320 n. 22; 361–362 nn. 1–4; 365 n. 9

FRASER, A. Campbell

Thomas Reid. Famous Scots Series. Edinburgh and London, 1898.

6 n. 1; 34 n. 96

⟨FREDERICK THE GREAT (King of Prussia)⟩

Military Instructions, Written by the King of Prussia for the Generals of His Army. London, 1762.

431 n. 47

New Regulations for the Prussian Infantry. Translated from the Original German Manuscript. London, 1757.

431 n. 47

Regulations for the Prussian Infantry. Translated from the German Original. London, 1754.

431 n. 47

GAIUS

. . . *Institutionum juris civilis commentarii quattuor,* or *Elements of Roman Law.* . . . With a translation and commentary by E. Poste. Third edition, revised and enlarged. Oxford, 1890.

323 n. 29

GELLIUS, Aulus

The Attic Nights. With an English translation by J. C. Rolfe. 3 vols. Loeb Classical Library. Cambridge, Mass., and London, 1927.

396 n. 14

GENTLEMAN'S MAGAZINE

The Gentleman's Magazine, or Monthly Intelligencer (London) 21 (1751): 522.

343 n. 84

GIBBON, Edward

Autobiography of Edward Gibbon, as originally edited by Lord Sheffield. With an introduction by J. B. Bury. London, 1962.

434 n. 59

The Decline and Fall of the Roman Empire. 3 vols. Chandos Library. London, n. d.

313 n. 12; 443 n. 11

GLASGOW COURIER

18 December 1794

84 n. 137; 464

GLASGOW EVENING COURANT
No. 642 (1758).
432 n. 47

GLASGOW MERCURY
No. 5, July 1791.
82 n. 131

GODWIN, William
Enquiry Concerning Political Justice, and Its Influence on Morals and Happiness. Harmondsworth, 1976.
445 n. 22

GRAVE, Selwyn A.
The Scottish Philosophy of Common Sense, Westport, Conn. , 1977.
34 n. 99; 39 n. 3

GRIFFIN-COLLARS, E.
La Philosophie écossaise du sens commun. Thomas Reid et Dugald Stewart. Brussels, 1980.
39 n. 3

GROTIUS, Hugo
De jure belli ac pacis libri tres . . . Cum annotatis auctoris . . . nec non Joann. Frid. Gronovii . . . notis . . . ex altera recensione Joannis Barbeyracii cum notulis eiusdem. . . . 2 vols. Amsterdam, 1735.
90; 336 n. 52; 359 n. 129; 396 n. 19; 399 n. 36; 429 n. 40; 430 n. 42
The Freedom of the Seas. . . . Translated with a revision of the Latin text of 1633 by Ralph van Deman Magoffin. Edited . . . by James Brown Scott. Carnegie Endowment for International Peace. New York, 1916.
327 n. 35
The Rights of War and Peace. . . . Translated into English. To which are added . . . the . . . notes of J. Barbeyrac. 3 vols. London, 1738.
314–315 nn. 1–2; 317–321 nn. 5–25 passim; 323 n. 29; 325–333 nn. 31–45 passim; 336–341 nn. 50–73 passim; 343–348 nn. 88–119 passim; 355–356 nn. 122–123; 358–359 nn. 127–128, 130; 361–367 nn. 138, 1–14 passim; 369 n. 1; 372–375 nn. 1–19 passim; 378 n. 3; 380–383 nn. 20–36 passim; 385 n. 47–393 n. 7 passim; 396 n. 14–401 n. 2 passim; 408–409 nn. 17, 3; 413–414 nn. 8, 14; 417 n. 19; 422–424 nn. 14, 19–20; 427 n. 26; 429–433 nn. 40–58 passim; 435–439 nn. 66–116 passim; 441 n. 153
True Religion Explained, And defended against the Arch-enemies thereof in these times. In six Bookes. Written in Latine by Hugo Grotius,

and now done in English for the common good. London, 1632.
378 n. 3

Haakonssen, Knud
"From Moral Philosophy to Political Economy: The Contribution of Dugald Stewart." In V. Hope, ed., *Philosophers of the Scottish Enlightenment*, pp. 211–232. Edinburgh, 1984.
85 n. 138
"Hugo Grotius and the History of Political Thought." *Political Theory* 13 (1985): 239–265.
32 n. 89
"John Millar and the Science of a Legislator." *Juridical Review*, June 1985, pp. 41–68.
22 n. 54; 81 n. 129
"Moral Philosophy and Natural Law: From the Cambridge Platonists to the Scottish Enlightenment." *Political Science* 40 (1989): 97–110.
49 n. 23
"Natural Jurisprudence in the Scottish Enlightenment: Summary of an Interpretation. " In D. N. MacCormick, ed., *Enlightenment, Rights, and Revolutions*, pp. 36–49. Aberdeen, 1989.
49 n. 23
"Natural Law and Moral Realism: The Scottish Synthesis." In *The Philosophy of the Scottish Enlightenment*, pp. 61–85. Oxford Studies in the History of Philosophy 1. Edited by M. A. Stewart. Oxford, 1989.
49 n. 23; 53 n. 44; 59 n. 57
"Natural Law and the Scottish Enlightenment." In *Man and Nature*, Proceedings of the Canadian Society for Eighteenth-Century Studies, vol. 4, pp. 47–80, edited by D. H. Jory and J. C. Stewart-Robertson. Edmonton, 1985.
32 n. 89; 59 n. 57
"Reid's Politics: A Natural Law Theory." *Reid Studies* 1 (1986): 9–27.
60 n. 61
"The Science of a Legislator in James Mackintosh's Moral Philosophy." *History of Political Thought* 5 (1984): 245–280.
82 n. 130
The Science of a Legislator: The Natural Jurisprudence of David Hume and Adam Smith. Cambridge, 1981.
61 nn. 64, 66; 62 n. 75; 68 n. 89; 79 n. 123; 81 n. 128

Harrington, James
The Political Works. . . . Edited, with an Introduction, by J. G. A. Pocock. Cambridge, 1977:

The Art of Lawgiving in Three Books
411 n. 4
Commonwealth of Oceana.
18 n. 42; 85; 394 n. 8; 404 n. 6
A Discourse upon This Saying.
394 n. 8
Pian Piano . . .
404 n. 6
The Prerogative of Popular Government.
404 n. 6

HARTLEY, David
Observations on Man, His Frame, His Duty, and His Expectations. London, 1749.
303 n. 3

HEINECCIUS, Johann Gottlieb
A Methodical System of Universal Law . . . Written in Latin . . . Translated, . . . with notes and supplements, by George Turnbull. . . . 2 vols. London, 1741.
8 n. 7; 90; 305–306 nn. 1, 4; 315 n. 3; 317 n. 7; 320–324 nn. 22, 25–26, 29; 329–331 n. 39; 337 n. 54; 339–341 nn. 60–73 passim; 348 n. 104; 351–354 nn. 110–119 passim; 359 n. 128; 361–365 nn. 1–7, 9; 367 n. 12; 372 n. 3; 374–375 nn. 8–9, 15–16; 385 n. 47; 387–389 nn. 1–7, 9; 396–400 nn. 16–42 passim; 409 nn. 3–4; 422–424 nn. 12, 19, 21, 26; 427 n. 26; 429–433 nn. 40–58 passim; 435–437 nn. 66–84 passim

HELIODORUS
An Aethiopian History. . . . Englished by Thomas Underdowne, anno 1587 with an introduction by Charles Whibley. London, 1895.
315 n. 3; 341 n. 71

HERODOTUS
[*The Histories.*] With an English translation by A. D. Godley. 4 vols. Loeb Classical Library. New York and London, 1921–25.
313 n. 12

HOADLY, Benjamin
The Original and Institution of Civil Government Dicuss'd, viz. I. An Examination of the Patriarchal System of Government. II. A Defense of Mr. Hooker's Judgment . . . To which is added a large Answer to Dr. F. Atterbury's Charge of Rebellion. . . . Second edition. London, 1710.
411 n. 4; 416–417 nn. 14, 17

A Sermon Preach'd before the . . . Lord-Mayor, Aldermen, and Livery-Men of the several Companies of London. . . . September 29th, 1705. London, 1705.
417 n. 16

HOBBES, Thomas
De cive, The Latin version, entitled in the first edition "Elementorum philosophiae sectio tertia de cive" and in later editions "Elementa philosophica de cive." A critical edition by Howard Warrender. Oxford, 1983.
272–273; 439 n. 114
De cive. The English version, entitled in the first edition "Philosophicall Rudiments Concerning Government and Society." A critical edition by Howard Warrender. Oxford, 1983.
306 n. 4; 315 n. 1; 317 n. 7; 320 n. 22; 338 n. 59; 363 n. 5, 365–366 nn. 9, 11; 370 n. 1; 384 n. 41; 409 n. 3; 414 n. 14; 420 n. 11; 427 n. 26; 429 n. 40; 439 n. 114
Leviathan. Edited with an introduction by C. B. Macpherson. Harmondsworth, 1968.
315 n. 1; 317 n. 7; 320 n. 22; 363–366 nn. 5, 9, 12; 384 n. 41; 409 n. 3; 414 n. 14; 420 n. 11; 429 n. 40

HOEVELER, J. David, Jr.
James McCosh and the Scottish Intellectual Tradition, from Glasgow to Princeton. Princeton, 1981.
35 n. 99

HOME, Henry (Lord Kames)
"Considerations upon the State of Scotland with Respect to Entails" (with letter to Lord Chancellor Hardwicke, 29 August, 1759). British Museum Add. MSS. 35, 449, folios 189a–194b. In W. C. Lehmann, *Henry Home, Lord Kames, and the Scottish Enlightenment: A Study in National Character and the History of Ideas,* pp. 327–332. The Hague, 1971.
333–334 nn. 46–47
Elements of Criticism. . . . The fifth edition. 2 vols. Edinburgh, 1774.
360 n. 135
Essays on the Principles of Morality and Natural Religion. Edinburgh, 1751.
42; 45; 314 n. 1
Essays upon Several Subjects concerning British Antiquities. Third edition. Edinburgh, 1763.
387 n. 4
Historical Law-Tracts. 2 vols. Edinburgh, 1758.

A Short Introduction to Moral Philosophy (translated from the Latin).
Facsimile of first edition, 1747. Hildesheim, 1969. In *Collected Works*, vol. 4.

> 30 n. 84; 67 n. 87; 70 nn. 97–98; 89; 305–306 nn. 1, 3–4; 312
> nn. 1, 7; 317–328 nn. 8–39 passim; 331–348 nn. 40–105 passim;
> 351–365 nn. 110–139, 2–9 passim; 367 nn. 12, 1; 374–377 nn.
> 13, 15–16, 21, 1; 379 nn. 3, 5, 7–9; 381–383 nn. 20–38 passim;
> 385 n. 43–389 n. 9 passim; 397–398 n. 23–28; 400–401 nn. 40–
> 43; 405–406 n. 9; 409 n. 3; 422–423 nn. 14, 17, 19; 427 nn. 25–
> 26; 429 nn. 41–43; 433 n. 58; 435–437 nn. 66–85 passim; 459

Synopsis metaphysicae, ontologiam et pneumatologiam complectens. Facsimile of second edition, 1744. *Collected Works*, vol. 7:203–333. Hildesheim, 1971.

> 30 n. 84; 32–33 n. 91

A System of Moral Philosophy. Facsimile of first edition, 1755. 2 vols. Hildesheim, 1969. In *Collected Works*, vols. 5, 6.

> 70 n. 97; 89; 305–306 nn. 1, 3–4; 312 n. 1; 317–329 nn. 8–39
> passim; 331–337 nn. 40–54 passim; 339–348 nn. 60–105 passim;
> 351–365 nn. 110–139, 2–9 passim; 367 nn. 12, 1; 374–377 nn.
> 13, 15–16, 21, 1; 379 nn. 3, 5, 7–9; 381–386 nn. 20–59; 397–398
> nn. 22–35 passim; 400–401 nn. 40–43; 405–406 n. 9; 409 nn. 3–
> 4; 412 n. 5; 422–424 nn. 14–19; passim; 426–427 nn. 41–43; 433
> n. 58; 435–437 nn. 66–85 passim; 459

Isidore of Seville

Etymologiarum sive originum libri XX, recognovit brevique adnotatione critica instruxit W. M. Lindsay. 2 vols. Lithograph reprint of the first edition. Oxford, 1971.

> 317 n. 3

Jack, Robert

"Dr. Reid's Lectures, 1774–1776." Glasgow University Library MSS. 116–118.

> 76 n. 110; 86; 305 n. 2; 362 n. 3; 364 n. 5; 366 n. 12; 397 n. 25;
> 409 n. 1; 412 n. 8; 414 n. 14; 419–420 nn. 8–9

James I (King of Great Britain)

The Workes. . . . Published by James, Bishop of Winton. Facsimile reprint of 1616 London edition. Anglistica & Americana 85. Hildesheim, 1971.

> 404 n. 7

Jardine, George

Outlines of Philosophical Education, Illustrated by the Method of Teaching the Logic Class in the University of Glasgow. Glasgow, 1825.

> 29 n. 81

⟨JENYNS, Soame⟩
Disquisitions on Several Subjects. London, 1782.
379 n. 3

JOHNSON, Samuel
"Introduction to the Proceedings of the Committee Appointed to Manage the Contributions begun at London, Dec. 18, 1758, for Clothing French Prisoners of War." In *Works of Samuel Johnson*, vol. 12. London, 1823.
436 n. 69

JONES, Peter
"The Polite Academy and the Presbyterians, 1720–1770." In J. Dwyer, R. A. Mason, and A. Murdoch, eds., *New Perspectives on the Politics and Culture of Early Modern Scotland*, pp. 156–178. Edinburgh, n. d.
11 n. 19

JUSTINIAN I (Roman Emperor). For the *Institutes*, *Digest*, and *Codex*, see under *Corpus Juris civilis*.

JUVENAL, Decimus Junius
Satires. In *Juvenal and Persius*. With an English translation by G. G. Ramsay. Loeb Classical Library. New York and London, 1918.
122; 145; 168–169; 307–308 nn. 10–11; 318 n. 16; 342 n. 77; 360 n. 136

KAEMPFER, Engelbert
Histoire naturelle, civile, et ecclésiastique du Japon . . . traduite en François sur la version Anglois de J. G. Scheuchzer . . . [by J. Neaulme] 3 vols. La Haye, 1732.
226; 394 n. 12

KAMES, Henry Home (Lord). *See* HOME, Henry (Lord Kames).

KENYON, J. P.
Revolution Principles: The Politics of Party, 1689–1720. Cambridge, 1977.
72 n. 101

KETTLER, David
The Social and Political Thought of Adam Ferguson. Columbus, Ohio, 1965.
24 n. 62

KIRK, Linda
Richard Cumberland and Natural Law. Secularisation of Thought in Seventeenth-Century England. Cambridge, 1987.
91 n. 11

KRIEGER, Leonard
The Politics of Discretion: Pufendorf and the Acceptance of Natural Law.
Chicago and London, 1965.
376 n. 29

KUEHN, Manfred
Scottish Common Sense in Germany, 1768–1800: A Contribution to the
History of Critical Philosophy. Kingston and Montreal, 1987.
35 n. 99

LAURIE, Henry
Scottish Philosophy in Its National Development. Glasgow, 1902.
34 n. 99

LEECHMAN, William
"The Preface Giving Some Account of the Life, Writings, and
Character of the Author." In Francis Hutcheson, *A System of*
Moral Philosophy, pp. i–xlviii. Facsimile of 1st ed., 1755, prepared
by Bernhard Fabian. 2 vols. Hildesheim, 1969. (Hutcheson, *Col-*
lected Works, vol. 5).
30 nn. 83–84

LEGUM, Richard
"An Updated Bibliography of Works on the Philosophy of Thomas
Reid." *The Monist* 61 (1978): 340–344.
39 n. 3

LEHMANN, W. C.
Henry Home, Lord Kames, and the Scottish Enlightenment: A Study in
National Character and the History of Ideas. The Hague, 1971.
John Millar of Glasgow, 1735–1801: His Life and Thought and His Con-
tributions to Sociological Analysis. Cambridge, 1960.
22 n. 52

LEHRER, Keith
"Reid's Influence on Contemporary American and British Philosophy." In S. F. Barker and T. L. Beauchamp, eds., *Thomas Reid:*
Critical Interpretations, pp. 1–7. Philadelphia, 1976.
35 n. 99

LEIBNIZ, Gottfried Wilhelm von
Die philosophischen Schriften. . . . Edited by C. I. Gerhardt. 7 vols.
Berlin, 1875–90.
The Political Writings. . . . Translated and edited, with introduction
and notes, by P. Riley. Cambridge, 1972. Includes his "Opinion
of the Principles of Pufendorf" (pp. 65–75).
320 n. 22

76; *260*; 320 n. 22; 322 n. 26; 324–326 nn. 29, 31–32; 328 n. 37;
363 n. 5; 365–366 nn. 9–10, 12; 381 nn. 21, 28; 383 n. 38; 399
n. 38; 409 n. 3; 411 n. 4; 413 n. 8; 415–416 n. 14; 418 n. 19;
424–425 n. 23

LONDON MAGAZINE
  Vols. 23 (1754) and 26 (1757).
  431 n. 47

⟨LONG, Thomas⟩
  *A Resolution of Certain Queries concerning Submission to the Present Gov-
  ernment.* Reprinted in *A Collection of State Tracts, Publish'd on Occasion of the Late Revolution in 1688 and during the Reign of King
  William III,* 1:439–465. London, 1705–7.
  411 n. 4

MacCORMICK, D. N.
  "Law and Enlightenment." In R. H. Campbell and A. S. Skinner,
  eds., *The Origins and Nature of the Scottish Enlightenment,* pp. 150–
  166. Edinburgh, 1982.
  32 n. 89

McCOSH, James
  *The Scottish Philosophy, Biographical, Expository, Critical, from Hutche-
  son to Hamilton.* Hildesheim, 1966.
  8 n. 7: 11 n. 19; 28 n. 78; 34 n. 99

McCRACKEN, Charles J.
  Malebranche and British Philosophy. Oxford, 1983.
  39 n. 3

MACHIAVELLI, Niccolò
  Discourses (on the First Ten Books of Titus Livy). Translated . . . with
  an introduction and notes by L. J. Walker, with a new introduction and appendixes by C. H. Clough. 2 vols. London, 1975.
  394 n. 8; 404 n. 6; 420 n. 11; 431 n. 47

MACKIE, J. D.
  The University of Glasgow, 1451 to 1951. Glasgow, 1954.
  28 n. 78

MACKINNON, K. A. B.
  "George Turnbull's Common Sense Jurisprudence." In J. Carter
  and J. Pittock, eds., *Aberdeen and the Enlightenment,* pp. 104–110.
  Aberdeen, 1987.
  8 n. 7

Mackintosh, James
Vindiciae Gallicae: A Defence of the French Revolution and Its English Admirers, against the Accusations of the Right Hon. Edmund Burke (1791). In *The Miscellaneous Works of the Right Hon. Sir James Mackintosh*, vol. 3. London, 1846.
82

Mackintosh, Robert James (ed.)
Memoirs of the Life of . . . Sir James Mackintosh. 2 vols. London, 1836.
82 n. 132

Macklin, Charles
Love à la Mode (1759). In *Four Comedies by Charles Macklin*, edited . . . by J. O. Bartley, pp. 44–77. London, 1968.
445 n.23

Macmillan, Duncan
Painting in Scotland: The Golden Age. Oxford, 1986.
37 n. 104; 85 n. 138

Macrobius, Ambrosius Aurelius Theodosius
Saturnalia. Translated with an introduction and notes by P. V. Davies. New York, 1969.
430 n. 42

Mandeville, Bernard
An Enquiry into the Origin of Honour, and the Usefulness of Christianity in War. Second edition with a new introduction by M. M. Goldsmith. London, 1971.
422 n. 11
A Letter to Dion. Edited by Bonamy Dobrée. Liverpool, 1954.
421 n. 11

Manuel, F. E., and F. P. Manuel
Utopian Thought in the Western World. Cambridge, Mass., 1979.
443 n. 7

Marcil-Lacoste, Louise
Claude Buffier and Thomas Reid: Two Common-Sense Philosophers. Kingston and Montreal, 1982.
39 n. 3
"The Seriousness of Reid's Sceptical Admissions." *The Monist* 62 (1978): 311–325.
41 n. 4

Mathew, W. M.
"The Origins and Occupations of Glasgow Students, 1740–1839."

Past and Present 33 (1966): 74–94.
28 n. 78

MEDICK, Hans
Naturzustand und Naturgeschichte der bürgerlichen Gesellschaft. Göttingen, 1973.
30 n. 84

MEIKLE, Henry W.
Scotland and the French Revolution. London, 1969.
84 n. 135

MIKHALEVSKY, Nina
"Bibliography." In S. F. Barker and T. L. Beauchamp, eds., *Thomas Reid: Critical Interpretations*, pp. 133–140. Philadelphia, 1976.
39 n. 3

MILL, John Stuart
An Examination of Sir William Hamilton's Philosophy and of the Principal Questions Discussed in His Writings. London, 1865.
34

MILLAR, John
"Lectures on the Institutions of the Civil Law, Glasgow, 1794 (Notes of a student)." Edinburgh University Library MS. Dc.2. 45–46.
334 n. 46
The Origin of the Distinction of Ranks. . . . The fourth edition, corrected. . . . Edinburgh, 1806.
334 n. 46; 365 n. 9; 368 n. 3

⟨MILLAR, John⟩
Letters of Sidney, on Inequality of Property. To which is added, A Treatise of the Effects of War on Commercial Society. Edinburgh, 1796.
81 n. 129

MILTON, John
The Doctrine and Discipline of Divorce. Restor'd to the Good of Both Sexes. . . . In *The Works of John Milton*, 18 vols. in 21 (vol. 3, ii). New York, 1931–40.
362 n. 3
. . . Paradise Lost. A new edition, by Richard Bentley. Facsimile reprint of 1732 London edition. New York, 1974.
396 n. 15

THE MONIST
Vol. 61, no. 2 (1978): *The Philosophy of Thomas Reid.*
39 n. 3

MONTAIGNE, Michel Eyquem de
  Essays. Translated by John Florio. Introduction by L. C. Harmer. 3
  vols. Everyman's Library. London, 1910.
    322 n. 26; 393 n. 7

MONTESQUIEU, Charles-Louis de Secondat (Baron)
  *Considérations sur les causes de la grandeur des Romains et de leur déca-
  dence.* In *Oeuvres complètes* . . . publiées sous la direction de M.
  André Masson. Vol. 1. Paris, 1950. (Facsimile reprint of 1758
  Amsterdam edition).
    394 n. 8
  Persian Letters. Translated with an introduction and notes by C. J.
  Betts. Harmondsworth, 1973.
    317 n. 7; 322 n. 26
  The Spirit of the Laws. Translated by T. Nugent, with an introduc-
  tion by F. Neumann. 2 vols. in 1. Hafner Library of Classics 9.
  New York, 1949.
    221; 313 n. 12; 362 nn. 2–3; 365 n. 9; 368 n. 3; 391 n. 21; 393–
    394 nn. 5–12 passim; 419 n. 8; 422 n. 11; 442 n. 3; 444 n. 12

MOORE, G. E.
  "The Nature and Reality of Objects of Perception. " In G. E.
  Moore, *Philosophical Studies*, pp. 31–96. London, 1960.
    35 n. 99

MOORE, James
  "Locke and the Scottish Jurists." Paper delivered at the Conference
  for the Study of Political Thought: "John Locke and the Political
  Thought of the 1680s," Folger Shakespeare Library, Washington, D.C., March 1980.
    53 n. 44

MOORE, James, and Michael SILVERTHORNE
  "Gershom Carmichael and the Natural Jurisprudence Tradition in
  Eighteenth-Century Scotland." In I. Hont and M. Ignatieff, eds.,
  *Wealth and Virtue: The Shaping of Political Economy in the Scottish
  Enlightenment*, pp. 73–87. Cambridge, 1983.
    30 n. 84; 32 n. 89
  "Natural Sociability and Natural Rights in the Moral Philosophy of
  Gerschom Carmichael." In V. Hope, ed., *Philosophers of the Scot-
  tish Enlightenment*, pp. 1–12. Edinburgh, 1984.
    30 n. 84; 32 n. 89

MORE, Thomas
  The Best State of a Commonwealth and the New Island of Utopia (1516).
  In *The Complete Works of St. Thomas More*, edited by E. Surtz and

J. H. Hexter, vol. 4. New Haven and London, 1965.
18 n. 41; 64; 69 n. 93; 384 n. 42; 443–445 nn. 7–22 passim

MÖRNER, Magnus
The Political and Economic Activities of the Jesuits in the La Plata Region.
Stockholm, 1953.
444 n. 12

MORRISON DAVIDSON, J.
Concerning Four Precursors of Henry George and the Single Tax. London, n. d. (ca. 1890).
81 n. 125

MURRAY, David
Memoirs of the Old College of Glasgow. Glasgow, 1927.
28 n. 78; 30 n. 84

NEWTON, Isaac
Optice: sive De reflexionibus, refractionibus, inflexionibus & coloribus lucis libri tres . . . Latine reddidit Samuel Clarke . . . Editio secunda, auctior. London, 1719.
126; 310 n. 18

NORTON, David Fate
David Hume: Common-Sense Moralist, Sceptical Metaphysician. Princeton, 1982.
8 n. 7; 38–39 nn. 1–2; 43 n. 11; 53 n. 43
"From Moral Sense to Common Sense: An Essay on the Development of Scottish Common Sense Philosophy, 1700–1765." Ph.D. dissertation, University of California at San Diego, 1966.
3 n. 1; 42–43 nn. 10–11
"Hutcheson's Moral Realism." *Journal of the History of Philosophy* 23 (1985): 392–418.
53 n. 43

OGILVIE, William
Birthright in Land. With biographical notes by D. C. MacDonald. London, 1891.
81 n. 125

⟨OGILVIE, William⟩
An Essay on the Right of Property in Land, with Respect to Its Foundation in the Law of Nature; Its Present Establishment by the Municipal Laws of Europe; and the Regulations by Which It Might be Rendered More Beneficial to the Lower Ranks of Mankind. London, n. d. (1781 or 1782).
81 n. 125; 445 n. 15

OLSON, Richard
Scottish Philosophy and British Physics, 1750–1880: A Study in the Foundations of the Victorian Scientific Style. Princeton, 1975.
35 n. 100

OTIS, James
The Rights of the British Colonies Asserted and Proved. In *Pamphlets of the American Revolution, 1750–1776,* edited by Bernard Bailyn . . . and J. N. Ganett, vol. 1: *1750–1765.* John Harvard Library. Cambridge, Mass., 1965.
425 n. 24

⟨OTIS, James⟩
A Vindication of the British Colonies, against the Aspersions of the Halifax Gentleman. . . . In *Pamphlets of the American Revolution, 1750–1776,* edited by Bernard Bailyn . . . and J.N. Ganett, vol. 1: *1750–1765.* John Harvard Library. Cambridge, Mass., 1965.
425 n. 24

OVID (Publius Ovidius Naso)
Metamorphoses. With an English translation by Frank Justus Miller, 2 vols. Loeb Classical Library. New York and London, 1916.
342 n. 77; 371 n. 3

PAINE, Thomas
Agrarian Justice Opposed to Agrarian Law and to Agrarian Monopoly. London, 1797.
445 n. 15
Rights of Man. London, 1791–92.
445 n. 15

PAMPHLETS OF THE AMERICAN REVOLUTION, 1750–1776
Edited by Bernard Bailyn . . . and J. N. Ganett, vol. 1: *1750–1765.* John Harvard Library. Cambridge, Mass., 1965.

PENELHUM, Terence
Butler. London, 1985.
10 n. 18

PENN, William
A Brief Account of the Province of Pennsylvania, lately granted by the King under the great seal of England to William Penn, and his heirs and assigns. (An abstract of the patent granted by the king . . . 4 March 1681.) London, 1681.
419 n. 8
A Call to Repentance, recommended to the inhabitants of Great Britain in

general etc. (Extracted from a book intituled An Address to Protes-tants. . . .) N.p., 1745.
420 n. 8

The Frame of the Government of the Province of Pennsil-vania . . . Together with certain laws agreed upon in England by the Governour and divers Freemen of the aforesaid Province. . . . N.p., 1682.
419 n. 8

The free-born Englishman's unmask'd battery . . . With some quotations from . . . William Penn . . . explaining the duty of a true Protestant Dis-senter to the King. . . . N.p., 1747.
420 n. 8

PERSIUS (Aulus Persius Flaccus)
Satires. In *Juvenal and Persius.* With an English translation by G. G. Ramsay. Loeb Classical Library. New York and London, 1918.

PETERSON, R.
"Scottish Common Sense in America, 1768–1850: An Evaluation of Its Influence." Ph.D. dissertation, University of Michigan, 1972.
35 n. 99

PHILLIPSON, N. T.
"Lawyers, Landowners, and the Civic Leadership of Post-Union Scotland." *Juridical Review,* n. s. 21 (1976): 97–120.
333 n. 46

PITT, William (1st earl of Chatham). *See* CHATHAM.

PLATO
Alcibiades I and II. In *Plato* . . . with an English translation by W. R. M. Lamb, vol. 8. Loeb Classical Library. New York and London, 1927.
122; 307 n. 10; 311 n. 1

The Collected Dialogues. . . . Edited by Edith Hamilton and Hunting-ton Cairns, with introduction. . . . Bollingen Series 71. New York, 1961.

Gorgias. Translated by W. D. Woodhead. In *Collected Dialogues.*
318 n. 16

Laws. Translated by A. E. Taylor. In *Collected Dialogues.*
311 n. 1

Letters. Translated by L. A. Post. In *Collected Dialogues.*
316 n. 6

Protagoras. Translated by W. K. C. Guthrie. In *Collected Dialogues.*
311 n. 1

Republic. Translated by P. Shorey. In *Collected Dialogues*.
311 n. 1; 313 n. 3; 315 n. 3; 319 n. 19; 341 n. 71
Socrates' Defense (Apology). Translated by H. Tredennick. In *Collected Dialogues*.
394 n. 9; 318 n. 16

PLAUTUS, Titus Maccius
Mercator. Miles gloriosus. Mostellaria. Persa. In *Plautus*. With an English translation by P. Nixon. Vol. 3. Loeb Classical Library. New York and London, 1924:
Mercator.
230; 396 n. 20

PLUTARCH
The Greek Questions. . . . With a new translation and a commentary by W. R. Halliday. Reprint of 1928 Oxford edition. New York, 1975.
327 n. 37
Lives. With an English translation by B. Perrin. Vol. 9. Loeb Classical Library. New York and London, 1914–21.
395 n. 14
Moralia. . . . Vol. 14, with an English translation by B. Einarson and P. H. de Lacy. Loeb Classical Library. Cambridge, Mass., and London, 1967.
392 n. 2

POCOCK, J. G. A.
Virtue, Commerce, and History: Essays on Political Thought and History, Chiefly in the Eighteenth Century. Cambridge, 1985.
72 n. 101

POLYBIUS
The Histories. With an English translation by W. R. Paton. 6 vols. Loeb Classical Library. Cambridge, Mass., and London, 1922–27.
371 n. 1; 389 n. 11

POPE, Alexander
An Essay on Man. . . . Scolar Press facsimile reprint of 1734 London edition. Menston, 1969.
413 n. 9

PRICE, Richard
A Review of the Principal Questions in Morals. Edited by D. D. Raphael (from the third edition, London, 1787). Oxford, 1948.
305 n. 1; 309 n. 14; 312 n. 7

RAPHAEL, David Daiches
The Moral Sense. Oxford, 1947.
    51 n. 34; 52n. 39; 58 n. 56

RASMUSSEN, S. V.
Studier over William Hamiltons Filosofi. Copenhagen, 1921.
    35 n. 99

⟨RASTELL, John⟩
    A new interlude and a mery of the nature of the iiii ele-
    ments. . . . Printed as *The Nature of the Four Elements.* Tudor Fac-
    simile Texts. Edinburgh and London, 1908.
    390 n. 19

REID, Thomas
    Philosophical Works. With notes and supplementary dissertations by
    Sir William Hamilton. Photographic reprint of eighth edition
    (1895), with an introduction by Harry M. Bracken. 2 vols in 1.
    Hildesheim, 1983.
    303 nn. 1, 3; 334 n. 46
    "A Brief Account of Aristotle's Logic, with Remarks." In *Philosoph-*
    ical Works.
    23
    Correspondence of Dr. Reid. In *Philosophical Works.*
    14 n. 33; 20; 23–24 nn. 60, 65; 26–28 nn. 72–76, 78; 33 n. 93,
    36 n. 102; 44 n. 14; 65 n. 82; 76 n. 110, 342 n. 86
    "Cura Prima. Of Common Sense," edited by D. F. Norton. In
    L. Marcil-Lacoste, *Claude Buffier and Thomas Reid: Two Common-*
    Sense Philosophers, Appendix. Kingston and Montreal, 1982.
    42 n. 9
    "An Essay on Quantity; Occasioned by reading a treatise in which
    simple and compound ratios are applied to virtue and merit." In
    Philosophical Works.
    11; 314 n. 1
    Essays on the Active Powers of Man. In *Philosophical Works.* (Abbre-
    viated A.P.)
    20–21; 31; 34–35; 41 n. 6; 44 n. 14; 47–64 nn. 18–74 passim; 64
    nn. 78–79; 66; 76 n. 110; 79–80 nn. 123–124; 88–89; 307–308
    nn. 10–11; 312–315 nn. 1, 7, 9, 1, 3; 317–319 nn. 7–19 passim;
    321 n. 25; 324 n. 29; 326 nn. 32, 34; 338–339 nn. 59–61; 342–
    343 nn. 74–87 passim; 349 n. 105; 360–362 nn. 135, 137, 2; 375–
    376 nn. 20–21, 29; 379–380 nn. 7, 13; 383–384 nn. 37, 40–41;
    394 nn. 9–10; 401–402 nn. 1, 4; 457

Essays on the Intellectual Powers of Man. In *Philosophical Works.* (Abbreviated I.P.)

9 n. 13; 20 n. 47; 21; 25; 30–31; 34; 38–39 nn. 1, 3; 41–42 nn. 5–9; 51–52; 303–304 nn. 1, 4–6, 46; 402 n. 4

Inquiry and Essays. Edited by Ronald E. Beanblossom and Keith Lehrer. Indianapolis, 1983.

34 n.99

An Inquiry into the Human Mind, on the Principles of Common Sense. In *Philosophical Works.* (Abbreviated H.M.)

9 n. 13; 14; 19–21; 31; 39 nn. 2–3; 43–44; 342–343 nn. 80–86 passim

"Observations on the Dangers of Political Innovation. " *Glasgow Courier,* 18 December 1794, pp. 518–523. Also in Archibald Arthur, *Discourses on Theological and Literary Subjects.* With an account of some particulars in [Arthur's] life and character by William Richardson. Glasgow, 1803.

464

Philosophical Orations of Thomas Reid. Edited, with an introduction, from the Birkwood Collection manuscripts by W. R. Humphries. Aberdeen, 1937.

17 n. 39; 39 n. 3; 42; 81

The Philosophical Orations of Thomas Reid delivered at Graduation Ceremonies in King's College Aberdeen, 1753, 1756, 1759, 1762. Edited . . . by D. D. Todd. Translated by S. M. L. Darcus. In *Philosophical Research Archives* 3 (1977): 916–990. (Abbreviated *Orations*)

14–18; 428 n. 32

"A Statistical Account of the University of Glasgow." In *Philosophical Works.*

26 nn. 72–73; 36

RICHARDSON, William

"An Account of Some Particulars in the Life and Character of Archibald Arthur, Late Professor of Moral Philosophy, in the University of Glasgow." In Archibald Arthur, *Discourses on Theological and Literary Subjects.* With an account of some particulars in [Arthur's] life and character by William Richardson, pp. 493–517. Glasgow, 1803.

33 n. 94; 84 n. 137

ROBERTSON, William

The History of Scotland. In *The Works of William Robertson . . .* with a sketch of his Life and Writings by R. A. Davenport, vols. 1–3. London, 1826.

334 n. 46

Ross, Ian Simpson
Lord Kames and the Scotland of His Day. Oxford, 1972.
22 n. 52; 23 n. 59; 45 n. 16; 333 n. 46
"Unpublished Letters of Thomas Reid to Lord Kames, 1762–
1782." *Texas Studies in Literature and Language* 7 (1965): 17–65.
23–25 nn. 59, 64, 66; 44 n. 14

Rousseau, Jean-Jacques
Oeuvres complètes. Edition publiée sous la direction de Bernard
Gagnebin et Marcel Raymond. 4 vols. Bibliothèque de la Pléiade.
Paris, 1959–69.
Discours sur l'origine et les fondements de l'inégalité. Texte établi et an-
noté par J. Starobinski. In *Oeuvres complètes*, vol. 3.
313 n. 13; 343 n. 84; 412 n. 6
Du contrat social. Textes établis et annotés par R. Derathé. In
Oeuvres complètes, vol. 3.
412 n. 6; 420–421 n. 11
Emile ou De l'éducation. Textes établis par C. Wirz. In *Oeuvres complètes*, vol. 4.
412n. 6
Lettres écrites de la montagne. Texte établi et annoté par J.-D. Can-
daux. In *Oeuvres complètes*, vol. 3.
420 n. 11

Ryan, Alan
"Locke on Freedom: Some Second Thoughts." In K. Haakonssen,
ed., *Traditions of Liberalism: Essays on Locke, Smith, and Mill*, pp.
31–55. Sydney, 1988.
53 n. 44

Schlenke, Manfred
*England und das friderizianische Preussen 1740–1763. Ein Beitrag zum
Verhältnis von Politik und öffentlicher Meinung im England des 18.
Jahrhunderts.* Freiburg and Munich, 1963

Schneewind, J. B.
Sidgwick's Ethics and Victorian Moral Philosophy. Oxford, 1977.
10 n. 16; 35 n. 99
"The Use of Autonomy in Ethical Theory." In *Reconstructing Indi-
vidualism: Autonomy, Individuality, and the Self in Western Thought*,
edited by T. C. Heller, M. Sosna, and D. E. Wellbery, pp. 64–75.
Stanford, Calif., 1986.
10 n. 16

Sciacca, M. F.
La filosofia di Thomas Reid. Milan, 1963.
39 n. 3

SCOTT, William Robert
Adam Smith as Student and Professor. New York, 1965.
27 n. 77
Francis Hutcheson: His Life, Teaching, and Position in the History of Philosophy. New York, 1966.
30 n. 83

SEGERSTEDT, T. T.
Moral Sense-skolan och dess inflytande paa svensk filosofi. Lund and Leipzig, 1937.
35 n. 99

SELDEN, John
De jure naturali et gentium juxta disciplinam Ebraeorum libri septem. In *Opera omnia,* edited (with vitam auctoris) by D. Wilkins, 1:1. London, 1726.
90; 310 n. 18; 375 n. 20
Mare clausum: The Right and Dominion of the Sea. . . . Formerly translated into English by M. Nedham and now perfected and restored by J. H. [James Howell]. 2 parts. London, 1663.
90; 327 n. 35; 375 n. 20

SENECA, Lucius Annaeus (the Younger)
Ad Lucilium epistulae morales. With an English translation by R. M. Gummere. 3 vols. Loeb Classical Library. Cambridge, Mass., and London, 1917–25.
306 n. 3; 315 n. 5
Declamations (Controversiae, Suasoriae). . . . Translated by M. Winterbottom. 2 vols. Loeb Classical Library. Cambridge, Mass., and London, 1974.
381 n. 21
Tragedies. With an English translation by Frank Jushes Miller. 2 vols. Loeb Classical Library. New York and London, 1917.
316 n. 3; 342 n. 77

SHAFTESBURY, Anthony Ashley Cooper (3rd earl of)
Characteristics of Men, Manners, Opinions, Times. Edited, with notes by John M. Robertson, with an introduction by Stanley Green. Library of Liberal Arts 179. Indianapolis, 1964.
124; 309 nn. 14–15; 360 n. 135; 421 n. 11

SHER, Richard B.
Church and University in the Scottish Enlightenment: The Moderate Literati of Edinburgh. Edinburgh, 1985.
6 n. 3; 12 nn. 24–25; 45 n. 16

the author the honour to expel him. Third edition. London,
1793.
445 n. 15

STAIR, James Dalrymple (1st viscount)
The Institutions of the Law of Scotland. . . . Edited by David M. Walker.
4 books. New Haven, Conn. , and Edinburgh, 1981.
329 n. 39; 339 n. 60; 355 n. 121; 365 n. 8; 399 n. 37

STATE TRACTS
*A Collection of State Tracts, Publish'd on Occasion of the Late Revolution
in 1688 and during the Reign of King William III.* 3 vols. London,
1705–7.
404 n. 8; 411 n. 4; 413 n. 8

STEIN, Peter
"From Pufendorf to Adam Smith: The Natural Law Tradition in
Scotland." In N. Horn, ed., *Europäisches Rechtsdenken in Geschichte
und Gegenwart*, pp. 667–679. Munich, 1982.
32 n. 89

STEWART, Dugald
Account of the Life and Writings of Thomas Reid. In Dugald Stewart,
*Biographical Memoirs of Adam Smith . . . , William Robertson
. . . , Thomas Reid. . . .* Edited by Sir William Hamilton, pp. 243–
328. Edinburgh, 1858.
4 n. 2; 6 n. 1; 10 nn. 14–15; 17 n. 39; 24 n. 62; 28 n. 79; 37 nn.
103–104

STEWART, M. A.
"Berkeley and the Rankenian Club." *Hermathena* 149 (1985): 25–
45.
8 nn. 7–8
"George Turnbull and Educational Reform." In J. Carter and
J. Pittock, eds., *Aberdeen and the Enlightenment*, pp. 95–103. Aberdeen, 1987.
7–8 nn. 6–8

STEWART-ROBERTSON, J. C.
" 'Horse-Bogey Bites Little Boys'; or, Reid's Oeconomicks of the
Family." In *Studies in Eighteenth-Century Culture* 16 (1986): 69–89.
69 n. 88
"Sancte Socrates: Scottish Reflections on Obedience and Resistance." In R. L. Emerson, G. Girard, and R. Runte, eds., *Man and
Nature.* Proceedings of the Canadian Society for Eighteenth-Century Studies, 1:65–79. London, Ont., 1982.
76 n. 110

"The Well-Principled Savage, or The Child of the Scottish Enlightenment." *Journal of the History of Ideas* 42 (1981): 503–525.
8 n. 17; 11 n. 19; 20 n. 47

STEWART-ROBERTSON, J. C., and D. F. NORTON
"Thomas Reid on Adam Smith's Theory of Morals." *Journal of the History of Ideas* 41 (1980): 381–398; 45 (1984): 309–321.
55 n. 52

SUETONIUS (Gaius Suetonius Tranquillus)
The Lives of the Caesars. With an English translation by J. C. Rolfe. Revised edition. 2 vols. Loeb Classical Library. Cambridge, Mass., and London, 1951.
312 n. 5

SWIFT, Jonathan
The Correspondence. . . . Edited by Harold Williams, vol. 3: *1724–1731.* 5 vols. Oxford, 1963–65.
343 n. 84

TACITUS, Cornelius
Agricola and *Germania*, translated by M. Hutton, revised by R. M. Ogilvie and E. H. Warmington, *Dialogus*, translated by W. Peterson, revised by M. Winterbottom. Loeb Classical Library, *Tacitus*, vol. 1. Cambridge, Mass., and London, 1970:
Germania.
396 n. 14

TALMUD
The Babylonian Talmud. Translated into English with notes, glossary, and indices under the editorship of I. Epstein. 34 vols. London, 1935–48. (Seder Nezikin: Sanhedrin)
310 n. 18

TERENTIUS AFER, Publius (Terence)
The Self-Tormentor (Heauton timorumenos). In *Terence*, with an English translation by John Sargeaunt, 1:113–229. Loeb Classical Library. Cambridge, Mass., and London, 1912.
315 n. 5

THOMAS, Peter D. G.
The House of Commons in the Eighteenth Century. Oxford, 1971.
382–383 n. 34

THOMAS AQUINAS
Summa theologiae (Latin and English). Blackfriars edition, vols. 23, 36–44. 61 vols. New York and London, 1964–80.
312 n. 1; 315 n. 2; 317 n. 3

Conduct and Affairs of Nations and Sovereigns. . . . Translated from
the French. 2 vols. London, 1759–60.
269ff.; 317 n. 7; 356 n. 122; 369–370 nn. 9, 1–3; 375 n. 19; 381
n. 20; 383 n. 35; 389–392 nn. 11–24 passim; 419 nn. 3–4, 5; 422
n. 13; 424 nn. 19, 21; 427–441 nn. 26–157 passim

VEITCH, John
"A Memoir of Dugald Stewart." In Dugald Stewart, *Biographical
Memoirs* . . . , pp. vii–clxxvii. Edinburgh, 1858.
24 n. 62; 83 n. 132

VIRGIL (Publius Vergilius Maro)
Virgil. With an English translation by H. Rushton Fairclough. 2
vols. Loeb Classical Library. New York and London, 1916–18;
rev. ed. 1934:
vol. 2:
Aeneid (books VII–XII) . . .
318 n. 16

VOLTAIRE, François Marie Arouet de
Oeuvres complètes. . . . Second edition. 75 vols. Paris, 1825–28.
Candide ou l'optimisme. Paris, 1959.
444 n. 12
Essai, sur les moeurs et l'ésprit des nations. In *Oeuvres complètes*, vols. 20–
25.
444 n. 12
Histoire de Russie. In *Oeuvres complètes*, vol. 31.
422 n. 12
Letters on England. Translated with an introduction by L. Tancock.
Harmondsworth, 1980.
420 n. 8
Prix de la justice et de l'humanité. . . . In *Oeuvres complètes*, 40:277–372.
322 n. 26

⟨WALLACE, Robert⟩
*A Dissertation on the Numbers of Mankind in Antient and Modern Times:
With an Appendix containing Observations on the same Subject, and
Remarks on Mr. Hume's Discourse on the Populousness of Antient Na-
tions.* Edinburgh, 1753.
366 n. 11
Various Prospects of Mankind, Nature, and Providence. London, 1761.
81 n. 128; 443 n. 7

WARBURTON, William
. . . *Works.* A new edition in twelve volumes. To which is prefixed a
discourse . . . containing some account of the life . . . of the au-

thor, by Richard Hurd. Vol. 7: *The Alliance between Church and State; or, The Necessity and Equity of an Established Religion, and a Test-Law, Demonstrated.* London, 1811.
    421–423 nn. 11, 14, 17

WEINSTOCK, Jerome A.
    "Reid's Definition of Freedom." In S. F. Barker and T. L. Beauchamp, eds., *Thomas Reid: Critical Interpretations*, pp. 95–102. Philadelphia, 1976.
    44–46 nn. 14–17

WESLEY, John
    The Journal of the Rev. John Wesley, vols. 4 and 6. Enlarged from original manuscripts. . . . Standard edition. Edited by Nehemiah Curnock. 8 vols. London, 1938.
    436 n. 69

WINKLER, Kenneth
    "Hutcheson's Alleged Realism." *Journal of the History of Philosophy* 23 (1985): 179–194.
    53 n. 43

WODROW, Robert
    Analecta, or, Materials for a History of Remarkable Providences. 4 vols. Edinburgh, 1842–43.
    30 n. 84

WOLFF, Christian Freiherr von
    Institutiones juris naturae et gentium. Edidit et curavit Marcellus Thomann. Halle and Magdeburg, 1750. Facsimile reprint in his *Gesammelte Werke* (in progress), Abt. II, Band 26. Hildesheim, 1969.
    356 n. 123; 438 n. 97
    Jus gentium methodo scientifica pertractatum, in quo jus gentium naturale ab eo, quod voluntarii, pactitii et consuetudinarii est, accurate distinguitur. Halle, 1749. Facsimile reprint in his *Gesammelte Werke* (in progress), Abt. II, Band 25. Hildesheim, 1972.
    370 n. 1; 438 n. 97
    Psychologia empirica, methodo scientifica pertractata. . . . New edition. Frankfort a.O. and Leipzig, 1740.
    91; 303 n. 3
    Psychologia rationalis, methodo scientifica pertractata. . . . New edition. Frankfort a.O. and Leipzig, 1740.
    91; 303 n. 3

WOLLASTON, William
    The Religion of Nature Delineated. . . . Sixth edition. London, 1738.

GENERAL INDEX

THIS INDEX covers the Introduction, Reid's *Practical Ethics*, and the Commentary. In entries for Reid's text the page numbers are printed in italics. This also applies to texts of Reid quoted in the Commentary—but *not* in the Introduction. In view of the many variations in Reid's spelling, it has been necessary to standardize the spelling in the index. Where not inappropriate, modern spelling has been adopted.

Apart from providing access to the details of each of the three main parts of the book, the index has two further functions. It indicates a large number of the particular links between Reid's text and the Commentary. It also gives an overview of Reid's linguistic usage. I have therefore sought to index Reid's text as non-interpretatively as possible. More particularly, I have reduced to a minimum the identification of synonymous expressions for the purpose of collective entries.

Names of authors are not included in cases of mere references and citations. For these the Bibliographic Index should be consulted. However, author's names are included here when something is said about the author.

aristocracy, *175*
Aristotle, 17; 311 n.1; 315 n.2; 319 n.19;
 399 nn.38–39
arithmetic, 7
arms, *116; 176; 205; 267–268*
 poisoned, 275
army, 80; *207; 237; 259; 275*
 British, 432 n.47
 standing, 432 n.47
Arnauld, Antoine, *106*
Arrian, 11–12; *122;* 307–308 n.10
Arthur, Archibald, 33; 85 n.137
art(s), 75; *103; 115–116; 258; 261; 285;*
 288
 advancement of, *265*
 curriculum, 6–8; 10–11
 fine, 15; 29; *108*
 liberal, 19
 manual, 18
 mechanical, *108*
 and power, 19
 progress of, *106*
 useful, *176*
artes, 189
artists, 85 n.138
Arts,
 course at Glasgow, 26–27
 at King's College, Aberdeen, 15ff.
Asia, *175*
Asiatics, *175–176*
assassination, *267; 274*
assertion and promises, 339 n.60
assignation, *215; 268*
assistance, right to, 381 n.20
associatio idearum, 188
 passionum, 188
Astraea, *156;* 342 n.77
astronomy, 13; *106*
atheism/atheist(s), 50 n.31; 320 n.22; 421
 n.11
Athens/Athenians, *227; 256;* 306 n.5;
 307 n.9; 393 n.6; 396 n.14; 420 n.10
Atlantic, the, *149;* 425 n.24
Atterbury, Francis, *178; 252;* 416 n.14
Attila, 313 n.12
attributes, divine, 306 n.4
Augustine, 344 n.88
Aurelius, Marcus, *122;* 308 n.10
Austrian Succession, War of, 434 n.59;
 436 n.73
Author,
 divine, *168; 235*

 of Nature, *204; 217; 219–220; 227–*
 228; 298; 307 n.6; 380 n.11
 of our Being, *231*
authority, 19; *147; 176; 248; 252; 277–*
 279; 289; 367–368 n.3; 405 n.9; 413
 n.14
 civil, *230;* 417 n.17
 and courage, 18–19
 despotic, *279; 284*
 divine/of God, *123;* 410 n.4
 and goodness, 18
 kingly, *242*
 of law, 319 n.18
 of master, *234–235*
 and military skill, 18
 offices of, *291*
 original, *171*
 papal, 416 n.14; cf. *442 n.158*
 parental, *253;* cf. 398–399 nn.36–37;
 417 n.17
 paternal, *151; 171; 243*
 of people, 411 n.4
 political and property, 81
 and power, 19
 principle of, 367 n.3
 public, *256*
 and resistance, 416–417 n.16
 and right, 18
 and wisdom, 18
authors, ancient, *156*
avarice, *275*
axioms, moral, *245–246*

Babylon, *252*
Bacchus, *256*
Bacon, Francis, 15; 38; *106; 304 n.5;* 421
 n.11
badges of rank, 78; *290*
Baird, George, 33; 86
balance of power, 441 n.144
Balguy, John, 56 n.52; 320 n.22
Bantam, *226*
banishment, *276*
barbarity, *115*
Barbeyrac, Jean, 7 n.6; 89; 91; *197; 202;*
 323 n.29; 346 n.96; 367 n.14; 374–375
 nn.7, 9, 10, 19–20; 381 n.22; 382 n.32;
 430 n.42
 and ages of children, 337 n.54
 and *agnati/cognati,* 391 n.21
 and creationism, 401 n.42
 and divinity of natural law, 320 n.22

moral, *126;* 310 n.18; 383 n.38
municipal, *228*
mutiny, *264*
of nations, 74; *114; 143; 182; 254–*
255; 260; 263; 268ff.; 368–370 nn.9,
1–3
arbitrary, 441 n.153
definition of, *273;* 318–319 n.18;
369 n.1; 419 n.1; 439 n.115
and of nature, *269–270*
necessary (natural), *270; 273*
obligation of, *273*
and slavery, 400 n.41
voluntary (conventional) *270; 273;*
276
writers on, *259*
natural, 59ff.; 64; 67–69; 72; 76; 79–
80; 85; *143–149; 231;* 326 n.31
and positive, 374 n.10
and revealed, 372 n.3
(theory of), 24; 53; 84. *See also* lawyers, modern natural
of nature 7; 71; 73; *113; 178; 192;*
197; 201; 213–214; 236; 246; 253–
255; 263; 340 n.66; 371ff.; 376 n.28
and acquisition, 381 n.28
and appropriation, 383 n.35
and *cessio,* 389 n.7
and children, 398 n.33
and compensation, 387 n.3
definition of, *273;* 318 n.18; 369
n.1; 379 n.3
and delict, 359 nn.128–130
ends of, 410 n.4
and entails, 66; *150–153; 214;* 333
n.46
and God, 318 n.17; 410 n.4
guidance by, 364 n.5
and happiness, 366 n.10; 378 n.3
and incest, 397 n.23
and moral agency, 410–411 n.4
and of nations, 15–16; *201; 269–*
270; 317 n.7; 376 n.29
obligation of, *181*
permissive, 7
in Selden, 310 n.18
and sociability, 378 n.3
and succession, 338 n.58
and usury, 353 n.118
and war, 430 n.42
new, *280*

of non-resistance, 417 n.18
of peace and war, *114*
penal, *292*
permissive, *216;* 392 n.24
pleas, *287; 294–296*
positive, 60; 69; 325 n.31; 328–329
nn.38–39; 331 n.41; 337 n.54; 338
n.58
and delict, 359 n.128
divine, 397 n.23
preceptive, *216;* 392 n.24
of prescription, *260*
of property, *296*
and right, *142*
of the Sabbath, *216;* 417 n.18
Scots, 91; *213;* 331 n.39; 354 n.121;
365 n.8
and slavery, 367 n.14
social, 310 n.18
of sovereigns, *273*
of the state, *146; 200; 229; 246*
of succession, *260;* 384 n.42
supreme, 71; *76; 252–253; 259*
of testaments, 384 n.42
and theft, 383 n.38
of Twelve Tables, *192; 216; 263;* 391
n.21; 393–394 n.8; 430 n.42
law of tithes, *216*
utopian, *295–296*
dislike of, 445 n.22
of war, *267*
of wills, *260*
lawsuits, *287; 297*
lawyers, 19; *142; 202*
law(yers), modern natural, 16; 59; 66;
71; 87; 89–91; 315 n.2; 317 nn.7–9;
318 n.17; 319 n.21; 321–322 nn.25–
26; 324–325 nn.29, 31; 327 nn.35, 37;
328–331 n.39; 332 n.42; 333 n.45
and atheism, 421 n.11
and animals, 378–379 n.3
and colonization, 427 n.26
and contract, 338 n.59
and deception of enemy, 435 n.66
and donation, 386 n.54
and economics, 350 n.106
founder of, 375 n.20
German, 74
and inanimate nature, 378 n.3
and interpretation, 355 n.122
and concept of justice, 375 n.21

States General (Dutch), *271*
station(s), *177; 234; 250; 282; 291–292*
  in life, 19; *133; 135; 235*
  private, *121;* 385 n.43
  in society, *110; 127–129*
status solutus, 200; 376 n.26
Stewart, Dugald, 4; 23–24; 28; 34; 36;
  80 n.124; 85
Stewart, John, 13; 23
Stillingfleet, Edward, 411 n.4
Stirling, 424 n.20
stock, common/public, *283–285; 293*
  mercantile, *294*
stocks, *166*
Stoics/Stoicism, 11; 17; 48–49; 57; *121–
  123; 131; 178;* 307–308 nn.9–10
  Christian, 21; 36; 58
  Roman, 322 n.26
  school of, 307 n.9
  Shaftesbury's, 8
Strachan, 6
Stuart, House of, 72; *242*
students, Reid's, 26–28; 34; 333 n.46;
  393 n.6
subjection, *243*
subjectivism, 53
subjects, 75; *173; 175; 180–181; 183;
  195; 233; 235; 243; 250; 254; 257–
  260; 273; 298–299;* 442 *n.158*
  British, *261; 263;* 425–426 n.24
  defense of, *275*
  of foreign state, *262; 265*
  French, *274*
  of great mogul, *240*
  happiness of, *261*
  Jesuits', *284*
  labor of, *293;* 427 n.25
  liberty of, 425–427 nn.24–25
  lives of, 75; *259*
  morals of, 69
  property of, 75; *258; 263;* 427 n.25
  rebellious, *268*
  rights of, *240; 252; 261*
  in Utopia, *288; 292; 295–297*
submission, *173; 175–176; 249; 252–
  253; 299;* 413 n.14; 442 *n.158*
  absolute, 413 n.8
subordination, *248*
  natural, *177*
subsidy (in war), *274*
subsistence, *247; 259; 285; 286; 291–*

293; 297
succession, 61; 66; *263;* 332 n.44; 338
  nn.56 and 58; 379 n.6; *386–387*
  to crowns and magistracies, *177*
  in entail, *211; 213–214; 386–387*
  nn.1–5. See also entails
  hereditary, *242*
  and intention, 336–337 nn.53–54
  intestate, *154–155; 211;* 336–337 n.54
  in land, *261; 295*
  laws of, *260;* 384 n.42
  testamentary, 66; *211*
suicide, *147; 258;* 322 n.26
sultan, *279*
superfluities, *161*
superior, *246–247; 265; 278*
superstition, *109; 123; 175–176;* 421
  n.11; 435 n.69
supplications, *255*
Supreme Being, *109; 117ff.; 193; 227;
  230; 255; 287*
  Governor, *120*
  Judge, *135*
  Lord, 310 n.18
  Mind, 15
swearing, *123; 159*
Sweden, *272*
  kings of, *270*
Swift, Jonathan, 343 n.84
Swiss, the, *264;* 431 n.47
sympathy, 54–55 n.52; *223*
Syracuse, *193*
system, legal, 321 n.25
  material, *178*

Tacitus, Cornelius, *227*
talents, *286*
  natural/acquired, *291*
  (social), *289–290*
Talmud, 310 n.18
Tamerlane (Tamburlaine), *132;* 313 *n.12*
Tarquinius Superbus, *215;* 393 n.8
  Collatinus, 393 n.8
Tarquins, *222*
taxation/taxes, *173; 176; 243; 246; 260;
  293–296*
  consent to, 75–76; *260*
  and legislation, 425–426 n.24
  right of, 76; 424 n.20
techne, 17; 31
temperance, 19; 48; 56; 58; *112; 127;*